LIGHT AND SHADOWS
A HISTORY OF MOTION PICTURES
THIRD EDITION

THOMAS W. BOHN
Ithaca College

RICHARD L. STROMGREN
University of Massachusetts — Amherst

Mayfield Publishing Company
Mountain View, California

Text and photo credits follow the index.

Library of Congress Catalog Card Number: 86-061131

International Standard Book Number: 0-87484-702-8

Manufactured in the United States of America
10   9   8   7   6   5   4   3

Mayfield Publishing Company
1240 Villa Street
Mountain View, CA 94041

Sponsoring editor: C. Lansing Hays
Developmental editor: David B. Andrews
Manuscript editor: Suzanne Lipsett
Managing editor: Pat Herbst
Production editor: Jan deProsse
Art director: Cynthia Bassett
Interior and cover design: Vargas/Williams/Design
Illustrator: Elaine Wang
Production manager: Cathy Willkie
Compositor: Progressive Typographers
Printer and binder: Malloy Lithographing, Inc.

CONTENTS

Undertaking an expanded and revised edition of a work like *Light & Shadows* presents both pains and pleasures. There are of course the pleasures of being able to add new material, and to amplify, modify, and correct old material. With the passage of almost ten years (a significant part of the history of this young medium), there is also the opportunity to reassess influences, redirect attention, and perhaps redress grievances—all done in response to research undertaken by the authors and others in the field and in acknowledgment of reactions we have received from students and colleagues to the original and second editions.

The pains are associated with trying to provide a clear, accurate, and readable text that is also reasonably complete within the limits of a single volume. We have probably not succeeded in all these things. Choices must finally be made between elaboration and succinctness, between complete documentation and keeping in focus the many crosscurrents of film's evolution.

But we *have* succeeded in preserving the core of a text that continues to win the respect of instructors and students alike—despite the emergence of other film histories in the wake of our own. What's more, we believe we know why our text has been well received. One reason is the strength of our overall approach, which remains unique. In this new edition, as in the previous two, we look at film history through a contextual "grid" —that is, we examine all the rich and varied influences that have shaped the evolution of a medium that in turn shapes the lives of us all. We feel strongly that the most enlightened history of motion pictures embraces the interrelationships of the film industry, film technology, film art, filmmakers of all definitions and of course the political, social, and cultural climate that is affected by this dynamic medium. We hope that immersing students in the context of earlier eras will help them to develop their own "context" as moviegoers of today.

Another reason for the success of this text is that the *Light & Shadows* grid lends form to a sprawling subject, an essential consideration for students who are unfamiliar with much of the material. In addition, the different grid elements allow us to consider a broad spectrum of points of view on the medium's evolution. This has been the key to preserving our text's reputation.

Balance remains the byword of our text. As in previous editions, no lengthy side tours are taken to tangential topics. Although we've considerably expanded our coverage of film's evolution as an art, we have also, for the most part, deliberately avoided extended analyses of individual films and directors, which would be intrusive and break up the flow of our narrative. This revision retains the balance and compactness that have pleased past users of the book.

In writing and revising our text, we've kept its primary users—the students—first in mind. *Light & Shadows* is still comprehensive and a valuable reference tool, but we've refrained from subjecting students to an encyclopedic barrage of birth and death dates, film titles, and footnotes. In short, we've not let data overwhelm and obscure what we think is an exciting story. We've made sure that *Light & Shadows* stays both entertaining *and* informative.

However, we have kept instructors in mind, too, and have been careful to retain ingredients that have particularly pleased them: the in-depth discussions of movies and morals, the rich material on the workings of the film industry (especially on the evolution of the studio system), and the stimulating coverage of film in the early age of television.

▶ CHANGES TO THE THIRD EDITION

Despite our belief in the original premise and promise of *Light & Shadows,* as authors we felt some changes were necessary in this edition. In the first and second editions, we divided our chapters up according to the various elements of our grid: the technical and industrial aspects of film, with some chapters treating the social and artistic aspects. This made developing a consistent narrative somewhat cumbersome. The major change in this third edition of *Light & Shadows* is a more strictly chronology-bound narrative. We've incorporated all the major elements of our grid within each individual chapter, but this restructuring has allowed us to expose and spotlight the major threads of the story as they occur, rather than being bound by an artificial division of film history into strictly technical, social, artistic, and industrial forces.

Though redistributed according to time period, most of the material dealing with film's function in reflecting social conditions and thought has been retained, as has the evolution of the production, distribution, and exhibition arms of the industry.

As we've already mentioned, we have considerably expanded coverage of film's artistic evolution — both in text and photographs. Notably, the material on the German and Soviet silent film benefited by this expansion; each now merits its own chapter.

Our coverage of American silent film has always drawn high marks. To this material we've added increased coverage of the landmark films of the day. Consequently, one of the book's strongest features is now even better. Similarly, the chapter on the emergence of sound now deals more specifically with the impact of sound on film art and aesthetics. The studio styles chapter, another that instructors applaud, has also benefited from a stronger emphasis on the aesthetic and artistic strengths and characteristics of the American studio film. Other major changes include an ambitious updating of trends in the genre film, increased coverage of recent U.S., European, and Third World movements, and a re-examination of what we call the "film experience" from the perspective of the mid-1980s.

Several other features are particularly noteworthy:

- More than double the number of photographs. As in previous editions, we've developed a mix of photographs that illustrate the classic films as well as capture the texture of the time being studied.

- Expanded captions with capsule descriptions that go beyond the text discussion. For many readers for whom only the title of a particular film is familiar, the captions explain something of its substance, style, or significance.

- In each chapter, to complement the text and photos, primary documents from the era being studied are spotlighted in a series of boxes. We've relied mainly on primary documentation for this material, to heighten the immediacy of the chapter, to reinforce our text's scholarship, and to provide an even richer variety of points of view.

- A detailed chronology that brings together in concise and graphic form the people, events, and films that have all contributed to the heritage and evolution of the medium. Many instructors have told us that students need a "time fix" on important events that actually occurred simultaneously but now must be covered in separate chapters. (One instructor said: "Sometimes my students get confused. They think *Potemkin* was made while the Keystone Kops were running around Sennett's studios.") In snapshot fashion, the chronology can provide students with a quick overall time orientation.

- Chapter overviews that bring into sharp focus the material about to be presented.

- Chapter summaries that recap and reinforce points made in the foregoing material.

- A completely updated bibliography.

Many instructors have told us they prefer our text because it is "teachable." We believe that these new features add considerably to our text's value as a teaching tool.

▶ INTRODUCTORY ASSUMPTIONS

The scope, design, and direction of this book are strongly influenced by the factors that make film unique. No other art is so interdependent with the worlds of commerce and technology. No other medium so completely fulfills the functions of both high art and popular culture. Film clearly reflects contemporary social thought — the fears, joys, obsessions, and taboos of its time — and it just as surely reinforces and modifies our understanding, attitudes, and beliefs about the world around us. In addition, for all this interaction, film is often a strongly personal medium reflecting the dreams, ideas, and inspirations of producers, directors, screenwriters, and actors as well as audiences themselves.

The history of motion pictures, then, is necessarily the history of an industry, of technology, society, art, and personality. Furthermore, this history reflects not only independent parallel events but strongly interdependent activities as well.

However, this book is more than a chronology of films and personalities. It is an integrated story of the experiences that influenced film's artistic expression, industrial advancement, and social interaction.

We believe that a history of this young and exciting medium should be more than an accounting of titles, synopses, and production notations. As authors, therefore, we have brought with us the biases that have been and remain a part of our movie experiences. Thus *Light & Shadows* is not an "objective" history: The authors have a point of view and present opinions as well as statements of fact. Behind these opinions and facts, however, is a history of motion pictures, the people who made them, and the people who viewed them. Above all else, this interaction between medium, maker, and audience defines the essence of film history and provides the structure of this particular narrative.

Several editorial decisions should perhaps be explained. We have dated films according to the year of release—that is, when they were first shown publicly. As for titles of foreign films, we have chosen to be inconsistent if not arbitrary in the use of original versus translated or U.S. release titles. Our reasoning here is that the titles of certain films have become so familiar to the reader/viewer in one form or the other that the introduction of the less-known or indeed obscure version of the title would add little to the usefulness of the text and would risk confusion. For example, de Sica's 1948 film is best known and therefore best identified as *Bicycle Thief* in this country; Fellini's film is *La Dolce Vita* and Buñuel's *Belle de Jour* for most people. So, in each case we have chosen the most recognizable title.

The reception by both students and teachers of film to the first two editions of this work has been especially gratifying. Our satisfaction with such enthusiastic response must finally be tempered with the responsibility to not simply polish the prose and document recent film happenings but to strive further in providing an accurate, readable, and insightful study of the people, films, and phenomena that have been a part of this medium's evolution.

ACKNOWLEDGMENTS

If we have succeeded at all in our endeavor it is largely through the efforts of a number of people whose assistance we would like to acknowledge. For their generous help and cooperation through succeeding editions we would once more like to thank John Kuiper, Rita Horowitz, Colin McArthur, Arthur Weld, and Marty Norden. For special help in finding the right words and pictures for the third edition we are grateful to Seymour Rudin, Walther Volbach and Mary Corliss at the Museum of Modern Art/Film Still Archive. A gracious thanks to Karen Davis, whose ability to "read between the lines" made for a typed manuscript that was both clean and functional. We give special thanks to David Andrews for his help and encouragement; his unflagging determination and "true grit" were vital in bringing this project to fruition. And for her keen perception and sensibility in the production of the new edition, our gratitude to Jan deProsse at Mayfield. Thanks also to Suzanne Lipsett for her editorial assistance and to the colleagues who reviewed portions of the manuscript for this edition: Charles F. Beadle, Jr., Texas Christian University; William D. Hannan, Black Hawk College; Stuart Kaminsky, Northwestern University; Frank Scheide, University of Arkansas; and Tom Stempel, Los Angeles City College.

We want to especially acknowledge Dan Johnson, not only for his chapter on documentary film in this edition, but also for his contributions to this book's previous editions. He has provided a sense of spirit and passion that has enlivened our discourse in this text.

DEDICATION

For their patience and understanding
through the light and shadows of revision,
we dedicate this third edition
with love to our wives,
Donna and Pip.

A Film Chronology

	TECHNOLOGY	INDUSTRY AND CONTROLS
1450–1500	Leonardo da Vinci produces his "camera obscura" theory.	
1600–1650	Kircher develops his magic lantern. ▶	
1822	Joseph Niepce produces the first photograph.	
1824	Roget presents his theory of "persistence of vision."	
1829–1850	Optical toys are produced using phase drawings to suggest motion. Louis Daguerre develops a workable system of photography (1839).	
1870–1887	The motion picture camera is invented and refined.	
1888	George Eastman begins to produce and market roll film.	Edison turns over the development of the motion picture to W. L. Dickson.
1889	W. L. Dickson projects film in the Edison Studio.	
1891	Edison patents the Kinetoscope "peep show."	
1894	The first motion picture studio, "The Black Maria," is constructed by Dickson in West Orange, N.J. ▼	The first Kinetoscope parlor opens in New York.
1895	The Lumière brothers demonstrate their projection system, the "cinematographe."	Edison fails to secure foreign patent for the Kinetoscope.

THE SILENT FILM ERA

1896		Charles Pathé founds the Pathé-Frères Company.
1897		In the first censorship case, a judge calls a wedding night pantomime "an outrage on public decency."

ART AND ARTISTS	KEY FILMS	SOCIOPOLITICAL ENVIRONMENT
		Gutenberg introduces printing with movable type, in Europe.
		Galileo makes a mathematical description of falling objects.
		The Remington Company begins manufacturing the typewriter.
		The first major exhibit of Impressionist paintings is held in Paris.
		Electricity is first used to drive machinery.
	Fred Ott's Sneeze (U.S.) ▲	
The first public showing of a motion picture takes place in Paris.	▶ *L'Arroseur arrosée* (France)	
The first public showing of a motion picture takes place in the U.S.	*The Kiss* (U.S.)	McKinley is elected U.S. president. The U.S. suffers severe economic recession. Utah becomes a state.
Méliès begins producing films in his Paris studio.		

TECHNOLOGY	INDUSTRY AND CONTROLS
1898	
1899	Federal law prohibits interstate transport of prize-fight films.
1900	
1901	Edison wins a patent-infringement suit against Biograph.
1902	Edison loses the patent suit on appeal.
1903	Georges Méliès opens a New York branch of Star Films.
1904	
1905 The first color films are produced through hand tinting.	A call is made for improvement in theater health and safety codes and supervision of children in attendance.
1906	
1907 Lumière invents color photography.	Official prior censorship of movies begins in Chicago.
1908	The Motion Picture Patents Company is formed.
1909	The National Board of Motion Picture Censorship is formed (it will become the National Board of Review).

ART AND ARTISTS	KEY FILMS	SOCIOPOLITICAL ENVIRONMENT
	Cripple Creek (U.S.) *Barroom* (U.S.)	The Spanish-American War begins. Hawaii is annexed to the U.S.
Edison hires Edwin S. Porter as electrician and handyman.	*Cinderella* (France)	
		The Boxer Uprising occurs in China.
		U.S. President McKinley is assassinated. J. P. Morgan forms U.S. Steel.
Screen narrative begins.	*A Trip to the Moon* ▲ (France)	The Wright brothers make the first flight.
	The Great Train Robbery (U.S.) *Uncle Tom's Cabin* (U.S.)	The first radio message is sent from the U.S. to England. The Russo-Japanese War begins.
		Construction on the Panama Canal begins.
The first nickelodeon opens in Pittsburgh.	*Rescued by Rover* (G.B.)	The St. Petersburg revolt and *Potemkin* mutiny occurs. Japan defeats Russia.
Single-reel film (nine to eleven minutes) becomes standard length.	*Dream of a Rarebit Fiend* (U.S.)	Industrial Workers of the World is founded in the U.S.
	Ben Hur (U.S.)	Oklahoma is admitted to the union. Immigration into the U.S. is restricted. Gorky's *Mother* is published.
The French *"Film d'art"* movement is founded. Griffith joins the Biograph Company.	*The Adventures of Dollie* (U.S.)	A New York journalist reports on a race riot in Springfield, Massachusetts, and describes the plight of U.S. blacks in *The Independent*. U.S. banks close as the economic depression continues.
Film companies begin migrating to Southern California.	*The Lonely Villa* (U.S.)	The U.S. and Japan make a gentlemen's agreement binding Japan to issue no further passports to Japanese citizens intending to immigrate directly to the U.S. The Westinghouse Company goes bankrupt. Half of all Americans live on farms or in towns of less than 2,500; the country has 6 million farms. The NAACP (National Association for the Advancement of Colored People) is organized in N.Y. Delaware forbids the employment of children under 14. The U.S. has 2,600 daily newspapers to serve 90 million people. U.S. automobile production reaches 127,731. Perry reaches the North Pole.

ADJUSTING FILM
Show Will Continue
in
a
Few
Minutes

No. C 6

TECHNOLOGY	INDUSTRY AND CONTROLS
1910 Pioneer work in animation using a "cell" system is begun.	William Fox wins a suit against MPPC, allowing him to distribute films. Open warfare ensues between MPPC and the independent film companies.
1911	The first state censorship law appears in Pennsylvania.
1912	An antitrust suit is brought against MPPC by the Taft administration. The Motion Picture Copyright Law is passed.
1913	Comprehensive censorship laws are enacted in New York City.
1914	A Chicago ordinance allows the showing of certain films to persons over 21. Paramount Pictures is formed.
1915	Legislation calling for federal censorship of movies is introduced in Congress. The Supreme Court disallows movies First Amendment protection on the grounds that motion picture production is "a business pure and simple." Ince, Sennett, and Griffith form the Triangle Company.
1916 Refinements in scenic design are introduced.	The Smith-Hughes bill is introduced in Congress, calling for establishment of a federal motion picture commission to censor films. The bill dies.

ART AND ARTISTS	KEY FILMS	SOCIOPOLITICAL ENVIRONMENT
D. W. Griffith produces *His Trust*, the first two-reel film. "Imp" Company begins the promotion of stars. ▼	*His Trust* (U.S.) *His Trust Fulfilled* (U.S.)	The U.S. population reaches 92 million, with 13.5 million foreign born. The average U.S. worker earns less than $15 per week; work hours range from 54 to 60 hours per week, and there is a wide irregularity in employment. The Mann-Elkin Act (Interstate Commerce Act) is passed. The Mann-White Slave Traffic Act is passed (making illegal the interstate transportation of women for immoral purposes). Freud's *Psychoanalysis* is published.
Griffith's *Enoch Arden* is the first two-reel film to be released.	*Enoch Arden* (U.S.) *The Lonedale Operator* (U.S.)	New York's Ellis Island has a record one-day influx of 11,745 immigrants. The U.S. population reaches 94 million. The population of Great Britain reaches 40.8 million; England and Wales, 36 million; Ireland, 4.3 million; France, 39.6 million; Italy, 34.6 million; Japan, 52 million; Russia, 167 million; India, 315 million; China, 425 million.
Sennett forms the Keystone Company. The first fan magazine, *Photoplay*, appears.	*Queen Elizabeth* (France) *Quo Vadis?* (Italy)	China is proclaimed a republic. Woodrow Wilson is elected U.S. president. New Mexico and Arizona are admitted to the Union.
Chaplin joins the Keystone Company. De Mille produces his first film.	*Nights of Cabiria* (Italy) *Judith of Bethulia* (U.S.)	The U.S. has 40 percent of world industrial production, up from 20 percent in 1860. Einstein reveals his theory of relativity.
The first movie palace, the Strand, opens in New York City.	*Tillie's Punctured Romance* (U.S.) *The Perils of Pauline* (U.S.)	Suffragettes march on Washington to demand voting rights for U.S. women. The assassination of Crown Duke Ferdinand sparks World War I. The Panama Canal opens. The term *birth control* is introduced by U.S. feminist Margaret Higgings Sanger in her publication, *The Woman Rebel*. U.S. auto production reaches 543,679.
The Birth of a Nation is shown at the White House.	*The Birth of a Nation* (U.S.)	U.S. racial tensions are heightened by Griffith's *The Birth of a Nation*, which has racist aspects. A new Ku Klux Klan is founded on Thanksgiving night at Stone Mountain.
	Intolerance (U.S.) *Civilization* (U.S.) *The Pawnshop* (U.S.)	World War I in Europe takes a heavy toll; U.S. remains neutral. President Wilson wins re-election in U.S. A polio epidemic strikes in the U.S.

TECHNOLOGY	INDUSTRY AND CONTROLS

1917

The MPPC is ruled an illegal conspiracy in restraint of trade and is dissolved.

A merger of major German film companies (Ufa) brings construction of huge new studios.

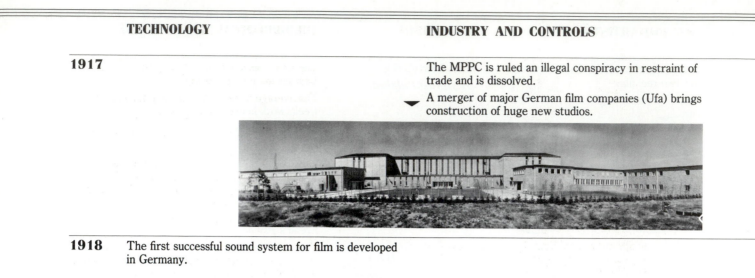

1918 The first successful sound system for film is developed in Germany.

1919

The first "Red Scare" hits Hollywood.

1920

1921

The Federal Trade Commission issues formal complaints against several film companies for their practice of block booking.

The film industry is rocked by scandals.

Wall Street begins substantial investment in the film industry.

ART AND ARTISTS	KEY FILMS	SOCIOPOLITICAL ENVIRONMENT
	◣ *Easy Street* (U.S.)	Russian troops mutiny following two days of strikes and riots at Petrograd. The February Revolution takes place in Russia. Kerensky proclaims Russia a republic. The Bolshevik Revolution begins at Petrograd on the night of November 6. The Kerensky government falls, and a new government, headed by Lenin, takes office on November 7 under the name of the Council of People's Commissions. The U.S. declares war on Germany.
	Blind Husbands (U.S.)	Russia's new Bolshevik government withdraws from the "Capitalist-Imperialist" war on March 3 by signing the treaty of Brest-Litovsk with Germany. Russia's royal Romanov family is shot to death July 16 by order of the Bolsheviks.
Pickford, Fairbanks, Chaplin, and Griffith form United Artists. The Soviet film industry is nationalized and a film school, headed by Lenin's wife, is founded in Moscow.	*Broken Blossoms* (U.S.) *Sir Arne's Treasure* (Sweden) ◣ *The Cabinet of Dr. Caligari* (Germany) *Male and Female* (U.S.)	The Treaty of Versailles is signed, ending World War I. A new German Republic is established with its constituent assembly at Weimar. The first direct trans-Atlantic flight takes place.
A print of Griffith's *Intolerance* is studied continuously at the Kuleshov workshop.	*Way Down East* (U.S.) *The Golem* (Germany) *The Phantom Chariot* (Sweden)	The world population reaches 1.86 billion. Abortion is legalized in Soviet Russia by a decree of the Lenin government. Berlin is seized on March 13 in a right-wing German *putsch* headed by the American-born Journalist Wolfgang Kapp. Transcontinental air-mail service begins in the U.S. The first public broadcasting stations open in England and the U.S. Prohibition takes effect in the U.S. Joan of Arc is canonized. The Nineteenth Amendment gives U.S. women the right to vote.
Buster Keaton establishes himself as a leading film comedian. Charlie Chaplin expands films to short feature length.	*Destiny* (Germany) *The Kid* (U.S.) *The Four Horsemen of the Apocalypse* (U.S.) *Orphans of the Storm* (U.S.) *Tol'able David* (U.S.)	Famine kills 3 million Russians. A Russian Famine Relief Act is passed by Congress ($20 million). Warren Harding becomes U.S. president. An Emergency Quota Immigration Act is passed. Fascists win the general election in Italy.

TECHNOLOGY	INDUSTRY AND CONTROLS
1922 Lee De Forest develops a sound system for film.	The Motion Picture Producers and Distributors Association (Hays Office) is formed for self-regulation of film.

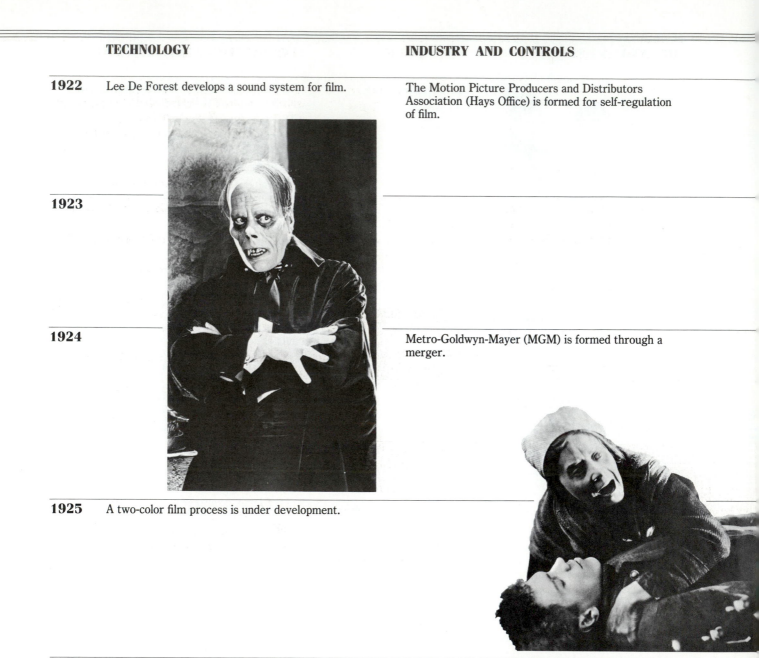

1923

1924

Metro-Goldwyn-Mayer (MGM) is formed through a merger.

1925 A two-color film process is under development.

1926

Renewed attempts to form a federal motion picture commission fail in Congress.

ART AND ARTISTS	KEY FILMS	SOCIOPOLITICAL ENVIRONMENT
Felix the Cat, the first popular cartoon character, appears.	 *Nosferatu* (Germany) *Foolish Wives* (U.S.) *Nanook of the North* (U.S.)	The German stock market collapses in August, and the mark falls in value from 162 to the dollar to more than 7,000 to the dollar. The German foreign minister is murdered by nationalist reactionaries. Pope Benedict dies. King Tut's tomb is discovered at Luxor.
Harold Lloyd joins Chaplin and Keaton as a top film comic. Ernst Lubitsch migrates to Hollywood.	*The Covered Wagon* (U.S.) *Safety Last* (U.S.) *The Ten Command-ments* (U.S.) *A Woman of Paris* (U.S.)	Adolf Hitler, 34, stages a "Beer Hall *Putsch*" at Munich on November 8. The Union of Soviet Socialist Republic (U.S.S.R.) is established. The U.S. resumes diplomatic relations with Mexico. Calvin Coolidge becomes U.S. president following the death of Warren Harding.
	The Marriage Circle (U.S.) *The Story of Gosta Berling* (Sweden) *Waxworks* (Germany) *The Last Laugh* (Germany) *Strike* (U.S.S.R.) *Greed* (U.S.) *The Iron Horse* (U.S.)	Lenin dies at age 53. Nationalists and Communists are defeated in German elections. A new bill further limits U.S. immigration (Japanese are barred). Calvin Coolidge is elected U.S. president.
The French avant-garde movement begins.	*The Joyless Street* (Germany) *Variety* (Germany) *Potemkin* (U.S.S.R.) *The Gold Rush* (U.S.) *The Big Parade* (U.S.) *The Phantom of the Opera* (U.S.) *The Freshman* (U.S.)	The Russo-Japanese Treaty is signed. Von Hindenburg is elected president of Germany. The Scopes "Monkey Trial" takes place in Tennessee.
A major migration of German film artists to Hollywood takes place.	*Metropolis* (Germany) *Mother* (U.S.S.R.) *Moana* (U.S.) *What Price Glory?* (U.S.) *Ben-Hur* (U.S.)	Stalin establishes himself as virtual dictator of the Soviet Union, beginning a 27-year rule. Berlin Treaty of reassurance between Russia and Germany is signed. A general strike takes place in Britain. Television is invented.

TECHNOLOGY	INDUSTRY AND CONTROLS

THE SOUND ERA

1927 Warner's Vitaphone ushers in the sound era.

Abel Gance introduces triple-screen projection with *Napoleon*.

The Federal Trade Commission orders Paramount to stop block-booking practices, but its ruling is overturned.

1928 The first Academy Awards are presented.

1929

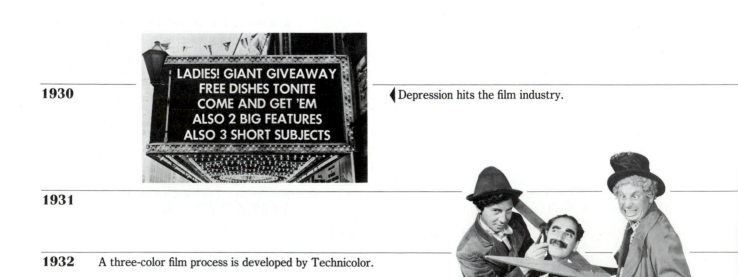

1930 ◄ Depression hits the film industry.

LADIES! GIANT GIVEAWAY FREE DISHES TONITE COME AND GET 'EM ALSO 2 BIG FEATURES ALSO 3 SHORT SUBJECTS

1931

1932 A three-color film process is developed by Technicolor.

1933

ART AND ARTISTS	KEY FILMS	SOCIOPOLITICAL ENVIRONMENT
The Jazz Singer opens in New York. William Fox initiates "Movietone News" for movie theaters. The Roxy, the world's largest movie theater, opens in New York.	*The End of St. Petersburg* (U.S.S.R.) *Ten Days That Shook the World* (U.S.S.R.) *The Italian Straw Hat* (France) *Napoleon* (France) *The General* (U.S.) *Sunrise* (U.S.) *Underworld* (U.S.) *The Jazz Singer* (U.S.)	Stalin expels Leon Trotsky from the Central Communist Party. Relations between Russia and China are broken off. "Black Friday" breakdown of the German economic system occurs. Military control of Germany is abolished. Lindbergh makes the first solo trans-Atlantic flight.
	The Passion of Joan of Arc (France) *Storm Over Asia* (U.S.S.R.) *The Lights of New York* (U.S.) *Un Chien Andalou* (France)	Stalin launches the first Five-Year Plan. Leftist parties win the German election. Herbert Hoover is elected U.S. president. Chiang Kai-shek is elected president of China. Amelia Earhart flies the Atlantic.
	Arsenal (U.S.S.R.) *Hallelujah!* (U.S.) *The Love Parade* (U.S.) *Wings* (U.S.)	Trotsky is expelled from Russia. The Soviet Congress approves a five-year plan. A stock market crash on Wall Street leads to worldwide depression. The airship *Graf Zeppelin* flies around the world. Unrest occurs between Jews and Arabs in Palestine. U.S. Congress limits immigration to 150,000.
	The Blue Angel (Germany) *Earth* (U.S.S.R.) *Anna Christie* (U.S.) *All Quiet on the Western Front* (U.S.)	Mahatma Gandhi begins his civil disobedience campaign.
Griffith directs his last film.	*M* (Germany) *Little Caesar* (U.S.) *The Front Page* (U.S.)	Japan invades Manchuria.
	Tarzan the Ape Man (U.S.) *I Am a Fugitive from a Chain Gang* (U.S.)	
The British Film Institute is founded.	*Duck Soup* (U.S.) *King Kong* (U.S.) *The Private Life of Henry VIII* (G.B.) *Zéro de Conduite* (France)	Franklin Roosevelt is inaugurated as U.S. president; he declares a bank holiday and establishes the National Industrial Recovery Act and other emergency measures. The 21st Amendment repeals the 18th (Prohibition) Amendment.

TECHNOLOGY	INDUSTRY AND CONTROLS
1934	The Catholic Legion of Decency is founded.
1935 *Becky Sharp* (U.S.) becomes the first feature film in Technicolor.	20th-Century-Fox is incorporated; Republic Pictures is founded.

1936	
1937	
1938	The average Hollywood feature film cost $125,000. An antitrust suit is filed against Paramount.
1939	The National Film Board of Canada is formed.

ART AND ARTISTS	KEY FILMS	SOCIOPOLITICAL ENVIRONMENT
	Man of Aran (G.B.) *It Happened One Night* (U.S.) *L'Atalante* (France) *Triumph of the Will* (Germany)	Hitler becomes Leader and Chancellor of Germany.
The Museum of Modern Art Film Library is established.	*The Thirty-Nine Steps* (G.B.) *The Informer* (U.S.) *Mutiny on the Bounty* (U.S.) ➤ *Top Hat* (U.S.) *Night Mail* (G.B.) *A Night at the Opera* (U.S.)	The Social Security Act is signed. The Nuremberg Laws make the swastika the official flag of the Reich and ban Jews.
La Cinemathèque Française, national archive of film, is founded in Paris. Irving Thalberg dies.	*Modern Times* (U.S.) *Mr. Deeds Goes to Town* (U.S.) *Fury* (U.S.) *Things to Come* (G.B.) *The Plow That Broke the Plains* (U.S.)	Edward VIII abdicates as King of England. Franco is appointed Chief of the Spanish state.
	Grand Illusion (France) *Captains Courageous* (U.S.) *The Life of Emile Zola* (U.S.) *Dead End* (U.S.) *The River* (U.S.) *The Good Earth* (U.S.)	Japan invades China.
Georges Méliès dies.	*Alexander Nevsky* (U.S.S.R.) *The Lady Vanishes* (G.B.) *Olympia* (Germany) *Bringing up Baby* (U.S.) *Snow White and the Seven Dwarfs* (U.S.)	The Munich Pact is signed, effectively turning Czechoslovakia over to Germany.
	Gone with the Wind (U.S.) *The Rules of the Game* (France) ◀ *Stagecoach* (U.S.) *The Wizard of Oz* (U.S.) *The Stars Look Down* (G.B.) *Ninotchka* (U.S.)	The German invasion of Poland begins World War II.

TECHNOLOGY	INDUSTRY AND CONTROLS
1940 RCA demonstrates stereophonic sound in Disney's *Fantasia*.	The consent decree abolishes block-booking and "blind selling."
1941 The first regularly scheduled television transmission begins in the U.S. 16 mm. color film begins to be used for some short subject films.	The U.S. Senate investigates the motion picture industry on charges of "war-mongering"; Joe Breen resigns as head of the Production Code.
1942	The U.S. Government orders censorship of all motion pictures, as a wartime security move. 22 percent of all Hollywood male personnel are in the armed forces.
1943	The War Production Board limits the cost of a motion picture set to $5,000; night photography is banned.
1944 Technicolor Monopack process allows the use of a standard camera for color photography.	
1945	The cinema is nationalized in Czechoslovakia, Poland, and Yugoslavia. Will Hays resigns as head of the MPPDA.

ART AND ARTISTS	KEY FILMS	SOCIOPOLITICAL ENVIRONMENT
Hattie McDaniel becomes the first black to win an Oscar, for her role in *Gone with the Wind*.	*The Great Dictator* (U.S.) *The Grapes of Wrath* (U.S.) *Gaslight* (G.B.) *Fantasia* (U.S.) *The Philadelphia Story* (U.S.) *Rebecca* (U.S.)	Roosevelt is re-elected for a third term as U.S. President. Germany occupies France and begins aerial bombardment of Great Britain.
	Citizen Kane (U.S.) *Meet John Doe* (U.S.) *Sergeant York* (U.S.) *The Maltese Falcon* (U.S.) *Listen to Britain* (G.B.)	The Japanese attack on Pearl Harbor brings the U.S. into World War II. Germany invades Russia; Stalin becomes Soviet premier.
The term "neo-realism" is coined in Italy.	*Mrs. Miniver* (U.S.) *In Which We Serve* (G.B.) *Ossessione* (Italy) *Yankee Doodle Dandy* (U.S.) *The Magnificent Ambersons* (U.S.)	World War II key battles fought: Coral Sea, Midway, Guadalcanal; more than 500,000 Americans are in the armed forces serving overseas.
Eisenstein publishes *The Film Sense*.	*For Whom the Bell Tolls* (U.S.) *The Oxbow Incident* (U.S.) *Casablanca* (U.S.) *Day of Wrath* (Denmark)	W-2 Withholding Tax Act is signed. Mussolini resigns as premier of Italy.
	Open City (Italy) *Wilson* (U.S.) *Going My Way* (U.S.) *Ivan the Terrible* (U.S.S.R.) *Meet Me in St. Louis* (U.S.) *The Miracle of Morgan's Creek* (U.S.)	The Allied invasion of Normandy takes place (D-Day). The GI Bill is signed. Roosevelt is re-elected for a fourth term.
UPA animation group is founded.	*Les Enfants du Paradis* (France) *A Walk in the Sun* (U.S.) *Mildred Pierce* (U.S.) *The Lost Weekend* (U.S.) *The Bells of St. Mary's* (U.S.) *Brief Encounter* (G.B.)	The atomic bomb is dropped on Hiroshima and Nagasaki. Germany and Japan surrender, ending World War II. The United Nations Charter is signed. Roosevelt dies; Truman succeeds him as U.S. President.

	TECHNOLOGY	**INDUSTRY AND CONTROLS**

1946

Film company revenues hit an all-time high.

Code Seal of Approval is withdrawn from *The Outlaw.*

1947 The zoom lens is developed.

The HUAC investigates alleged Communist subversion in the motion picture industry.

Britain imposes a 75% import tax on foreign films.

1948 The transistor is invented.

Columbia Records introduces the 33⅓-rpm long-playing record.

The "Hollywood 10" are found guilty of contempt of Congress and blacklisted from the motion picture industry.

The Supreme Court outlaws block-booking.

1949

1950

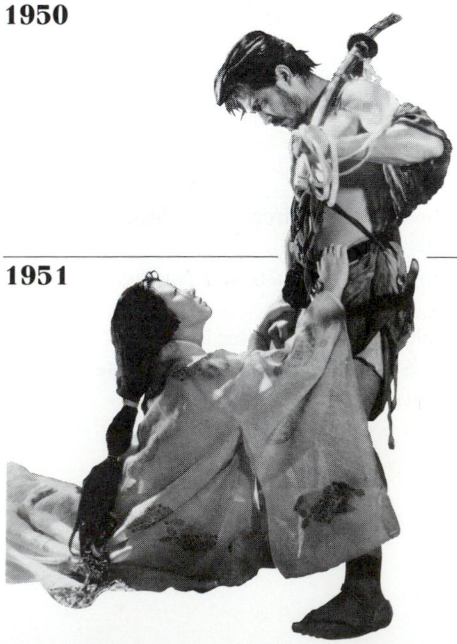

The "Paramount decision" orders studios to sell their theaters.

1951

Arthur Krim and Robert Benjamin take control of United Artists from Mary Pickford and Charles Chaplin.

Decca Records buys Universal.

Columbia establishes Screen Gems.

ART AND ARTISTS	KEY FILMS	SOCIOPOLITICAL ENVIRONMENT
First Cannes Film Festival is held. W. C. Fields and William S. Hart die.	*The Best Years of Our Lives* (U.S.) *My Darling Clementine* (U.S.) *Shoeshine* (Italy) *Great Expectations* (G.B.) *The Spiral Staircase* (U.S.) *The Big Sleep* (U.S.)	Calculation by computer begins at the University of Pennsylvania. Winston Churchill delivers his "Iron Curtain" speech.
Lee Strasberg founds the Actor's Studio. Ernst Lubitsch dies.	*Odd Man Out* (G.B.) *Gentleman's Agreement* (U.S.) *Crossfire* (U.S.)	India gains independence. The Loyalty Oath act is signed. The World Bank is established. The Taft-Hartley Labor Law is passed by Congress.
D. W. Griffith dies.	*Red River* (U.S.) *The Snake Pit* (U.S.) *Louisiana Story* (U.S.) *The Red Shoes* (G.B.) *Hamlet* (G.B.) *Key Largo* (U.S.) *The Treasure of the Sierra Madre* (U.S.)	Mahatma Gandhi is assassinated. Israel achieves independence. The U.S. Supreme Court abolishes teaching of religion in the classroom. The Marshall Plan is enacted. Harry Truman is elected U.S. president.
A cycle of anti-racial prejudice films emerges.	*The Bicycle Thief* (Italy) *On the Town* (U.S.) *Intruder in the Dust* (U.S.) *White Heat* (U.S.) *All the King's Men* (U.S.) *The Third Man* (G.B.)	The Chinese People's Republic is proclaimed. The NATO pact is signed. The Berlin blockade crisis takes place.
The "Zagreb School" of animation is founded in Yugoslavia.	*The Miracle* (Italy) *Sunset Boulevard* (U.S.) *All About Eve* (U.S.) *The Men* (U.S.) *Rashomon* (Japan) *Orpheus* (France) *The Gunfighter* (U.S.)	The Korean War breaks out.
Robert Flaherty dies.	*A Streetcar Named Desire* (U.S.) *The Lavender Hill Mob* (G.B.) *African Queen* (U.S.) *An American in Paris* (U.S.) *Miss Julie* (Sweden) *The Diary of a Country Priest* (France)	General MacArthur is dismissed. 250,000 U.S. troops are sent to Korea.

	TECHNOLOGY	INDUSTRY AND CONTROLS
1952	Cinerama debuts.	The HUAC investigate and report on Communism in the industry.
		The Miracle Supreme Court decision is made.
		FCC Sixth Order reports on television licensing and expansion.
1953	*Bwana Devil* becomes the first 3-D film. CinemaScope is introduced. ▶	Otto Preminger releases *The Moon Is Blue* without Code approval. 
1954	VistaVision wide screen is introduced by Paramount.	The U.S. Supreme Court strikes down censor's use of "immorality."
		Will Hays dies.
		The Federal excise tax on motion picture tickets is cut from 20% to 10%.
1955	Todd-AO process is used for *Oklahoma*.	RKO sells its feature films to television.
		Howard Hughes sells his studio to General Tire.
1956		The Fund for the Republic publishes a blacklisting study by John Cogley.
		Nicholas Schenck resigns from MGM after fifty years in the industry.
		Major studios sell pre-1948 films to TV.
1957		All weekly U.S. newsreel companies give up theatrical service.
		Louis B. Mayer dies.
		The new Production Code goes into effect.

ART AND ARTISTS	KEY FILMS	SOCIOPOLITICAL ENVIRONMENT
	High Noon (U.S.) *Singin' in the Rain* (U.S.) *Forbidden Games* (France) *Umberto D* (Italy) *The Wages of Fear* (France)	Dwight Eisenhower is elected President of the U.S. Queen Elizabeth ascends to the British throne. The hydrogen bomb is exploded by the U.S.
V. I. Pudovkin dies.	*The Moon Is Blue* (U.S.) *Shane* (U.S.) *From Here to Eternity* (U.S.) *Mr. Hulot's Holiday* (France) *I Vitelloni* (Italy) *The Great Adventure* (Sweden)	Stalin dies and is succeeded by Malenkov. The Rosenbergs are executed for treason. The Korean War ends.
Science fiction films represent a new cycle.	*A Star Is Born* (U.S.) *Rear Window* (U.S.) *Gate of Hell* (Japan) *On the Waterfront* (U.S.) *La Strada* (Italy)	The U.S. Supreme Court declares racial segregation in U.S. schools unconstitutional. The McCarthy hearings begin.
▼ James Dean dies. 	*Marty* (U.S.) *Rebel Without a Cause* (U.S.) *Diabolique* (France) *Pather Panchali* (India) *The Blackboard Jungle* (U.S.) *Night and Fog* (France)	The U.S. and Nationalist China sign a defense pact. Churchill resigns as Prime Minister of Great Britain. The Salk polio vaccine is tested. South Vietnam is declared a republic.
	The Man with the Golden Arm (U.S.) *Giant* (U.S.) *Around the World in 80 Days* (U.S.) *Baby Doll* (U.S.) *The Searchers* (U.S.) *The Seventh Seal* (Sweden) *The Burmese Harp* (Japan)	Eisenhower is re-elected president of the U.S. Blacks engage in sit-in and boycott of buses in Montgomery, Alabama. Britain gives up rule of Suez Canal Zone. Russia crushes the Hungarian rebellion. Israel attacks Egypt.
Eric von Stroheim, Humphrey Bogart, and Max Ophüls die.	*The Ten Commandments* (U.S.) *The Bridge on the River Kwai* (U.S.) *The Cranes Are Flying* (U.S.S.R.) *Throne of Blood* (Japan) *Wild Strawberries* (Sweden)	The first earth satellite (Sputnik I) is placed into orbit by the U.S.S.R. Black students are prevented from enrolling in Central High School, Little Rock, Arkansas.

TECHNOLOGY	INDUSTRY AND CONTROLS
1958	Republic Studio closes.
	Harry Cohn, President of Columbia, dies.
	Fifty percent of U.S. features are now made by independents.
1959	Japan leads world film production with 493 features.

1960	The Writers Guild of America and the Screen Actors Guild strike studios.
	Studios lease post-1948 films to TV.
1961	The U.S. Supreme Court upholds local censorship of motion pictures.
1962 Telstar launches trans-Atlantic television.	The U.S. produces only 138 feature films.
	MCA buys Decca Records and, with it, Universal Studios.

ART AND ARTISTS	KEY FILMS	SOCIOPOLITICAL ENVIRONMENT
	South Pacific (U.S.) *Cat on a Hot Tin Roof* (U.S.) *Gigi* (U.S.) *The 400 Blows* (France) *Paths of Glory* (U.S.) *Room at the Top* (G.B.) *Ashes and Diamonds* (Poland)	Khrushchev becomes premier of Russia. Explorer I, first U.S. satellite, launched. Pope John XXIII elected.
Cecil B. De Mille dies. "Nouvelle vague" emerges in France.	*Anatomy of a Murder* (U.S.) *Look Back in Anger* (G.B.) *Hiroshima, Mon Amour* (France) *Ben-Hur* (U.S.) *Rio Bravo* (U.S.) *Breathless* (France) *The Virgin Spring* (Sweden)	Fidel Castro gains control of the government in Cuba. Alaska becomes the 49th state; Hawaii becomes the 50th state. TV "quiz scandals" revealed.
Mack Sennett, Clark Gable, and Victor Sjöström die.	*L'Avventura* (Italy) *Spartacus* (U.S.) *Psycho* (U.S.) *The Apartment* (U.S.) *Never on Sunday* (Greece) *Saturday Night and Sunday Morning* (G.B.)	John F. Kennedy is elected U.S. president. "Sit-down" protest begun by blacks in Greensboro, North Carolina.
Gary Cooper dies.	*Jules and Jim* (France) *La Dolce Vita* (Italy) *West Side Story* (U.S.) *Two Women* (Italy) *Last Year at Marienbad* (France) *Viridiana* (Spain)	Building of the Berlin Wall begins. The Peace Corps is created. Russia puts the first man in orbit. The first U.S. military companies arrive in Vietnam.
Marilyn Monroe dies.	*Lawrence of Arabia* (G.B.) *The Manchurian Candidate* (U.S.) *The Longest Day* (U.S.) *Lolita* (U.S.) *Knife in the Water* (Poland)	The Soviet missile crisis takes place in Cuba. John Glenn becomes first U.S. astronaut to make orbital flight. James Meredith denied admission to U. of Mississippi.

TECHNOLOGY	INDUSTRY AND CONTROLS

1963

1964 | The U.S. Supreme Court calls into question the concept of ''community standards'' as a definition of obscenity.

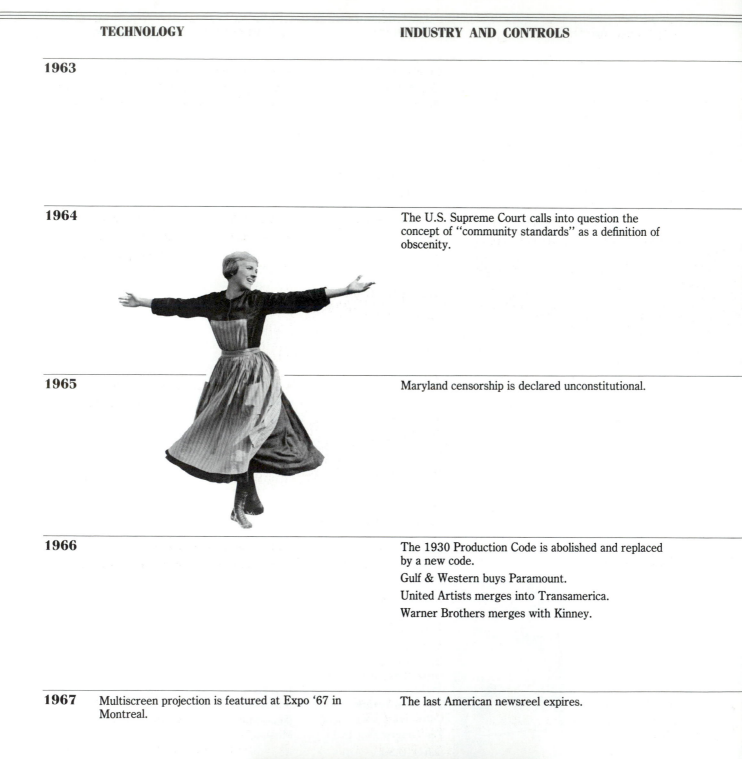

1965 | Maryland censorship is declared unconstitutional.

1966 | The 1930 Production Code is abolished and replaced by a new code.
Gulf & Western buys Paramount.
United Artists merges into Transamerica.
Warner Brothers merges with Kinney.

1967 | Multiscreen projection is featured at Expo '67 in Montreal. | The last American newsreel expires.

ART AND ARTISTS	KEY FILMS	SOCIOPOLITICAL ENVIRONMENT
Jean Cocteau dies.	*Cleopatra* (U.S.) *Hud* (U.S.) *Dr. Strangelove* (G.B.) *This Sporting Life* (G.B.) *Tom Jones* (G.B.) *8½* (Italy) *David and Lisa* (U.S.) *Winter Light* (Sweden)	President Kennedy is assassinated. The civil rights march on Washington, D.C., ends with Martin Luther King, Jr.'s "I Have a Dream" speech.
	My Fair Lady (U.S.) *The Red Desert* (Italy) *A Hard Day's Night* (G.B.) *Woman of the Dunes* (Japan) *Diamonds of the Night* (Czechoslovakia) *The Married Woman* (France)	The Civil Rights Bill is signed into law. Lyndon Johnson is elected U.S. president. The Gulf of Tonkin Resolution is passed by Congress.
David O. Selznick dies.	*The Sound of Music* (U.S.) *The Pawnbroker* (U.S.) *Repulsion* (U.S.) *Darling* (G.B.) *Doctor Zhivago* (U.S.) *Juliet of the Spirits* (Italy) *Help* (G.B.) *Tokyo Olympiad* (Japan)	Watts riot takes place in Los Angeles. U.S. begins air attacks on North Vietnam.
Buster Keaton, Walt Disney, and Robert Rossen die.	*A Man for All Seasons* (G.B.) *Fahrenheit 451* (France) *Persona* (Sweden) *Who's Afraid of Virginia Woolf* (U.S.) *Blow-up* (Italy) *The Shop on Main Street* (Czechoslovakia)	Indira Gandhi becomes Prime Minister of India. Racial riots erupt in Chicago and Cleveland.
The American Film Institute is founded. Spencer Tracy, G. W. Pabst, and Paul Muni die.	*Bonnie and Clyde* (U.S.) *In the Heat of the Night* (U.S.) *The Graduate* (U.S.) *In Cold Blood* (U.S.) *Belle de Jour* (France) *Cool Hand Luke* (U.S.)	The Arab-Israeli Six-Day War takes place. The world's first human heart transplant is attempted. Riots or disturbances erupt in 127 U.S. cities over the summer.

TECHNOLOGY	INDUSTRY AND CONTROLS

1968

The MPAA film rating system is introduced.

As many feature films are now shot in New York as in Hollywood.

1969

1970

Presidential Commission on Pornography releases report.

1971

U.S box office receipts at all-time low.

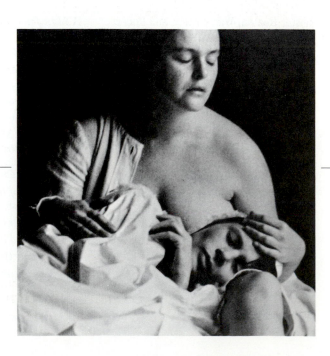

1972

ART AND ARTISTS	KEY FILMS	SOCIOPOLITICAL ENVIRONMENT
	2001: A Space Odyssey (U.S.) *If. . .* (G.B.) *Romeo and Juliet* (Italy) *Z* (France) *Planet of the Apes* (U.S.) *The Lion in Winter* (U.S.) *Rachel, Rachel* (U.S.) *Hour of the Furnaces* (Argentina)	Martin Luther King, Jr., and Robert Kennedy are assassinated. Richard Nixon is elected U.S. president. The Democratic Convention in Chicago is marred by riots. President Johnson signs Civil Rights Act. Pierre Trudeau sworn in as Canadian Prime Minister. Czechoslovakia invaded by Russia.
Judy Garland, Josef von Sternberg die. 	◀ *Easy Rider* (U.S.) *Butch Cassidy and the Sundance Kid* (U.S.) ◀ *Midnight Cowboy* (U.S.) *M*A*S*H* (U.S.) *Alice's Restaurant* (U.S.) *The Wild Bunch* (U.S.)	American astronauts walk on the moon. Woodstock Music Festival is held. Massive student protests on U.S. campuses. Warren Burger becomes Chief Justice of U.S. Supreme Court.
	Catch 22 (U.S.) *Tristana* (Spain) *Women in Love* (G.B.) *Patton* (U.S.) *Five Easy Pieces* (U.S.) *Love Story* (U.S.)	Student protest and killings take place at Kent State University. U.S. troops enter Cambodia. First jumbo jets placed in service.
	Klute (U.S.) *A Clockwork Orange* (U.S.) *Clair's Knee* (France) *The French Connection* (U.S.) *Harold and Maude* (U.S.) *The Last Picture Show* (U.S.) *Straw Dogs* (U.S.) *Little Big Man* (U.S.)	China becomes a member of the U.N. *The New York Times* publishes The Pentagon Papers. Lt. William Calley found guilty of My Lai murders. War erupts between India and Pakistan.
Over two dozen black genre films are produced.	*The Godfather* (U.S.) *The Discreet Charm of the Bourgeoisie* (Spain) ◀ *Cries and Whispers* (Sweden) *The Emmigrants* (Sweden) *Blazing Saddles* (U.S.) *Deliverance* (U.S.) *The Sorrow and the Pity* (France)	President Nixon visits China. Dow-Jones average reaches 1,000.

TECHNOLOGY	INDUSTRY AND CONTROLS
1973	MGM and 20th-Century-Fox sell their back lots. Supreme Court establishes community standards censorship criteria for films.
1974	Supreme Court declares that films may not be frivolously censored.
1975	A hard-core sex film, *Exhibition,* is shown at New York Film Festival for first time.

ART AND ARTISTS	KEY FILMS	SOCIOPOLITICAL ENVIRONMENT
American Film Theatre initiates a subscription series of distinguished filmed plays.	*Last Tango in Paris* (Italy) *Aquirre, The Wrath of God* (Germany) *Sleeper* (U.S.) ◢ *The Sting* (U.S.) *Mean Streets* (U.S.) *The Exorcist* (U.S.)	An agreement is signed to end the Vietnam War. The energy crisis hits the U.S. Televised Watergate hearings begin. Spiro Agnew resigns as U.S. Vice President.
	Amarcord (Italy) *The Godfather II* (U.S.) *Young Frankenstein* (U.S.) *Chinatown* (U.S.) *Scenes from a Marriage* (Sweden) *The Conversation* (U.S.) *Harry and Tonto* (U.S.)	President Nixon resigns; Gerald Ford becomes U.S. President.
	Tommy (G.B.) *The Rocky Horror Picture Show* (G.B.) *Nashville* (U.S.) ◣ *Jaws* (U.S.) *Hearts and Minds* (U.S.) *Alice Doesn't Live Here Anymore* (U.S.)	Top Nixon aides convicted in Watergate hearings.
Toronto Film Festival is established.	*Marathon Man* (U.S.) *All The President's Men* (U.S.) *One Flew over the Cuckoo's Nest* (U.S.) *Rocky* (U.S.) *Network* (U.S.) *Taxi Driver* (U.S.) ▲ *Seven Beauties* (Italy) *Cousin, Cousine* (France)	Jimmy Carter is elected U.S. President. U.S. celebrates Bicentennial.
Charlie Chaplin dies.	*Annie Hall* (U.S.) *The Goodbye Girl* (U.S.) ◀ *Star Wars* (U.S.) *Saturday Night Fever* (U.S.) *That Obscure Object of Desire* (Spain) *Close Encounters of the Third Kind* (U.S.)	Death penalty revived in U.S.

TECHNOLOGY	INDUSTRY AND CONTROLS

1978

Cliff Robertson accuses David Begelman of theft; sets off industry investigation.

1979

1980

Screen Actors Guild conducts longest strike in its history.

1981

Heaven's Gate is a box-office disaster.
United Artists sold to MGM.
Largest box-office receipts in history.

ART AND ARTISTS	KEY FILMS	SOCIOPOLITICAL ENVIRONMENT
Mickey Mouse is 50 years old.	◀ *Coming Home* (U.S.) *Interiors* (U.S.) *Autumn Sonata* (Sweden) *The Deer Hunter* (U.S.) *An Unmarried Woman* (U.S.) *Bread and Chocolate* (Italy) *Animal House* (U.S.) *Grease* (U.S.)	U.S. establishes diplomatic relations with China.
Jean Renoir, Mary Pickford, John Wayne die.	*Hair* (U.S.) *The China Syndrome* (U.S.) *Being There* (U.S.) *Apocalypse Now* (U.S.) *Superman* (U.S.) *The Marriage of Maria Braun* (W. Germany) *Manhattan* (U.S.)	
Alfred Hitchcock, Mae West, Raoul Walsh die. 	*The Blues Brothers* (U.S.) *My Brilliant Career* (Australia) *Coal Miner's Daughter* (U.S.) *The Elephant Man* (G.B.) *The Tin Drum* (Germany) *Kramer vs. Kramer* (U.S.) *The Empire Strikes Back* (U.S.) *Ordinary People* (U.S.)	Ronald Reagan is elected U.S. President. Sakharov is exiled from Russia. The prime rate reaches 20% in the U.S. Cuban refugees stream into the U.S. Solidarity is formed in Poland.
William Holden, William Wyler, Melvyn Douglas, Paddy Chayefsky die. ▲ Abel Gance's *Napoleon* (1927) is restored and exhibited to universal acclaim.	◀ *Raiders of the Lost Ark* (U.S.) *Superman II* (U.S.) *Man of Iron* (Poland) *Gallipoli* (Australia) *Ragtime* (U.S.) *Reds* (U.S.)	Iran frees U.S. hostages. Labor unrest escalates in Poland. President Reagan is shot; Pope John Paul II is shot. The U.S. launches the first space shuttle. Sandra Day O'Connor becomes the first female U.S. Supreme Court Justice.

TECHNOLOGY	INDUSTRY AND CONTROLS

1982 *Tron* uses computer technology to provide settings and props.

Coca-Cola buys Columbia Pictures.
Box-office receipts surpass record set in 1981.

1983

HBO begins feature-film production.

1984

1985

ART AND ARTISTS	KEY FILMS	SOCIOPOLITICAL ENVIRONMENT
Ingrid Bergman, Werner Fassbinder, Henry Fonda, Grace Kelly, Jacques Tati, King Vidor die.	*Tootsie* (U.S.) *Gandhi* (G.B.) *On Golden Pond* (U.S.) *E.T.* (U.S.) *Chariots of Fire* (G.B.) *Das Boot* (Germany) ◀*Diner* (U.S.)	Barney Clark is the first recipient of a permanent artificial heart. Argentina seizes the Falkland Islands. Canada gets its first constitution. Israel invades Lebanon. The Equal Rights Amendment fails to get approval in Congress. Poland bans Solidarity.
Luis Buñuel, George Cukor, Gloria Swanson die.	*Return of the Jedi* (U.S.) *Country* (U.S.) *Silkwood* (U.S.) *Local Hero* (G.B.) *War-games* (U.S.) *Zelig* (U.S.) *Risky Business* (U.S.) *Mr. Mom* (U.S.) *The Big Chill* (U.S.) *The Year of Living Dangerously* (U.S.) *The Dresser* (G.B.)	The U.S. Embassy in Beirut is bombed. AIDS is named the U.S. government's top health priority. A report criticizes U.S. public school education. The U.S. invades Grenada.
Richard Burton, Janet Gaynor, James Mason die.	*Cotton Club* (U.S.) *Indiana Jones and the Temple of Doom* (U.S.) ◀*Ghostbusters* (U.S.) *Once Upon a Time in America* (U.S.) *Romancing the Stone* (U.S.)	Ronald Reagan is re-elected U.S. President. Divestiture of AT&T takes effect. The world responds to Ethiopian famine. Indira Gandhi is assassinated.
Colorization of vintage MGM/UA classics begins, prompting a storm of protest.	*Back to the Future* (U.S.) *Rambo* (U.S.) *Prizzi's Honor* (U.S.) *Desperately Seeking Susan* (U.S.) *Witness* (U.S.) *The Killing Fields* (G.B.) *Ran* (Japan) *The Color Purple* (U.S.) ◀	Riots erupt in South Africa. U.S.–Soviet Summit takes place in Geneva.

Technology, Industry, and Form (Beginnings to 1907)

Focus

The first steps in the technological, artistic, and commercial development of film are not traceable to a single person or even a particular nation. It is true that film's beginning in the late nineteenth century was clearly linked to the development of technology and equipment required to photograph and project a silent screen image. Moreover, early standardization of equipment plus brisk trade between Western Europe and the United States permitted the trans-Atlantic exchange of early inventions and films, which partially explains the international nature of film's early growth. Less easy to document, however, is the influence early inventors, scientists, and filmmakers had on one another, and the extent to which they themselves were affected by the "archaeological" work of the unacknowledged pioneers who preceded them.

Archaeology

Most historians face the question of where to begin their narratives. The film historian is no exception. One might argue that since the motion picture is less than 100 years old, the film historian should find it easier to begin than other kinds of historians. But only the technology known as cinematography has yet to reach its centennial; the first attempts to represent reality in motion date back to prehistoric man.

Why should a history of motion pictures be concerned with events and discoveries that preceded the existence of the medium? Why not simply start in 1895, with the first public showing of a motion picture? In part, the answer rests on the fact that the motion picture medium depends on technology to communicate. Without cameras, film, and projectors, there would be no such communication. This does not imply that people have been unimportant in creating and designing the messages conveyed and in operating the machines. After all, a camera photographs only what someone "tells" it to photograph. But only a camera can reproduce reality in the form of a photograph or motion picture.

Therefore, in a history of the medium, we must tell the story of the technology that made it possible. Although we view technology along with the aesthetic, industrial, and social aspects of motion pictures, we must acknowledge that technology comes first. The motion picture is the child of science. We begin with cinematography and the scientific and technical discoveries fundamental to it, because only after the technology was realized could the artistic and industrial developments take place.

Our search of the past for a beginning might lead in many directions—for example, to cave paintings of boars with eight legs or to Chinese shadow plays. Many film historians agree that motion pictures came into existence in the nineteenth century, a period of vast scientific and technical achievements during which the discoveries and inventions of the past were brought meaningfully together. However, to begin with the nineteenth century would be to ignore our early fascination with reality in motion and our myriad attempts to duplicate it in art and science. Further, it would mean focusing almost exclusively on the technology of the medium and bypassing the human needs and desires behind its development. In an effort to encompass those ancient motivations, we begin with a look at some of the significant steps leading up to the nineteenth century.

Not one evolutionary line but a maze of ideas and discoveries concerned with reproducing physical reality is discernible throughout human history. In addition, the individual lines detectable in this maze are broken, diffused, and at times contradictory. We can say with certainty, however, that cave paintings, such as the 20,000-year-old Lascaux drawings of animals in suspended motion, represent the most primitive examples of human attempts to recreate motion. However, such attempts were individual and random efforts, not symbolic of a larger cultural or artistic consciousness. Chinese shadow plays were another matter. In these entertainments, animated, two-dimensional figures were "projected" on a screen to tell simple stories in serial form. These plays represented a culture's conscious attempt to recreate reality and present an interpreted event in motion.

Another significant step was taken around 340 B.C., when Aristotle noted that sunlight passing through a square hole cast a round image on a wall. This "dark room," as he referred to the phenomenon, was in reality a camera, with a square hole acting as an aperture. As Martin Quigley notes in his book *Magic Shadows*, Aristotle's observation was the first important contribution by a single individual to the science of reproducing reality. From this time on, hundreds of individuals studied, experimented with, and wrote about various phenomena regarding light and motion. Several individuals and their efforts stand out, because they advanced the existing technology toward the capability to accurately *duplicate reality*. Once this capability existed, human beings were liberated from the need to rely exclusively on *remembering* reality. The contributions of these central figures are briefly reviewed in the following subsections.

Leonardo da Vinci (1452–1519)

In 1500, Leonardo da Vinci developed a theory of the *camera obscura,* or "dark room." Da Vinci produced the phenomenon by cutting a hole in one wall of a dark room so that light from the hole fell onto the opposite wall. If the scene outside was bright enough, an image was visible on the wall, upside down and right for left. Whereas Aristotle had observed the same phenomenon almost 2,000 years earlier and had regarded it as a scientific oddity, da Vinci's work formed the theoretical basis for photography.

Giambattista della Porta (1540–1615)

Giambattista della Porta, an Italian entrepreneur, popularized and refined da Vinci's work. Della Porta borrowed freely, usually without credit, from many previous works, but his significant contribution was the way he used the camera obscura. Rather than confining himself to scientific descriptions, he created hunting and battle scenes, substituting artificial objects for pictures of reality. He even refers in his writings to presenting "little shows" for important people. In using the tools of the scientist to entertain and amuse, Della Porta took a new direction in motion picture prehistory.

Athanasius Kircher (1601–1680)

Perhaps the most important discovery preceding 1800 was Athanasius Kircher's magic lantern. The magic lantern is the only pre-nineteenth-century ancestor of a contemporary motion picture device—in this case, the projector. In fact, magic lanterns similar to those used in the 1600s were still used by traveling showmen in the twentieth century.

Although conflicting claims somewhat obscure the origin of the magic lantern, the invention most likely dates from Kircher's 1646 publication *Ars Magna Lucis et Umbrae* ("The Great Art of Light and Shadow"). In this work, Kircher describes, among other things, the *magia catoptrica,* a device using mirrors and a light source to project an image. Kircher developed the lantern to the point where it could project a series of slides to tell simple stories, and it came to be used in permanent theaters and traveling shows for the amusement of both rich and poor. The magic lantern remained popular for more than 200 years. Kircher's invention represented yet another significant step in the evolution of the motion picture process, since it served as a source of entertainment for the masses, not simply the rich and well educated, to whom such pleasures were limited until its appearance.

Johannes Zahn (16? – 17?)

The first step in linking projection with motion was taken at the end of the seventeenth century by Johannes Zahn. Zahn used glass slides mounted on a circular disk that revolved in front of a magic lantern. The resulting "motion" was crude, however, since Zahn's device lacked a shutter, used a candle for a light source, and projected pictures that were simple phase drawings (illustrations of an object or person in various stages of animated motion).

E. G. Robertson (1763 – 1837)

Following Zahn's innovation, the magic lantern was used for increasingly elaborate productions. Perhaps the ultimate theatrical experience was E. G. Robertson's *Phantasmagoria.* Using a rear-projection method coupled with a complex system of lenses and reflectors, Robertson illustrated the macabre stories he told with witches, ghosts, and other apparitions. He mounted these performances for startled audiences assembled in old ruins and deserted mansions. The magic lantern of the late eighteenth century was the natural predecessor of Georges Méliès, who used motion pictures for the same purposes a century later.

By the end of the eighteenth century, optics and projection had developed to the point at which elaborate and complex amusements could be presented to a paying public. However, the images presented were drawn pictures of still life. Photography and cinematography—motion photography—were yet to be conceived.

The Invention of Cinematography

Any attempt to construct an overview of the major nineteenth-century discoveries leading up to the development of cinematography must acknowledge the importance of Kurt W. Marek's book, *Archaeology of the Cinema* (1965). Marek, writing under the pen name C. W. Ceram, stated that the basic change characterizing

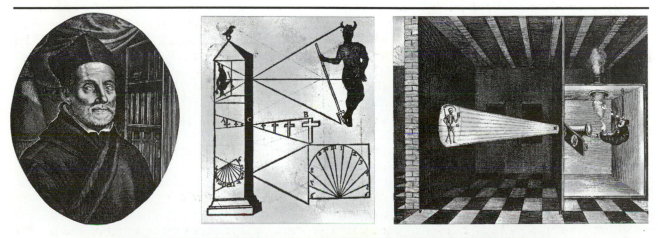

▲ A portrait of Athanasius Kircher and two illustrations from Kircher's *Ars Magna Lucis et Umbrae* (1646) showing the properties of the lens and the projection of a slide.

nineteenth-century thinking was a shift from the mechanical, which is static, to the technical, which is dynamic. His observation suggested that the thrust behind the inventions of the nineteenth century was not so much utility and the solving of existing problems as a sense of scientific curiosity.

Marek might better have used the word *explosive* to describe the tremendous technological advances of this "age of invention." Again, the profusion of dynamic ideas, discoveries, and inventions makes a linear historical narrative difficult since development rarely proceeded along straight lines. Although the period comprises only seventy years of development, a number of independent, parallel movements can be discerned within it that do not form an orderly pattern.

The invention of the motion picture was one of many problems solved, concepts realized, and inventions perfected during this fruitful time. From our perspective as film historians, a primary motivating force in the nineteenth century was the driving need to discover the essence and solve the problem of recreating life in motion. The actual steps in the evolution of cinematography took place in various locations and often simultaneously. The motion picture was clearly a child of its time. Those who helped develop the many aspects of the motion picture were often individuals working alone, pursuing their particular fields of research out of a sense of discovery and personal interest. They were generally willing to share the fruits of their labors, and eagerly accepted any opportunity to demonstrate the results of their often unacknowledged efforts. As a result, inventions were developed, disseminated, and quickly adopted. Only after these inventions became the basis for financial gain did the developmental process become bogged down in the disputes over patents and control that were to characterize the early motion picture industry.

Although cinematography resulted from many discoveries and ideas, five major concepts and inventions form its technological and theoretical base:

1. persistence of vision
2. photography
3. the motion picture camera
4. film
5. the motion picture projector

We cover each of these elements in turn in the following subsections.

Persistence of Vision

Motion pictures do not actually move. What we see is simply an illusion: a moving image created by projecting a sequence of individual still photographs (frames) at a fixed speed. The frames are held in place for a fraction of a second, and the eye/brain phenomenon called *persistence of vision* helps to create the illusion of motion. By means of this phenomenon, the viewer retains an image of the projected frame for a fraction of a second longer than the image actually appears on the screen. A shutter mechanism masks the actual movement of the still frames, while the projector and the viewer's brain (again, through persistence of vision) work in tandem to create the illusion of motion. One can produce an elementary example of this image retention by whirling burning sticks around in a circle. If the sticks are whirled fast enough, observers perceive an unbroken circle of flame. Although this phenomenon had been observed and commented on for centuries, a theory to explain it did not emerge until the early 1800s.

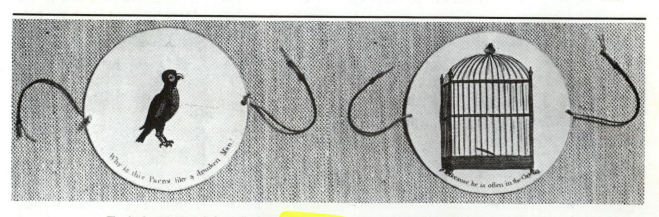

▲ The little spinning disks called the Thaumatrope, invented by Dr. John Paris in the 1820s. When the disks were spun, the pictures on either side merged into a single image.

Several people are credited with developing the theory of persistence of vision, beginning in 1818 with a Czech inventor, J. E. Purkyne. Six years later, in 1824, an English physician, Peter Mark Roget (known principally for his thesaurus), presented a paper developing the same theory. At about the same time, Dr. John Paris described a toy he constructed called a Thaumatrope, which worked on the principle of persistence of vision. Paris quickly realized the commercial value of the principle and arranged to have various motion devices made and sold in London.

Following Paris's Thaumatrope, a number of toys and devices appeared. The most important and popular of these were Joseph Plateau's Phenakistoscope (1832), Simon von Stampfer's Stroboscopic Disk (1832), and George Horner's Zoetrope (1834). These were the first devices based on a realized theory of the persistence of vision. They soon became the core of a new industry, as many companies were formed to build and sell them to an enthusiastic public.

Photography

While motion toys were becoming popular parlor entertainments, developments in photography were reaching fruition. Once again, experiments dating back several centuries preceded the actual invention. It was not until 1813, however, when French physicist Nicéphore Niepce began to experiment with transferring lithographic drawings by means of light, that photography as we know it appeared. Niepce teamed with Louis Jacques Mandé Daguerre in 1829, and the two worked together to perfect a photographic process. When Niepce died in 1833, Daguerre continued the research, and in 1839 he produced a workable system of photography.

Now, for the first time, humans had the technological capability to duplicate reality in its natural form. However, each photograph produced by Daguerre's method was unique and irreproducible. Improvements in the process by William Henry Fox Talbot in England soon made it possible for any number of positive prints to be made from a single negative, and photography thus became a method not only of duplication but of multiplication as well. Exposure time was soon reduced to three minutes, but it was not until the development of a dry-plate process in 1871 that exposure time was reduced to the seconds-long periods we are familiar with today.

The importance of photography to the development of motion pictures is obvious. Even with sophisticated motion toys, the phenomenon of reproducing motion was limited as long as it was based on drawings. With the photographic process, true images were substituted for phase drawings and reality in motion became possible.

The Motion Picture Camera

The best impressions of motion were fairly crude, despite the increasing use of photographs in motion toys, since the individual "frames" in these devices consisted of posed stills. The development necessary to improve the flow of motion was a method of taking photographs of a subject in a natural state of movement.

The process of solving this problem was lengthy and involved. It began in 1872 with a man named Eadweard Muybridge and a former governor of California, Leland Stanford. Although popular myth holds that Stanford was involved in a bet as to whether all four legs of a galloping horse were ever off the ground at once, recent research reveals that Stanford was primarily interested in the question from a breeding and training perspective. Stanford hired Muybridge to help resolve the matter, and the latter attempted various methods of photographing a galloping horse but met with little success. Stanford and Muybridge then went their separate ways. Stanford subsequently became familiar with the work of Dr. E. J. Marey in France and, his interest revived, rehired Muybridge in 1877 for another try. Muybridge realized that no single camera could do the job. He arranged twenty-four cameras side by side along a track. Twenty-four strings were stretched across the track, and as the horse galloped down the track it broke the strings and tripped the cameras' shutters. The result was a series of twenty-four phase pictures, which, when put together, formed a series picture. Muybridge's experiment showed that at a certain point in the motion all four legs of a galloping horse are indeed off the ground at one time. Muybridge was $100,000 richer, and motion picture technology had advanced another step forward. Muybridge continued to use his multicamera method to conduct motion studies of animals and humans, although later he replaced the strings with a timing device that tripped the shutter automatically.

Obviously, Muybridge's method did not solve the problem of how to reproduce motion photographically. A single camera was needed, and a number of researchers began working in this direction. The most significant development occurred in France in 1882 when, after more than ten years of experimentation, the French physiologist Marey, now clearly influenced by Muybridge, developed a photographic gun capable of taking twelve pictures a second. He soon began to work with rolls of paper film, and then celluloid, and ultimately he

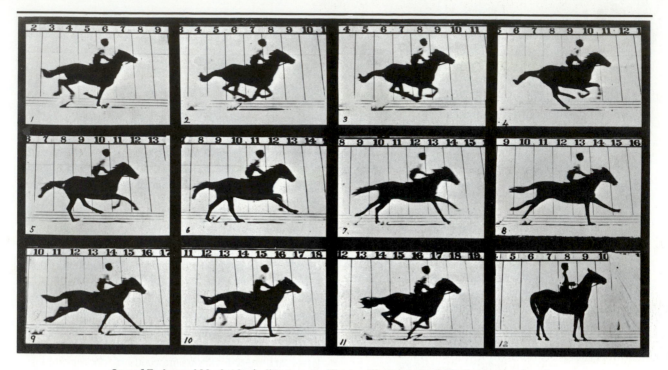

▲ One of Eadweard Muybridge's "Automatic Electro-Photographs." Muybridge produced thousands of these series in the 1870s and 1880s, with subject matter ranging from horses galloping and cats leaping to children dancing and men and women (often nude) climbing ladders and stairs. The purpose of these motion studies was to illustrate and advance the knowledge of human and animal locomotion.

increased the capacity of his camera to 100 pictures a second. Marey, however, was concerned primarily with animal locomotion for scientific study, and did little to develop the commercial potential of his work.

Film

Marey's development of a crude motion picture camera brought cinematography to an intersection with another line of scientific development. One of the major obstacles confronting those working on instantaneous photography was the necessity of using glass plates. Plates were bulky and incapable of reproducing long sequences of action. This problem was solved in 1887, when an American preacher and amateur inventor named Hannibal Goodwin developed celluloid film. However, in 1888, George Eastman, with his famous Kodak camera, perfected and promoted film.

Eastman, however, was not concerned with cinematography. The idea of using Eastman's film for making motion pictures is credited to William Kennedy Laurie Dickson, an associate of Thomas Edison. A good deal of controversy surrounds Edison and his work on motion pictures. Popular legend has long established him as the "father" of motion pictures. Others suggest that he left most of the work to Dickson while claiming credit for the invention. Strong support for Dickson's primary role has surfaced in recent years, and his place in film history as the inventor of motion pictures is well established.

As a sidenote, it is important to mention that, in weighing Edison's contributions to the evolution of motion pictures, we should look beyond the laboratory to acknowledge the full range of his activity. His work was a combination of invention and consolidation. That he employed associates or developed others' preliminary ideas should not detract from his deserved reputation as one of those responsible for the invention of motion pictures. In fact, Edison contributed more as a promoter of the technology and as one of the first important American motion picture executives than as a pure inventor. We might view his major role in motion picture history as that of a bridge or, more appropriately, a catalyst between the world of business and the world of science. He moved as comfortably in the board room as he did in the laboratory.

Using celluloid film, Dickson worked on the motion

▲ Thomas Edison's Kinetoscope. This was a peep-show device holding a fifty-foot loop of film.

▲ *Fred Ott's Sneeze,* one of the earliest motion pictures and perhaps the most famous film sneeze ever. The action involved one of Thomas Edison's assistants, Fred Ott, sneezing for Edison's kinetograph in his studio in West Orange, New Jersey, in 1889.

picture camera, developing the first useable model in 1888. By October 1889, Dickson had filmed and projected motion pictures on an experimental basis in Edison's studio in West Orange, New Jersey. Soon part of the laboratory was turned into a studio for the shooting of brief film clips, such as *Fred Ott's Sneeze.* In 1891 Edison applied for patents on the Kinetograph, a motion picture camera, and the Kinetoscope, a viewing device. The latter device was not a projector, but simply a cabinet containing a fifty-foot loop of film viewable by only one person at a time looking into the top of the machine.

By 1894, the Kinetoscope was being marketed internationally. As the demand for Kinetoscope films grew, Edison found it necessary to build a separate motion picture studio. Dubbed the Black Maria, the studio was little more than a tar-paper shack with openings in the roof to let in the sun. The shack was hung on a pivot so it could be turned to catch the sun, but even so, most of Edison's films were reportedly shot around noon to allow for maximum light conditions.

Edison filmed a great variety of subjects, including a barbershop scene, a Chinese laundry scene, and such celebrities as Buffalo Bill, Annie Oakley, and a dancer

▲ The Black Maria, Edison's first motion picture studio, so named because it was covered with black tar paper. The whole studio could be rotated on a pivot to catch the sun so that a scene would be well lit.

▲ *The Serpentine Dance* by Annabelle, shot in 1896 by the American Mutoscope company. The film had the twin appeals of beauty and motion upon which so much of motion picture art is based even today.

known as Annabelle. By 1894, Edison's catalog listed sixty subjects, most of them determined by what could be filmed most easily in a cramped studio space of the Black Maria without putting too great a strain on the heavy immobile camera.

The Kinetoscope was a great success, and other inventors, most notably Edison's assistant Dickson, developed competing peep-show systems. The most successful was the mutoscope, perfected in part by Dickson; its invention led to the formation of the American Mutoscope Company. Edison soon turned his attention to other scientific inquiries and failed to develop a projection system. By the time he got back to the idea, several others had beaten him to the punch.

The Motion Picture Projector

Kircher's magic lantern had been around for more than 200 years when an Austrian military officer named Baron Franz von Uchatius combined it with the Plateau Phenakistoscope disks to achieve moving images on a screen. However, the Uchatius machine used phase drawings rather than photographs, and its light source moved past the pictures, achieving a dissolve rather than shutter effect. The idea of using photographs on disks and projecting them was developed by several people,

including Jules Dubosq in France and Charles Wheatstone in England. Around 1870, an American, Henry Heyl, developed a projector using posed motion photographs and gave public showings before large audiences in Philadelphia.

All this early experimentation was limited, however, by the lack of true motion pictures. As soon as film became available and motion picture cameras began recording life in motion, projection, the last step in the development of cinematography, became a reality.

As we have seen, many of the inventions associated with cinematography appeared simultaneously. This was no less true of projection, and as a result there are many conflicting claims of credit. William Friese-Greene of England patented a camera in 1889, but apparently he did little with projection even though a plaque perpetuates his name and memory as "the inventor of commercial Kinematography." Louis Aimé Augustin Le Prince holds a more substantial claim, as it has been documented that he was taking and projecting motion pictures between 1888 and 1890. However, in 1890, Le Prince boarded a train to Paris and disappeared without a trace. Other pioneers include Georges Demeny, Max and Emil Skladanowsky, Birt Acres, and Robert Paul.

The most important contributions to the final step that completed the process of cinema photography, however, were made by two brothers, Auguste and Louis

Lumière, who perfected a camera and a projector that they called a Cinématographe. The Lumières began exhibiting films before a paying public in Paris on December 28, 1895, thereby mounting the first exhibition of motion pictures to a paying audience. Their critical contribution was a claw device that moved the film strip in front of the light source. The Cinématographe was also portable, a distinct advantage over the Kinetograph. The claw was replaced by the so-called Maltese Cross, developed by Oskar Messter, which created the intermittent-movement effect basic to modern projectors.

The Lumière brothers began producing films at a rapid rate, and in 1897 they published their first large catalog, which listed more than 350 different films. By 1898 they had several catalogs, listing more than 1,000 films. These short films covered an amazing range of forms, including documentaries, short stories, and trick films. The most dominant form, however, was the simple recording of reality—for example, workers leaving a factory, a train entering a Paris station, and one of the Lumière children eating breakfast.

All this activity soon made it apparent to Edison that he had used poor judgment in failing to develop a projection system. It was clear that his Kinetoscope would soon be obsolete and that his embryonic motion picture empire was in danger of crumbling. In response to the situation, Edison's agents came to him with a projection system based on the work of Thomas Armat and C. Francis Jenkins. Edison incorporated a loop in the film-lead apparatus, developed by Woodville Latham, that helped ease the strain on the film strip, and used his new projector, which he called a Vitascope, for the first time on April 23, 1896, at Koster and Bial's Music Hall in New York. This marked the first public projection of motion pictures in the United States, and the event was greeted with tremendous enthusiasm by both the viewing public and the fledgling motion picture industry. As J. Austin Fynes recalled about another early showing,

I never saw a more startled audience than that which, on Monday night in June of that eventful year [1896] saw the Lumière Cinématograph exhibited for the first time in America.

My advanced advertising had been liberal and quite florid in tone; the house was packed; a fairly strong vaudeville entertainment was half completed when the picture-screen—then an ordinary white sheet—was lowered, and the first motion-photograph was thrown on. . . . They increased the business of that playhouse [Keith's Union Square Theatre] from an average of $4,000 a week to $7,500 a week—and this without Sundays. They brought into the atmosphere of "vaudeville" a new class of patrons, the most select that had ever visited that style of show. . . . All

through that long, hot summer the motion pictures at Keith's held the town enthralled. Packed to its utmost capacity, day after day, the theatre established what I believe to be the highest record of any out-and-out vaudeville theatre in New York City; for its net profits that season figured close to $125,000!

Within twelve months from the first exhibit, every vaudeville theatre in this land had a picture machine of some sort or another as part of its programme . . . shrewd businessmen soon perceived that here was a new field for a profitable investment. And an innovation, which had at first appeared to be ephemeral, rapidly assumed a very sustantial permanency.

With the development of projection, cinematography existed as a technical reality. All the technological principles and devices had been discovered and invented, and the focus of film history moved quickly from the world of science and technology to the new arenas of art and business.

The Single-Shot Film

The first experimental clips made by Edison and Lumière from 1888 to 1895 and the first public showings in Paris and New York in 1895 and 1896 make a good starting point for discussing film history in terms of form and function. In the case of the earliest films, which were strict recordings of what came before the camera lens, there is little to be said of form. But the function of these pioneer works was clearly to exploit early viewers' fascination with the moving images of both real and dramatized activities. One need only look at a few of the earliest Edison and Lumière efforts to appreciate their commonality of purpose. *The Black Diamond Express,* a brief clip made by the Edison Company in 1896, records the hurtling movement of an oncoming train; *Fatima,* produced by Edison the following year, captures the gyrations of an exotic dancer. During the same time, the Lumière brothers in Paris were using their Cinématographe camera to record *Workers Leaving the Lumière Factory, Boat Leaving the Harbor,* and *Fish Market at Marseilles.*

The natural way to extend these clips was to expand upon their brief glimpses of activities, real or staged, providing somewhat more elaborate routines and historical events. The Edison studios captured *Gold Rush Scenes in the Klondike* in the 1890s and recorded *The Funeral of Queen Victoria* in 1901. These, along with countless other special-event clips made by both American and French studios, formed the beginning of newsreel film. Although staged films usually showed brief vaudeville routines — Edison's *Fun in a Bakery Shop* (1902) is an example — attempts were also made to recreate actual events, as illustrated by Edison's *Execution of Mary Queen of Scots* (1895) and the *McGovern-Corbett Fight,* staged in the Biograph Studios in 1903.

At the turn of the century, with films still running no more than a minute, it is questionable that the infant industry would have continued to woo audiences had not several pioneers extended the medium beyond its original peep-show function. In the early years of the first decade, the rudiments of narrative construction gradually evolved and movie makers began to discover that film could be used to tell a story.

Although the Frenchman Georges Méliès and the American Edwin S. Porter are generally given the lion's share of credit for beginning to use films to tell stories, several "idea men" and directors working anonymously in the Edison and Lumière studios in the late 1890s were actually the first to start exploring film's narrative potential. Though still no more than a minute long and limited to actions that could be recorded from a fixed camera position, some clips by these early experimenters definitely revealed progression and causal relationship between actions. *Washday Troubles* (1895) was a short routine by Edison in which a prankster upsets a washtub and is chased by the irate washerwoman. In the same year the Lumières produced a clip in a similar vein. This was *Watering the Gardener,* (L'Arroseur Arrosé), which shows a gardener becoming the victim of a boy who crimps a garden hose and then releases it when the gardener brings the nozzle closer for inspection. For Edison, James H. White photographed a short film called *Love and War* (1899), in which he developed four separate scenes, each in a different location. However, the narrative development of films composed of a single shot, or one "take," of the camera was clearly limited.

Biograph — Best of Them All

*A*nybody who thinks that the enthusiasm of the modern music hall audience is all for European singers of questionable propriety should have been at the Olympia Music Hall last night. The audience went fairly frantic over pictures thrown on a screen. Several machines for the throwing of moving pictures have been shown here, but the new biograph, for all its horrible name, is the best of all of them. The biggest part of enthusiasm began when a view of a McKinley and Hobart parade in Canton was shown. The cheering was incessant as long as the line was passing across the screen, and it grew much greater when the title of the next picture appeared: "Major McKinley at home." Major McKinley was seen to come down the steps of his house with his secretary. The secretary handed him a paper, which he opened and read. Then he took off his hat and advanced to meet a visiting delegation.

The biograph showed some other interesting pictures, notably one of the Empire State Express rounding a curve, which was one of the best, if not the very best, moving picture that has yet been exhibited here. Seven boxes were occupied by members of the National Republican Committee and their friends, who came to see Major McKinley walk across the lawn.

—New York Tribune
(October 13, 1896)

Electric Theater 262 S. Main, Opp. 3rd St. New Place of Amusement

Up to date high class moving picture entertainment especially for ladies and children. See the Capture of the Biddle Bros., New York in a Blizzard, and many other interesting and exciting scenes. An hour's amusement and genuine fun for 10 cents admission.
Evenings: 7:30 – 10:30

From *L'Arroseur Arrosé* (1895). This Lumière comic skit reveals the rudiments of narrative within a single shot.

Georges Méliès

The next important step in narrative construction was to link a series of shots, making it possible to record actions requiring more than a single location or time period. In 1896, Georges Méliès, theater producer, actor, designer, and professional magician, became fascinated with the Lumière camera and its possibilities, and it was he who realized the true beginnings of storytelling in motion pictures.

When Méliès purchased his first motion picture camera, he was a successful professional magician and owner of the Robert Houden theater in Paris. Thus, it was natural that Méliès's first exploration of the medium centered around the capability of films to create magic. His early films revealed a wide range of trick effects used to produce imaginative fantasies. These films involved miraculous appearances and disappearances, transformations, and the coming to life of inanimate objects. Méliès explored all the tricks of his magical trade and expressed them cinematically through such devices as double exposure, the superimposition of images, fast and slow motion, and optical effects, all transitional devices soon to become basic in film narrative along with fading an image to black and dissolving one image into another.

Méliès quickly outdistanced his fellow filmmakers on both sides of the Atlantic with his carefully planned and fancifully executed bits of film magic, and by the turn of the century his richly inventive fantasies were being enjoyed by American as well as European audiences. But not until after 1900 did Méliès's films begin to reveal a more significant step in the development of narrative

Georges Méliès, one of film's pioneering artists and the master of film fantasy.

construction. Until this time, his films had been limited to action that could be developed within a single setting and during an uninterrupted time period. But now he began to explore the camera's ability to record, through multiple scenes, a series of events that combined to tell a unified story. Méliès fashioned in sequence and *linked* together a series of action tableaux, which he himself labeled "artificially arranged scenes," thus combining the several units of action required to tell a story. He drew from both original narratives and those adapted from literature in these more structured films. Primitive

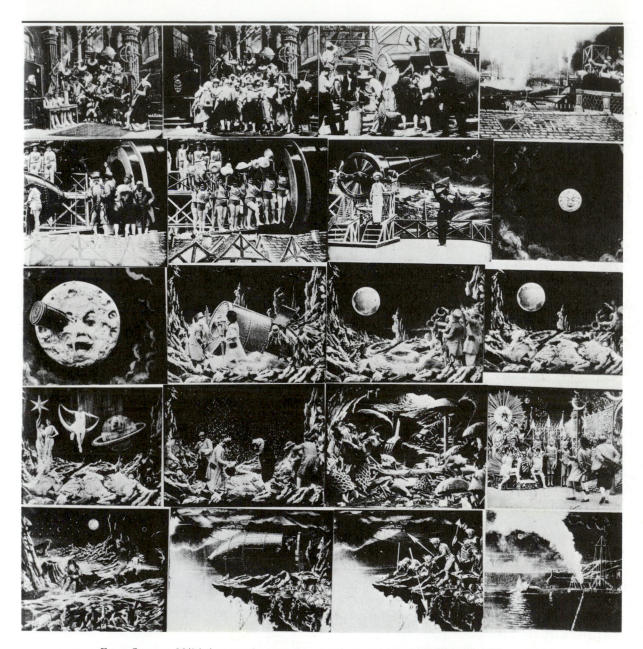

▲ From Georges Méliès's most famous film, *A Trip to the Moon* (1902). This photo montage illustrates the visual charm characteristic of most of Méliès's films. Using elements ranging from a chorus line to a "man in the moon," Méliès wove a magical tapestry of action based on his special effects.

though the films were at first, they illustrated the fundamental techniques of narrative cinema and marked the beginning of a creative use of the medium. As writer and producer, Méliès planned the tableau sequence to provide continuity and progression; as scenic designer, he produced the setting appropriate to each unit of action; and as director, he orchestrated movement and action within each of the scenes. Obviously, Méliès was his own special effects man as well. The result was a distinctive, immediately identifiable style.

Cinderella (1899), the first of Méliès's "action tableau" films, was composed of twenty scenes. This film clearly illustrates not only Méliès's advances in cinematic construction, but also the rich, theatrical style that

From *The Impossible Voyage* (1905). Here Méliès explores the world of science fiction and reveals his talents as scenic designer.

would quickly become his trademark. More inventive and elaborate films followed, and Méliès's imaginative wit, along with his growing technical control, reached a peak in 1902 with *A Trip to the Moon.* Here, in thirty scenes, Méliès created a wildly fanciful version of the Jules Verne story that shows scientists in an "astronomic club" planning and constructing a rocket and flying it to the moon. The group has a bizarre series of lunar experiences, including an encounter with the "Selenites," and finally returns to earth and a triumphal reception. The film is a humorous romp with a distinctive charm, and the visual rendering of both setting and action is highly imaginative. Méliès took the opportunity to weave into the simple narrative a good-natured spoof of scientific and technological interests of the day and thus further distinguished himself as one of film's first satirists. He exploited contemporary social foibles and preoccupations in several subsequent films, but always in the service of fantasy. Méliès's objective was dream building, not social persuasion.

For the next few years, Méliès continued to delight audiences with his fairy tales and fantasies as well as the occasional realistic depiction of an historical event — for example in *Paris to Monte Carlo* (1905). By the close of the decade, however, his popularity was declining. It is true that he suffered from the primitive state of production and distribution methods, but he was also a victim of his own limitations in the use of the medium. For all his inventiveness and imagination in planning and execution, and ultimately in the linking of scenes for storytelling, Méliès was never able to use the camera for anything beyond the recording of staged action. He had quickly seen the many trick possibilities of the camera, but he was apparently blind to its potential as a creative and fashioning tool. He would aim the camera from one end of his studio at entire scenes being played in typical theatrical fashion. Actors would enter and leave the scene from left and right, occasionally bowing to the camera audience. No change in perspective or break in action would occur until the scene had run its course. To put it simply, Méliès created a richly inventive style of storytelling, but he left unexplored the unique properties of the medium for plastic expression — the control of time and space. As Georges Sadoul, one of the foremost authorities on Méliès, has written, "With Méliès the gimmick is always trying to startle us: it is the *end,* and not a *means* of expression." But perhaps the best summary of Méliès's strengths and weaknesses is found in his own writing:

> The composition of a scene, an episode, a drama, a fairy story, a comedy or an artistic tableau naturally requires a scenario taken from the imagination. Then there is a search for ways of affecting the audience: drawings and models for costumes and scenery; the setting on a chief attraction, without which there is no chance of success. And as for tales of illusion or fairy stories, the tricks and processes must be studied with particular care. The rendering on film must be prepared in advance, just as much as the groupings and movements of the players. It is exactly like preparing a stage play. The only difference is that the author must know how to do everything himself and, consequently, be author, director, designer and, sometimes, actor, if everything is to be as he wishes it. The author of a scene must direct it himself, because it is absolutely impossible if two people meddle in it.

Although this limitation does explain Méliès's decline and eventual obscurity by 1914, it does not diminish the fact that he brought planning, selection, and control to moviemaking; started the medium on its way to storytelling; and served as an inspiration to filmmakers who followed. His influence is most clearly seen in the French chase and trick films that became a staple of the industry by 1910. And one need only look at Edwin S. Porter's *Dream of a Rarebit Fiend* (1906) — to say nothing of the countless lesser efforts by imitators both in Europe and America — to appreciate the influence of Méliès's infectious and fanciful style. It has been reported by historians that the American film genius D. W. Griffith said of Méliès, "I owe him everything." In view of both Griffith's revolutionary approach to the medium and Méliès's distinct limitations, this remark might seem excessive, but in fact it acknowledges that important first step that begins any long journey — in this case the linking of scenes necessary to breathe visual life into a story.

Edwin S. Porter

The person most responsible for taking film narrative techniques beyond the work of Méliès was the American Edwin S. Porter. Unlike Méliès, whose background was in theater, Porter was a machinist whose expertise drew him to a series of jobs related to the motion picture industry. Throughout the 1890s, Porter worked intermittently as projectionist, inventor of motion picture equipment, and free-lance newsreel photographer, much of the time for Edison. He was on hand at Koster and

▲ Edwin S. Porter, the most prominent innovator in American cinema in the early 1900s.

Bial's Music Hall on April 23, 1896, to assist in the first American public projection of motion pictures. Porter was hired full time by the Edison Company in 1899, initially to work as a mechanic. Soon, however, he began to direct, and by 1902 he had become an important director for the company with an impressive list of films to his credit.

In addition to continuing his work in newsreels, Porter became increasingly involved in producing the short, single-situation comic routines that had become a staple of the industry. Though uninspired in terms of dramatic quality, these films exhibited some technical advances. Stimulated both by Méliès and his own interest in machinery, Porter began to experiment with such devices as double exposure, split screen (two images projected side by side), panoramic shooting, a primitive form of animation, and shooting film at night with incandescent light. His *Uncle Josh at the Moving Picture Show* (1902) employs double exposure to combine the antics of a country hick's reaction to his first movie with an image representing the action on the screen. (He used, among others, excerpts from Edison's *The Black Diamond Express* [1896] in the film within a film.) And in 1901, in two documentary films Porter shot at the Pan-American Exposition at Buffalo, New York, he employed both night shooting and a complete 360-degree pan of the camera.

Toward the end of 1902 Porter produced *The Life of an American Fireman*. This film, along with his *The Great Train Robbery* (1903), established the foundation of cinematic narrative construction and earned for Porter the title "father of the story film."

The Life of an American Fireman (not *Policeman*, illustrated in the accompanying photo, which came later) seems crude by contemporary standards. The film is a simple story of race and rescue, beginning with a fire chief's dream of a mother and child in danger. An alarm sounds, the fire department races to the fire, and mother and child are rescued — all in seven scenes and less than two minutes' running time. With the exception of the final scene, which depicts the arrival of the force at the

▶ Scenes from Edwin S. Porter's *Life of an American Policeman* (1905). These scenes contrast sharply with Méliès's artificially created "motion tableaux." Here Porter uses the natural environment of the city to bring screen realism to his audience. Scenes 5 and 17 further illustrate Porter's expanded use of action and camera perspective, as characters move toward and away from the camera.

Life of an American Policeman
(Scene 2)

Life of an American Policeman
(Scene 5)

Life of an American Policeman
(Scene 7)

Life of an American Policeman
(Scene 17)

fire and the rescue, all the scenes are composed of single shots from a fixed camera position. Some were actually stock shots of real fire department activities from Edison files, though how much of the footage was borrowed is still debatable. But what made the film a significant breakthrough in narrative construction was that each successive shot drew meaning from those preceding it, and the arrangement of the scenes followed the traditional pattern of dramatic progression: exposition, development of the action, suspense, crisis, climax, and resolution. Porter, like Méliès, was demonstrating that the action of a film need not be completed within a single scene. He discovered that he could establish progression and draw meaning from a combination of scenes, and represent a longer period of time than the actual running time of the film.

Though Porter probably did not fully understand the potential of the technique at the time, another basic tool of cinematic construction is revealed in the final scene of *The Life of an American Fireman* — the viewing of a scene from multiple vantage points. Porter dissolves from the arrival of fire apparatus to the fate of mother and child within the burning building, and then dissolves again to the exterior for the rescue. In subsequent films, however, Porter reverted to single-shot scenes, and the use of the shot as the basic building block in narrative construction had to wait for D. W. Griffith's work nearly a decade later.

In view of the inferior quality of his next few films such as *The Gay Shoe Clerk* (1903), Porter's revolutionary use of the medium in *The Life of an American Fireman* might be seen more as an incidental experiment than some sudden awakening to the true method of film construction. But these films were simply tasks assigned to Porter by Edison to meet a heavy production schedule. Even *Uncle Tom's Cabin* (1903), which was the longest and most ambitious film to come from the Edison studio to that time, was a photographed stage play, much in the Méliès tradition. Despite a certain charm of dressing and decor, it lacked any real development in narrative construction.

Among his other tasks, Porter was assigned to make a promotional film, *A Romance of the Rail* (1903), commissioned by the Delaware Lackawanna and Western Railroad, and intended to sell the joys — in particular, the services and cleanliness — of train travel. This project, coupled with the dramatic potential he saw in a currently popular road show entitled *The Great Train Robbery,* spurred Porter to produce a film by the same name, which was to prove a legendary contribution to the development of screen narrative plus a pioneer classic of the American Western.

Released late in 1903, *The Great Train Robbery* quickly became a sensation. It also helped to ensure the success of the nickelodeons (motion picture theaters so named because of their five-cent admission charge) that were springing up across the country (see box, page 26). What made this film a new experience for movie audiences, and a critical influence on the development of the medium, was its closely knit construction and narrative flow. Composed of fourteen scenes and running nearly twelve minutes, the film builds a simple, tightly woven narrative concerning a train hijacked by outlaws. After stealing both the mail and passengers' belongings, the robbers flee the train and are pursued and killed by a posse in a desperate gun battle. The film, of course, has the intrinsic drama of railroading and the built-in momentum of the chase. But Porter's major contribution was in developing the action within each scene to create a natural association and flow among the combined scenes. Freeing himself from the limits of the single situation and real time, he introduced three distinct units of action: two in fixed locations — the interior of a telegraph office and a dance hall, where the posse is alerted — and a third whose location changes as it follows the fleeing bandits. The result of linking the several scenes together was a natural progression of action in time and space.

In itself this scene-linking technique was not new, having been accomplished by Méliès in *A Trip to the Moon* and by Porter himself in *The Life of an American Fireman.* What made the construction unique was the cross-cutting, or interweaving, of critical units of action that were going on simultaneously and that climaxed with a final gun battle, when two units of action — the bandits and the posse — were brought together within a single scene. This cross-cutting, in addition to moving the action forward, created tension by leaving each phase of the action momentarily unresolved.

Such a key formative work naturally inspires accolades, and *The Great Train Robbery* has come to be known as a veritable catalog of film firsts. Camera movement in the film is often mentioned, for example. Noted in particular are the short tilt of the camera to follow the fleeing bandits and the close-up of the outlaw leader firing directly at the audience. According to a suggestion in the Edison catalog, the latter might be used either to begin or end the film — the exhibitor had the choice. In fact, however, camera movement in *The Great Train Robbery* is negligible, and the close-up, though perhaps startling in its effect on early audiences, is not an integral part of the narrative. Porter did employ a Méliès-inspired special effect when he showed the train coming into the station through the window of the telegrapher's office. The designation of the film as the first Western is also misleading, since short, single-scene vignettes, such as the Edison Company's *Cripple Creek Barroom* (1898) and Porter's own *The Life of an American Cowboy* (1902), preceded it.

The strength of basic structural editing in the film also leads to the assumption that Porter used shot breakdown — that is, he built the action in a given scene by means of a series of shots taken from varying angles and distances. In fact, Porter did not use shot breakdown, and this is the key limitation of the film. The camera simply records activities designed for the scene from a fixed, medium-shot, eye-level position. Though the intercutting of scenes helps to build suspense, the potential for adding pace or tempo created by controlling shot length remains unexplored.

Soon after the *The Great Train Robbery,* however, Porter made a further contribution to narrative construction by using contrast editing in *The Ex-Convict* (1904) and *The Kleptomaniac* (1905). By extending the simple cross-cutting of separate but related actions that he used in *The Great Train Robbery,* Porter developed the direct comparative study of two parallel events. The story in *The Ex-Convict* compares the lifestyles of a rich industrialist and a poverty-stricken ex-convict; in *Kleptomaniac* he shows how justice serves the rich and the poor.

With the release of *The Great Train Robbery,* Porter's reputation as a leader in moviemaking was secure. The rapidly expanding nickelodeon circuit brought ever-increasing demands for film, and short narrative films began to flood the market. Porter's own rigorous production schedule plus his continued fascination with the technological end of the industry left him with little time or inclination for further experimentation in narrative technique. By 1907, the year that D. W. Griffith joined the Edison studio and began his own impressive rise to director stardom, Porter was becoming more supervisor than director. The remainder of his career, though distinguishing him, oddly enough, as both executive and inventor, had little to do directly with the course of film form and function.

Other Pioneers

Although their work in shaping the development of screen narrative is less easily documented, a number of other early directors were making popular and even influential contributions to film form. By 1907, in France, Méliès was joined by several filmmakers pioneering in the documentary animation, melodrama, and, most significantly, comic fantasy. Individual artists such as Ferdinand Zecca, Emile Cohl, Louis Feuillade, and Jean Durand explored the trick potential of the camera and found a basic narrative framework — usually a chase sequence — on which to hang their fancies. Both French and American schools of silent screen comedy, particularly the early works of René Clair and the original Sennett Keystone films, show clear evidence of their influence. The pursuit of a disappearing criminal in Zecca's *Slippery Jim* (1905), the runaway pumpkins in Cohl's *The Pumpkin Race* (1907), and runaway time in Durand's *Onésime Horloger* (1910) illustrate that the manipulation of time and motion through trick effects was central to these pioneer directors of screen slapstick and farce. In the latter work, a young man who is to inherit a fortune from an uncle in twenty years shortens the waiting time by tampering with a clock and thereby speeding up his life.

In England, the "School of Brighton" was making equally significant progress in developing the form. Men such as G. A. Smith, James Williamson, and Cecil Hepworth helped to make the English films among the most innovative in the world. As early as 1900, in such films as *Stop Thief* (1901) and *Fire* (1901), Williamson demonstrated a crude form of parallel editing. However, it was Cecil Hepworth who developed most of the early innovations, and his pioneering efforts in editing certainly paralleled Porter's and in several instances predated him. Hepworth worked with intercutting news footage with other film to create a story in such early films as *Peace With Honour* (1902) and *Alice in Wonderland* (1903).

In *Rescued by Rover* (1905), Cecil Hepworth extended his basic blueprint for narrative and provided a preview of the rescue formula Griffith would perfect. This film, made up of twenty individual shots, is about a gypsy's abduction of a child from its pram. The drama unfolds as the family dog, alerted to the crisis, takes up the trail of the infant. Following the scent across a stream and into a house and an attic room, he discovers the child, races back to the family home to alert the master, and leads him to the kidnapper's hideout. Although the action is not a chase in the strict sense of the word, the feats of the canine hero, together with Hepworth's own work in building a story from a collection of shots, makes the film a significant accomplishment. Particularly dynamic are the several shots in which Hepworth records action moving directly toward or directly away from the camera. Twice alone, and once leading the master to the rescue, Rover is seen racing toward the camera lens. Such movement contrasts with the horizontal orientation of most movement within the frame to this time. Notable exceptions, of course, are shots of onrushing locomotives of the early Lumière and Edison clips. *Daylight Burglary,* produced by the Sheffield Photo Company in 1903, and *The Pickpocket,* produced the same year by Gaumont, further illustrate the early use of multiple camera positions by British filmmakers and the beginnings of the movie chase.

Both in France and Italy, by the end of the century's first decade, the stage was being set for the costume spectacles as well as the chase. Although ponderous and basically uncinematic, these films extended Méliès's early attention to scenic design. Such films as *The Fall of Troy* and *The Sack of Rome,* from Italy, provided audiences with glamorous and spectacular scenery that was both decorative and appropriate to their historical period. Similarly, by 1908 the French Film d'Art Company was bringing to the screen a series of classic plays performed by the French National Theater. Though faithful recordings of stage pieces and therefore limited in their cinematic style, especially acting, these filmed plays nevertheless helped to push films beyond the single-reel length while introducing more prestigious dramatic material to the screen than had as yet been seen.

Industrial Development

As the first films of Edison, Lumière, Méliès, Porter, and others began to attract large audiences, the economic potential of this revolutionary new medium became apparent. The various cinematic devices that were invented became the basis of a thriving industry, and the first years of development were dominated by a concern over patents and a jockeying for position in the new get-rich-quick world of motion picture production and exhibition.

The Beginnings of an Industrial Identity: 1895–1900

The first five years of industrial growth were closely tied to technological development. During that period, no manufacturer was able to supply a complete equipment package for motion picture photography and exhibition. Edison could not make enough projectors, Biograph (an early rival) would not sell them, and neither Edison nor Biograph would rent nor sell cameras. With equipment in short supply and the public clamoring for more films, the fledgling industry was in a state of chaos. Most of the early developers did not anticipate the tremendous popularity of motion pictures, and when the explosion came they were caught unprepared.

Edison is a good example of this "only a novelty" thinking. As noted earlier, he ignored projection until others had already entered the field and had to depend on the work of others and his own industrial strength to catch up with a rapidly developing industry. For others, the situation was similar. The industrial and technological advances in these first years were basically forced by the public's eager acceptance of motion pictures.

Although the incredible popularity of motion pictures was not foreseen, the hindsight of history shows us that society was ready for the new medium. As Nicholas Vardac demonstrates in his book *From Stage to Screen* (1949), nineteenth-century theater had, by its emphasis on realism, unwittingly provided a "climate of acceptance" for motion pictures. Theatrical realism was expressed in elaborate spectacles involving actual chariot races, real forests, and live animals, including camels and elephants, on stage. Of course, such staging was only possible in large theaters in major cities. Audiences in small towns heard about these performances but never saw them. And theatrical realism could only go so far before it ultimately had to bow to the limitations of the stage. When motion pictures arrived, they immediately addressed themselves to both issues. They not only replaced elaborate stage realism in large cities, but, more importantly, they brought new dimensions of realism to the towns of rural America.

For the first but certainly not the last time, motion pictures met the needs of society. It is true that motion pictures were a novelty. But forces more far-reaching and deeper than novelty helped the new amusement industry gain acceptance. Urbanization, industrialization, immigration, the growth of a strong middle class, and increased leisure time all helped to create this climate of acceptance for motion pictures. America had large cities filled with an immigrant working class that had limited amounts of time and money and a limited knowledge of English but a growing desire for entertainment. Silent pictures made few demands on that restricted language capability.

Edison and Biograph, their positions solidified by patent holdings and strong financial backing, were the two dominant companies. Biograph was initially a competitor of Edison's in the peep-show business with its mutoscope viewing device. Edison's former key associate, William Dickson, helped to found Biograph by building a camera and projector designed to circumvent Edison's patents. Vitagraph came into existence in 1897 through the efforts of J. Stuart Blackton and Albert E. Smith, who also designed apparatuses that circumvented Edison's patents. However, Smith and Blackton based their system more closely on Edison's, and therefore Vitagraph films could be used in Edison projectors, greatly expanding their potential market.

Industrial development was not confined to the United States, however. In Germany, Oskar Messter invented an "independent projector." He soon began producing films, and by 1897 published his first cinema catalog, containing eighty-four films. Even more significant was the Frenchman Charles Pathé, who founded Pathé Frères in 1896 with a total capital of 24,000 francs. By 1913 the firm had a capital of more than 20 million francs. Pathé soon became the dominant company in Europe and firmly established itself both in Russia and the United States.

Within these organizations there was little evidence of structure or division of labor. Few of the producers had experience or training. Actors, writers, editors, and directors were rare if they were to be found at all. And there was no organized film-distribution system and no middlemen. Companies simply set up their cameras, shot simple scenes, printed the films, and sold them directly to vaudeville houses or storefront exhibitors. Despite this often chaotic state of affairs, however, several individuals were conscious of the tremendous commercial potential of the medium.

One factor holding back commercial, technical, and artistic development, however, was the lack of film stock. The manufacturers of raw film stock, most notably Eastman, made most of their film for amateur still cameras and did not immediately begin producing motion picture film once the need arose. As a result, the fifty-foot length of film originally used by Edison's Kinetoscope and functionally dictated by the Latham Loop, became standard. In order to create longer programs, exhibitors had to splice together fifty-foot (one-minute) films. Since it was difficult to produce complex stories under such conditions, narrative development became closely tied to the development of longer film stock. It was not until 1900 that 250-foot film lengths with a running time of three to four minutes became available.

Refinement and Progress: 1900–1907

By 1900 production quality began to improve. Audiences expressed their dissatisfaction with films that provided little more than snapshots of reality, and films soon began to function as "chasers," filling in the time between vaudeville acts. A certain degree of quality began to emerge as a few talented cameramen, such as Porter and others, became directors, and professional actors were sought for more demanding roles. Henry Marvin of Biograph, for example, began training photographers and actors. He also organized scenario writing as a separate phase of production.

Motion picture exhibition was developing rapidly as well. At first, motion pictures fit into the existing entertainment structure to become part of vaudeville presentations, but it was not long before the urgency of growing public demand became a sign to certain showmen that motion pictures could be exhibited as a separate attraction. The 1904 World's Fair brought motion pictures to St. Louis, but in less than grand fashion. The theater consisted of 94 camp chairs and a bed sheet for a screen.

◀ A mutoscope peep-show machine. The mutoscope was an early rival of Edison's Kinetoscope; it operated with a wheel containing photographic flip cards, as compared to the fifty-foot celluloid loop in the Edison device. These machines were very popular in penny arcades even as late as the 1960s, and a few are still in use today.

▲   A motion picture theater in Tacoma, Washington, in 1903.

The World's Dream opened in St. Louis two years later with 140 folding chairs and room for 200 more. Operating costs amounted to slightly more than $50 a week, including $25 for films, $12 for the projectionist, and $15 for a barker.

Blacktop tents were among the first theaters, as motion pictures extended beyond large cities into rural areas. These theaters were generally crude affairs with coal-stove heat and boards laid in the aisles to prevent patrons from sinking up to their ankles in mud. However, their large seating capacity, up to 3,000 people in some cases, compensated for their primitive state. Soon, however, permanent buildings were converted into crude theaters. There was little concern for quality in these early years, as the largely working-class audiences were not accustomed to the luxury associated with legitimate theater or even vaudeville. As an *Architectural Record* of the time noted, "The decoration of the hall is usually simple. No great elaboration is necessary as the waits between reels are usually short and the audience has little time to admire the auditorium."

It was motion pictures themselves that were fascinating, not their viewing environment. The experience of three young men in New Orleans was typical. William Rock, R. J. Wainright, and William Reed opened up Vitascope Hall on Canal Street in 1896, charging ten cents admission, another ten cents if the audience wanted to

see the projection booth, and yet another ten cents for a single frame of film to take home.

Soon other theaters were opened. Thomas Tally, a pioneer exhibitor on the West Coast, opened his first theater in 1897, but it was not until 1902 that he ran an advertisement announcing the debut of motion pictures as independent entertainment.

In 1898, Herbert Miles opened one of the first specially adapted motion picture theaters in New York, and soon people all over the country were busy converting stores into theaters. Even this development was limited, however, by the availability of films. It was not until around 1900, when the Edison/Biograph stranglehold on equipment was broken, that exhibition emerged as a truly separate, independent branch of the industry. This emergence was possible primarily because of Edison's mistakes and the eagerness of other companies to get in on what appeared to be an industrial bonanza. Edison's failure to develop projection and take out an international patent allowed several companies to enter the fields of both exhibition and production, mainly with the help of foreign equipment.

While fixed theaters were being developed, motion pictures were being exhibited in rural areas by entrepreneurs and itinerant showmen. An article by Calvin Pryluck suggests that this "separate infrastructure" of motion picture exhibition was more widespread than previously assumed. In "The Itinerant Movie Show and the Development of the Film Industry" in the fall 1983 *Journal of the University Film and Video Association,* Pryluck notes:

> Movies easily became part of the entrepreneurial, itinerant, undifferentiated, and flexible structure of the entertainment industry as it existed at the end of the nineteenth century. Wherever there was entertainment there were movies. There were movies on showboats. There were movies at the height of the gold rush of 1898 in the Klondike near the Alaska-Canada border, thousands of miles from any other settlement.

Pryluck offers a specific illustration documenting the "roadshow" concept well:

> A five person company calling itself E. Gorton and Stewart's Cinegraph was also touring Michigan that season; their plans were more localized. Following a three week tour in April, their plans were to open a store show for five weeks in Kalamazoo, Michigan, a town whose population in 1900 was 24,000. "Then we will go by wagon, [performing in] small towns."

Despite certain improvements, the quality of production was limited by the haphazard operations of many corporations. Most producers made little conscious effort to create a quality product. The chief concern of most companies was quantity, since exhibitors were constantly clamoring for more films to fill what seemed to be an insatiable public appetite. Films were sold by the foot, and production was therefore geared to manufacturing so many feet per week.

Motion pictures were also an expensive product, and producers were reluctant to try anything new. Films longer than 400 feet were not produced until 1903. With production geared to a cost-per-foot philosophy, longer films meant more money, and if the public was satisfied with short films, why rock the boat? However, 1903 saw the appearance of perhaps the most significant film in motion picture history, *The Great Train Robbery.* This *was* something new, and the industry reacted to it with incredible speed. The film's 740-foot length, outdoor location, cinematic structure, and sense of realism spurred the industry into creating longer story films. By 1905, 1,000 feet, or "one reel" (nine to eleven minutes), became the standard length of most films.

By 1907 the motion picture industry was alive and surging with new business. New companies were springing up daily, and theaters were spreading across the country. *The Motion Picture World's Buyer's Guide for 1907,* an early trade journal, listed ten major manufacturers of equipment and films. Almost all of them

The Value of Film Negatives

*T*he costliest negative ever taken by one moving picture concern shows the occupation of Peking by the foreign soldiers during the Boxer rebellion. A photographer took the pictures of the allied troops as they scaled the walls of the city. That film cost $7,000. Many of the films taken of the Boer and Japanese wars were almost as costly.

The greatest picture ever taken was that of the fight between Jeffries and Sharkey, at Coney Island, in 1898. The film was 37,125 feet long—over seven miles. On this were 198,000 photographs, and the machine ran continuously for 110 minutes.

Some idea of the cost of this film may be had when one learns it is estimated that the total expense per minute of running the machine is $50. The film is used at the rate of 74 feet a minute and costs 25 cents for each foot.

Usually in taking pictures of long duration three machines are used, two in operation, one in reserve. The films come in lengths of 250 feet, and the machines alternate.

—Moving Picture World
(March 23, 1907)

achieved their prominence because of original patent holdings. However, these pre-eminent firms were being pressed to maintain their position by companies that were producing exciting films in spite of the fact they did not hold any key patents.

As production and exhibition facilities expanded, many companies began issuing two or three films (reels) a week. Well-known novelists such as Rex Beach and Richard Harding Davis began writing film scenarios. Sigmund Lubin built a new glass studio in Philadelphia in which four companies could work simultaneously. Edison

The Open Letter

*W*hat a story of progress in screen pictures the past quarter century tells! I wonder if any of the older Mentor readers remember the picture shows and panoramas of the days, or, rather, the nights of the seventies and early eighties! Does anyone recall Professor Cromwell and his picture lectures? For years Professor Cromwell exercised the spell of the "magic lantern"—we came to know it later as the "stereopticon"—and he enhanced the charm of his entertainment with a piano at one side of the stage and a melodion at the other, on which he discoursed sweet musical strains, while he revealed the melting beauty of "dissolving views,"— a new thing then in picture shows. In days before Professor Cromwell's innovations there were screen pictures that replaced each other abruptly, one after another, and panorama pictures that moved on rollers. How vivid and gaudy were the pictures of that time! How bold and brave were the colors— colors that proclaimed in uncompromising tones, the courage and determination of the artisan that painted them on. And the audiences of those simple days were delighted with the riot of color on the panorama screens—whether the colors were true or not. A purple cow was pleasing just because it was purple.

And, in those wonderful old panoramas, the greatest illusion of all was "night-lighting." Never will I forget the effect on my youthful mind of the panorama of "St. Peters and the Vatican, Rome," first by day, and then—by a simple trick of lighting from the back—the same scene illuminated at night. The twinkling of lights in a thousand little windows held us young people spellbound. What thrilled us most was the thought that the spectacle of the superb Cathedral and the Papal palace should be all lit up just for us. I have often wondered since whether St. Peters and the Vatican ever actually looked as gorgeous at night as our youthful eyes saw it on the screen of Professor Cromwell.

The day of Professor Cromwell, and all the other "Professors," passed and then came the treat of a perfected stereopticon. Progressive, intelligent, enterprising men like Stoddard, Burton Holmes, Elmendorf, and Newman traveled the world over and brought their treasures of splendid photography back to us. As soon as the vitascope entered the field they took that on—and also the "kinemacolor" process that gives us colors that closely reproduce nature's own. These men have become our chief travel-picture benefactors. Through the winter evenings they have taken us nearly everywhere and shown us nearly everything. The Elmendorf and Newman pictures are well known to Mentor readers for they are published in our pages; so, we enjoy the rich benefits of the experience of both of these distinguished camera artists.

. . .

And now we have the crowning achievement of modern photography, the Motion Picture Play— perhaps we might better say the picture plays have us, for they are about us everywhere. They are well named "movies," for, in the final analysis, that is their commanding appeal. *They move.* Some might contend that the film pictures hold us because they show us great life-dramas. But, if any of those very same life-dramas were presented in a series of "still" pictures, the essential appeal would be lacking. It is because they *move.* Throw some bits of crumpled paper on a table in a crowded room, and they will attract little attention. Tighten those bits of paper with twisted elastic so that they jump around in a lively fashion, and everybody will crowd about the table and watch them with interest. What is the answer? Motion. Motion means life—and life is the supreme interest of human beings.

It was a great day for us mortals when Galileo said of the earth, "It moves." Everything on the earth has been more interesting since then.

The Mentor *(July, 1921)*

built a new studio in 1907, at a cost of more than $100,000, and had it equipped with underground water tanks to create everything from a brook to an ocean. By this time, however, Edison had slipped in popularity. The two dominant companies were Biograph and Vitagraph,

primarily because they concentrated on attracting talented writers and actors.

Major production companies were located almost exclusively on the East Coast, although several companies, such as Selig and Essanay, operated out of Chicago.

At first, the major studios, such as Edison, Vitagraph, and Biograph, set up their studios in residences with outdoor sets located on the roof. However, as the demand for films grew, especially those with outdoor scenes, the companies were forced to leave these locations and move to the suburbs. West Coast production was limited to occasional sporadic trips, when an on-location Western or aquatic adventure was to be shot. William Selig supposedly shot the first film in California in 1907 when he photographed the water scenes for *The Count of Monte Cristo*. However, it was not until the Motion Picture Patents Company forced certain "independent" companies to move west, chronicled in Chapter 2, that California production assumed any significance.

However, in a pattern similar to exhibition development, hundreds of small companies sprang up in many different locations, including San Antonio, Texas; Ogden, Utah; and Jacksonville, Florida. Many more small companies set up shop throughout the East — for example, in Providence, Rhode Island, and Ithaca and Saranac Lake, New York. Kathleen Karr writes about some of these studios in *American Film Heritage* (1968) and relates a fascinating history of tiny independent companies struggling to survive in isolated locations. "Caribou Bill" Cooper's Arctic Film Company in Saranac Lake, New York, was an example. Most of these companies did not last long, and their largely unexplored history is a fascinating footnote to the development of motion pictures in the United States.

With production increasing both in quantity and quality, exhibition facilities began to improve as well. Progress was slow, however, because cost criteria dominated every aspect of exhibition. The cheaper the theater, the better. Any structure that could hold 100 people and be darkened was "converted" into a theater — which usually involved, at best, renting 100 folding chairs; throwing a sheet across a wire; begging, borrowing, or stealing a projector; and projecting films for a paying public. The following announcement in an early trade publication for exhibitors, *The Moving Picture* (1906), gives some indication of the state of exhibition between 1905 and 1907:

> Housewives of Knoxville, Mt. Oliver, and Carrick boroughs, Pa. are mourning the abandonment of the garden truck stands and the meat stalls at the Knoxville market house in Bausman street. The space formerly occupied by the stands is now being used for a moving picture show on the first floor and a roller skating rink on the second floor.

Audiences, however, ultimately tired of dirty, airless rooms and grainy prints. Something else was needed to attract audiences, and several people began to experiment in new exhibition patterns. One of the most unusual experiments was that of George C. Hale, who first exhibited his "Hale Tours" at the St. Louis Exposition of 1904. "Hale Tours" consisted of travel pictures projected in tiny theaters built to resemble railway coaches. A conductor took tickets inside and the car rumbled and swayed as the awed and sometimes frightened spectators watched Yellowstone Park's "Old Faithful" erupt before their very eyes. The accompanying box is a trade advertisement promoting Biograph film stock for use on Hale Tours.

By far the most significant development, however, took place in Pittsburgh in 1905, when two brothers,

---

HALE TOUR RUNS

ATTRACTIVE RAILROAD PICTURES
WHICH HAVE BEEN FOUND
Highly Successful With Tour Car Schemes

Biograph pictures are generally considered by far the most desirable for Hale Tour Cars, as they are printed on the hardiest stock, with the steadiest perforations, and show the finest photographic qualities. Out of our enormous stock we have selected the following subjects of varying lengths, and can heartily recommend them.

NO.	TITLE	LENGTH	CODE WORD
301	*Through the Haverstraw Tunnel*	54 feet.	Tessitrite

The most delightful bit on the West Shore Railroad. First view of the Hudson on the northbound trip.

879	*New York to Brooklyn over Brooklyn Bridge*	140 feet.	Fuocara

Shows all the details of the big structure, the passing trains, pedestrians, carriage traffic, etc.

885	*Elevated R. R., 110th St. Curve, New York City*	65 feet.	Furabatur

Known as "The Big Loop," the highest and most dangerous section on the New York Elevated. View shows Columbia College and the new Cathedral of St. John the Divine.

1082	*Queenstown Heights, M. C. R. R. (Niagara)*	52 feet.	Fuscorum

Niagara Falls Series. Taken from a trolley car. Picturesque suburban scenery on the Canadian side of the Falls.

1083	*Niagara on the Lake, M. C. R. R.*	52 feet.	Fuscous

Another bit of trackage on the same line as 1082.

1084	*Falls View Station, M. C. R. R.*	53 feet.	Fusculo

Magnificent panoramic view of the Falls.

1110	*Lower Rapids, Niagara*	52 feet.	Fusionando

Splendid view of the rushing waters from the Gorge Road.

1111	*Whirlpool Rapids, Niagara*	54 feet.	Fusionar

Scene of all the "barrel" exploits. Taken from the Gorge Road.

NOTE—The above eight films may be combined in a Trip from New York to Niagara Falls.

1285	*The Gap, C. P. R. R.*	78 feet.	Gabacha
1288	*Under Shadow of Mt. Stephen, C. P. R. R.*	54 feet.	Gabado
1289	*Down Kicking Horse Slide, C. P. R. R.*	78 feet.	Gabael
1307	*Frazer Canon, C. P. R. R.*	63 feet.	Gabazola

Four splendid scenes on the picturesque Canadian Pacific near Banff.

Biograph Bulletin *(June 30, 1906)*

The Nickelodeon

*T*here is a new thing under the sun—at least new within a short period of time—and entirely new in the sense that the public is waking up to what it means.

It is the 5-cent theater. . . .

One of its chief attractions is the knowledge that if you are stung it is for "only a nickel, five pennies, a half dime," as the barker says, and that if you don't like the show they can inflict only fifteen minutes of it on you.

Here are the ingredients of a 5-cent theater:

One storeroom, seating from 200 to 500 persons.

One phonograph with extra large horn.

One young woman cashier.

One electric sign.

One cinematograph, with operator.

One canvas on which to throw the pictures.

One piano.

One barker.

One manager.

As many chairs as the store will hold.

A few brains and a little tact. Mix pepper and salt to taste.

After that all you have to do is to open the doors, start the phonograph and carry the money to the bank. The public does the rest.

It makes little difference what time of day you go to a 5-cent theater. The doors are opened as early in the forenoon as there is a chance of gathering in a few nickels, the downtown theaters opening earlier than those in the outlying districts to accommodate the visitors. Each "performance" lasts fifteen minutes. At the end of each a sign is thrown from the cinematograph on the canvas announcing that those who came late may stay for the next "performance. . . ."

The name of the play is flashed on the canvas, so that it may be identified if ever seen again. Understand that the young men who sing the "illustrated songs" are the only live performers in these theaters. The rest is moving pictures; and that is the startling part of the great favor with which these theaters have been received by the public.

The plays that are put on at the 5-cent theaters are for the most part manufactured abroad. Paris is a great producing center. London has numerous factories that grind them out. They are bought by the foot.

This system of buying drama and comedy by the foot has its distinct advantages. If the piece grows dull at any point the manager can take a pair of shears and carve out a few yards or rods, thereby enlivening the whole performance. . . .

Moving Picture World (May 4, 1907)

Harry and John Harris, opened their first "nickelodeon," or five-cent theater (see the accompanying box). The idea caught on immediately. Soon the Harris brothers had fourteen nickelodeons in Pittsburgh, open from 8:00 A.M. to midnight six days a week. Since the program would change every fifteen minutes, up to 8,000 people could see it every day. In 1907, attendance in Chicago's nickelodeons averaged 100,000 a day. By 1910, there were more than 10,000 nickelodeons in the United States.

The nickelodeon became the first permanent home of motion pictures, and its importance should not be underestimated. Its development had as much to do with keeping the industry vital and alive as any individual's artistic contributions.

All this activity in production and exhibition was an indication of the industry's growing professionalism and maturity. By 1907 many future patterns of production and exhibition had been set. The last area of industrial development to emerge as a separate phase was distribution. In the early years, exhibitors simply bought films by ordering them from a catalog. Films were priced by cost per foot, and the going rate was usually around 10 cents a foot. Once purchased, films were then informally circulated by exhibitors among their various theaters.

Producers disliked this practice, however, and soon a new distribution pattern evolved in the industry. The first step involved setting up an organization, renting an office, and inviting exhibitors to come and trade films. Soon the idea of a more formal method of distribution

▲ The exterior and interior of a typical nickelodeon of the period 1905–1910.

An Honest Living

*T*he nickelodeon shows have furnished occupation for young women, many of them girls, who, after they have practiced the piano for years, found they could not earn a living as well as the girl who had learned nothing but to wash dishes. There must be two score of the moving picture shows in Pittsburgh, not to speak of those in Allegheny and McKeesport, and every one of them has a piano player.

The piano players at the nickelodeons of a year or so ago furnished excruciating music, for they were usually girls who played at street carnivals and the attractions in the private parks. As the shows became known and people of taste learned that frequently very interesting scenes were represented, the managers sought girls of another social class, with the result that the quality of music has improved and the higher class selections indicated as appropriate by the manufacturers of the most artistic films are played with taste and precision in many of the shows. With the coming of these girls facilities for withdrawal from the public eye had to be provided. Even now one sees, at a few of the shows, the girl piano player boldly face the incoming audience, with the light turned up; flirting with the ushers and altogether comporting themselves with the same freedom as members of a peripatetic German band; but at other places, as soon as the film has passed through the machine and a new audience is coming in, the piano player slips under the stage and is not visible until the lights are turned down and the film starts again. It is said that some of the girls have a very good social standing, and that their friends do not dream that they are earning an honest living by playing the piano in a public place.

—Moving Picture World, *April 27, 1907*

emerged. Harry Hiles, a San Francisco exhibitor, bought films from producers and rented them to exhibitors for a week at a time at about half the original price. Soon other men caught on to yet another big-money scheme, and distribution companies, or "exchanges," as they were called, began opening up across the country. By 1907, between 125 and 150 exchanges existed. Once established, the exchange (formal-distribution) method of getting films from producer to exhibitor remained the same throughout the history of the motion picture, although later the production studios would assume distribution as an automatic arm of production.

Wrap-Up

The history of motion pictures up to 1907 centered around the development of a technological reality, an industrial empire, and an emerging film aesthetic. These first several years were years of groping and grasping, years filled with new ideas and rapid development. Motion pictures were pulled into the twentieth century by an enthusiastic public that demanded new forms of entertainment. Motion pictures began their history as scientific curiosity and ==ultimately became the core of an industrial empire.==

However, along the way individual artists began to make their own contributions. Men such as Emile Cohl, Cecil Hepworth, Georges Méliès, and Edwin S. Porter worked independently but simultaneously in discovering the language of film. Throughout this journey, the developing of form and function was clearly linked to the larger social arena. Individual inventiveness and problem solving soon gave way to corporate mass production, largely owing to public response and demand. The relationships among artist, industry, and audience would continue to shape and define the motion picture throughout its history.

CHAPTER

2

Industrial Development and Emerging Film Styles (1908 – 1916)

Focus

By 1906, just a decade after the first public showing of motion pictures in the United States, it was clear that the movies were destined to be much more than a passing novelty. Production centers were desperately trying to meet the demands of an enthusiastic and ever-expanding audience, an extensive distribution system was in place, and exhibition had found a permanent home in the nickelodeon. Production, distribution, exhibition — the three components of the business model — had transformed the motion picture from a technological curiosity and supplement to the vaudeville theater into the product of a full-fledged industry.

Realizing the greater potential of film in terms of business (if not art), the pioneer producing companies such as Edison, Vitagraph and Biograph protected their interests by forming a collective trust company that would limit film production to its membership, control exhibition, and thus freeze out the upstart independent companies that were now proving a constant threat. The more progressive independent companies, while challenging the Trust, were also creating a climate for more innovative business practices and more creative films.

In surveying the film styles and content during this period, we find that the most significant contributions were coming from producers, directors, scenarists, and major performers who had the vision and the determination or commanding presence to extend film beyond the routine "photoplay" of the early narrative years. Under the ever watchful eye (and occasional guidance) of the protectors of public morals, these creative talents expanded and refined the art of screen storytelling, set down an entire lexicon of film technique, and developed what would become the staples of silent film — the serious drama or melodrama, the Western adventure, and the highly artful silent screen comedy.

The Trust and the Independents

Motion Picture Patents Company (Trust) Members

Biograph	Lubin
Edison	Méliès
Essanay	Pathé Frères
Kalem	Selig
George Kleine (distributor)	Vitagraph

Major Early Independent Production Companies

Original Firm		*Resulting Studio*
Famous Players (Adolph Zukor)	▶ Famous Players-Lasky	Paramount Pictures
Feature Play Co. (Jesse Lasky)		
Fox Film Corp. (William Fox)		20th-Century Fox
Goldwyn Pictures Corp. (Sam Goldfish, later "Goldwyn")	▶	Metro-Goldwyn-Mayer*
Metro Pictures Corp. (Louis B. Mayer)		
Selznick Pictures Co. (Lewis J. Selznick)		Selznick International Pictures
Independent Moving Picture Co. (IMP) (Carl Laemmle)		Universal Pictures

* Loew's Inc. was the exhibition chain founded by Marcus Loew and Joseph Schenck. It became the parent company and exhibition division of Metro-Goldwyn-Mayer.

▶ A Biograph theater wagon. A cameraman perches on the rear of this horse-drawn wagon, which advertises offerings of Biograph Pictures (a Trust Company), at a local Boston Theater: "Highest Grade Specialties" in continuous performance.

The Industry

The Trust

Most of the industry's problems in its years of infancy stemmed from patent disputes. Rather than trying to control the business by making the best films or hiring and promoting popular performers, the pioneer companies, which held patents on major camera and projection equipment, attempted to maintain control by denying access to the means by which films were made and exhibited. However, as entrepreneurs came to realize the tremendous financial potential of moviemaking, the patent-holding Trust companies began turning out as many lawsuits as films. In late 1908, George Kleine, a major company head, suggested a solution — a patents pool. In response, in 1909 the ten companies pooled sixteen patents controlling film, cameras, and projectors to form the Motion Picture Patents Company (MPPC).

The patents pool granted uniform licenses to the ten member companies to manufacture and control the use of cameras and projectors and to manufacture and lease motion pictures. The ten participating companies agreed to lease their films only to exchanges and exhibitors using licensed machines and only to those exchanges dealing exclusively in their films. They also agreed to charge prices no lower than those stipulated in the agreement. "The Trust," as the group came to be called, collected royalties of two dollars a week from all exhibitors using projection machines based on its patents. It issued licenses to make and sell such machines upon condition that they be used solely for exhibiting films leased by one of the ten participating manufacturers. Had it come five years earlier, the MPPC may well have succeeded in gaining control of the industry. By 1909, however, with motion picture attendance growing at a phenomenal rate, many small "independent" film companies were being formed to cash in on this latest economic bonanza. These companies were simply not about to stand aside and let the Trust take over. They fought back and they fought hard.

A Trust Company

*A*d copy in the trade press described the film wares of the original trust companies. Here Vitagraph advertises two weeks' worth of "Life Portrayals."

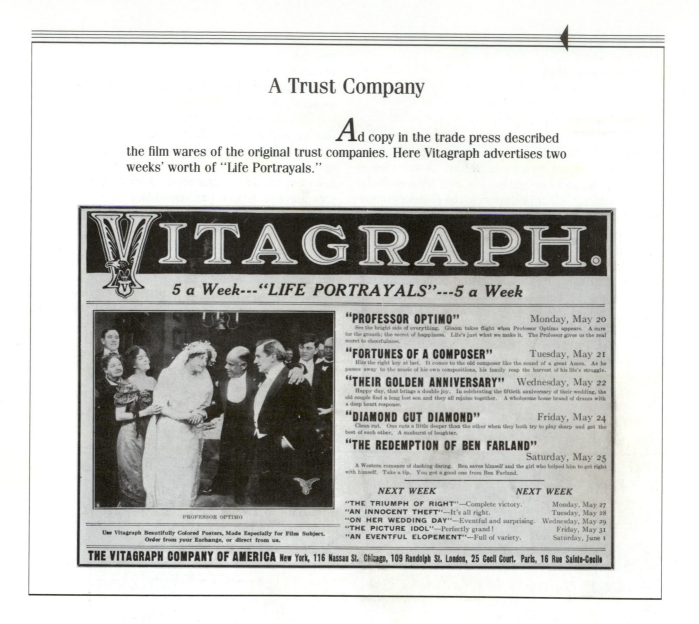

Obviously, the Trust was a restrictive monopoly. Between 1909 and 1914 open warfare ensued in the industry as independent producers, exchanges, and exhibitors engaged the Trust in a battle for the American audience. Much to the amazement of the Trust, these "independents" found a ready market for their films. And despite the Trust's efforts at controlling the industry, several independents kept fighting, both legally in the courts and illegally by making motion pictures with "borrowed" equipment.

Consolidating and regulating film distribution was the next step in the Trust's attempt at control. In 1910 the Trust organized the General Film Company as a distribution subsidiary. Distribution became the key to

fighting the system, and because the General Film Company became the distributor for most exhibitors, the independents had to work hard to get their films accepted.

The exhibitors themselves did not like the Trust because of the weekly two-dollar license fee and other restrictive practices, and they encouraged the independents by renting or buying their films. Given this stimulus, the independents continued the fight against overwhelming odds, and between 1909 and 1914 they struggled savagely for survival. Chief among their several important advantages was the attitude of the Trust itself. The MPPC saw films as a commodity sold by the foot, regardless of players, story, or size of theater. For the most part, the men who controlled the Patents Company were inventors and businessmen out of touch with the growing demand for better and longer films. As for the independents, they were such men as William Fox, Carl Laemmle, and Adolph Zukor. Most were uneducated immigrants who got their start operating local theaters and who knew what the public wanted. Labeled "outlaws" by the MPPC, they were free from restrictions, which provided a second great advantage—the chance to experiment. The Trust studios were not without their visionaries—in fact, the independents were eventually able to raid the Trust studios for their best talent. And in valuing the artistic over the product orientation, the "outlaws" soon began developing films devoted to story, and drawing on the appeal of their players.

The Trust was legally dissolved in 1917, but it actually died almost three years earlier. There were a number of reasons for this, but three developments became major factors in the decline of the Trust: (1) the establishment of a star system, whereby popular screen personalities were promoted and featured in advertising films and the studio; (2) the emergence of the feature-length film; and (3) the geographical shift of the industry's center to California. The first two factors were innovations that enabled the independents, especially Carl Laemmle and Adolph Zukor, who exploited these developments brilliantly, to market their films successfully. The third factor allowed the independents the freedom to make films far away from the Eastern-based Trust.

The Trust refused to identify actors and actresses in order to avoid any "unreasonable" salary demands from suddenly established "stars." Feature film was another innovation used by the independents to fight the Trust. In their commitment to cost-per-foot consciousness and the resultant two-reel length standard, the Trust studios severely limited their own commercial and artistic development. However, the potential for innovation and experimentation in the longer story format suddenly became clear. The independents, especially Adolph Zukor, seized upon the extended-length feature film as another way to compete with the Trust, and by 1914 several other independents had joined Zukor in the rush toward feature-length production.

These new developments were occurring in a place unfamiliar to most Americans—Hollywood, California. The move West began around 1908, and by 1910 several companies had established studios in California. However, the big rush occurred around 1913, when the independents began to look for locations where production could continue without harassment of court injunctions and "goon squads" hired by the Trust to interfere with

A Competitor of the Trust

*C*arl Laemmle's "Imp" Company and Adolph Zukor's Famous Players are among several independent and foreign companies that were advertising in the trade press by 1912.

production. San Francisco at first seemed to be the logical spot, as it was an established community with many advantages. However, the actual choice was the "frontier" town of Los Angeles and its sleepy suburb Hollywood, primarily because of the year-round sunshine and warm climate, and the varied geographical environments nearby — mountains, deserts, and ocean. Some historians cite the proximity to the Mexican border as an advantage, because it supposedly provided an escape from the Trust's litigation. This was probably not a real factor, however, since the border was at least four or five hours away, offering plenty of time for legal papers to be served. Nevertheless, the move West, begun as a fearful flight by a few independent companies, soon reached avalanche proportions as more and more production companies found the climate and geography of the East too confining. The simple inexpensive outdoor sets available in Los Angeles were a clear advantage over elaborate glassed-in studios, and the 365-day shooting schedule allowed many more films to be shot.

The Trust continued the fight on the movie set and in the courts, but ultimately it lost both battles. Most of the original Trust studios either quietly faded away or were absorbed by the stronger independent companies. By 1920 not one of the original Trust companies was a major force in the industry. Through the efforts of Carl Laemmle, Adolph Zukor, William Fox, and other independents a new system was formed, based not on patents and equipment but on stars and popular stories. As Benjamin Hampton notes in his detailed study of the early industry, *A History of the Movies,* "The story of the patents company and of General Film deserves to be remembered as a perfect illustration of the futility of laws that lack the support and sympathy of the populace."

The independents gambled on the public's taste and won. They created a new system based on this single great intangible, a system that ultimately suppressed the

▶ An interior and exterior set.
(A) Before the era of the Kleig light, interior sets were frequently constructed in the open air, with natural sunlight used to solve illumination problems. Here a construction crew pauses for a photograph during the construction of a roofless hotel lobby for Wharton Pictures.
(B) This exterior, used in the film serial *Patria*, shows Warner Oland (with cane) in a pre–Charlie Chan role.
(C) The *Patria* set was actually a replica of a house on 23rd Street in New York City.

Edison on Motion Pictures

"*T*he moving picture will endure as long as poor people exist. It fills the same want in the lives of the masses that the five cent trolley car filled. The motion picture fits into their income. The workers deserve and must have more amusement than the richer folk, who are able to afford the regular theater and other expensive pleasures.

The next steps of advancement will center about better photography, with less flicker, the production of multiple reel screen dramas, colored pictures and possibly stereoscopic films with the effect of actual depth.

We do not know yet how to attain the stereoscopic effect. I have no less than four suggestions a day from all parts of America, but yet have I found one process which is practical.

I have long been working on a method to secure photography in all natural colors in their right value."

—*From an interview with Thomas Edison,*
The New York Dramatic Mirror *(July 9, 1913)*

dominant Trust. The Trust failed because of its conservative attitude toward production and marketing methods, its preoccupation with its competitors, and its refusal to acknowledge the public's tastes in film. In 1913 Edison had visions of further technological development that may have been prophetic, but they were not enough to stem the tide of imaginative and aggressive independent producers.

The Independents

The important organizations in this immediate post-Trust period were Adolph Zukor's Famous Players Company (later incorporated into Paramount), the Mutual Film Company, Carl Laemmle's Universal Company, Richard Rowland's Metro (later incorporated into MGM), and VLSE (a combination of four former Trust companies—Vitagraph, Lubin, Selig, and Essanay). Notable individuals included Lewis J. Selznick and William Fox. In addition, hundreds of small companies jumped in to fill the void created by the Trust's decline, and by 1916 there were well over 150 production companies manufacturing between 1,200 and 1,500 films a year. Most of these early post-Trust companies developed

their own financial resources, were fiercely independent, and fought savagely for survival. Furthermore, most of them failed. Those independents that survived, however, would be the backbone of the American studio structure for the next four decades.

Adolph Zukor and his Famous Players Company dominated this early stage of development. The formation of Paramount in 1914 by Zukor, Lasky, and W. W. Hodkinson was a good example of how quickly power in the industry had shifted. Only a few years before, Hodkinson had been an employee of General Film, and Zukor had sat for hours in a reception room of the same company trying to get permission to exhibit his film *Queen Elizabeth* (1912). Zukor had originally come to the United States in 1888 from Hungary with, as the legend goes, $40 sewn into the lining of his coat. After achieving some success manufacturing furs, he became interested in penny arcades, and in 1902, after "observing the interests of the customers," he and two partners opened their own arcade in New York. He opened his first motion picture theater, the Crystal Palace, in 1904, and "finding the show business very much to my liking" began what was perhaps the longest career as a studio chief in film history. (Zukor died in 1976 at the age of 103.)

▶ Carl Laemmle, who emigrated from Germany to the United States in 1884; he opened his first theater in Chicago in 1906. He was a key pioneer among independent producers, and Universal Pictures, which he formed with associates in 1912, was to become a major Hollywood studio.

Zukor's history is typical of the men who would soon come to dominate the industry. William Fox was a garment worker who became a partner in a theater that he developed into a major production organization. Carl Laemmle, an emigré who managed a clothing store for a time in Oshkosh, Wisconsin, went to Chicago and was given a vacant theater which he expanded into a chain of theaters, and ultimately formed Universal Pictures, a major Hollywood studio. Marcus Loew was a fur dealer who bought a penny arcade and expanded it into the most powerful studio (MGM) in the industry. It is not accidental that most of the men who emerged victorious in this early struggle for control got their start in exhibition. Running penny arcades and store theaters gave them a knowledge of the public and what it wanted. In his autobiography, *The Public Is Never Wrong,* Adolph Zukor put it this way:

> In the Crystal Hall it was my custom to take a seat about six rows from the front. . . . I spent a good deal of time watching the faces of the audience, even turning around to do so. . . . With a little experience I could see, hear, and "feel" the reaction to each melodrama and comedy.

When Zukor and others began producing films, it followed quite logically that they would use the criteria of public taste in determining the types of films their companies should make.

Alongside these success stories were many failures. Two of the most powerful independents to fall were the Mutual Company, destroyed by internal dissent and a reluctance to make feature-length films, and the Triangle Company, destroyed because its corporate heads were out of touch with public taste. Triangle especially had great initial promise. It wanted to bring the stories and stars of the legitimate stage to the screen. However, the public did not want Sarah Bernhardt, Lily Langtry, or James O'Neil when it could see Mary Pickford, Bronco Billy Anderson, and Charlie Chaplin.

On the eve of World War I, Zukor, Fox, Laemmle, and other independents were ready to take control of and create a new structure for the rapidly expanding motion picture industry. Their methods, unlike the Trust's, were not restrictive or negative. Instead, they achieved control by promoting new ideas: feature-length films, actors and actresses publicized as "stars," and higher quality motion pictures. As Terry Ramsaye said of the new breed, in his account of the American silent industry, *A Million and One Nights,* "They bettered the art to better their own business. Pictures improved to improve the power of the box office."

The Feature Film

One of the most important methods used by the independents to break the Trust's monopoly was to produce longer films. The feature-length film as defined by today's standards had not yet arrived. In 1913, however, when the Italian spectacle *Quo Vadis?* was imported into the United States, it was a huge success, running twenty-two weeks in New York at $1 a ticket. The film had an enormous impact, and its nine-reel length (slightly more than two hours), spectacular content, and $1 admission price prompted some of the bolder independents to begin experimenting with a feature-length format.

Copyright Law and Lost (and Found) Films

*I*t is an anomaly in the task of preserving our film past that today we can view many of the films produced before 1912, yet a great percentage of films made between 1912 and 1951 are irretrievably lost. In the early years it was standard practice in film copyrighting to deposit with the Library of Congress entire copies of films transferred onto unprojectable paper rolls. The original films, made on highly unstable and inflammable nitrate stock, eventually deteriorated, but these paper copies remained on file and intact. In 1953 Kemp Niver undertook to transfer more than 3,000 of these early films onto modern safety stock so they could be viewed.

The Motion Picture Copyright Law enacted in 1912 made it unnecessary to deposit entire prints on paper rolls in the copyrighting process, so many films made from that date until 1951, when safety (acetate) film stock came into use, deteriorated and were lost. For several years, the Library of Congress, with the American Film Institute, has been engaged in transferring what remains of the old nitrate films onto safety stock. However, the Library of Congress estimates that between 80 and 90 percent of the films made during the teens and twenties are gone forever.

D. W. Griffith, a young director employed by Biograph, a Trust studio, was eager to attempt the new format. Partially inspired by *Quo Vadis?* but also, and more importantly, compelled by a need to develop his own style and content, Griffith made *Judith of Bethulia* in 1914. Its $36,000 cost proved to be too much for the conservative Biograph owners, however, and Griffith soon departed to begin preparations for his next film, *The Birth of a Nation,* as an independent producer.

The man who had the most impact on beginning a regular system of feature production, however, was not a director, but the producer Adolph Zukor. By 1914 he and Jesse Lasky were releasing three to four features a week through the independent firm, Paramount. This was a significant step. Motion pictures were beginning to attract a more sophisticated audience, one that was accustomed to literature and long plays. One-reel shorts were inadequate for the treatment of complex and sophisticated stories. Meeting this need brought about tremendous growth in the industry. Entire departments were established, employing thousands of people. Huge studios and back lots were constructed. The specialization of skills became more important than ever. As production became more complex, one person could no longer do everything.

Obviously, costs rose as well. Prior to 1910 a one-reel film cost approximately $2,000 to produce. By 1915 the cost of an average feature-length film (three to four reels) was between $20,000 and $40,000. However, the rise in cost was more than compensated for by higher gross earnings. The average net profit was $10,000 to $20,000 per picture. These profits spurred even greater expansion of the feature format, and by 1920, therefore, the entire industry had switched to feature production, though serials and comedy shorts were still produced. It was ultimately the public's acceptance of both the format and the increased admission price that made this transition possible.

The Star System

Even more important to the independents' rise to power was their willingness to sell motion pictures through the appeal of certain men or women who "starred" in them. If there was a beginning, it might well have been in April

The Developing Cinematic Arts

*T*he most important advancement in direction has been the attention to detail — the carefulness with the finer points of a picture. . . . Things thought unessential in the early days of action stories are now carefully studied. . . .

Realism in scenery is another keynote of the advance. The tendency all around is towards greater naturalness and towards the elimination of artificiality. A criticism, however, in many scenarios is that a strong situation, so called, is brought in, simply for the sake of the situation, and without being a logical part of the plot. That is all wrong. The story must develop plausibly.

— *From an interview with Horace G. Plimpton, Thomas A. Edison, Inc.,* New York Dramatic Mirror *(May 21, 1913)*

*I*n the matter of acting, of course, you have observed that important action now takes place closer to the camera, in order that all expressions may register. This means that the director must rehearse his people more thoroughly than of old.

The picture player is a specialist to a more marked degree than the actors and actresses of the stage. Every motion picture stock company must have a number of people who represent distinct types. They must really possess those characteristics which can be assumed by an actor in the drama through skill at make-up.

— *From an interview with Alice Joyce of the Kalem Company,* New York Dramatic Mirror *(June 18, 1913)*

1910, when a young woman named Florence Lawrence left the Trust company Biograph to join Carl Laemmle's IMP. Lawrence had been earning $25 a week at Biograph, and, like many other "faces," was beginning to accumulate a large public following. Biograph and other Trust companies clearly recognized that if these "faces" acquired "names" they might start to demand more money. Since the Trust sold their films by the foot regardless of who appeared in them, having to pay higher salaries to popular faces would disrupt the entire system. The independents, and Carl Laemmle in particular, perceived this restrictive philosophy as a way to create dissension and desertion among the actors and actresses

working for Trust studios. Laemmle therefore offered Miss Lawrence $1,000 a week to "star" in his IMP productions. He followed this with an extensive publicity campaign, and audiences were soon clamoring for more of Lawrence, "The IMP Girl."

Even more significant than Laemmle and Lawrence was another producer-star team, Zukor and Pickford. In his climb up the competitive ladder, Zukor did not follow the usual method of dominating by corporate consolidation and merger. Rather, he gained power by absorbing the strength of his competitors, most importantly star actors and actresses. Zukor's primary asset in this struggle was Mary Pickford who was, along with Charlie

Chaplin, the most popular screen personality up to 1920.

Dubbed "America's Sweetheart," Pickford presented an image of youthful womanhood. She started her career with D. W. Griffith at Biograph in 1909 and moved on to Paramount in 1914. Between 1914 and 1919, Mary Pickford made more than twenty films, ranging from low comedy to high drama. What is often lost in the stereotyped historical image of her as a pre-1920 Shirley Temple are her remarkable versatility and range as an actress.

In spite of her freshness and exuberance (or perhaps because of it), the Jazz Age of the twenties was not the proper climate for Pickford's continued growth. She did make several successful films in the twenties, but American audiences identified her with another age, and after only three talking films, she retired.

With Zukor, Laemmle, and an increasing number of stars showing the way, most of the major film producers quickly jumped on the star bandwagon, and by 1914 nearly all feature films were being made with star personalities. The feature film was of great benefit to the star system, since the longer a popular star was on the screen the better the audience liked it. But the feature form also allowed certain stars time to develop and demonstrate their talents. Stars became the pegs upon which producers could hang the whole system of mass feature production. Within three years the industry had undergone a profound shift in its balance of power. Not only had a new breed of independent producer replaced the old conservative Trust leaders, but, and perhaps just as important, control had shifted from employer to employee.

The leaders of this revolution, Chaplin and Pickford, closely paralleled each other in their careers. In fact, Pickford, with the help and guidance of her mother Charlotte, seemed to base her increasing salary demands on what Chaplin was earning. The accompanying chart shows the meteoric rise of these two young people, and at the same time indicates the growing strength of the industry, which was quite able, although not always willing, to pay these fantastic salaries.

According to Benjamin Hampton, prior to 1920 most stars earned between $500 and $1,000 a week. Lead players earned $150 to $500, and character actors $75 to $250. Even these salaries were not universal and perhaps not even typical. Mae Marsh, a major star in the silent period, remarked in a recent interview that when she appeared in *The Birth of a Nation* in 1915 she was still making $35 a week and was grateful for the sum. However, at the end of World War I salaries increased dramatically. As the industry expanded to keep up with public demand, more and more stars, sensing their own importance, asked for and received huge salaries. Indeed, the well-publicized weekly salaries of Tom Mix ($10,000), Geraldine Farrar ($10,000), and Alla Nazimova ($13,000) clearly illustrate that the star system reigned supreme.

As the public demand for stars increased, the film industry found it could no longer rely on the natural evolution of personalities to fill its films, and an effort was launched to find and promote new stars. By 1915 audiences were seeing such new discoveries as Theda Bara, Lillian and Dorothy Gish, Tom Mix, Norma Talmadge, and William S. Hart, among many others. Although Chaplin and Pickford led the parade, they were never

▶ Mary Pickford, in a typical "girl with the golden curls" pose. Although she was considered a major star of the silent screen, she was known to moviegoers as "Little Mary," the name of the character she usually portrayed.

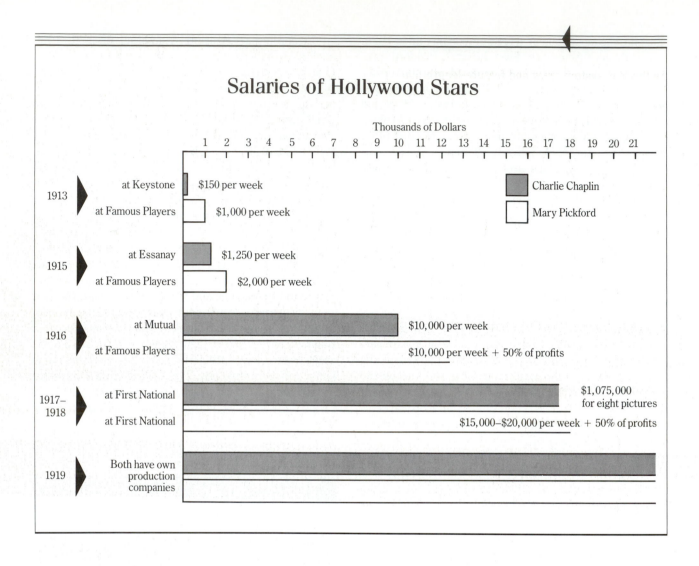

Salaries of Hollywood Stars

Thousands of Dollars

1 2 3 4 5 6 7 8 9 10 11 12 13 14 15 16 17 18 19 20 21

Charlie Chaplin
Mary Pickford

1913
at Keystone — $150 per week
at Famous Players — $1,000 per week

1915
at Essanay — $1,250 per week
at Famous Players — $2,000 per week

1916
at Mutual — $10,000 per week
at Famous Players — $10,000 per week + 50% of profits

1917–1918
at First National — $1,075,000 for eight pictures
at First National — $15,000–$20,000 per week + 50% of profits

1919
Both have own production companies

really part of it in the first place. They were natural phenomena, as much the cause as the symbols of the whole system.

More interesting in terms of what the star system finally came to mean for American motion pictures were the stars created and nurtured by the studios. The story of Theodosia Goodman is a case in point. She first appeared in a 1915 production called *A Fool There Was,* in which she played a siren and attracted strong public attention. The studio publicity machine swung into full gear and ultimately produced Theda Bara, who became one of the most popular stars of the time. She starred in more than forty pictures for Fox in three years, and made *vamp* a household word. The industry had created a star and then geared its production system around her. Her appeal was carefully nurtured, and ultimately she became the prototype of the seductress. As the *New York*

Times remarked in 1916, "Since Miss Bara is so well fitted by looks to act this sort of creature [vampire] before the camera, it would be squandering her resources to cast her in a Mary Pickford sort of role."

Other personalities were typed just as religiously: Lillian Gish was the sweet, fragile heroine; Clara Bow the wild, reckless flapper; Greta Garbo the femme fatale; Ramon Novarro the perfect troubadour; Lewis Stone the aristocrat; Reginald Denny the perfect athlete; and so on. There were clowns, vamps, flappers, villains, Latin lovers, and almost anything else the audience wanted. This "typing" of certain personalities was another indication of the size and complexity of the industry. Freezing a star's screen image and repeating it in film after film was of obvious economic advantage, since studios could produce formula films with standard appeals quickly and cheaply on a mass-production basis.

New Forms of Exhibition

As the star system grew and feature-length films prospered, exhibitors began expanding their operations beyond the nickelodeon stage, and by 1910 elaborate new theaters were being built. In Louisville, Kentucky, for example, a marble-and-glass-front theater, constructed for $35,000, contained 700 upholstered tip-up chairs, a mechanical piano and barrel organ, and uniformed ushers equipped with syringes used to kill germs and sweeten the air. By 1910 national attendance figures were an estimated 4 million people daily and 25 million a week, many of them children.

In the 1909 article entitled "The Spirit of Youth and the City," Jane Addams remarked:

> "Going to the show" for thousands of young people in every industrial city is the only possible road to the realms of mystery and romance; the theater is the only place where they can satisfy that craving for a conception of life higher than that which the actual world offers them. In a very real sense the drama and the drama alone performs for them the office of art as is clearly revealed in their blundering demand stated in many forms for "a play unlike life." The theater becomes to them a "veritable house of dreams" infinitely more real than the noisy streets and the crowded factories.

In 1912 there were approximately 13,000 motion picture theaters in the United States, most of them still nickelodeons. However, in 1914, Mitchell Mark opened the Strand Theater in New York, and the age of the motion picture palace began. Designed for motion pictures exclusively, the Strand occupied an entire block and seated 3,500 people. It was equipped with a huge pipe organ and could accommodate a symphony orchestra. The Strand was not simply another new theater. It symbolized a turning point in motion picture history. The article from the *New York Times* (April 22, 1916) reporting the opening of the Rialto, a major theater in New York's Times Square, is an excellent reference point for the time (see page 44).

Theda Bara, the first screen "vamp" and one of the most popular stars of the pre–World War I period.

The first home of Famous Players Film Company, the forerunner of Paramount.

Film Exhibition in Major U.S. Cities in 1910

City	Population	Approximate Number of Theaters	Seating Capacity
New York	4,338,322	450	150,000
Chicago	2,000,000	310	93,000
Philadelphia	1,491,082	160	57,000
St. Louis	824,000	142	50,410
Cleveland	600,000	75	22,500
Baltimore	600,000	83	24,900
San Francisco	400,000	68	32,400
Cincinnati	350,000	75	22,500
New Orleans	325,000	28	5,600

—Adapted from "The Moving Picture and the National Character," American Review of Reviews *(September 1910)*

Rialto Theatre Opens Its Doors

Luxurious Motion Picture House Begins Business in Times Square

With Fairbanks as Star

Stageless Theater, Handsomely Appointed and Seating 2,000 Has Replaced the Old Victoria

The Rialto Theatre, which for nearly a year has been building on the spot in Times Square where Hammerstein's old Victoria used to stand, opened its doors last evening to a specially invited and very imposing audience. Today and daily hereafter the clamorous public will be admitted, and so another motion picture house has been added to the thousands which dot the map of the United States. But the difference between the queer, jiggly films that used to serve as chasers on the Keith programs fifteen years ago and the elaborate photoplays of 1916 is no greater than the difference between the evilly ventilated little nickelodeons and the luxurious theatre which was opened last night.

—New York Times (April 22, 1916)

Guarding Movie Morals

*I*n my opinion nothing is of greater importance to the success of the motion picture interests than films of good moral tone. Motion picture shows are now passing through a period similar to that of vaudeville some years ago. Vaudeville became a great success by eliminating all of its once objectionable features and, for the same reason, the five cents theatre will prosper according to its moral attitude. Unless it can secure the entire respect of the amusement loving public it cannot endure.

—Thomas A. Edison, Moving Picture World
(December 21, 1907)

*T*he motion-picture business is a competitive one. There is the general trade injury coming from a single bad picture. If the manufacturer forces this condemned picture on the market, his rivals will make vigorous use of the fact that our board has refused to pass it. But, at any moment, if a majority of manufacturers should want to stop censorship, they could instantly end the board's existence.

—From an interview with John Collier,
General Secretary of the National Board of
Censorship, The New York Dramatic Mirror
(August 6, 1913)

*W*oe betide the screen if it cannot arouse interest in any other way than by a display of a woman's nakedness. I do not share the belief of certain motion picture producers and exhibitors, that the American public demand plays in which nudity laughs at conventions. Take the amusement "ads" in any newspaper, from Maine to California, and you will find that people are interested in the harmless, the uplifting, the entertaining, rather than the salacious, the prurient, and the pornographic. In New York, where wickedness is supposed to be the eternal sentinel of the city, there is but one show which makes a candid bid for the patronage of the baldheads.

—From "Nudity on the Screen" by Stephen
Bush, Moving Picture World *(January 1, 1916)*

Content Control

The expanding production and exhibition of film by the end of the first decade brought with it growing concern, both within and outside the industry, over film content, particularly subject matter that reached the limits of moral acceptability. As early as 1897 a brief clip of the exotic dancer Fatima was being doctored to mask the pelvic region of the gyrating performer. By 1907 the first municipal boards were established in New York and Chicago to see that movies met what were presumed to be community standards of morality.

In 1909 the fledgling industry took the first of what would be many steps toward self-regulation. To stem the

Regulations and Controls

1907 Jane Addams presents a resolution to the Chicago City Council calling for the regulation of motion picture theaters.

A Chicago ordinance empowers the police with controlling the content of films shown in the city, instituting official prior censorship of the movies.

1908 The Motion Picture Patents Company (MPPC) is formed by ten major producing companies to control all production and exhibition of films in the United States.

The mayor of New York City orders all movie theaters closed during Christmas week, and nickelodeons are placed under police jurisdiction. The City Board of Aldermen passes an ordinance barring children under age sixteen from attending any movie unless accompanied by an adult.

1909 Industry-supported regulation of movies is initiated in response to public criticism of film content. Called the National Board of Film Censorship, the new regulatory body is composed of "public spirited men and women," representatives of social organizations and of the industry.

1910 In a court fight with the MPPC, William Fox wins the right to distribute films as an independent producer.

A duty is imposed on all imported films.

1911 The Chicago Vice Commission publishes a study on vice in the city that contains a section on the evils of the nickelodeon entitled "Cheap Theaters."

The first state censorship board is established in Pennsylvania.

1912 The Taft administration files suit against the MPPC, charging it with restraint of trade in violation of the 1890 Sherman Antitrust Act.

Congress bars the interstate commerce of films of boxing matches after black heavyweight champion Jack Johnson beats the white former champion Jim Jeffries. It was thought that the ring victory by the "dark menace" might create racial tension.

1913 The first comprehensive municipal censorship law is enacted in New York City.

The Tariff Act gives the Secretary of the Treasury the power to censor imported films.

A state censorship board is established in Ohio.

1914 The first rating system is established in Chicago when the city ordinance is amended to prohibit the showing of certain films to persons under the age of twenty-one.

A state censorship board is established in Kansas.

1915 The MPPC is dissolved by a federal court as an illegal conspiracy in restraint of trade.

Legislation to establish federal censorship of movies is first introduced in Congress.

In a case involving the Mutual Film Corporation, the Supreme Court upholds the constitutionality of prior restraint of movies by disallowing its protection under the First Amendment on the grounds that it is "a business pure and simple, originated and conducted for profit."

1916 A state censorship board is established in Maryland.

The Smith-Hughes Bill, which calls for the establishment of a federal motion picture commission, is introduced in Congress but fails to pass.

In an effort to avert federal censorship, movie producers form the National Association of the Motion Picture Industry and announce a self-censorship program. It is the forerunner of the production code and the current rating administration.

tide of municipal and state censorship, the Motion Picture Patents Company—comprising manufacturers of two-thirds of the films produced in the United States—agreed to submit all its films to the newly formed National Board of Censorship of Motion Pictures. This New York-based board, made up of a number of private organizations concerned with the public welfare and supported financially by producing companies, became a national organ for prerelease censorship. Under the board's policy, films were screened and then approved, rejected, or returned for recommended changes. Reviewed films were then listed in the board's weekly bulletin as "Passed," "Passed with changes as specified," or "Condemned." The board's guidelines supported the censorship of obscenity, senseless morbidity, and the detailing of crime—particularly violence and brutality, scenes that might be considered offensive to recognized religions, and scenes that were contrary to "basic moralities."

In 1915 the most profound and far-reaching, if indirect, control of exhibition came in the form of a Supreme Court ruling. In a case known as *Mutual Film Corporation* v. *Ohio,* a distributor challenged the state statute providing for censorship of films prior to release. The high court ruled in favor of the state of Ohio:

> The exhibition of motion pictures is a business pure and simple, originated and conducted for profit . . . not to be regarded, nor intended to be regarded by the Ohio Constitution, we think, as part of the press of the country or as organs of public opinion.

It was not until 1952, thirty-seven years later, that the high court was again to consider the matter of film censorship. Its ruling in the *Miracle* case reversed the earlier decision and placed movies under the protection of the First Amendment.

By 1916, in addition to the proliferation of local censorship boards, mechanisms were in place for state regulation of films in Kansas, Maryland, Virginia, Ohio, Pennsylvania, and Massachusetts. In the latter state, Sunday blue laws dictated what was appropriate film fare for showing on the Sabbath.

Griffith and the Art of Film Construction

During this period of increasing concern over appropriate film content, one of the most controversial early creators was emerging as a visionary film artist and reactionary social observer. When David Wark Griffith was hired by the American Mutoscope and Biograph Company in the spring of 1908, the single-reel narrative film, with a running time of five to twelve minutes, had been established as standard fare. In addition to the continued production of filmed records of actual topical events, the films of this period were generally of two types: comedies, which were made up of a single comic routine or incident and usually ran for about five to six minutes, and stock melodramas, which were further developed in terms of story and ran for about twelve minutes. The comedy films, shown in pairs, or "split reels," because of their length, were slapstick routines that did not go much beyond recording of vaudeville skits, with perhaps an occasional shift in location. The melodramas were designed in traditional format, with hero and villain in battle or chase over the heroine, and the inevitable rescue providing climax and resolution. Though subject material came from a variety of sources, both original and borrowed from literature and stage, the plots were remarkably similar, with costumes and settings providing the major variation.

Films were still being sold outright at this point, on a per-foot basis, and with nickelodeons and storefront theaters now spreading well into the hinterlands, the mar-

▶ David Wark Griffith, here a young director of the American Biograph Company.

ket for films was increasing sharply. Biograph was struggling to keep pace with the other major companies in output while trying to freeze out the upstart independents. To meet the demands for competition, Biograph found it necessary to hold to a production schedule calling for two to three films per week.

The Formative Years

These "bullish" market conditions were prevailing, then, when D. W. Griffith came to Biograph in 1908. His background was in stock company acting and he had aspirations as a playwright. He came to New York with his actress wife, Linda Arvidson, in hopes of selling some of his stories to the film companies. Like most self-respecting theater people, Griffith considered acting in films to be demeaning, but after an unsuccessful attempt to sell a synopsis of *La Tosca* to the Edison studio, he acquiesced, and accepted Edwin S. Porter's offer of the

lead role in *Rescued from an Eagle's Nest*. This led to acting assignments from Biograph, and when the call went out for someone to help Biograph's only director, Wallace McCutcheon, meet the two-a-week schedule, it was to the energetic young actor, Griffith, that the studio turned.

Griffith's first assignment as director was *The Adventures of Dollie,* which he shot in two days. It consisted of about twelve scenes, all single-shot affairs taken from a fixed, full-shot position. The melodramatic action involves the kidnapping of an infant by gypsies, concealment of the child in a barrel that tumbles off a covered wagon and into a stream, and the final rescue by a boy fishing. There was little in the film to suggest the revolutionary effect its director was soon to have on the medium save for an interesting high-angle shot of the search for the missing child and the "planting" of the boy fishing early in the film, but the effort impressed Biograph's front office, and Griffith was quickly assigned to another picture. After directing some eighteen films and two

▲   From *Rescued from an Eagle's Nest* (1907). This tale of abduction and rescue features Griffith as rescuer and shows Porter's command of special-effects cinematography.

months after his directorial debut, Griffith signed his first contract. His films to this point showed no real breakthrough in technique but were respectably crafted within the limits of the two-a-week schedule that Griffith was obliged to meet. They show perhaps more care than usual in the staging of action, since Griffith resisted the rather extemporaneous fashion of shooting scenes that was customary and began to insist on adequate rehearsal time for run-throughs. In general, better acting and more attention to detail resulted.

Once under contract to Biograph, Griffith, like other filmmakers of the period, set about to tell stories visually. Following patterns established by Porter, he began to produce single-reel melodramas and comedies consisting of from two to twenty or more scenes, carefully selected and arranged to provide for natural association and forward flow. But within his first year of directing for Biograph, Griffith began to sense a need to exploit those characteristics peculiar to film.

Recognizing the dramatic impact that cross-cutting between actions of a story could have, Griffith began to extend and refine this device, which Porter had brought to film in *The Great Train Robbery*. Concerning himself not only with the selection and relationship of shots, but with controlling the length of shots themselves, he began to provide films with a kind of visual rhythm that was consonant with the emotional quality of the scene. The device, which became a trademark of the Griffith style, was particularly well suited to the concluding scenes of melodramas, those usually involving a chase, rescue, or both. He found that increasing the rate of cross-cutting as he approached the climactic point of the story could greatly intensify the suspense and general thrust of the film. Referred to as the "Griffith last-minute rescue," this technique became the hallmark of screen melodrama and, some years later, a key ingredient of the serial film. Thus we see in the stock melodrama situation of *The Lonely Villa* (1909)—where mother and children are being threatened by robbers while the alerted father and police are racing to the scene—the twofold use Griffith makes of the cross-cut, or "cutback," as the technique was called then. He found he could bring the separate but converging story elements into closer proximity while simultaneously reinforcing the emotional tone through the rhythmic cutting.

Griffith's even more fundamental contribution to screen narrative, and a distinct departure from anything that had gone before, was his conscious control and change of visual perspective within the scene. Earlier we noted Porter's use of a three-shot scene at the conclusion of *The Life of an American Fireman* and his close-up of the gunman in *The Great Train Robbery*. This was more a primitive form of cross-cutting than shot breakdown,

since technically there was a change in location from exterior to interior, and the latter, as already mentioned, was not an integral part of the action. Griffith gradually began to explore the possibility of changing the perspective of the camera within the scene or unit of action from the fixed, eye-level, middle-distance position that was a holdover from theatrical tradition and an expression of the belief that the camera was simply an instrument for recording action.

Even Griffith probably failed to realize the implications of the multiperspective approach to narrative construction at the time. There is no evidence that he theorized to any extent over the true nature of screen storytelling. Rather, he appeared to solve individual problems in exposition, dramatic reinforcement, transition, and resolution as they came along. The result, however, as revealed through the more than 450 films he made for Biograph, was a fundamentally original approach to film narrative. For Griffith the camera, not the actor, became the key to exposition and dramatic development. He treated it not simply as an instrument for recording staged business, but as the interpretive eye of the storyteller. As such the camera had to be free to choose its own perspective, to change its angle and distance from the central action, to be selective and search out significant detail, and then to step back and survey all elements of the action as they related to one another. Consistent with this approach, and indeed a necessary realization of it, was the breaking down of scenes into a series of individual shots. Using the shot—running the camera at a particular distance and angle from the action—as the basic building block in construction, it became possible to shift perspective instantaneously a number of times within the scene so that action could always be observed from the best vantage point. With the camera in a close-up position and free to move into the scene, details of the scene began to take on greater significance. Not only could more subtle nuances of gesture and movement of actors help convey the meaning of a scene, but inanimate props and details of the setting itself could be used both to develop the narrative line and enhance the mood of the scene. The setting for a particular action, which until this time had been treated mostly as "scenery" to fill the frame, now became a functional part of the action and an integral and supportive part of the narrative.

The implication of shot breakdown went beyond manipulation of the camera and opened up for Griffith and his followers the whole field of constructive or creative editing that was to become the foundation of the Soviet school of film construction almost two decades later. Just as the camera had become the key creative instrument for the filmmaker, so the unity of theme and the natural association of images rather than slavish adherence to unities of time and place became central to building the drama. Though his application of the principle is best illustrated in Griffith's feature films made after his apprenticeship years with Biograph, his introduction of the cut-away for a momentary shift in action in *After Many Years* (1908), and his subsequent use of the flashback for past-tense exposition, illustrate his early determination to extend screen storytelling beyond the single-setting, single-time-period scene.

In *After Many Years,* which Griffith based on Tennyson's *Enoch Arden,* a close-up of Annie Lee waiting for her husband to return is followed by a cut-away scene of Enoch cast away on a desert island. Like his use of cross-cutting for parallel action, Griffith's original use of such creative editing devices would solve the practical problems of providing necessary exposition and building suspense.

Of the many other innovations Griffith brought to film during his years with Biograph, the most significant, in terms of their influence on the further development of the medium, continued to be those directly related to his conception of basic narrative design. Two innovations that represented a further break with theatrical tradition were his movement of actors toward and away from the camera on entrances and exits from the scene and, as an outgrowth of his cross-cutting technique, allowing a scene to begin with action already in progress. Other devices, for which at least part credit should go to Griffith's cameraman Billy Bitzer, included moving the camera and such optical techniques as freezing the action within the frame ("freeze frame"). The origins of the latter seem to be in theatrical tableaux, and today the device is a stock-in-trade of television comedy and drama. Other optical techniques included the fading to a dark or blank screen to conclude a scene, and use of the "iris," a circular frame for the action that could open or close and that Griffith used both to focus attention and to close out one scene and introduce the next.

With respect to the total dramatic effect of a scene, Griffith's important contributions were his use of lighting, tinting, and soft-focus photography, and the attention he gave to such details as costuming, make-up, and set design. His use of lighting to establish mood and reinforce the emotional tone of a scene was particularly

significant. Until this time lighting had been considered a technical problem — simply getting enough light upon the action to expose the film adequately — rather than a dramatic tool. With the help of improved incandescent lighting, Griffith was able to fashion light and shadow for both general composition and special effects.

Unlike other film pioneers, whose contributions are usually associated with several films or even a single film, Griffith developed and refined his art of screen storytelling while making such a large number of single-reel films that it is difficult and misleading to point to a handful as representing milestones in the development of screen narrative. Many techniques were not original with Griffith but adopted and fashioned by him to become an integral part of the film's fabric, and not simply as a gimmick or addendum. Certain films from his Biograph years do, however, represent peaks of his creative energy and have come to be known as minor classics of his early period. In addition to *After Many Years,* already mentioned, these include *Pippa Passes* (1909), which Griffith based on the Robert Browning poem and which was heralded for its significant content and dramatic use of lighting; *The Lonely Villa* (1909), a model of cross-cutting; and *A Corner in Wheat* (1909), which employs a combination of freeze frame and contrast editing, and

▶ From *A Corner in Wheat* (1909). Frank Powell is the unscrupulous wheat trader who brings despair to farmers and poor consumers, and meets a just and ironic end when he trips into a grain elevator pit.

The First Two-Reel Films

His Trust (1910) and *Enoch Arden* (1911) were the first two-reel films to be distributed. Although each reel of *His Trust* was a complete story, Griffith had intended both parts to be shown together. Studio pressure resulted in their being released separately as *His Trust* and *His Trust Fulfilled.* *Enoch Arden* was a single, complete narrative and, despite studio attempts to release one reel at a time, exhibitor and audience pressure resulted in a single showing of what was to be the first multireel film.

which includes social commentary worked out to an ironic conclusion when the villainous wheat tycoon is buried in one of his own grain elevators. *Pippa Passes* also illustrates Griffith's interest in more complex structures for film narrative, with its four separate sections and linking motif foreshadowing the design Griffith was to use later in *Intolerance.*

Although Griffith began to find the single-reel length restrictive by 1910, the Patents Company practice of limiting films to one reel checked his ambition toward more complex stories and more expansive themes. Two films that have the distinction of being the first, and in fact among the few, two-reelers that Griffith made for Biograph were *His Trust* and *His Trust Fulfilled* (1910) and *Enoch Arden* (1911). Although each reel of *His Trust* was a complete story, Griffith had intended both parts to be shown together, but studio pressure resulted in their being released separately. *Enoch Arden,* a remake of his earlier *After Many Years,* was even more clearly a single entity, and despite studio attempts to release one reel at a time, exhibitor and audience pressure won out, and the film became one of the first multireel films to be exhibited as a single unit.

The Lonedale Operator, a single-reel melodrama produced in 1911, is among Griffith's best-crafted and most popular short films. In addition to its carefully edited cross-cuts, it uses both camera movement and movement within the frame to provide a kind of visual orchestration that was to become the key to the movie chase and rescue. A train engineer's race to save a telegraph operator from robbers sets the pace for cuts between a hurtling train and a telegraph office, where the frantic heroine vainly tries to barricade the door. It was a pattern often repeated in Griffith films.

Of the sixty-odd films Griffith made in 1912 (all but three were single reelers), the two that stand out, more for their stories and social themes than for particular techniques, are *The Musketeers of Pig Alley* and *The New York Hat*. The first is especially effective in its representation of New York slum life and is considered a vintage gangster film. *The New York Hat* combines the talents of Griffith with those of the film's sixteen-year-old screenwriter, Anita Loos, and those of its stars — Mary Pickford, Lionel Barrymore, Mae Marsh, and the Gish sisters (Lillian and Dorothy).

By 1913 pressure exerted by the Patents Company against multireel film had dissolved under the rush of "feature films" from independent producers and foreign exchanges, particularly the Italian historical pieces. Stimulated once again by the challenge of the longer film, particularly the nine-reel *Quo Vadis?* from Italy, Griffith produced his own first feature and his last film for the Biograph Studio, the four-reel biblical epic *Judith of Bethulia*. By the time Griffith began production of *Judith,* he had mastered most of the narrative tools of film. What this film provided was the training ground in large

cast and multiscene scope and spectacle that were to follow. It served as a kind of warm-up exercise for the epic spectacle that Griffith would give full expression in the Babylonian section of *Intolerance* three years later.

The release of *Judith of Bethulia* in 1913 marked the end of Griffith's association with Biograph and the close of his years of apprenticeship filmmaking. Although the films for which he would be best known were yet to come, it was the Biograph one-reelers that had allowed Griffith to develop an approach to visual expression while giving the art of screen narrative its foundation and early direction. By 1913, when Griffith left Biograph to begin work as an independent on his monumental *The Birth of a Nation,* the American film industry was about to launch an important new phase in its growth and development. The formative years had passed, and the years between 1913 and 1919 were to become years of refinement in which the term *art* could legitimately be associated with the medium.

With the multireel film, more intricate, more fully developed stories could be told. The "photoplay" had established itself as a popular form with audiences and a lucrative one for producing companies. The challenge now was to refine visual storytelling by tailoring screenplays that went beyond the bare bones of narrative and provided some sense of mood, emotional tone, and characterization. If indeed film had any claim to artistry at this point, it was in the successful visualization of dramatic incidents, both historical and contemporary and both originally conceived and adapted from literature and the stage. And it was Griffith who once again led the way.

When Griffith left Biograph in 1913, he joined the Mutual Film Corporation as head of production, bringing with him his cameraman, Billy Bitzer and the best of Biograph's talent. At Mutual he rushed production of four films while occupied with the planning of his next spectacle film, a story of the American Civil War and the Reconstruction period based on the Thomas Dixon novel *The Clansman*. Additional inspiration came from another Dixon work, *The Leopard's Spots*. Even while absorbed in this project, however, Griffith was able to

▲ From *The Lonedale Operator* (1911). Blanche Sweet uses the telegraph key in a desperate attempt to signal her plight at the hands of railroad bandits.

▶ From *Judith of Bethulia* (1913). The biblical epic casts Blanche Sweet as Judith and Henry Walthall as the Assyrian general, Holofernes, whom she is about to assassinate.

break new ground in such films as *The Avenging Conscience* (1914). Here he developed a psychological theme in a story adapted from Edgar Allan Poe's story "The Telltale Heart" and the poem "Annabel Lee," foreshadowing the style of Jean Epstein and others of the avant-garde who were to explore expressionist and other nonnaturalistic modes.

The Birth of a Nation

Griffith's Civil War epic went into production in 1914. Unable to find studio support, he had to finance the film independently, raising a sum that turned out to be five times the amount of money expended on any film to that date. Working without a shooting script, he produced and edited the film virtually single-handedly,* save for the invaluable aid of his cameraman, Bitzer. The result was

---

* Griffith continued to edit the film after its Los Angeles showing, and followed its opening in other major cities, still adjusting the print.

the twelve-reel (nearly 2½ hour) *The Birth of a Nation,* which had its premiere showing in Los Angeles in February 1915.

The film's reception, both critical and popular, can only be described as monumental, not just immediately but over the years as well. *The Birth of a Nation* brought to the scene a consolidation and refinement of Griffith's storehouse of techniques in cinematic construction and dramatic representation. Here was superspectacle—a kind of cataract flow of history blended with an emotionally charged, intimate story that had the grand sweep of great legend. Also introduced were sterotypical patterns and attitudes toward events of the Reconstruction period that proved inflammatory.

The setting is the South during and after the Civil War. The first half of the film portrays incidents of the war itself, while the second half is devoted to the postwar Reconstruction era, during which political power is given to former black slaves and the Southern whites become the victims of black terrorists and their Northern sympathizers (carpetbaggers). The final sequences portray the formation of the Ku Klux Klan as an instrument of self-protection.

Onto this historical panorama is superimposed a biographical story. It concerns two families—the Stonemans of Pennsylvania and the Camerons of South Carolina. Growing friendship and romance among the Stoneman and Cameron sons and daughters are interrupted by the conflicts of war. Phil Stoneman and Ben Cameron actually come face to face on the battlefield. It is in the postwar period, however, that conflicts deepen. Ben, in love with Elsie Stoneman, finds that her father, a powerful figure in Washington politics, is plotting with black terrorists to ravage the Southern whites. Ben finally provides the inspiration and leadership for the formation of the Ku Klux Klan, which rides, in the best tradition of the Griffith last-minute rescue, to save the Cameron family from marauding blacks breaking into a hut where the family has taken refuge.

Initially, what is most impressive is the film's overall design—the blending of historical events and personal drama. Neither Griffith nor any other filmmaker had ever attempted to re-create history—especially history so recent and, for Griffith, so personal—on such a grand scale, and the director obviously took pride in his role as historian and the son of a Confederate colonel. In the title that introduces the fateful Ford Theater sequence where Lincoln is shot, Griffith states, "An historical facsimile of Ford's Theatre as on that night, exact in size and detail with the recorded incidents, after Nicolay and Hay in *Lincoln, a History*." Griffith provided similar notes in introducing other key historical scenes, such as that showing Lee and Grant at Appomattox.

Beyond the general construction, what is impressive even today is the composition, the camera work, and the editing of individual scenes. It is here that Griffith proves himself the master craftsman: his cross-cutting between units of action while varying shot length to create rhythm; his integration of long, medium, and close shots to build a scene; the cutting away from an action before it is completed to build suspense and increase tempo. This mastery of editing, together with Griffith's handling of actors, gives certain individual scenes—battlefield struggles, Ben Cameron's return to Piedmont, the Lincoln assassination, and, of course, the ride of the Klan—tremendous dramatic force and has made them individually famous.

But beneath these intense scenes, masterfully conceived and executed, was a sentiment and theme many viewers found repugnant. As the son of a Confederate colonel, Griffith had grown up on romantic tales of the Old South, and he saw in the Dixon novel and other accounts of the period what he believed to be a true picture—the "black stranglehold" on the South after the war and the benevolent crusades of the Klan. This theme, together with the stereotypes Griffith either consciously or unconsciously introduced—the black mammy and faithful darkies on one hand, and a wide assortment of lust-crazed, arrogant, whiskey-drinking blacks terrorizing the white community on the other—made the film immediately explosive. It was barred from exhibition in a dozen states, and where it was shown in the North, protests and demonstrations followed. In at

◄ This composite photo of featured players was part of the souvenir booklet produced for a 1915 showing of *The Birth of a Nation*.

► From *The Birth of a Nation* (1915). The depiction of Ku Klux Klan activities was one of the film's most controversial ingredients.

Editorial and Response to *The Birth of a Nation*

*T*he very name of The Birth of a Nation is an insult to Washington, who believed that a nation, not merely a congeries of independent states, was born during the common struggles of the Revolutionary War, and devoted himself to cementing the union. It is an insult to Lincoln and the great motives inspiring him when he was called on to resist the attempt to denationalize a nation. This nation of ours was not born between 1861 and 1865, and no one will profit from trying to pervert history. To make a few dirty dollars men are willing to pander to depraved tastes and to foment a race antipathy that is the most sinister and dangerous feature of American life.

—New York Globe *(April 6, 1915)*

*Y*our editorial is an insult to the intelligence and the human kindness of nearly 100,000 of the best people in New York City, who have viewed this picture from artistic interests and not through any depraved taste such as you try to indicate. Among those you have insulted are your contemporaries on the newspapers of New York, whose expert reviewers were unanimous in their praise of this work as an artistic achievement.

—*D. W. Griffith*, New York Globe *(April 10, 1915)*

least one instance, at the film's opening at the Tremont Theatre in Boston, the showing led to a full-scale riot. Controversy continued to surround the film years after its initial release. Charges and countercharges of racism filled the press and periodicals, some written by Griffith himself. He wrote a forty-five page pamphlet, *The Rise and Fall of Free Speech in America,* from which he invited the press to quote freely. Subsequent releases of *The Birth of a Nation* continued to provoke protests, and as late as 1931 the film was banned in Philadelphia.

Sensitivity to the film's inflammatory subject is evident even today. The introductory notes to a pamphlet issued by the Museum of Modern Art in New York in connection with its series several years ago, "The History of the Motion Picture, 1895–1946," reads,

It is by our decision that D. W. Griffith's *The Birth of a Nation* will not appear in this cycle. Fully aware of the greatness of the film and its artistic and historic importance, we have also had sufficient and repeated

evidence of the potency of the anti-Negro bias and believe that exhibiting it at this time of heightened social tensions cannot be justified.

Ironically, along with the film's obvious artistic merits, the controversy surrounding it has helped to make it a hit at the box office.

Intolerance

Before the release of *The Birth of a Nation,* Griffith was already hard at work on a film that he called *The Mother and the Law,* which centered on modern industrial strife and the miscarriage of justice. This project, however, lacked the spectacle and epic proportions of *The Birth of a Nation* and such Italian period pieces as *Quo Vadis?* so Griffith conceived and added to the original project two period pieces that had more of the epic quality — the fall of the ancient city of Babylon and the events surrounding the Huguenot slaughter in Paris that has come to be known as the St. Bartholomew's Day Massacre. The result was his monumental 1916 release, *Intolerance.*

In the modern segment, the focus is on a young man and woman who, as the result of a factory strike, are forced to leave their home for the city. They marry, and soon afterward the boy is falsely imprisoned. Meanwhile the girl has a baby, which is taken from the young mother by community "do-gooders." No sooner is the boy released from prison than he is once again, though innocent, implicated in a crime — this time, murder — and is convicted and sentenced to death. The climax to this episode is constructed on the Griffith chase formula — desperate wife and friends rush to overtake the governor's train to secure a pardon as the boy is being led to the gallows.

This story of *The Mother and the Law* is reminiscent of Griffith's earlier one- and two-reel melodramas for Biograph. Its distinguishing feature, in addition to its place in the overall design of the film, is its pointed social commentary. The plight of the young couple illustrates the suffering that results from legal injustice, industrial turmoil, and hypocritical philanthropy. The story is also notable for its composition and the internal construction of certain scenes, which, like scenes from *The Birth of a Nation,* have come to be revered as classic Griffith: Mae Marsh wandering the streets in search of her child, and the frantic attempt to secure a pardon as the boy is being administered the last rites.

The Babylonian sequence is more in the tradition of *Judith of Bethulia.* It traces the attacks of Cyrus and his Persian horde on the city of Babylon (circa 539 B.C.), which is ruled by the benevolent monarch Belshazzar. Betrayal by the city's priests brings about the invasion of Belshazzar's court, despite the valiant efforts of a loyal mountain girl to warn her king.

Griffith may well have been inspired by the Italian spectacles of this period in conceiving his spectacle but he shunned the confining traditions and limitations of the stage. He showed here that spectacle need not be weighted down by the slow solemnity of the triumphal march. The camera was free to roam, and with the aid of editing, to cut from detail to detail. Characters, both principals and supernumeraries, were part of the action rather than of some theatrical design.

Considerably less developed, but no doubt of particular interest to Griffith as an historical document, was the French segment of *Intolerance,* which deals with Catherine de Medici's instigation of the massacre of the Huguenots in Paris in 1572. Here the intrigue within the court of Charles IX gives way to the personal story of two lovers, Prosper and Brown Eyes, who become victims of the slaughter. Though undistinguished in structure and lacking dramatic force, this segment is of interest for the carefully selected details of the French court and the Paris streets of the period.

Griffith included a fourth motif to the three stories to further expand the theme of intolerance through the ages. This is a series of scenes depicting key events in the life of Christ. Although generally referred to as the "Judean Story," this portion hardly constitutes a narrative. It is rather a series of vignettes (often just single shots) showing Christ with his disciples, his entrance into Jerusalem, the way of the cross, and finally the crucifixion. Introducing this motif gave Griffith an opportunity to use a great and familiar theme as both parallel and counterpoint to the other three tales.

What made *Intolerance* revolutionary was the complex interweaving of the four units. Griffith, still smarting from the "racist" criticism of *The Birth of a Nation,* wanted to show intolerance through the ages. He attempted to isolate the intolerance theme and, at the same time, weld together the separate period pieces by introducing, at key transitions, a scene of a woman rocking a cradle accompanied by the Walt Whitman line "endlessly rocks the cradle, uniter of here and hereafter." Thus, the viewer was swept from life in a present-day city to ancient Babylon and then to the Christian era and on to sixteenth-century France. And so the cross-cutting continued throughout the 4½-hour film, sometimes with but often without the cradle motif, until the four eras come rushing together in final resolution. An epilogue provided a vision of a future world of love and harmony where prison walls are replaced by flowering fields and heavenly angels look down upon a world of peace and tranquility.

This complex structure brought Griffith under the gun of some critics, who found the work heavy-handed and difficult to follow. Others, however, saw the liberating potential in the new design. A critic for the Boston *Transcript* expressed the hope that "American producers [would] take the technical freedom of *Intolerance* to heart and get away from many of the stiff conventions of the present-day method of telling a story on the screen."

One convention of storytelling that Griffith had helped to develop and refine was the writing of explanatory titles for silent films. These were used to provide a line of dialogue, explain the action of the scene, or to alert the audience to a transition from one scene to the next. But if Griffith was moving away from stiff conventions, as the Boston critic claims, he was also revealing, through his titles, a sentimental, even maudlin, attitude toward his subject. Besides being out of fashion for a nation at war, this stance was also losing its appeal for audiences developing some sophistication about screen drama.

A

B

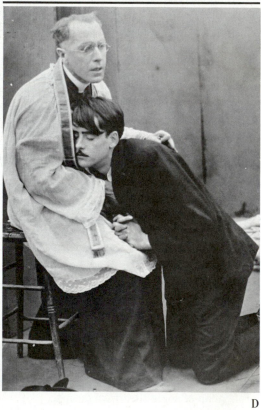

D

C

Audiences Everywhere Spellbound by

D. W. GRIFFITH'S COLOSSAL $2,000,000 SPECTACLE

"INTOLERANCE"

LOVE'S STRUGGLE THROUGHOUT THE AGES

Most Massive, Awe-Inspiring, Thrilling, Beautiful Production the World Has Ever Known. The Crowning Achievement of the World's Greatest Producer.

12 organizations now touring America and breaking the marvelous "Birth of a Nation" records everywhere.

INTERESTING → **3**RD   Month at the Colonial Theatre, Chicago
SIGNIFICANT   Month at the Chestnut St. Opera House, Phila.
                     Month at the Pitt Theatre, Pittsburgh

Direction WARK PRODUCING CORP.,   General Offices, 807 Longacre Bldg., New York

Intolerance appears to have been overwhelming, if not confusing, for most audiences, and it failed to do business. Shortly after its release, Griffith recut it, and the film was released as two separate films — *The Fall of Babylon* and *The Mother and the Law.* Catherine de Medici and Christ were left by the wayside.

From *Intolerance* (1916).

(A) The court of Belshazzar in the city of Babylon before it is stormed by Cyrus and the Persian horde.

(B) Catherine de Medici plots the massacre of the Huguenots in Paris.

(C) Christ in Jerusalem on his way to Calvary.

(D) The "boy" receives the last rites before his scheduled execution on the gallows.

Though a financial failure, the film proved to be an inspiration and a guide for the young Soviet filmmakers who were soon to make their own mark on the film world. In spite of its poor public showing and some adverse criticism, it became the second great monument to its creator's genius. If *The Birth of a Nation* was "like writing history with lighting," as Woodrow Wilson is supposed to have said, then *Intolerance* was a moral tract in the manner of a grand fugue. Its spectacle and structural bravado perhaps overshadow the mastery that Griffith was once more able to display in visualization and the cinematic rendering of individual scenes.

The Later Years

By 1916, eight years after joining Biograph as an actor in single-reel "potboilers," Griffith was the world's foremost director. Besides producing the medium's first two masterworks, he had established an entire system of narrative technique that would serve as the foundation for screen storytelling to this day. His films in the years that followed proved to be an odd mixture of brilliance (*Broken Blossoms,* 1919), strained competence (*Way Down East* [1920] and *Orphans of the Storm* [1921]), and pedestrian romantic larks (*Hearts of the World* [1917] and *True Heart Susie* [1919]).

Broken Blossoms was the first film to be released through United Artists, the distribution company Griffith formed with Douglas Fairbanks, Mary Pickford, and Charlie Chaplin in 1919. This film effectively illustrated Griffith's ability to return to a simple story of intimate relationships after the scope and complexity of *Intolerance.* Here Lillian Gish plays the London waif who is befriended by a Chinese boy (Richard Barthelmess) and as a result becomes the victim of her cruel father's wrath. In place of action reinforced by editing techniques and spectacle is a poetic atmosphere created through soft-focus photography, an intimate and searching camera, and exceptionally sensitive acting. As in *Intolerance,* the photography was embellished by use of tinted

film stock and carefully worked out lighting designs, with the final touch being the pervasive London fog. And *Broken Blossoms,* though not unique in this respect, also demonstrated the potential for achieving realism and atmospheric effects within the confines of the studio. This film inspired one writer for an exhibitors' trade review to suggest that Griffith "paints the lily. He adds another hue to the rainbow."

Orphans of the Storm gave Griffith the opportunity to return to the historical spectacle, this time using the French Revolution as a backdrop for personal drama. In the integration of historical pageantry with personal conflict, Griffith continued to reveal his dedication and control—the film showed surging crowds, the storming of the Bastille, and the rescue of Lillian Gish from the guillotine.

With *Way Down East,* an adaptation from a popular stage work, Griffith never quite reached the levels of artistry he achieved in other major works, though the

▲ From *Broken Blossoms* (1919). With *Broken Blossoms,* Griffith returned to the stark realism of city slum life that he had evoked years earlier in *Musketeers of Pig Alley.* He used the Thomas Burke story *The Chink and the Child* to continue his plea for tolerance, this time with an interracial tone. Scenes of rage and cruel treatment by the waif's father (Donald Crisp) are combined with scenes of tender love between the slum child (Lillian Gish) and a Chinese boy (Richard Barthelmess).

film was a popular and profitable addition to Griffith's "big pictures." The turgid plot and Victorian morality make this film almost a caricature of the stage "mellerdrama." What sustains the film as a more than routine contribution to silent cinema, however, is the portrayal of the heroine by Lillian Gish, Griffith's use of natural settings, and a particularly fine example of the last-minute rescue accomplished by Richard Barthelmess on the ice floes at the brink of a waterfall. The latter shot obviously presented some filming problems. Griffith's solution was to shoot the action at four different locations and then to intercut the shots. Shots of the heroine stumbling on a frozen river during a blinding snowstorm were photographed near the filmmaker's studio at Mamaroneck, New York. Cast and crew went next to White River Junction, Vermont, to film long action shots on the churning, ice-choked river. A more placid stream in Farmington, Connecticut, provided a safer setting for close-ups of the last-minute rescue. As a kicker, Griffith spliced in a stock shot of Niagara Falls.

Gish also managed to add some luster to the uneven *Hearts of the World* (1917), which was Griffith's contribution to the war effort. The film once again displayed his special skill in blending the personal story with the spectacular background. It is a propaganda piece that dramatizes the plight of a woman and her children in a French village who become victims of the hated "Huns." Gish's anguish at the death of her mother is unsurpassed. Perhaps even more to her credit is the ability to carry off the rather contrived scene in which she wanders through the battlefield in a state of shock searching for her love while clutching the wedding dress she was to have worn that very day. Finding him and presuming him dead, she lies down beside the "body" as a title reads, "and so they spent their wedding night." Initial enthusiasm for this first panoramic treatment of the Great War quickly waned with the signing of the armistice, however, and the film has since been generally ignored.

Griffith had come under fire earlier for his maudlin sentimentality, particularly in *Intolerance,* but in the postwar era it was even more out of tune with what was to be the Roaring Twenties. By 1925 he no longer commanded the singular reputation of master director. And in 1930, his career as a director ended with the release of his first sound film, *Abraham Lincoln.* Younger men with new ideas for film (if not new techniques) were arriving on the scene. And by this time Griffith was becoming a victim of the system he helped to create — the big studio operation. The unit system of production was a big-studio system under which specialized crafts were turned into distinct units. Under this system Griffith no longer had control over all stages of production. His innovations, however, continued to influence a host

Griffith on location at White River Junction for *Way Down East* (1920). What must have particularly impressed Soviet filmmakers like Eisenstein about *Way Down East* was Griffith's use of "creative geography"—assembling shots made at different locations to create a single scene.

of directors both at home and abroad. Erich von Stroheim, Cecil B. De Mille, Rex Ingram, Henry King, and King Vidor all show the Griffith influence in their early work. European directors who acknowledged his influence include Carl Dreyer and Sergei Eisenstein. Years later, Eisenstein said of Griffith,

I wish to recall what David Wark Griffith himself represented to us, the young Soviet film-makers of the twenties. To say it simply and without equivocation: a revelation.

An Essanay Ad

This 1914 Essanay advertising copy in the trade press reflects the popularity of the three staples of the period—comedies, Westerns, and romantic dramas. It also features performances by two early male stars, "Broncho Billy" Anderson (a cofounder of Essanay) and romantic lead Francis X. Bushman.

FIVE-A-WEEK ESSANAY

Coming October 24th!   Coming October 24th!

"The Love Lute of Romany"
(IN TWO PARTS)

A dramatic story of the Gypsies, photographed at Ithaca, New York. Many exciting and thrilling scenes throughout this production make it a box-office attraction of more than ordinary pulling power. The theme is new and one to be remembered long. A splendid cast, excellent backgrounds and climacteric events of unusual number. *Book this feature now. Heralds and posters ready.*

Released Tuesday, - - - October 21st
"The Way Perilous"
A beautiful love drama featuring Francis X. Bushman.

Released Wednesday, - - - October 22nd
"Day by Day"
A comedy that is new from start to finish. A real treat for any audience.

Released Thursday, - - - October 23rd
"The Kid Sheriff"
A Western comedy-drama of merit. Book this feature today.

Released Saturday, - - - October 25th
"Broncho Billy's Elopement"
A "Broncho Billy" picture that will long be remembered, featuring G. M. Anderson.

Coming Friday, October 31st!   Coming Friday, October 31st!
"The Toll of the Marshes"
(IN TWO PARTS)

A dramatic story of a land grafter who unmercifully robbed the poor to gain his goal—rich independence. His daughter is the innocent means of bringing about a novel and eccentric plot for this remarkable photoplay. Francis X. Bushman, Beverly Bayne and Frank Dayton featured. *Posters and heralds ready.*

WHAT DO YOU THINK OF OUR NEW POSTERS? AREN'T THEY GREAT? They will boom your business. Posters are lithographed in full four colors, 35c. each. You can secure these from your Exchange or direct from ESSANAY MFG. CO., 521 First National Bank Bldg., Chicago. Your lobby display will look attractive if you use photographs of ESSANAY players, 8x10, $3.00 per dozen. You can secure these from the PLAYERS' PHOTO CO., 177 N. State St., Chicago, Ill.

ESSANAY
FILM MANUFACTURING COMPANY
521 First National Bank Bldg., - - Chicago

Dramas, Melodramas, and Westerns

The formation of the Triangle Film Corporation in July of 1915 represented an important consolidation within the American industry. The name Triangle referred to the three production units that were to produce the three staples of the American silents: the regular dramas and melodramas that were pushing beyond the single-reel length; the specials, or large-budget, multireel showcase films, and the comedy shorts. The new company also brought together the three men who were establishing reputations as masters of these forms. Griffith, of course, was the champion of the specials. In charge of the bread-and-butter genres—regular dramas and comedies—were Thomas Ince and Mack Sennett respectively.

The Aesop of Inceville

Thomas Ince, like Griffith, had come to film initially as an actor with a background in theater. He starred in a Griffith-directed film in November 1910, wrote and directed his first film the following month, and by 1915 was a major creative force in the industry. His rise as a star director was actually the result of his combined talents as creative filmmaker and studio ruler.

When hired by the New York Motion Picture Company in 1911 to produce that company's first two-reel film, Ince was already engaged in both studio building and filmmaking. It was at his suggestion that the company leased an 18,000-acre tract of diverse topography along the Pacific for the filming of *War on the Plains* (1912). Under Ince's direction, this film became a prototype of the many epic Westerns that were to follow, and the California real estate on which it was shot, the largest back lot in Hollywood history, was soon known as Inceville. Here separate villages were constructed to provide Spanish, Dutch, Japanese, Irish, and Canadian locations. For *War on the Plains* Ince hired his own Wild West Show, and a group of Sioux Indians was also in residence.

Ince followed *War on the Plains* with more than two dozen double-reel films the same year, 1912. Able to personally supervise both the planning and execution of film projects, he entered into his most creative period—between 1912 and 1916. Major films of the period included *The Battle of Gettysburg* (1913), *The Italian* (1915), *The Coward* (1915), and *Hell's Hinges* (1916). Ince's reputation as a director came to be linked strongly with the Western film, but, as the foregoing titles show, his films were actually diverse in subject and stylistic approach. In addition to the Westerns, Ince made an ambitious historical piece, a saga of the South Pacific, and a caustic and heartrending social document on the fate of the American immigrant (*The Italian*).

Still, it was in the Western that Ince's special talents for the direct-story approach and tight dramatic structure were best displayed. The Western was a natural for film, because action was its stock-in-trade: riding, roping, jumping, brawling, the chase of runaway gunmen, overland stage rides, and stampeding cattle. The Western was the closest thing that Americans had to a national legend. It represented the rough-and-tumble action of the opening of the frontier, action that had a romantic quality about it while still permitting realistic detail and lean and direct progression. In the hands of Ince, and with the help of Western star William S. Hart, the genre was on its way to becoming a national institution.

What is impressive about Ince's two-reel Westerns is how remarkably simple and direct they are. Every incident, every action, is directly related to the basic plot structure, and exposition both through action and titles uncluttered and unambiguous. Even the longer films display this Spartan approach. *Hell's Hinges,* made by Ince and Hart for the Triangle Company in 1916, is a model of shoot-from-the-hip storytelling. The romantic image of the West has brought the weak-willed Reverend Henley and his sister Faith to Placer Center—"Hell's Hinges," as the town is affectionately known to its inhabitants. Blaze Tracey, local gunslinger, is turned from his job of intimidating the new arrivals by the sweet innocence of Faith. (The title for this scene reads, "A different kind of smile—sweet, honest, and trustful, and seeming to say, 'How do you do, Friend?'") The weak parson becomes a victim of the mob and is shot in the struggle that develops between the "petticoat Brigade" and the saloon mob bent on setting fire to the church. In the closing scenes, daybreak finds Blaze and Faith by the simple grave of the parson, while smoke drifts over the ruined town of Hell's Hinges. Blaze's final words: "Over yonder hills is the future—both yours and mine. It's callin' and I reckon we'd better go."

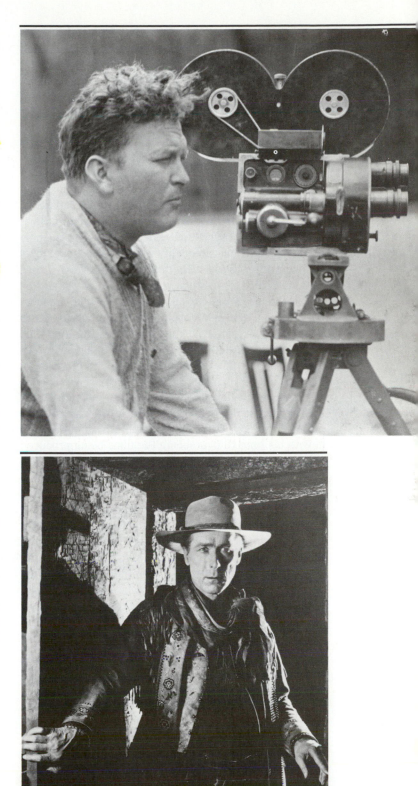

Thomas Ince, who came to be known as Hollywood's first "creative producer."

William S. Hart, who made a significant contribution to the mystique of the Western hero.

The titles in *Hell's Hinges,* which today seem stilted, have a simplicity and directness about them that is consistent with Ince's filmmaking style. Also well represented in this film is the simple, uncluttered, and realistic setting, which has an interesting textural appeal. The only suggestion of complexity comes in the characterization of Blaze Tracey himself. There is an enigma about the personality that is summed up in another title: "An embodiment of the best and worst in the West." Blaze resolves to keep law and religion out of Hell's Hinges, but dissolves in the face of kindness and purity. Ince may have kept his plot simple, but in the characterization, particularly in the Western hero as portrayed by Hart, there was some suggestion of depth. This was an enormously popular characterization and it became a model for many other heroes of both the East and West. These men lived clean, rode rough, were kind to animals and old folks, were shy with women, and often seemed preoccupied with a troublesome past or some personality quirk (akin to the character flaw in classic tragedy). And they all lived according to some personal code that audiences might not have understood but were perfectly willing to accept.

As Inceville developed as a major production center with an increasingly heavy schedule, Ince began to share more of the directorial chores with others in order to devote his time to overseeing the films being produced simultaneously on the lot. To maintain control of each production, Ince replaced his customary brief synopses with marginal notations with comprehensive shooting scripts detailing shot and scene breakdowns, camera positions, descriptions of action, and even lines for the actors to speak. Ince was thus able to shift from the director's role to producer's and still administer quality control. He also managed to produce films that, although directed by others, were very much in the Ince mold.

Under this new system, most of the work of producing a picture was completed once the scenario had been finished and put into the hands of a director. When the script writers had done their work, the scenario would come under Ince's careful scrutiny and then go back to the scenario department for changes, sometimes several times, before being given to the director with the instructions to "shoot as is." This method was to form the basis for the Hollywood "unit system" of production, with individual specialists overseeing various stages of production under the watchful eye of a production chief.

The system did not encourage creative contributions on the part of directors. Many working under these ties argued that such a procedure produced a mechanical effect devoid of any distinctive style. Ince films, however, provided the best evidence that in the case of this creative producer at least, the argument would not hold.

In actuality Ince was directing all films on the lot, but from his office and in his mind's eye rather than from behind the camera lens. It was his combined talents of knowing every aspect of production thoroughly, using a keen visual sense, and being able to give orders without giving offense that made Ince's method work for him. Though others tried to adopt it, few realized the same success.

With the formation of the Triangle Company in 1915, Ince became increasingly involved in production supervision and thereafter did little of his own directing. When Ince broke with Triangle in 1918, William S. Hart was still under contract to him. The two joined Adolph Zukor at Paramount, but Ince had little direct involvement in the Paramount production.

Silent Comedy and the Art of Mime

By 1913, with Griffith and Ince leading the way, the dramatic film reigned supreme. Major trust and independent companies had all experimented with comedy, but with few exceptions these films were little more than extensions of vaudeville and circus routines. Vitagraph, Lubin, and Essanay, in particular, were producing comic skits in fair number, but American screen comedy had not yet found a true form and was still a minor genre. However, the next few years would bring changes resulting in what may well stand even today as the American film's most enduring contribution—silent screen comedy. The coming together in Hollywood of major comic talents and the production personnel who knew how to exploit it made American comedy in the teens and early twenties unrivaled.

The inspiration was largely European, however. Both comics and filmmakers (Chaplin, Stan Laurel, and Ernst Lubitsch, among others) came from abroad and had been strongly influenced by pioneer works in England, Germany, and France. Of particular importance were the early French chase and trick films of Lumière, Méliès, Zecca, and Durand, and the singular Max Linder, who by the early teens had become an international favorite and Pathé's star attraction. Few of Linder's films have survived, and he is almost forgotten today, but his presence in evening dress or morning coat with mustache and cane was both a joy to audiences and an inspiration to later comic stars. Both Sennett and Chaplin acknowledged their debt to Linder, Chaplin calling him his teacher. Like Chaplin's, his routines were in clear contrast to the frantic style of other comedians, and his invention of bits of business with the most ordinary props was a preview of Chaplin's own special comic approach.

Sennett: The Fastest Fun on Earth

The man who became the catalyst for the development of silent screen comedy and gave it an identifiable style was the Canadian-born Mack Sennett. After an unsuccessful stint in musical comedy, Sennett began his career in film in 1908, appearing in many Griffith-directed films. Biograph was doing little in the comedy field when Sennett first arrived, but the young actor could not look at the tragedies and melodramas being turned out without seeing the potential for pure farce. Gradually, Sennett began directing comedies for Biograph and developing his frenetic comic style—a combination of vaudeville, circus, pantomime, and the classic Italian commedia dell'arte. By the time he became head of the Keystone Company, in 1912, he had a wealth of experience in comic forms both in and outside of film.

But if Sennett had been influenced by a number of comic forms, the film critics by this time were showing the kind of conditioning that screen narrative was having on them. A review of Sennett's first Keystone film, *Cohen Collects a Debt*, reads,

> As one sits through this eight or ten minutes of senseless, idiotic horseplay he wonders what it is all about. Never once is the spectator allowed to grasp the thread of the story, if there is a thread. . . . (*New York Dramatic Mirror*, September 25, 1912)

If lacking in continuity in the usual story sense, Sennett's films did exhibit an incredible economy of film time in working out various bits of action. Cutting was central to the Sennett style, tightening up the *action* (a more appropriate word than *narrative*) and propelling it forward.

The immediate popularity of Sennett's comedies with unsophisticated audiences is understandable. His work was screen comedy in the simplest form: completely visual, depending neither on narrative nor characterization but simply on visual incongruity and surprise. Although it created a world in which conventional logic had to be suspended, it dealt with people, objects, and conventions of the real world rather than with fantasy and illusion, as the French pioneers had done. It was a distorting lens that perhaps grossly exaggerated but still reflected real policemen and tramps and dowagers rather than showing complete fabrications. Sennett ingeniously converted people into character types, and these in turn he transformed into machines.

Unlike Ince and Griffith, each of whom in his own way carefully planned a film's action in advance, Sennett was a master of improvisation. He allowed gag routines to develop out of basic situations that had been scripted, but only with the barest suggestion of a location or bit of business. At the heart of the formula was *pace*. Often with a meager indication of what motivated it, a chase would begin: an automobile careening through busy city

▶ **Mack Sennett.** As head of the Keystone Company from 1912 to 1915 and pioneer and catalyst for American silent screen comedy, Sennett was responsible for launching the careers, or at least influencing the styles, of a score of film comics, including Charlie Chaplin, Harry Langdon, Harold Lloyd, Marie Dressler, Wallace Beery, and W. C. Fields.

▲ From a Keystone comedy. Charlie Murray makes his entrance into a dress shop in a variation of the Sennett chase.

traffic would miraculously escape demolition, leaving behind a nightmare of confusion and wreckage. Passing within inches of an oncoming locomotive, it would charge through pond and brush, demolish at least one frame building along the way before taking to the air at cliffside or dockside and landing in the Pacific Ocean. The occupants would then regain their composure for the next phase of the chase; they might be bruised and shaken but they were seldom badly injured.

There were, of course, many variations to the chase sequence, ranging from Griffith's melodramatic last-minute rescue to the nihilistic antics of the Keystone Kops. One sequence that became a trademark of Keystone slapstick was the pie-throwing battle. A key ingredient here was to explore every angle or variation on the basic gag, and when these had been exhausted, to find one more, with the whole thing occurring in about two-thirds the time physically possible.

Keystone films were usually group efforts. Sennett's idea men would come together to discuss possible routines for a film. They would pass suggestions around, modify and embellish them, and gradually develop a general "plot" outline. It was always an outline that Key-

stone directors worked from, not a script. Thus, much of the action could be worked out and even invented on the set. Often a production unit would be sent out to take advantage of some scheduled community activity, and once there would work out comic routines that the event itself suggested — a street parade, a beauty contest, a carnival. It was a children's soapbox derby held in Venice, California, that prompted Sennett to develop a single-reel comedy around that event. The result was Charlie Chaplin's second Keystone film, *The Kids' Auto Race at Venice* (1914).

If gag routines and pace were at the heart of Keystone comedy, it was the preposterous characterizations that provided the finishing touch. So it was that Sennett, through the Keystone years, groomed an entire stable of comic stars. Top among these in the early years were Ford Sterling and Mabel Normand, whose mimic abilities were the central focus of many of the studio's single-reel romps. In a sense, Sterling and Normand were among the straightest of the Keystone comics. Many were endowed with physical characteristics that could be exploited to serve the slapstick formula. Mack Swain, with imposing frame, bushy mustache and eyebrows, and withering stare, was the perfect foil. Chester Conklin, who could rival Keaton for his deadpan expression, had a quality of movement that might be likened to that of a mechanical rag doll. With Ben Turpin it was all in the wild, cross-eyed stare, and with Roscoe (Fatty) Arbuckle the extraordinary size. If, individually, in ordinary dress these actors had comic potential, then together, as a befuddled police force, the possibilities were even greater. So reasoned Sennett, and so were born the Keystone Kops. As the Kops became famous, Sennett found that sex appeal lent an even greater attraction. His equally famous bathing beauties were the result.

Keystone created a surreal world of characters and situations with the special qualities of the incongruous and of surprise that film could so effectively capture. It was a form that borrowed from other comedic arts as well as pioneer screen works. Sennett had been schooled by Griffith, Max Linder, Méliès, and other early French directors. Like Méliès he used camera tricks to exploit the absurd; from Linder he learned how to develop plot or situation to suit the personality and bearing of his actors. And from Griffith he learned pacing, adding to the effectiveness of a scene by building it up through shot selection and arrangement. But it was his particular genius to extract so much fun from the same basic melodramatic situation that was the hallmark of so many Griffith works.

Just as Sennett had been a pupil of Griffith, Méliès, and Linder, so his Keystone studio became the schoolroom for both comic stars and directors to follow. Charlie Chaplin, Harry Langdon, and Harold Lloyd all worked under Sennett at some point in their careers; other members of the company who eventually reached stardom were Marie Dressler, Wallace Beery, W. C. Fields, Gloria Swanson, Bebe Daniels, and Carole Lombard. Directors such as Frank Capra and George Stevens also had their basic training under Sennett.

By 1915, when Sennett joined the Triangle Company, he had established himself as the top producer of screen comedy, with an unrivaled stable of comic talent. As independent production companies proliferated and the market for comedy continued bullish, production expanded under an array of banners, with a host of performers. By this time, routines were being repeated many times over and little was being added to the form. In addition to borrowing ideas and situations, some comedians adopted the styles of comic stars who had found formulas for success. Imitation Chaplins were naturally the most prevalent. With the market remaining strong, earlier comedies were recut, regrouped, or simply retitled to play along with successors and imitators.

If the "idea men" and gag writers were unable to provide much that was original, the stars themselves, through the late teens and twenties, brought new vigor and artistry to silent comedy. But not all screen comedians were able to make the grade. Those who survived through the twenties were essentially those who could develop personalities or characterizations revealing some emotional make-up. Pure slapstick, physical incongruity, and mechanical gags would no longer suffice; it was now necessary to convey visually some reflection of internal conflicts and aspirations.

Charlie Chaplin: "The Mob God"

Of the comics who were to reign during what has come to be called the golden age of silent screen comedy, the names Buster Keaton, Harry Langdon, and Harold Lloyd are prominent in terms of popularity and artistry, but Charlie Chaplin was the undisputed champion. Chaplin's contribution to the art of mime has been so often, and sometimes so eloquently, described that it has established its own art of superlatives. (Even George Bernard Shaw ranked Chaplin as "the only genius developed in the motion pictures.") Most of the accolades were well earned. What Chaplin brought to the screen, in addition to the adored characterization of the little tramp— wistful underdog and foil of pomposity — was a rare gift of mime and a seemingly boundless imagination in exploring the comic and pathetic possibilities of any situation, any object, any shade of human reaction.

While touring the United States with an English vaudeville troupe, the Karno Pantomime Company, Chaplin was called by Keystone to replace Ford Sterling, who was threatening to quit the company. Chaplin's first film for Keystone, *Making a Living,* was released in February 1914. The film is in the true spirit of most Keystone films, with Charlie dressed as something of an English dandy, complete with monocle and cane, showing a dashing way with the ladies but no visible means of support. He finds employment with a newspaper and manages to make the big scoop on an auto accident by stealing the story from another reporter. Even in this earliest of Chaplin films, an occasional gesture or expression and a way of embarking on the inevitable chase sets him apart from the other stars of the Keystone lot.

As was apparent almost immediately, Chaplin's own tradition in comic mime was at odds with the frenetic and slapdash style of the Sennett studio, and after playing in a dozen films directed by others, he began to write and direct his own material. He adopted the costume of the little tramp in his second Keystone film, *Kids' Auto Race at Venice,* and as he began to take over the control of his films, a slower, more studied, and more disciplined style began to develop. But Chaplin was still obliged to meet a

The Keystone Stars

*T*he Sennett comic stars featured in this 1915 advertising copy include Charlie Chaplin's brother Syd. Charlie had already left for Essanay.

production schedule of nearly one film a week, which gave him little time for reflection and refinement. His Keystone films were mostly improvised, dependent on fast-paced action and showing little attention to characterization. Several of them were collaborative efforts with Mabel Normand, which gave her equal billing. In his one year with Keystone, Chaplin made thirty-four shorts and one six-reel feature, *Tillie's Punctured Romance* (1914), in which he costarred with Marie Dressler, who had created the role of Tillie on the stage.

The lure of a less demanding production schedule and a handsome increase in salary brought Chaplin to the Essanay Company, a chief rival of Keystone in the production of comedies. It was in his sixteen films for Essanay that Chaplin began to develop the distinctive style of tragicomedy that was to link the term *pathos* forever with his screen characterizations. *The Tramp* (1915), his sixth film for Essanay, clearly shows the development of the sad clown. Here Charlie, a tramp, comes to the rescue of Edna Purviance (the female lead in most of his subsequent shorts), who is being robbed. He is rewarded by a job on her father's farm, where he once more routs the robbers but loses the girl to her handsome lover. The film's sad ending shows Charlie walking down the road away from the camera, with a shrug of the shoulders. This closing action was used in other of his shorts and became a Chaplin trademark.

Another outstanding and popular work of his Essanay period was *The Bank* (1915). Here Chaplin illustrates perfectly how the simple action that relates to characterization can be the most rewarding. Charlie enters a bank looking for all the world like the manager, with calm self-assurance and cocky gait. He walks over to the huge bank vault, deftly twirls the combination, swings open the door, enters, and emerges with mop and pail, ready to start the day's work. Chaplin himself quickly became aware of the importance to his screen personality of small bits of by-play. Just a year after making his first film, he reflected in an interview with *Motion Picture* magazine that "to pull off an unexpected trick, which the audience sees is a logical sequence, brings down the house. It is always the little things that bring the laughs. It's the little actions suited to the situation, that make the hit."

By the time Chaplin joined the Mutual Company in 1916, his films were becoming increasingly rich in such little actions. As a confirmed alcoholic in *The Cure* (1917), his almost catatonic reaction to a drink of "health water" offered him by Edna Purviance is inspired. In *The Rink* (1916), the invention is equally rewarding. Here Charlie, a waiter, uses traces of various dinner courses a customer has spilled on his person as a helpful reminder in preparing the bill. In *The Immigrant* (1917), Chaplin

From *Making a Living* (1914). Chaplin portrays an English dandy in his first film appearance. Henry Lehrman, here with Chaplin, also directed the film.

takes advantage of camera angle to gain surprise. Charlie, presumably seasick, is seen heaving at the rail. Not until he straightens up and the camera comes around to a new vantage point do we realize Charlie is enthusiastically engaged in hauling in a big fish.

Although Charlie was in the process of refining the basic tramp characterization, he did not limit himself to the familiar costume or the social status it represented. Many variations were slight and simply adapted to the professional role in which Charlie was engaged— waiter, clerk, even policeman were still unmistakably the little tramp. Occasionally, however, Chaplin's social status would be noticeably improved and the costume would show more marked modification. In *One A.M.* (1916), Charlie is in evening dress when he does battle with a revolving table and a Murphy bed. In *Carmen* (1915), he dons the costume of a toreador for his role as Don Hosiery. But the most pronounced transformation comes in *The Woman* (1915), in which he plays the title role in appropriate finery. Though roles shifted at times, basic attitude and invention remained undisturbed. Adopting a professional air, Charlie could charm a man in the post office into sticking out his tongue, presumably so Charlie could check his health. The motive was actually to get a stamp licked for posting a letter.

The Mutual films still showed vestiges of slapstick humor, but a slower, more controlled pace began to evolve. Routines were more carefully worked out and a subtler style of mime came into play. This marked the extension and refinement of bits of business into classic routines, which themselves became famous, even when the particular film in which they appeared were forgotten. *The Pawn Shop* (1916), which became the most popular of the twelve Mutual films, and *Easy Street* (1917) illustrate how far Chaplin had come in perfecting his style. In *Easy Street,* Charlie, a reformed derelict turned policeman, has his big confrontation with Eric Campbell, the strong-man bully who has been terrorizing the neighborhood. To demonstrate his strength, Campbell bends the post of a gas street lamp until the globe is nearly to the ground. This provides Charlie with his weapon. Maneuvering the bully's head into the globe, he turns on the gas, and Campbell is efficiently put to sleep. Each time he begins to revive, Charlie lowers the globe over his head with the calm self-assurance of an anesthetist.

The same deft and "professional" handling of the situation marks his famous clock routine in *The Pawn Shop*. Here Chaplin undertakes the examination of an old-fashioned alarm clock that has been handed to him by a customer. Charlie begins his examination with a stethoscope, then taps the ailing instrument with all the expertise of a crack diagnostician. For the operation on the timepiece that follows, he turns to hammer, brace and bit, and, finally, a can opener. Peeling back the cover, he judiciously sniffs at the innards and begins his extraction using a pair of pliers and periodically squirting the interior with oil. He removes the mainspring, which he carefully measures from nose to extended fingers like a piece of yardage, and finishes the operation by squirting and hitting the moving parts until all have been stilled. He then shovels the remains into the owner's hat and completes the routine by hitting the already stunned customer on the head with a rubber mallet.

In addition to the refinement of such visual routines, the Mutual films give more attention than do the earlier films to the character of Charlie himself. No longer simply the initiator or victim of visual gags, the little tramp emerges as an emotional being. He aspires to some role in life that will afford him a particle of prestige (which Charlie can usually find, no matter how lowly the job). He falls in love and suffers the anxiety of the quest and the heartbreak of rebuff or disillusionment. In *The Vagabond* (1916), Charlie is once again seen walking the lonely road, but now he is a personality whose actions reflect the inner state rather than the physical resolution to mechanical routines.

With the link between character and action thus established, a unity and cohesiveness is present that is not found in the earlier films. But Chaplin was not primarily a storyteller, and narrative simply provides a framework or setting for his various trials and aspirations. In fact, even with the polish of the Mutual films, many routines — his bit as a waiter in *The Rink* (1916), the superb ballet sequence with a masseur in *The Cure* (1917), and his drying of dishes in a clothes wringer in *The Pawn Shop* (1916) — might easily be interchange-

◀ From *Easy Street* (1917). With Charlie as a rookie cop and Edna Purviance providing the love interest, this film remains the popular favorite among the twelve films Chaplin made at Mutual in 1916–1917.

A Review of the Chaplin Style

*T*he author gives the stage comedians amusing lines, and Chaplin has no lines. Elaborately humorous plots are invented for the spoken drama, and Chaplin's plots are so simple that the popular legend credits him with improvising them as he goes along. He is on a stage where the slapstick, the "knockabout," the guttapercha hammer and the "roughhouse" are accepted as the necessary ingredients of comedy, and these things fight against the finer qualities of his art, yet he overcomes them. In his burlesque of Carmen he commits suicide with a collapsible dagger, and the moment of his death is as tragic as any of Bernhardt's. His work has become more and more delicate and finished as the medium of its reproduction has improved to admit of delicate and finished work.

—*Harvey O'Higgins,*
"Charlie Chaplin's Act,"
The New Republic
(February 3, 1917)

able. The films' unity is traceable to character motivation rather than a smooth narrative progression.

By the time Chaplin completed his twelve films for Mutual, his tramp had become an international star and even a household word. Of the period, he writes in his autobiography, "Fulfilling the Mutual contract, I suppose, was the happiest period of my career. I was light and unencumbered, twenty-seven years old with fabulous prospects and a friendly, glamorous world before me."

Virtually all twelve Mutual films have become mini-classics and make up the bulk of contemporary retrospectives of Chaplin's short films. In addition to the more elaborate routines he had begun to develop, rare moments of seemingly spontaneous by-play enriched the films. Much of this involved a precision in gesture and movement that made Chaplin a master of ballet in addition to his other talents. His stand-off with the masseur in *The Cure* is a masterpiece in choreography and shows the discipline of his style. But refinement of routines in no way robbed the films of the freshness and vigor of earlier works.

Wrap-Up

By 1916, with the official demise of the MPPC and the establishment of such independent producers as Fox, Laemmle, and Zukor as founders of large corporate entities, the motion picture was brought into the circle of big-business interests. Hollywood, with its ever expanding production facilities, including its huge "back lots," was becoming the motion picture capital of the world. And a world of dreams, both on screen and off, was being created in the movie palaces now springing up in major cities across the United States.

With four state and many municipal censorship boards in place, 1916 brought with it the spectre of federal film control by way of a censorship bill introduced in Congress. In response, the movie industry established its own self-censoring agency, the National Association of Motion Pictures, a forerunner of the Production Code and the current Rating Administration. But the industry's problems with regulation and control of film content and their exhibition were only beginning.

American audiences had been introduced to foreign films early in the century through Lumière's news and views and the Méliès fantasies. Italian spectacles and Zukor's introduction of such classic French fare as *Queen Elizabeth* as part of his "Famous Players in Famous Plays" plus the promotion of exotic foreign stars continued to give film exhibition in this country something of an international flavor. Considerably more significant, in spite of wartime restrictions, was the exposure of audiences around the world to American stars, settings, customs, and values by way of the Hollywood film.

By 1916 Griffith was at his peak and the multireel film established as the model for serious screen storytelling. Thomas Ince had fashioned the Western into an indigenous and indispensable part of American film. And with Sennett and Chaplin leading the way, the year marked the beginning of the golden age of American screen comedy, which would unfold for the next two decades.

American Silent Film (1917 – 1927)

Focus

When Griffith departed Biograph and Chaplin arrived from London in 1913, the American film was already set on a new course in its evolution. While still under the conservative influence of the Motion Picture Patents Company, American filmmakers had cautiously engaged in narrative construction with single- and double-reel films. The end of the Trust's influence and the establishment of Hollywood as the center of filmmaking meant that a new era of big business, individual enthusiasm, and stylistic opulence was under way. The feature-length film had arrived, stars were being discovered weekly, film budgets were expanding astronomically, and the first movie palaces were rising above the walls of the nickelodeon.

With this new industrial spirit and new-found respectability came new and more specialized talents in both the business and creative professions. During the golden age (1917 – 1927) of silent film, the most significant talents were those men and women — usually studio heads, directors, and major stars — who had not only the vision but the determination or commanding presence to extend film beyond the routine "photoplays" of the early narrative years.

Charlie Chaplin, Buster Keaton, and Douglas Fairbanks led the way in showing that storytelling could be used to accommodate the talents of the stars. As this point of view gained momentum, Mack Sennett, Griffith, and Ince, who nurtured the staple genres of comedy, drama, and period spectacle, were overshadowed by directors such as von Stroheim, Lubitsch, and De Mille, men who were able to capture the imagination and satisfy the moods of the time.

But if Griffith was the "father of film technique" and Ince the first "creative producer," it was the legion of creative spirits, anonymous as well as internationally acclaimed, who gave film its form and direction between the mid-1910s and the late 1920s. The pantheon included, in addition to the screenwriters, directors, and actors mentioned here, hundreds of production workers who, in increasingly discrete areas of specialization, were learning to master a new medium and a new art.

While the creative environment evolved, the industrial environment in which these people worked changed as well. The Trust companies, for the most part, were gone by 1916, replaced by the victorious independents. The change went beyond one simply in the corporate cast of characters: new maturity and strength were clearly evident in the industry that were not present before 1916.

New Strength in the Industry

Exhibition

By 1916 motion pictures occupied a new position characterized by strength, grandeur, and sophistication. They were no longer simply vaudeville "chasers" or the working folks' amusement.

There were several principal causes for this change. One was the feature film. Audiences were now viewing two-hour films, so the wooden chairs and cramped conditions of the nickelodeon quickly proved to be uncomfortable and inadequate. Theater quality became important, not only in showcasing the films themselves, but also in making audiences comfortable.

Perhaps the major cause of change, however, came from the audience itself. In 1914, Americans spent almost $300 million at the motion picture box office. Middle-class America had discovered motion pictures and was able and willing to pay for them. This new audience exercised greater discretion and demanded higher film and theater quality than earlier film viewers. When *The Great Train Robbery* played to a largely lower-middle-class audience, a store theater filled with wooden benches inspired no complaints. With such people as President Wilson making up part of the audience for *The Birth of a Nation,* however, wooden benches would no longer do. Moreover, the sophisticated musical scores in the longer silent films required more than simply a piano, and soon theaters were being equipped with elaborate organs. In large cities symphony orchestras played original scores for important productions.

By 1916, then, there were more than 21,000 new or

remodeled theaters across the country, one or some in every major city. These theaters had an average seating capacity of 500 and an average admission price of 8¢. In 1917 the Riviera Theater opened in New York with all the latest innovations, including a playroom equipped with a sandbox, slides, seesaws, and attendants. In 1919, the $2 million Capitol Theater opened in New York with room for 5,300, compared to the Metropolitan Opera's 3,000 and Carnegie Hall's 2,632. At least in terms of

GRAND FOYER
The Paramount Theatre

The **Theatre of a Thousand Wonders**

New York, city of wonders, will experience a brand-new sensation when the Paramount Theatre opens on Saturday, November 20th.

Here is a theatre so beautiful, so luxurious, so different, that *just being inside* is sheer, unalloyed pleasure!

Beauty meets the eye at every step, rugs as lovely as rare museum fabrics lie upon the marble floors and softly in the air everywhere is the sound of music of unseen origin.

The playground of the millions, in a Palace worthy of a King, yours to enjoy any time, any day or night! It will conquer New York in a day!

*Formal Opening Tonight
Regular Performances begin Tomorrow, 10:45 A.M.*

POPULAR PRICES!
10:45 to 1 P. M., *Weekdays and Saturday;* 40c
1 P. M. to 6 P. M., *Weekdays except Saturday;* 65c
After 6 P. M., " " " 75c
1 P. M. to closing, *Saturday;* 90c plus 9c tax 99c
10:45 A. M. to closing, *Sunday and Holidays;*
90c plus 9c tax 99c

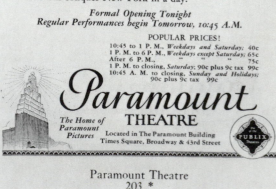

Paramount THEATRE

The Home of Paramount Pictures

Located in The Paramount Building
Times Square, Broadway & 43rd Street

PUBLIX

Paramount Theatre
203 *

seating capacity, the motion picture had surpassed the established culture.

Hundreds of new motion picture theaters were being constructed, and their interiors were designed to match the sets of the motion pictures being shown in them. All types of designs were being incorporated in theater construction. *Architectural Record* even began to note some of the more unusual ones—for example, the all-redwood theater in Scotia, California, with its entrance vestibule supported by eight redwood trunks two feet in diameter.

In the twenties, atmospheric houses became the rage. A rural French village was evoked in a Rochester, Minnesota, theater; a $500,000 Egyptian theater took shape in Milwaukee, Wisconsin; and in Portland, Oregon, an Indian temple appeared. These new theaters boasted crystal chandeliers, Oriental rugs, original paintings, statuary, and elaborately uniformed attendants.

The peak was reached in 1927, when S. L. "Roxy" Rothapfel opened the Roxy Theater in New York. This was the ultimate in exhibition. This "cathedral of motion pictures," with its 6,200 seats and elaborate facilities, was a perfect illustration of Rothapfel's philosophy. In describing the opening of another New York theater, the Capitol, Rothapfel said:

> Not so many years ago, fifteen to be exact, I was running a little movie show behind a barroom in a mining town in Pennsylvania. It was a one-man show. I painted my own displays, ran the projection machine, and sometimes walked to the nearest exchange to get pictures.
>
> If someone had predicted a dozen years ago that an orchestra, a chorus, soloists of international reputation, scenic artists, and a large mechanical staff would one day be part of the organization of a "movie" house, the prophet would have been called an irresponsible visionary.
>
> And yet this very thing has come to pass.
>
> The Capitol Theatre, New York, has 5300 seats. Its grand orchestra numbers eighty musicians. There is a chorus and a ballet. When we presented the master photoplay, "Passion," 175,000 came to see it during the two-week run.

▶ A 1916 advertisement for the opening of New York's Paramount Theater. As the ad states, "*just being inside* is sheer unalloyed pleasure," making the motion picture itself almost a secondary attraction.

▶ An artist's drawing of the interior of the Roxy Theater. This "cathedral of motion pictures" provided a total experience, more than simply a film on a screen.

Stepping Out

*G*oing to the new Strand Theatre last night was very much like going to a Presidential reception, a first night at the opera or the opening of the horse show. It seemed like everyone in town had simultaneously arrived at the conclusion that a visit to the magnificent new movie playhouse was necessary.

I have always tried to keep abreast of the times and be able to look ahead a little way, but I must confess that when I saw the wonderful audience last night in all its costly togs, the one thought that came to my mind was that if anyone had told me two years ago that the time would come when the finest-looking people in town would be going to the biggest and newest theatre on Broadway for the purpose of seeing motion pictures I would have sent them down to visit my friend, Dr. Minas Gregory at Bellevue Hospital. The doctor runs the city's bughouse, you know.

— Victor Watson, New York Times *(April 12, 1914)*

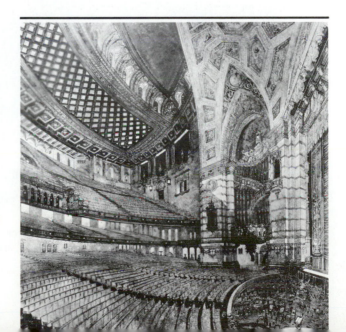

Production

As the industry expanded to keep up with public demand, more and more stars, sensing their own importance, asked for and received huge salaries. Indeed, the well-publicized weekly salaries of Tom Mix ($10,000), Geraldine Farrar ($10,000), and Alla Nazimova ($13,000) clearly illustrate that the star system reigned supreme.

The inevitable outcome was the formation of personal production companies by certain major stars. The companies represented the formalization of the process in which motion pictures were sold on the basis of the stars they featured. As the films grew more popular, these stars demanded more and more money. The studios found it increasingly difficult to pay these huge salaries, despite increased profits. However, the public seemed willing to pay almost any price to see certain stars, so the stars who could went into business for themselves. Doing so, however, was only possible for those few whose power matched that of the studios. "Ordinary" stars did not have this type of strength.

Some of the major personalities who went into production for themselves were Harold Lloyd, Norma Talmadge, Buster Keaton, Gloria Swanson, and Harry Langdon. Only a few, such as Lloyd and Keaton, were successful. The majority failed—not because they suddenly became unpopular, but because they had no knowledge of what made their films successful.

United Artists was the most successful production organization outside the major studios. This group was formed in 1919 by Mary Pickford, Charles Chaplin, Douglas Fairbanks, D. W. Griffith, and William S. Hart, with the advice and consultation of B. P. Schulberg. Hart soon dropped out, but became very successful at producing films on his own. The remaining four worked out a system whereby they financed everything themselves and earned producer profits as well as a share from distribution. Fairbanks and Pickford, soon to become partners in marriage as well as business, subsequently bought their own studio, as did Chaplin. Among them the three actors made about eight films a year. Griffith was kept busy satisfying other contracts and his production for the company was limited.

The forming of United Artists represented the fullest expression of the star system. By 1920 the system had reached a proportion out of scale with reality, as

▲ Charlie Chaplin, with pen in hand, and three other founders of United Artists. From left to right, D. W. Griffith, Mary Pickford, and Douglas Fairbanks. The two men in the back are unidentified.

Salary Sampling

*I*n my opinion, the greatest portion of the expense going into the production of a motion picture today is the salaries of the stars, directors and supporting cast. These salaries are clearly out of proportion to the services rendered in similar professions, and should be readjusted immediately. With these tremendous salaries paid to stars, directors and supporting casts, the average picture is boosted way above its normal cost, necessitating a corresponding increase in exhibition value, with a corresponding increase in film rentals which the exhibitor cannot assimilate, so that the entire matter backwashes to the producer.

Our reports recently contained the story that Baby Peggy, a child of 5 years, was receiving a guarantee of $500,000 a year for appearing in motion pictures. Contrast that with the salary that the President of the United States of America is receiving, which is $75,000 a year, and it can readily be seen what a tremendous impression the contrast has upon the outside world.

One thing is certain. The only ones in the entire industry that are getting the money at present are the actors.

An immediate adjustment must come, and that at once. And if those who are receiving these tremendous salaries are reluctant to meet a readjustment of an economic condition in the film industry, then, I say, by all means get new faces for the screen immediately. The exhibitor will be glad to help.

Just an example of what a few are receiving may be found in the following list:

Lewis Stone	$2500	House Peters	2500
Rockliffe Fellowes	1800	Florence Vidor	2000
J. Warren Kerrigan	1500	George Walsh	1500
Milton Sills	2500	Tom Mix	4000
Richard Dix	1250	Mabel Normand	3000
Conrad Nagle	1250	Elliot Dexter	2000
Jack Holt	1500	Elaine Hammerstein	2500
Lon Chaney	1750	Larry Semon	5000
Conway Tearle	2750	Shirley Mason	1500
James Kirkwood	2500	Viola Dana	2000
May McAvoy	3000	Al St. John	1000
Anna Q. Nilsson	1500	Priscilla Dean	3000
Wallace Beery	2500	Norma Talmadge	10,000
Noah Beery	1500	Constance Talmadge	5000
Mary Astor	750	Pauline Frederick	5000
Lila Leo	1500	Dorothy Dalton	7000
Betty Compson	3500	Richard Barthelmess	2500
Gloria Swanson	500	Lillian Gish	5000
Barbara La Marr	3500	Mae Marsh	1500
Patsy Ruth Miller	1500	Walter Long	1250
Kenneth Harlan	1000	Wyndham Standing	1500
Hope Hampton	1000	Betty Blythe	2500

— *William Brandt, President, Motion Picture Theatre Owners, New York State,* Moving Picture World *(November 10, 1923)* stars assumed more importance than the studios employing them. This changed very quickly, however, as film costs soared and the industry expanded. The studios could no longer afford to pay astronomical salaries when other costs were rising as well. Outside financial backing was required and, as conservative businesspeople entered the scene, stars were forced out of their dominant position. In 1919 *The Miracle Man* was made starring a group of relatively unknown actors and actresses, including Betty Compson, Joseph Dowling, Thomas Meighan, and Lon Chaney. The film cost $120,000 and grossed more than $3 million. The film proved to be something of a watershed in convincing the studios that competent but relatively unknown and reasonably salaried players under solid direction could turn a profit in a well-scripted film. Soon producers and directors were making films without stars. Cecil B. De Mille, for one, emphasized elaborate sets and sexual themes, and his films were successes. The system began to produce films based on content, theme, and production value as well as stars.

Once again the balance of power shifted. The result was the decline of a star-*dominated* system, though not the star system itself, by 1920. Stars were still powerful and would remain a major factor in the making and selling of films. However, once again they were employees working under lucrative, though at times restrictive, contracts. It was not until the 1960s, when the studio system crumbled under its own weight, that the employer/employee relationship turned around again.

As pioneers, however, Chaplin and Pickford did not drop back into the system. They continued to produce their own films, as did a few others such as Buster Keaton and Harold Lloyd. However, stars no longer dominated the system. Again, as with the Trust, the industry had grown too quickly and too large to be controlled by any one part of it. A new system emerged, one that defined itself more in terms of the latest stock market quotations than the salaries paid to a young mustachioed man named Charlie or a little blonde-haired girl named Mary.

The Establishment of Hollywood

Along with the changes in the industry came a geographical shift. As explained in Chapter 2, the move West was initially a result of the independents' conflict with the Trust. Soon, however, the appeals of year-round sunshine and inexpensive outdoor sets began to attract more companies. As Kevin Brownlow has pointed out in his book *The Parade's Gone By,* the coming of motion pictures to the West Coast in general and to Hollywood in particular took the form of a gradual infiltration rather than a direct invasion. The industry was once again displaying its natural reluctance to depart from established procedure.

In 1908–1914, the pioneer period, many companies went West, some to succeed but most to fail. Still, by 1916 enough had prospered to give Hollywood the appearance of a major industrial center. And by 1919 approximately 80 percent of the world's motion pictures were being made there. Gertrude Jobes, in her book *Motion Picture Empire,* describes this metamorphosis well:

> Well-paved boulevards extended for miles where for generations muddy paths had been the only roads. Building after building covered what had been pasture land fifteen years before. Palatial studios replaced tottering shacks. Millionaire's Lane supplanted Poverty Row. The world's most glamorous city emerged on the site of an unknown sleepy village.

By 1921 and 1922 there were 49 studios in and around Los Angeles and about 175 production units. And studio payrolls had reached almost $40 million.

The shift West was mental as well as geographical. The West Coast, with its air of newness, enthusiasm, and unfulfilled growth and size, was ideal for the rapidly expanding industry. The East was staid, conservative, heavy, and established. No such adjectives applied to Hollywood, and as a result the industry was free to create its own image. The sense and feel of the West in American heritage and tradition have always been powerful. There was always new land, new opportunity, and new life in the West, and this "newness" was just as real for the motion picture industry as it had been for those arriving in wagon trains fifty years earlier. The word *Hollywood* became synonymous with *motion pictures.* The city symbolized the appeal and glamor of motion pictures for the public as much as the films themselves. As Richard Griffith and Arthur Mayer state in *The Movies,* "Hollywood in the Twenties was garish, extravagant, ludicrous, acquisitive, ambitious, ruthless, beautiful — which was just what its world public wanted it to be."

A New System

The result of the individual changes in production, exhibition, and location was a new system of making, distributing, and exhibiting motion pictures. What emerged was not only a new style of making films but a new *form* for film, one that had the characteristics of an industrial product. Standardization was a goal eagerly sought by the new system, and motion pictures were soon brought into line.

One of the key individuals in establishing this new system was Thomas Ince. As described in Chapter 2, Ince was accomplished as a director, especially of Westerns, but he made his real contribution as the industry's first production supervisor. His importance in standardizing the production of motion pictures cannot be over-emphasized. Some have felt that his contributions to production style were ultimately negative in that he took motion pictures away from the control of individual directors. However, whether negative or positive, his contribution was overall necessary. By 1916, the motion pictures being produced by the studios required more efficiency in production.

Until 1916 motion picture financial practices were fairly sane and businesslike despite the war with the Trust, the rise of the star system, and the gradual conversion to feature films. Costs were kept at a reasonable level, primarily because most companies were self-sufficient and required no outside capital. However, the ultimate impact and influence of stars such as Chaplin and Pickford plus the feature film made financial sanity not only difficult, but risky. While conservative companies pondered new salary demands and looked hesitantly at feature production, bold competitors rushed in and gambled their resources on stars and stories.

Adolph Zukor continued to lead the parade. By 1916–1917, through consolidation, merger, and the acquisition of competing companies' stars, he had become the largest producer and distributor of motion pictures in the world. His most significant accomplishment, and one of the most important developments in this early period, was the consolidation of distribution and production under one corporate structure as opposed to separate companies all fighting for a piece of the action. The rest of the industry soon followed in his footsteps, and by 1917 the profits made from distribution were financing production.

This consolidation left the exhibitor in an extremely vulnerable position because he had no bargaining power in the selection of motion pictures for his theater. Zukor, especially, made life difficult for exhibitors by instituting and promoting a policy known as block booking. This procedure forced exhibitors to rent their films in blocks from certain companies and, in effect, required that they accept a number of "bad" films to get the studio's major films. Zukor's studio, Paramount, was especially secure in this practice, because it employed most of the major stars of the period. As the plan went, an exhibitor might have to take three or four films of lesser quality to get a Mary Pickford film. The scheme was of tremendous value to industrial standardization, because a production company was guaranteed exhibition for virtually all its products, regardless of quality.

Exhibitors complained bitterly about the practice, but were powerless to break it until 1917, when Thomas Tally and other exhibitors formed the First National Company. First National was an independent production company that, at least in the beginning, neither employed actors nor owned a studio, but rather allowed players and directors to act as their own producers and then distributed and exhibited their films. Charlie Chaplin was the first major star to join followed by Mary Pickford. Soon, First National acquired its own production facilities and began signing actors and actresses to contracts. Soon it was second in power only to Paramount.

This activity was taking place against the background and drama of World War I. The war was the most important factor in establishing the world dominance of American films. From the earliest days, American audiences had patronized the nickelodeon where foreign-made films danced upon the screens. But the war interrupted the product flow. While European energies were brought to bear upon survival, and then upon reconstruction, the American industry was evolving toward world domination. In 1914 American films accounted for approximately 50 percent of the world's market. In 1918 they accounted for 80 percent. Most of Europe's major industries were decimated by the war, and the American industry rushed in to fill the vacuum.

"Naturally," said Lewis J. Selznick in 1920, "the most important thing that has happened since the beginning of the war is the ending of the war. The reopening of the European market is the big opportunity we have been awaiting for four years." American corporations began setting up foreign subsidiaries and raiding native European industries for their best talent. By 1925 American films had captured 95 percent of the British market and 70 percent of the French and Italian screen time. Foreign films, in turn, had little chance in the American market. In 1922, for instance, U.S. companies purchased more than 400 foreign-made titles, but only six were released for exhibition.

A temporary recession occurred in the American film industry at the end of the war. Three factors combined to cause it: the reduction of the European market, a large backlog of war films, and an influenza epidemic. This combination spelled disaster for many small independent American companies, but the large organizations came through relatively unscathed. The industry was simply too strong at this point to be permanently crippled.

Major Studios of the Twenties
Silent Feature Production

	Paramount	MGM	Universal	UA	Fox	First National	Warner Bros.
1921	101	——	55	9	64	——	4
1922	84	——	46	8	64	——	5
1923	55	——	60	4	52	——	11
1924	57	19	50	4	53	15	22
1925	74	27	51	10	43	52	26
1926	64	34	57	6	51	52	32
1927	67	42	64	13	49	58	43
1928	60	42	59	14	51	47	28

In the postwar period, the Hollywood dream factories were in full production. The studio system was in the ascendancy, feature-length films were the norm, and only in America were both capital and personnel available in quantities necessary to satisfy the demand and meet the production values to which the world was becoming accustomed. President Coolidge summed up the mood of America: "The business of America is business." In the case of the movies, business was booming, for the product involved — which was slick, smooth, and well-made — was apparently desired by the public both at home and abroad. In contrast, the health of the European industry was so weakened by the war and ensuing changes, and the prognosis was so dim, that one American businessman suggested that embargoes be placed upon all American imports to *force* European industries to revive and find a solid base once again.

As the American motion picture industry geared up for one of the most glorious and extravagant periods in its history, a new order of men and organizations emerged to sustain it. As Benjamin Hampton states,

> The movie business was no longer an infant industry in which anyone might find fame and fortune. It had passed the middle period in which men with moderate capital might establish themselves. Within a few years it had grown to maturity and had become one of America's greatest industries, subject to large capital necessities and the financing rules and regulations of big business and Wall Street. Twilight was descending on independent control of theaters, studios, and exchanges.

In a sense, the industry had come full circle, and, though composed of independent companies, it was now similar in organization and structure to the Trust it had displaced only eight years earlier. Men such as Zukor, Laemmle, and Fox had worked hard to establish this new order and were not about to lose control. And control — of both distribution and exhibition — became vital as merger, consolidation, and interlock became watchwords of the new system.

At the beginning of the twenties, the major studios were Paramount, First National, and Fox. Second-level companies included Universal, Selznick, Metro, and Goldwyn. Bringing up the rear were thirty or forty "poverty row" companies, such as Columbia and Monogram. Although Universal, under the leadership of Carl Laemmle, had been one of the strongest companies in the fight against the Trust, it did not attempt to compete with the majors in elaborate, star-studded feature films; instead it emphasized low-cost features, comedies, Westerns, and serials. Universal became known as the family studio, both for the type of films it produced and for the nepotism that "Uncle Carl" Laemmle established as the basic organizational structure for his studio.

Industry statistics for 1919–1920 reveal a gross industry income of $750 million, 15,000 theaters with a seating capacity of 8 million people, and another 1,200 theaters under construction. These figures, however, represented only the tip of an iceberg of feverish financial activity. In addition to the money required to buy theaters, film costs were rising at an incredible rate, and

De Mille Film Costs

Title	Cost	Gross Earnings
Male and Female (1919)	$170,000	$1,250,000
Why Change Your Wife? (1920)	74,000	300,000
Forbidden Fruit (1921)	340,000	850,000
Adam's Rib (1922)	400,000	880,000
Manslaughter (1922)	385,000	1,200,000
The Golden Bed (1925)	440,000	800,000

the industry was turning into a monetary madhouse. The primary factors were theater acquisitions, salaries, feature-length films, and an emphasis on spectacular sets, costumes, and design. As the postwar boom continued, many companies felt that since the public seemed willing to pay to see almost anything, there was no limit to the amount of money they could spend on production. In 1915 Griffith made *The Birth of a Nation* for $100,000; three years later he reportedly paid $175,000 just for the rights to *Way Down East*. MGM spent $4.5 million on *Ben Hur* in 1926. Other costly films of this period included *The King of Kings* (1927), made at a cost of $2.5 million, and *Wings* (1927), which cost $2 million. According to film historian Benjamin Hampton, a 1,500 percent increase occurred in the cost of producing an average feature film between 1914 and 1924. Much of this spending was stimulated by the example set by Cecil B. De Mille, who, while at Paramount in 1919, devised a production formula based on a combination of money and sex. Using this formula, he produced a number of extremely successful films, some of which are listed in the accompanying table. The industry quickly took notice of these figures, especially the cost-to-profit ratios. Whereas *Male and Female* (1919) grossed almost eight times its cost, however, *Ben Hur* (1926), *Thief of Baghdad* (1924), or *King of Kings* (1927) would have had to set new box office records to duplicate this feat. Indeed, while *Ben Hur* was one of the top grossing films of the era, it lost money owing to its heavy production costs and other contractual obligations. Overproduction was a problem as well, as the industry was making 600 to 800 features a year. In Hollywood in 1922, there were more than 200 production units and 52 studios employing more than 15,000 people.

The year 1922 was something of a high-water mark in terms of industry excess, aptly symbolized by Douglas

The castle set from Douglas Fairbanks's 1925 production of *Robin Hood*. This picture gives some indication of the extravagance of Hollywood productions in the boom years of the 1920s.

Fairbanks's $2 million spectacle, *The Thief of Baghdad*. Following the diminished returns from this and other films, producers began to realize that increased cost did not automatically result in increased profits.

The 1923 *Film Daily Yearbook* signaled the end to this monetary extravaganza with its headline "Production Orgy Over," followed by this statement: "Until 1923 the motion picture industry was the spoiled child among American industries, spending as lavishly as it pleased on more and more costly productions, knowing that the generous public would foot the bills." The industry discovered there was a limit to the public's ability and willingness to spend money on motion picture tickets. In addition, other leisure activities, made possible by radio and the automobile, were taking increasing amounts of the public's time and money.

Scandal and Sin

Hollywood's meteoric rise into prosperity and worldwide popularity was also brought up short by a series of public scandals that occurred in the early 1920s. These episodes seemed to mirror events in public life, such as the Teapot Dome Scandal in the Harding administration. The scandal involved the secret leasing of naval oil reserves to private companies by Secretary of the Interior Albert Fall. Fall was convicted amidst great publicity. Three events in the film industry, dealing with sex, drugs, and murder, shocked the American public and brought demands for control and censorship of motion pictures. Although motion pictures treated sex with increasing candor, the public was basically tolerant of exposure to sexuality as long as it stayed on the screen. The reaction was different when sex moved off the screen into real life.

The first and most notorious scandal occurred in 1921. It involved Fatty Arbuckle, a major silent film comedian, at the time probably second in popularity only to Chaplin. Arbuckle was accused of causing the death of a young actress at a party that soon became a "wild orgy." In the ensuing publicity, Arbuckle was characterized as a sex fiend. The case dragged through three court trials and the nation's press before Arbuckle was eventually declared innocent. By this time, however, the publicity was so unfavorable that Arbuckle never worked in films again, except under an alias in a few cheap potboilers.

The second incident involved the murder of the well-known director William Desmond Taylor. This time two leading actresses were implicated through their personal relationships with Taylor. One was Mary Miles Minter, hailed as the new Mary Pickford, and the other was Mack Sennett's leading comedienne, Mabel Normand. As in the Arbuckle case, neither woman was convicted of anything more than indiscretion. However, the public was outraged, and two more careers were ruined.

The final tragedy occurred in 1923 and involved the popular actor Wallace Reid, who died while trying to cure himself of drug addiction. Although no one else was implicated in his death, the publicity served to fan the flames of censorship even higher.

The public outrage at these and other scandals was enormous, primarily because they confirmed to many that Hollywood was indeed a den of sin and iniquity. Censorship pressure started to come from all quarters, including the federal government. By the end of 1921, thirty-six states were considering censorship legislation, and the word *Hollywood* was commonly heard in congressional speeches, usually accompanied by unfavorable adjectives.

In desperation, the industry leaders got together and hired Will Hays, Postmaster General under President Harding (and, ironically, involved in the Teapot Dome Scandal) to head up a new industry self-regulatory agency, the Motion Picture Producers and Distributors Association of America, Inc. (MPPDA). Hays's powers to "censor" more often took the form of consultation than confrontation. The Hays Office, as the MPPDA came to be known, functioned effectively in fending off local, state, and federal censorship legislation. It persuaded the studios to tone down sexual content and applied pressure on stars to avoid public scandals. More importantly, it reviewed summaries of screenplays and passed judgment on their acceptability.

All this activity was conducted on an informal basis until 1930, when sound films brought new problems with dialogue, and studio competition became increasingly fierce. As public concern grew, the industry responded by adopting the Motion Picture Production Code, a set of content standards that would remain the basic self-regulatory mechanism of the industry for almost forty years.

▶ Fatty Arbuckle, in a typical role in one of his pre-1920 comedy shorts.

▶ Will Hays (left) seen here with Carl Laemmle, head of Universal. Hays served as head of the MPPDA from 1922 to 1946.

Stabilization

On the heels of the public outcry over morals and increased concern over costs and content, several studios closed. However, the most important result of these developments was production standardization. Among the many changes brought about was the rigid inspection of scenarios and preproduction cost analyses by production executives and corporate finance men. Efficiency experts were brought in and, although not always successful, they at least helped to bring some degree of sanity to this ephemeral world of shadows and emotions. Not everyone agreed, however, that the type of sanity introduced was good. James Morrison is quoted in Kevin Brownlow's book, *The Parade's Gone By:*

> I left the Vitagraph in 1918 when they brought in efficiency experts. When that happened the art of the company disappeared. Here were three people dividing two million dollars a year—and yet they brought in efficiency experts. These people limited the amount of film that directors could shoot . . . and they even had people straightening nails.

An even more significant change was the introduction of the executive producer as a key job in the industry. Although pioneered by Thomas Ince, the idea took one of its most dominant forms in the person of Irving Thalberg, who joined MGM in 1925 and proceeded to revolutionize the business of making motion pictures. No director, regardless of previous reputation, was safe from Thalberg's supervision and revision, and he quickly became a model used by the entire industry. Many directors and players rebelled, but with little effect.

Fortunately for MGM, Thalberg was an intelligent, creative man. Thalberg, and with him the position of executive producer, was here to stay. In the best sense of Thalberg's tradition, executive producers curbed artistic excess and helped make many films successful by watching a film's "bottom line" and keeping up with what audiences were watching in the theaters. In the worst sense, executive producers were unnecessary and uncreative burdens. As Kevin Brownlow notes, "Hollywood summed up their value by calling them 'glacier watchers'—they stand around making sure the studio isn't engulfed by a glacier."

A further sign of the industry's attempt to achieve some form of financial stability is found in a 1923 report by the National Bank of Commerce, which stated, "The motion picture industry is slowly getting out of the class of a game and more in the class of a business." By 1924 most studios had adopted a budget system, and the average cost of a feature had stabilized at $150,000 to $200,000. In addition, some studios instituted special features, such as giving a director a certain amount of money to make a picture and letting him keep what was left over. Most studios went to a diversified plan, making a variety of films and refusing to put all their eggs in one basket.

As studios grew in size and more elaborate and expensive films went into production, the planning and scripting of films became increasingly important phases of production. These changes inspired increasing resentment on the part of many directors, who saw their role as diminished to that of stage manager. In big production companies in particular, heavy production schedules did not allow directors time to collaborate on scenarios, even when they were so inclined. Ince had helped make the producer the person who called the shots, which relegated the director to the position of glorified cameraman. The directors who were to make their names as creative artists were those who could summon the independence and creative energy to participate in the planning and scripting process.

If Ince's role as producer showed that creativity in film could be centered elsewhere than in the imagination of the director, it also helped indirectly to encourage the talent of the legions of screenwriters who labored in obscurity for the major companies. The filmwriter became a fixture of studio operations several years before the big-studio assembly-line techniques began developing in the mid-teens. Ince employed scenarists to hammer out scripts for him, albeit under close supervision. Among the many scenarists Ince used, his favorite was C. Gardner Sullivan, who many regard as the dean of screenwriters during the period 1914 through 1924. Sennett, meanwhile, had his stable of "idea men"— often female—who brainstormed the early Keystone antics. Even earlier, Griffith collaborated with several scenarists, such as Frank Woods, Gerrit J. Lloyd, and Anita Loos, the teenage girl who provided him with his script for *The New York Hat.* Most Griffith works, however, were shot "off the cuff," and he seldom used a continuity or shooting script once involved in production.

Anita Loos was one of the first and most important scenario writers. As noted, she began her writing career at age fourteen, and by the end of the silent era she had 200 scenarios and countless title-writing assignments to her credit. With a ferocious appetite for literature and aspirations to become a writer, Loos began submitting scenarios to the major film companies when she found that it was lucrative enough to provide her with the financial independence to pursue a literary career. By 1916 she had an impressive list of film credits at Biograph, Reliance, Lubin, and Metro. In her scenarios, she created dramas of people and places around the world even though she herself had never been out of California.

Loos's special gift proved to be writing in a wry comic vein. Douglas Fairbanks found himself on the way to stardom with the Loos script *His Picture in the Paper,* and after that Loos wrote most of his screenplays as well as several of Mary Pickford's. She also wrote several films for Constance Talmadge between 1919 and 1925, and when she joined MGM and Irving Thalberg in 1929, she began writing screenplays for Jean Harlow.

For MGM she took on the added job of "film doctor," working on faltering scripts by other scenarists. *San Francisco, The Women,* and *I Married An Angel* are among her more prominent feature film credits, but it was her novel *Gentlemen Prefer Blondes* that brought her the cheers and admiration of world statesmen and the literary elite. This work also proved to be one of the most durable properties in the history of the arts, having gone from novel (1925) to Broadway play (1926) to movie (1928) to stage musical (1949) to movie musical (1953), with Loos writing or collaborating on each version.

Loos also made important contributions to film by writing titles—silent films' substitute for the spoken word. In addition to writing titles for most of her own screenplays, she also supplied titles for many films she didn't script, including *Intolerance.* Through titles, Loos found it possible to introduce verbal humor to the silent screen, and one wonders, although it is difficult to document such speculation, whether the florid style of titles in many of the early silents did not represent Loos having some private fun with the melodramatic form and Victorian sentiment.

Loos, of course, was only one of the many unsung creative spirits who gave birth to film stories. Sonya

▶ Pioneer screenwriter Anita Loos, in 1923. Loos specialized in clever lines rather than plot and character development.

Levien, who began writing screenplays in 1919, later produced scripts for *State Fair* (1933), *In Old Chicago* (1938), *Drums Along the Mohawk* (1939), *Cass Timberlane* (1947), and *Hit the Deck* (1955). Frances Marion, who scripted some of the best of the Rudolph Valentino and Mary Pickford films, went on to write the screenplays for *Anna Christie* (1936), *Stella Dallas* (1937), and *The Big House* (1930). Jeanie MacPherson wrote many of the De Mille scenarios, while Jane Murfin, who began writing for film in 1917, went on later to create screenplays for Howard Hawks, William Wyler, and George Cukor. Screenwriting in the teens was a training ground for many who were to labor, virtually unnoticed by filmgoers, on films large and small, sound and silent—and significantly for the time, a large proportion of them were women.

As Hollywood filmmaking in the twenties became more standardized, the quality of individual films and directors dropped significantly. Nothing similar to the "age of Griffith" asserted itself during the 1920s. Rather, there emerged a series of company directors who made films using assembly-line methods with little opportunity to break new ground in the medium or otherwise distinguish themselves as screen artists.

The films produced in this manner were characterized by stars and plot formulas. Although the studios produced a variety of films, most of the films of the twenties could be characterized as modern, reflecting the postwar decade with all its exuberance and spirit. This was the Jazz Age. It was also a production age: industrial production in the United States increased 50 percent between 1920 and 1929. America moved from the farm of *Tol'able David* (1921) to the city of *The Jazz Singer* (1927). In between, more than 5,000 feature films were made.

These films reflected both the time in which they were made and the system that produced them. There were, for example, almost 100 films on alcoholism and more than 150 on automobiles. Bigamy was the subject of 49 films, bigotry the subject of only 6. Bootlegging appeared as a major theme in 87 films and chorus girls were the subject of more than 100 pictures. Farming, on the other hand, was a theme in only eleven films.

Most of these were studio formula films produced in cycles with distinct patterns. For example, there were more than 60 films dealing with flappers, and about the same number glorifying aviation, but the production pattern with respect to these films is more interesting than the numbers alone. As the accompanying graph reveals, the system was responsive to both internal and external influences. In the case of flappers, as soon as one studio began to achieve success with the theme, the other studios followed suit. With aviation, the key was Charles

Lindbergh's flight in 1927, which the studios jumped on with glee.

In other areas, Chaplin was joined by other comic geniuses—Buster Keaton, Harold Lloyd, and Harry Langdon, among others—and silent screen comedy was enjoying its golden age. The genre would be further enriched in the course of the decade by a new sophisticated style fashioned by director Ernst Lubitsch and actor Douglas Fairbanks, among others. In the dramatic film, where the creative energy was less likely to be consolidated in a single writer-star-director, the films that distinguished themselves and influenced the course of screen drama were those by the few directors who managed to break stride, pull themselves out of the assembly-line routine, and, while fighting off constant studio pressures, follow their own creative instincts.

Hollywood's First-String Directors

Erich von Stroheim

Erich von Stroheim, both as actor and director, possessed the kind of individuality and determination that enabled him to stand above the crowd, and in so doing he drew himself into a critical crossfire between producers and the public. His own real-life career as an Austrian army officer became a recurring role for him when he

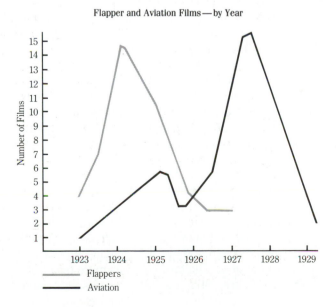

Flapper and Aviation Films—by Year

◄ Erich von Stroheim, one of film's authentic geniuses. He had a passion for detail unmatched in history.

▶ From *Greed* (1924). Trina and McTeague's wedding feast, like many scenes in the film, is a treasure of symbolic visual detail.

Devil's Passkey (1920). A $75,000 ceiling was stipulated that von Stroheim exceeded by $100,000. This film also took an unprecedented nine months to produce. In spite of his continued extravagance in both time and money, von Stroheim somehow prevailed upon Laemmle once again, and the result was *Foolish Wives* (1922). The finished film came in at thirty-two reels (about seven hours running time), and cost more than $1 million to produce. In spite of the commercial success of these films, Universal finally lost patience with von Stroheim's extravagance and fired him.

Within the industry von Stroheim's reputation was well established as both an accomplished screen artist and a reckless squanderer of time and money. His films were long, expensive, and slow to produce, but they were also popular and helped keep Universal solvent. So MGM was willing to risk the excesses of Hollywood's *enfant terrible* and hired him to direct an adaptation of the popular Frank Norris novel *McTeague*. The novel's grisly image of human avarice was well suited to von Stroheim's developing sense of naturalism, and in *Greed*, released in 1924, he produced his longest, costliest, and most impressive work. Following the Norris story closely, von Stroheim once again so magnified and extended details that the film ran more than forty reels in length (nearly nine hours). It brought to life the adventures of McTeague, the brutish self-styled San Francisco dentist who marries the miserly Trina. Hoarding her lottery fortune, and grasping for spare change from her struggling husband, she is finally murdered by McTeague. The setting shifts in the final scenes from squalid San Francisco interiors to the scorching expanse of Death Valley, where McTeague, with his wife's gold coins in hand, is stalked by Trina's former sweetheart.

The original film was basically emasculated by outside film cutters assigned to pare it down to a viewable ten reels, so any analysis of *Greed's* overall structure is impossible. What survives in the shortened film, however, are masterful moments of action in an atmosphere that is as much tactile as visual. Erich von Stroheim's dedication to detail is seen in the grimy walls, drab fur-

began acting in early Hollywood films. His American screen-acting debut actually began with several minor roles in *The Birth of a Nation* (he appeared in blackface) and *Intolerance*. In the latter film, in addition to assisting Griffith, he appeared as the Pharisee. But it was his image of the suave and seductive count, prince, and Prussian officer in the films he directed himself that made him known to audiences — and helped earn him a reputation as a panderer and corrupter of morals. His early films brought him under fire. *Photoplay,* in reviewing *Foolish Wives* (1922), called the film "an insult to American ideals and womanhood" while nevertheless speaking of von Stroheim's "genius for detail and artistic talents nothing short of incredible." Even his later films, in which he does not appear, have a pervasive erotic quality that is sophisticated and elegant, and at times sordid, but that always seems a bit perverse.

This very "genius for detail" made von Stroheim's relations with producers strained at best. His career is a case study of the independent and uncompromising director at odds with an industry increasingly concerned with production schedules and cost accounting. The first film he directed in Hollywood, *Blind Husbands* (1919), was budgeted at $25,000 by Carl Laemmle, president of Universal Pictures. The final cost was more than three times that figure. Still, the film's success convinced Laemmle to give von Stroheim another assignment, *The*

nishings, and unmade beds that are so much a part of *Greed*. Forty years later, this kind of atmosphere came to be known in the British film movement as "kitchen sink" realism. As a result of this painstaking detail, *Greed* is virtually a document of social realism in America at the turn of the century. This approach did not reflect pure self-indulgence on von Stroheim's part, as some suggested, but rather served as a means of revealing the total environment of the characters. Von Stroheim had said that "a shot of an inanimate object accentuates its dramatic importance." This was a lesson he had learned from Griffith and that now became the essence of his own style.

Social realism was a trademark of von Stroheim's later work as well. *The Wedding March* (1927) and the unfinished *Queen Kelly* (1928) were both drawn from the director's impressions of Vienna royalty, and although fantasy at times mingled with realism (the common girl in love with the prince), the films reflected the gradual dissolution of the Hapsburg Empire. Even *The Merry Widow* (1925), based on the operetta by Franz Lehár, became a sardonic satire on the Austrian royal family.

The blending of naturalistic detail with ironic imagery gave von Stroheim's work added power. In *Greed*, this characteristic approach was represented in the spilling of life-sustaining water and useless gold as McTeague

and his adversary die in the desert, in the glimpse of a funeral procession during Trina and McTeague's wedding reception, and in the murder of Trina beneath the branches of a Christmas tree. Some of von Stroheim's most grotesque and ironic images are found in *The Wedding March*, which he made for Paramount in 1927. The attempted rape of Mitzi takes place in a slaughterhouse, with a boar's head gazing down from the wall and carcasses hanging from the ceiling. The cruelest of von Stroheim's imagery appears in the scene where the crippled princess limps down the aisle in her wedding, forced upon her, to an unwilling prince. In this picture, gay Vienna becomes a place of misery for the poor, and one of decay for the excessively rich and privileged. As MGM did with *Greed*, Paramount gave *The Wedding March* to professional film cutters to cut down, and it is therefore the impact of individual scenes rather than the work as a whole that remains impressive.

Both von Stroheim's virtues and shortcomings as a director seem bound to the spirit of extravagance for which his work became known. At its best, the work showed uncompromising detail that was the essence of screen realism and resulted in scenes incredibly rich in meaning. At its worst, the work revealed an excess that resulted in films of staggering length and complexity whose coherence, once the studio editors were finished with them, remained questionable.

Josef von Sternberg

The seamier side of realism and the lower-class milieu that were so much a part of von Stroheim's work were further explored by Austrian-born director, Jonas Sternberg, who later adopted the more imposing name of Josef von Sternberg. His first film, *The Salvation Hunters* (1925), brought critical plaudits for its dreary, realistic settings (the mud banks of San Pedro Harbor) and its sordid story of a couple who exchange their home on a river scow for a room in town and the wife's services as a prostitute. Von Sternberg was able to make a virtue of the economic stringencies under which he was forced to work, producing a stark study of aimlessness and despair through striking pictorial compositions. Although void of the visual detail of von Stroheim's work, the film revealed much of the same city squalor that characterized *Greed* and the modern sequence in Griffith's *Intolerance*.

On the strength of this first directorial effort, MGM signed von Sternberg to an eight-picture contract. After two unsuccessful efforts for MGM and an abortive script by Chaplin starring Edna Purviance, von Sternberg was finally rewarded with both popular and critical acclaim for *Underworld* (1927) and *The Last Command* (1928), both of which he made for Paramount.

His next film, *Docks of New York* (1928), confirmed his reputation as a visual stylist and revealed his special talent for creating a darkly poetic mood and sordid atmosphere to complement his stories of degradation, disillusionment, and despair. Having developed his own brand of social realist film, or "street film," von Sternberg was ready to take on the German studios and film star Marlene Dietrich in the land where dark drama was having its finest hour.

Ernst Lubitsch

Another director who soon joined the ranks of star directors and made important contributions to screen elegance and sophistication was a German, Ernst Lubitsch. Lubitsch is best known today for his comedy/romances of the thirties, but he was a major creative force in the industry, first in Germany and subsequently in Hollywood, before the movies learned to speak.

In Germany, Lubitsch had been a cabaret and music-hall actor and had trained as a classical actor under Max Reinhardt before he began his film career in 1913. Appearing first as a Jewish comic in a popular series that he wrote and directed himself, he continued as writer, director, and actor in short comedies throughout the war years until *Carmen* (1918), his first big picture, plus *Madame Du Barry* the following year, put him into the international spotlight.

Although the foreign invasion of screen talent did not peak in Hollywood until the close of the silent era, Lubitsch's trip from Germany to Hollywood in 1923 to direct Mary Pickford in *Rosita* marked the beginning of the European exodus. The enthusiastic reception of the early films he worked on in Hollywood, first as director and later as producer, won him a place among the industry's top film creators. Turning from period costume pieces, he began to make his own contributions to so-

phisticated comedy in 1924 with *The Marriage Circle,* and continued to explore the more intimate and "tasteful" approaches to the genre with *Kiss Me Again* (1925), *Lady Windermere's Fan* (1925), and *So This Is Paris* (1926).

Lubitsch was the kind of director who could not be bound by a script, and his films reveal his talents as set designer, choreographer, and cameraman. The charm and sophistication that became the hallmarks of his work are found as much in the decor, dress, and movement of actors as in the handling of the story itself. Sets were uncluttered and functional, and stage business was laced with subtle insight into human relationships. The racetrack sequence from *Lady Windermere's Fan* (1925) and the wedding procession in *The Love Parade* (1929), Lubitsch's first sound film, are particularly extravagant examples. Precision and elegance, no matter how inane the plot, were at the heart of what came to be known as "the Lubitsch touch."

As with von Stroheim, sex was a major ingredient of Lubitsch's films. He believed that "you cannot ignore one of the most important and profound relations in life." His delicate handling of the subject was in clear contrast to the works of the other directors, however. Where von Stroheim displayed a strong feeling of the naughty and even perverse, Lubitsch treated sex as delightful, healthy fun and set up most American attitudes on the subject as rather silly. He was able to carry this off by maintaining a special attitude himself and a style of production that exuded a sense of good-natured, well-mannered, and well-bred sophistication. The result was a series of glittering images that had romantic rather than erotic appeal.

Lubitsch used titles sparingly in his silent films and relied instead on innuendo, at which he became a master. His control of both actors and camera enabled him to convey ideas with subtlety and wit in perfect harmony with the era of sophisticated sex. Though he went on to an equally distinguished career in sound film, his place in the silent cinema remained undiminished, earning him a position among the handful of directors in Hollywood who brought the art of silent filmmaking into full flower.

Cecil B. De Mille

Although von Stroheim's films emphasized realism, and often eroticism, in screen drama, his works could never be called spectacle films, despite their length and budget excesses. The distinction for carrying on the tradition of screen spectacle as well as furthering the expression of sophisticated sex goes to Cecil B. De Mille, whose film career spanned forty-six years and included seventy feature films. Though he never earned a place among the serious visual stylists and storytellers of either the silent or sound periods, De Mille became Hollywood's super-

◀ Ernst Lubitsch and Mary Pickford during a break in the filming of *Rosita* (1923). *Rosita* was Lubitsch's first Hollywood film.

▶ Cecil B. De Mille directing a camera crew in the filming of *The Ten Commandments* (1923).

showman, known especially for the biblical spectacle and the exotic bedroom drama.

De Mille had some experience as a bit actor and playwright, and in 1913 he joined Jesse Lasky, an ex-cornet player and vaudeville producer, and Sam Goldwyn, an ex-glove salesman, to form the Lasky Feature Play Company. De Mille's first film, *The Squaw Man* (1913), made the young company a profit in spite of the fact that the original print was destroyed by sabotage, a casualty of the continued patent war with the Trust. *The Virginian* (1914) and *Call of the North* (1914) proved to be even more successful, and with *The Cheat* (1915), which won a particularly warm reception in France, De Mille began gaining international recognition. These early films covered a broad range of subjects and styles, ranging from the amours of a sheik in *The Arab* (1915) to the exploits of a Bowery tough in *Cimmie Fadden* (1915).

With *Joan the Woman* (1917), De Mille moved into historical spectacle, using the dual-story structure he would employ again in *The Ten Commandments* (1923). Here the story of Joan of Arc was introduced as the vision of a World War I officer about to go into battle. Even the otherwise acerbic Alexander Woollcott, in reviewing *Joan* for the *New York Times,* spoke glowingly of "the beautiful and exalted pageantry of the coronation [which] is the sort of spectacle that takes the breath away and lingers always in the memory."

By 1918 bucolic frontier settings and the sweet innocence of Mary Pickford were being traded for the drawing room, bathroom, and bedroom in a succession of sophisticated and intimate dramas whose very titles suggest De Mille's concern for popular appeal: *Old Wives for New* (1918), *Don't Change Your Husband* (1919), *For Better, For Worse* (1919), *Male and Female* (1919), *Why Change Your Wife?* (1920), and *Forbidden Fruit* (1921). Burns Mantle, in reviewing *Why Change Your Wife?*, speaks of "a rare concoction—the most gorgeously sensual film of the month; in decoration the most costly; in physical allure the most fascinating; in effect the most immoral." *Male and Female* (1919), though titled to fit the new image of its director's films, is actually a more moral and substantial work, based on the James Barrie play *Admirable Crichton.*

It was *The Ten Commandments* (1923) that ultimately brought De Mille to the forefront as a director. Like Griffith's *Intolerance,* the film brought together historical spectacle and contemporary conflict. Scenes showing Moses receiving the tablets, the pillar of fire, and the parting of the Red Sea were coupled with a modern parable of good and evil in which an evil son who cuts costs in the building of a cathedral causes the death of his mother when she wanders into the crumbling

From Cecil B. De Mille's *The Ten Commandments* (1923). This scene graphically illustrates how De Mille successfully combined sex and religion into a winning formula, which reflected the fact that he took a greater interest in sin, scenery, and sex than in any moral fable.

structure. Though the story is melodramatic nearly to the point of self-parody, the piety and pomp of the film won the favor of audiences and critics alike. *Photoplay* magazine called it "the greatest theatrical spectacle in history," concluding that "it will last as long as the film on which it is recorded. It wipes the slate clean of charges of an immoral influence against the screen." Keeping within the industry's code of morality, De Mille had found a formula for showing erotic and otherwise sinful pleasures, while keeping the plot and its characters clean through appropriate condemnation and punishment of sins. The formula worked for De Mille again in *The King of Kings* (1927). This time the New Testament was the source, and after paying deference to the sinning woman in the person of Mary Magdalene, the film followed the major events of the life of Christ. Mordaunt Hall, *New*

Beheading the Sphinx

*I*f, a thousand years from now, archaeologists happen to dig beneath the sands of Guadalupe, I hope that they will not rush into print with the amazing news that Egyptian civilization, far from being confined to the valley of the Nile, extended all the way to the Pacific Coast of North America. The sphinxes they will find were buried there when we had finished with them and dismantled our huge set of the gates of Pharaoh's city. Pharaoh almost had to get along without sphinxes, however. They were made in Los Angeles and transported by truck to Guadalupe; but no one had thought to measure the clearances of the bridges along the route. There were some anxious moments when our majestic and mysterious sphinxes were ignominiously halted by a bridge too low for them to pass under. No one lost his head, though, except the sphinxes, who were decapitated long enough to pass under the bridge and then had their heads restored for the remainder of their progress.

— *Cecil B. De Mille*, The Autobiography of Cecil B. De Mille

York Times film critic, called it the "most impressive of all motion pictures."

Such critical excesses notwithstanding, De Mille's silent films suffer by comparison with the other major works of key American and foreign directors, and today he is either ignored or attacked by critics for "puerile" and "pretentious" works that catered only to the mass appeal of the moment and have worn badly over the years. Though such charges are probably deserved, De Mille's prominence and final influence on film's development are undeniable. He was clearly a master technician in building spectacle and in organizing and visualizing historical material in a way that could be easily under-

stood and enjoyed. No other director of this period, save Griffith and Chaplin, was able to draw audiences on the strength of his direction alone. De Mille's stardom as director is suggested by the number of times he appeared on screen playing himself. But more significant in terms of long-range influence than his own stardom was his role in launching many important screen actors in their careers. These included Gloria Swanson, Bebe Daniels, Wallace Reid, Fredric March, Claudette Colbert, Gary Cooper, Barbara Stanwyck, and Loretta Young. As Maurice Bardeche and Robert Brasillach wrote in *A History of the Motion Pictures,*

> De Mille taught Babbitt how to kiss a countess's hand, how to peel a peach, use finger bowls and keep his hands out of his pockets. Cinema attitudes, cinema drawing rooms, cinema society women, cinema sentiments, cinema adulteries and forgivenesses were established.

The Second String

The overpowering presence of such stars as Pickford, Fairbanks, and Chaplin tended to obscure the names of such directors as Allan Dwan, Fred Niblo, Rex Ingram, and Raoul Walsh, who were faced with both handling the constant pressures of the studio front offices and accommodating the temperaments and creative inspirations of their actors. Though many such associations undoubtedly resulted in compromise on the directors' part, the contributions of these "second-string" directors were still significant. They represented a new breed of filmmakers whose talents were often more closely associated with the successful handling or display of stars than with story invention or camera and editing technique. Nonetheless, some became more than star-handlers and stood above the array of contract directors under salary to the major studios.

Henry King

Several notable films mark the career of Henry King in silent features, including *Ramona* (1924) and *Stella Dallas* (1925), but *Tol'able David* (1921) alone places King among the decade's distinguished directors. This David and Goliath tale of a country boy who sees his family shattered by a hateful clan of mountain thugs shows how well-schooled King had been by both Ince and

Griffith. The general story line and attitude of the film are clearly in the Griffith mold, though both are mostly free of the cloying sentimentality of Griffith's work. The quality of gentle and loving rural life is accentuated through both the sensitivity of the characterizations and the extraordinary visual appeal of the settings. Coupled with this is a tight, lean narrative design that displays all the momentum (and often the brutality) of the Ince Westerns.

James Cruze

As with King, James Cruze's reputation in silent films rests primarily on a single film. *The Covered Wagon* (1923), which lifted the Western melodrama to epic stature, showed the director's facility for using a frontier setting to infuse the drama with a sense of national and natural history. Cruze's subsequent films, *Ruggles of Red Gap* (1923), *Old Ironsides* (1926), and several sound features, showed his ability to work with at least moderate success in a variety of styles and genres and to avoid the single-track syndrome of many of his contemporaries.

Rex Ingram

Rex Ingram did not fare as well in longevity, but he did escape obscurity and enjoy some critical tributes for such films as *The Four Horsemen of the Apocalypse* (1921) and *The Prisoner of Zenda* (1922). Ingram believed that, along with narrative techniques and characterizations, an important part of screen storytelling was to create an atmosphere consistent with and complementary to the mood of the film. He was less interested in slavishly rendering realistic detail than in suggesting meaning through a bit of set decoration or an actor's gesture. But this flair in direction seems to have been placed more at the service of popular appeal than true exploration, and Ingram is best known today for making an international hero of Rudolph Valentino. Ingram retired from film shortly after the coming of sound.

King Vidor

The Big Parade (1925) and *The Crowd* (1928) were two films of sufficient technical stature and strong enough social conscience to place their director, King Vidor, in the ranks of solid directors of the late silent era. In *The Big Parade,* Vidor created a panorama of war's imprint on lifestyles while avoiding the overinflated look of the spectacle film. *The Crowd* provided Vidor with a more intimate focus and became a human-interest study of the central character and his struggle against the unfeeling masses. In terms of continued success through the sound era, Vidor ranks at the top of the second-string directors.

◀ From *Tol'able David* (1921). In stark and dramatic contrast to De Mille's spectacle-filled films, this Henry King film pays homage to rural life and basic values. In this scene, David (played by Richard Barthelmess) struggles to ''do his duty'' in getting the mail through despite grievous injuries.

◥ From King Vidor's *The Crowd* (1928). James Murray plays in a symbolic scene from this classic silent drama.

decade and included fifty features in addition to early shorts, his reputation as a major American director was not established until he worked in sound films. However, his silent works were received favorably by the public and critics, and they gave the Western a new hero in Harry Carey, who appeared in most of Ford's early features. The silent film for which Ford is best remembered today is his 1924 *The Iron Horse,* which, along with James Cruze's *The Covered Wagon,* helped to usher in the panoramic Western. Where Cruze had dramatized the crossing of the continent by the wagon train, Ford showed the building of the first transcontinental railroad.

Alfred Hitchcock

Alfred Hitchcock was another visual stylist who pioneered in silent films. His career extended far beyond any of those of his contemporaries identified here. He was to become a star director *extraordinaire* in his long and successful association with the American industry, but he took longer than any of them to bring his talents to the American scene.

Beginning as a graphic artist for Famous Players-Lasky at the Islington Studios in London, Hitchcock moved through the jobs of scriptwriter, art director, and assistant director. In 1925, he finally made his first solo effort at directing—in *The Pleasure Garden,* made in Munich. Eight more silent features followed before he turned to sound in 1929 with *Blackmail,* the first British talking picture.

Outstanding among Hitchcock's silent films, and responsible for his early rise to fame as the "master of suspense," was *The Lodger* (1927). Here, as with most of his early works, Hitchcock joined scenarist Eliot Standard in preparing the screenplay, which was based on a novel about the famous Jack the Ripper murders. In style and story, *The Lodger* is clearly a prototype of the Hitchcock thriller. It opens with a close-up of a woman screaming while a neon sign flashes the words "Tonight —Golden Curls." With a telegraph typewriter providing the necessary exposition of the murder, the film centers on the suspicion of the star boarder of a London family. The apprehension of Daisy, the victim, sets the mood as she watches the chandelier sway to the lodger's pacing on the floor above. The audience can only feel terror when the lodger picks up a poker as Daisy bends over to retrieve a chess piece (his motivation is actually to stoke the fire).

Hitchcock's portrayal of the lodger in the film is even more frightening. Attending a fashion show, this character's eyes remain riveted on the models. He never averts his gaze, even when he lights the cigarette of the woman

Silent Beginnings to Brilliant Careers in Sound

A number of filmmakers who made their major contributions after the arrival of sound had their basic training in the silents. William Wellman began making films in 1923 and won an Academy Award for his 1927 *Wings,* the first Oscar ever awarded for best picture. An important phase of Frank Capra's training came in directing Harry Langdon. And Howard Hawks, whose prolific and versatile career in sound features was to range from *Bringing Up Baby* (1938) to *Rio Bravo* (1958), had his start as scriptwriter and editor in the late 1910s.

John Ford

John Ford, whose work was to become synonymous in the sound era with rugged individualism and poetic images of the West, learned the fundamentals of filmmaking and developed his style in the late silent era. He started directing in 1917, making two-reel Westerns for Universal, and although his silent film credits spanned a next to him. And a shot down a stairwell that shows only his hand sliding on the railing is as supremely Hitchcockian as any scene from any period in the director's career.

The tightness of the script of *The Lodger* is reinforced in the economy of the film's titles. In fact, one title sums up the whole plot when Daisy's boyfriend/detective says, "When I put a rope around the avenger's neck, I'll put a ring around Daisy's finger." And, as a model in lean and tight structure, the film closes with the same shot seen at the opening: "Tonight — Golden Curls."

The Stars

Major refinements in silent screen art are usually attributable to insightful and independent directors. However, the actors themselves often provided the creative energy necessary not only to ensure the success of individual films but also to help set the direction of styles and genres. Most stars, such as Mary Pickford, Richard Barthelmess, Emil Jannings, and Pola Negri, were groomed by skillful directors and producers, and the extent of their influence often depended upon how they were handled by a particular director. Others, such as Douglas Fairbanks, William S. Hart, and Rudolph Valentino, had personalities and styles that were so pervasive and so distinctive that directorial credit became incidental, and their own dynamic influence reigned over virtually every aspect of production. And, some, such as Charlie Chaplin and Buster Keaton, quickly took over the direction of their own films, whereupon their contributions as directors and as actors soon became indistinguishable.

As William Everson has pointed out, in the mid-1920s the stars assumed far greater importance for the public than ever before. The look of films had changed, according to Everson, and with technique being stressed less, a pattern emerged of slower plot development and longer scenes. All of this made stars more important to both the style and success of films.

Mary Pickford

Mary Pickford continued with her pre-1920s mixture of romance and melodrama but added measures of maturity and strength that took her beyond strictly Pollyanna roles. It was not an easy transition, however, and in 1923, when she was thirty, she ran an appeal in *Photoplay* for suggestions about parts she might play. The answers she received were disappointing: Cinderella, Heidi, and so on. She attempted a few mature roles, but being an expert businesswoman, she realized that to maintain her popularity and income she had to bow to public opinion, and she quickly settled back into more familiar roles with such films as *Little Annie Rooney* (1925), *Sparrows* (1926), and *My Best Girl* (1927).

Pickford attempted a few sound films, but retired in 1933, stating, "I left the screen because I didn't want what happened to Chaplin to happen to me. . . . The little girl made me. I wasn't waiting for the little girl to kill me." She continued her work as an executive with United Artists until she and Chaplin sold their control in 1953. Her importance to film history rests as much on her role as an executive with United Artists as on her role as "Little Mary," everyone's childhood sweetheart.

Pola Negri

Quite the opposite of Mary Pickford in style and appeal was Pola Negri. She was the first European actress courted by Hollywood and, teamed with the director Ernst Lubitsch, she helped launch his career. Born in Poland, Negri trained as a dancer, and during World War I she went to Berlin and quickly became a major star in the German cinema. *Madame Du Barry* (1919) was very successful in America, and in 1922 Paramount invited her to Hollywood. She played a woman of mystery and sophistication, a cross between Theda Bara and Clara Bow. The titles of her films alone provide evidence of her appeal — for example, *Forbidden Paradise* (1924), *A Woman of the World* (1925), *Good and Naughty* (1926), and *Loves of an Actress* (1928). With the coming of sound, Negri's heavy accent drove her out of Hollywood. She returned to Germany where she enjoyed great popularity in the mid-1930s. At the beginning of the war, she left Germany again and retired.

Richard Barthelmess

If Pickford and Negri were represented as polar opposites on the spectrum of female stars in the 1920s, Richard Barthelmess and Rudolph Valentino were clearly their male counterparts. Barthelmess, unlike many of his contemporaries, was college educated and trained in theater. He made his film debut in 1916 and soon achieved stardom in Griffith's *Broken Blossoms* (1919) and *Way Down East* (1920). However, he is perhaps best remembered for his role in Henry King's *Tol'able David* (1921). Barthelmess was not quite a male Pickford, but he was the role model for the earnest hero of romantic melodrama. His best work was opposite Lillian Gish for Griffith and King in the early 1920s.

Tom Mix astride his famous horse Tony.

A lantern slide advertising Pola Negri in *Gypsy Blood* (1921). Lantern slides were an early form of previews/ trailers and were displayed on the screen before the main feature. Note how the ad skillfully combines Negri's sex appeal with an appeal to high culture by informing the reader that the film is from the "original French version" of *Carmen*.

Rudolph Valentino in *The Sheik* (1921). Here he displays the smoldering intensity that made him the romantic idol of the twenties. The film was a huge box-office success; it not only elevated Valentino to major stardom, but introduced the word "sheik" into the romantic slang of the Jazz Age twenties.

Like many of the major stars of the time, Barthelmess formed his own production company and made a number of successful films. He also made a reasonably successful transition to sound as an actor, appearing in several key films of the 1930s, including Howard Hawk's *The Dawn Patrol* (1930), William Wellman's *Heroes for Sale* (1935), and, most notably, Howard Hawk's *Only Angels Have Wings* (1939). Barthelmess retired in 1942.

Rudolph Valentino

For many, Rudolph Valentino was *the* male star of the 1920s. More than any other actor of the time, he represented in both his on- and off-screen life, the very personification of modern sexuality. Valentino's meteoric rise from obscurity and his tragic death at the height of his career in 1926, made him the stuff of legend. He was perhaps the silent screen's greatest lover and surely one of the most popular stars of the time. His first great role was in Rex Ingram's *The Four Horsemen of the Apocalypse* (1921), and he was quickly catapulted to prominence in such films as *The Sheik* (1921), *Blood and Sand* (1922), *The Eagle* (1925), and *The Son of the Sheik* (1925). His basic screen presence was that of a foreign adventurer with oiled body and dark, heart-stopping eyes. Smoldering passion was his stock in trade. His death (from acute appendicitis) and funeral in 1926 were media events rivaled only by Lindbergh's flight; yet in retrospect he seems badly out of date, even for his time. He was purely a creature of the moment created by the system — a product to be consumed and then discarded.

Tom Mix

Tom Mix was also a product of the system and the time. Unlike Valentino, however, Mix was the real thing — a cowboy, Texas Ranger, and rodeo star. The system exaggerated all these characteristics, of course, but Mix was an authentic Western hero. Still, Mix's screen life contrasted sharply with his rugged personal life. On screen he stressed daredevil stunts, fancy costumes, and a light-hearted semicomic character. In this sense he was a western Douglas Fairbanks. With Tony the Wonder Horse, Mix filled the screen with marvelous stunts — all done without a double — involving everything from horses to trains to cars and airplanes. He was the Fox Company's biggest money maker of the 1920s, and though he did not make a successful transition to sound, he developed an enormously successful rodeo and circus act that he performed until his death in 1941.

William S. Hart

If Tom Mix was art imitating life, William S. Hart was his opposite. Hart, born in rural New York and trained as a classical stage actor, represented all the western "reality" that Mix ignored. He began his film career in 1914, making two-reelers for Thomas Ince, and he continued with Ince for most of the decade before going to Paramount in 1918. He concentrated on feature-length Westerns and exerted great control over his films. Among Hart's best works are *Hell's Angels* (1916), *The Toll Gate* (1920), and *Tumbleweeds* (1925). Hart's importance in film history, however, does not depend exclusively on his playing of a stern, steely-eyed cowboy of strong moral courage and strength. Hart made sixty-nine films between 1914 and 1925. He directed thirty-six of these, wrote the screenplays for more than

twenty-five, and in general was in complete charge of every film he made.

In assessing Hart's style as a director, one must look closely at the man himself. His film style reflected and grew out of the content of his films, but it also reflected his personal vision of the West. Hart's West was both realistic and romantic — realistic because he lived in it at an early, impressionable age, and romantic because of his basic personality and nineteenth-century mores. His personality and emotional make-up combined with his own Western experience of the region worked to create his vision of the West as both a physical playground for dramatic action and an arena for moral conflict.

Part of Hart's view of the West was his personal moral code. His character was rarely completely good or evil, but rather was a man standing *between* good and evil, and usually moving from evil toward good. But a basic morality, inner strength, and belief in a code of honor were critical factors that allowed audiences to accept the fundamental ambiguity of the character.

William S. Hart has been overlooked and almost forgotten as a film director of great ability. Even *Tumbleweeds,* a classic film of epic stature, has done little to enhance his directorial reputation, because his strong screen presence overshadowed his direction and because it was his last film. However, perhaps the greatest limitations on Hart's reputation as a director are the plots and themes of his films. Hart was a nineteenth-century romantic who insisted on total control of his films. This rigidity was ultimately self-destructive, since Hart was unable and unwilling to adjust the style and content of his films to the demands of a 1920s Jazz Age audience. The harsh surface realism in Hart's sets and costumes, his hopelessly romantic view of women, and the essential sameness of his plots combined to blind the public to his overall ability as a director. He remained unrecognized in this role during his lifetime and is still generally ignored as a director in the history of film.

Lon Chaney

Most of the other major stars of the 1920s, such as Clara Bow, Colleen Moore, John Gilbert, and Ramon Novarro, fell into certain types associated with Pickford, Fairbanks, Valentino, Mix, and Hart. However, one star of the time not only broke with these basic stereotypes, but created a role unique in film history. That star was Lon Chaney, and such was his artistry that despite the fact that he was almost totally identified with the horror-film genre, he transcended the essential mediocrity of most of the films in this category to achieve almost universal

William S. Hart as Blaze Tracey in *The Toll Gate* (1920). His steely-eyed gaze in combination with the naturalism/realism of setting, action, and costume produced a Western character unrivaled in originality and dramatic intensity.

Lon Chaney, in perhaps his most famous role, as the phantom in *The Phantom of the Opera* (1925). Though Chaney based his horror largely on physical and mental deformity, through his acting ability he transformed his monsters from crude stereotypes into characters having genuine emotion and appeal.

critical acclaim. Known as "the man of a thousand faces," he began acting in films in 1912, and throughout the teens he made more than 100 films at Universal, mostly playing character parts that capitalized on his skill with make-up. He gradually took on larger leading roles, and as Quasimodo in *The Hunchback of Notre Dame* (1923) Chaney established himself as a major star. His work at MGM for the rest of the decade consisted of one tour de force performance after another. Especially notable was his classic performance in *The Phantom of the Opera* (1925). Chaney made one sound film before he died of throat cancer in 1930 at the age of forty-four. As one critic summed up Chaney's career, "He had laid down the basis of horror. No one has surpassed his convictions."

Douglas Fairbanks

Perhaps with the exception of Fred Astaire, who in the following decade would dance his way through a series of films without the least fear of competition, no screen personality had the exclusive control and the universal appeal of Douglas Fairbanks. Fairbanks brought a new type of hero to the silent screen—the suave, dashing swashbuckler whose charm was exceeded only by his acrobatic derring-do. He established the screen's first one-man genre, thereby carving out for himself his own distinctive brand of screen entertainment.

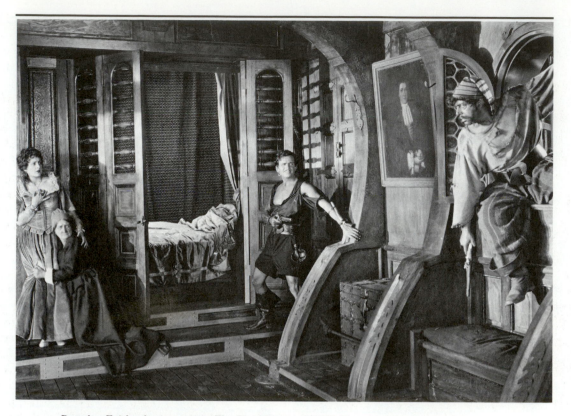

▲ Douglas Fairbanks (center) in *The Black Pirate* (1926). The stage is set here for another flash of grace, dexterity, and derring-do by Fairbanks, the movie screen's original "swashbuckler."

As early as 1915, Fairbanks was working under Griffith in a variety of comedies and period pieces. Later in the decade, he began to settle into light, good-natured comedies of American manners such as *His Majesty, The American* (1919), and *Mollycoddle* (1920). In the comic/romantic adventure films of the twenties, however, Fairbanks came to excel—combining superhero with clown as Zorro, Robin Hood, the thief of Baghdad, and Dumas's D'Artagnan.

Fairbanks's uniqueness as a romantic hero stemmed from the incredible array of athletic skills he mustered for his various roles. For his characterization as D'Artagnan, "the best swordsman in France," in *The Three Musketeers* (1921), he spent months in training with the foil. In his dual role of father and son in *Don Q, Son of Zorro* (1925), he displays dazzling balletic movement and whip handling. And for general athletic prowess, his aerial antics in *Robin Hood* (1922) and *The Black Pirate* (1926) set a standard that was challenged, but never beaten, by later swashbucklers such as Tyrone Power and Errol Flynn. Fairbanks's major appeal was in physical attractiveness rather than any real depth of character. In addition to his displays of grace and dexterity, he showed both a joy of life and a hint of self-parody that audiences found irresistible. And the Fairbanks image extended beyond the screen to articles in fan magazines, some written by the star himself, extolling the virtues of clean living and the body beautiful.

The overall flow and tempo of the Fairbanks films of the twenties made them more than popular oddities. Sparked by the star's exuberant, exacting personality and acting style, such films as *The Three Musketeers* (1921) and *The Mark of Zorro* (1921), which were both directed by the otherwise undistinguished Fred Niblo, exhibit dynamism and control, especially in the action sequences.

Charlie Chaplin

With his style already established, Chaplin's association with the First National Company between 1918 and 1923 marked a transitional period in his development. Until 1923, with the exception of the Sennett-directed adaptation of *Tillie's Punctured Romance* (1914) and Chaplin's four-reel spoof of *Carmen* (1916), all his films had been either one or two reels long. With *A Dog's Life* (1918), *Shoulder Arms* (1918), and *Sunnyside* (1919), Chaplin's films went to three reels, with *The Pilgrim* (1923) to four, and with *The Kid* (1921), to six reels, short feature length. The increase in length was not in itself much of an innovation, but it provided an extended view of Chaplin's wistful and lonely but always resourceful and outgoing little fellow. The individual routines, rather than the narrative itself, continued to make such films as *Shoulder Arms* (1918) and *The Pilgrim* (1923) memorable. In *Shoulder Arms,* for example, Chaplin finds he is the only soldier who does not receive a letter at mail call. Pathos turns to glee and then to a mixture of tragedy and comedy when a package arrives—it is a cheese so overripe that Charlie must put on his gas mask before hurling it over enemy lines. In *The Pilgrim,* Chaplin provides another sampling of mimic artistry when, masquerading as a minister, he delivers a sermon on the story of David and Goliath, all in pantomime.

Contractual obligations with the First National Company prohibited Chaplin from appearing in films of United Artists, the company he formed in 1919 with Pickford, Fairbanks, and Griffith. By 1923, when he finally began appearing in films for his own company, he was devoting himself exclusively to feature films, pro-duced at an average rate of only one in four years. In fact after making and/or appearing in seventy films between 1914 and 1923, he made only three more before the sound era and only ten more total before his retirement in the early 1950s.

A Woman of Paris (1923), Chaplin's first film for United Artists, represented an abrupt change of pace. Abandoning his tramp character and role as actor except for a minor walk-on, he produced what he called "a drama of fate," an ironic and sophisticated tragicomedy that spawned a whole series of suave and sparkling comedies of manners. Although a disappointment to audiences who wanted more of the little tramp, the film foreshadowed the sardonic social commentary that became a central element of Chaplin's later works. It also suggested that Chaplin the screenwriter and director could make it alone, without the help of Charlie, the little tramp.

The film by which Chaplin himself said he wanted to be remembered is *The Gold Rush* (1925). Here was his princely gift to Hollywood's golden age of comedy, a full display of his by now polished style and a showcase of comedic poetry. The film is a treasure house of classic mime. Perhaps the most memorable sequence is Charlie's Thanksgiving dinner, when near-starvation in a snowbound cabin forces him to cook and serve up a boot, which he proceeds to tackle with all the dexterity and relish of a true gourmet. Another example is the New

From *The Gold Rush* (1925). Chaplin's shoulders could be as expressive as his face. Here he looks on admiringly as Georgia Hale entertains.

A Review of *The Gold Rush*

*T*here is more than mere laughter in "The Gold Rush." Back of it, masked by ludicrous situations, is something of the comedian's early life — the hungry days in London, the times when he was depressed by disappointments, the hopes, his loneliness and the adulation he felt for successful actors. It is told with a background of the Klondike, and one can only appreciate the true meaning of some of the incidents by translating them mentally from the various plights in which the pathetic little Lone Prospector continually finds himself. It is as much a dramatic story as a comedy.

Throughout this effort there runs a love story, and one is often moved to mirth with a lump in one's throat. Chaplin takes strange situations and stirs up tears and smiles. He accomplishes this with art and simplicity, and in his more boisterous moments he engineers incidents that at this presentation provoked shrieks of laughter. You may analyze some of them and think them absurd. They are, but it does not alter the fact that you find yourself stirred by the story, gripped by its swing and filled with compassion for the pathetic little hero. You forget the ridiculous garb of the Lone Prospector and he grows upon you as something real.

—*Film review*, New York Times *(1924)*

tion, but what finally enriches and caps the experience is our satisfaction at the consistency of the action with the characterization itself.

Although Chaplin did not characteristically use a carefully crafted screenplay, *The Gold Rush* and *City Lights* (1931) both demonstrate that he could work effectively within the feature-length format. In these longer films he gave more attention to narrative links than in the one- and two-reelers, and he allowed routines and by-play to grow more naturally out of basic situations. But it was finally the details in human behavior and the consistency of his mimic style that satisfied the viewer's need for unity.

By 1928, when Chaplin released the silent *The Circus,* the sound era had arrived, and when *City Lights* appeared in 1931 the silent era was already a memory. The fact that Chaplin dared to remain silent — except for background music and sound effects — not only in *City Lights* but even *Modern Times* (1936) shows the strength of his convictions about silent comedy. And the public enthusiasm over these films is perhaps the best testament to the durability of Chaplin's art. As screenwriter, director, and even composer of film music, he was to continue his work in film on a less frequent but still regular basis on into the sixties. But with the coming of sound, the days of the little tramp were numbered.

What is finally most significant about Chaplin's film legacy is what it eschews or simply ignores. Though the multireel film had new narrative potential, Chaplin never really concerned himself with plot; with the coming of sound he continued successfully in silence. Even the storehouse of cinematic technique — camera composition, editing, set design — that Griffith had bequeathed and others had anxiously adopted Chaplin employed in a functional and unassuming manner. It would be difficult to find another filmmaker of any era, then or now, who showed as much independence in his approach to film art as Charlie Chaplin did.

Buster Keaton

If Chaplin was the undisputed king of comedy in the late teens, by the twenties there were at least contenders for the crown. Chief among these was Buster Keaton, who, like Chaplin, was his own *auteur* of silent comedy, writing and directing his own material. Keaton too had started in vaudeville, but he had the edge on others with similar backgrounds by having been initiated into stage life when less than a year old by his parents, who toured the circuit with an acrobatic routine. He began his screen career in 1917 with several shorts for Joseph Schenck, followed by an association of several years with Metro,

Year's Eve party, when Charlie, anxiously awaiting the arrival of Georgia, with whom he has fallen in love, sits at the festive table he has prepared and dreamily creates a dance with the "oceana rolls" on the end of two forks. At the heart of his mime is the precise and painstaking attention to the detail of an action and its relationship to some incongruous and unexpected situation. We are delighted with the surprise and impressed with the inven-

From *The Navigator* (1924). Buster Keaton strikes a characteristic pose, revealing solemn dedication to the task at hand.

first in shorts and eventually in feature-length films. By 1921, while still making two-reel shorts, Keaton was establishing himself as one of the industry's top comic artists, though the number of films to his credit was much smaller than either Chaplin's or Harold Lloyd's, the third of the major comic stars.

Like Chaplin, Keaton dramatized the unassuming fellow who struggles against the big and unpredictable world; unlike the little tramp, however, the role he played was essentially unsentimental, and he displayed a greater pessimism in the face of unending adversities. Yet the earnestness, calm assurance, and lonely detachment of his character had a strange comic appeal, although the term *clown* hardly seemed to apply.

His careful, methodical approach seemed the antithesis of Keystone slapstick, yet, as in the Sennett comedies, Keaton's adversaries were often from the mechanical world—a runaway train, a balloon, a foundering boat, or a thrashing paddlewheel. In *Cops* (1922), Keaton was already displaying creative virtuosity in his portrayal of the well-meaning young man who becomes the victim of his own contrivance. In this film his character equips a delivery wagon with a directional signal fashioned out of a retractable clothes rack and a boxing glove. The pride he takes in his own ingenuity is subtly revealed in the way he operates the mechanism—until he unknowingly knocks down a policeman directing traffic. In *The Boat* (1921), Keaton's pride in workmanship once again produces a solemn posture of self-esteem—he stands at the helm of the boat he made as it slips down the skids into the water, slowly sinking out of sight until only his hat floats on the surface. The situations are funny in themselves, but what provides for more than the superficial laugh and makes the film a richer experience is the humanity that even Keaton's masklike expression—that frozen blankness that came to be known as the Great Stone Face—cannot hide. A complete range of expression reflecting emotional tone is present; it is simply concentrated in the eyes and subtle shades of gesture and movement.

By 1923 Keaton had launched into feature films and in these his special talents as director as well as mime are best revealed. *The General* (1926), his most impressive work, reveals a unity and tightness in narrative structure not present in any other silent comedy. Keaton based the film on an actual Civil War episode in which a Confederate train engineer gave chase and recovered a locomotive named "The General," stolen by Union spies. Keaton plays the role of Johnny Gray, a loyal Confederate son who has been rejected for military service because of his vital job as engineer. In accomplishing the great train rescue, he also wins his lovely, if dim-witted, Southern sweetheart, Annabelle Lee.

An important feature of *The General* is the strength of the story itself. Unlike Chaplin, who in even his most polished works used the film narrative as a framework for his routines, Keaton was interested in telling a story. In Keaton's work, being drawn into *events* and not simply surprised by *gags* provides added delight to the audience. *The General* is more than a showcase for Keaton the comic star; it is a splendidly conceived screenplay. Rarely, if ever, has an entire film been devoted to a chase with such rewarding results.

Keaton's basic framework in *The General* displays a flawless arrangement and impeccable pacing of visual gags to exploit the fortuitous. If we are amused at one moment by Keaton unknowingly sending a pursuing engine off onto a siding, we are delighted by the unexpected ingenuity he shows in clearing railroad ties off the tracks at another. It is the constant shifting from active to passive roles, whereby Keaton is the victim one moment and the master of the situation the next, that satisfies our love of surprises and makes the character seem more human. Adding to our difficulty in anticipating the direction of the next routine is that Keaton's active role often proves hopeless. When he tries to load a tender with firewood, the trees teeter on the edge of the car and bounce to the ground. In *Sherlock, Jr.* (1924), his struggle with a piece of paper stuck to his shoe is equally frustrating. On the other hand, when he is unaware of the situation, or unable to respond, the fateful link of circumstances often wins the day. In *The General,* he accidentally knocks out a Union soldier when he turns around with a piece of firewood in his hand, and, in *Sherlock, Jr.,* he manages to miss several booby traps that have been planted for him in a billiard room.

This careful plotting of routines in order to keep an audience constantly off guard is certainly not unique with Keaton. It is at the heart of Chaplin and is even found in the broader styles of slapstick comedians. Rather, what best distinguishes Keaton's style from Chaplin's is the concentration of comic invention in the mechanical gag —the endless battle with gadgets and infernal machines. What makes Keaton's style so rewarding is that it

fits smoothly into the general design of his films and the characterizations being portrayed.

An added bonus in Keaton's films is an interest in humanity that goes beyond the central character and leads to the gentle spoofing of character types and institutions. In *The General,* Keaton has fun with military ritual and heroism. The Union troops fall like dominoes each time the train comes to a stop, and the general orders a train onto a burning trestle that collapses, sending the train into the ravine below. Nor do the honors of the Confederate victory escape spoofing: Johnny draws his sword only to have the blade fall off. And when he finally gets a kiss from his girl, he carries on the romance while saluting an entire passing battalion. Even Annabelle Lee is depicted as a hare-brained young thing — she retrieves a splinter to help feed the firebox of the train. Nothing is sacred, and all characters and actions are carefully designed to fit not just the moment but the narrative and the theme.

By the middle of the decade Keaton had become one of Metro's biggest attractions, ranking second only to Chaplin among the comic stars of the silent age. But like

▲ From *The General* (1926). Keaton played one of his classic roles in this tightly structured film.

many other actors, Keaton found the transition to sound a difficult hurdle. Silent suffering and solitary wonder were too much a part of the character he had developed. After several sound shorts and features, he became a gagman and script doctor for MGM. He filled out the last years of his career with cameo appearances in several films that provided little opportunity to further extend his creative spirit and disciplined style. But his contributions to the great comedic outpouring of the silent period stand alongside those of Chaplin as singular achievements in film art.

Harold Lloyd

Though he never enjoyed the acclaim that Sennett received, Hal Roach was another important producer of silent screen comedies. In fact, by the early twenties, Roach was giving Sennett stiff competition in the production of two-reelers. A major part of Roach's success came from launching Harold Lloyd on a screen career that itself was to complement and rival those of Chaplin and Keaton. The Roach-Lloyd association began with a series of shorts in which Lloyd portrayed his own version of the little fellow, Willie Work. After a brief stint with Keystone, Lloyd was signed by the American Pathé Company, which was interested in promoting a new comic star to compete with Chaplin. The result was a long series of one-reelers featuring Lloyd as a character called Lonesome Luke. The films appeared between 1915 and 1917, and were made under Roach's supervision.

Lonesome Luke displayed at least two elements of the Chaplin formula in his use of comic suspense and ingenuity in handling of props. Some early criticism that Lloyd was a mock Chaplin gave way to adulation as Lloyd found his own screen personality. In oversized glasses with tortoise-shell rims, he portrayed the innocent and mild-mannered young man who, despite an initially bland appearance, reveals a zest for life and a tenacity to succeed. Still, he was the straightest of the major comics. With the exception of the glasses, there were no distinctive visual characteristics to identify him; he could easily have been lost in a crowd. Indeed, this became a major part of his comic formula. But when that blandness of character was put into bizarre and hair-raising circumstances, the result was an incomparable comic style.

Safety Last (1923) and *The Freshman* (1925), two of Lloyd's most popular films, clearly illustrate this juxtaposition of character and situation. In *Safety Last,* Lloyd

▲ From *The Freshman* (1925). Shy innocence in the face of adversity proves once again to be Harold Lloyd's magic formula.

Lloyd on Lloyd

*B*ecause we did have pretty good gags in our pictures right straight through, and because I didn't have on comedy clothes, a lot of people got the idea that you were the kind of act where you could just do gags. But that's not true, because gags are done from inside. You must feel them, you must know how they are, you must time them, you must react to them. There's just one thing after another that a comic, to get a piece of business over, has got to know. And you could generally prove that if you could get ten comics doing the same piece of business, one will invariably do it much funnier if it suits him, if it's his type of business, than someone who doesn't know that technique and doesn't have that feeling. You must have that feeling of comedy within you; and my character, you see, was a funny character in that. That's the reason I used him: He belied his appearance, especially in the early days, when somebody put horn-rimmed glasses on for a mollycoddle type.

—*Harold Lloyd,*
CAFS Seminar
(September 23, 1969)

twirling a loose thread around his finger, he unravels the stitching and the suit begins to fall apart as he stands on the dance floor. Entanglement in a dance partner's dress and a tablecloth completes the destruction and humiliation despite the efforts of an on-the-spot tailor to sew him back together.

Though he trusted somewhat in the kind intervention of fate, Lloyd's reaction to the calamities that befell him was not resignation or blind faith. He was continually aggressive in the face of the most unpredictable and seemingly insoluble problems. What Lloyd's character may have lacked in emotional depth he made up for in his unflagging determination to succeed. And though seriously determined to make a go of it in society, his aggressive behavior was never rebellious or even questioning of prevailing social values, as were the works of Chaplin and Keaton. Rather, his character simply adopted a role that would place him most comfortably and advantageously within the social order.

Lloyd, too, failed to make an effective transition to sound. He starred in a few sound films for Fox and Paramount, but stopped acting in 1938, returning to his Beverly Hills mansion, where he was content to be active in civic organizations and to re-issue compilations of his silent work.

Harry Langdon

In terms of both critical and popular reception, as well as the test of time, Chaplin, Keaton, and Lloyd are secure in their positions as the leading comics of the period. And owing to their personal control over their material, they also rank as the most influential forces in silent screen comedy. Yet there were other actors who enjoyed a tremendous following, and who, though less directly in control of total production, remain major contributors to the form.

Sennett's own choice of the greatest comedian of them all was Harry Langdon. This actor too had come to film shorts for Sennett in 1924, via the vaudeville route. In a film career that was to end in virtual obscurity barely five years after it began, Langdon was able to develop a characterization that brought him close to, if not within, the circle of major comic stars. Langdon's style comes closest to that of Chaplin in its suggestion of innocence and pathos, but it did not mimic Chaplin's. With his large dark eyes and pretty face, Langdon invariably played the part of a child who had never grown up. His innocence was trusting — he had an unalterable faith in people and a humble belief in finding his way in a sometimes hostile world. Still, the deep emotional sensitivity present in

is employed by a store to climb the outside wall of a building as a publicity stunt. Nearly half of the film is taken up with the climbing sequence, a motif that had also been central to Lloyd's earlier *High and Dizzy* (1921) as well as other shorts. The controlled frenzy he displayed while hanging from an awning, a flagpole, or the hand of a gigantic clock proved far more hilarious than the hysteria of a cross-eyed cop or other slapstick antics. In *The Freshman,* it is shy innocence in the face of adversity that proves to be the magic formula. Here Harold comes to a school dance in a tuxedo that has been only temporarily stitched together. Absent-mindedly

◄ Harry Langdon in one of his most famous films, *Long Pants* (1927), directed by Frank Capra. Langdon was at his best in the role of simple man-child, a character who mixed innocence with maturity and who was forever being flattened by fate and bouncing back with child-like faith.

Other Comic Stars

Along with Harold Lloyd, two more great comic stars came from the Roach lot in the silent era — Stan Laurel and Oliver Hardy. Laurel had arrived from England with Chaplin on the Karno Pantomime Company tour, where he occasionally worked as an understudy for Chaplin roles. After a stint in vaudeville, he worked for Universal, Vitagraph, and finally Hal Roach. Hardy joined Roach in 1924. His earlier film career had included a portrayal of a Mack Swain-type character as a foil for Billy West. (Swain was a large bully often pitted against Chaplin.) In their first films together they did not appear as a team. Once they began to work together, however, they built a relationship that was to span twenty-five years and make them the first and probably the most durable of the screen's many comedy teams.

There is little that is refined or emotionally endearing about Laurel and Hardy's early comic style. Early shorts such as *Big Business* (1929) resemble a Sennett romp with zany physical (and often destructive) antics. Here the pair attempts to sell a Christmas tree to an uninterested homeowner — Jimmy Finlayson, a favorite antagonist in many of their films. Their persistent ringing of the doorbell to release a branch caught in the door brings Finlayson back with hedge clippers, which he uses to top the tree. This brings instant retaliation from Stan and Ollie, who begin to dismantle the house, and this in turn prompts Finlayson to demolish their car. Where Laurel and Hardy surpass Sennett's free-wheeling patchwork of gags is in the slow progression that develops as they build on a basic routine.

Unlike the other major comics, their early characterizations are thin and more reflective of types than individuals — Stan, the delicate, nervous, whimpering, and uncoordinated mouse; and Ollie, the fat, pompous bully who is easily cowed and equally clumsy. Like Langdon, both are characterized as outsized children. But

Chaplin's tramp and even in Keaton's wooden stare was never revealed in Langdon's characterization. More child than man, he had a passivity that prevented strong audience empathy.

Like Lloyd, Langdon did his finest work when guided by another director. His best films, *The Strong Man* and *Long Pants,* were produced in 1926 and 1927 under the direction of Frank Capra. As Capra relates in his autobiography, *The Name Above the Title,* "The tragedy of this supreme talent is that he never knew what made him great, nor why the world forgot him. Quick fame, and the consequent barnacles of conceit that clogged his ego, made him impervious to help from those who *knew* the secret of his magic." His eclipse came with attempts to write and direct his own material and to move into feature-length films, which could not effectively support his simple, low-key style. He appeared, on and off, during the thirties in several shorts and a few features, but he never achieved anything like his previous fame.

growing throughout the association, and ultimately helping to ensure their success, especially in the sound era, was a sense of balance between them as perfect foils for each other. This was teamwork *par excellence*. The unity of a film's structure was revealed in Stan and Ollie's continued interplay as they kept one another in line while together conquering their frightfully disordered world.

It was the two working together that was funny, and this comic pairing was never equalled, although in their better efforts Abbott and Costello and Hope and Crosby came close. Their sound work, with the exception of the superb Academy Award-winning short, *The Music Box* (1932), was primarily feature length. Although not as crisp and unified as their silent shorts, the duo's sound features, such as *Sons of the Desert* (1933), *Babes in Toy Land* (1934), and *Way Out West* (1938), displayed their comic inventiveness to good measure.

There were many other notable contributors to American silent screen comedy. Ben Turpin, Chester Conklin, Snub Pollard, Larry Semon, and Al St. John were among the many who seldom enjoyed center-ring status but were nevertheless creators of screen characterizations that greatly enriched the genre. What enabled the stars of the first magnitude to stand out among the many lesser comics were their individual identities, the resulting unity of their films, especially when comedy began to push toward feature length.

For Sennett, the individual gag was the basic unit of construction. As each developed, it was strung together with as many others as could be created from the basic situation, and even then each gag was extended, repeated, modified, and repeated again to fill out the single- or double-reel length. For the major comic stars, the basic unit became the characterization itself. Even here, narrative development often remained only a framework on which comic incidents were hung. And even feature-length silent comedies, when used to illustrate refinement in form, must be looked at in terms of discipline and consistency in style rather than the dovetailing of plot lines.

Dream Building, Cinemorality, and the Formula Film

The feature-length narrative film emerged as the dominant form of silent film in the mid-1920s. It was a complex and interesting form with multiple and often conflicting functions. Here, in the full-length feature, the influence of other art forms was most clearly at work,

here social concerns were developed and given dramatic emphasis, and here the profit motive exerted its strongest influence. In the same way, the history of the silent film, as it was produced by the American industry, reflected the often conflicting motivations of producer, filmmaker, and viewing public.

In any given project, for example, the director might want to represent an original dramatic incident or one borrowed from a stage or literary work, striving for that elusive quality of screen realism. Meanwhile, the producer, conscious both of cost accounting and audience mood, was sure to be dedicated to efficiency and budgetary control. And the audience, by means of patronage, had its own opinion — and its own power via the box office.

Two other motivating factors were also at work from the very beginning, and they became increasingly important as motion pictures became a major industry: production demands and the demands, or at least what were thought to be the demands, of audiences. Together these demands resulted in the need for efficient *dream building*. *Efficient* meant meeting the production demands of cost and time while still developing visually intelligible narratives in the prescribed single-, double-, or multireel length. *Dream building* meant satisfying audience appetites for familiar structure in comedy and melodrama in emotionally satisfying films that reflected current moral standards.

These combined factors resulted in the development of standard forms and formulas that had profound effects on films' structure and style and on what films said about the world they represented. The key ingredients for efficient dream building were being discovered, tested, and made permanent up through the 1920s.

The first necessity was motion, any kind of motion, and this key ingredient soon evolved into the motion of the chase.

Next, the chase with a Western setting was developed, and it became the Western star vehicle. With William S. Hart's emergence as a frontier hero in 1917, the formula of the Western hero was being carefully made to fit the basic framework of existing melodrama. With minor variations, the Western hero was endowed with key physical and moral attributes that served both the style of drama and the expectations of fans. Basic requirements were skill, particularly in the handling of firearms; resourcefulness in finding water, lost cattle, or villains; and the ability to endure fatigue and pain. In terms of personality and moral stature, the hero showed particular kindness to old people, children, and animals; was shy with women; and was unshakable in his sense of justice and loyalty. His strength of character was often made more appealing by the fact that his past was in some way blemished (he was a reformed outlaw) or his personal code was not completely revealed. These and other characteristics of the Western formula facilitated efficient visual storytelling while exploring the appeal of an open and unregimented life, far removed from the convention-bound existence of most urban audiences.

The same kind of standardization occurred in non-Western melodramas and comedy as well. The comic chase, for example, provided the perfect kind of routine for the deflation or upsetting of pomposity and petty authority. Once again the affinities of the medium were developed and audiences were satisfied with slightly irreverent fun.

The melodrama, however, best illustrates the flourishing formulas for dream building and cinemorality (films that make strong moral statements). The prestige and popularity of comedy in the teens and twenties tend to obscure the fact that the majority of American films produced were melodramas. They had proven their durability since they were first introduced and were still the popular art form of the masses. Mind-boggling plot complications notwithstanding, the stories portrayed in full-length features were the essence of simplicity in terms of characterization, motivation, and general attitude. Most had their roots in one of a surprisingly few key situations, and, with the simplest of modifications, they were ground out easily to meet heavy production schedules. Themes that proved particularly popular were repeated again and again with only the slightest changes in location, season, or nationality of characters to distinguish the resulting films.

Keeping the narrative simple—a requirement of the studios and a demand of most viewers—meant reducing all variables to the lowest common denominator. It was a great game of rounding off fractions. East was East, West was West, heroes wore white, villains wore black, Irish women took in washing, Jews ran pawnshops, Indians were on the warpath or, if peaceable, were forced into action by the villain's gift of firewater and firearms. It was as impossible to be a little good, a little perverse, or a little Italian as it was to be a little dead. This rounding off naturally favored stereotypes, and resisted unwieldy, unpopular, or otherwise uncomfortable subjects. And, besides perpetuating a simplistic vision of manners and morals in general, it helped establish and reinforce stereotypical patterns of thought and behavior in specific circumstances for specific character types. Movies developed not only their own code of morality but also a set of attitudes on a great variety of social issues.

The extent to which a film seriously reflected social thought and examined specific social issues depended on which of three general kinds of social commentary it contained: incidental, gratuitous, or conscious.

Incidental social commentary was usually a passing reference to a people, place, or time meant to place the film in space or time or to otherwise embellish or refine a setting. Thus, a South Sea island, a Union Civil War camp, or a Chinatown opium den might provide the appropriately exotic, heroic, or sinister social milieu in which a particular story could thrive. Though such setting choices might seem to have little social reference and to be simply a part of the visual backdrop, they clearly express stereotyped impressions of people, events, and locations. For example, the choice of a New York tenement might reinforce an oversimplified image of Irish immigrants and give a film a humble ambience. And, clearly, the presence of a doting black servant ultimately does more than merely establish the affluence and cozy comforts of a Southern plantation.

Gratuitous social commentary is more than social window dressing. Here social conditions were used to trigger or "enrich" dramatic conflict but never as a means of exploring issues seriously. The social condition would simply be plugged into the formula as an acceptable factor affecting the twists and turns of plot, and the goal would be to find an acceptable plot resolution rather than to discover something about human nature.

Films characterized by gratuitous social commentary are legion. The Western provides a perfect example. Makers of Westerns needed both conflict and a way of proving the hero's gallantry, and they found both in "the menacing Redman." They showed little concern for motivation or characterization; they simply accepted that when a wagon train moved West, it would be besieged by a whooping mass of painted savages who would kill and scalp all the settlers—all except the heroine. She would be taken hostage until the hero (usually the wagon-train guide or cavalry officer) came to the rescue. Likewise, it was always the corrupt political boss who made life miserable for the aspiring statesman, and the Oriental opium smoker who caused the downfall of the young virgin.

In the final category, conscious social commentary, the film's dramatic development was integral to or an outgrowth of social circumstances. Though the treatment of the social issue might be superficial, the filmmaker consciously made some realistic observations on social thought and true conditions and, at times, even sought to reinforce or alter existing attitudes and beliefs. The "message picture," as a film of this sort was popularly called, is represented by many classics of the silent screen. Nevertheless, the formula method of filmmaking usually discouraged social commentary that had any dimension, shading, and direction. Therefore, message pictures represented a very small fraction of the overall output of films. But those that were made in the 1920s were the roots of what was called social realism in later decades.

The films of the 1920s, even the most pedestrian and formulaic, were often socially significant not only for what they said but also for what they ignored about the social order. A brief survey follows of some of the major social issues of the time and the films that reflected those issues.

Institutional and Public Issues

One of the most pervasive and timeless areas of concern, expressed in both the arts and politics, is the function or failure to function of social institutions. Issues that were both sufficiently broad and potentially dramatic to be represented in the earliest silent films had to do with law, justice, and the penal system; the young, old, sick, handicapped, and disadvantaged; and people at work, particularly regarding working conditions and labor/management relations. Where films went beyond the incidental or gratuitous reference and focused on issues themselves — say, capital punishment, prison reform, child welfare, mental illness, the plight of migratory workers — they were sometimes able to make responsible observations on how the social system was working and how the individual related to it. But within the American film industry, the formula system favored the uninvolving and simplistic reference.

Capital punishment is a particularly good example of an issue that is timeless and controversial on the one hand and excellent thematic material for melodrama on the other. The first screen treatment of the subject dates back at least to a clip produced by Biograph in 1902 called *Career in Crime*, which shows an electrocution. Scores of crime melodramas can be found throughout silent films, many of which are built around false sentencing and last-minute rescues. The modern sequence of Griffith's *Intolerance* is the classic example, but many others use such miscarriages of justice as plot devices without pretending to examine social problems in any manner. Occasionally, circumstances surrounding an execution, or a near-execution, are bizarre. In De Mille's *The Forbidden Woman* (1927), Zita is allowed to be executed as a spy while two brothers who have both loved her look on. In *The Daring Years* (1923), it is the combination of a last-minute confession and a power failure that saves the innocent, and in *The Last Hour*

(1923), it is a malfunction at the gallows. Few films get beyond such machinations. Universal's *Legally Dead* (1923) managed to make its point and throw in the plot twist as well. Here a newspaper reporter gets himself arrested so he can interview inmates to support his theory that most victims of capital punishment are innocent. He is later wrongfully convicted of a murder; he is executed, declared legally dead, but restored to life by a shot of adrenalin.

Prison conditions and the need for reform likewise received no very serious consideration in the silent film, although as early as 1903, in *A Convict's Punishment*, Biograph showed a prisoner being accosted, tied, and whipped by two prison guards. Cruel wardens were convenient heavies, and wretched prison conditions helped to supply motivation for dramatic escape attempts, but films that dealt with the penal system as an issue were rare. Thomas Mott Osborne, a former warden of Sing Sing Prison, produced one in 1921. Titled *The Right Way*, it told the story of two boys who became members of a "Mutual Welfare League," a prisoners' organization that attempted to save prisoners from execution. For its time, Porter's *The Ex-Convict* (1907) was rare in exploring the problems facing the person with a prison record, but serious and central focus on the issue was scant until Mervyn LeRoy's sound film, *I Am a Fugitive from a Chain Gang*, in 1931.

Child labor and child welfare issues were treated in Mary Pickford's 1926 *Sparrows*, made for United Artists. In this film, a farm for unwanted children in the southern swamps is run by a brutal family that mistreats and starves its charges. Though hardly a tough look at the issue of child abuse, it is at least free of the romantic characterization of waifs common to the screen. The assorted abandoned and orphaned children represented in motion pictures were usually depicted as tenacious street urchins (*The Heart of a Waif*, [1915] and *The Gutter-Snipe*, [1915]), true to the spirit of Dickens. Often they straightened out their elders' predicaments and were especially adept at sparking romance, as in De Mille's *Let 'er Go Gallagher* (1928), in which a waif helps her friend capture a notorious criminal and save his romance. Chaplin's *The Kid* (1921) is the darling of this genre.

▶ From *Sparrows* (1926). Mary Pickford valiantly rescues mistreated orphans in a southern swamp.

Problems of mental illness, particularly insanity, were so heavily exploited in early silent comedies and dramas that a highly stereotyped and grotesque screen image of the disturbed individual emerged. As early as 1904, in *The Escaped Lunatic,* the comic chase was set in a mental institution, where an inmate thinks he is Napoleon. The topic was fair game even for such comic stars as Harold Lloyd who, in *Doctor Jack* (1922), portrays a doctor who cheers up a despondent girl by acting like an escaped lunatic. In *The Lunatic at Large* (1927), most of the farcical action takes place on the grounds of a private sanitarium for the wealthy. This tendency toward affluence on the part of the insane seems to sug-

gest a belief that making the inmates well-heeled rendered the subject inoffensive.

In melodramas, nervous breakdowns or temporary insanity provided convenient plot devices. Causes ranged from mental cruelty to Chinese water torture, but in the case of the mad scientist no explanation seemed necessary. Half-wits were convenient for taking murder raps and otherwise helping to work out the plot without risk of protest. Insanity began to appear with some regularity in Gothic horror pieces, such as Metro's *The Monster* (1925), which starred Lon Chaney, or *The Cat and the Canary* (1927) and *The House of Secrets* (1929). Some sobriety and distinction, if not seri-

ous exploration of the subject, came with Victor Sjöström's *The Tower of Lies* in 1926.

Poverty was another major ingredient of melodrama and even romantic fantasy. The real-life and contemporary problems of the city poor—the slum dwellers—and of the country poor—tenant farmers and migratory workers—received little serious attention. However, Griffith's *The Musketeers of Pig Alley* (1912) was something of a pioneer work in this area. With much of the film's footage shot in New York City streets, it emphasized the milieu of the city slum and its effects on people. *Means and Morals* (1915) dramatized young people's moral lapses when faced with a life of poverty, and *The Rose of Italy* (1916) depicted the dangers confronting an immigrant girl from Little Italy at the hands of an ex-Mafia member who is himself an organization target. Most films on the topic tended in the direction of *Sally in Our Alley* (1927), in which a tenement orphan is adopted by three neighbors—a Scotsman, an Italian, and a Jew—and later taken to the home of a wealthy aunt, who almost succeeds in teaching her snobbery and social embarrassment with respect to her old friends.

The tenant farmer was virtually ignored until King Vidor's *Hallelujah,* in 1929, and the obscure musical *Georgia Rose,* in 1930. Though Griffith had tentatively begun examining problems of the farmer versus big business in *A Corner in Wheat* (1909), and the effects of strikes in the modern sequence of *Intolerance,* the following decade saw little follow-up. *The New Disciple* (1921) dealt directly with the exploitation of factory workers, using passages from Woodrow Wilson's *The New Freedom.* Other than that, labor strife was treated as the by-product of melodrama, with labor agitators hired to induce workers to strike and otherwise cause trouble for the company bosses.

Private Issues and Taboos

Marital complications and extramarital intrigues were so much a part of silent screen drama that it is difficult to discern any meaningful grouping or patterns to suggest trends. What is clear, though, is that even in the prewar and prefeature decades (1895–1915) sex was a popular and highly salable commodity, despite the hanging on of Victorian morals. The boudoir film, for example, which is usually associated with De Mille, probably had its beginning with Méliès's *Apres Le Bal—Le Tub* (1897), in which a woman disrobes and steps into her bath assisted by her maid. As she steps out she is wrapped in a towel, and then she exits from the scene. In *The Bride's First Night* (1898), a bride is shown entering a bedroom, un-

dressing, getting into bed, and then being joined by her husband, who begins kissing her. In a 1903 clip, Méliès even recorded the antics of a peeping Tom in a hotel corridor. Edison's contribution to the risqué if not erotic early films includes the famous *Irwin-Rice Kiss* (a close-up of Broadway stars May Irwin and John Rice kissing) and the censored dance in *Fatima.* Fallen women and worldly, if sometimes depraved, men became very much a part of screen melodrama. Their function was to provide the evil influence and keep such innocents as Mary Pickford, Robert Harron, Mae Marsh, Richard Barthelmess, and the Gish sisters in mortal danger to keep the plot brewing.

The twenties brought a more liberal and sophisticated treatment of sex-related topics, and with the appearance of Theda Bara and Rudolph Valentino, the term erotic became applicable.

Despite a new sophistication and liberation from Victorian values, particularly in the works of De Mille, sex issues did not come under serious examination during the twenties, and under the influence of the Hays Office many subjects remained distinctly taboo. However, infidelity was second to none as the dramatic complication in films of the late teens and twenties, and with the arrival of the vamp (*A Fool There Was* [1915]), even healthy marriages were in jeopardy. But despite all the extramarital hijinks constantly being paraded, common-law marriages were rarely shown, and mixed marriages (both religious and ethnic), with the exception of the ever popular *Abie's Irish Rose,* were few. Miscegenation, when it was treated, was almost always portrayed as having occurred in the past as a "sin of the father." It was a taboo subject that could serve as a plot device or reinforcement in characterization—in *The Wise Virgin* (1924), for example, the villain is revealed to have had a Burmese mother—but it never came under careful examination as a social issue.

Divorce—or "Popular Sin," as it was called in a 1926 Paramount film by that name starring Florence Video—was a constantly reappearing theme. Pressures from the Hays Office, however, restrained major companies from treating divorce frivolously and showing retribution, resolution, or reconciliation. Mate swapping, though suggested by some titles, turned out to be the innocent fun of romantic comedies. Prostitution was a frequent and accepted plot ingredient as long as it was properly condemned.

Other sex-related topics that were buried even deeper among the array of plot devices, if they were not completely skirted, included abortion, incest, rape, and sexual perversion. Abortion was rarely suggested, and then only as a thought, a bad dream, or the act of a completely depraved woman. In *The Road to Ruin* (1928), Sally begins with liquor and cigarettes, graduates to a love affair with an older man, and, after becoming pregnant, has an abortion. She finally dies of shock when she finds she is paired off in a whorehouse with her own father. Incest, as this synopsis might suggest, was a good plot device; the last-minute discovery of the true relationship of a pair of lovers would either avert the union or make it legal, and viewers could be appropriately repelled and titillated by the anticipation. But incest was much too delicate a topic to be used often, even when properly condemned. Rape also occurs in a surprisingly small number of films. When treated, it is in the past tense or, like incest, as an event to be anticipated and averted by a last-minute rescue. Sexual perversion or deviant sexual behavior did not exist either in act or thought in films produced for general release.

Other social evils, such as alcohol and narcotics, were represented more widely but fared no better than most other issues in terms of realistic appraisal. The evil of drink was more of a plot requirement or embellishment than a meaningful focus, and, though sermonizing was frequent, most films were void of any substantive inquiry. Alcoholism served the plot necessities in Griffith's *A Drunkard's Reformation* (1909) and *What Drink Did* (1908); it also made a hit of *A Fool There Was* in 1915 and boosted Theda Bara to stardom and vamp status. References to narcotics became stereotyped, with a favorite theme being the smashing of the dope ring responsible for a loved one's death. *The Spirit of the Poppy* (1914) was an early attempt to dramatize the effects of drug addiction. In 1923 a flurry of films that approached a more direct and "straight" treatment of the topic were released. *The Drug Traffic,* an independent picture, featured a doctor whose despondency leads to drug addiction and death. In *The Great Menace,* a district attorney's son becomes implicated in drug traffic and murder while investigating the evils of addiction, and in *Human Wreckage,* which was produced by Thomas Ince with the cooperation of the Los Angeles Anti-Narcotics League, a family is driven to ruin through addiction to morphine.

Racial Issues

In many respects race produced the most interesting examples of efficient dream building through the use of social attitudes and accepted images. Racial stereotypes served the formula film because they provided the necessary motivation or helped trigger conflict without the need of complex explanations. Accepted mores regarding race relations were also useful plotting devices, because they could be used to explain a sudden twist of a story quickly and efficiently. In *The Red Rider* (1925), both requirements of speed and efficiency were met. The Indian chief discovers he is white. He wins the white girl when the Indian princess to whom he was originally betrothed offers herself as a sacrifice by taking the white girl's place in a canoe that the tribe sets adrift above a waterfall. The taboo of miscegenation and the myth of the Indian princess who sacrifices herself for love help to bind together the tortured narrative while satisfying the romantic and moral notions of the audience.

Obviously, most of the silent screenplays that dealt in any way with race did so in an incidental or gratuitous manner. In the case of the American Indian, the building and reinforcing of stereotyped images is particularly significant, for the relative isolation of the Indian from other cultural groups plus the Indian's constant appearance on the screen gave film a corner in image building.

Stereotyping was not necessarily limited to a single image, and the continual reappearance of Indians in film after film resulted in a variety of "redskin" types and situations. Of this array, the image that most quickly comes to mind is the whooping savage who threatens the pioneer settlement or wagon train. As early as 1904, the American Mutoscope and Biograph Company had produced a short narrative clip entitled *The Pioneers,* in which a pioneer family is surprised by Indians, the parents slain, and the children captured. The heroes of the drama are a group of trappers who rescue the children and kill the Indians. Biograph and other companies continued throughout the decade to exploit the Indian massacre theme, sparking protests from various Indian tribes to the Bureau of Indian Affairs in the period 1908–1912. Whether these objections had any effect on American filmmakers is questionable, but gradually films began to show some justification for the Indians' savage behavior. *A Mohawk's Way,* directed by D. W. Griffith in 1910, showed a white woman treating an Indian child after her doctor husband refuses aid. The settlers' cruelty to Indians later brings on an attack in which the wife is spared while many of the settlers, including the husband, are massacred. In another Biograph film made in 1910, *The Indian Runner's Romance,* the daughter of an Indian chief is abducted by three white men shortly after her marriage to a brave. One of the three, who has won her at gambling, is pursued by her husband, who kills the white man and walks off into the sunset with the woman. Although many other films of the period showed a more understanding attitude toward the Indians, sometimes even affording them the status of a hero, the massacre continued to be a favorite theme. Even

Griffith—who in 1908 dramatized a chief's rescue of a wounded son from white kidnappers, whom the chief slays *(The Redman and the Child)*—showed a murderous attack on a wagon train in his 1912 *The Massacre*. Half-breed gun smugglers and renegade guides were popular plot ingredients, and Bison's 1913 *Early Days in the West* was almost a caricature of the genre. It is the typical story of a Sioux attack on a wagon train and a cavalry rescue, complete with a treacherous Indian guide who kidnaps the daughter of one of the settlers. *How Lone Wolf Died* (1914) tells of the renegade whose savagery against whites leads to a miserable death in the desert. That savage ways could be changed was illustrated in a number of films of the period. In *The Heron Converts* (1916), a group of Jesuit Fathers tame the treacherous Heron tribe and give them religion as well.

The noble savage was almost as popular an image of the American Indian as the scalp hunter. Favorite themes expressing this idea included sympathetic accounts of the sacrifices made by chiefs, young braves, and maidens for their own honor and the survival of the tribe. *The Redman's View* (1909) showed the separation of Indian lovers and the death of the girl's father in

the advance of the ever-encroaching whites. In *Seminole's Sacrifice* (1911), a trader invites a Seminole tribe to battle with an American garrison. After the Indians' defeat, they are offered amnesty if they will surrender their chief, Red Jacket. Their refusal leads to the chief's voluntary surrender to save the tribe.

Other sympathetic types that sometimes attained hero status were grateful Indians eager to return favors (interactions with the Northwest Mounted Police were especially amicable to this variation), the faithful Indian companion (who reached stardom in Tonto, the Lone Ranger's friend), and the selfless sacrifice of the Indian maiden (often played by Mona Darkfeather, born in Los Angeles of a Spanish family). Here *Ramona* (1928), *The Red Rider* (1925), and *The Heart of Night Wind* (1915) serve as striking examples. *The Vanishing American* (1925) gives the honor of sacrifice to a Navajo brave (Richard Dix), who falls in love with a white schoolteacher, beats an evil Indian agent, warns the whites of an Indian attack, and dies in the arms of the schoolteacher. But first place should probably go to the heroine of *An Apache Father's Vengeance* (1912). Here an Indian woman is dressed up and taken to a dance by some

From *The Vanishing American* (1925). Richard Dix as Nophaie leaves tribal customs and dress to join his tribe at war.

officers' wives. Indians attack the unprotected garrison and, when the girl rides to warn the cavalry, she is shot by her own father. The film ends with cavalry soldiers covering her body with the American flag.

By the 1920s another popular image was that of the Indian college graduate whose exposure to white man's ways and women often led to integrated romance. However, a continuing sensitivity to miscegenation, even between whites and native Americans, usually resulted in a last-minute change of heart or revelation of true parentage. In *Blazing Arrow* (1922) a Columbia student loses the girl when his Indian identity is revealed, but he wins her back when it is discovered that he was only adopted by an Indian chief. *The Great Alone* (1922) has as its star a Stanford University football star who is scorned by fellow students because he is a half-breed. He repays the kindness of a white girl by rescuing her, but falls in love with a half-breed girl. First National Pictures made its variation on this theme in 1925 with *The Scarlet West,* in which the son of a chief is rebuked by his people after he pursues an eastern education and joins the cavalry. He falls in love with the commandant's daughter, but eventually gives her up, along with his army commission, to rejoin his own people. The most elaborate of the group was doubtless Cecil B. De Mille's offering, *Braveheart,* also made in 1925, in which Rod La Rocque stars as the young brave who goes to an eastern college to study law and help protect the tribe's fishing rights. He makes All-American playing football and becomes a scholar, but is expelled from college and disgraced by his tribe when he confesses, in order to save a friend's reputation, to selling football signals to an opposing team. He finally wins back his tribe's respect (and their fishing rights), but denies his love for a white woman and marries an Indian instead.

The image of the American Indian in American silent films was strongly influenced by plot requirements and stereotypes that had already become well established. Collectively Indians were shown as threatening pioneer expansion; individually they were used to trigger personal conflict and interracial intrigues. These latter dramas were simplistic and exploitative, but they occasionally suggested something of the struggle that the coming of whites produced for both races. Few films attempted to explore the internal affairs of Indians or to seriously inquire into the effects of westward expansion. Those films, such as Griffith's *The Squaw's Love* (1911), that dramatized aspects of Indian life without depending on conflicts with whites were mainly romantic idylls. Attention to militant racism on an individual and personal level was rare, though it arose as early as 1912 in *The Vanishing Tribe* and again, more elaborately, in Universal's *Red Clay,* made in 1927.

Uncle Tom and Others

Blacks, like Indians, were very much a part of the film scene from the beginning. In contrast to the Indian's usual portrayal, however, a popular early role for the black was a kind of surreal buffoonery of the most exploitative kind. Showing white actors in blackface and the trick potential of the camera, a variety of shorts appeared early on that involved bizarre transformations of blacks into whites and vice versa. Méliès's *Off to Bloomingdale Asylum* (1902) is the vintage and oft-cited example, but it was only the beginning of an extended series that continued into the twenties. Another early variation was the British-made *The Negro's Revenge* (1906), in which a Negro who has been insulted by a white woman employs two boys to blacken the woman's face while she sleeps so she will be jeered at by passersby. A soaking by a gardener finally turns her white again. *His Darker Self,* made nearly two decades later, repeats the basic gag:

> Unlucky in love, the despondent Claude tries to enter a cafe for colored people. Turned away, he goes home and blackens his face. Returning, he is admitted and offered a job as target in a knife-throwing act. Forced to flee when he starts to throw the knives back, he hides in a religious meeting on the beach. Thrown into the water to be baptized, he emerges white, to the horror of the rest of the congregation, who flee in terror.

In 1925 Universal produced a series based on the comic strip "The Gumps." One episode involved a pair of black servants turning white in terror when an escaped lion approaches them. Less fantastic, but hardly less demeaning, was the image of the black in comedies not dependent on color change. Characterized as shiftless, thieving, or terror-stricken darkies, they reappeared in countless films whose titles alone are insults. *A Nigger in the Woodpile* (1904) ends with two blacks being blown up in their cabin—dynamite had been hidden in firewood they have stolen. *The Wooing and Wedding of a Coon* (1905) is described by its producers as "a genuine Ethiopian Comedy," and *Coon Town Suffragettes,* produced by Sigmund Lubin in 1911, shows black "mammies" organizing a movement to keep shiftless husbands out of saloons. *The Chicken Thief,* made by Biograph in 1904, is described by its producers in a film bulletin as follows:

> From the opening of the picture, where the coon with the grinning face is seen devouring fried chicken, to the end where he hangs his head down from the ceiling, caught by a bear trap on his leg, the film is one continuous shout of laughter.

Meanwhile, Lubin was producing his *Rastus* and *Sambo* series, slapstick shorts that characterized blacks as complete fools. Even when not characterized as clowns, blacks were portrayed as the cause of consternation and chagrin for whites. In *The Masher* (1907), a lady-killer who flirts with a veiled lady runs away in embarrassed shock when he discovers she is black. *A Fool and His Money* (1914) is described in a contemporary film guide as "a brilliant comedy featuring James Russell, the American cakewalk king. Acted entirely by niggers."

Such blatant racist humor became less evident by the twenties. The black image then tended to be of the good-natured, superstitious servant—Snowball, Excema (sic), Diploma—dedicated to pleasing the mistress or master and perhaps yearning to be just a little bit white. In *Topsy and Eva* (1927), based on the characters from Harriet Beecher Stowe's *Uncle Tom's Cabin,* Topsy, who has been bought by Little Eva for a nickel, prays, "I won't ask you to make me white as Eva—just a nice light tan will do."

Segregation, like slavery, was virtually ignored by the silent film except in an occasional comedy such as *Spyin' the Sky* (1917), a racist romp with action involving a Klan-type group, or Paramount's *The Palm Beach Girl* (1926), in which a farm girl who has been covered with soot is hustled onto a black bus in Palm Beach by a bellhop. Any serious treatment of the subject took a specific form: the trials and tribulations of a girl or boy thought to be the product of a mixed marriage, who wins a lover when his or her real white birthright is discovered. *Symbol of the Unconquered* (1921) provided a more realistic treatment of race—a black woman is thrown out of a hotel in a Western town. But it is doubtful that any white audiences saw this film, since it was produced by a black company without general distribution.

In serious films, blacks were generally the faithful darkies on the antebellum plantation. When not part of the scenery, they were part of intrigues that involved miscegenation and the woes of mulattos and octoroons. Griffith became with *The Birth of a Nation* a central figure in portraying blacks on the screen. He made many other shorts both before and after this film that were less controversial but that contained stereotyped roles of servants and occasionally villains. In a film that has been interpreted as Griffith's atonement for his earlier racist portrayals, *The Greatest Thing in Life* (1918), a dying black man is shown crying for his mother. After his death, a white comrade bends over and kisses him. But four years later, in *One Exciting Night,* Griffith again portrayed a black man as a frightened, superstitious, weak-kneed dolt.

By the time the 1914 version of *Uncle Tom's Cabin* went into production, blackface was beginning to give way to black actors, and the role of Tom in that film was played by a Negro. Black companies began to produce their own films in 1916, initiated by the Lincoln Motion Picture Company, founded by George P. Johnson, and the Colored Players Film Corporation in Philadelphia. These films were intended for black audiences, however, and never received general distribution. In 1929 Fox released *Hearts of Dixie,* the first all-Negro production by a major studio. It helped usher in the era of the screen musical and a new role for blacks—that of the song and dance players.

The Cohens and the Kellys

The portrayal of Jews in silent films is virtually one long Jewish-Irish joke. The pattern was set as early as 1903, when Biograph made a short entitled *Levi and Cohen, "The Irish Comedians."* This image thrived for a quarter of a century, suggesting that just as the Negro's fondest dream was to be white, the Jew's aspiration was either to marry into a good Irish Catholic family or to have an Irish business partner, or both. In IMP's *Levi and McGinnes Running for Office* (1914), a contest for

▶ From *The Cohens and the Kellys in Scotland* (1930). The Universal Pictures series featured George Sidney and Charlie Murray as business partners, here on a search for Scottish plaids.

local alderman brings Patrick, Moshey, and their families into conflict.

Jewish-Irish relations continued to be treated by films throughout the silent era, but the topic got a special boost with the phenomenal success of the Anne Nichols play *Abie's Irish Rose,* which opened in New York in 1924. Although the screen version was not produced until 1929, with the coming of sound, the success of the play spawned several silent comedies centered on business and filial relations between Jew and Irishman. Most notable among these was Universal Picture's series *The Cohens and the Kellys,* which began in 1926 and continued into the sound era with the families' escapades in Africa, Paris, Scotland, and Atlantic City. Once the children had been happily married off in the original, the several sequels found the two fathers, now business partners, off to distant lands in search of ivory, plaids, and bathing suits.

Few serious screenplays centered on Jews in the silent period, even though melodrama was the predominant form. Those that did appear are not locked into the single-theme syndrome of the comedies, but focus on myths and stereotypes and virtually ignore anti-Semitism. As in the comedies, Jews in the melodramas are usually stereotyped by occupation—as pawnbrokers, tailors, moneylenders, or proprietors of delicatessens. Conflicts usually involve business crises or family estrangement. Griffith's early entry was *Romance of a Jewess* (1908), in which the daughter of a pawnbroker falls in love with a gentile bookstore owner. Father and daughter are estranged at the marriage but are finally reconciled at the tragic death of the husband. Griffith wrote the script for *Old Isaacs the Pawnbroker* the same year, about a kindly Jewish pawnbroker who comes to the aid of a destitute mother and child.

A sympathetic attitude toward Jews found expression throughout the teens, with the plight of Russian Jews becoming a prominent theme by the early twenties. The discrimination against American Jews, however, was not given an airing until well into the sound era. A notable exception was *The Women He Loved* (1922), in which a California rancher shows dislike for a Jewish immigrant who has established a small ranch nearby. With the conflicts resolved, he finally consents to his daughter's marriage to the Jew's son. And in *Welcome Stranger* (1924) a shopkeeper is driven from a small New England town by the mayor, but is later honored by the town when he helps bring a power plant to the community. Even where the drama was serious, it still portrayed a world of dreams.

Religion and Politics

A popular aphorism holds that it is useless to argue about religion and politics. Hollywood, as already suggested, was not doing much arguing about any social issue, and in the case of these two it ignored politics and used religion repeatedly for setting, plot intrigue, and general moral tone.

The earliest and most enduring of the religious-theme films were the historical pageants and passion plays that brought to the screen personalities and events of early Christendom. These prenarrative tableaux ranged from pseudo-documentary clips of well-known biblical settings to more fanciful visions of religious pursuits, tribulations, and persecutions. In 1898, Méliès, in *The Temptation of St. Anthony,* depicted the trials of the saint at the hands of a group of seductive naked women, one of whom comes down from a cross. An angel then appears to save St. Anthony from his torment. Pathé's *The Persecution of the Christians* (1905) shows two less fortunate Christians brought into an arena, tied to a stake, and left to the lions. Once the narrative form was established, Pathé was able to make the first film version of the journey to the Promised Land and the receiving of the Ten Commandments in *Moses and the Exodus from Egypt* (1907).

American studios, like those in France and England, began with the tableau, and with the coming of storytelling turned to the parable and allegory, which permitted the dramatization of both historical and contemporary themes. In 1907, the Biograph Company undertook *The Life of Christ,* which its bulletin describes as a passion play in twenty-five scenes, from Bethlehem to the Resurrection.

By the twenties, however, it was the biblical spectacle and the melodrama revealing the consequences of godlessness that best represented Hollywood's contributions to religious inspiration and education. *My Friend the Devil* (1922), *A Woman's Faith* (1925), and *The Road to Glory* (1936) were typical of the many films in which a character regains religious faith after renouncing God at some moment of personal tragedy. Although De Mille himself is better known for the historical spectacle, he also made contributions to the little moral drama. His *The Godless Girl* (1929) shows the daughter of an atheist organizing a high school club called the Godless Society. And the modern segment of his *The Ten Commandments* (1923) represented his contribution to the modern religious screenplay. But for all the preaching found in the historical spectacle and intimate parable of the silent film period, little was said of the pressures and anxieties of individuals and groups in their everyday contact with prejudice, persecution, and self-doubt.

Antiwar sentiment, another politically sensitive issue, was given sporadic attention through the silent and early sound periods. Such works as Griffith's *Intolerance* and Ince's *Civilization,* and later *All Quiet on the Western Front* and *The Big Parade,* were among the more prominent works on this subject. But these were compromised in their treatment of the issue either because they were fanciful period pieces, as with the Griffith and Ince films, or because their message was neutralized through heroics, as with the latter two works. Lesser-known films on the subject tended to be similarly afflicted.

Direct war propaganda became particularly fashionable during World War I. *The Battle Cry of Peace* (1915) was a star vehicle for Norma Talmadge and one of the earliest true war propaganda films. But the inevitable star of subsequent films of the genre was the Kaiser himself, the arch villain of the war. *The Kaiser, the Beast of Berlin, To Hell with the Kaiser,* and *The Kaiser's Shadow,* which Ince produced for Paramount, are among the studies of the most hated of the Huns. Even Chaplin's *Shoulder Arms* in its original version had a concluding scene showing Charlie capturing the Kaiser. In 1918, when all these films were released, the motion picture industry was recognized by the War Office as the major medium for propaganda. In "Wid's Yearbook" (an industry annual) for that year, Cecil B. De Mille suggests that "had pictures accomplished nothing throughout their short history but to bring the great war home to the people of the United States, they would have vindicated, eternally, their right to live."

With the conclusion of World War I, events and political strains resulting from the Russian Revolution came to be a popular political subject, if not a preoccupation, of the Hollywood industry. The end of Czarist rule provided romantic potential, and Bolshevism, a new type of screen heavy. Numerous films featured the Russian countess who sought refuge from the Bolsheviks with the aid of Russian peasants. In *The Face in the Fog* (1922), a revolutionary terrorist is in search of the Romanov jewels. Lionel Barrymore plays the reformed crook, Boston Blackie, who exposes the Bolshevik and returns the jewels to the grand duchess. The following year Barrymore starred as the Bolshevist himself in *The Eternal City,* which centered on a Communist-Fascist conflict. Here an Italian orphan and the daughter of his foster father become estranged when he joins the Fascists and suspects her of becoming the mistress of a secret leader of the Communist party. He becomes Mussolini's right-hand man and leads the Fascists against the Bolsheviks. In key scenes of this First National film, directed by George Fitzmaurice, Mussolini is shown reviewing his troops with the king at the royal palace. Although politics still served melodrama here, this film was a rare example of American attention to a Fascist theme.

As is clear in this brief overview, filmmakers found ample ways of meeting audience expectations for readily identifiable characters and morally acceptable conclusions, while still using the silent screen to mirror attitudes on private and public issues.

Wrap-Up

By 1927 the motion picture industry had reached huge proportions. The investment in studios and equipment since 1912 had grown to more than $2 billion, and the number of theaters had doubled, from 10,000 to 20,000. Just as important, theaters had changed in character.

Attendance figures had risen to almost 100 million per week. Supplying this audience with films were almost 2,500 producer/exhibitor corporations. Southern California alone contained 54 studios, employing more than 42,000 workers.

The motion picture industry of the silent era had been built on a foundation of ashes and dreams — the ashes of a monopoly and the dreams of ambitious business people. Incredible changes had taken place by the end of the twenties, and opinion was — and still is — divided on the value of most of them. Many believed that the commercialization and industrialization of a potential art form had irreparably damaged motion pictures. Others felt that the necessary and useful function of entertaining a mass audience, which only a large industry could perform, sufficiently justified the changes. Mae Marsh, a major silent film star, stated: "Looking back, there's surely been a change in the film business over the decades. First it was a little family, then it became an industry, and then it became a match factory."

The German Silent Film (1919 – 1932)

Focus

In his *Language of Film,* Ron Whitaker observes that "the most casual student of film history cannot fail to notice that great film movements germinate during periods of economic and political chaos." There is no better example of this phenomenon than the emergence of a German industry between the end of World War I in 1919 and the rise of Fascist rule in the early thirties. During this period, Germany, defeated in war, became recognized throughout the world as a center for creative filmmaking. These years, called the golden age of German cinema by many film historians, yielded films characterized by refinements in cinematic technique coupled with bold experimentation in style, both in basic narrative construction and visual detail. Among the more celebrated screenplays were those devoted to traditional expressionist themes, often drawn from deeply subjective and highly stylized theatrical and literary sources. At the other end of the spectrum were equally distinguished themes reflecting contemporary realism that capitalized on the camera's ability to record physical detail faithfully.

Besides producing works that were quickly recognized as major achievements in film aesthetics, the movement provided a training ground for producers, directors, screenwriters, and scenic designers who were eventually lured to Hollywood. Their migration not only had a significant influence on Hollywood filmmaking but also resulted in a gradual decline of the German film throughout the early thirties, the years of the Fascist takeover. Still, a legacy in both screen fantasy and social realism endured. This legacy significantly helped to elevate the motion picture to a level of respectability and aesthetic substance.

An Emerging Industry

Early development in both film technology and the industry had put Germany among the pioneering nations in the promotion of the new motion picture medium. In 1895, the Skladanowsky brothers were showing their "Bioscopes," or "living pictures," to Wintergarten audiences in Berlin. Oskar Messter began producing films the following year, using the camera and projector apparatus he had himself developed to produce and exhibit first short and then feature films of some technical and artistic merit. In his features he introduced screen performers who were to become the stars of the German silent film. And in 1908 the first International Cinematographic Industry Exhibition was held in Hamburg.

Actualities (filmed real-life events), Méliès-style fantasies, and productions patterned after the French Film d'Art models characterize the early period of German film production, and by 1910 the German industry had joined the international pool as a source of film. By the early teens, talent from the theatrical fields had been drawn to the new medium, as noted, raising film's status as a cultural entity but limiting its styles and techniques to those of the theater. In 1913, there were 28 producing companies in Germany, and in 1917, 245. But until the end of World War I, German-produced films in distribution, even within Germany, were outweighed by films from France, Italy, Denmark, and the United States. At the start of the war fewer than one in five films shown in Germany had been produced there.

The war stopped the flood of films from the Allied nations and provided the opportunity for a dramatic expansion of the German film industry. At the same time, the conflict was fostering a home audience greatly in need of diversion and escape. With the joint efforts of an increasingly profitable industry and a government recog-

nizing the propaganda potential of the medium, a film-making combine was formed under the sponsorship of the German government. This centralization of film production was intended not only to command stronger financial backing, more rigorous production schedules, and stronger movement in the export market, but also to help support the war effort and promote German interests and ideology both at home and abroad.

By 1917 all film production was centralized within the combine under the propaganda ministry. With the blessing (and substantial financial support) of the German High Command, Ufa (Universum Film A.G.) emerged as the largest and most powerful film company in Germany and eventually Europe.

The end of the war brought a return to social democracy and an end to government control. It also brought a rapid expansion in the film market, particularly the export trade. Financial stability, a vigorous export market, and huge, well-equipped physical plants allowed Ufa to absorb small companies Emelka-Konzern, and Terra-Film A.G. (the three largest firms) to absorb smaller companies, expand, and dominate all aspects of the industry.

A vigorous, financially sound, and carefully managed industry emerged. Although it did not assure quality in production, the industry did provide the right climate for an outpouring of creative talent. From 1919 to about 1925, the association of aggressive studio heads such as Erich Pommer with some very talented production personnel (screenwriter Carl Mayer; directors G. W. Pabst, Fritz Lang, and F. W. Murnau; scenic designer Walter Rohrig; and performers Emil Jannings, Werner Krauss, and Lya de Putti) provided the creative force that won Germany an international reputation in film production and won for the medium itself the status of a serious art form. In spite of the unemployment, inflation, and political instability plaguing the country, a sound, well-disciplined organization combined with imaginative and

◄ The Ufa Studio, outside Berlin. In 1917, German film production was merged under a national umbrella known as Ufa (Universum Film A.G.). In this enormous, efficient, and technologically advanced studio center, located at Neubabelsberg, all the major German silent and early sound films were made. Later, under Nazi control, the studio was forced to produce National Socialist films, and after World War II it became the center for East German production.

energetic screen artists not only to put German film into the lead as an industrial and aesthetic entity, but also to affect profoundly the American art and industry up to and even through the second World War.

An Emerging Art

The old styles and themes — the historical spectacles — provided the initial creative thrust in German feature films of the teens. Toward the end of the war, companies quickly moved to revitalize the industry by restaging the popular prewar spectaculars derived from ancient Teutonic myths and legends. The music of Richard Wagner, especially the "Ring Cycle," suggests a parallel to the grand action and massive emotions of many of these films.

From the very beginning, German films had featured some of the key personalities of the theater world, and it was common practice for actors and actresses to move freely from stage to screen. As a result, motion pictures were being accepted as a legitimate form of entertainment and social activity (if not great art) long before such status was granted to American motion pictures, and even before the truly creative force emerged in German cinema that would be in evidence by the end of the decade.

A creative team of production personnel with Ernst Lubitsch at the helm began producing such costume dramas as *Madame Du Barry* (1918) and *Carmen*

(1918). Though hardly visionary in their content, these historical spectacles showed a growing technical mastery of the medium and set standards in acting and directing and in the design and execution of setting and decor that were to be emulated by production people both inside and outside Germany. These standards centered on discipline and careful control over every element of production, within the confines of the studio where better control was possible and little was left to chance.

One group of films quickly drew critical attention and survived as a central part of the legacy of German silent film: the macabre fantasies that dealt with the supernatural. A tradition in German arts and letters that emphasized the influence of dark forces on human life was a precursor and ultimate model for this important group of films, which themselves were the roots and inspiration for a variety of horror studies and psychological thrillers to follow. Two hundred years before, Goethe had speculated that man finally becomes used to cruelty, and "in the end makes a law of that which he despises." Goethe's *Faust* and E. T. A. Hoffmann's *Tales* had set

► From *Siegfried* (1924). This first part of Fritz Lang's two-part treatment of the Nibelungen legend follows the betrayal of Siegfried by Brünhilde and his murder by Hagen. Together with the second part, *Kriemhild's Revenge*, it reflects the dedication in German art, literature, and film to the dark legends of supernatural powers.

A Review of *Caligari* on Its American Release

*T*he original decrees of futurism, post-impressionism, and cubism have now invaded the film world. If artists can paint houses upside-down, windows aslant, and mountains wider at the top than at the bottom, the designers of scenery can create similar effects for the motion pictures.

The fantastic is in vogue in Germany, popular because it is a change from the eternal masses marching back and forth thru the same villages. The German film industry, tho it is prosperous, has not the unlimited means that are at the disposal of the American companies today. The German movie public is just as fed up with the old commonplace films as is the rest of the world and it has welcomed the change. Life in Germany is now unbearably intense, a turmoil seemingly without beginning or end. In a world that is upside-down, what is more natural than that the films, too, shall metaphorically, stand on their heads?

The public has now developed a taste for futuristic films, fantastic architecture, exotic plots, and eccentric acting. The large firms are beginning to rival one another to keep up with the public, which flocks to the latest futurist sensation.

—*From* Shadowland *(January 1921)*

the tone for gothic studies of demonic forces, and expressionism had become a pervasive force in German arts and letters. After the war, this traditional homage to the supernatural was combined with a fascination with Freudian psychology and the workings of the subconscious mind. The highly subjective and stylized environment possible in films was well suited for representing the experience of the subconscious, and filmmakers, like painters, composers, and writers, began to experiment in stylized representations of the world of individual human perception—frequently of the less stable variety.

Certain traditions in German—and American—film emphasized the influence of supernatural and mystic forces on human life, even questioning the whole notion of free choice. Selig-Polyscope had presented *Dr. Jekyll and Mr. Hyde* in 1908. Edison released *Frankenstein* in 1910. *The Golem,* made in Germany in 1915 and again in 1920, had introduced a form of robot, and the Faustian *Student of Prague,* also in an original version (1913) and a remake (1926), ended with the damnation of a student

for consorting with the devil. The American Draculas and Frankensteins of the 1930s, however, lacked the despair, horror, and doom that was so heavy in the German films of the previous two decades.

The Student of Prague

Danish director Stellen Rye introduced the genre of dark legends with the original *Student of Prague* in 1913, with noted stage actor Paul Wegener in the title role. Based loosely on the Faust legend, this film concerns a young student who sells his mirror reflection to a sorcerer, who in turn brings the image to life to carry out murderous schemes. In addition to its narrative and visual design, the film is of interest for some exceptional special effects. At one point, when Baldwin, the student, has made the contract with the demonic Scapinelli, a ghostly mirror image is seen leaving his body. Later in the film we see Baldwin gazing into a mirror in which no reflection appears. And in the film's climactic moment,

Baldwin fires a shot at the apparition (his alter ego) and he himself falls dead from the bullet wound. *The Student of Prague* established a model for supernatural creatures, which were let loose in countless horror films over the next three decades. The 1926 remake featured Conrad Veidt (shown in the accompanying photograph) and Werner Krauss under the direction of Henrik Galeen.

The Golem

Galeen had collaborated earlier with Paul Wegener on a film that provided another prototype of a sinister screen creature. *The Golem* (1920), also set in Prague, is a mystical fantasy noted for its impressionistic setting and special effects. Based on a Jewish legend, it tells the story of a rabbi who makes a clay statue that he brings to life by means of a secret formula. The clay figure becomes the rabbi's servant, fighting against persecution of Jews in the royal court. The film's major action unfolds in the ancient ghetto of Prague. After completing the bidding of the rabbi, the Golem is turned back into clay, but an ambitious student restores it to life, and the Golem now stalks the countryside, isolated, rejected, and seething with malice and revenge. The film concludes with a spectacular shot of the Golem as spurned lover, jumping to his death and disintegrating into the clay from which he was originally molded.

In *The Golem,* Wegener applied what was known as the futuristic style to material drawn from medieval lore. Distorted and unrealistic visual design and highly stylized lighting, costuming, and acting combined to produce nightmarish scenes. The image of the Golem, played by Wegener himself, manifested the power of evil in a supernatural creature who was himself the victim of human

From *The Student of Prague* (1926). This German remake of the 1913 Danish film, based loosely on the Faust legend, tells of a student who loses his reflection in a barter made with an evil sorcerer. Removing and giving a separate existence to student Baldwin's mirror image provided the director Galeen with several opportunities for special visual effects.

From *The Golem* (1920). Paul Wegener played the Golem and directed the film, bringing to the screen a haunting image of terror in human form unleashed on an unsuspecting public.

misadventure. This was the same basic formula that would provide the model for the *Frankenstein* cycle in the United States as well as many other horror fantasies on both sides of the Atlantic. *The Golem* was popular in the United States as well as in Europe and ran for ten months in its initial engagement at New York's Criterion Theater.

The original version of *The Golem,* produced by Wegener in 1915, is no longer extant, but the 1920 remake received international recognition for its rendering of the ancient medieval ghetto and cabalistic rites performed there. The unusual screenplay was matched by the extraordinary setting created by Poelzig, a designer in the theater of the celebrated German producer-director Max Reinhardt. Medieval Prague is given an appropriately sinister character — dark passages and mazelike alleys wind among a confusion of slanted windows and up-thrusting roofs that represent the tumble of houses that make up the ghetto. The *New York Times* (June 20, 1921) speaks of "a combination of exceptional acting and the most expressive settings yet seen in this country."

The Cabinet of Dr. Caligari

The fullest, perhaps most extreme rendering of German expressionism on film came in 1919 with the production of *The Cabinet of Dr. Caligari.* Like his precursors, Frankenstein and the Golem of 1913, Caligari was a dark study in evil power run amok. As a monster who wreaks havoc and destruction on society and ultimately on himself, he was the personification of evil.

The idea for the film was hatched in the minds of two young leftist artists, Carl Mayer and Hans Janowitz, devotees of the radical expressionist art movement who were embittered by their experiences in the war. The film concept harmonized perfectly with leftist theory of the time, which held that the common man was but a tool in the hands of power-mad leaders. Mayer and Janowitz visualized an evil man, Dr. Caligari, who would symbolize these power-mad leaders, a man who could cast spells over simple folk to make them do his dirty work. They devised to show poor Cesare, a somnambulist, made to commit various criminal acts under the demonic and hellishly evil Dr. Caligari.

▲ From *The Cabinet of Dr. Caligari* (1919). The awakening of another of German film's supernatural creatures told of the upside down world of Cesare, the somnambulist (Conrad Veidt) and his creator, the evil Caligari (Werner Krauss).

The Safety of the Studio

Caligari initiates a long procession of 100 per cent studio-made films. Whereas, for instance, the Swedes at that time went to great pains to capture the actual appearance of a snow-storm or a wood, the German directors, at least until 1924, were so infatuated with indoor effects that they built up whole landscapes within the studio walls. They preferred the command of an artificial universe to dependence upon a haphazard outer world. Their withdrawal into the studio was part of the general retreat into a shell. Once the Germans had determined to seek shelter within the soul, they could not well allow the screen to explore that very reality which they abandoned. This explains the conspicuous role of architecture after *Caligari*.

—*Sigfried Kracauer,* From Caligari to Hitler

From *The Cabinet of Dr. Caligari* (1919). Wild distortion in scenic detail is enhanced by stylized movement and painted shadows made to reflect the world of a madman.

"Really something new—different," they said in explaining their idea to Erich Pommer, powerful production head at Ufa. The film proved to be more than that. It stylized, distorted, and played havoc with images. It aimed to destroy, with political intentions, Griffith's romantic naturalism and sentimental perspective on human nature.

Few members of the German mass audience were impressed, except for the intellectuals, and in America the masses were not flocking to the latest sensation either. *The Cabinet of Dr. Caligari* was macabre, morbid, threatening, and grotesque—a horror show reflecting the spirit of the times.

What distinguished *Caligari* as a film, despite its failure at the box office, was not only its story pattern and basic expressionistic style, but also the overall artistic control, the resulting continuity, and the precision in execution. This film made artists and intellectuals as well as thrill seekers sit up and take notice. It showed that film could be more than simple recording or mere entertainment.

The visual realization of a madman's world—transforming the everyday details of life into their subjective, and demented, counterparts—gave *Caligari* its major strength. Stark white streets and sky stood in contrast to the distorted dark shapes and angles of the hovering buildings, trees, and the characters themselves. The sets were designed in forced perspective so that walls, floors, and ceilings seemed to have no relationship with the horizontal or vertical. Windows and doors were trapezoidal, and acutely gabled roofs were topped with precariously mounted crooked chimneys.

▶ From *Warning Shadows* (1922). In this film, directed by Arthur Robison, a wizard who entertains with shadow plays hypnotizes a group involved in a love intrigue and allows them to follow their shadows into the future. The play of light and shadows becomes a central motif and enhances the film's mystical mood.

Extending the expressionistic design even further was the painting of light and shadows directly on the set. Though it has been rumored that the "artificial light" effects were the result of economic stringencies that required cutting electricity costs, it is far more likely that the painting of light and shadows permitted yet another dimension in expressionist design and permitted complete control of composition.

Although the design and "lighting" of sets may have been central to the vision of a madman's world, this vision was ingeniously extended by the costuming, make-up, and even the movement of the actors. The white featureless mask of the somnambulist, Cesare; the black lines that streak the white gloves and hair of Caligari; the slow, unearthly movement of the sleepwalker as he creeps along a wall—all these suggest the inner horrors of the unbalanced mind.

Also making *Caligari* more than an intriguing exercise in expressionistic style was its unconventional narrative. The film's creators and screenwriters Mayer and Janowitz had portrayed the film's central figure as a representation of mad authority. "They saw an 'experiment' in the script," states the Ufa studio producer Erich Pommer, "I saw a comparatively cheap production." Pommer doubtlessly also saw trouble with audiences' acceptance of the film's radical view of institutions and their leaders. Before the film's release, he saw to it that a framing device be used to place the entire story in the mind of a young asylum inmate who is the real raving lunatic. The radical perspective of the film was thus reversed and the monster leader tamed. This reversal in perspective permitted the addition of a final scene, in which the kindly Caligari suggests to his associates at the asylum that he is aware of the young patient's problem and thinks he can help him.

Caligari made film fantasy and horror not only acceptable but even respectable among world critics. Following its release in the early twenties were a number of decendants of *The Golem,* the sorcerer of *The Student of Prague,* and of course *Caligari* and his somnambulist servant. In 1920, F. W. Murnau adapted Robert Louis

Stevenson's *Dr. Jekyll and Mr. Hyde* to the screen (in *Der Januskopf*), while Paul Wegener remade *The Golem*. Arthur Robison's *Warning Shadows* (1922), Paul Leni's *Waxworks* (1924), and Galeen's remake of *The Student of Prague* (1926) all contributed to the on-going parade of sinister characters in other-worldly settings.

Nosferatu

Galeen adapted the Bram Stoker novel *Dracula* to the screen in 1922, and with director F. W. Murnau, created one of the more popular and enduring of the screen's monsters to follow *Caligari*. *Nosferatu,* a title made necessary because of copyright restrictions, presented another man possessed by satanic powers. He appears by day as the respected Count Orlock, but by night, under the curse of vampirism, he stalks the deserted streets in search of fresh victims. In one particularly memorable scene, Nosferatu boards a sailing vessel and, after infecting the crew with pestilence, sails the rat-infested phantom ship into the Bremen harbor. Here, in another striking scene, we see Nosferatu dissolve in the morning sunlight, for he is under a curse that will not allow him to survive the light of day. It is for such ingenious and macabre camera effects that this film remains a classic of haunting and grotesque imagery. *Nosferatu* is also distinctive as the first important film of the timeless and prolific vampire genre.

Metropolis

The most sustained contributions to screen expressionism during the period came from the husband-wife team of Fritz Lang and Thea von Harbou. Their collaboration as screenwriter and director started with *Der müde Tod (Destiny)* in 1921. They continued with *Dr. Mabuse* (1922); *Siegfried,* a cinematic rendering of the popular Teutonic legend, in 1923; and *Kriemhild's Revenge* in 1924. Their dual career culminated with the futuristic drama of a totalitarian society, in *Metropolis* (1926). In visualizing both the legendary past and a visionary future, Lang used strikingly original designs, from a curious Chinese garden in *Der müde Tod* to a menacing forest in *Siegfried.*

Fritz Lang conceived of *Metropolis* when he was denied permission to land in New York. He gazed at the panorama of the city from the ship's deck and envisioned the world of the year 2000, a world of class warfare and robots tracking about in a kind of science fiction set never before seen on film. To Lang, the future was but an extension of his contemporary experience. In *Metropolis,* he used futuristic design and the highly stylized orchestration of movement to symbolize the class struggle that the film dramatizes. He moved masses of people in triangular or rectangular formation ascending and descending enormous stairways. It took eighteen months to shoot the film; several thousand people were involved in the production.

From *Nosferatu* (1922). Another creature with supernatural powers to grace German silent films is the vampire Dracula, called *Nosferatu* in the Murnau film. A memorable scene in this first of many screen appearances shows him sailing a deserted, rat-infested ship into the German port of Bremen.

From *Nosferatu.* Highly stylized settings, costumes, make-up, movement, and lighting were the legacy of German expressionism and a hallmark of the horror films in particular. *Nosferatu* followed the original *Student of Prague* (1913), *Caligari* (1919), and *The Golem* (1920) in the tradition.

From *Destiny* (1921). In this Fritz Lang metaphysical/fantasy film, the settings of ninth-century Baghdad, seventeenth-century Venice, and this exotic Chinese garden are featured in a nightmare journey by a girl who must bargain with the Angel of Death for a reunion with her lost love.

Metropolis is the story of a banker's son who rejects the comforts and security of the "upper city" to join the struggles of the workers in the "lower city." Here he falls in love with Maria, the film's proletarian heroine. In spite of the machinations of an evil scientist, who uses a robot (in the image of Maria) to incite riots and destroy the city, Maria suggests that love be the mediator between management and labor—"the heart must mediate between head and hand"—and saves the workers' city.

The geometrical patterns Lang made using both men and machines are a continuous display of intriguing visual design. They also suggest a totalitarian perspective that is said to have placed the film, along with the early outdoor spectacles of Leni Riefenstahl, among Hitler's favorites. From a cinematic point of view, the simplistic political theme of *Metropolis* plus the sometimes stultifying effect of viewing human drama as lifeless geometric design are among the film's liabilities. What makes the film noteworthy, in addition to the ingenuity of its overall structure, is the precedent it created for the futuristic adventures that followed it. Indeed, one might even see a link over time between the robotlike Maria in *Metropolis* and the robot C3PO in *Star Wars*, the space age spectacle made in 1977.

From *Metropolis* (1926). Few effects were beyond the capabilities of the Ufa studio. Here the crew is filming the dramatic flooding of the workers' underground city, a scene that German film historian Sigfried Kracauer calls "cinematically an incomparable achievement."

Metropolis as Propaganda

*I*n fact, Maria's demand [in *Metropolis*] that the heart mediate between hand and brain could well have been formulated by Goebbels. He, too, appealed to the heart—in the interest of totalitarian propaganda. At the Nuremberg Party Convention of 1934, he praised the "art" of propaganda as follows: "May the shining flame of our enthusiasm never be extinguished. This flame alone gives light and warmth to the creative art of modern political propaganda. Rising from the depths of the people, this art must always descend back to it and find its power there. Power based on guns may be a good thing; it is, however, better and more gratifying to win the heart of a people and to keep it." The pictorial structure of the final scene [of *Metropolis*] confirms the analogy between the industrialist and Goebbels.

—*Sigfried Kracauer*, From Caligari to Hitler

The New Realism and the Social Milieu

It was not the horrific fantasies of the supernatural alone that gave the German film prominence and respect as a new art form in the early twenties. Another group of films, which fell under the heading of *Die neue Sachlich-keit* (the new realism), began to draw the attention of audiences and artists alike. Unlike the horror fantasies, these films were set in contemporary German cities. In fact, they have frequently been referred to as "street films," because much of their action is set in lower-class neighborhoods and concerns the struggles — social and emotional as well as physical — of the common man.

Like the expressionist fantasies, these social realist dramas were marked by their impressive visual design: controlled lighting and composition and an incredible degree of detail in setting, conjured up exclusively within the confines of the studio. They were impressive also for the exceptional acting of such major performers as Werner Krauss, Emil Jannings, and Greta Garbo. What set these films apart, however, was the use of the camera as a creative instrument in storytelling and character delineation. No longer was the camera allowed to sit on the tripod and simply record the action placed before it. Instead it explored the action, at one moment taking on the role of an unseen, inquisitive observer looking in on the "magic circle of action," the next moment actually becoming the eyes of one of the characters. Where the subjective experience had been suggested through expressionistic setting and decor in *The Cabinet of Dr. Caligari,* now the first-person subjective view was realized through the expressive positioning and movement of the camera.

Murnau — *The Last Laugh*

An early example of such visual exploration was produced in 1924, when director F. W. Murnau teamed up with scriptwriter Carl Mayer, cameraman Karl Freund, and the noted stage actor Emil Jannings to produce *The Last Laugh.* The film's narrative was deceptively simple — this was the story of a proud hotel doorman crushingly humiliated by being demoted to washroom attendant. What made the film unusual was that it was completely free of explanatory titles and its story was told entirely through picture progression. What made it an extraordinary screen drama was the tour de force acting by *both* Jannings and the camera.

In *The Last Laugh* the camera was everywhere. To film the opening scene in one shot, without cuts, cinema-

The Last Laugh (The Last Man)

"*T*he Last Man" is a film without titles. Not for theoretical reasons. But for the sake of an art. Which is the best expression of this age. It is said that motion pictures cannot be supreme art because titles are used. And titles are but an expression of literature.

Therefore, in "The Last Man" an attempt has been made. To use the medium of pictures. To express action and thought. Without words. Without titles.

A number of foreign directors have come to this country within the last few years and showed us something in the way of directing. But if F. W. Murnau ever starts directing in this country it would seem almost a certainty he would show us additional directorial feats, for his "The Last Man" gives every indication that he is a past master at the art of making pictures.

—Variety *(December 10, 1924)*

tographer Karl Freund followed the actor by sitting on a bicycle with his camera inside an open-grilled elevator, filming as the elevator descended into the open lobby, and riding through the lobby and out through the hotel's large revolving doors, camera rolling all the while. To make the scene more subjective, a medium shot was followed immediately by an extreme close-up of Jannings's eyes, so that the viewer was able to see what the character was seeing. To give the camera this point of view, various contraptions were designed enabling the camera to dolly in. Freund recalled that to help the audience feel Jannings's drunken despair, "I strapped the camera to my chest (with batteries on my back for balance) and played drunk!"

The American-born Emil Jannings had played in the earlier Lubitsch production of *Madame Du Barry* (1919), but with *The Last Laugh* he emerged as a star in his own right. His performance as the strutting hotel doorman, so proud of his braid-bedecked uniform and his

▲ From *The Last Laugh* (1924). *The Last Laugh* illustrates how unreal effects created by the "futurists" could be modified to give depth to the more traditional story film. Emil Jannings's performance here made an impact on American audiences, and Jannings was lured to Hollywood, with the film's director, producer, cinematographer, and scenic designer.

▲ From *The Last Laugh*. The final sombre scene shows the film's hero in utter humiliation and despair after his family and friends discover that he has been demoted from doorman to washroom attendant at a posh Berlin hotel.

central function, remains compelling and is impressive even by today's standards.

The acting, plot direction, and camera work in *The Last Laugh* were all widely praised. In fact, the camera work was considered so unusual that the film came to be regarded as a "cinematic curio." In addition to the international recognition the film enjoyed, the popular appeal of *The Last Laugh,* particularly with American audiences, was also assured by a change in the film's ending. The original story ended with Jannings in complete despair, huddled in a corner of the deserted washroom. But the tacked-on happy ending has him inheriting a millionaire's entire fortune, making him the guest to whom everyone must bow. Perhaps the fact that writer Carl Mayer made the millionaire an American represents a well-placed punch at the demand for tailoring Ufa products to fulfill American wishes.

Dupont — *Variety*

Pommer, Jannings and Freund were reunited in the following year, 1925, to work with director E. A. Dupont

on a second "social realist" study. *Variety* (*Vaudeville* in its original release) came to be noted for the combination of sinister theme and bold use of camera. This film served Jannings as a vehicle for expressing inner turmoil and emotional anguish, this time as a circus performer whose wife becomes the lover of a handsome young aerial artist. It also gave Freund the chance to further explore the possibilities of subjective camera work by using unusual angles, multiple exposure, and fluid movement. A notable example comes near the film's climax, when Freund once again strapped the camera to his chest, this time while swinging from a trapeze. Thus he manages to suggest not simply the physical perspective of the protagonist, but also the psychological imbalance the aerialist experiences as he swings over the crowd in the Berlin Winter Garden.

In general, the control of camera, action, and special effects in *Variety* is subtle and complex, and this control is responsible for a kind of dramatic tension that pervades the film. In one emotionally charged scene, Artinelli, a handsome trapeze artist attracted to the young wife of "Boss Müller," stops by her hotel room after her husband has left. The couple stands just inside the open bedroom door, and the window curtain flutters in the breeze created by the draught. Then, rather than focusing on the actors or subsequent action (the closing of the door), the camera stays on the open window as the curtains become still. In another scene, tension reaches a peak when Boss Müller, in a beer garden, sits down at a table on whose tablecloth someone has drawn a caricature of the new "lovers" and the cuckolded husband. Müller is kept from discovering the insult by a series of distractions and by the concealment of the drawing by a tray that a waiter has placed over it.

The skilled timing and integration of such cinematic devices made *Variety* more than the maudlin melodrama that its screenplay suggests. Here was another Ufa production so effective in its visual design that titles were almost unnecessary. Like *The Last Laugh,* despite its showy technique, the film ultimately became absorbed in the emotional drama of an individual falling victim to his own pride, jealousy, and final humiliation. This psychological bent of the social realist films provided such actors as Jannings and Werner Krauss with meaty roles through which to exercise their considerable talents. Such films were also able to satisfy current interests in Freudian psychology in a more natural and identifiable way than the expressionistic films about madmen and the subhuman.

A Review of *Variety*

In this picture [*Variety*] there is a marvelous wealth of detail; the lighting effects and camera work cause one to reflect that occasionally the screen may be connected with art. While there may be some speculation concerning the appeal of this striking piece of work, because of the tragic climax of the actual story, there is no doubt regarding its merit. Scene after scene unlocks a flood of thoughts, and although the nature of the principal characters is far from pleasing; the glimpses one obtains are so true to life that they are not repellent.

—*Film Review,* New York Times *(December 21, 1924)*

From *Variety* (1926). This dark intrigue involved illicit love and mad jealousy in a vaudeville setting.

Pabst—*Secrets of the Soul* and *The Joyless Street*

Another of the major German directors of the period, George Wilhelm Pabst, further contributed to this group of psychological studies with his *Secrets of the Soul* (1926). This film actually becomes a psychoanalytic case study of a professor (Werner Krauss) who is beset by repressed feelings of inferiority when a boyhood friend, a favorite cousin of his wife's, arrives from India. The psychosis takes the form of nightmares in which the professor attacks his wife with a dagger. The dream sequences here provide an interesting link with the expressionist films of the period and serve as forerunners of the cinema psychodrama to follow, in films ranging from Hitchcock's *Spellbound* and *Marnie* to Bergman's *Persona* and *Through a Glass Darkly.*

In German social realism, the psychological drama was frequently combined with a study of the social milieu in urban settings. As noted earlier, *Die neue Sachlichkeit* is in fact usually given the label of street films. The

▶ From *The Street*. In the social realist films, the action was frequently set in the streets, workplaces, and general milieu of the lower middle classes.

label referred to the location of the action (*not* where the films were shot), but it was also linked to the recurrence of the word *street* in the titles (*The Street, The Tragedy of the Street, The Joyless Street*).

Pabst's *The Joyless Street* (1925) perhaps best exemplifies this group of works, in which social rather than psychological stresses are central to the dramatic development. The characters of this film leave the psychological interior of the mind for the *angst* represented by the exterior and physical world, experiencing the social and economic terror of the period, with its destitute masses and merciless profiteers. Here Pabst naturalized the "street" genre even further by exploring the vices of the management class and the brute selfishness of the petty bourgeoisie. A simple secretary (Greta Garbo) is caught between the forces of moral degeneracy and an inept social institution. Garbo's naturalness and sheer beauty captured the hearts of the world. With Asta Nielsen, the pin-up of World War I, also featured in the film, *The*

▲ From *The Joyless Street* (1925). Entire city blocks were built within the Ufa studios for this film, so that complete control could be exerted over the material.

Joyless Street was a success despite its portrayal of American relief agents living it up in cabarets while talking clinically about the poor they were sent to relieve. Like *The Cabinet of Dr. Caligari* and *The Last Laugh* before it, *The Joyless Street* was given an upbeat ending — an American Red Cross worker arrives on the scene to save the damsel in distress.

Migration

When foreign audiences had a choice between seeing a movie made in their own country and one made in the United States, it was usually the American offering that won at the box office. To protect its own emerging industry, Germany had established quotas on American imports, and there were demands in the United States for reprisals against the former enemy. But when Germany's *Madame Du Barry* (*Passion* [1919]), directed by Lubitsch, reached America in 1920, the premiere at Philadelphia's Bellevue-Stratford Hotel was hailed as the social event of the year. Twelve hundred of the city's socialites crowded into the ballroom to acclaim the "emotional actress," Pola Negri.

When the next Lubitsch picture became available, Paramount grabbed it for American distribution. As *Passion* had brought to life the French story of Madame DuBarry, *Deception* (1920) offered the biography of the English queen, Anne Boleyn, and King Henry VIII. The American industry took notice of Lubitsch's name, and critics praised *Deception*. They cited particularly Lubitsch's understanding of historical fact and his ability to blend it with fictitious details, his control of the spectacular crowd scenes, his manipulation of the tempo, his sensitive handling of the tragic and violent scenes, and his "discriminative" use of the close-up. American directors, it was said, had something to learn from Lubitsch.

Gypsy Blood (1918), drawn from *Carmen,* arrived from Germany in 1921, and *The Loves of Pharaoh* (1921) in 1922. Exhibitors were advised to sell these pictures by linking them with the successful *Passion.* And in 1923 Warner Brothers signed Lubitsch to direct a series of eighteen adaptations from "classic" literature.

Some in the industry became worried by these developments, and Congress was again petitioned to place a stiff tariff on German imports. "Let the hysteria stop because it makes us as an industry look rather silly before the world," urged one trade magazine. The Germans began to wonder if after all they might be destined to

Film's Secret Attractions

*W*hat is it in the films of some foreign manufacturers that makes them in such demand in this country? It certainly is not the subjects, the plots of which are, as a rule, mentally (and often morally) below the level of those attempted by American producers. It cannot be said, either, that our home manufacturers are behind in the tricks of stagecraft and scene painting, nor are they at a disadvantage in the choice of outdoor settings. What is this mysterious something in certain films which attracts, while others are insipid, notwithstanding that the subject may be of greater merit?

—Moving Picture World
(October 17, 1908)

dominate world cinema. If American audiences could so easily be entertained by Hollywood's naive films, why couldn't Germany come to dominate even the American screen with more complicated, sophisticated, and realistic films? From Universal Studios, Carl Laemmle was heard to exclaim, "Let it come. Healthy competition never did any man or organization any harm." But the steady stream of unique Ufa products would worry some Americans throughout the 1920s. And as *Passion, Variety,* and *The Joyless Street* continued to draw substantial American audiences, it was even proposed that the export of raw film stock be reduced to put a crimp in German production. However, the eventual eclipse of the prestigious and popular German silents was not the result of limiting film stock. In April 1925, Murnau was hired by Fox. Lang and Pommer soon followed to other U.S. studios. Screenwriter Carl Mayer and cinematographer Karl Freund left Ufa in 1927 to begin work on *Berlin: Symphony of a Great City,* a camera study of a day in the life of Berlin. The film reflected a radically different style of filmmaking that would eventually lead to documentary filmmaking. Freund was soon to join the exodus to Hollywood, where, for the next two decades, many films were to exhibit a strikingly Germanic style.

▶ From *Berlin, The Symphony of a Great City* (1927). This film marked a new direction for a production team noted for the "street films" it heretofore produced entirely within the studio. Conceived by Carl Mayer as a "melody of pictures," it gave cinematographer Karl Freund the opportunity to escape the confines of the studio. Walther Ruttmann, collaborated with Edward Meisel on a symphonic composition for this early sound documentary.

The End of the Golden Age

Although the migration to Hollywood drained Germany's talent pool, a few distinguished works were made during the twilight of Germany's golden age.

von Sternberg — *The Blue Angel*

The Blue Angel (1930), Ufa's first major sound film, was based on the book by Heinrich Mann. The film was directed by Josef von Sternberg, who was brought from the United States to Germany by Erich Pommer. Besides marking a high point in its director's career, *The Blue Angel* also extended the distinguished acting career of Emil Jannings (already established in Hollywood). Jannings here played a spiritless professor who is suddenly ignited by a sexy Lola, a nightclub singer and dancer played by Marlene Dietrich.

Visually, the film reflects the style perfected by the German system. Its use of sound, however, was unlike the "all talking, all singing, all dancing" format that was already monotonously commonplace. When the professor walks into his classroom, it is filled with undisciplined students and chaotic noise; when he leaves, it is deadly silent, and pity for the old man flows out of the room on the screen and into the theater. This film demonstrated that silence can strengthen nonverbal expression. The professor falls hopelessly—mindlessly—in love with the performer, leaves the profession he has come to hate, and becomes a clown in Lola's troop. Former students now in the audience boo him from the stage. With a Shylock-like howl, he tries to kill his Lola—who never was "his"—and we see him at the end slumped over his teacher's desk. *The Blue Angel* led Germany into the sound era and also extended the darker brooding qualities of the social realist film.

Lang — *M*

Fritz Lang made his own contribution to social realism in the real world with his 1931 movie *M*, a remarkable experiment in early sound that used a chilling story of the underworld in pursuit of a pathological killer as an extension of the "street film." Peter Lorre plays the child murderer from Düsseldorf who is hunted by both the police and the underworld. As the pressure builds and the need to kill again mounts sickeningly in his mind, he whistles a melody from Grieg. Thereafter, even when we cannot see him, his whistled madness signals his presence.

M preserved all the best of silent film technique while its makers plotted functions for sound that must have impressed D. W. Griffith and other pioneer filmmakers. Composition, lighting, camera movement, set design—all the traditional hallmarks of silent German cinema are kept in place. It is the function of sound (and silence) that made the movie both a masterpiece *and* a box-office success.

A little girl named Elsie plays in the street. The psychopath approaches, casting his shadow on the poster advertising a reward for his apprehension. Meanwhile, the girl's mother prepares lunch: the clock ticks, the table is set, the soup is hot, but no Elsie. Concern shows in the mother's face. The clock strikes twelve, and no little girl appears. The mother rushes into the hallway, calling Elsie's name, and the camera looks down the empty stairwell. Silence. The child's balloon drifts up and away but is caught in utility wires. And we know that the child murderer has struck again.

There is an atmosphere of futility and inevitability in *M* that echoes the feeling in *The Blue Angel*. The child murderer, like the professor, is on a path to destruction. *M* shows a police force using all the latest techniques in criminal investigation but unable to root out the psychopath. Only members of the underworld, under the leadership of a leather-coated, black-gloved figure—the

A Song Popular Among German Film People in the Early 1930s

Es geht der Dolly gut   For Dolly everything is OK
Sie sits in Hollywood   Sitting at a table
An einen Tish   With Lilian Gish in Hollywood
Mit Lilian Gish   And where am I?
Und wo bin ich?   And where am I?
Und wo bin ich?

         —*La Biennale di Venezia*

Nazis?—are able to find the killer. When they do, they drag him into a deserted brewery where they try and convict him in their own underworld court. It must have been eerie to see the film in Germany while "Brown Shirts" sang the Horst Wessel song, which commemorated a slain Nazi hero, outside in the street.

M illustrated a fusion of the psychological drama and the social realist drama, or street film. Like the Freudian case studies in repression, it focuses on the individual and internal stress. And like the street films such as *Variety* and *The Joyless Street,* it draws on the social milieu of lower-class urban life for its setting. *M* ushered in the age of sound in Europe and at the same time provided something of a reprieve and extension for the golden age of silent cinema, already in decline by the mid-twenties.

Pabst — *Kameradschaft*

In 1932, the year before Hitler became Chancellor of Germany, G. W. Pabst produced *Kameradschaft,* which provided an ironic conclusion to the era. This film was a documentarylike drama about a mine disaster and rescue involving international cooperation on the Franco-German border. Pabst used the story as a plea for international understanding and peace. French miners are trapped in the mine, and on the other side of the border, German miners, despite the reluctance of the officials, break down a barrier in a long-abandoned tunnel to rescue their French counterparts. After the rescue, the barrier is replaced, cutting off the light that was briefly allowed to shine. Here Pabst seems to be anticipating the dark days of German isolation that were to follow.

Wrap-Up

Germany's loss of its distinguished "place in the sun" may have happened partly because the movement had simply run its course. Innovations in technique and originality of theme no longer had the appeal of daring experiments. Some filmmakers were feeling cramped by working strictly within the confines of the studio. There is little doubt that Germany's demise as a filmmaking center was hastened by the migration of much of the country's top talent. It is also clear that the government sealed the fate of German film by imposing new sociopolitical requirements on the industry.

In 1933, Hitler was named chancellor of Germany. He called on Goebbels to head his propaganda ministry, and all the mass media were put under the control of the dictatorship. The film industry's purpose became "to receive those tasks which it has to fulfill in the National Socialist State."

With the exception of a few documentaries and newsreels (see Chapter 14), no films of interest were produced under the Nazi regime. Indeed, German audiences abhorred the blatantly propaganda-ridden features that were produced in the early Nazi years. The few Hollywood "B" pictures that were allowed into the country drew large audiences in comparison. Goebbels relented in pressuring the film industry, and the Propaganda Ministry began to depend mainly on the press and radio. And as the power and direction of the "1000-year" Reich became clear, another exodus of German talent took place.

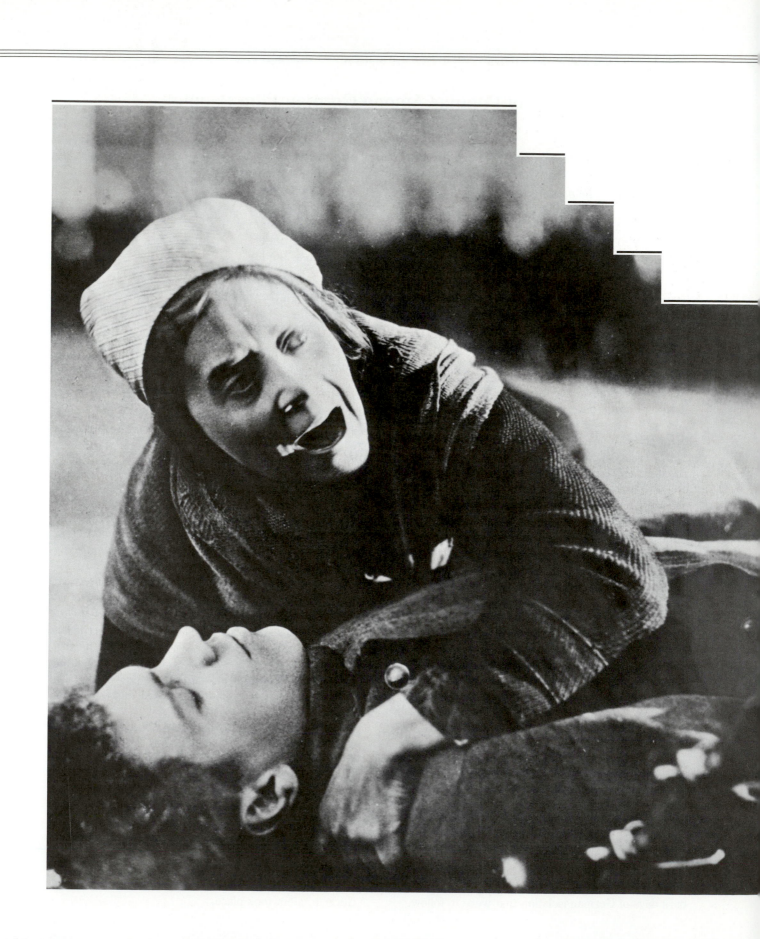

5

The Soviet Silent Film (1918–1930)

Focus

On October 15, 1926, David O. Selznick, an MGM producer and director, dictated one of his numerous memos to his boss, Harry Rapf:

> It was my privilege a few months ago to be present at two private screenings of what is unquestionably one of the greatest motion pictures ever made. *The Armoured Cruiser Potemkin,* made in Russia under the supervision of the Soviet Government. . . . It possesses a technique entirely new to the screen, and I therefore suggest that it might be very advantageous to have the organization view it in the same way that a group of artists might view a Rubens or a Raphael.

Selznick noted that there were no individual characters and no studio sets in this piece of "superb craftsmanship"; he also noted the strength of character types, lack of make-up, "exquisite pieces of photography," and "starkly realistic dramatic scenes."

In what had become standard studio procedure, Selznick suggested that his organization "consider securing the man responsible for it, a young Russian director named Eisenstein."

Who was this Eisenstein, and what was going on in the Soviet Union that gathered comment from Hollywood moguls and American critics? New film ideas had burst forth from a defeated Germany, and now again they were emanating from Red revolutionaries just recovering from civil war and devastating famine.

What Selznick saw at a private screening, New Yorkers were soon seeing on their downtown movie screens — despite prevailing Red-scare mongering and a general distrust of things and people foreign. The film on the screen was shockingly different from American and

A Russian Perspective

*T*o the American adventure film with its showy dynamism and to the dramatizations of the American Pinkertons the kinoks [a nickname for Russian filmmakers and theorists] say thanks for the rapid shot changes and the close-ups. Good . . . but disorderly, not based on a precise study of movement. A cut above the psychological drama, but still lacking in foundation. A cliché. A copy of a copy.

—*Dziga Vertov, "We: Variant of a Manifesto"*

German productions. Unlike the Germans, the Soviets emphasized real locations, not expressionist or studio renderings. But even though the Soviets had returned to Lumière's world of surface reality, they were obviously able to penetrate to deep emotional and psychological levels. Rather than probing subterranean, Freudian depths, these films were uplifting, inspiring experiences.

Nevertheless, because their production system was in harmony with the creative impulse, Russian filmmakers had little preoccupation with box-office appeal and mass entertainment values. They did not cater to American audiences' needs for escapist entertainment (see accompanying box), but such films as *Potemkin* by Eisenstein and *Mother* by Pudovkin were to generate among those viewers who responded to the aesthetic and cultural values of films the same kind of excitement that *The Cabinet of Dr. Caligari* had generated. In 1923 Lenin had asked Griffith to come to the Soviet Union to head Soviet production; soon Hollywood studios were planning to draw Soviet filmmakers to Hollywood.

Before the Revolution

*T*he year 1896 marked the first public showing of motion pictures in Petrograd as well as New York. Among the Russian film clips on display was one on the coronation of Czar Nicholas II. Still, until 1908 Russian movies rarely showed Russian events or told Russian stories. Dominated by the French film companies, the movies shown to Russian audiences were imported on a large scale. However, news bits, like the crowning of Nicholas, were hits, and soon many such recordings of actual events were making their way onto the screen. But Russian audiences tired of these Lumière-type bits and pieces, and the first narratives of Russian material, although made by foreigners, were immediately successful. Soon Pathé was exporting to the United States topical dramas about Jewish life and the pogroms of czarist days. Meanwhile, the Russian police were keeping a close watch on all newsreel materials and film dramatizations of Russian events.

Filmmaking in Russia during the final days of the Romanov Dynasty was not marked by the kind of experimentation and invention that characterized the work of Ince, Griffith, and Chaplin during this period. Rather, feature films in production by the early teens were mostly an undistinguished assortment of costume spectacles and adventure films patterned after the Italian spectacles and early American Westerns.

Romanov rule ended in March 1917 with the deposition of Czar Nicholas. On March 8 the czar had received a telegram from David Selznick offering him a job in the movies. At the same time, events surrounding the revolution were duly recorded on motion picture film in the streets of Moscow and Petrograd, and on May 1 of the following year Edward Tissé, soon to become the most celebrated of the Soviet cinematographers, was filming the first May Day celebration in Red Square.

While in exile in Switzerland, Lenin had spent considerable time in newsreel theaters, marvelling over the medium's potential for documenting real events and molding public thought. He returned to Petrograd to declare that "of all the arts, for us the cinema is the most important." Ironically, the czar spent his last days in isolation, watching films at his private theater in the Winter Palace.

The central role that movies were to play in the development of the new Soviet state is revealed in the events that followed the 1917 revolution. By June 1918, a Cinema Committee had begun production of the first Soviet film, *Signal*. August of the following year marked the centralization of the Russian film industry under the People's Commissariat of Propaganda and Education. And 1920 saw the opening of the State Film School in Moscow. These events not only solidified the government's control over the medium but also infused the films produced with a strong sense of Soviet nationalism and revolutionary spirit. Besides serving as a vehicle for artistic expression, motion pictures now assumed a new role — as tools for expressing Soviet ideology.

Creative Geography

L. V. Kuleshov assembled in the year 1920 the following scenes as an experiment:

1. A young man walks from left to right.
2. A woman walks from right to left.
3. They meet and shake hands. The young man points.
4. A large white building is shown, with a broad flight of steps.
5. The two ascend the steps.

The pieces, separately shot, were assembled in the order given and projected upon the screen. The spectator was presented with the pieces thus joined as one clear, uninterrupted action: a meeting of two young people, an invitation to a nearby house, and an entry into it. Every single piece, however, had been shot in a different place; for example, the young man near the G.U.M. building, the woman near Gogol's monument, the handshake near the Bolshoi Theatre, the white house came out of an American picture (it was, in fact, *the* White House), and the ascent of the steps was made in St. Saviour's Cathedral.

—*V. I. Pudovkin*, Film Technique and Film Acting *(1958)*

The universal appeal and dynamic quality of film made it a perfect government tool in the sociopolitical education of the people, particularly the vast, multilingual, and largely illiterate masses. To make the medium and its revolutionary message available to everyone, particularly people in remote areas, the government converted trucks, trains, and even ships at pierside into movie theaters. These *agitpoeza* or *agittrains* rumbled across the far reaches of the Soviet Union, establishing the presence of the Bolshevik government and espousing Communist party propaganda by means of such "instructive newsreels" as *October Revolution* and *The Festival of Communist Youth,* which toured extensively via Russian rail through 1919 and 1920.

Kuleshov and Vertov: Soviet Film Pioneers

The three years following the Russian Revolution and the birth of the Soviet state saw civil war within the Russian army, invasion of Russia by Western powers,

trade embargos, extensive famine, and finally economic collapse. During the chaos of the Revolution, many in the Russian film industry fled to Western Europe, and a great many of those went to Paris. One who remained to become a dominant figure in the training of new talent at the State School was Lev Kuleshov.

When *The Birth of a Nation* and *Intolerance* reached the Soviet Union, smuggled in from Germany, Kuleshov and others were amazed by the use of close-ups and parallel action (the superb battle scenes of *The Birth of a Nation* and the four themes worked into *Intolerance*). Already these Soviet filmmakers were getting a good deal of experience with editing. Unable to shoot the films they wanted because they lacked equipment and film stock, they set about re-editing shots in existing films, both of fictional stories and real-life events, to make them say what they wished. The Russian filmmakers were already fascinated with the possibilities and the power of the editing process, and they recut the earlier American masterpieces time and again, each time delighted with the effects produced.

Kuleshov began to wonder if the reality of a shot's context was at all important. To test his idea, he conducted what was to become a noted experiment in cinematography. First he filmed a close-up of veteran actor

Mosjukhin, who showed no particular emotional expression. Then he shot a bowl of soup, a child at play, and an old woman lying in a coffin. To each of these he attached a section of the close-up of the actor, and when he projected the results, viewers noted the superb acting. The old man's face and the bowl of soup created a new meaning: hunger. Old man plus child at play equals the pleasure and delight of a grandfather. Old man plus woman in coffin equals sorrow.

And so, working from Griffith's pioneering efforts, Kuleshov concentrated on shot juxtaposition, finding that he could greatly intensify emotional response. He achieved something like what Franklin Schaffner did in *Patton* (1970). When the figure of Patton is first introduced, a series of extreme close-ups follows: shots of the medals on the chest, the helmet, the riding crop, the holster, and other such details. With these juxtapositions, the figure of Patton takes on heightened emotional qualities that could never have been achieved with merely a long or medium shot.

Russian cinema had begun with documentary films—newsreels recording the end of the Romanov Dynasty, the drama of the Revolution, and the glories of the Soviet Communist movement and the leaders. Theorists and filmmakers alike were singing the praises of the new medium and the way it allowed a view of real-world drama through the eye of the camera. And Dziga Vertov discovered new ways of photographing and editing documentary material. "The basic and most important thing is the 'cine-perception' of the world," wrote Vertov. "The starting point is the use of the cine-camera as a 'cinema-eye,' more perfect than the human variety, in order to explore the chaos of visual phenomena filling space."

Throughout the early twenties, in *Leniniana, Kino-Eye, March On, Soviet, The Man With a Movie Camera,* and *Three Songs About Lenin,* Vertov experimented with his approach to documentation, which he considered a complex method that led to great simplicity. Through his "Kino-Eye" approach, he led the experimental study of the real world by using montage — the creative assembling of film material — to put life into some coherent and meaningful pattern.

Vertov carried on his experiments in documentary in 1922, giving them the collective title *Kino-Pravda. Kino-Glaz* (Film Eye) was the name adopted by Dziga Vertov and his brother Mikhail Kaufman for the group they formed to produce these twenty-three newsreels between 1922 and 1925. Through each of these episodes, made up of a mixture of footage from various sources, he attempted to show that the scientific precision of the camera (or "mechanical eye"), which perceives the world "without a mask, as a world of naked truth," could be used by means of creative editing to

I Am an Eye

*W*e are taking untrodden paths. Inventing and experimenting, we made films that were newspaper leaders, satirical articles, essays or poems.

I am eye, I am a mechanical eye. I, a machine, am showing you a world, the likes of which only I can see. . . . My road is toward the creation of a fresh perception of the world. Thus I decipher in a new way the world unknown to you.

—*Dziga Vertov, quoted in* Soviet Film *(July 1967)*

produce an expressive kind of truth. Vertov recognized the implications of the Kuleshov experiments and combined footage shot in different places at different times to produce meaningful sequences. Through several feature films as well as subsequent installments of *Kino Pravda,* Vertov developed a method of creating structural symmetry into which diverse images could be brought together to emphasize parallel or contrasting relationships. In *Kino-Eye* (1924), the arrangement of contrasting images takes on a political dimension, as old and new, youth and age, disease and health, and progressive and reactionary methods are contrasted.

Vertov's formalism reached a peak with his *Man with a Movie Camera* (1929). The film is ostensibly a tour of Moscow but is also a tour de force of technical virtuosity in which the camera and cameraman (Vertov's brother, Mikhail Kaufman) are the stars. The film is a full-blown study of the relation of film and reality: a movie audience is shown watching the film we are seeing; the cameraman is shown photographing a scene; this scene is followed by alternating shots of the scene as viewed by the camera and by the subject being photographed. We are finally shown the shots we have just viewed being edited in the laboratory.

Both Kuleshov and Vertov realized that, up to their time, little of the medium's potential had been realized. They saw that by editing shots as "plastic material" they could extend the range of relationships among individual shots and the overall function of the editing process.

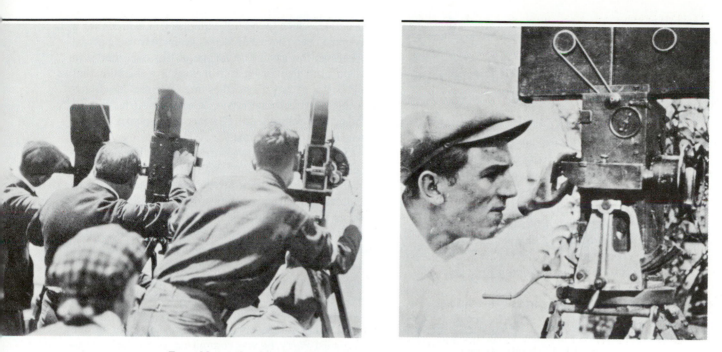

▲ From *Man with a Movie Camera* (1929). This film was Kino-Glaz's best-known work. It was as much a display of cinematic technique as it was film journalism: Eisenstein called it "purposeless camera hooliganism." Dziga Vertov was assisted in cinematography by his brother Mikhail Kaufman who, as cameraman for the movie, also became its star. *Kino-Glaz (Film Eye)* was the name Vertov and Kaufman adopted for the group they formed to produce twenty-three newsreels between 1922 and 1925 known as *Kino Pravda (Film Truth).*

Excited by the possibilities, Vertov would go on with his experimental editing and film theories, leaving production for the masses to others.

As this overview of the pioneers' work suggests, despite the centralization of all Russian film production under the People's Commissariat of Propaganda and Education in 1919, filmmakers in Russia had the freedom to pursue their inventiveness unhampered by political factors.

Eisenstein and the Collision of Images

Sergei Eisenstein, born in Riga, Latvia, in 1898, began his studies in engineering and architecture, but after service in the Red Army, he was gradually drawn to the arts. He went from poster design to set design, and finally to a position as a director of the Moscow Proletkult Theater. Here, under the tutelage of producer Vsevolod Meyerhold, he developed a radical style in theater

▲ Sergei Eisenstein, seen here clowning on the czar's throne, where events of the past were re-enacted for his film, *October* (1928).

A Gathering of Talents

*E*ach of us has come to the world of film-making by his own way. For instance, there is Pudovkin, a chemist; Dovzhenko, a teacher; here I am, an engineer; Dzigan, whom I remember as an actor at the Rakhmanova Studio; Kozintsev, Yutkevich, Kuleshov, all painters; Alexandrov, a cinema operator, theatre props-man and electrician; Ermler, of the Cheka; Shengelaya, a poet, and so on. . . .

The all-powerful storm of the October Revolution uprooted all of us from the most diverse activities and occupations, swept us away with its mighty streams and, combining into one whole everything we had brought with us from various fields of knowledge and activity, set us working at a great and collective endeavour—our cinematography.

—*Sergei Eisenstein,
quoted in* Soviet Film
(July, 1967)

production, which found full expression in *Gas Masks,* a play staged in an actual Moscow gas factory using actual workers as the cast. The failure of this experiment in realism propelled Eisenstein into film, a medium that could better satisfy his need to integrate real-life drama into the theatrical experience. At this point in his career, as he himself remarked, "The cart fell to pieces and the driver fell into the cinema."

Strike! (1924), which *Pravda* called "The first genuinely revolutionary film," was also Eisenstein's first film effort. It was intended to document (and dramatize) the prerevolutionary struggles of the Russian working class as they challenged industrial leaders by resisting factory owners, pursuing underground activities, and finally going on strike. The film began a tradition in the use of actual locations for setting, and was the first film in which the masses appeared as the collective hero. *Strike!* also marked the beginning of the extraordinary association of Eisenstein and cinematographer Eduard Tissé.

Although Eisenstein was never a member of the Communist Party, he was committed to the ideals of the Revolution. He turned to the material of the collective experience and the historical events that formed the new political experiment. And to this material he brought the thinking and techniques formulated by Kuleshov and others. By shooting and editing selectively, he produced his own documents and his own arguments, much as a historian does with selected facts and selected words.

Even in *Strike!,* Eisenstein had begun to experiment with the complex method of montage construction that would become a hallmark of his work. Intellectual montage for Eisenstein was the creation of a visual metaphor through the combination of two or more shots to communicate an abstract idea that eludes visual representation through a single image. When shots of butchers killing a bull were combined with czarist cavalry cutting down the masses of workers in the street, the intended metaphor became crystal clear. The result was anything but the smoothly edited matching-action material that Russian filmmakers saw as characterizing the passivity-inducing Hollywood films. This combination of images agitated, shocked, and compelled the viewer into participation.

◀ From *Strike!* (1924), Eisenstein's first film, and a showcase for the filmmaker's complex theory of montage construction. Oppression and despair in a czarist factory lead to a strike and ultimately to open warfare between capitalists and the labor force.

Said Eisenstein, "Any two pieces of film stuck together inevitably combine to create a new concept, a new quality born of the juxtaposition." Japanese calligraphy had actually inspired the idea: combine the symbols for heart and dagger to get a symbol of sorrow. Soon filmmakers everywhere were talking about "montage," that "technique entirely new to the screen," as Selznick had noted.

Though *Strike!* and the several epics to follow were based on historical events, they were history much manipulated and altered. Soviet films were no longer newsreel recordings; rather, they were political treatises in dramatic dress. And it was editing, or montage, that held the key to generating revolutionary ideas through the manipulation of historical incidents. Using the abortive revolution of 1905 as a backdrop, Eisenstein set about in his next film to dramatize a key incident involving the mutiny of a ship's crew at the port city of Odessa. In the five-part *Potemkin,* constructed with mathematical precision, the themes of revolution and brotherhood are combined as the ship's crew and Odessa citizens join to challenge czarist oppression. Eisenstein was offering his own challenge to the old methods of constructive editing and linkage in favor of diverse and radical means of joining images. Here was editing for shock, attention, interpretation — he juxtaposed visual symbols to produce a shock of recognition and a new meaning through the association of images. An officer's sword in a close-up revealing the elaborate hilt is followed by a close-up of the Orthodox chaplain holding a crucifix; the point is that one barrier to social change is the close relationship between the czarist regime and the church, which reinforced government control over the people.

Given his fascination for shot combinations, Eisenstein developed another technique. A crew member on mess duty is setting the tables. Fury is growing, because the meat intended for the meal is full of maggots. A critical moment in the life of the sailor comes as he picks up a plate. The moment of his radicalization occurs when he notices, perhaps for the first time in his life, the phrase, "give us this day our daily bread" painted on the edge of the dish. Eisenstein takes this moment and breaks it down into a number of separate shots — the man grabs the plate, raises it over his head, and slams it

▶ From *Potemkin* (1925). The arousal of the masses in response to czarist oppression is shown through a montage of three shots of stone lions.

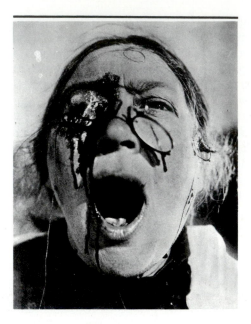

◢ From *Potemkin*. The director himself describes the construction of the Odessa Steps sequence: "And then, as the *downward* movement reaches its culmination, the movement is suddenly reversed: instead of the headlong rush of the *crowd* down the steps we see the *solitary* figure of a mother carrying her dead son, *slowly* and *solemnly* going up the steps."

◀ From *Potemkin*. Eisenstein writes: "Suddenly the tempo of the running crowd leaps over into the next category of speed—into a rolling baby-carriage."

▲ From *Potemkin*. "Close-ups leap over into long-shots," Eisenstein writes of the Odessa Steps montage.

down, breaking it into pieces. The truth Eisenstein was after was the psychological condition at a moment of crisis—which in retrospect *seems* to have lasted forever. The film experience evokes the feeling, common in dreams, of being unable to move except in slow motion.

Griffith had done a masterful job of reducing real time to make screen time tolerable for the viewer. After all, most experience in life is quite dull. Eisenstein, on the other hand, *expanded* real time on the screen, finding a way to communicate visually a psychological reality that everyone has experienced. This expansion of time occurs at several points in *Potemkin,* most dramatically in "The

Odessa Steps Sequence," in which the townspeople who have come out in support of the Potemkin's mutinous crew are slaughtered. This sequence effectively illustrates Eisenstein's use of the "collision of images" to complement the collision of forces within the narrative.

What fascinated Eisenstein was not complicated and abstract film theory, but a quality worked into the film itself, a quality that was apparent to the viewers, however far removed they might be from the process of its construction. The *New York Times* noted "an excellent conception of rhythm . . . a sort of purr to this picture as it is unfurled."

Two Views of the Odessa Steps Sequence

A cripple moves suddenly. The armed guard press slowly, pitilessly, down the broad stone steps, abreast. Only terror now. A woman rushes down the steps with her child. She misses him. He has been shot down. She runs with the boy in her arms, chattering, pleading, into the fire from the guard. A beautiful young mother in a mantilla wheeling a baby carriage, falls on the stones. Down, down, gathering speed in its flight, whistles the carriage.

—The action on the Odessa Steps as described by Evelyn Gerstein in her New Republic *review of October 20, 1926*

*F*irst, there are *close-ups* of human figures rushing chaotically. Then, *long-shots* of the same scene. The *chaotic movement* is next superseded by shots showing the feet of soldiers as they march *rhythmically* down the steps.

Tempo increases. Rhythm accelerates.

And then, as the *downward* movement reaches its culmination, the movement is suddenly reversed: instead of the headlong rush of the *crowd* down the steps we see the *solitary* figure of a mother carrying her dead son, *slowly*, and *solemnly going* up the steps.

Mass. Headlong rush. *Downward.* And all of a sudden—

A *solitary* figure. Slow and solemn. *Going up.* But only for a moment. Then again *a leap in the reverse direction. Downward* movement.

Rhythm accelerates. Tempo increases.

The shot of *the rushing crowd* is suddenly followed by one showing a perambulator [baby carriage] hurtling down the steps. This is more than just different tempos. This is *a leap in the method of representation*—from the abstract to the physical. This gives one more aspect of the downward movement.

Close-ups, accordingly, give place to *long shots*. The *chaotic* rush (of the mass) is succeeded by the *rhythmic* march of the soldiers. One aspect of movement (people running, falling, tumbling down steps) gives way to another (rolling perambulator). *Descent* gives place to *ascent. Many* volleys of *many* rifles give place to *one* shot from *one* of the battleship's guns.

At each step there is a leap from one dimension to another, from one quality to another, until, finally, the change affects not one individual episode (the perambulator) but the whole of the method: the risen lions mark the point where the *narrative* turns into a *presentation through images.*

The visible steps of the stairs marking the downward progress of action corresponds to steps marking qualitative leaps but proceeding in the opposite direction of mounting intensity.

—As described by Eisenstein in The Film Form, *1949*

Although Max Reinhardt, Douglas Fairbanks, and many audiences and critics sang *Potemkin's* praises, and many American leftists joined in, others were shocked and worried over its strong and affecting revolutionary edge. Germany and England were initially opposed to the film's exhibition, and in America there was concern that *Potemkin* would be banned by the industry's own watchdog committee. However, the film was not banned but was shown in large cities to critical acclaim. The *New York Times* listed it as one of the top ten films for 1926. In Russia, *Potemkin* was billed by the Commissariat as "the pride of the Soviet Cinema." In just two years, its director had become both the foremost spokesman for Soviet film propaganda and the central and revolutionary force in Russian film theory and aesthetics.

Eisenstein's next film, *October* (known in the United States as *Ten Days That Shook the World*) was inspired by American journalist John Reed's historical account of the 1917 revolution. The film was commissioned by the Central Committee of the Communist Party in 1927 to commemorate the tenth anniversary of the Bolshevik Revolution. Eisenstein chose to center the action on the rise and fall of the provisional government under Alexander Kerensky, using actual locations in Petrograd (now Leningrad) for settings. The film lacks the unity of *Potemkin* and also sacrifices emotional involvement, becoming a rather cold intellectual exercise in the service of its ideology. But Eisenstein used the film to further extend the possibilities of montage construction.

We watch the people, small in scale, attaching long ropes to an enormous statue of the czar. As in the sailor's smashing of the plate and the shooting of the mother standing near her baby carriage in *Potemkin,* multiple shots are used to show the statue falling to the ground in expanded real time. Shortly afterwards, when Alexander Kerensky is in power, the statue returns to its former position, arms and other pieces coming back into place (the first shots run again, backwards), to demonstrate symbolically that Kerensky's attempt at democratizing the government is a return to all the Bolsheviks had fought against.

Having restored the death penalty, Kerensky stands at the head of the palatial staircase, arms folded (he was previously compared to a mechanical peacock spreading its fanning tail). Cut: a statue of Napoleon in a similar posture. Here, in solid Marxist fashion, Soviet montage displays thesis, antithesis, and synthesis. Thesis: Ker-

▲ *Ten Days That Shook the World (October)* (1927). Here Eisenstein reruns the scene in which the czar's statue is pulled down — seen earlier — this time backwards, to symbolize the return of autocratic rule under Kerensky's provisional government.

ensky, new head of state; antithesis, Napoleon, symbol of vain, despotic rule; and synthesis, a new meaning given to the character of Kerensky.

In a feverishly dramatic sequence involving a drawbridge, Eisenstein creates intense pity and terror. The people are trying to escape from the city's center and return to their houses in the working-class suburbs, but they must cross the drawbridge to make good their escape. Metric and rhythmic montage cut between the people and the objective — the bridge — which is slowly rising to cut off their escape. At the end of the rising sections of the bridge lies the body of a girl, and at the other end a horse hitched to a carriage. Each time the shot returns to the slowly rising bridge, our anxiety for the escaping people, the horse, and the body of the girl (her soft hair slowly tumbling into the crevice of the parting roadway) continues to rise. Then the bridge sections come almost upright, preventing any escape. The horse, dangling in its harness and hanging over the edge, suddenly breaks loose from the carriage and plunges into the water below as the carriage careens down the roadway. Then, in a long shot, the body of the girl drops through space and into the Neva River, which divides the workers' quarter from the rest of the city.

Metaphor through montage is further extended by the intercutting of shots of trilling harps and balalaikas with those of Mensheviks — Congress members who advocated compromise, according to Eisenstein — speaking before the Soviet Congress. Here the tiresome strumming of the musical instruments is equated with "the empty speeches in the face of the gathering storm of historical events," in Eisenstein's own words.

Eisenstein came under increasing attack at home for "barren intellectualism" and personal indulgence in expression whose meaning escaped the general Soviet audience. *October* was attacked for its "formalist excess," and Eisenstein's aesthetics and Soviet ideology began to show increasing strain. A new Stalinist regime brought the expulsion of Leon Trotsky from the Politburo of the Communist Party and required that the considerable footage devoted to this central figure in the film be expurgated.

Eisenstein's final silent film, *The General Line* (1929; renamed *Old and New*), was a tribute to the new agricultural collective, an attempt, according to its director, "to exalt the pathos of everyday existence." Unlike his previous works, this film centers on a single character — a peasant woman, Marfa, who leads the way in progressive farming. Memorable scenes include Marfa's fascination with the newly arrived cream separator and her vision of the flower-bedecked mating of cow and bull.

The Inspiration for a Filmic Metaphor

*I*t must have been God's will that prompted me one early dawn, after an all-night session of shooting interiors of Tsar Nicholas's library, to look out the window and see the gigantic jaws of the Palace Bridge raised to the sky like the arms of a drowning man. And all at once, there on the blades of the bridge appeared the vision of the battered buggy and the wounded horse, and the golden sunbeams playing on it became the strands of a dying girl's golden hair.

That is why the ex-engineer was crawling inside the mechanical bowels of the Palace Bridge and calculating with its operators how to maintain a certain rhythm and tempo in raising the bridge, resulting in one of the most powerful scenes in *October.*

Later, the bridge grew into a symbol. The symbol of separation between the center of the city and its working-class suburbs.

—*Sergei M. Eisenstein,* Immoral Memories: An Autobiography *(translated by Herbert Marshall)*

Despite its lovely imagery and the refinement in montage technique the film reveals, *Old and New* is frequently ignored in reviews of the Eisenstein legacy. Although the film was popular in Russia at the time of its release, it was bitterly denounced by the party, and at a time when both Eisenstein's creative energy and his international reputation were at their peak.

Before the release of *Old and New,* it had been rumored that Eisenstein would be coming to America to work for United Artists. Indeed, there was a great affinity between the work of Soviet filmmakers and that of

Eisenstein on His Films

Strike! **(1924)** "We brought collective and mass action on the screen, in contrast to individualism and the 'triangle of drama of the bourgeois cinema.'"

Potemkin **(1925)** "*Potemkin* looks like a chronicle (or newsreel) of an event, but it functions as a drama."

October **(1927)** "Kerensky's essential nonentity is shown satirically. We have the counterpoint of a literally expressed conventional idea with the *pictured* action of a particular person who is unequal to his swiftly increasing duties."

Old and New **(1929)** "It was on the cutting table that I detected the sharply defined scope of the particular montage of *Old and New*. This was when the film had to be condensed and shortened. The 'creative ecstasy' attending the assembly and montage—the 'creative ecstasy' of 'hearing and feeling' the shots—all this was already in the past. Abbreviations and cuts require no inspiration, only technique and skill."

Que Viva Mexico! **(1932)** "Do you know what a *'Serape'* is? A Serape is the striped blanket that the Mexican indio, the Mexican charro—every Mexican wears. And the Serape could be the symbol of Mexico. So striped and violently contrasting are the cultures in Mexico running next to each other and at the same time being centuries away. . . . And we took the contrasting independent adjacence of the [Serape's] violent colors as the motif for constructing our film."

Bezhin Meadow **(1935)** [Uncompleted]

Alexander Nevsky **(1938)** "One of the most successful scenes in *Alexander Nevsky* [is] the attack by the German wedge on the Russian army at the beginning of the Battle of the Ice. This episode passes through all the shades of an experience of increasing terror, where approaching dangers make the heart contract and the breathing irregular."

Ivan the Terrible, Part I **(1944)** "In him [Ivan] we wished chiefly to convey a sense of majesty, and this led us to adopt majestic forms."

Ivan the Terrible, Part II **(1946)** "The most important thing is to have the vision. The next is to grasp and hold it.

"Direction becomes drawings; the voices and intonations of various characters are drawn as series of facial expressions. Whole scenes first take shape as batches of drawings before they take on the clothing of words.

"One of the absorbing aspects of film-making, compensating for much that is irksome, difficult and unpleasant, is the constant variety and novelty of the subject matter. Today you film a record-breaking harvest. Tomorrow a matador in the bull-ring. The next day, the Patriarch blessing the new Tsar. And each subject requires its own peculiar and strict technique."

From *Que Viva Mexico!* (1932). After Eisenstein's return to the Soviet Union, this film was recut in Hollywood and released in 1933 under the title *Thunder Over Mexico.*

Charlie Chaplin. But it was Jesse Lasky, of Paramount, who succeeded in bringing Eisenstein to America. At Paramount Eisenstein produced a script for Theodore Dreiser's *An American Tragedy* that was never filmed.

Meanwhile, the infamous Fish Committee, organized to identify and expel Communists from Southern California, was calling Eisenstein the "international Judas of the cinema," and an official representing the organization of Hollywood Technical Directors applied to him such epithets as "Red Jew" and "Jewish Bolshevik." One pamphlet of the time was entitled *Eisenstein, Hollywood's Messenger from Hell.* Eisenstein was even arrested in Mexico as the most "dangerous agent Moscow has ever sent on a mission." But the evidence most revealing of the differences between film as commercial product and film as art is found in another Selznick memo to Paramount's general manager, B. P. Schulberg, for whom Selznick was now working. Having read Eisenstein's treatment for *An American Tragedy,* Selznick found it "a memorable experience; the most moving script I have ever read. It was so effective that it was positively torturing." However, he added, "As entertainment, I don't think it has one chance in a hundred."

Before Eisenstein's return to the Soviet Union, he was to experience yet another misadventure—his Mexican project (*Que Viva Mexico!,* 1932), a celebration of contrasts in Mexican culture which he undertook with funds raised by Upton Sinclair. This uncompleted epic was intended to evoke the diversity of Mexican culture and heritage. But it too eschewed traditional entertainment values and was never released in its original form.

Pudovkin: Linkage and the Plastic Material

Vsevolod Pudovkin became enamored of cinema when he saw Griffith's *Intolerance* in Moscow in 1920, and he gave up his career as a chemist to join the Kuleshov workshop. Over the next eight years, he was able to establish himself, side by side with Eisenstein, as a major force, both theorist and practitioner in silent Soviet cinema. In his three silent features, *Mother* (1926), *The*

End of St. Petersburg (1927), and *Storm Over Asia* (1928), he refined montage construction by exercising his own approach. Unlike Eisenstein's intellectual and dialectic work, Pudovkin's method was based on the linkage of shots and the overall emotional force of their combination.

In *Mother,* the major difference between Eisenstein and Pudovkin is immediately apparent: Pudovkin's dramatization of revolution focuses more on the individual human drama than do Eisenstein's mass epics. *Potemkin* resembles the spontaneous recording of an uncontrolled event; *Mother* represents more traditional storytelling, following a narrative line, with events hinging upon the relationship of a mother and son. Within the framework, an array of jolting images is presented: the imprisoned boy's agony, reflected in close-ups of his hands; his quiet joy in anticipating his release joined to shots of melting snow and ice, representing the promise of spring and new life. The film also juxtaposes shots of the populace going through the streets to liberate the political prisoners with shots of river ice churning under spring's thaw — and the idea comes through that nothing could withstand the inevitability of either. In another scene, shots of the cavalry coming from the left are joined with shots of the masses coming from the right, suggesting the inevitable conflict. Viewers are forced to feel deeply for the son and to experience exhilaration when the mother finally picks up the Red flag. Even though events have been plotted around these two characters, and both are killed, we are still left with heady emotions of inevitable victory. No sniveling private agonies here, but bigger issues — ideology moving a nation toward ultimate victory.

Pudovkin's *The End of St. Petersburg* (1927), like *October,* was commissioned to celebrate the tenth anniversary of the Bolshevik revolution. In subject and setting, it is a companion piece to the Eisenstein work (much

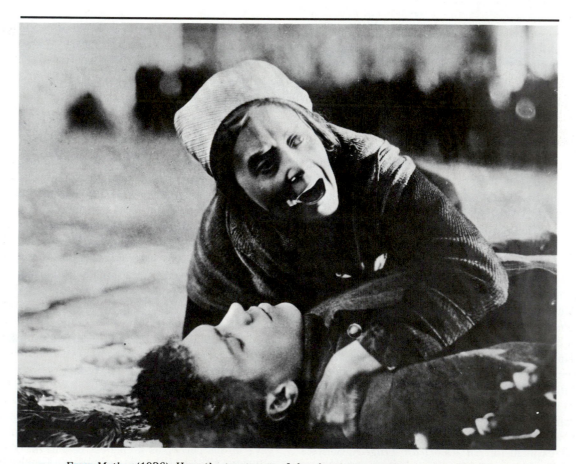

▲ From *Mother* (1926). Here the treatment of the abortive peasant revolt of 1905 is based on the Gorky novel about a peasant woman who unwittingly betrays her own son to the police and sees him shot down in a May Day street demonstration just after his escape from prison.

Plastic Expression in Creating a Film

*T*he scenario-writer must bear always in mind the fact that every sentence he writes must appear plastically upon the screen in some visible form. Consequently, it is not the words he writes that are important, but the externally expressed plastic images.

To the film director each shot of the finished film subserves the same purpose as the word to the poet. Hesitating, selecting, rejecting, and taking up again, he stands before the separate takes, and only by conscious artistic composition at this stage are gradually pieced together the "phrases of editing," the incidents and sequences, from which emerge, step by step, the finished creation, the film.

The expression that the film is "shot" is entirely false, and should disappear from the language. The film is not *shot,* but *built,* built up from the separate strips of celluloid that are its raw material. . . .

— *V. I. Pudovkin, quoted in* Soviet Film *(July 1967)*

---

of the action of both films was shot at the Winter Palace at the same time), but its method differs, particularly its weaving of personal drama into epic events. "The film is not *shot,* but *built,*" Pudovkin wrote in his *Film Technique and Film Acting* in 1926. The two directors continually challenged one another's methods, with Eisenstein reducing their differences to a simple equation: "Linkage — P, and Collision — E."

In reality, though, both directors explored both the linking and contrasting possibilities of montage, and both were subjected to harsh official Soviet criticism. Pudovkin's third feature, *Storm over Asia* (1928), is the story of a Mongolian trapper turned Soviet partisan who is shot by a member of a British interventionist detachment. Identified as a descendant of Genghis Khan, he is nursed back to health and set up as a puppet ruler over Mongolia. But the young captive ruler recognizes his true mission as leader of his people, revolts against his British captors, and, in the film's stirring climactic storm sequence, rides at the head of the Mongolian hordes against the oppressors. At one point, to dramatize the suffocating effect of his "imprisonment," Pudovkin shows the Mongol leader collapsing and, as he falls, overturning a fish tank. By combining the image of the stricken man with that of the fish, floundering out of water, the director suggests the suffocating restraints of the man's situation. The scene is one of many striking filmic metaphors for which the director is noted. But for this, his last great silent film, Pudovkin was denounced by the party for failing to follow Communist ideology closely enough and for engaging in self-indulgent excesses. With reactionary forces gaining control of the Politburo, the experimental era of Soviet cinema was coming to a close.

Dovzhenko: Cinema Poetry

Alexander Dovzhenko (*Arsenal* [1929] and *Earth* [1930]) carved a middle ground between Eisenstein and Pudovkin by uniting the epic story lines of the former with the personal stories of the latter. While the other two directors came from mathematical and theatrical backgrounds, Dovzhenko was more rooted in the poetic humanism of the nineteenth century. Dovzhenko's special gift to cinema was his discovery of the lyric qualities in the most ordinary and homely of happenings. His characters are simple Ukranian peasants bound to the soil and dedicated to building a new world in farm and factory.

Arsenal is an epic poem that embraces both reality and fantasy. Grim scenes of trench warfare and the revolt of the workers in a Kiev munitions factory lead to a lyric conclusion in which the young hero stands against the firing squad and poetically remains defiant and impervious to the bullets. Such fundamental themes as life and death, the indomitable spirit of man, and fertility and rebirth within the land and human life were essential to Dovzhenko's work. In *Earth* the death of old reactionary farming traditions and the birth of new Soviet collectives are dramatized in incidents involving a young hero in love who is inspired by the arrival of a tractor for plowing the fields. As he walks along the dusty moonlit road, he begins to dance, supremely happy, raising the dust in clouds around him, and then — a shot rings out, horses

Dovzhenko's Role as "Ukrainian Bard"

*I*n my film, *Arsenal*, I considerably narrowed the range of my cinematic goals. The assignment to make the film was entirely political, set by the Party. I wrote the scenario in a fortnight, filmed and edited it in six months. In making *Arsenal* I had two tasks: to unmask reactionary Ukrainian nationalism and chauvinism and to be the bard of the Ukrainian working class, which had accomplished the social revolution.

I conceived *Earth* as a film that would herald the beginning of a new life in the villages. But collectivization and liquidation of the small landowners class — events of tremendous political significance that occurred when the film had been completed and was ready to be released — made my statement weak and ineffectual. I went abroad for about four and a half months.

—Alexander Dovzhenko,
Arsenal and Earth *(1939)*

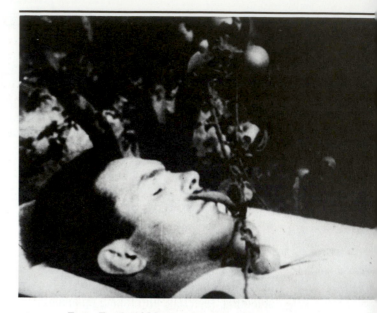

From *Earth* (1930). Dovzhenko's celebration of the new agricultural collective is particularly rich in symbolic imagery. *Earth* was filmed in the director's own Ukrainian countryside and evokes a sense of rebirth, fruition, and abundance.

It should be noted that in spite of the emphasis placed on montage, much of the artistry in Soviet film-making resulted from the creative use of the camera and the combined talents of director and cinematographer. In Germany Karl Freund provided the striking images for such films as *The Last Laugh* and *Variety*. In Hollywood G. W. (Billy) Bitzer composed the shots that helped make Griffith's work memorable. And in the Soviet Union, such director/cinematographer associations also emerged. Dovzhenko's poetry was clearly enhanced by the camera work of Daniel Demutski, and Pudovkin's emotionally charged images were at least in part the work of his cinematographer, A. N. Golovnia. But the most formidable among these associations was that of Eisenstein and Eduard Tissé, with the director providing the inspiration and basic design and cinematographer Tissé composing memorable images from behind the camera lens.

Other Notables

The contributions of other notable directors to Soviet silent cinema came closer to the more traditional narrative forms. Abram Room brought sophistication and wit

grazing in a nearby field raise their heads, and the boy falls dead, the victim of a vengeful reactionary farmer. Earlier in the film Dovzhenko had juxtaposed shots of a pregnant woman with those of the death of an old man. Now he brings together shots of the boy's simple funeral (he is carried shoulder high through an orchard with branches of fruit trees brushing his face) with those of a life-giving rain shower.

Before turning to film, Dovzhenko had been a painter, absorbed in the possibilities of visual composition within the frame. As the son of Ukrainian farmers, he felt a strong attachment to the land and the simple values of his people. In film he discovered a way of expressing, through a series of stunning images, the hope that social and agrarian reform could bring. But his films were marked by lyricism and humanism rather than ideological fervor, and his method was tied more to the poetry that could be evoked by individual images than to politics as reflected through complex forms of montage construction.

to Russian movies of the period in his *Bed and Sofa* (1927). This film is a satire on the postwar Moscow housing shortage and how it affects a young couple and the male boarder who shares their small apartment. Its lack of austerity and use of simple, realistic settings prefigure the lighter of the Italian neorealist films.

In *Fragment of an Empire* (1929), Friedrich Ermler told the story of a wartime amnesia victim who returns to Leningrad and, through the reconciliation of the old and new of the city, has his memory restored. This film is less politically charged and self-conscious about its style than the revolutionary epics and it is frequently comic in intent. It started Ermler on a career that was to place him among the major Soviet directors in the early years of sound.

Grigorie Kozintsev, whose filmmaking extended into the 1970s, began his career in film before the arrival of sound. His association with Leonid Trauberg began in 1921, when the two men founded the Factory of Eccentric Actors. After a series of experimental shorts, the team produced one of the last outstanding Soviet silent films, *The New Babylon*. This is a highly stylized drama about the establishment of a commune in Paris at the end of the Franco-Prussian War in 1871. Though appropriately Marxist in its perspective, *The New Babylon* has a sardonic wit and elegance about it and is free of the heaviness of the acknowledged masterworks.

One woman gained recognition among major contributors to Soviet silent cinema. The feature-length chronicles by Esther Shub were also of epic proportions, but they followed the documentary tradition of Vertov rather than the dramatizations of Eisenstein and Pudovkin. Schub's *The Fall of the Romanov Dynasty* (1927), like *October* and *The End of St. Petersburg*, commemorates the tenth anniversary of the Bolshevik Revolution. It also serves as a prototype of the compilation documentary, which combines existing newsreel with footage from other films.

Politics and Compromise

Though Soviet films were never widely distributed in America, they provided filmmakers themselves — plus critics and others interested in film's development — with memorable filmgoing experiences and mightily enriched the history of film. Unfortunately, these exciting and positive events were now tempered by another dimension. Compromise was a way of life in Hollywood. Germans faced economic limits, and the Soviets faced ideological restraints. If a particular production manager had had sympathy for Eisenstein's vision, for example, last-minute changes would not have been allowed. A studio official trusted Pudovkin enough to force cooperation out of a bureaucratic bookkeeping department. Eisenstein, returning from the abortive *Que Viva Mexico!* project, found himself in a dangerous position. Under the repressive demands for socialist realism imposed by the new head of state, Josef Stalin, one could not know from one minute to the next which points of view were to be perceived as heresy or truth.

In March 1928, the First All-Union Party Conference on Film Questions was convened in Moscow. "Formalist" and other "decadent" uses of the film medium were now being openly attacked. Even the simple poetry of Dovzhenko came under fire. Soviet officials charged *Earth* with reflecting ambiguity of attitude, and of being "defeatist" and "counterrevolutionary."

The Stalinists of the 1930s made sure that inventiveness had run its course in the Soviet Union — with a few fortunate exceptions. Eisenstein was permitted to teach but not to make films. He was charged with "barren intellectualism." The government ordered films that would reinforce changing policy doctrine, history, and dedication to the work ethic. During the same period, however, Pudovkin's *Deserter* (1933), Vertov's *Three Songs About Lenin* (1934), and Dovzhenko's *Frontier* (1935) came into being, proving that the progress made in the 1920s had not been entirely lost in the 1930s.

By 1938 Eisenstein had found his way again with *Alexander Nevsky*. In this film he replaced the people *en masse* with a hero of the people, Grand Duke Alexander Nevsky, who in the thirteenth century had driven first Swedish and then German invaders out of Russia. The film concerns itself with repelling the latter. The Nevsky folk epic from the dim mists of the ancient past must have seemed a safe scenario — until Stalin signed a pact with Hitler. The completed film was not released in the Soviet Union until the pact had been broken. Suddenly, with Germans almost at Moscow, all the appeals to nationalism and to the motherland were valuable, and *Alexander Nevsky* was called into service.

Alexander Nevsky is highly theatrical and formal. Each shot was so carefully planned and plotted before production that the film might as easily have been made as an animation film as a feature. The German enemy is encased in iron masks, devoid of humanity. Greatness is demanded of the kindly Nevsky, whose heroic leadership drives the Teutons into retreat. And the primitive reed instruments used to play Sergei Prokofiev's score only add to the strange power of Eisenstein's images.

In 1943, Eisenstein began work on what was intended as a massive trilogy on the life of Czar Ivan IV. He completed and released *Part I* of *Ivan the Terrible* in 1944, winning the Stalin Prize for the film's artistry. But

Some Initial American Press Reactions to Soviet Films

Potemkin

As this screen version of the mutiny aboard a Russian cruiser now stands it may interest a few Russians in this country, but it is utterly devoid of entertainment and box office value.

The authorities need not fear that the showing of this picture will cause any unrest among the lower classes in this country, for not enough of them will see it to make any difference. Those that are out-and-out reds, and those that are inclined to socialism will undoubtedly find great things about the picture, but hardly anyone else will.

To Russians this may all mean something. As a pictorial historical record for the archives of the Soviet Government it may also mean something, but to the average American, unless he be an out-and-out red, it doesn't mean a damn. And that's that.

—*Variety (December 8, 1926)*

Ten Days That Shook the World

And so to the film. It is clever, but a bore.

—*New York Times (November 3, 1928)*

Arsenal

Imaginatively conceived and cleverly photographed though the scenes undoubtedly are in "Arsenal," a Soviet symbolic argument against war which is now holding forth at the Film Guild Cinema, a little of this sort of thing goes a long way.

—*New York Times (November 11, 1929)*

Mother

This very dramatic film was done by a lyrical director, V. Pudovkin. He interpolated many landscape pictures among the scenes of action, reflected the unrest of humanity and of nature, made the dawning of freedom coincide with the coming of Spring and linked the parade of the May "Day" demonstrants with the breaking up of the ice in the river.

It is idle to compare "Mother" with "Armored Cruiser Potemkin." The exceptional case of "Potemkin" cannot remain for all time the standard by which to measure Russian films. "Potemkin" was a supreme piece of work which cannot be duplicated even by the Russian film art every day.

—*New York Times (January 8, 1928)*

the director's interpretation of Russian history in *Part II* was not looked upon favorably by the Party Central Committee, and the film was condemned and refused release. The third part of the trilogy was never produced. Eisenstein died of a heart attack in 1946 with *Part III* still in the planning stage.

Disillusionment had marked the end of Eisenstein's career as it had other notable Soviet filmmakers. Vertov said of himself, "The tragedy of Vertov is that he didn't know how to grow old." Before Dovzhenko died in 1956, he mourned the loss of vision that had "given way to the narrow-minded speculations in realism and indifference of petty reptiles who lack ideas and principles." He said, "There is no love; there is no passion." But for a few short years, there was, as Eisenstein said, a time for artistic expression free from the ruts of the past.

Wrap-Up

Today the films of Eisenstein, Pudovkin, and Dovzhenko — and even Vertov's *Man with a Movie Camera* — are impressive monuments to a new order, absorbing dramas, and compelling experiments in visual style. The great outpouring of films of which they were a part was accompanied by another outpouring — of ideas on how films could be constructed. In both the films themselves and the writings of their creators, a body of film theory evolved. At the center is the concept of montage — the assemblage of individual pieces of footage. The fundamentals of montage construction existed, of course, in the works of Griffith — he built scenes by selecting and arranging shots to give varying perspectives and angles on the same action. Cross-cutting between contrasting and parallel actions and creating tempo and rhythm by carefully controlling the length of each shot were also techniques that the Russian filmmakers adapted from early American films and refined.

The more experimental and complex implications of montage involved the natural association in the viewer's mind between images that are spliced together, no matter how disparate or "illogical" that association might seem. Beginning with the simple Kuleshov experiment, and extending through the theory and practice of Eisenstein's "intellectual montage," Soviet cinema came to offer a method of film construction that yielded visual metaphors and the visual representation of abstract concepts. Whether through "collision," as Eisenstein maintained, or "linkage," as Pudovkin suggested, it became possible to create figurative, symbolic, and other nonrepresentational imagery in a medium that until then had been mostly limited to realistic, literal, and concrete imagery.

German films seemed hypnotized by their own reflections, and innovation in them was eventually crushed by goose-stepping Nazis. The Soviets, however, exalted the medium and came to celebrate a new order founded on new ideals. Eventually, though, this movement also atrophied in the face of regimentation. Both movements were born out of chaos. Both burned brightly and long enough to affect the medium fundamentally and permanently. But for both the conjunction of forces that fostered them were soon out of phase, and the creative spirit moved on, capriciously perhaps, in search of a new place and a new time in which to make more cinema magic happen.

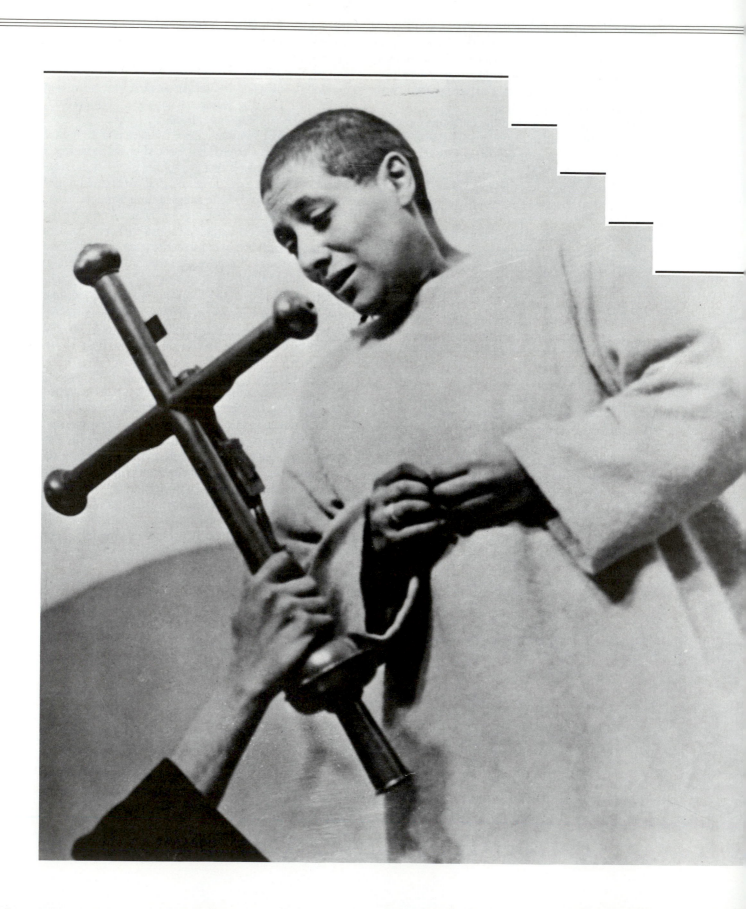

6

Other International Influences (1919 – 1927)

Focus

As it had been in the United States, so it was in France, Britain, Scandinavia, Italy, and everywhere else where electricity and technology were present. That first Lumière brothers' export spurred national production everywhere: films made for home consumption soon warranted sales offices in foreign capitals. The evolution of narrative forms increased the popularity of films as consumer goods. With demand consistently greater than supply, production centers blossomed throughout the world in the first decade of the twentieth century.

But by the end of 1918, the European film industry was in disarray. Europe had been at war for four years. Americans had joined in the fight "over there" only during the last six months. The European film industries had either been all but destroyed or had been in government service for four years. And Hollywood had rushed in with exports to fill the product void. European audiences often preferred Hollywood's exports over native movies, a factor that added to the difficulty of re-establishing the European film industries.

However, many of Europe's film industries eventually found their feet again. French filmmakers during the 1920s produced film art and experimentation that rivaled that of the Soviets and Germans. Expressionism, impressionism, Dadaism — moviemakers drew these art forms from painting and applied them to the *moving* picture art. Such films were not appreciated by mass audiences, but the American business world kept a close watch to see whether any of these new ideas would catch the public's fancy.

Hostility among European businesspeople towards American imports eventually led to protective tariffs and quota systems, and France, Britain, Italy, and Scandinavia began to work toward restoring prewar conditions.

However, with the exception of France, Germany, and Russia, most European industries never regained their prewar vitality. First Germany and then the United States attracted leading talent away from native lands. And with respect to non-Western films, Americans simply paid no attention, but continued to gaze at their own images, mesmerized.

The European Film Industries in Decline

"**T**he American invasion of the foreign screen was a walk-over," said a former war correspondent. "It was tantamount to 'conquering' a world where the inhabitants were unarmed." But as the two preceding chapters make clear, the Soviet Union and Germany were exceptions. The Soviet film industry was organized and budgeted to serve the political system. Thus, an aesthetically vital nationalized film industry flourished in Russia, totally protected from Western competition. In Germany the film industry was also developed by the government, in the effort to gain some measure of international esteem through the country's film art. The German government used quotas and other means to protect the quickly maturing industry and, of all the film-producing countries in the world, only Germany was feared by Hollywood as a potentially serious competitor.

At the turn of the century, British, French, Italian, and Scandinavian movie companies had all opened booking offices in New York. In the 1920s producers would recall the "1907 mentality" with sadness, mourning a time when an insatiable market accepted anything thrown onto the screen. Producers learned to tell more complicated stories; length increased and character development became more important. But World War I arrested European film evolution and production between 1914 and 1918. Hollywood had the field to itself, and after the war American films flooded European markets, where national industries were in shambles.

Quotas were imposed on American imports, and reciprocity agreements were forged between foreign and American distributors to protect struggling industries. But still the prewar glory days were not to be regained. By 1921, Dansk Astra Film, a Danish company, had simply folded up. Italian producers were dreaming "away the sunny days of spring," reported an American sarcastically, while they passed resolutions demanding more protection from U.S. imports "in order to build up the home industry." No one in Europe, this writer contin-

ued, is able "to account for the flood of American pictures . . . while their own productions cannot gain the desired foothold in the United States."

The precise reasons for American domination mystified observers on both sides of the Atlantic. Having watched European developments for three years, W. Stephen Bush thought he had it figured out. In 1925 he wrote in the American trade magazine, *Moving Picture World,*

> Time and again I have seen a delightful theme or a strong subject or uncommon dramatic values simply ruined by incompetent direction in European studios. The average European film has a touch of coarseness, of heaviness, often of vulgarity that creeps into the celluloid like a pestiferous germ. Also there is a lack of vim and life and a perfect vacuum as far as real humor is concerned. Pessimism and various forms of dramatic melancholia, utterly out of place in an entertainment dependent upon the plain people, infest the European film apparently beyond remedy.

So much for the "average" European film. According to Bush's sources, "the American film in Europe is popular not merely because it is first class entertainment but because it carries a message of hope and cheer and enlightenment in almost every reel." Two years later, as more and more unusual German, French, and Soviet films were reaching the United States, another columnist speculated,

> We are a light-hearted lot as a rule, and we want primarily to be amused when we go to the movies. Artistry appeals to us but we don't want artistry alone, a little symbolism goes a long way, the sordid seamy side of life does not entertain the average man nor does the allegorical. . . . We are optimistic and much prefer to gaze upon the brighter side of life. We are an energetic people and we want dash, vigor, vim, go, vitality, pep, action.

Not only were the story lines in European efforts too complex and depressing, but who in America knew anything about the players? The cult of the star personality had been raised to a high art by studio publicity departments, and newspapers as well as fan magazines perpetuated the myths carefully crafted to guarantee box office receipts. Foreign pictures released in the United States usually lacked the benefit of celebrity-generating machinery. Stories and stars, said the Americans: "When these foundation stones are missing or weak the entire entertainment structure falls no matter how superb the decorations of the building may be."

By the mid-1920s it was estimated that Hollywood

movies accounted for 50 percent of the exhibitors' business in France and Germany, and 85 to 95 percent of the box office in Western and Central Europe as well as Central and South America. In 1927 only 75 foreign features were in American distribution, and in 1928 there were fewer than 200.

From the thousands of foreign titles urged upon American distributors, the public chose films that critics and historians decades later found to be the most important. Again, in 1927 and 1928, *Dr. Mabüse, the Gambler* (1922), *Nosferatu* (1922), *Warning Shadows* (1922), *The Street* (1923), *Siegfried* (1924), *Berlin: The Symphony of a Great City* (1927), *Metropolis* (1926), and other German productions were in distribution. Britain sent a number of minor films, and also a thriller from a new director, *The Lodger* (1927), directed by Alfred Hitchcock. From France came *Les Misérables* (1926); *Napoleon* (1926), a remarkable spectacular by Abel Gance that incorporated multi-image, color, and wide-screen effects; and the startling, unforgettable *The Passion of Joan of Arc* (1928). *The End of St. Petersburg* (1927), *Potemkin* (1925), *Mother* (1926), and *October* (*Ten Days that Shook the World* [1928]), were admitted from the Soviet Union.

Occasionally one of these foreign "allegories," often labeled "pessimistic" and "seamy," received wide distribution. More often these films were shunted to a few ethnic theaters, and to a growing chain of autonomous art houses and cine clubs usually associated with museums and universities. An industry survey in the early 1920s pretended to prove that Americans did not like foreign films. It reported that 82 percent of respondents rated German films as poor, 87 percent thought the same of French films, and 89 percent placed Italian films in that category.

Although European labor costs were much lower than in the United States, profits often derived only from distribution outside the country of origin. Because technology was improving, it was essential to purchase costly new equipment. But postwar reconstruction claimed much of the available capital at a time when studios needed outside financial backing to produce competitive feature films. Never before had foreign markets been more important to production companies in Britain, France, Scandinavia, and Italy.

Industry representatives estimated that only 15 to 20 percent of the European population went to the movies regularly. American industry analysts, ever mindful of increasing their own potential audiences, advised their European cousins to expand exhibition facilities, since many towns and villages had no movie houses. Where theaters did exist, American travelers were appalled by hard wooden seats in small dingy halls with "contemptible accommodations for patrons, no service,

1928 Feature Imports

Germany	83
Britain	37
France	31
Soviet Union	16
Sweden	7
Italy	6
Poland	4
Austria	2
Argentina	1
Canada	1
Czechoslovakia	1
Egypt	1
India	1
Norway	1
Syria	1

—*Film Daily Yearbook 1929*

or only foolish pretense of it, no ventilation, no comfort of any kind." Even in America's smallest towns, upholstered seating and other conveniences were becoming the norm, as the influences of the metropolitan movie palaces rippled across the nation.

The Europeans were also said to lack an understanding of promotion. Savvy promoters criticized European advertising copy, saying it harkened back to "the dull lustre of mid-Victorian essayists," where "verbosity is the sure sign of genius." In France, where it was a tradition for a movie house to include a bar, one American wag reported that "the theater is used to draw customers to the bar, rather than the reverse." (However, Britain's trade magazine, *The Bioscope,* tartly noted that "the American buyer is not likely to buy a good thing unless he is told beforehand that it *is* good. It is a frame of mind which the advertising fraternity in America have cultivated in buyers and is not to be criticized.")

Of course, it was not in the interest of American studios to promote foreign film distribution in the United States. But more than that, the 1920s was a period of rising postwar suspicion of all things foreign. Hearst newspapers warned about the "yellow peril," and California passed a law barring Asian Americans from own-

Monster Demonstration Staged by Ex-Soldiers Drives "Caligari" off Screen in Los Angeles

*A*s a result of a demonstration against German films by members of the American Legion, the management of Miller's Theatre, Los Angeles, shelved "The Cabinet of Doctor Caligari" after a run of only a few hours on the day of its opening, Saturday, May 7. The protest, which was started immediately after the opening of the film, by picketing the theatre, was kept up all afternoon.

By night the demonstration had assumed monster proportions. The streets in the neighborhood of the theatre were packed for blocks and street car and automobile traffic was interfered with. Long lines of protestants armed with banners bearing patriotic legends marched up and down in front of the theatre. At 8:30 o'clock, Fred Miller, manager of the theatre, announced that the film would be taken off and "The Money Changers" substituted.

F. J. Godsol, chairman of the board of directors of Goldwyn Pictures Corporation, which released the picture, said in an address to a convention of exchange managers now in session at the Goldwyn studio, that "The Cabinet of Doctor Caligari" was the only German picture that Goldwyn was interested in and that this film was merely distributed and not owned by Goldwyn. Godsol said further that Goldwyn had no intention of releasing any other German pictures.

—Motion Picture World *(May 21, 1921)*

ing land. Congress voted to reduce immigration quotas for Asian and Southern Europe and Mediterranean countries. As for those who were already here, the appreciation for ethnic traditions that was to emerge decades later did not yet exist. Many immigrants worked diligently to eliminate traces of ancestral origin. To patronize "foreign" films was, for them, almost un-American.

Art critics and film aesthetes could praise the German and Soviet film, and even American tradesmen admired the direction and editing in *Strike!* (1924) and *Potemkin* (1925). It was admitted that "nine out of ten directors will study *[Potemkin]* as an example of something new in the handling of mobs." For the most part, however, the American mass audience was not impressed with the foreign allegories.

About *The Cabinet of Dr. Caligari* (1919), exhibitor C. C. Johnson, owner of the A-Muse-U Theatre in Melville, Louisiana, advised his peers, "Why did Gold-

wyn ever allow his name to be placed on this specimen of junk? Absolutely rotten. . . . As the reels unwound the audience departed."

For R. X. Williams and the Lyric Theatre in Oxford, Mississippi, *The Golem* (1920) "is the kind that you wish you had a Dark House in place of the picture. . . . By the third reel the house was empty." "For me, the biggest piece of cheese I ever ran," said O. W. Harris, St. Denis Theatre, Sapula, Oklahoma.

Arthur B. Hancock had tried to put on *The Loves of Pharaoh* at his Columbia Theatre in Columbia City, Indiana. "European made, it is true, but the picture has merit; sets and acting are wonderful; action, as much as in the average Western, but different." Hancock previewed the import for local opinion leaders, but even with their word-of-mouth praise he only broke even. Unless patrons "know the stars they will not support a picture," he concluded.

France

Beginning with the Lumière brothers, the French film industry remained productive and innovative in the years prior to World War I. Like most European countries, France's film industry was essentially destroyed in World War I. In 1920, however, Charles Pathé left his American film interests to give all his energy to reviving production at home. At the same time, other French filmmakers visited Hollywood to observe production methods, study new postwar technological advances, and explore the possibilities for cooperation. Louis Nalpas, a successful director, and Abel Gance, a producer praised by D. W. Griffith, were among the French visitors. Unlike many other German and Scandinavian filmmakers, the Frenchmen returned home where, as an American reporter observed, they "learned to be sufficient unto themselves."

Jean Sapene, publisher and entrepreneur who had been hired by Mr. Pathé to manage the Pathé Frères production companies, said that since Americans did not want their pictures, so be it. "But we will keep on making them—five, ten, twenty a year, as many as we can make well—until they come to us and say they want them."

The trouble with French pictures, American exhibitors claimed, was they were "too stagey." Even some French exhibitors were said to prefer American pictures, because, while their countrymen liked sentimental stories, nevertheless "they cannot be expected to do nothing but cry for a couple of hours." Publisher Sapene huffed that French story lines were not suitable for American and British mass audiences, because "the taste of your public, especially in the small towns and villages, is too crude to appreciate the delicacies and subtleties of our art."

Six years later, Universal asked for American distribution rights to several French films. *Michael Strogoff* (1926) was based on a popular Jules Verne novel. It had been produced by a Pathé subsidiary in Latvia. A reviewer in *The Film Daily* noted that "there has been some talk that France was about to step out as a producer; that a bid for a place in the international market would be made." As for *Strogoff,* all the American box-office requirements were present: "love interests, heroics, lavish and colorful spectacle, effective battle scenes, and a corking good fight with the villain." Best of all, "It moves rapidly."

Les Misérables (1926) came to American screens in 1927 along with four other French films that year. In 1928, thirty-one features were imported, but only nineteen came over in 1929, as sound technology arrested

Finding a Market

*Y*ou must remember that, owning to the enormous market in the United States, American companies are assured of sufficient receipts within their own country, and what they make in the foreign field is over and above their assured profits at home. On the other hand, French companies must find a market abroad for their products, for the market at home is not sufficient. The two markets in which the French industry is particularly interested are the United States and Great Britain.

—*Robert de Simone, editor of the French* Scenario, *quoted in* Motion Picture World *(June 26, 1920)*

the brief revival. Although the American market did not become a significant source of profit for the French industry, much of the prewar vitality was restored. French film companies were at work throughout France, and from Spain to India.

Napoleon (1926) came to America in 1928, released in this country by MGM. This picture was directed by Abel Gance, whom Griffith had praised. The epic used standard and wide-screen projection—and not only wide screen, but a panorama that occasionally broke into three content areas. Eisenstein had complained about being limited to the standard screen size. Why not, he had asked, use whatever screen area is most appropriate to the visual idea? Use the standard area, but if a panoramic wide screen—or a tall vertical screen—would better serve the purpose, then use it. *Napoleon* was restored in 1981 by Francis Ford Coppola, and in that year it opened in New York's Radio City Music Hall with a new orchestral score composed by Coppola's father, Carmine Coppola. In his nineties, Gance accompanied the film to its American rerelease.

The French predisposition for experimentation and camera tricks had not passed with the brothers Lumière or Méliès. The Paris milieu of the 1920s encouraged experimentation. The city attracted an influx of expatriot writers, artists, philosophers, and hangers-on. Manifestos were declared among the ruins of monarchies and empires ended by World War I. The atmosphere was thus conducive to revolt and discovery.

Film societies and clubs had sprouted to show both old classic films and the short new films made by artists who were turning from their traditional materials to study moving images. The work of some of the explorers was underwritten by private patrons.

These new filmmakers were primarily visual artists, and their work was not linked to narrative traditions. But Louis Delluc had been a writer before he turned to the cinema. He advocated a cinematic style that was different from American, German, and Soviet models. He and his compatriots, including Abel Gance, retained familiar story lines but applied to them an impressionistic camera style. Often the plots were sad, involving characters caught in circumstances beyond their control. *Fièvre* (1921) is an example. In this film a single flower on a bar-top signifies a beauty and sensitivity that the pathetic wife of a crude sailor wishes for but will never have.

René Clair applied Dadaist perspectives to his delightful films. *The Crazy Ray* (1923) revels in a sense of the absurd. A mysterious ray has frozen time and motion, freezing the people of Paris in their various activities — from picking pockets to pursuing romance. When the ray's inventor is finally persuaded to permit a return to normalcy, time and motion resume — but first at too fast and then too slow a pace. Clair's *Entr'acte* (1924) makes sport of the funeral as social ritual. His funeral procession speeds to the cemetery, the mourners wear white, throw rice, and eat the decorations pulled from off the hearse, which is being pulled by a camel. An apparently legless man propels himself along the street in a low car — from which he later leaps to run on his own legs in Laurel and Hardy style. The frenzied procession ends Méliès-fashion as the funeral director uses a magic wand to make everyone, even himself, vanish.

In Germany, Hans Richter opted for the abstract as he experimented with camera, lenses, exposures, form, rhythm, motion, and animation. As an abstract painter, he was fascinated by the options opened up by motion pictures that were impossible to pursue via static images painted on a canvas. The films *Rhythmus 21* (1921) and *Film-studie* (1926) are examples of his work. Fernand Léger was doing similar work in France. Filmed by Americans Dudley Murphy and Man Ray, Léger's *Ballet Mécanique* (1924) presents ballerinas dancing up and down in slow motion on a glass floor just above the cam-

Ballet Mécanique

A few weeks ago we went to the Cameo Theatre to see "The Grand Duchess and the Waiter." There following that most excellent piece of work, a strange motion picture was thrown upon the screen. . . . It had no story, no plot, no actors. It consisted of shapes and patterns, in a constant motion, being broken up, assembled in new form, fanning out again, approaching, receding, seeming for all the world like the animation of a cubist painter's dream. . . .

So we found Mr. Murphy and asked him what was behind this extraordinary film.

"I made it," he said, "because I wanted to make a *moving picture*. . . . Take the typical chase scene. Whether it is a yacht chased by a destroyer, an automobile by an airplane, a horse by another horse, the image is not so important. It is a question of tempo."

Mr. Murphy's definition is certainly exemplified in his work. For we have never seen, outside of the "Big Parade," a moving picture with such rhythmic and dynamic tempo as is contained in "Ballet Mécanique."

"Ballet Mécanique" should certainly be put into country-wide distribution. But more important still, one of the big producers of full length pictures should grab young Mr. Murphy and lead this son of Erin and America gently and firmly by a contract to a more or less secluded studio spot where he can have an opportunity to advance the art and the attraction power of the *moving picture*.

— *William J. Reilly, "When Is It a Moving Picture?"* Moving Picture World *(May 15, 1926)*

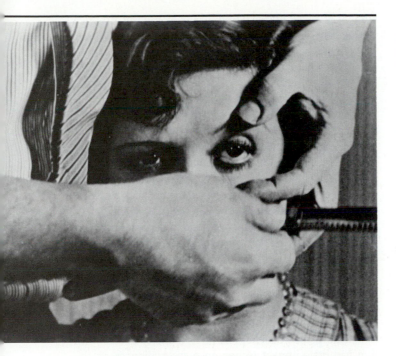

From *Un Chien Andalou* (1928), Buñuel and Dali's surrealist masterpiece.

From Ivens's *Rain* (1929), an impressionistic vision of city life during a rain shower.

À Propos de Nice

*I*n this film, the description of a whole town begging from sheer laziness, we are spectators at the trial of a particular world. After indicting this life and atmosphere of Nice — and, alas, elsewhere — the film proceeds to a generalized impression of gross pleasures, to different signs of a grotesque existence, of flesh and of death. These are the last twitchings of a society that neglects its own responsibilities to the point of giving you nausea and making you an accomplice in a revolutionary solution.

—*Jean Vigo, about his*
À Propos de Nice *(1930)*

era lens; gears and levers are synchronized with camera angle and editing to produce a Freudian cubist symphony of forms in motion.

Surrealists took the experimental stage when Luis Buñuel and the controversial Salvador Dali, both from Spain, combined forces to create *Un Chien Andalou* (1928). The horrible images from the subconscious con-

tained in this film — ants crawling from a hole in the palm of a hand, a slaughtered donkey slung across a grand piano as someone pulls both across a room, and a razor slicing across a woman's eyeball — scandalized audiences then as they still do. Dali boasted that the film "ruined in a single evening ten years of pseudo-intellectual post-war avant-gardism." Later, Dali and Buñuel's *L'Age d'Or* (1931) scourged political and Roman Catholic institutions in devastating images. Negative reaction was so strong that the government removed the film from exhibition.

Impressionistic imagery is the material of another approach influenced by the Russian Vertov. Alberto Cavalcanti's *Rien que les Heures* (1926) and Walther Ruttmann's *Berlin: The Symphony of a Great City* (1927) helped to establish a tradition for the "city" film, a documentary form that redeemed reality for the intelligentsia through a high cinematic style. Cavalcanti takes us through one day — that is the convention usually employed, although that is not how such films were shot — revealing the conditions of slum dwellers, a part of the reality of Paris that filmgoers normally avoided. Ruttmann cuts from a crowded street to a herd of cattle. Images collide, and one image breaks into multiple reflections of itself.

Joris Ivens began his career with a wondrous cinematic poem, *Rain* (1929), an impressionistic study of a rainy day in Amsterdam. He then turned to impressionistic realism with *Borinage* (1933), concentrating on conditions in Dutch slums. Thereafter Ivens grew increasingly committed to social change, which remained at the center of his work though he never lost his impressionistic vision. Rain, cobblestones, and umbrellas: he could never resist such images, whether in Amsterdam or a village in the People's Republic of China.

To a committed socialist like John Grierson, who believed that documentary should be useful rather than serve as an excuse for artistic high jinks, Ruttmann's *Berlin* (1927) was a failure except for a brief moment during an afternoon rain shower. "The people of the city," he admitted, "got up splendidly, they tumbled through their five million hoops impressively, they turned in; and no other issue of God or man emerged than the sudden bespattering spilling of wet on people and pavements."

Jean Cocteau referred to his films, such as *The Blood of the Poet* (1930), as cinematographs — personal images and statements recorded on film. Centered for the most part in France, the 1920s were a sometimes outrageous but certainly vital and exciting ten years for the *moving picture.*

The earlier discussed René Clair abandoned the anarchy of Dadaism to work more in the mainstream of feature production. In 1927 he adapted a play, *The Italian Straw Hat,* for the screen. The play had been set in the mid-1800s, a period in Europe when a hat was a symbol of social status. (Immigrant women in America during that time were astounded that in the New Land any woman regardless of class could put away her kerchief for whatever kind of hat she wanted and could afford.) Clair turned the script into a more contemporary, wittier satire on the foibles of the bourgeois.

In Clair's version, a proper man is on his way to be married when his horse munches on a straw hat left on a bush. The hat belongs to a married woman whose lover demands the groom replace the hat so the woman's husband will not become suspicious. One comic event and character follows hard upon another as the search for the hat continues apace, only ending with the wedding. Of course there is a madcap chase, and a denouement that leads to a happy ending for all the characters involved. *The Italian Straw Hat* failed at the box office, yet it is regarded as one of the best European comedies of the 1920s. It presents the essence of the art of mime and frothy theatricality "so expertly timed and choreographed," as Pauline Kael said, "that farce becomes ballet."

What these French filmmakers of the 1920s did with film had little impact either on mass audiences or the mass-entertainment industry. But they established a new kind of film movement, one that was to spread to other countries: the experimental, or underground, cinema. The American Man Ray was part of the French movement from the beginning; his *Return to Reason* (1923) created a riot among French viewers. And his counterparts in America learned from these experiments. However, the Hollywood-dominated 1930s were not a fruitful time for experimental cinema. After World

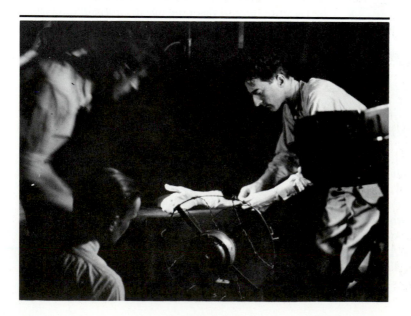

◀ Jean Cocteau arranging the Hermophides set for *The Blood of the Poet* (1930).

▲ From *The Italian Straw Hat* (1927). The film is a classic example of René Clair's sense of humor combined with his innate visual sense. This film represents Clair's Dadaist heritage at its best.

War II, the underground cinema was even alive and strong in America. It was to learn what Vertov had shown with his *Man with a Movie Camera* (1928): that the potential for meaning is limitless. When the intention is not merely to tell a story, but to explore the meaning of images — drawn either, like Vertov's, from the surfaces of reality, or, like those of the French filmmakers described here, with images conjured from the subconscious — anything can happen.

Jean Vigo had juxtaposed economic disparity between rich and poor in *À Propos de Nice* (1930). In 1933 he began working with sound in *Zéro de conduite,* which was banned in France for twelve years. The content of the film was drawn from his own experience in private school. In the film he balances the playfulness that can lead children to break rules with students' loneliness and alienation — and their interactions with humorless authority figures.

French experimentalists turned their attention to other pursuits with the coming of sound. Buñuel's bizarre *Land Without Bread* (1932) is a good example of what artist/filmmakers did with the element. A narrator drones on throughout, mimicking the typical travelogue sound track: "As the sun sinks slowly in the West, we bid a fond adieu. . . ." As for music (since all travel films have music), a Brahms symphony seems to have been selected at random. It is jarringly clear that the music does not fit the imagery — which is the point.

René Clair emerged as the French sound genius. *Le Million* (1931) and *À Nous la Liberté* (1931) are wonderful fantasies. They exhibit all the pleasurable characteristics of Clair's earlier works, particularly *The Italian Straw Hat.*

À Nous la Liberté introduces two convicts who escape from prison. One becomes a wealthy tycoon and the other a bum and free spirit. But the assembly line faced by both is not much different from prison routine, and by the end both tycoon and bum take to the open road, rejecting prisons of both kinds. The theme and spirit of this movie must have influenced Lewis Milestone's *Hallelujah, I'm a Bum* (1933) and Chaplin's *Modern Times* (1936). Milestone's film made viewers happy to be poor in the midst of a terrible economic depression, but Chaplin's seems a poor, heavy-handed imitation of a world that for Clair, was a ballet in which the dancers' feet never touch the floor.

Clair remained true to his avant-garde roots, poking fun at social and economic values, but with grace, wit, and a light and easy heart. Along with numerous others, Clair left France when the German intentions became clear. He worked for an American studio located in England. Here he made *The Ghost Goes West* (1936), which traces the adventures of a *nouveau riche* American who buys a Scottish castle and moves it to Florida, block by block.

Feyder's *Carnival in Flanders* (1935), Allegret's *Heart of Paris* (1935), and Duvivier's *They Were Five* (1936) all express a last-minute hope that the inevitable might occur. Marcel Carne had learned the craft from Clair and Feyder, and under Nazi occupation produced a theatrical masterpiece set in the nineteenth century, *Les Enfants du Paradis* (1945). After the war, the French New Wave, *la nouvelle vague,* would renounce Clair's staged fantasies and the theatrical retreats from occupation to confront contemporary issues.

Jean Renoir

Auguste Renoir was an impressionist painter whose subjects radiated sweetness and grace. His son, Jean Renoir, was a potter who became a filmmaker. Jean's gift for identifying those attributes and values from the past that were ennobling made his work valuable enough. But he was also able to bridge the gap between past and the future, and the future he saw offered humans the chance to express their care one for another. In special ways, Renoir films, particularly those from the 1930s, belong to the human family everywhere.

Renoir began his career in film as a part of the avant-garde community, but he moved away from its preoccupations with technique, form, and rebellion. He controlled mood, atmosphere, and light as carefully in his films as his father controlled these elements in his paintings. His Little Match Girl in the film of that name (1928) did not dance happily into the future, but disappeared beneath the snow in a deserted street. Renoir made a film for the French Communist Party, thought lost until the discovery of a print in 1969, and went on to direct his own version of Maxim Gorky's *The Lower Depths* (1936).

In his *Toni* (1934), Renoir used legal records to trace the plight of Italian laborers working in a French quarry. This film is in a naturalistic style, both in characterization and locale, and thus it is a precursor to the neorealism that would develop in Italy following World War II.

Contrasted with the despair of the Germans, the romanticism of his fellow French artists, and the use of montage in the Soviet Union, Renoir's work and style offer the relief of a humanistic intelligence. Truffaut called this film realist the "least eccentric" of his time.

Renoir's *Grand Illusion* (1937) rejects montage and affirms "composition in depth," as the French film critic Bazin called the technique of deep focus, which was to find its ultimate expression in Orson Welles's *Citizen Kane* (1941). In *Grand Illusion,* Renoir also favored smooth panning shots to avoid cutting from one actor to the other for a response. Here was naturalism transformed by an impressionistic approach. The style complemented his theme.

Renoir's subject in *Grand Illusion* was World War I, the conflict between German and French soldiers and the end of an era. He saw the film as a way to offer suggestions about the future. Erich von Stroheim played a German commander, von Rauffenstein, who lives, in Prussian style, by the fading chivalric rules of war. Renoir shows von Rauffenstein not as a caricature but as a deeply complex, thoughtful person who appreciates beauty, form, and discipline. The German's French counterpart is De Boeldieu, his prisoner, who shares his values. The two are caught in the catch-22 of their world, a rule that demands that prisoners attempt to escape and that captors punish such attempts with death. To allow his prisoners to escape, von Rauffenstein draws the German's fire. His heart rebels against the action, but his training permits no alternative. In the scene where the old Prussian sits by the deathbed of his French prisoner and counterpart, Renoir created one of the most deeply affecting moments in film.

The two Frenchmen who escape from the German fortress represent another level to be analyzed. Renoir portrays the pair as a Gentile mechanic, Maréchal, and a cultured Jew, Rosenthal. When the two men make their escape, both their religious and class differences are explored. These differences erupt in conflict, but the conflict is sublimated in the interest of crossing the border.

Renoir shows that survival is paramount for the modern soldier. In the new order, a rich man who might have been a von Rauffenstein under the old rules cares not a shred more about decorum than does the lower-class soldier. And as the two escapees make their successful run, they face an uncertain future. In shaping this story, Renoir reveals himself not as an armchair revolutionary who revels in the passage of an era and its seeming hypocrisy, nor a sentimentalist who mourns the passing of an age of grand illusion. Rather, he is a humanist who understands the fullness of the time, who sees with sympathy the passing of the old, who cautions restraint, and who cares about the future.

The Rules of the Game (1939) extended Renoir's analysis of human nature by studying the master and servant classes, both hopelessly bound by traditional behaviors and values. Both classes resist understanding the meaning of the signals that point to the emptiness of their games. French audiences resisted as well, and when the war began the censors banned the film. The film's exposure of artifice was too extreme for the time;

From *Grand Illusion* (1937). The film depicts the passing of an era.

national unity, not divisiveness, was needed. *Grand Illusion* was banned, too, because of its pacifism. Renoir escaped from France as the Germans invaded and then settled in America, where he found work at 20th Century-Fox. However, he came into conflict with Darryl Zanuck, and he was removed from his first American project, *Swamp Water* (1941).

Renoir was to have an impact far greater than that of the probing and thoroughly modern French films of his period. When working on *The Lower Depths* in 1936, Renoir hired an Italian named Luchino Visconti. This name was to be associated with Italian neorealism, a naturalistic approach to filmmaking that emerged in Italy even before the Allies had cleared out the Fascists. Before leaving France for the United States, Renoir visited Visconti and his friends — Vittorio de Sica, Roberto Rossellini, Cesare Zavattini, and others — at the Centro Sperimentale in Rome, the only place in Italy where foreign pictures were tolerated, and for purposes of study and analysis alone. The center, though isolated within Italy, was yet tolerant enough of ideas to allow these young filmmakers to devote time and thought to the nature of film, thus permitting a new idea to take wing.

Jean Renoir said, "No, I don't believe there are such things as absolute truths; but I do believe in absolute human qualities — generosity, for instance, which is one of the basic ones." Integrity is another quality Renoir might have believed in, for in his relentless cinema ideas and their truth guide his quest and the function of his characters. Under his hard gaze, the universals of human experience were allowed to shine forth, marvelous and true. Renoir paved the way for modern films, those motion pictures that were to emerge from most of the countries that had film industries, after the bloodbath that was World War II.

Scandinavia

By 1910 thousands of Scandinavian short films had unwound before American audiences. In the 1920s relatively few films from Scandinavian countries were distributed here, although Swedish distribution in Europe remained substantial. German studios attracted some of the Scandinavian talent, and so did Hollywood. Swedish directors Victor Sjöström and Mauritz Stiller went to Hollywood, the latter bringing along two of his most well-known actors, Lars Hanson and a young woman named Greta Garbo.

The Danish actress Asta Neilsen performed brilliantly in her last Danish film, *Toward the Light* (1918), and then joined other Danes already at work in German studios. Hers was an acting style that would later be identified as highly appropriate to the screen — simple, spare, and natural. Also, Scandinavian techniques had earlier demonstrated the functions of shadows and focus by means of lighting control, techniques that were being copied by the Germans.

Samuel Goldwyn secured the services of Sweden's Victor Seastrom to participate in producing American "super-features," and his company trumpeted the event as proof of "the sincerity of American producers in their determination to secure the finest artistic motion pictures obtainable." The event, said Goldwyn, was "one of the most significant happenings in recent motion picture history."

"Nobody knows how Seastrom does it," heralded the advertisements for Goldwyn's production of *Name the Man* (1923). The studio made this boast of its new Swedish prize: "See it and be convinced how great a miracle the mechanism known as a motion picture camera is capable of when there is a heart, intelligence, humility and sincerity in the driving force back of it — the mind which directed it."

Garbo's first and last film in Sweden was *The Story of Gösta Berling* (1924). In theme, *Berling* fell well within the Scandinavian tradition. It reflected a preoccupation with the attitudes of Kierkegaard, Ibsen, and Strindberg, a tradition within which Ingmar Bergman would develop thirty years later.

Garbo's Countess Elizabeth Dohna, the rather innocent wife of a repressed, prudish, and emotionally stunted aristocrat, captured attention worldwide. Garbo had "it" — star quality, presence, and the mystery of gesture and facial expression that fired dreams.

In the film, Reverend Berling is a man on fire, full of passions and emotions that conflict with society's laws and conventions. Because he is an alcoholic, he is defrocked, and he swings between extremes of behavior, unable to find motives in a life gone sour. But Garbo lifts him up from the abyss — and lifts up the viewer as well. Though romantic, this is not a formula film. An undercurrent of modern *angst* pervades the story. Social conventions that no longer serve modern needs, barren religious puritanism, psychological ills, and primitive superstitions pervade this work. Given their similar backgrounds and traditions, it was perhaps fitting that Neilsen from Denmark and Garbo from Sweden should be featured in G. W. Pabst's German *Joyless Street* (1925).

▶ From *The Passion of Joan of Arc* (1928). The film starred the Italian actress Falconetti.

If it is true, as is commonly noted, that international coproduction marked the 1960s, then the pattern merely repeated that of the 1920s. In 1928, Carl Dreyer, originally from Denmark but soon working for Ufa, made *The Passion of Joan of Arc* — in France. This picture was designed by Hermann Warm of *Caligari* fame; was photographed by Rudolph Maté of Poland; and featured the Italian actress Falconetti as Joan.

World audiences were deeply affected by *The Passion of Joan of Arc*. The camera recorded what was probably the largest collection of remarkable compositions ever assembled in a motion picture, and the film remains a lasting testament to the power of the silent screen. Falconetti was so drained by the experience that she never appeared in a motion picture again. The picture was banned in Britain because of the effectiveness and pathos built into the final sequence, in which flames and smoke consume the body of the French maid. Wrote Mordaunt Hall in the *New York Times,*

> When one leaves the theatre the face of that peasant girl with all its soulfulness appears to leap from one to another in the throng. Long afterward you think of the tears welling from the eyes, of the faith that seemed to stay any suggestion of attrition. . . . [As] the smoke streaks up birds are seen in the heavens.

If any work of art has the power to lift off the top of one's head, Dreyer's film does. Falconetti's face persists in one's memory long after the final credits. Her face and the faces of the authorities, both secular and religious, are shown in a most remarkable series of portraits. These views are striking in both composition and tonal contrasts — contrasts in facial details and costumes — and all are set within whitewashed walls and corridors.

The camera is steady when fixed on Falconetti, but it shows her enemies, moving constantly, in both medium and close range. As viewers watch, they begin to feel enclosed, driven beyond empathy toward shared experience. Knowing the outcome makes watching all the more compelling.

The Passion of Joan of Arc represented the culmination of European movements. The film expressed Dreyer's vision and direction, which itself reflected the expressionists' control of surfaces, textures, and light. It showed the Germans' fluid, objective/subjective camera

work and, as shot duration decreased toward the climax, their refinement of montage. Finally, in the reduction of the frame information to the bare minimum and the infusion of the whole with a brooding, Nordic sense of fate, *The Passion of Joan of Arc* fell into the Scandinavian tradition as established in skaldic literature.

England

Even in the 1920s, the British film industry was so destitute and so completely overwhelmed by Hollywood that a quota system was instituted as part of the Cinematographic Act of 1927, allowing British companies to distribute American films only if they produced a certain number of their own films. Thus, "quota quickies" were produced for a fast profit, and not with the intention of revitalizing a national industry. In desperation, the English brought in the German filmmaker E. A. Dupont to add luster to the moribund industry. But neither his *Piccadilly* nor *Atlantic* (1929) brought the hoped-for miracle, and Dupont returned to his fatherland.

The 1927 act also required that American studios planning to release their products in Britain make some movies in Britain. To satisfy the demand, however, Hollywood merely sent to England a number of people who had already fallen from the firmament or who failed to make a successful transition from silent to sound produc-

tion. The infusion of has-beens hardly served to energize the British film. By the end of the decade, the British industry had fallen into another severe slump, and MGM was using British studios and technicians to produce such films as *A Yank at Oxford* (1928) and *Goodbye, Mr. Chips* (1939). These films featured American talent and directors and were released as American productions — which did little to stimulate the English industry's recovery.

In 1930 Paramount dispatched one of its European-imported directors, Alexander Korda, back across the Atlantic, this time to England. Within a year, Korda had cut his ties with Paramount and had formed his own company. He had learned the Hollywood style and was convinced that the matrimonial exploits of Henry VIII offered good material for a film. With Charles Laughton as Henry, he launched *The Private Life of Henry VIII* (1933) as what appeared to be a successful model. Soon other talents from America were making frequent trips between the two countries, and British production picked up.

But Korda and his investors knew they could not depend upon the United Kingdom alone for the necessary gate receipts. His budgets increased, but box-office returns from America did not. American companies failed to conduct exciting promotional campaigns for Korda's films. The films were booked into a few large cities where the limited audiences remained unimpressed, since the films did not bear the image of middle America.

One British director, however, did captivate audiences. His unique handling of the whodunit in *The Lodger* (1926) attracted interest, and *The Thirty-nine Steps* (1935) and *The Lady Vanishes* (1938) realized excellent box-office returns in both Britain and the United States. But Hollywood offered him a contract, and Alfred Hitchcock left for America.

Except for a dedicated band of documentary filmmakers, only the work of Carol Reed stands apart from the confused and disjointed production of the period in England. Reed's *The Stars Look Down* (1939) was a simple and straightforward story set in a Welsh mining town. Its uncompromising realism and the accurate reflection of issues and attitudes suggest influence of the documentary movement, and its approach would eventually be developed by the neorealists in Italy after the War. Twenty years later, after the release of *The Stars Look Down,* the Angry Young Men movement in Britain would hark back to Reed's maverick piece. The film was withheld in America until 1942, after John Ford's similar but pale version of the same story *How Green Was My Valley* (1941) had run its course. Even then, because the miners were antagonistic toward their own union, *The*

Stars Look Down was not received kindly by American unionists fresh from a decade of intense and bloody conflict with management.

What the British were unable to accomplish during the 1930s was swiftly, though indirectly, rectified by Hitler. The Nazi threat quickly established a British cinema reflecting uniquely British values and concerns. Once again the film industry was harnessed to the task of unifying a country and supporting a national will — first in the interest of survival and then of victory.

Italy

The situation in Italy paralleled that in England with respect to several issues. Here the industry had once produced as many as 450 features a year and had enjoyed vast world markets, but by 1919 it had fallen on bad times. By 1920 only half as many titles were released as in prewar years, and in 1927 fewer than a dozen features were issued. Unable to discern the temper of the times, the Italian studios continued to grind out the old spectaculars in which the grand-opera style of acting was employed. Italy invited the Germans to perform for their industry whatever magic the Germans had used in their own film industry to bring German cinema to world attention. But a remake of the 1912 *Quo Vadis?* (1924) did nothing to help the situation. MGM was invited to Italy for a remake of *Ben Hur* (1926), but the studio scrapped the project and the crew returned to Hollywood, where the horrendously expensive (and ultimately profitable) production was shot.

The Fascist government under Mussolini centralized all film production in 1925 and tried to breathe new life into the industry by drawing from American, German, and Soviet theories and practice. That organization, known as LUCE, was functioning by 1927. In 1935, Centro Sperimentale was trying to develop an Italian "school," but nothing was to come of the organization except a remarkable complex of equipment and studios. Clearly, these and other attempts were stimulated by a national need for recognition and esteem in the world community. The film medium had become, perhaps unintentionally, a yardstick by which national images were measured. Unfortunately for the industry, however, creativity and experimentation cannot be summoned at will by industrialists or politicians.

But there was in Italy a faint voice being raised, a voice beyond the pale of Fascist structures, which contained the seeds of revolutionary change. During the thirties, writers and critics began to plead for a rejection of studio fakery and a return to the natural settings of the real world. They wanted an end to the pompous veneer, the sumptuous settings, and the inflated characters, which together amounted to only passive entertainment. The final collapse of fascism and the end of World War II set free uninhibited creative forces that would generate the necessity, impulse, and will to develop an authentic vitality. In film, this vital energy took the form of neorealism. Cesare Zavattini describes it this way:

> A return to man, to the creature who in himself is "all spectacle": this would liberate us. Set up the camera in a street, in a room, see with insatiable patience, train ourselves in the contemplation of our fellow-man in his elementary actions. We will abandon trick photography, process shots, the infinite subterfuges so dear to Méliès. The wonder must be in us, expressing itself without wonder: the best dreams are those outside the mist, which can be seen like the veins of leaves.

The Far East

Lumière shorts were exhibited in Japan in 1897, and Japanese production was soon underway. American Western themes were immediately popular in China. But American audiences saw virtually nothing from the Far East and what had become in the 1920s a thriving and serious film industry there. Later, in 1929, Tokyo's Shochiku Studio and China's Great Wall Film Company each had a feature in American distribution. And in the 1950s, Americans would learn of Kenji Mizoguchi when his Academy Award winning foreign film *Ugetsu* (1953) circulated through art houses. Mizoguchi began his directing career in the 1920s.

Wrap-Up

The upheavals of the 1920s and 1930s produced one of the most fascinating periods in film history. Concepts of the nature of film were shaken and potentials for artistic manipulation of the medium were forever enriched. And the period saw international cross-fertilization on a grand scale. Buñuel, from Spain, was working in France;

Feyder, born in Belgium, was working both in Hollywood and in France; Dreyer, from Denmark, was working in Germany and France; Robison and Man Ray, from the United States, were working in France; and Eisenstein was working, if unsuccessfully, in America and Mexico. A continuous interchange of directors, technicians, and actors took place throughout the filmmaking world. Serious cinema finally tapped the resources of the other arts during this time, and with intentions other than entertaining the masses, filmmakers carved out new territory on the film landscape.

The fires of passion, and sometimes of love, continually poured forth from the individual and collective visions. And oppressive reactions, policies, and pressures continually inhibited the filmmakers' purposes. As the intensity of the period diminished, a new factor, sound, entered the scene to cause new responses and generate new problems.

Not until after World War II would movements with the intensity of those of the 1920s occur again in Europe. For the next decade contributions to the growth and development of the medium would come from just a few individuals, whose vision would transcend the economic collapse and political terror appearing on the horizon.

Uncertainty marked the decade of the 1930s. Basic premises of Western thought were shaken to their roots. The chaos threw institutions and traditions, even whole film industries, into complete disarray. But such responsiveness was appropriate in a medium that reflected the raw pulse of its time, both in terms of mass diversion and serious analysis. It was up to the individual free spirits who rose above the chaos to point the medium, in existence for barely forty years, in new directions. Beginning in 1927, new sound approaches were explored and integrated, and American film was further influenced by talent from elsewhere in the film world.

Sound:
A New
Beginning
(1927 – 1933)

C H A P T E R

7

Focus

We have emphasized throughout this book that motion picture technology has been critical historically, economically, and artistically to the total development of the form. It seems necessary, however, to reassess the contribution of technology as we turn to the most dramatic and revolutionary technological development in film. All artists must work within the physical parameters of their media. Therefore, all film artists must begin with an understanding of technology and its role in defining the essential nature of motion pictures.

In film, the raw materials of reality are shaped by and for the mechanical apparatuses that record, arrange, and project filmed images. Control is the essence of any art, and indeed, of almost any experience, and film is no exception. Even in the most improvisational films, and in so-called cinéma vérité, where the films supposedly simply record reality, the filmmaker exerts control by arranging and shaping specific realities. To exercise control over their work, filmmakers must conceive films as totalities, from the script through the projected image. In the process, they must also take into account the fundamentally mechanical nature of the medium.

As we have seen, motion pictures were born of research in a scientific age. Cinematography was a culmination of many discoveries and inventions, mostly mechanical and technological. This historical reality is continually reflected in film history. Although many historians might not equate the contributions of D. W. Griffith and Lee De Forest, pioneer radio and electronics inventor, it is important to realize that both individuals had enormous impacts on motion picture history.

The effects of technology take several forms. First, and most important, technology sets motion pictures apart as an art form. In this respect, film is similar to other mass media, such as television, photography, radio, and audio recordings. The technological dependency inherent in motion pictures has many effects. For example, technology is often the criterion in a director's selection of a particular performer or face. D. W. Griffith used young actresses, such as Lillian Gish and Mae Marsh, primarily because the film stock used at that time revealed every line and fissure in the human face. Thorold Dickinson explains:

> By the time [the actresses'] figures were fully developed, their faces . . . were already assuming the look of the *femme fatale;* by twenty-five they were regarded as character actresses, by forty as grandmothers.

Expense is a second major impact of technology. Though much of a film's cost derives from nontechnical expenditures, such as story costs and salaries, approximately 20 to 30 percent of total cost is directly related to the technology required to create a film. And the basic mass-audience orientation of film is a third impact of technology, one related to cost. Film is fundamentally a mass medium trying to reach as many people as possible. One of the justifications for this mass orientation is the cost imposed by films' technological base.

Yet another effect of technology on motion pictures had to do with production complexity. The efforts of thousands of people involved in creating such spectacles as *Intolerance* (1916), *Robin Hood* (1924), *Gone with the Wind* (1939), *Spartacus* (1960), and *Gandhi* (1982) result in tremendous expense. In part because of the technology involved, making a film is a team — not an individual — effort.

Technology has also contributed to the domination of film by business organizations rather than the filmmakers themselves. Both patent rights on inventions and the huge costs required to produce films on a mass basis have resulted in the development of powerful industrial organizations driven solely by the profit motive. Such men as Adolph Zukor, Irving G. Thalberg, and Louis B. Mayer may have represented or symbolized a company, but few individuals, even at the height of their power, have ever controlled the medium.

A less obvious but important effect of technology has been its impact on the historical patterns discernible over time. Throughout its history, whenever the industry has felt threatened and concerned about its dominance in the mass entertainment field slipping, it has turned to technology to restore the pre-eminence of motion pictures. This pattern was especially clear at the two major turning points in film history — the introduction of sound and the appearance of television. These

Edison on Sound

*I*n the year 1887, the idea occurred to me that it would be possible to devise an instrument which should do for the eye what the phonograph does for the ear and that by a combination of the two all motion and sound could be recorded and reproduced simultaneously.

—*Thomas A. Edison*

major technological changes significantly affected the state of the medium at times when the industry needed a boost.

We must consider the technology of sound and its impact on motion picture history, therefore, in the context of the overall impact and meaning of technology to motion pictures. The coming of sound was not an isolated phenomenon in motion picture history, but rather the continuation of the interplay between technology, art, and commerce.

Early Attempts at Sound

Sound motion pictures were conceived in principle from the very beginning. Films were not silent because people wanted them to be; the silents were always a compromise. The two factors that delayed the advent of sound were lack of technical knowledge and the industry's resistance to "rocking the boat" by creating a new motion picture form that would involve great expense.

The first thirty years of motion picture history saw few attempts to actively exploit silence and make it an integral part of films. With the exception of the best films of Chaplin, Keaton, and a few other artists working primarily in comedy, most silent films attempted to compensate for the lack of sound by using frequent titles, by depending on live and often elaborate musical accompaniment, or both.

Movie Palace Organ

*T*he Hope-Jones organ costing $22,000 is capable of furnishing all the accompaniment, but it is augmented at night by an orchestra of eight men, conducted by the organist, Carl Stalling.

This organ is run by electric motor with pipes incased in two separate swell boxes at either side of the stage. This swell box for all pipes gives greater variety of tone, the loudest stop thus being turned into the softest of tones without change of manual. The stops — open diapason, clarinet, kinura, orchestra violin, violin celeste, flute, vox humana and tuba horn, are made more effective by the "borrowing system" by which four or five different tones may be produced. The numerous traps are accessories for making the "silent drama" realistic. Besides the imitation of the various instruments of the orchestra such as the chrysoglott, harp, chimes, bells, snare drum, tambourines, castenets, Chinese block, glockenspiel and xylophone, there are the equally important auto horn, blown at the dramatic moment; steamboat whistle; beat of horse's hoofs, used for the inevitable horse chase in the Western drama; clanging of fire gong; the troublesome telephone bell; tom-tom; and bird whistle. All these are necessary accessories, although a little out of the realm of music. But they are all performed from the organ.

—Moving Picture World *(July 26, 1919)*

Of course, as many observers have pointed out, silent films were never silent. Directors, producers, and exhibitors were constantly seeking ways to add an aural dimension to films. One of the most popular early methods was to place actors behind the screen and have them speak or sing in synchronization with the projected image. Even D. W. Griffith used this method in some road-show presentations of *The Birth of a Nation.* James Limbacher, in his book *Four Aspects of Film,* quotes one of the sound men who worked in this manner:

I was given instructions to slap two boards together when a certain red light flashed on. We could see the film through the back of the screen to be sure we got our synchronization correctly. But I was glued to that red light. When it came on, I slammed the two boards together. When I looked at the screen, I discovered I had just shot Abraham Lincoln!

The most common method of adding sound to motion pictures was piano, organ, or orchestral accompaniment. Pianos were a fixture of the earliest store theaters and nickelodeons, and by 1912 elaborate organs, with a variety of sound-effects equipment, were being installed in many new theaters.

Finally, the golden age of movie palaces brought about an equally golden age in motion picture music. Complete orchestras were standard in many theaters and people sometimes claimed they went to the movies just to hear the music.

Most theater musicians operated from a standard repertoire, which meant they played certain selections for various moods and tempos. They were aided in this by cue sheets issued with the films; these indicated standard pieces for particular moments in a film (see the box on page 177). In addition, certain major films — for example, most of Griffith's major works, including *The Birth of a Nation, Intolerance,* and *Broken Blossoms* — had original musical scores. In fact, the characters in *Way Down East* all had musical themes identified with them in the score.

Despite the elaborate and at times satisfactory use of sound in motion pictures, there was constant experimentation with synchronous sound, and the basic inventions necessary for sound motion pictures began to

▶ S. L. Rothapfel, owner of the Roxy Theater, admiring a new addition to his picture palace. Huge organs like this one provided a wide variety of music and sound effects for silent motion pictures.

▶ From Cecil B. De Mille's *The Ten Commandments* (1923). This production still shows how music was used in silent film to help create mood and "environment" for a scene. Ruth Dickey and her orchestra were "morale makers" at Camp De Mille, not only playing on the set for atmosphere but also furnishing music for dancing at night. As the picture also illustrates, moviemaking could be very unglamorous and, especially with on-location shooting, often harsh and difficult.

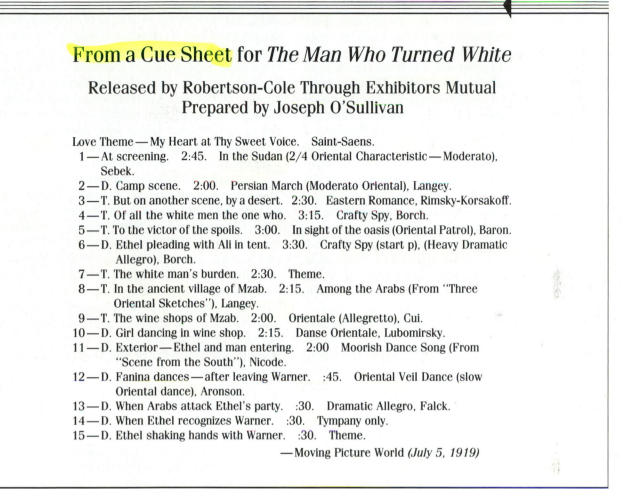

From a Cue Sheet for *The Man Who Turned White*

Released by Robertson-Cole Through Exhibitors Mutual
Prepared by Joseph O'Sullivan

Love Theme — My Heart at Thy Sweet Voice.   Saint-Saens.
1—At screening.   2:45.   In the Sudan (2/4 Oriental Characteristic — Moderato), Sebek.
2—D. Camp scene.   2:00.   Persian March (Moderato Oriental), Langey.
3—T. But on another scene, by a desert.   2:30.   Eastern Romance, Rimsky-Korsakoff.
4—T. Of all the white men the one who.   3:15.   Crafty Spy, Borch.
5—T. To the victor of the spoils.   3:00.   In sight of the oasis (Oriental Patrol), Baron.
6—D. Ethel pleading with Ali in tent.   3:30.   Crafty Spy (start p), (Heavy Dramatic Allegro), Borch.
7—T. The white man's burden.   2:30.   Theme.
8—T. In the ancient village of Mzab.   2:15.   Among the Arabs (From "Three Oriental Sketches"), Langey.
9—T. The wine shops of Mzab.   2:00.   Orientale (Allegretto), Cui.
10—D. Girl dancing in wine shop.   2:15.   Danse Orientale, Lubomirsky.
11—D. Exterior — Ethel and man entering.   2:00   Moorish Dance Song (From "Scene from the South"), Nicode.
12—D. Fanina dances — after leaving Warner.   :45.   Oriental Veil Dance (slow Oriental dance), Aronson.
13—D. When Arabs attack Ethel's party.   :30.   Dramatic Allegro, Falck.
14—D. When Ethel recognizes Warner.   :30.   Tympany only.
15—D. Ethel shaking hands with Warner.   :30.   Theme.

—*Moving Picture World* *(July 5, 1919)*

emerge early in the twentieth century. León Gaumont exhibited talking pictures at the Paris Exposition of 1900 by combining a projector with a phonograph. Most early efforts were attempts to solve the two major obstacles to sound motion pictures — amplification and synchronization. Many individuals contributed to the development of sound films, but, as with cinematography, it was an American who made the first and perhaps most significant contribution. This was Dr. Lee De Forest, and his invention, the audion, initially had nothing to do with motion pictures.

De Forest's audion tube made possible, among other things, the amplification of electrical signals, which in turn provided the stimulus for radio broadcasting. With this basic discovery in 1907, the age of electronics was born. As one contemporary account put it, the audion performed the task of "unlocking the door to progress and improvement in almost every phase of sound transmission, recording, and reproduction." De Forest later

developed an interest in motion pictures, and in 1922 he produced a sound system called Phonofilm. However, this system met with little success, owing partly to technical problems, but more significantly to a cool response from the industry, which had no use for sound at this time. Nevertheless, research on sound systems began in earnest after World War I, stimulated in part by the War and the role of electronic communications in it.

The next research problem concerned how to synchronize sound with picture. Research centered on two different types of systems — photographic/electronic sound on film and mechanical disk. Each system had its advantages, and as a result both were developed to commercial status almost simultaneously. The sound-on-film system, which ultimately became the industry standard, was expensive and complicated. The disk method, while less expensive and relatively simple, was decidedly less reliable and more cumbersome.

The earliest successful work in sound on film took

place in Germany in 1918. In the United States, Western Electric developed a system that reproduced sound photographically on the same strip of film on which the visual images were photographed. A light in the projector then picked up the various striations, and these signals were pushed through an amplifier, emerging as sound. Initially cooperating with De Forest, Western Electric developed a number of experimental machines between 1922 and 1925, and by 1926, now separated from De Forest, had produced a commercially viable system. The method was demonstrated to representatives of the Fox Film Corporation, who subsequently purchased it and gave it the name Movietone.

The first use of sound on film was a throwback to the principle of the earliest motion pictures—the simple recording of reality. Sound newsreels focused on such subjects as Charles Lindbergh taking off for Paris and, in a later edition, Lindbergh accepting a medal from President Coolidge. In both films the camera was virtually locked into place, simply recording the scene in front of it. There was no attempt at composition, and the only editing was done when the camera had to be stopped for a change of reels. Everything was dictated by the microphone. Despite the absence of traditional filmic values, these newsreels were very popular and remain valuable today as historical records.

The disk system of sound motion pictures was directly linked to the development of the phonograph, and it produced sound movies by synchronizing a record with the film. Edison developed the first disk system. He discarded his initial attempt, but picked up the idea again in 1913, and his company made several films that year using round cylinder records connected to a projector by a pulley. However, the project was soon dropped and there was little further development until 1926, when the Vitaphone system was introduced. Vitaphone used seventeen-inch disks played at 33-1/3 rpm on a turntable synchronized with the projector. The disk system was superior to sound on film, primarily because it was cheaper and produced higher quality sound.

Warner Brothers and Vitaphone

As noted previously, one of the obstacles to the development of sound film was the film industry's reluctance to encourage and become involved in costly experimentation when business was stable. Despite the general aura of indifference surrounding sound, however, one company found it practical to become interested in sound

very quickly. Warner Brothers, barely two years old in 1926, was on the verge of bankruptcy and desperately in need of some kind of competitive edge to stay alive. The company lacked the extensive theater holdings of the other major firms and found it difficult to find a first-run market for its films. In 1925, Sam Warner saw a demonstration of Western Electric's sound disk system, became enthusiastic, and quickly convinced his three brothers that sound would give them the edge they needed to stay competitive. In April 1926, the Vitaphone Corporation was formed, with Sam Warner as president.

Don Juan (1926), starring John Barrymore, was the first major film to use the Vitaphone process. In the theaters, the film was preceded by one twenty-minute short, featuring a talk by MPPDA "czar" Will Hays, and several other shorts, including one on the New York Philharmonic Orchestra, demonstrating the potential and attractiveness of sound. The sound in the feature itself, however, was limited to music provided by the New York Philharmonic. Since musical accompaniment was nothing new to silent film audiences, the "miracle" of sound was going to have to do better than this to revolutionize the industry and keep Warner Brothers from bankruptcy.

Following Don Juan, Warner and Vitaphone both produced a series of short films specifically designed to demonstrate the potential of sound. These short subjects are comparable to the "demonstration" records that accompanied the introduction of stereophonic music in the late 1950s. They were worth little except as illustrations of how the system worked, and they were therefore usually given away by dealers rather than sold. Most of these shorts ran less than an hour and presented seven to ten variety skits and musical numbers, the latter performed by various orchestras, singing groups, and soloists. These films were simple recordings of vaudeville acts, demonstrating little camera movement, composition, or editing. The emphasis was on "showing" people what sound "looked" like.

Warner Brothers continued to produce these shorts along with silent features, constantly trying to gauge audience response. Meanwhile, Fox Films was producing their sound-on-film Movietone newsreels with increasing regularity. Consequently, by mid-1927 sound in its several forms was making tentative but definite strides forward. For sound to develop beyond the experimental

▶ The sound-projection system developed by Western Electric and used by Warner Brothers under the name Vitaphone.

stage, however, the industry as a whole was going to have to accept and use it for feature presentations. Fortunately, circumstances were gradually forcing the industry to do just that.

Competitive Media

By 1926 the boom of the early twenties was coming to a close. Business was spotty, and a reader of *Variety's* December 15, 1926, issue would have gleaned from the following headlines that something was going wrong:

NEW ORLEANS CAN'T ENTHUSE OVER ITSELF
MINNEAPOLIS IN BAD SHAPE WITH HIGH GROSS
LAST WEEK $12,000
BUFFALO SUFFERS BAD DROP
15% AND 20% DISCOUNT COUPONS BY RIVAL
MILWAUKEE HOUSES

There were several definite reasons for the decline. The first was radio. Although less than six years old as a broadcast medium, radio boasted 732 stations and three national networks in 1926. The new medium was especially strong in large cities — New York had more than 40 stations and Chicago 58. And the stations were competing directly with the first-run theaters, the keystones of the studio empires. *Variety* headlined this competition in 1927 with "Radio Aces Hurt Theaters." The city was

Minneapolis, Minnesota, which had 25,000 sets and several strong stations offering many kinds of programs, including symphonies, musical variety programs, and talk shows. The same atmosphere prevailed in every large city in the country, and for the first time in its young history motion pictures felt the direct force of competition from another mass medium.

In addition to radio, many other media attractions contributed to popular culture in the 1920s. Vaudeville was not yet dead, and various forms of tent entertainment, such as plays, religious revivals (Billy Sunday and Aimee Semple McPherson, in particular), and circus and carnivals shows also lured big audiences. And legitimate theater, symbolized most aptly by Florence Ziegfield's "Follies" revues, was enormously popular. Newspapers and magazines (especially the new "tabloids") represented another commanding popular medium; records and sheet music rounded out the environment. All these forms of entertainment plus spectator sports and the automobile, both of whose popularity was increasing, provided stiff competition for movies.

A second reason for declining movie attendance was the high cost of admission to most theaters. The nickel had been buried and the dime had one foot in the grave. Rising admission prices were a direct consequence of the high production costs brought on by Hollywood's spectacle binge of the early 1920s. Most audiences gladly paid their quarters, half-dollars, and dollars for super productions such as *Ben Hur, The Ten Commandments, The Trail of '98,* and *Wings.* However, they were reluctant to pay the same prices for ordinary studio potboilers. The studios, on the other hand, were accustomed to enthusiastic responses to everything they produced. Attendance figures had climbed rapidly throughout the early and middle twenties, and the studios had grown fat and complacent about both their products and their audience. When the bubble burst, it hit the second-line studios, such as Warners, which were struggling hardest to gain a foothold in the industry. The firms that had come in during the boom days were now finding it difficult to keep their heads above water.

The Jazz Singer

Despite the studio's success with sound shorts, Warner Brothers continued to struggle. The company found that more was needed than the New York Philharmonic and Will Hays to lure audiences away from Buster Keaton, John Gilbert, and Mary Pickford. Sound by itself was obviously not enough. Warners desperately needed something unique to break into first-run theaters. They found that Al Jolson, combined with a heart-rending

▲ From *The Jazz Singer* (1927). Al Jolson displays some of the vitality that made his personality important to the film's appeal.

drama, met that need precisely. *The Jazz Singer* opened in New York on October 6, 1927, and motion pictures were never the same.

Only portions of *The Jazz Singer* had synchronous sound (see the accompanying box), but where it did occur, sound was used here for the first time as an integral part of a film, not simply as accompaniment or window dressing. The moment Al Jolson uttered the phrase, "Come on, Ma! Listen to this," audiences began to cheer wildly.

Still the other studios held back. In addition to sound, other technological wonders, such as color and the wide screen, were being introduced. The studios were reluctant to convert to a mode of production that might prove to be merely a passing fancy. The winter of 1927/1928 saw the studios perched on a very uncomfortable fence.

However, by the spring of 1928 public response to *The Jazz Singer* and to Warners' first all-talking feature, *Lights of New York,* was sufficient to convince the major

studios to sign contracts for recording equipment. With the new production season beginning in September, the summer of 1928 was one of great activity. Studios hired construction crews to work round the clock building sound stages. In a typical move, Carl Laemmle of Universal spent $1.2 million for four sound stages in Fort Lee, New Jersey. And a great rush was on to hire engineers, voice coaches, dialogue writers, musicians, and singers. Anyone who had any possible sound-related skill was immediately put to work by the studios. MGM, for example, developed plans for a school where its foreign players could learn English.

Meanwhile, silent film production was quickly disappearing. In less than three years, more than 95 percent of what was once the base of a huge industry attracting millions of people each week simply vanished. Few tears were shed, however, especially by the studios. Sound was indeed the magic they had needed to restore financial vigor to the industry. Profits were up for all the major studios, but for none more dramatically than Warner

Sherwood on *The Jazz Singer*

*T*here is one moment in *The Jazz Singer* that is fraught with tremendous significance.

Al Jolson, appearing as a Jewish youth, returns to his old home after years of wandering around the Pantages circuit. His strictly orthodox father disowned him because he chose to sing mammy songs in music halls rather than chants in the synagogue; his mother, however, welcomes the prodigal with open arms.

Al sits down at the piano and sings "Blue Sky" for his mother. Thanks to the Vitaphone attachment, his marvelous voice rings out from the screen, the sound agreeing perfectly with the movements of his mobile lips, the wriggling of his shoulders, the nervous tapping of his feet.

After the song, there is a brief bit of spoken dialogue, and then Al bursts into "Blue Sky" again. When he is halfway through the chorus, his father enters the room, realizes that his house is being profaned with jazz, and shouts, "Stop!"

At this point, the Vitaphone withdraws and *The Jazz Singer* returns to a routine of pantomime punctuated with subtitles.

Such is the moment referred to in paragraph one—and when it came, I for one suddenly realized that the end of the silent drama is in sight.

There is no question of doubt that the Vitaphone justifies itself in *The Jazz Singer*. Furthermore, it proves that talking movies are considerably more than a lively possibility: They are close to an accomplished fact.

The Jazz Singer isn't much of a moving picture, as moving pictures go. It has a good idea (taken from Samson Raphaelson's play), but it has been hoked and sugared to a regrettable extent; and Al Jolson as an actor on the screen is only fair.

But when Al Jolson starts to sing . . . well, bring on your super-spectacles, your million-dollar thrills, your long shots of Calvary against a setting sun, your close-ups of a glycerine tear on Norma Talmadge's cheek— I'll trade them all for one instant of any ham song that Al cares to put over, and the hammier it is, the better I'll like it.

—*Robert E. Sherwood*, Life
(October 27, 1927)

Brothers, whose $17.2 million profit in 1929 represented a 745 percent increase over 1928 profits. Weekly attendance figures for the industry climbed to close to 100 million.

By early 1929, MGM had only five silent films in production. That same year Fox discontinued silent production completely. The activity at the studios was duplicated by the theaters. When it finally became apparent that sound was here to stay and the studios were going to produce nothing but sound films, theater owners began their frantic renovation process. In 1927 only 157 theaters were equipped for sound. At the end of 1928 there were more than 1,000 sound theaters, and by the end of 1930, more than 13,000 theaters, most of them capable of handling both sound on film and disk. Approximately 8,000 theaters were still silent, but these were theaters in rural areas whose owners could not afford to convert to sound. Many of these theaters played silent films well into the thirties and then went out of business. By 1930 only 5 percent of the films produced in Hollywood were silent, and these few were made by small companies that could not afford to convert to sound and were simply running out their string by supplying the remaining silent theaters with new products.

Clear reasons for the immediate and almost universal public acceptance of sound are difficult to pinpoint. Nicholas Vardac, in his book *From Stage to Screen,* notes that nineteenth-century theater produced a "climate of acceptance" for motion pictures both by its emphasis on realism and, in most cases, its ultimate inability to produce complete realism. Much the same could be said about the sound film. Both radio and the phonograph had stimulated audience interest in sound entertainment and had created various dramatic forms that audiences readily accepted. By 1926–1927, the phonograph and radio had become established in households—45 percent of all American homes had phonographs and 40 percent had radio sets. So sound as entertainment was an accepted reality for a majority of American homes, and extending sound to motion pictures was quite natural. Perhaps, once again a "climate of acceptance" had been prepared that made sound films welcome.

Another factor in the rapid and total acceptance of sound film was that, even given elaborate musical scores and varied sound effects, silent motion pictures had always been considered incomplete and artificial. Titles, even when intelligently and sparingly used, were intrusive and usually broke the rhythm of a film. A study in 1914 demonstrated that one-fourth of the audience could read a printed title in one-third the time required by the rest of the audience. As a result, most titles were designed for the slower three-fourths. As literacy increased, viewers increasingly found the time that titles were on screen intolerably long. Also, the mass audience was not used to mime as a standard way of communicating. Furthermore, most actors and actresses were relatively unskilled in mime; only Chaplin, Keaton, and several other silent comedians were capable of using it as a natural and effective means of communication. Thus, silent film was basically an incomplete medium, and most people accepted the addition of sound as natural.

Problems and Impacts

Despite the tremendous expansion in sound production, in 1928 the industry was still undecided about which system to adopt, disk or sound on film. Most studios and theaters hedged their bets and used both. However, the advantages of sound on film soon became obvious, and, once the problems associated with editing were solved,

this became the industry standard. But a number of other problems involving sound still confronted the industry. Most of them were technical, but these difficulties often had severe ramifications in the artistic realm.

The Impact on Technology

One fundamental problem involved camera placement. Sound basically immobilized the camera, since microphones picked up and amplified camera noise when the camera came within range. The short-term solution was to encase the camera in a sound-proof booth. This eliminated the noise, but it also eliminated most camera movement. Microphones were also immobile, which further compounded the problem. As a result of these constraints, most early sound films were static stage pieces. Edward Everett Horton recalled those days vividly in Kevin Brownlow's *The Parade's Gone By:*

> In those days there was no boom that followed you all around. The microphones hung down, all wrapped around with material to make them look like part of the backdrop. We had three or four cameras. In a great big ensemble scene these cameras were sort of coffins covered with tarpaulins so that you couldn't hear the buzz of the camera. They were on turnstiles. . . . We were instructed not to talk until we felt ourselves in center of the camera. So the scene would go around: "You see this man?" . . . Camera turns . . . "Yes." . . . Camera turns . . . "You know what happened?" . . . Camera . . . "No." . . . Camera . . . "Killed." . . . Camera . . . "What?" . . . Camera . . . "Who did it?" . . . Camera.

Desperate to achieve some mobility, cameramen resorted to a variety of measures, including using four cameras for a single take. At times such a set-up could require ten or more changes of the close-up camera's direction for a single ten-minute scene.

Microphones presented their own problems. All the early ones were stationary, as noted, and most were crude and had little directional control. They picked up any and every sound on the set. The result was a new art: the ability to hide microphones in flowers, vases, clocks, tables, and costumes. Actors and actresses suddenly became aware of new patterns in stage direction that stressed walking over to a bush or a table simply to be heard. An authentic and amusing example of such microphone follies appears in MGM's 1952 musical *Singin' in the Rain.*

Although the problems caused by stationary microphones were irritating, they were small compared to those created by the microphones' overall sensitivity to normal sound. Knock-kneed extras, talkative directors, silk bloomers—virtually anything that created sound was a potential problem. Rubber suddenly became the latest in fashion as filmmakers discovered that conventional jewelry and shoes created too much noise. A new style of manicuring was developed to eliminate the clicking of long nails. Sugar cubes and matchsticks had to be handled with great care. People learned to eat and kiss all over again, and chewing gum was instantly abolished. "Voice dynamics" became a term to be feared, as Clara Bow learned in her first sound film, *The Wild Party* (1928). She entered a room, hollered "Whoopee!!" and all the sound tubes died. Even noise outside the studio had to be controlled. Garbage trucks on studio lots were equipped with balloon tires, and men were stationed on rooftops with flags warning airplanes to stay away. When King Vidor was filming his first sound film, *Hallelujah!,* (1929), he had lookouts stationed all over the lot, and even so was still restricted to about ten minutes of shooting a day. The lights themselves made noise, and as a result incandescent lighting soon replaced arc lights.

Most of these technical problems were solved within a year or two. However, the artistic problems involving sound took longer. Part of the explanation for this disparity lies in the mental attitude of various technical and artistic groups. Technicians were enthusiastic about the new developments; they were eager to solve problems and develop new and better methods of recording and reproducing sound. However, many artists were reluctant to embrace the new medium. They had developed a unique art form in silent film and resisted the idea of abandoning it completely. Many critics were certain that sound was the death of everything artistic in cinema. This remark by British filmmaker and critic Paul Rotha was typical of the time:

> It may be concluded that a film in which the speech and sound effects are perfectly synchronized and coincide with their visual images on the screen is absolutely contrary to the aim of the cinema. It is a degenerate and misguided attempt to destroy the real use of the film and cannot be accepted as coming within the true boundaries of the cinema. Not only are dialogue films wasting the time of intelligent directors, but they are harmful and detrimental to the culture of the public.

Charlie Chaplin was among those most violently opposed to sound and, as noted earlier, he continued to make silent films, including *City Lights* (1931) and *Modern Times* (1936), throughout the thirties. These films

▲ Charlie Chaplin in his "man versus machine" film *Modern Times* (1936). Chaplin aimed his satiric wit at the machine age in his last "silent" film—silent only in speech, since Chaplin composed the music, including the popular song "Smile," and added numerous special sound effects.

were silent, however, only in that they lacked dialogue. Chaplin made rich use of music and sound effects, much in the fashion of René Clair. In his autobiography, Chaplin states,

> Occasionally I mused over the possibility of making a sound film, but the thought sickened me, for I realized I could never achieve the excellence of my silent pictures. It would mean giving up my tramp character entirely. Some people suggested that the tramp might talk. This was unthinkable, for the first word he ever uttered would transform him into another person.

Ultimately Chaplin did turn to sound with *The Great Dictator* in 1940. By then, however, his tramp was gone, forever silent.

Despite reluctance by some and outright hostility from others, many directors saw great possibilities in sound and welcomed it. The accomplished Russian director Pudovkin put it this way:

> [T]he sound film is a new medium, which can be used in entirely new ways; sounds and human speech should be used by the director not as a literal accompaniment, but to amplify and enrich the visual image on the screen. Under such conditions, could the sound film become a new form of art whose future development had no predictable limits?

Pudovkin was, of course, pointing to a basic problem that plagued almost all makers of early sound films — the literal reproduction of every sound shown on the screen. Although it affected all aspects of film production, sound had its greatest impact on editing. At first, the changes in editing were beneficial. No longer was it necessary to cut to an object making a sound in order for the audience to "hear" it. An excellent example of this new editing freedom occurs in *Rain* (1929), where the camera focuses on Joan Crawford's face while Walter Huston recites the Lord's prayer.

Despite these benefits, however, many restrictions on editing derived from the early sound techniques as well, owing to the necessity to synchronize sound and image. This constraint, coupled with the camera's immobility, resulted in single-perspective shooting. The only way to create multiperspective shooting and introduce some editing was to shoot all scenes with several cameras — one for long shots, one for medium shots, and one for close-ups. Not until the development of the Movieola in 1932 was editing made simple and clean in design.

However, even with the potential for more freedom in editing, the simple fact that people in a scene could now talk made establishing relationships much easier and simpler. Editing became less of an artistic tool and more of a functional device. The "invisible" editing style of most Hollywood pictures in the thirties, where individual shots and entire scenes flowed together in smooth uninterrupted patterns, was clear evidence that meaning could now be carried by sound, without the need to emphasize so heavily the visual elements of the motion picture process.

The Impact on Content

The influence of sound on the content of films was immediate and dramatic. Because audiences wanted to hear any and every sound, and because music was cheaper and easier to produce than dialogue, the musical film was quickly established as a new genre. If words were going to dominate, the thinking went, they might as well be put into the most pleasing and dynamic form possible. At first the genre consisted simply of Broadway musicals and operettas transported intact from New York to Hollywood. *Rio Rita* (1929), starring Bebe Daniels, was a big success, and was quickly followed by dozens of others, including *The Desert Song* (1929), *Sunny* (1929), *Sally* (1929), *Showboat* (1929), and *Gold Diggers of Broadway* (1929).

With the appearance of MGM's *Broadway Melody* in 1929, a faint trace of originality began to creep into the form. *Broadway Melody* was a huge success; it grossed more than $4 million and won an Oscar for best film (the first sound film to do so). The natural reaction on the part of the studios was to follow with more of the same. *Hollywood Revue* came along the same year featuring a new twist, "all-star" lineup. Paramount's *On Parade,* Warner's *Show of Shows,* and Universal's *King of Jazz* imitated the pattern and the first wave of what would become a flood broke on the shore. A sidelight to this development was the rapid increase in the sale of film songs as records and sheet music. As *Photoplay* noted in 1929, within a month of a film's release the average motion picture song was selling almost 100,000 sheet copies and records. For example, *Fox Follies* opened in late 1929, and within three weeks "Breakaway," "That's You, Baby," and "Walking with Susie" each sold 100,000 sheet copies and records. This tremendous economic potential was not lost on the studios, and Warner Brothers quickly spent $5 million to acquire Witmark, Inc., one of the oldest music publishing firms in the country. Virtually every major studio imitated the move.

Sound affected film content in two other ways of note, one permanent and one only temporary. The most dramatic and lasting impact involved comedy. Silent

To: Mr. A. A. Kaufman   August 13, 1929

Dear Al:

   May I suggest for the Revue [*Paramount on Parade* (1930)] that we
might do something very amusing on the contrast of silent pictures and talking pictures? As an initial idea along these lines, we might have a very
romantic love scene played without the voices being heard, first advising the
audience to put their own interpretation on the dialogue, which they cannot
hear; and then playing the exact same scene with ridiculous and amusing
dialogue, completely contrary to what the audience has thought it to be.

   An idea something along these lines was used in the *Music Box Revue* in
New York some years ago, when a very melodramatic scene was played with
nonsensical dialogue. We have an excuse for such a scene, which they did
not have.

   You know from experience that often in silent pictures very romantic
love scenes were played with the actors talking about a party the night
before, or some other totally irrelevant subject.

                                             David O. Selznick

comedy, including the work of Chaplin, Keaton, and Lloyd, had achieved a uniqueness and universality that is still evident today. However, today's audiences are amused by a style and form that disappeared more than fifty years ago. Sound brought an end to the genre and helped create new comedic forms based on verbal humor. Mime and visual slapstick were still part of sound comedy, but a unique art form — silent film comedy — had ceased to exist almost overnight. The Marx Brothers and W. C. Fields became prototypes for sound comedy and, although some of their humor depended on physical action or gesture, Fields's "grumbling" and misanthropic asides and the Groucho and Chico's Dada-istic, stream-of-consciousness dialogue provided the true comic dimension to their characters.

   Other, more subtle forms of sound comedy emerged throughout the thirties, as writers, directors, and performers felt their way through the new medium. In one shift, light banter came to replace verbal assault. *The Thin Man* series, starring William Powell and Myrna Loy, featured a dry, urbane wit and the technique of overlapping dialogue. Frank Capra's "screwball" comedies, such as *It Happened One Night* (1934), *Mr. Deeds Goes to Town* (1936), and *Mr. Smith Goes to Washington* (1939) reflected a solid, *Saturday Evening Post*, middle-class writing style.

   The other genre affected by sound was the Western. Although the ultimate effect was only temporary, the immediate impact was catastrophic. The Western is inherently visual, as most of its action takes place outdoors. But sound-imposed limitations on camera movement and editing greatly restricted outdoor shooting. As a result, no important Western films were made for the first two years of sound. However, *In Old Arizona* (1929) proved to be popular and set the tone for future Westerns by demonstrating that while *speech* could add somewhat to the Western form, *sound* could add a great deal more. The sounds of bacon frying, cattle stampeding, and campfires crackling were highly dramatic to audiences who had not heard such sounds before in film, and these sounds pleased audiences as much as talk and song did.

The Impact on People

New forms and changes in content required new people, and soon performers who could sing and talk were brought West from New York. As in any industry, when supply is low, the price is high, and this principle applied to performers who could provide the new medium with high-quality speech and song. The singers were among the first to arrive. John McCormack, the well-known Irish tenor, was paid $50,000 for ten weeks' work. Marilyn Miller was paid $1,000 an *hour* for her singing. Dozens of other performers with varying degrees of talent were pushed in front of cameras to delight audiences with recreations of their original roles on Broadway. These included Fanny Brice, in *My Man* (1928); Texas Guinan, in *Queen of the Night Clubs* (1929); and Sophie Tucker, in *Honky Tonk* (1929). This influx of stage players making their individual attempts at screen immortality was vaguely reminiscent of the original Film d'Art movement, and many of these actors ultimately met the same fate as their predecessors. After the novelty wore off, only those performers who had some screen presence remained. The rest went back to Broadway.

People who could talk came next. Although one might assume that there were plenty of talented performers who could already talk, the studios found, to their dismay, that huge investments in faces and figures did not guarantee voices as well. The following list of "New Faces," as it appeared in a 1929 issue of *Photoplay,* indicates the new orientation:

Carlotta King — graduate of stage operettas
Charles King — Broadway musical comedy
Joan Bennet — sister to Constance and Barbara
Morton Downey — tenor soloist with Paul Whiteman
Lee Tracy — Broadway actor
Jeanette MacDonald — musical comedy
O. P. Heggie — English stage actor
Marilyn Miller — Ziegfield's leading musical star

These "new faces" quickly populated America's screens and became stars almost overnight, but many "old faces" just as quickly disappeared. Myths developed concerning silent film performers whose careers were ruined by inadequate voices. And it is true that some individuals had "bad" voices, voices that simply did not sound right in films. Most foreign performers were dismissed immediately, although a few, such as Greta Garbo and Marlene Dietrich, did succeed. However, the faces and figures of both these stars did a great deal to compensate for their accents.

Some American players faded very quickly as well. The story of John Gilbert is well known and typical of what happened to many silent performers. Gilbert, one of the silent film's biggest romantic stars, was unsuccessful in sound films, not because his voice was necessarily *bad,* but rather because it was *inappropriate.* Had Gilbert's image as a performer been light and comedic rather than heavy and romantic, the public might have accepted his relatively high-pitched voice readily.

Another reason many silent performers dropped

from sight was that sound films required a new sense of realism and naturalism in acting. What was needed was a soft, subtle style, not the broad, sweeping, sometimes deliberately exaggerated styles of such performers as Douglas Fairbanks, Lon Chaney, and John Gilbert. In fact, this acting style appeared foolish and overly dramatic in sound films. Historian Leslie Halliwell estimated that 90 percent of all silent stars faded with the appearance of sound. Such major stars as Milton Sills, Mary Philbin, Aileen Pringle, Blanche Sweet, Renée Adorée, Joblyna Ralston, and hundreds of others were dropped from studio rosters and faded from the public mind with astonishing speed.

Not every star could be retired, however, and with musicals and plays being produced at a frenetic pace, many performers were forced into speaking and singing roles for which they were ill-suited. Until new talent could be developed or imported, the studios used various techniques to enable actors and actresses with poor or inappropriate voices to continue performing. The most common technique, and one still used today, was voice dubbing: substituting an off-screen voice for that of an on-screen performer. Paul Lukas's heavy German accent required a double for all his speaking parts, and Lawford Davidson was paid $500 a week as Lukas's voice. Today dubbing is most common in foreign films, where, as an alternative to subtitles, the dialogue is recorded in English and dubbed in to replace the voices of the original performers. Dubbing is also used in some musicals to replace the voice of a well-known performer who cannot sing, to retain the star appeal. This latter practice was more common in the early years of sound than it is today. Richard Barthelmess, who made several excellent sound films in the 1930s, was initially forced into a singing role in the film *Weary River* (1930), and the critical reaction to his dubbed and obviously artificial singing was not kind.

Overall, sound resulted in a shift in perspective. Suddenly men and women were being evaluated in terms of beautiful voices rather than beautiful faces. Studio casting offices added new classifications to their card indexes on players, listing type of voice, accent, and such notes as "cultured" or "lisper." Fan magazines featured articles on "The Sex Appeal Voice of Ann Harding," "Baby Talk of Helen Kane," and "Vamping with Sound." Many performers, such as Conrad Nagel, Will Rogers, and Claudette Colbert, who possessed the all important "phonetic value," experienced tremendous boosts to their careers with the advent of sound.

Off-screen performers and artists were affected as well. Certain types of occupations, such as title writers and pit-orchestra musicians, simply ceased to exist. But the gains were more important than the losses. Perhaps the two most important new personnel categories were

Casualties of Sound

*T*he consternation among silent players with the advent of sound was naturally very great. But the stories of sudden wreckage of careers has been vastly exaggerated. This is shown by a glance at the list of our major players as the silent era closed.

Among them were William Powell, Richard Dix, Bebe Daniels, George Bancroft, Clara Bow, Clive Brook, Nancy Carroll, Gary Cooper, Jean Arthur, Fay Wray, Florence Vidor, Emil Jannings, Adolph Menjou, Evelyn Brent, and Paul Lukas.

There were tense moments, of course, while voice tests were being made.

Jean Arthur listened to her playback and cried in despair, "A foghorn!" It was that foghorn quality which made her a greater star than she might have become on the silent screen.

William Powell heard his voice and raced out the door, shouting over his shoulder that he planned to go into hiding. Powell had been on the stage but, like many others, was amazed to hear his own voice.

It is true that the microphone helped some voices and took away from others. But most of those with real ability and determination adjusted to the new medium. There are always stars on their way down, and it was easy to blame sound for those who happened to be slipping.

It is widely believed, for example, that Clara Bow was finished by the "talkies." Her voice was actually quite good and she made talking pictures. But the unrestrained vitality which had been her great asset now was a curious handicap. The technicians had not learned to use the microphones as skillfully as they do today, and the players had to manage to stay near one of them, which was likely as not concealed in a bouquet of flowers, without giving the impression that the voice was being aimed into it.

Clara was too restless. She would be all over the set, and then, realizing that the microphone was not picking up her voice, would sometimes stand and curse it. Besides, the day of the flapper was over. Clara might have made a new career as an emotional actress or a mature comedienne. But the row would have been a hard one and she chose instead to retire.

The one great tragedy of sound was John Gilbert, Metro-Goldwyn-Mayer's sensational romantic star. His voice was too high—not effeminate, but with a piping note which all the efforts of the voice instructors could not bring into line with his screen appearance. His failure upset him emotionally and doubtless had much to do with his early death.

—*Adolph Zukor*, The Public Is Never Wrong

---

sound technician and writer. The technicians were not really welcomed with open arms, since they placed new, exacting demands on creative personnel. Thorold Dickinson expresses this attitude quite clearly in his book, *A Discovery of Cinema:*

> And all the time, those interlopers, sound engineers aiming at scientific accuracy, interfered with the temperamental atmosphere of film-making, vetoing voices of unusual character, insisting on flat clarity of speech and precise levels of volume of sound, unable to record a real shout or a real whisper, demanding compromises to meet the narrow limits of tolerance of their yet primitive equipment. It was a hell of mediocrity until the non-conformists began to find a way.

Still, owing to the crudeness of the early equipment, the technicians were absolutely necessary for achieving reasonable sound quality. Much of their early work consisted of electronically adjusting the voices of various performers to acceptable levels. At times, however, they became overzealous in their efforts. Dickinson describes such an effort:

> Tallulah Bankhead, the late actress, had a low voice and the early attempts by sound engineers to "tinker" with it met with disaster. As Miss Bankhead herself said: "They made me sound as if I'd been castrated! I told the studio that if they tampered with my voice I'd walk off the set. After that they never twiddled any more knobs to change my voice again."

Although this new breed was looked upon by many as a necessary evil, talented engineers, such as Douglas Shearer at MGM, made many significant and lasting contributions to the art and science of motion pictures. Shearer was responsible for several important technical achievements in sound; over his long career he won twelve Academy Awards for "best sound." His work on the "munchkins'" voices in *The Wizard of Oz* was one of the highlights of his career.

Writers of both dialogue and song were another vital group. Both types were imported from Broadway and Tin Pan Alley — a euphemism for popular song writers of the teens and twenties in America. Writers had almost as much power in early sound films as engineers, with dialogue writers carrying the most weight.

Given the critical function that dialogue played in sound films, writing departments started requiring a variety of specialists. And though screenwriters remained anonymous throughout the early years of sound, they soon became key members of a production team, responsible for supplying the narrative voice. A studio's stable of stars was now complemented by its stable of writers, which included men and women from the literary world who joined filmmakers both in writing original screenplays and adapting plays and books. Adaptations had always been a significant part of the industry's output, but the talking film opened new horizons for representing existing works, particularly stage plays. By 1930 Universal had inaugurated a policy of purchasing the screen rights to plays and novels in advance of publication.

The narrative design of films changed immediately and significantly when dialogue became important. Whereas story had given a film its raison d'être in the silent era, narrative development now served to move characters into new sets of circumstances that could be verbalized. In George Cukor's *Dinner at Eight* (1933), for example, the dialogue by Edna Ferber from the original stage play is central. In screen comedy throughout the silent era, narrative design played a subordinate role to visual routines and by-play — with story merely serv-

ing as a framework for the visual elements. Now other genres became similarly affected, and sophisticated or earthy repartee and the verbal duel became ends in themselves. The importance of the well-turned phrase and other attributes of clever dialogue tended to keep both cinematic style and the story in check. Camera angle, lighting, editing, and even the design of settings were calculated to serve the speaking actor, and much of what had been learned about visual statement and inference was forgotten.

As suggested earlier, the addition of music to the sound track did more than replace the pit piano as a source of background music; it ushered in a new genre of film — the musical. In this form, visual storytelling usually took the shape of a flimsy narrative framework on which musical production numbers could be hung. Less prominent than music and speech but equally self-conscious was the screen's reproduction of natural sound effects, which gave the promise of greater realism, but which, in the formative years, usually resulted in noisy artificiality.

Words in the form of songs became as important as dialogue, with the "all talking, all singing, all dancing" film dominating the nation's screens. Songwriters, such as Irving Berlin, Jerome Kern, Harry Warren, Mack Gordon, and others, contributed as much to the new rhetoric of film as anyone. Suddenly films became known on the basis of songs as well as stars.

The Impact on the Industry

Although less visible and dramatic, the effects of sound on the structure of the motion picture industry itself were perhaps the most important. Along with the stock market crash of 1929, sound basically reorganized the industry. Moviemaking was still big business, but in contrast to the early years, when many small companies participated in film production, the beginning of the sound era witnessed a concentration and centralization of capital, resulting in fewer companies.

Throughout the 1920s, film companies had merged and consolidated into fewer and larger producer/distributor/exhibitor organizations. However, sound resulted in enormous costs that only the largest, most economically secure companies could afford.

In their research, film scholars Douglas Gomery and Michael Conant reveal that in addition to the royalties charged by AT&T (which held most of the sound patents), these sound-related costs included studio, laboratory, and theater conversion, plus higher costs for labor and materials. According to various figures, in 1928 the cost to install sound in a theater ranged from $5,000 to

$12,000. Other estimates relate to the total cost of sound conversion for the entire industry. At the time, the MPPDA projected the cost at $500 million; later Gomery estimated $30 million.

These figures refer to expenditures other than those for theater construction and film production. In his excellent study *Antitrust in the Motion Picture Industry,* Michael Conant found that in 1928 alone $161,930,000 was spent on new theaters. By 1935, according to a group of architects, $1,460,000 had been spent in theater construction, exclusive of sections of theater buildings devoted to office space. Meanwhile, by 1930 the average production cost for a film was between $200,000 and $400,000.

With costs increasing in these ways, small companies and theaters either fell prey to the larger corporations and chains or simply faded away. The introduction of sound, therefore, stimulated even more consolidation in the industry. It also attracted more financiers and bankers, people who were ready to supply the necessary capital, arrange mergers, and share in the increased profits.

And those profits were at peak levels. In 1930 total assets were reported to be more than $1 billion, while net income for the five major corporations—MGM, Paramount, Warner Brothers, Fox, and RKO—totaled $70,703,000. By the end of the 1920s, the industry had developed into a mature oligopoly, with these five corporations, now totally integrated, diversified, and operating worldwide, dominating the business. The big five controlled 77 percent of the first-run theaters and the production and distribution of 50 percent of the feature films in the United States.

Solutions and Progress

The magic of sound had carried the industry through the first years of the Depression in excellent shape. One even heard the film business referred to as "Depression-proof." However, as the Depression moved along its grinding, unrelenting path, audiences began to stay home. Attendance figures dropped from 100 million per week in 1930 to fewer than 70 million per week in 1931. Again, the industry began to get restless and started searching for new formulas and solutions.

Meanwhile, an artistic restlessness was occurring in Hollywood. Although sound had wiped out silent film as an art form, it could not eliminate the feelings and talents of the many creative artists who had worked in it those

first thirty years. Such individuals as Rouben Mamoulian and King Vidor realized that although sound had destroyed something unique and placed severe technical limitations on the state of the art, the more positive side of the situation still needed to be developed. They determined to supply what was missing: the creative use of sound coupled with a full realization of film's visual potential, which had been lost, owing to sound-imposed limitations on camera work and editing.

One of the first challenges was to restore camera mobility. Much of the credit for meeting it belongs to Rouben Mamoulian. Perhaps more clearly than any other director of the time, Mamoulian recognized the basic distinction between stage and screen and attempted to reinforce this difference. Mamoulian began his career directing plays in London, but he emigrated to the United States, where he worked in both opera and legitimate theater. He became well known through his work in the Experimental Theater Guild and for his staging of the first production of *Porgy and Bess* in 1929. His "symphony of noise" sequence in *Porgy* perfectly illustrated his stylistic blend of sound and movement, and it greatly impressed the critics. He caught the attention of Hollywood, and was soon brought in from the East. Paramount initially wanted to sign him to a long-term contract in which he would spend several years learning the trade. But Mamoulian insisted on a one-film contract and went off to study and absorb what he could about the process of filmmaking. He was not satisfied with what he saw. As he stated some years later,

> The camera technique then was to shoot a film as a stage play, with ready-made dialogue. They would put two cameras on the set, and shoot two close-ups and a long-shot, then cut them together: all you *could* call these films were talkies!

Although Mamoulian's best work was in the musical genre—for example, *Love Me Tonight* (1932), *Summer Holiday* (1947), and *Silk Stockings* (1957)—his first sound film, *Applause* (1929), was a harshly realistic story about an aging burlesque queen. In this film, he liberated the camera by shooting several scenes silent and adding sound later. He shot one scene involving a huge crowd in Penn Station in New York. This scene ended with a remarkable crane shot that would have been impossible to shoot in the normal sound manner. Mamoulian also conceived of recording sound on two channels instead of one. In a scene from *Applause,* the burlesque queen is singing a lullaby to her daughter while the girl is saying her evening prayers; Mamoulian used two microphones to record each actress on a separate channel (see box on page 191). In later films, such as *City*

Helen Morgan as an aging burlesque queen in Rouben Mamoulian's innovative *Applause* (1929). Morgan's powerful performance and Mamoulian's use of sound and camera movement combined to create a moving and revolutionary early sound film.

Streets (1931) and *Dr. Jekyll and Mr. Hyde* (1931), he experimented with overlapping dialogue, sound flashbacks, and synthetic sound. Still, his most important contribution to the developing art of sound film was his restoration of a sense of movement to the medium.

King Vidor was another pioneer in using sound artistically. Whereas Mamoulian had been a novice and had come to film with little background or orientation, Vidor was an accomplished director with several silent "classics" to his credit. He began his career by producing two-reel comedies in Houston, Texas; he made several documentaries and then came to Hollywood, where he directed religious films (*The Turn of the Road* [1918]), Jazz Age films (*Wine of Youth* [1924]), classic literary films (*La Bohème* [1925]), and climaxing his silent film career, two realistic dramas (*The Big Parade* [1925] and *The Crowd* [1928]). In both these films, but especially in *The Crowd,* his camera work was highly mobile, a style that was greatly influenced by the Germans, as he himself acknowledged.

Thus, unlike Mamoulian, who was free of stylistic habits and idiosyncracies, Vidor brought to sound film a broad background rich in silent film technique. This was reflected in his first sound film, *Hallelujah!*, made in 1929 with an all-black cast. The theme was taken from his youth in Texas, where he watched the black workers at his father's sawmill participate in religious meetings, revivals, and baptisms. Much of the film was shot on location in Tennessee and Arkansas. Vidor's basic method, like Mamoulian's, was to shoot silent and dub sound in later. However, Vidor was primarily concerned with achieving high sound quality, and he attempted to achieve a balance between a "free" camera and a wide variety of sounds. This balance is nowhere more brilliantly developed than in *Hallelujah's* gripping climax, a remarkable chase sequence through an Arkansas swamp. The camera relentlessly tracks a pursued man as he flees in terror through the swamp, but it is the "sound" of the swamp that creates the scene's atmosphere. Vidor shot the scene silent and then, back in the studio, added such sounds as a branch breaking, a bird screaming, and a foot being pulled out of quicksand. He integrated these sounds with the tracking movement of the camera to produce an atmosphere of impending doom and terror. Thus, the bird call becomes a hiss, the broken branch a broken bone, and the sound of quicksand the sound of a man being sucked down into the depths of

From King Vidor's all-black film *Hallelujah!* (1929). A gospel meeting provided an excellent showcase for sound.

Mamoulian on Sound

*T*here are a lot of things you do for the first time, and the question always is: Why wasn't it done before? Take sound. What always fascinated me about films was the magic of the camera. When sound came in, I thought that the imaginative things you can do with the camera you should be able to do with sound. You don't have to be bound by naturalism. In *Applause* I took a scene with Helen Morgan singing a lullaby to her little girl. She is a burlesque queen; the girl has just come out of a convent and seen her mother perform at the burlesque theater. She is terribly upset about it. Then they come to that dingy little hotel and the girl can't sleep, so Helen Morgan sings her a burlesque song, but in the manner of a lullaby.

I wanted the girl to take a rosary and whisper her prayers. In those days we only had one microphone hanging from the center. And the sound man was the dictator. If he said an actor was too far away, well, then bring him in. Or if you can't be sitting, then stand up. Don't open the letter, because it breaks the microphone, so you soak the letter in water so that it won't make a sound. It was dreadful.

So the sound man said, "Well, you can't do it." Naturally, on the stage or in life, if somebody is singing loud, you can't hear someone else whispering a prayer. I said, "Why don't you have one microphone for Helen Morgan and another one under the pillow for the girl, and record it on two separate channels so that you can boost the whisper and keep the sound under control? Then you take these two pieces of film and print them together in the laboratory." They thought I was crazy.

I also wanted to do this whole scene in one shot. The problem there was not only the lens, but the fact that when the first talkies started, they used three cameras on the set, each enclosed in a bungalow. They said, "You can't move it, it's a big bungalow." So I said, "Why don't we put little wheels on it? I'm going to use only one camera for this scene; get six strong men and they will push it and move it, as necessary. You will start with the long shot, close-up, then medium shot, again in close-up, and so on." They said, "It can't be done."

—Interview with Rouben Mamoulian
American Film *(January–February 1983)*

hell. Also, Vidor used music, especially Negro spirituals, to convey mood and meaning. By synchronizing the musical rhythms to the visual action, Vidor fused sound and picture into an integral whole.

Two other important pioneers in establishing an expanded perspective for sound films were Lewis Milestone and Ernst Lubitsch. Both concentrated on freeing the camera from the constraints of the microphone by shooting silent and dubbing sound in later. Milestone worked with realistic themes in the antiwar film *All Quiet on the Western Front* (1930) and the behind-the-scenes newspaper story *The Front Page* (1931). The battle scenes in the former are remarkable—the camera follows the action as huge waves of men move across open battlefields. Meanwhile, the sounds of shells "crumping" into the ground and "whining" overhead, rifles "cracking," and tanks "rumbling" add realism and set a tone of chaos and destruction. In *The Front Page,* Milestone worked primarily with dialogue, creating tempo and pace through rapid speech and quick cutting. Milestone's ability to integrate sound and movement made his films unique in a time when themes and settings typically involved little movement.

Ernst Lubitsch worked in a lighter métier, using music and song in romantic fantasies, such as *The Love Parade* (1929) and *Monte Carlo* (1930). In both these films, he used a silent camera in order to create movement and establish a distinct visual rhythm. He was especially concerned with integrating sound effects, music, and dialogue—for example, in one particularly memorable sequence from *Monte Carlo.* The scene involves a train, the Blue Express, moving away from a station, and Lubitsch integrates the sound and tempo of the train wheels into the song "Beyond the Blue Horizon," sung by the passengers and the peasants in the surrounding countryside. Critics used the phrase "sound montage" to describe this scene. Sounds and music performed the same function for the ear that an assembly of shots did for the eye, uniting several distinct parts to create a whole.

Walt Disney, in his animated cartoons, did some of the most innovative work in early sound films. Disney came to Hollywood in 1923 from Kansas City and, along with animator Ub Iwerks, produced a number of silent animated shorts. But it was sound that propelled Disney into the mainstream of Hollywood producers. Because cartoons are free from space and time relationships as they exist in nature, meaning can be created in them in ways impossible in "normal" films. Disney began to experiment with sound in the same ways he had earlier manipulated visual reality, and in his first sound film, *Steamboat Willie* (1928), he achieved a freedom with sound impossible in other films. In *Steamboat,* Mickey Mouse creates a symphony out of the song "Turkey in the Straw" by using animals on a boat as various instru-

▲ From Walt Disney's 1928 production, *Steamboat Willie.* The most famous mouse in the world makes his debut here by playing a tune.

ments. He squeezes a duck's throat, twists a cat's tail, and taps on a cow's teeth to produce various sounds. Disney followed this film with *The Skeleton Dance* (1929), in which he further refined and perfected his fantasy use of sound.

European Developments

Just as the invention of the motion picture camera occurred simultaneously in various countries, so did the perfection of sound technology in the form adopted by Warner Brothers. The sound film was acclaimed by international audiences immediately, and by 1930 the medium had been fitted for sound almost everywhere.

Eight sound pictures had been made in Germany before *The Blue Angel* in 1930, and in 1931, the year of Fritz Lang's *M,* 146 sound pictures were released. During the same period in France, René Clair was spinning his delightful fantasies, which preserved the visual integrity of the medium and wove the element of sound into his fabrics, both affirming the German applications and demonstrating further uses of the new element.

European contributions to the development of sound film were in no way to parallel the stylistic breakthroughs of the previous decade, however. A handful of directors made certain creative demonstrations of sound applications and singular refinements of style and personal statements, but no surge or breakthroughs marked this early period. However, several key films and certain directors deserve special mention.

Germany

When *The Blue Angel* opened at New York's Rialto Theatre in December 1930, additional screenings had to be scheduled to accommodate the crowds waiting to see Emil Jannings and Marlene Dietrich. The German picture used Klangfilm technology, and while the sound track's hissing and distortion were problems for projectionists, the audiences did not mind.

The Germans had demonstrated an early intuition for integrating sound and visuals. In *The Blue Angel,* the powerful composition and lighting control evoked an atmosphere that, in retrospect, suggests parallels between the cruel schoolboys and the rising tide of cruelty within Germany; between the released passions of Marlene Dietrich's Lola and the repressed passions—and hope—of the German people; between the increasing incompetency of Professor Unrat (played by Emil Jannings) and the disintegration of order in the country at large. The film was a joint Hollywood-German production, and two versions were filmed, one in German and one in English.

Fritz Lang's *M* (1931) further demonstrated a masterful utilization of sound, as described in Chapter 4. No camera techniques were sacrificed to the sound element in this film. Lips moved, but we did not necessarily hear the words spoken. In some instances other sounds better revealed the intended meaning of the shot. And Lang realized that the existence of sound technology did not require every screen moment be filled with sound. He understood that silence itself was a meaningful dimension that deepened in the context of the sound film itself.

France

In France, by 1930 the experimentalists had turned away from their adopted medium and back to their former pursuits. The desire to shock and outrage and to stage radical attacks upon the feature film that told a story (which is to say, the accepted social norm) seemed to have run its course. Jean Epstein turned his impressionistic camera upon real life. In his 1929 film *Finnis Terrae,* he studied the lives of the simple and primitive

kelp gatherers off the French coast, giving dramatic import to and inspiring empathy for their simple dignity within a harsh environment.

Ideas about uses for sound were generated by the score in René Clair's fantasy films. *Le Million* (1931) and *A Nous la Liberté* (1931) preserved the humor and dalliance so evident in Clair's earlier *Paris Qui Dort* (1923), *Entr'acte* (1924), and *The Italian Straw Hat* (1927). Like Lang in Germany and Vidor in America, Clair demonstrated that silence could be tolerated in the sound film. And, again like Lang and Vidor, his primary emphasis was on vision, shots, and editing. To that he *added* sound, but with restraint. He used not only synchronous sound, but also asynchronous, contrapuntal sound. His camera was free to roam and probe, his action motivated by energy and sudden cuts in time and space. Sound was incorporated as an element that could be used in a sense similar to montage. The Soviets had shown what one shot in relation to another could trigger in the mind; Clair was adept at bouncing a shot against a sound to do the same thing. So when we see a mantel clock with cupid figures blowing trumpets, we hear not the chiming of a clock but the sound of blowing trumpets. It is not the fight scene barely visible in the shadows that suggests the ferocity of the battle, but the sound of chugging locomotives and the screams of passing trains. The girl we and the hero think is singing a beautiful song is revealed to be a phonograph record.

Both in the United States and abroad, developments and improvements in sound continued to evolve through a combination of technological and artistic developments. The invention of the sound Movieola greatly simplified the editing of sound film. Improvements in microphones, booms, printers, and sound mixers greatly extended the artistic possibilities of sound in film. Individual artists such as Alfred Hitchcock, Walt Disney, Jean Renoir, and Orson Welles used the new technology to make many artistic advances and produce memorable films. However, despite these improvements, it took years for sound to be taken for granted and used without self-consciousness.

The Development of Color

Like sound, color existed in motion pictures from the very beginning. As early as 1894, C. Frances Jenkins projected hand-tinted color films. For the first twenty-five years, tinting and toning were the standard methods of producing color in film. Filmmakers achieved the effect by hand-coloring each frame, by coloring the positive print, or by using tinted film stock. Porter's *The Great Train Robbery* (1903) was released in a version that contained various color scenes, including a red-tinted gunshot blast at the end of the film, tinted in by hand. Hand tinting, of course, was very expensive, and as films became longer and more sophisticated, this process became obsolete. However, Robert Paul in England did produce a colored version of *The Miracle* (1910) by hand-tinting 112,000 individual frames.

The next step was the development of a process whereby color either existed in the film stock or was added through optical or mechanical means after the film was exposed. The first practical "natural" color process, Kinemacolor, was developed in 1906 by two British inventors, Edward R. Turner and G. Albert Smith. Kinemacolor created color by means of an additive process—the film itself had no actual color but color values were revealed through appropriate filters in filming and projection. Encouraged by financier Charles Urban, the inventors gave public demonstrations of Kinemacolor in 1908, and in 1909 Urban showed the process to the Motion Picture Patents Company. The MPPC considered buying the American rights to the process, but ultimately decided against it. This decision was not surprising, since millions of dollars were being made with black-and-white film. The MPPC saw no need to upset the status quo.

About the time that the MPPC decided against color film, several American inventors were developing a new color system they called Prizma. This was a subtractive process, in which the color was in the film and the picture became a complete self-contained color record, requiring no special projection equipment. Several films, including J. Stuart Blackton's feature-length *The Glorious Adventure* (1921), were filmed in the Prizma process.

However, this early development was superseded by the introduction of Technicolor in 1916–1917. Essentially the brainchild of two MIT graduates, Herbert T. Kalmus and Robert Comstock, Technicolor was a two-color (red and green) subtractive process. The first film made with this new process was *Toll of the Sea* (1920), later followed by *Ben Hur* (1924).

The quality and clarity of Technicolor soon established it as the leader in the field. However, its high cost—twenty-seven cents a foot—was a major obstacle in the way of widespread commercial development. The industry wanted to spend less than ten extra cents a foot to add color, and it needed faster service than Technicolor could provide. Work continued in various quarters through the twenties with various degrees of success. *Cythera* (1924) became the first color film shot under artificial light. Douglas Fairbanks's film *The Black Pirate* (1926) was the most elaborate vehicle for early color; this critical comment is an indication of its success:

. . . while the spectator fails to find any carnival hues shooting across the canvas where this cinema is shown, still the deep rich brown of his pirate ships is there, the faded gray and brown clothing of the players are there; the weak, green waters of the sea are there.

Extensive color work was done in short subjects, as the process was constantly being improved while costs dropped. By 1927–1928, a commercially feasible system had become available. Interestingly, though, concern over whether *sound* film could survive on its own merits in the first years led to a boom in the production of color films during 1929–1930. Even though shooting in color increased film cost, many studios felt the gamble was necessary to attract audiences to sound. In 1929 Technicolor contracted for seventeen features, and by 1930 the number for the year was thirty-six. Lab crews were working three eight-hour shifts, and since the Technicolor process required special cameras operated by trained men, the pressure on Technicolor was great. *On With the Show* (1929) was the first all-talking Technicolor film, and it was quickly followed by many others, most of them from Warners.

One major obstacle persisted, however. Technicolor was still a two-color process. Red and green produced passable color registration, but more natural color required the addition of a third color—blue. Meanwhile, another problem arose from outside the lab; when it became obvious that sound film could succeed on its own merits the demand for color films disappeared. By 1932 the boom in color had come and gone.

Despite the decline in demand, work on a three-color process continued. By 1932 a system was perfected, but Technicolor was finding it difficult to convince the industry, now safe and secure with sound, to try it out. However, in a situation analogous to Warner Brothers' gamble with sound, a struggling Walt Disney, desperately needing something to save his studio, opted to make his 1932 film *Flowers and Trees* with Technicolor. The result was a success for both Disney and Technicolor. The film demonstrated the beauty and appeal of the three-color process, and Disney's fortunes soared. The first feature to be produced in the three-color process was Mamoulian's *Becky Sharp* in 1935. However, the two films that really showcased the Technicolor process were *The Wizard of Oz* and *Gone with the Wind*, both released in 1939. Public and industrial acceptance of color films was now certain, and Technicolor became the established industry standard.

Eastman Kodak developed color negative film stock in 1949, further revolutionizing color filming. With this advance, studios could now film color features with a 35 mm camera rather than Technicolor's specialized equipment. The savings inherent in this step made low-cost color features possible. Simultaneously, the threat of television created panic in the industry and the studios once again turned to technology as a cure. Wide screens, 3-D (three-dimensional), and color were the magic this time. Although screen size stabilized and 3-D films never became common, color continued to dominate.

With the increase in color production, filmmakers tried to use it more intelligently and artistically. Color, like sound, had first been used as a gimmick, a novelty that audiences soon tired of. It was often used in musicals and other light genres but at first few filmmakers attempted to develop its dramatic value. Some attempts at integrating color artistically were made in such films as *An American in Paris* (1951), but it wasn't until the 1960s, through the work of Michelangelo Antonioni, Igmar Bergman, Federico Fellini, and others, that color was used naturally as a dramatic and aesthetic element in film. The word *natural* in this context does not mean "real" color, but rather color used as part of the symbolic language of film. These innovations of the 1960s used color to make statements and create meaning rather than simply to dress up films to make them more attractive.

Wrap-Up

Sound changed motion picture history in significant and fundamental ways. Technology, as one of the pivotal arms of the medium, reigned supreme. Sound and concurrent advances in other aspects of motion picture technology, such as lighting and color, heralded a new beginning for the motion picture. Soon filmmakers started using technical innovations to create and communicate rather than simply as window dressing or gimmicks on display for their own sake. The 1930s, although dominated by an industry that was often responsible for limiting the potential of film, saw this technology brought under control and used to great advantage.

The impact of sound on the business of film was profound, and represented a clear turning point in film history. In a way, history was repeating itself. As occurred when the MPPC lost its fight against the independents, an old established order gave way to a new one. The single unique aspect of this revolution was that no major established company—with the possible exception of First National, which was absorbed by Warners—was hurt. Conversely, several new corporate "stars" emerged either through sound-stimulated growth (Columbia), consolidation and merger (20th Century-Fox), or outright creation (RKO). Most small, independent

studios, however, died quick and unceremonious deaths. The huge amounts of capital necessary to retool for sound required even the biggest studios to seek outside funding, and, as a result, Wall Street became more firmly entrenched in Hollywood than ever. With millions of borrowed dollars riding on the flimsy wings of motion pictures, the tolerance for and acceptance of personal grandeur was gone. The organization replaced the individual, and that organization extended all the way from New York to Hollywood. It is interesting to note the geographical shift in direction, which again symbolized a broad, deep change in the industry. The control of the industry was back East again, and this meant less flexibility, more financial responsibility, and an obligation that stretched beyond the studio walls.

The psychological effect that sound had on the industry was profound as well. As the industry grew bigger it grew more self-important. The business became standardized, complex, and technical. A whole new way of making films emerged. In the creative realm, because films cost more money, content became more conservative—a new, safe rhetoric emerged shaped by corporate values. Also, the medium exhibited less artistic freedom.

Even the most exploitive and banal use of sound, however, could not completely obscure the sound film's potential for creative storytelling and, ultimately, for developing realism on the screen. Even aside from the singular contributions of such creative pioneers as Clair, Lubitsch, and Mamoulian, the positive implications of sound became clear. Speech not only replaced the clumsy intrusion of titles, it also made exaggerated gestures and movement unnecessary and allowed for more naturalistic acting. Through the combination of voice and subtleties of visual response, characterization could be more finely drawn, and a quality of realism and intimacy could emerge that was seldom displayed in silent films save in the performances of such masters as Chaplin and Jannings.

Besides expanding the ability to delineate character, sound also increased the possibilities for basic narrative exposition and plot detail. Though screenplays did not necessarily have more significant content, as is sometimes claimed, sound did provide an additional channel by which information could readily be conveyed. The result was an increase in specificity and detail that supported more intricate plotting.

Perhaps *Variety* best summed up the impact of sound on the motion picture business:

> It didn't do any more to the industry than turn it upside-down, shake the entire bag of tricks from its pocket and advance Warner Brothers from last place to first in the league.

8

Studio Styles (1933–1945)

Focus

The changes in industrial structure brought about by sound resulted in equally significant changes in the types of films produced. As suggested in Chapter 7, a new rhetoric began to emerge—a corporate rhetoric influenced by big business, big money, big stars, and big audiences.

With the new rhetoric began what some call the golden age of American film—a period lasting from the early 1930s to 1946. The dates and the adjective are arbitrary, to be sure. For some, only the silent era was golden, and for them sound brought with it a tarnish, a lowering of aesthetic standards. For others, the golden years begin now. For them, the words *freedom* and *independence* refer specifically to a break with an old, outdated Hollywood tradition. But whichever era one treasures, Hollywood and motion pictures were more firmly established and more deeply rooted in the American consciousness from the early thirties to the end of World War II than at any other time in history. In a time of economic depression and international conflict, motion pictures, as Hortense Powdermaker observed in *Hollywood: The Dream Factory,* eased people's loneliness, helped them escape their anxieties, provided them with vicarious experiences, portrayed solutions to problems, created models for human relationships, and developed new value systems and new folk heroes.

The Studio System

As John Baxter stated in *Hollywood and the Thirties,* "Without the studios, Hollywood could never have existed." The system rested on the already well-estab-

Feature-Length Production, 1930–1939

	All	Paramount	Loew's	Fox	Warner	RKO	Columbia	Universal	UA	Other
1930–31	510	58	43	48	69	32	27	22	13	198
1931–32	490	56	40	46	56	48	31	32	14	167
1932–33	510	51	37	41	53	45	36	28	16	203
1933–34	480	55	44	46	63	40	44	38	20	130
1934–35	520	44	42	40	51	40	39	39	19	206
1935–36	517	50	43	52	58	43	36	27	17	191
1936–37	535	41	40	52	58	39	38	40	19	208
1937–38	450	40	41	49	52	41	39	45	16	127
1938–39	526	58	51	56	54	49	54	45	18	141

—*United States* v. *Paramount Pictures Inc., et al.,* Civil Action no. 87-273 in the District Court of the United States for the Southern District of New York, amended and supplemental complaint (14 November 1940)

lished studio foundations of the silent period. However, the introduction of sound created even more specialization and a greater division of labor, because music and the writing and speaking of dialogue called forth entire new departments and hundreds of additional people.

For filmmaking to take place, the studios were an economic necessity. Like television today, Hollywood in the thirties and forties faced the weekly pressure of entertaining a mass audience. Consequently, the studio system grew up as a necessary industrial response to the huge public demand for more of its product. Harry Cohn, president of Columbia, in talking to a young film editor, remarked,

> Listen kid, . . . I make fifty-two pictures a year here. Every Friday the front door opens on Gower Street and I spit a picture out. A truck picks it up and takes it away to the theatres, and that's the ball game. Now, if that door opens and I spit and nothing comes out, you and everybody else around here is out of work. So let's cut out the crap about only good pictures. How many of those pictures I spit out do you think that I think are any good? . . . I run this place on the basis of making one good picture a year . . . The rest of them I just have to keep spitting out.

The 500 films a year produced by the major studios in this period were products of a sophisticated industrial system, and as such they reflected not only the attitude of the system, but the mood of the time and audience. Films reflected the time precisely *because* they were products of an industrial system. Few aspects of our society are more attuned to the pulse of society than industry. Individuals and small groups often think and act independently of the system. D. W. Griffith and William S. Hart, for example, did not really produce films that were in tune with society. Rather, their films were the result of strong personal vision. This vision contributed both to the greatness of these directors and their ultimate failure to maintain top status in the industry. Hart's firm stand against "showmanship and nonrealism" and Griffith's Victorian view of manners and morals were clearly at odds with what audiences of the time wanted. The studio system of the thirties and forties, however, was completely in tune with what the paying public wanted. As a result the films of this period have meaning more as social documents than personal works of art.

Studio Profiles

When one speaks of Hollywood studios, the names that immediately come to mind are MGM, Paramount, Universal, RKO, Columbia, Warner Brothers, and 20th Century-Fox. Without question, these majors dominated production. Together with United Artists they accounted for more than 60 percent of all feature film production. However, the other 40 percent did exist, and indeed there were other active production studios. In 1935, according to *The Film Daily Yearbook,* there were 46 production companies, 26 active studios, 174 enclosed stages, and 19,000 permanent employees in Hollywood. Some companies, such as Burroughs-Tarzan Enterprises, Superior, and Supreme Pictures, produced only one feature film a year. Others, such as Chesterfield, Invincible, Alliance, and Tiffany, produced from 10 to 25 features a year. More important, studios such as Monogram and Republic were responsible for entire genres of film, most significantly serials and the "B" (low-budget) Western. Despite this activity, the seven major studios named above dominated the scene and set the tone and style of the era. Some historians place United Artists among the majors. However, UA was never a studio as such. It was simply a distribution arm for various independent producers.

The only independent producers able to maintain some degree of production parity with the majors were Samuel Goldwyn and David O. Selznick. Goldwyn did his most important work in association with William Wyler — their films included, for example, *Dodsworth* (1936), *Wuthering Heights* (1939), and *The Best Years of Our Lives* (1946). Goldwyn's great value lay in the example and precedent he set for other independents. He was not well educated or greatly talented. However, he was able to recognize talent in others and knew the audience as well as any studio head. He brought cinematographer Gregg Toland and choreographer Busby Berkeley to Hollywood, gave them their starts, and provided an economic and artistic climate that allowed both to develop their unique and highly personal styles.

Although David O. Selznick was like Goldwyn in some ways, his artistic temperament was vastly different. Selznick came up through the studio system and in the early thirties was one of MGM's top producers. At MGM he made such films as *Dinner at Eight* (1933), *Anna Karenina* (1935), and *A Tale of Two Cities* (1935). Increasingly annoyed at studio restrictions and spurred on by the example of his late father, Lewis, an early motion picture producer, Selznick became an independent producer in 1935. Taking as his studio motto "In a Tradition of Quality," he produced some of the most outstanding films of the period, including *A Star is Born* (1937), *Nothing Sacred* (1937), *Rebecca* (1940), and *Duel in the Sun* (1946). His most memorable and significant film was, of course, the monumental *Gone with the Wind* (1939), and in a sense he spent the rest of his life (he died in 1965) trying to live up to it. Unlike

▸ Clark Gable and Vivian Leigh in *Gone with the Wind* (1939). To get Gable on loan from MGM, Selznick had to give MGM distribution rights to the film. Leigh was the winner of a highly publicized national talent search, and this role established her as a major star.

Selznick on *Gone with the Wind*

*A*l Lichtman shares my hopes that the picture is turning out so brilliantly that its handling will have to be on a scale and of a type never before tried in the picture business. The only close approach to it would be *The Birth of a Nation*. Al has a lot of wonderful ideas as to different experiments in road showing and shares my hopes that the picture will be road shown in every town and hamlet in America, undoubtedly not reaching the regular theaters for a year, most probably not reaching them for two years, and quite possibly not reaching them for three years or longer. Al has stated on several occasions that there is no telling what the gross of the picture may be — perhaps ten million dollars, perhaps twelve or thirteen million, perhaps fifteen million. I know all this sounds like Hollywood insanity to you, but if these expectations and hopes are insane, then I have been insane in the manner in which I have approached the picture (which I grant you is possible), because I have staked everything on it, including my personal future and the future of my company. For your confidential information, the cost is presently only a little under three and a half million dollars — how much more than this it will go we don't know. This means that its cost is almost twice that of any other picture ever made, with the possible exception of *Ben-Hur* [1925, silent], the cost of which I don't know (and I doubt that anybody else does: the boys were still charging luncheon checks to it a couple of years ago!). You can see that we're going to have to have the largest gross any picture has had in the last ten years simply to break even.

Incidentally, it will be the longest picture ever made — running somewhere between three and four hours. Obviously, the very least we will have to have will be two intermissions. Plans I have discussed with Al include showings with two intermissions; and perhaps even experiments with the picture running in two theaters simultaneously — the first half in one theater and the second half in another theater, with one admission ticket sold for both theaters. . . .

—*David O. Selznick (May 2, 1939)*

Goldwyn, who usually left his talent alone, Selznick constantly interfered with the makers of his films, making suggestions about everything from editing to music. As a result, most of his films have a curiously uneven quality, with form and content seemingly pieced together by Selznick from what others had originally created.

MGM

MGM was the dominant studio of the period. Actually, its corporate name was Loew's, Inc.; MGM was used simply as a trademark. Marcus Loew was a pioneer exhibitor, and in the course of expanding his theater holdings he organized his enterprises as Loews, Inc., in 1919. Together with his partner, Nicholas Schenck, he acquired Metro Pictures in 1920, the Goldwyn Company in 1924, and later in the same year Louis B. Mayer Pictures. With Schenck heading up the corporation in New York and Louis B. Mayer and Irving Thalberg teaming up to run the studio in Hollywood, MGM quickly grew into the most successful studio of the thirties. The firm continued to dominate during the war years, concentrating on romantic and idealistic stories. With their still-powerful

▲ A 1935 aerial view of MGM's back lot. The shot reveals a conglomerate environment of cities, castles, villages, and lakes.

stable of stars, at this time headed by Mickey Rooney, MGM reigned supreme for most of the forties as well.

As head of the studio, Louis B. Mayer was a power not only at MGM but throughout the entire industry. He was a public figure in every sense of the word, delighting in escorting distinguished visitors around the set and dabbling in politics and fine racing horses. Mayer ran the studio primarily on an emotional level, alternately weeping and laughing as he "discussed" star's contracts or future productions. Had Mayer total control over the studio, it is unlikely that MGM would have achieved its dominant position in the industry.

Fortunately, Mayer's "instincts" were balanced by Irving G. Thalberg's calculated judgment. Beginning as secretary to Carl Laemmle at Universal, Thalberg came to MGM in 1924 at the age of twenty-five and quickly established a reputation as a boy wonder. Thalberg had the official title of Vice President in Charge of Production. Unlike Mayer, he perferred to work in the background. However, it is generally accepted that Thalberg was the one individual responsible for MGM's consistent high quality. Thalberg supervised every aspect of studio production. Bob Thomas, in his book *Thalberg,* describes this supervision very well:

▼ Two of Hollywood's leading "moguls" and a Hollywood leading lady. Louis B. Mayer (left) and Irving G. Thalberg were opposites in appearance, style, and taste, but they nevertheless provided MGM with dynamic and often inspired leadership throughout the 1930s. The leading lady is Norma Shearer, one of MGM's top stars and the wife of Thalberg.

He made the selection of story material. He assigned his associates to supervise the myriad of details necessary to put a movie before the cameras. He retained the responsibility for selecting the writers and directors. He thrashed out the scripts with the writers, repeatedly offering his own original solutions to narrative problems. He cast the films and approved the costumes and sets. He made himself available for problems that arose during shooting. After the picture was assembled, he often made important changes in the cutting. He previewed the film and ordered extensive retakes if the public's reception was not favorable. He even oversaw the publicity and advertising campaign.

He was neither a director, writer, actor, editor, designer, composer nor any other craftsman ordinarily associated with film making. He came closest to being a producer, yet he was not like today's producer, who follows a single film from beginning to end, then commences another one. Thalberg fulfilled the functions of a dozen producers.

Thalberg died in 1936, having established himself not only as the model creative Hollywood producer, but also as a legend. The memory of this powerful figure continues to stimulate and occasionally inspire the industry.

MGM's reputation as "the home of the stars" was well deserved. The studio employed the greatest array of production talent of any studio in history. The MGM system was a well-constructed, smoothly operating machine. At the top was Thalberg, supervising and controlling many associate producers, all of whom were attuned to his method of operation. Thalberg would assess the particular talents of these men and then place them in positions he felt suited their interests and skills. Hunt Stromberg, for example, specialized in "sexy" subjects, such as *Our Dancing Daughters* (1929) and *Red Dust* (1932), which starred Jean Harlow and Clark Gable. Albert Lewin assumed control over many of MGM's literary works, such as *Private Lives* (1936), starring Noel Coward, and *The Guardsman* (1931), starring Alfred Lunt and Lynn Fontanne. Harry Rapf specialized in melodrama, such as *The Champ* (1934), and oversaw all "B" picture production.

These men reported directly to Thalberg and formed an "inner council" by which the vast production empire was controlled. It was a highly efficient system, as Thalberg did not have to waste time and effort with MGM's myriad directors and stars. Only when Stromberg, Lewin, and the others had problems they couldn't handle did Thalberg step in. This work style allowed Thalberg time to analyze almost all of MGM's output and gave the directors the power to directly control the films themselves.

Next in command were the contract directors, and here MGM was fortunate to have people with both talent and long-term contracts. These men included Clarence Brown, who directed the highly styled Greta Garbo films — *Anna Christie* (1930), *Anna Karenina* (1935), and *Conquest* (1937) — as well as such typically "American" films as Eugene O'Neill's *Ah, Wilderness!* (1935) and *Of Human Hearts* (1936). William S. Van Dyke was a versatile director responsible for "The Thin Man" series, starring William Powell and Myrna Loy; he also directed the Jeanette MacDonald/Nelson Eddy musicals. Sam Wood directed Marx Brothers comedies as well as such other efforts as *Goodbye, Mr. Chips* (1939), *Our Town* (1940), and *King's Row* (1942). Sidney Franklin directed MGM's literary films, such as *The Guardsman* (1931), *Private Lives* (1931), *The Barretts of Wimpole Street* (1934), and *The Good Earth* (1937). Victor Fleming was in charge of (though he did not personally direct) some of MGM's biggest productions, including *Captains Courageous* (1937) and *The Wizard of Oz* (1939).

All these men, and many more, were highly talented individuals, as the diversity of the films they directed makes clear. The overall directorial image at MGM was one of variety rather than strong personal style. There were simply too many other powerful and talented artists involved in films to allow one individual, such as a director, to stand out. The MGM directors were, in effect, supervisors and coordinators of talent. Each imprinted his films with a certain style, but his was only one of several "prints."

MGM's pool of technical and artistic personnel also contributed significantly to the studio's style. The costumer was Adrian, whose influence was seen in everything from elaborate costume spectacles such as *Mutiny on the Bounty* (1935) and *The Barretts of Wimpole Street* (1934) to the flowing satiny gowns worn by such stars as Jean Harlow, Norma Shearer, and Greta Garbo. His styles set a standard for motion pictures and the fashion industry and became symbolic of the era.

The set designer was Cedric Gibbons, whose work ranged from the huge, elaborate sets for *Mutiny on the Bounty* (1935) to the smaller but intricate and detailed backgrounds for *Dinner at Eight* (1933). Gibbons's sets were difficult to characterize, though they were known to impart a "glow" and "polish" to the films he worked on. *New York Times* film critic Bosley Crowther remarked that for the 1936 production of *Marie Antoinette* Gibbons was instructed to produce the most

▶ The ballroom scene from MGM's *Marie Antoinette* (1936). The scene illustrates the high style of the studio as well as the individual efforts of costumer Adrian and set designer Cedric Gibbons.

exquisite and impressive sets that could be conceived. According to Crowther, "Versailles itself was slightly tarnished alongside the palace Gibbons whipped up."

Sound was supervised by Douglas Shearer, brother of leading MGM actress Norma Shearer, who also happened to be Thalberg's wife. Shearer, however, didn't need connections to ensure his place at MGM, or in the industry as generally. He was, as was noted in Chapter 7, one of the leading innovators in motion picture sound technology.

This multitude of detail—whether involving costume, set, or sound design—was representative of the system itself. Films were constructed and totally controlled events, usually made entirely within sound-stage environments. Even when a film was shot on location, the reality was controlled as much as possible. Indeed, the "reality" of MGM's films *was* that of Gibbons, Adrian, Shearer, and others.

Despite the array of production talents at MGM, however, it was the studio's stable of talented actors and actresses that, more than anything else, generated its reputation and success. Among the best known and most talented stars under contract to MGM in the thirties and forties were Ethel and John Barrymore, Wallace Beery, Jackie Cooper, Joan Crawford, Marion Davies, Clark Gable, Spencer Tracy, Robert Montgomery, Mickey Rooney, Jean Harlow, Helen Hayes, Walter Huston, Myrna Loy, Robert Young, Robert Taylor, William Powell, Nelson Eddy, Greta Garbo, Norma Shearer, Jeanette MacDonald, Rosalind Russell, and Luise Rainer. As a number of critics have noted, MGM had a distinct feminine emphasis, and it is clear that top female names dominate the foregoing list. Only Gable, Tracy, and Taylor were superstar male leads. Eddy, Powell, Rooney, and others were primarily character stars who played a relatively limited range of parts. By accumulating all this talent, MGM cornered the market on stars, and, by placing a certain type and number of stars in a film, the firm could virtually ensure a film's success.

MGM's films were built primarily around their stars and are best characterized as vehicles for specific performers. Greta Garbo made fourteen sound films for MGM, including *Anna Christie* (1930), *Grand Hotel* (1932), *Queen Christina* (1933), *Anna Karenina* (1935), *Camille* (1936), *Ninotchka* (1939), and *Two-Faced Woman* (1941). She portrayed the remote goddess, aloof but passionate, with the ability to seem utterly unaware of the camera. With the exception of Garbo's foreign presence, however, MGM was primarily known for its middle-class American melodramas, comedies, and romances.

Gable was Metro's top male star. He embodied the sense of American idealism that permeated so many of MGM's films. Gable was the embodiment of the no-nonsense, rugged, All-American man. His roles covered a wide variety of types, but all centered on his inherent manliness. From *Red Dust* (1932) to *Mutiny on the Bounty* (1935) to *Test Pilot* (1938) to his ultimate role as Rhett Butler in *Gone with the Wind* (1939), Gable passed through MGM's films with a cheerful good humor and gruff manliness that earned him the title "King of Hollywood."

Greta Garbo and John Barrymore, two of Hollywood's most famous "profiles," in MGM's *Grand Hotel* (1932). Garbo as a lonely ballerina and Barrymore as her jewel-thief lover provided audiences of the thirties with classic images of power and beauty.

ety of roles and films, including Puck in *Midsummer Night's Dream* (1935), *Ah, Wilderness!* (1935), *Boys' Town* (1938), *Babes in Arms* (1939), and many others. Like most stars of the time, Rooney was typecast, and he found it difficult to expand into more challenging roles. He has always been underrated as an actor, and only in recent years has his talent really been appreciated.

Despite all this individual brilliance, it is important to remember that it was the system that dominated production, as director Joseph Mankiewicz makes clear in a recent interview.

I'd be willing to bet that in all the years I worked at Metro it would be hard to name a film done by one of the Metro stable of directors, say Woody Van Dyke, Victor Fleming, Bob Leonard, Clarence Brown, Jack Conway, and so on, which some *other* director didn't complete. People forget. Production in those days was such an assembly line, with so many films being turned out that by the time a film was previewed the guy who'd originally directed it would have already gone on to another. After the preview, there'd always be changes and retakes, and the front office would assign another director to handle them. Nobody ever thought anything of Sam Wood, who was a fine director, coming in to do the retakes on a Victor Fleming picture.

Gable survived by essentially playing himself; Spencer Tracy succeeded as a skilled actor who created a variety of memorable roles. Tracy wandered through several studios in the early thirties until he signed on with MGM in 1935. Once established he created some of MGM's most compelling roles—the wronged hero in *Fury* (1936), the priest in *San Francisco* (1936), the Oscar-winning Portuguese fisherman in *Captains Courageous* (1939), another best-actor role as Father Flanagan in *Boys' Town* (1938). Tracy was easily Metro's most versatile male star; he allowed the studio greater content variety than was possible with Gable, Robert Taylor, Mickey Rooney, or others.

Taylor was MGM's glamorous romantic lead. He played opposite most of Metro's top female stars in such films as *Camille* (1936), *This Is My Affair* (1937), *A Yank at Oxford* (1938), *Lady of the Tropics* (1939), and *Lucky Night* (1939). He chafed somewhat under the one-dimensional casting and worked hard in the early forties to establish a tougher image with such roles as the boxer in *The Crowd Roars* (1938), the title role in *Billy the Kid* (1941), and a war-hardened veteran in *Bataan* (1943).

In some seventeen films made about the adventures of a small-town boy growing up in typical American fashion, Mickey Rooney *was* Andy Hardy. But ultimately Rooney proved himself more than Andy Hardy. Diminutive, aggressive, and talented, Rooney appeared in a vari-

Paramount

Paramount was second in power and prestige only to MGM. Unlike MGM, which was headed by a triumvirate, Paramount was primarily the product of one man, Adolph Zukor. Zukor began with his Famous Players Company in 1912, and, after waging a successful fight against the MPPC, he formed Paramount in 1914, by merging with the Jesse Lasky Feature Play Company. Zukor built his empire through theater acquisitions and several complicated mergers. He acquired an impressive stable of stars and other artists, many of whom came from Europe. The latter included Eric von Stroheim, Ernst Lubitsch, Josef von Sternberg, Pola Negri, Marlene Dietrich, and Maurice Chevalier.

Owing largely to vast theater holdings, Paramount was the dominant studio of the silent era, but financial problems and internal dissension caused it to slip to second place. It went bankrupt in 1932, and was reorganized in 1935 with Barney Balaban as studio head. Paramount's style was the opposite of MGM's. Its films included the comedies of manners of Ernst Lubitsch, the lavish spectacles of Cecil B. De Mille, and the continental intrigues of Josef von Sternberg.

At first, primarily through the pioneering work of Lubitsch and Mamoulian, Paramount was the acknowledged leader in sound experimentation and development. This was at least partially due to its dominant position in the twenties, when it easily made the financially hazardous transition to sound. The contributions of Mamoulian and Lubitsch to the development of sound have already been discussed, but it is important to note that not just their sound work but their whole careers at Paramount were significant. In the early thirties, Mamoulian departed radically from his early realistic efforts and began to specialize in fantasy and musical films such as *Dr. Jekyll and Mr. Hyde* (1932), *Love Me Tonight* (1932), and *Song of Songs* (1933). He soon moved on to work at MGM and for Sam Goldwyn, but he never managed to recapture his early brilliance. Lubitsch, on the other hand, maintained a consistent profile with his sophisticated, fast-paced comedies and musicals. Using two of Paramount's early stars, Maurice Chevalier and Jeanette MacDonald, he produced some of the period's wittiest, most charming musicals — *The Love Parade* (1929), *One Hour with You* (1932), and *The Merry Widow* (1934). His nonmusical efforts were characterized by the same sophisticated charm and continental gaiety. Lubitsch's humor was distinctly European, emphasizing sly glances, sharp repartee, and peeks behind closed doors. Some of his most successful films were *Trouble in Paradise* (1932), *Design for Living* (1933), and *Angel* (1937).

Two more directors who represented the Paramount style were Mitchell Leisen and Cecil B. De Mille. Leisen is not particularly well known today, but his work in the thirties and early forties was well done and responsible in great part for the lustrous look of Paramount films. Leisen was one of the few directors to come up the studio ladder from costume design. His origins there greatly influenced his work, especially his light comedies, such as *Death Takes a Holiday* (1934), *Murder at the Vanities* (1934), *Hands Across the Table* (1936), and *Midnight* (1939). His strong visualization powers transformed stock romances and melodramas into charming films deserving of renewed critical focus. De Mille, of course, achieved a lasting reputation as the great showman, the master of the spectacle film. His work for Paramount beautifully illustrated the coordination between individual and studio. With heavy emphasis on set design, costumes, and casts of thousands, De Mille produced a remarkable number of "big" films, including *The Sign of the Cross* (1932), *Cleopatra* (1934), *The Crusades* (1935), *The Plainsman* (1937), *The Buccaneer* (1938), and *Union Pacific* (1939). De Mille's style is difficult to define. He was primarily concerned with three major elements in all his films — sex, sin, scenery — and he managed to integrate and manipulate all three regardless of whether the content was the Bible, ancient Egypt, the Middle Ages, or the American West.

However, of all the directors who worked for Paramount in these years the one who best represented the studio's style was Josef von Sternberg. He set a tone of high style and continental romance that came to be known as *the* Paramount style. Most of his best work was done with Marlene Dietrich, beginning in 1931 with *Dishonored* and followed by *Shanghai Express* (1932),

▶ Marlene Dietrich and Cary Grant, in Josef von Sternberg's classic film *Blonde Venus* (1932). As the still illustrates, in this film style triumphed over content. However, as a vehicle for Dietrich and Sternberg, as director, it is a cinematic masterpiece.

Blonde Venus (1932), *The Scarlet Empress* (1934), and *The Devil Is a Woman* (1935). In all these efforts, von Sternberg displayed a visual style that can only be described as exotic, with its emphasis on lighting and decor. He has been characterized as a "lyricist of light and shadow." Few of his films are distinguished by plot, since content was not really important to him. In fact, von Sternberg is quoted as saying, "The best source for a film is an anecdote." He is a classic example of a talented director who needed a studio within which to create his best work. He required total control over his environment and used all Paramount's technical and artistic resources to achieve his results. And he was a good example of the dominating power of the star system, since Paramount was willing to put up with many of his eccentricities because of his "special" relationship with Marlene Dietrich; as long as she appeared in his films, they were virtually guaranteed financial success.

Technical personnel also contributed greatly to Paramount's effectiveness. Perhaps the key individual here was set designer Hans Dreier. His work is especially evident in most of De Mille's and Sternberg's films. In a recent interview, Garson Kanin described Dreier's style as "rococo," and then quoted Ernst Lubitsch's remark that he had been to Paris, France, and Paris, Paramount, and preferred the latter.

Although Paramount had relatively few contract stars, it employed some of the most striking and individual personalities of the period. Marlene Dietrich was perhaps the most glamorous of these. In seven films, ending in 1935, von Sternberg created of Dietrich a woman of calculated beauty and frank sexuality. However, equally if not more valuable to the studio was the glamorous and sexy Mae West. Beginning with *Night After Night* (1932), she starred in eight films over the next six years, all of which were very successful at a time when Paramount desperately needed income. Her films, like her personality, fill the screen with sexual suggestions. However, West always played a lady. Sex for her was a private act, and even with such lines as "It's not the man in my life, but the life in my man," she conveyed sex more as a suggested presence than a physical act. Though most fans were unaware of the fact, she controlled her own scripts and wrote her own dialogue. Her

▲ Cary Grant and Mae West, in Paramount's *She Done Him Wrong* (1933). West repeated her Broadway hit role of Diamond Lil and also coscripted the film, easily her best. Grant is the man she invites to come up and see her sometime.

best films, made in the early thirties, included *She Done Him Wrong* (1933), *I'm No Angel* (1933), and *Night After Night* (1932). Her visual and verbal sexuality prompted attempts at censorship and hurried the Motion Picture Production Code and the Catholic Church's Legion of Decency into place. After new rules of conduct were laid down, her films no longer had the same impact and, sensing frustration to come, she gradually withdrew from active filmmaking.

Gary Cooper was the studio's top male lead. He was used in everything from foreign intrigue to high society to light comedy. Another Paramount personality was Bing Crosby, a major radio star, whose efforts in the thirties helped the studio tremendously. However, it was not until he teamed up with comedian Bob Hope in *Road to Rio* (1940) that Paramount began to push him as a major star. As a result of the success of the "road films" and Paramount publicity, Crosby and Hope were top box-office attractions throughout most of World War II. During the early forties, Lubitsch remained a top director, with such comedies as *Going My Way*. Another director, Preston Sturges, came into his own during that time as a master of light comedy and satire with such films as *The Lady Eve* (1941), *The Miracle of Morgan's Creek* (1944), and *Hail the Conquering Hero* (1944).

It is difficult to get a solid grip on Paramount. Its profile was a mixture of light comedy, continental intrigue, and lavish spectacle. Perhaps this multiple personality resulted from a shaky financial base and front-office politics, but it may have been simply due to the fact that the studio employed many different talented artists. Whatever the reasons, the profile of Paramount's output was among the most fascinating and diverse of any studio.

Edward G. Robinson, in his classic role as Rico in Warner Brothers' *Little Caesar* (1930). Directed by Mervyn LeRoy, the film established Robinson as a major star but also cast him as a "tough-guy gangster" a stereotype from which he was never able to completely break away. The film helped establish Warner Brothers' screen image of social realism.

Warner Brothers

Unlike Paramount, whose personality was hard to define, Warner Brothers had a distinct and consistent profile. It quickly became known as the studio with a hard, fast big-city style. Warners was a "Depression studio," and its films and overall style reflected the mood and atmosphere of the time more clearly than any other company.

Begun in 1917 as a film distribution company by Harry, Jack, Al, and Sam Warner, the company expanded into film production in the early twenties. It catapulted into the major-studio ranks through its pioneering role in sound and was soon acquiring other companies and its own theater chain. Jack Warner ran the studio in Hollywood with an iron hand, while Al and Harry stayed behind the scenes. Sam Warner, the force that propelled the company into sound, died the day before *The Jazz Singer,* the first sound feature, opened in 1927.

During the thirties and forties, Warners was best known for four types of films: gangster films, social-conscience movies, backstage musicals, and biographies.

Key films establishing Warners' gangster and social-conscience style were *Little Caesar* (1930), starring Edward G. Robinson; *The Public Enemy* (1931), starring James Cagney; *I Am a Fugitive from a Chain Gang* (1932), starring Paul Muni; and *The Maltese Falcon* (1941), starring Humphrey Bogart. In addition, scores of lesser-known films were produced, such as *Heroes for Sale* (1935), *Wild Boys of the Road* (1934), *Confessions of a Nazi Spy* (1939), and *Mission to Moscow* (1943), all of which resulted in one of the most prominent cycles of social realism in film history. The content of these films was seemingly torn from newspaper headlines, and several (including *I Am a Fugitive from a Chain Gang*) were based on fact. Equally important to this sense of realism was the fundamental style of the films, characterized most clearly by the hard, flat, black-and-white photography pioneered and perfected by Warner cinematographer Sol Polito. Editing also played a key role, since most Warners' films were cut to a maximum of 90 minutes, with many running just over an hour.

Another type of "Depression film" developed at Warners was the backstage musical. The form took the Depression as a basic theme, but spent little time in detailing the reality of it. Society simply served as a

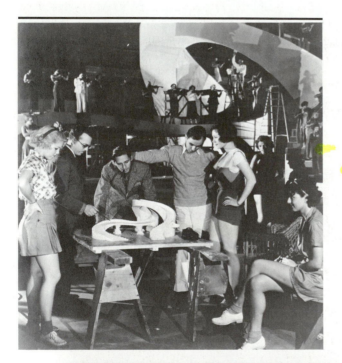

springboard from which to launch elaborate musical numbers. Key films included *42nd Street* (1933), *Gold Diggers of 1933* (1933), and *Footlight Parade* (1933). These and several other films were known primarily for the work of choreographer Busby Berkeley. Famous for his stylized nonrealistic production numbers, Berkeley became better known than most of the directors he worked under. Berkeley used squadrons of people, usually scantily clad young women, in intricate and complex designs that often resulted in an almost surrealistic atmosphere. The Depression was still present in these films, but it was presented as "fun," in contrast to the graphic settings of such social realist films as *Little Caesar* and other "gangster movies." The plots generally revolved around attempts to produce a musical without adequate money, with an air of imminent disaster hanging over the entire company. Despite underlying themes of fear and paralysis, the endings were always happy — the music played on, the boy got the girl, and light was always in view at the end of the tunnel.

These types of films best represented the basic Warners style. However, like any studio, Warners had a large pool of talent, and diversity, therefore, was almost a built-in quality. Warners' diversity centered primarily around three talented and totally unique stars — George Arliss, Errol Flynn, and Paul Muni. These three starred in a number of biographical films, which often had strong classical overtones.

◀ Busby Berkeley at work designing one of his patented production numbers for Warners and (below) the end result as it appeared in *Gold Diggers of 1933*.

Arliss was a veteran of many years on the legitimate stage and was used by the studio in such prestigious vehicles as *Disraeli* (1929), *Old English* (1930), and *Voltaire* (1933). Arliss won the Academy Award for Best Actor for his performance in *Disraeli,* but in retrospect most of his films are quite dated, and his individual performances are heavy and obviously influenced by his stage experience.

At the opposite end of the continuum was Errol Flynn, Warners' answer to Douglas Fairbanks. Less talented than Fairbanks, especially in handling light comedy, Flynn was the epitome of the virile, handsome individualist, battling all types of enemies, from pirates to Indians. Flynn moved through his films with a steely-eyed stare and unswerving demeanor but rarely dominated as Fairbanks did. Most of his films, such as *Captain Blood* (1935), *The Charge of the Light Brigade* (1936), *The Adventures of Robin Hood* (1938), *The Dawn Patrol* (1938), and *The Sea Hawk* (1940) stressed broad, impersonal action rather than intense personal drama. Nevertheless, Flynn was one of Warners' most productive and popular stars, appearing in more than thirty films between 1935 and 1946.

Besides Spencer Tracy, Paul Muni was one of Hollywood's most talented and versatile actors. He was used initially in typical Warners films such as *I Am a Fugitive from a Chain Gang* (1932), *Bordertown* (1935), and *Black Fury* (1936). However, he soon began to branch out with a series of biographical studies that included an Academy Award-winning performance in *The Life of Emile Zola* (1937) followed by an equally powerful performance in *Juarez* (1939). Muni supplied Warners with most of their prestige during this time and became one of the industry's most respected craftsmen.

The two leading stars at Warner Brothers were Edward G. Robinson and James Cagney. Their careers resembled each other and suffered from similar problems. Though both actors were versatile, both were typed early in their careers as "tough guys." And, although they both tried, neither was ever able to escape the image and role stereotype completely. Cagney was slightly more successful than Robinson, because of his dancing ability, which he parlayed into an Academy Award-winning performance in *Yankee Doodle Dandy* (1942). Both men's stories illustrate how the system was built and how it depended on personalities while manipulating and controlling these same personalities for its own benefit.

As should be clear by now, Warners was a "male" studio. It had few female stars, and those it did have all seemed to be cast from the same mold — that of a tough, wise-cracking "dame." The most typical female stars at Warners were Joan Blondell, Glenda Farrell, and Bette Davis. Davis, who consistently fought for better roles,

▼ From *The Life of Emile Zola* (1937). Paul Muni in the title role plies the trade of a fishmonger in this film biography.

achieved a measure of creative independence and versatility. The studio soon regarded her as their "female Muni," and she amply rewarded them with an Academy Award-winning performance in *Jezebel* (1938) and nominations for the next four years running in *Dark Victory* (1939), *The Letter* (1940), *The Little Foxes* (1941), and *Now, Voyager* (1942).

Warners' directors received little attention, and with good reason. Warners' system of production placed less emphasis on directing than on acting, editing, and photography. To be sure, several good contract directors worked for Warners. Lloyd Bacon, for example, was responsible for several of the Berkeley musicals and churned out more than forty films between 1928 and 1943. Like many of Warners' directors, he had a strong sense of pace and an ability to handle crisp dialogue. His best films were *Footlight Parade* (1933), *42nd Street* (1933), and *Marked Woman* (1937). William Dieterle was best known for his well-mounted biographical dramas, including most of Muni's prestige vehicles. Michael Curtiz was the most prolific and talented of Warners' directors, directing everything from *Jimmy the Gent* (1934) and *Yankee Doodle Dandy* (1942) to *Casablanca* (1942), for which he received the Academy Award as Best Director. Between 1930 and 1946, Curtiz directed more than sixty films for Warners, including most of Errol Flynn's pictures, and he achieved a light, almost winsome style despite being responsible for action pictures that involved more coordination of people and equipment than artistic direction.

Mervyn LeRoy was Warners' other "major" director, besides Curtiz, and he was responsible for some of the studio's most ambitious productions of the thirties, including *Little Caesar* (1930), *I Was a Fugitive from a Chain Gang* (1932), *Gold Diggers of 1933* (1933), and *They Won't Forget* (1939). As this partial list makes clear, LeRoy was a perfect studio contract director, able to serve different themes and work with different people easily. Like others of his ilk, such as Lewis Milestone, LeRoy seemed to need a firm central theme and strong crew to do his best work.

Garson Kanin, in an interview some forty years later, provided some insight into the Warner system and how it functioned in relation to its directors:

> There were Warner directors, for instance, who never got near a script. It's no secret that Michael Curtiz sometimes started shooting a script without reading it. He would make about four pictures a year, which at those studios wasn't unusual. They would be prepared almost entirely by the front office, they'd be cast and the sets would be designed. And then they would say, "Well Mike Curtiz, he's finishing Thursday. . . . Do you want him to start on Monday? No, make it Tuesday." They'd call him in and say, "You're going to start this on Tuesday." He'd say, "What is it?" And they'd say, "Well, it's *The Charge of the Light Brigade.*" "What's that?" "Well, you'll see. . . ." He would then maybe read it, maybe not. The director would do his part of the job and the film went to the cutter and he put it together. Frequently a director at Warners wouldn't even see his assembled stuff. It was all organized, assembly line stuff, and I think that's one reason why the general run of pictures was so bland . . . in all my years in Hollywood, and later, I never knew a director who had final say on his work. Not one. . . . And if you talked to producers and heads of the studios, they would say, "Why should they? It's our money. . . ." For the most part, they (directors) were employees who got paid so much per week. Not even by the year; they were paid by the week on Fridays, like employees. That's what made the world go around. . . .

In summary, other studios had bigger stars, bigger movies, and bigger budgets. But Warners displayed a crisp professionalism. This resulted in movies with a texture and style that audiences immersed in the Depression and World War II could use to escape from everyday realities. These films are still some of the freshest, most invigorating examples of studio filmmaking.

20th Century-Fox

Although 20th Century-Fox was organized in 1935, its founder, William Fox, started his studio in 1915. Fox continued to operate the studio until 1932 but was eased out following a series of court actions and stock mergers. He was replaced by Sidney Kent, and in 1935 the organization was merged with 20th Century Pictures.

20th Century-Fox achieved its reputation primarily through the efforts of Darryl F. Zanuck who, in 1935, became Vice President in Charge of Production at the age of thirty-three. Zanuck, like MGM's Thalberg, supervised virtually every aspect of production. Mel Gussow's biography of Zanuck, *Don't Say Yes Until I Finish Talking*, gave a good description of Zanuck's style:

> He announced assignments, assigned credits, including his own (whether a picture should be "produced by DFZ" or "DFZ's production of"), suggested old movies to be rerun as guides for new movies, rewrote dialogue, canceled projects, moaned about the state of Hollywood and the state of the world, welcomed new employees

(to Charles Brackett: "the steam room downstairs is at your disposal, and also Sam, the barber"), distributed praise as well as scorn, changed titles, and changed his mind (depending on the grosses, a picture could go from great to terrible in a swirl of memos). Except to his top personnel and specific producers, directors and writers he was working with, he was accessible largely through memos.

Zanuck placed his emphasis on stories. This priority was determined by both chance and necessity, since 20th Century-Fox had relatively few stars. In 1935, Zanuck inherited Will Rogers, Shirley Temple, and Charlie Chan. Rogers died less than a year later, so Zanuck came up with the motto, "Stars don't make pictures, pictures make stars." This was Zanuck's version of whistling in the dark. The Fox output in the thirties and forties simply did not create many stars. Had it not been for Temple, Chan, and, later, Betty Grable, Fox might not have survived.

The Charlie Chan series began in 1931 with Warner Oland in the title role. More than a dozen films were produced in six years, most of them similar in plot and style. The only changes seemed to be in the title, which found Charlie in different parts of the world: *Charlie Chan in London, in Paris, in Egypt, in Shanghai; Charlie Chan at the Circus, at the Race Track, at the Opera, at the Olympics, on Broadway,* and *at Monte Carlo.* Following Pearl Harbor, however, Orientals were out as sympathetic characters, and Charlie quickly disappeared.

Almost as prolific as Chan and far more popular, Shirley Temple was one of the most remarkable phenomena of the entire period. She took the American public by storm, starting in 1934 with *Carolina,* and for the next six years reigned as one of the industry's top box-office attractions. During this time she starred in twenty-three films for Fox, all of them highly successful. For all practical purposes, her career was over by the time she was ten years old. Fox placed her in a number of films as a teenager, but she never regained the success she had as a child star. She made her last film, *A Kiss for Corliss,* in 1949 at the tender age of twenty-one. Fortunately for Fox, Betty Grable arrived on the scene to pick up the slack left by the decline of Chan and Temple. Grable headed up the so-called "Fox girls," who were basically nameless but all looked alike. They were placed in films primarily to reveal their physical attributes, and the films were very successful with a male population separated by war from normal female companionship. Grable, of course, became the prototype of all pin-up girls during the war and was one of the most popular stars of the war period.

▲ Lionel Barrymore and Shirley Temple, in Fox's 1935 production *The Little Colonel.*

If Fox had a major director, it was John Ford. He could hardly be called a studio contract director, however, since his work often transcended the studio and, besides, he worked sporadically for other studios. Ford's most important films for Fox during this time were *Judge Priest* (1934) and *Steamboat Round the Bend* (1935), both starring Will Rogers; *Young Mr. Lincoln* (1939); *The Grapes of Wrath* (1940); and *How Green Was My Valley* (1941). Ford's career is discussed in detail later in the chapter.

Henry King also made several major films for Fox, including *In Old Chicago* (1938), *Alexander's Ragtime Band* (1938), *Jesse James* (1939), and *Song of Bernadette* (1943). And Fox developed and spotlighted several major screenwriters, including Nunnally Johnson (*Jesse James* and *The Grapes of Wrath*), Philip Dunne (*The Rains Came* [1939] and *How Green Was My Valley*), and Lamar Trotti (*Young Mr. Lincoln* and *The Ox-Bow Incident* [1942]).

Fox was not a major studio; it didn't match MGM or Paramount in style, substance, or output, but it developed a distinctive yet eclectic form and was home to several of the era's best known filmmakers.

Jane Darwell, in her Academy Award winning performance as Ma Joad in John Ford's *The Grapes of Wrath* (1940). As the determined head of a family, Darwell created a performance of great dignity and force, symbolizing for many hope in a time of national depression.

Columbia

Harry and Jack Cohn started Columbia in 1924, beginning on what was known in Hollywood as "poverty row." However, through the bulldog tenacity and instincts of Harry Cohn, the administrative ability of Jack Cohn and Joseph Brandt, and the films of Frank Capra, Columbia emerged in the thirties as an important studio, though below the level of MGM, Paramount and Warners. Like most of the so-called "minor" studios, Columbia had few stars and even fewer assets for indulging on lavish productions. It was not until Rita Hayworth emerged in the early forties that Columbia had a star of international magnitude. Before Hayworth, Columbia's films were populated by such people as Ralph Bellamy, Jean Arthur, Grace Moore, and Lee Tracy. However, Cohn developed a plan for hiring stars for individual pictures and managed to produce several important films, including Howard Hawks's *Twentieth Century* (1934), with John Barrymore and Carole Lombard, and George Cukor's *Holiday* (1938), with Cary Grant and Katharine Hepburn. And in most of Frank Capra's films the leads were borrowed from other studios—for example, Clark Gable and James Stewart from MGM and Gary Cooper and Claudette Colbert from Paramount.

Rather than stars, Columbia relied heavily on writers and directors, both of whom they also borrowed or briefly lured from other studios. Important directors employed by Columbia included Lewis Milestone, Howard Hawks, George Cukor, George Stevens, and Leo McCarey. Writers of reputation included Dorothy Parker, Robert Riskin, Herman Mankiewicz, and Jo Swerling. Few of these people stayed long, however. This policy of quick departure was due mainly to Harry Cohn. Legends have grown up around "King" Cohn. As the only person in the history of Hollywood to be both president of the company and chief of production, he totally dominated the studio and its personnel. However, Cohn also had an instinct for recognizing talent. And he maintained a healthy respect for the talent he discovered, as evidenced when he offered to directors the unheard-of opportunity of sharing in their pictures' profits. Although almost 70 percent of Columbia's product was "B" (low-budget) quality, such "A" features as Capra's *Lost Horizon* (1937) and *You Can't Take It with You* (1938), Leo McCarey's *The Awful Truth* (1937), and Charles Vidor's *A Song to Remember* (1945) provided Columbia with prosperity, reputation, and up to 60 percent of its profits. Columbia's films were mostly contemporary in content, which related both to Cohn's personal tastes and the lack of money required for expensive period pictures.

Although Capra did his best work as a contract director for Columbia, he deserves special recognition beyond his value as an asset to the studio. Most of his films bear

From Frank Capra's 1939 production *Mr. Smith Goes to Washington*. Here James Stewart as Mr. Smith makes an impassioned plea for justice on the floor of Congress.

the stamp of an individual creator, although screenwriter Robert Riskin and cameraman Joe Walker deserve some of the praise for such Academy Award-winning films as *It Happened One Night* (1934), *Mr. Deeds Goes to Town* (1936), and *You Can't Take It with You* (1938). Capra's films display a boisterous sense of humor and a knack for improvisation. However, the most striking characteristic of his work in this period is what one reviewer called "the fantasy of good will" — a philosophy inherent in Capra's films that the little man could triumph over all odds, whatever they might be. This philosophy was especially popular in the Depression with such films as *Mr. Smith Goes to Washington* (1939). In his autobiography Capra expresses a need to be a spokesman for the little man; his films had to contain a message and not simply entertain. His approach was very successful — in four years (1934–1938) Capra won three Academy Awards for best director and his films won the Best Picture Award twice.

RKO (Radio-Keith-Orpheum)

RKO was actually a top holding company that integrated various production-distribution and exhibition organizations, among them RKO Radio Pictures, Inc. Organized

in 1931, RKO was originally conceived by RCA, which was seeking a place in the development of sound pictures. However, the Depression soon took its toll, and RKO went into bankruptcy in 1933. But the studio survived, due mainly to the efforts and talents of Fred Astaire and Ginger Rogers, who starred in an eight-film series of smart, fashionable musicals beginning with *Flying Down to Rio* in 1934. The most popular films of the series and some of the most engaging musicals ever made were *Top Hat* (1935), *Swing Time* (1936), *Shall We Dance* (1937), and *Carefree* (1938). Plot was never particularly important or even relevant to most of these films. Narrative served simply as the thread that strung the individual Astaire-Rogers numbers together. Although some attempts were made to integrate individual production numbers with the rest of the film, once a production was started it took on a life of its own. Unlike Busby Berkeley's tightly edited fantasies, Astaire performed in a real environment with the camera usually recording him dancing alone or with Miss Rogers in full figure and in one take. Astaire was an original and an unduplicated creator, not so much in his choreography (Hermes Pan did much of this work for RKO), as in his completely natural, almost eerie physical grace. He used these natural abilities to interpret both dance and song (Astaire did not possess a great voice, but Irving Berlin

Fred Astaire's First Screen Test

*P*lease arrange for the executives, including Brock, to see the test of Fred Astaire. I am a little uncertain about the man, but I feel, in spite of his enormous ears and bad chin line, that his charm is so tremendous that it comes through even in this wretched test, and I would be perfectly willing to go ahead with him for the lead in the Brock musical. I should like to have Brock's opinion; but even if he is opposed to Astaire, I would be in favor of signing him for this part if some of the other studio executives have any enthusiasm for the man.

—*David O. Selznick (January 26, 1933)*

called him the best interpreter of his music of any singer), projecting the very essence and spirit of all that was light, gay, and debonair.

The rest of RKO's product was a hodgepodge of "B" potboilers, serials, and comedy shorts (most starring Edgar Kennedy and Leon Errol) and the occasional "A" film, usually starring RKO's major star Katharine Hepburn. Hepburn made fourteen films for RKO between 1932 and 1938, beginning with *A Bill of Divorcement* (1932), which also starred John Barrymore, and ending with Howard Hawks's classic comedy *Bringing Up Baby* (1938) with Cary Grant. Other occasional major films of the period included the granddaddy of all monster films, *King Kong* (1933); John Ford's *The Informer* (1935), featuring a masterful performance by Victor McLaglen as the half-witted brute who betrays his friend for a handful of silver; and, of course, Orson Welles's *Citizen Kane* (1941) and *The Magnificent Ambersons* (1942).

Universal

Universal was one of Hollywood's oldest studios; it was founded by Carl Laemmle in 1912. The studio established itself as one of the top silent companies, primarily because it created films for which there was little competition. Universal was known as the home of the "B" film. In 1927–1928, for example, the studio produced silents of four types—twenty-six Westerns, four serials, fifty-two comedies, and several feature novelties. It continued this pattern into sound and, in the thirties, became known primarily for horror films and "B" musicals. A teenager named Deanna Durbin was the key to Universal's musical success. She made a number of very popular films, including *Three Smart Girls* (1936), *100 Men and a Girl* (1937), *Mad About Music* (1938), and *That Certain Age* (1938). The slapstick comedy of Abbott and Costello also helped to fill Universal's coffers, but its major creative efforts were in the horror genre. Begin-

◄ From *Top Hat* (1935). Fred Astaire and Ginger Rogers danced and sang their way through the Depression in films whose tone and mood contrasted sharply with the harsh social realism of *Public Enemy* and *The Grapes of Wrath. Top Hat* was one of the brightest and freshest of the nine films the two made together, and it contains some of Irving Berlin's best songs, including "Cheek to Cheek," and "Top Hat, White Tie, and Tails."

▶ From James Whale's 1931 production of *Frankenstein*. Boris Karloff, as the monster, plays tenderly with a little girl.

ning in 1931 with *Frankenstein,* Universal produced some of the classic horror films of all time, including *Dracula* (1931), *The Mummy* (1932), and *The Invisible Man* (1933). Most of these films were not great commercial hits, perhaps because they did not simply exploit the grotesque visual nature of the genre, but also presented a moral and philosophical point of view. *Dracula,* for example, as played by Bela Lugosi, was not simply some bizarre caricature, but the very embodiment of evil. And Frankenstein's monster, as played by Boris Karloff, was not some insane creature, but a driven animal who evoked feelings of both compassion and terror. The genre was further enriched by director James Whale's *The Old Dark House* (1932), *The Invisible Man* (1935), and *The Bride of Frankenstein* (1935), plus Edgar Ulmer's *The Black Cat* (1934) and Rowland Lee's *Son of Frankenstein* (1939).

Like most of the other minor studios, Universal produced an occasional "A" picture that captured both the critics' attention and the audiences' wallet. Included among these infrequent major films were Lewis Milestone's *All Quiet on the Western Front* (1930), James Whale's *Showboat* (1936), and George Marshall's *Destry Rides Again* (1939), starring James Stewart and Marlene Dietrich in a brilliant performance as Frenchy.

Republic — A Minor Case

As noted, a number of minor studios coexisted with the majors. These included such organizations as Monogram, Grand National, and Eagle-Lion. However, one studio, formed by the merger of several smaller ones, was, along with Universal, king of the "B" film, especially the "B" Western. This studio was Republic, founded in 1935 by a number of small-time independent producers and located in the old Mack Sennett studios. Under the leadership of Nat Levine, Republic specialized in the rapid-fire production of Gene Autry and Roy Rogers Westerns, twelve-chapter serials, detective stories, and country-style musicals starring Judy Canova.

Speed and cost-cutting were the specialty of Republic and Levine in particular. Republic pictures played every Saturday afternoon in thousands of neighborhood

theaters. The pace of production at Republic was so fast that writers would often find themselves hard at work typing dialogue for scenes being shot twenty feet away.

The key to Republic's success was churning out a low-cost product quickly and efficiently with a few major stars sprinkled in — in this case, Autry and Rogers. This work style illustrates once again the major dividing line between success and failure in Hollywood: hundreds of minor studios had the same characteristics as Republic — except for the one or two popular personalities under contract who carried the day.

Short Subjects

Clearly, as we have seen, the period of 1933 to 1945 was dominated by a system of production that subordinated the individual creator to the demands of producing for a mass audience. The system resulted in the creation of certain patterns and formulas. Feature-length films were the most conspicuous of the studios' products. However, the production of nonfeature material perhaps illustrated more clearly how the system worked. Only a system anticipating and subsequently geared toward meeting a huge public appetite for film could afford to produce so much nonfeature material.

Shorts were the most important of these nonfeatures. All the major studios made them as part of their regular production schedules. They were usually created by separate, autonomous units, staffed by people who did nothing but make a particular kind of short. For example, Columbia made the Three Stooges shorts in a short-subject unit headed by Jules White and Del Lord. Most of the films made in this unit were shot in three to five days and relied heavily on stock footage and material from previous films in the series. Between 1934 and 1958, Columbia turned out 190 Three Stooges shorts, a record for both longevity and productivity.

Jack Chertok was head of short subjects at MGM, where he produced, among many others, the famous "Pete Smith Specialties." Chertok's comment that "we had access to most facilities so long as we didn't get in the way" is representative of the studios' attitude toward shorts. They relied on shorts for overall studio profit but only reluctantly recognized their legitimacy in the total studio structure. The longevity of shorts proved their money-making ability and it was only in the mid-1950s, when the total audience for film had declined and the costs for all film, including shorts, had risen, that studios dropped these nonfeature products from their schedules. In effect, the television series became the short film, and many of the major studios dropped short production in order to make television series.

Only four studios — Universal, Columbia, Republic, and Mascot — produced serials. The other five major studios did not find it necessary or feasible to devote time, money, and personnel to serials because of their predominantly "A-feature" schedule. Serials covered almost every conceivable area of content, including outer space (Flash Gordon, Buck Rogers), the West (the Lone Ranger, Red Rider), the jungle (Tarzan, Jungle Jim), and detectives (Flying G-Men, Dick Tracy). They were usually issued in installments, ten to fifteen to a series, and were enthusiastically received almost every Saturday afternoon by millions of cheering children. In 1946, *Film Daily Yearbook* estimated that the weekly audience for serials was 12 million.

Like everything else that was produced in the studios, serials had a strong economic basis for existence.

One of their key functions was to provide a testing ground for new talent and a burying ground for old talent under long-term contract. John Wayne, for example, began his career playing in serials for Mascot. Walter Brennan, Mickey Rooney, and Lloyd Bridges all had serial experience before achieving stardom. On the other end, several major silent stars, such as Henry B. Walthall (the "Little Colonel" in *The Birth of a Nation*) and Francis X. Bushman, wound up working in serials in the late thirties.

Although of feature length, the series film bore a strong resemblance to shorts and serials because of its repetitive nature. Just as the need to program continually for a mass audience makes the series program a necessary staple of the television industry today, so the series film was a staple of the studio system of the thirties and forties. Perhaps no other film form suggests so well the place Hollywood occupied in American life as the series film. In producing a number of films with the same characters in similar plots, studios exhibited confidence that the public would accept what they offered. They also demonstrated the system's dependency on formula and its willingness to repeat a proven concept. Some of the most popular series included "Hopalong Cassidy" (sixty-six films); Columbia's budget series, including "Ellery Queen," "Boston Blackie," and "Blondie"; and Paramount's "Road" series, starring Bing Crosby and Bob Hope (six films). Perhaps the most famous and successful series of all was "Andy Hardy." Beginning in 1937 with *A Family Affair*, MGM produced seventeen Andy

▶ From *Andy Hardy Meets a Debutante* (1940). Mickey Rooney gives a typical Andy Hardy kiss to his best girl.

Hardy films, ending with *Andy Hardy Comes Home* in 1958. Produced by George Seitz's economy unit and starring Mickey Rooney and a host of stock characters, the series made more than $25 million for MGM.

Animation

Animation in the form of the short cartoon was yet another feature of the system. Animation had existed in a number of countries almost from the beginning of motion pictures. In fact, the motion toys of the nineteenth century were animations. The strip cartoons used in the Zoetrope and Phenakistoscope were drawn by the thousands, but with the development of photography phase pictures replaced them and animation declined.

Animation, by definition, is film created frame by frame. It normally takes three forms: the cartoon, puppet animation, and pixillation (animation of the human form). The basic technique is simple but arduous; it consists of creating twenty-four different phase pictures for every second of screen time. A ten-minute cartoon requires 14,400 different drawings.

Animation did not develop rapidly at first, since most filmmakers were fascinated with their newfound power to record reality in motion. Emile Cohl of France was the first major producer of animated films. He made more than 200 cartoons between 1908 and 1918. His standard character was Fantoche, a type of comic everyman, ill-fated but resilient. Most of his early work used jerky matchstick figures often outlined in white on a black background.

Cohl's work was followed in the United States by that of Winsor McKay, who created the short cartoon *Gertie the Trained Dinosaur* (1909). Cartoons were popular with audiences despite the increasing sophistication and popularity of feature films with flesh-and-blood stars. During the 1920s, several cartoon series were created around popular characters. These included Betty Boop and Koko the Clown, both created by Max Fleischer; Krazy Kat; and, perhaps the most important, Pat Sullivan's Felix the Cat. However, the lack of sound and color greatly hampered cartoon development. Audiences could accept a silent Douglas Fairbanks or Charlie Chaplin, because they were dynamic human characters. But silent cartoons containing stick figures and crude backgrounds had great difficulty competing with the human form.

Into this tentative and relatively undeveloped field came a man from Kansas City who revolutionized the animated cartoon. Walt Disney began his career making one-minute black-and-white animated commercials. With his partner and chief artist, Ub Iwerks, Disney soon gravitated to Hollywood, where he experimented with a mouse character. But he met with little success initially, and not until Mickey, as the mouse was later called, began to talk and sing, in *Steamboat Willie* (1928), did Disney's cartoons find an audience.

After the success of *Steamboat Willie,* Disney began to expand his operation. He succeeded primarily because of his willingness to gamble and experiment with technical innovations, primarily sound and color, and his ability to create appealing characters with which audiences could associate and identify. Disney was also a perfectionist, and his films achieved a quality new to the field of animation. As noted briefly in Chapter 7, his first color film was *Flowers and Trees,* made in 1932; soon afterwards he was filming exclusively in color. He continued this success with his "Silly Symphony" films. In 1937 Disney began making feature-length animated films with *Snow White and the Seven Dwarfs.*

The keys to Disney's success were stories and characters. All his films had carefully constructed plots, and most of them preached a moral or delivered some sort of message. His characters were humans in animal disguise. Each one, whether Mickey Mouse, Donald Duck, Pluto, or Goofy, had a clearly identifiable personality. Mickey was the eternal optimist—a personification of Disney himself. Donald Duck was an angry protagonist, quickly taking offense and ready to fight at a moment's notice.

In 1940, Disney made his one attempt at serious art in cartoon form with the production of *Fantasia.* This is a complex and serious film with many brilliant and visually stunning sequences. However, *Fantasia* was not financially successful, at least not at first. Its attempt to raise animation to a higher, more philosophical level while maintaining the popular appeal of Mickey Mouse worked against audience expectations and predispositions. But reissued in the late sixties, the film succeeded greatly with a more visually literate and filmically sophisticated audience who saw the film as some sort of inner reality—a mind-expanding trip.

After a successful war effort in which Donald Duck taught American soldiers how to handle an M-1 rifle and informed other Americans about South America, Disney turned to live-action nature films, such as *Seal Island* (1948) and *Beaver Valley* (1950).

Walt Disney dominated the cartoon field during the thirties and forties, but almost all the major studios had cartoon divisions. Columbia produced "Scrappy" cartoons, using a staff of 200 people. Universal's 100-person cartoon unit was headed by the creator of Woody

Woodpecker, Walter Lantz. Warner Brothers had its "Merry Melody" series and introduced the two most famous non-Disney characters, Bugs Bunny and Porky Pig. Twentieth Century-Fox distributed Terry Toons, created by independent Paul Terry. And Paramount distributed Max Fleischer's "Popeye the Sailor."

With the exception of Disney, however, the industry viewed cartoons as simply program fillers, a little extra frosting on the cake. For the audience, though, children and adults alike, cartoons became an expected and special attraction and the characters became stars in their own right. After the war, television began to saturate the audience with hundreds of new cartoon characters and old stories, and the theatrical cartoon, already weakened by the general industry collapse, died.

In essence, the nonfeature film was perhaps the most typical and representative form of film produced by the studio system. Shorts came about as a result of the double-feature practices of exhibitors during the Depression and the studios' efforts to satisfy their agreements with the exhibitors. The studio system was the perfect place for these films. Contract players were in abundance, and shorts gave new actors and actresses a safe, obscure testing ground, since most series and shorts were virtually ignored by the critics. The studios employed staff producers, directors, and writers by the year rather than by individual pictures, and this helped to make shorts inexpensive to produce.

The Sound Film as Social Document

Any assessment of the films of this time must look beyond the internal intrigue and structure of the studio. Certainly, the industrial system symbolized by the studio was the dominating feature of this period. However, outside the industry the time was dominated by two of the century's most dramatic episodes, the Depression and World War II. Motion pictures were highly influenced by these events, and it is therefore worthwhile to briefly examine the motion picture as social document.

With the arrival of sound came an increasing battle over the direction film should take to satisfy aesthetic and social needs. Clifford Howard, in appraising "American Tendencies" for *Close Up* in 1932, observed that "Hollywood today is more nearly in tune with the normal honesties of life than it has been since the days when Jesse Lasky and Sam Goldwyn made pictures in a barn and ate their lunches from paper bags."

Veteran critic Harry Potamkin was less optimistic when he wrote, in the same issue,

> At last the movie, being a topical medium too, must recognize the depression as subject matter. The audience is lured to see a film pretending to tell the truth and they are shown another picture of the glib studio formula, *American Madness*. With a grand flourish this film opened at the Mayfair. There was a spotlight on the theatre but not a flashlight on the truth.

Much of the criticism of movies during the period was tied to a recognition of the greater potential of the medium, particularly as a social instrument. Archibald MacLeish, writing for *Stage* in 1939, stated that "the real problem was whether a form of art which ignored everything comprehended under the term 'social issue' in this time could have vitality, could have the fourth dimension of life."

It was not just that film had progressed so little, even with voice, that brought it under fire, but that it could accomplish so much more. Only a few exceptional works, such as Orson Welles's *Citizen Kane* and Jean Renoir's *The Grand Illusion* and *Rules of the Game,* were establishing an aesthetic base and social function for the medium, thereby raising standards and the expectations for other works.

But most films were not being produced for social philosophers, theorists, and critics, and, despite criticism, they continued to satisfy the requirements of the industry itself and, at least partially, the needs of the public. As Sinclair Road observed in his essay, "The Influence of the Film," in 1946, "The typical Hollywood film has given people all over the world an opportunity to slip away from the disappointment and inadequacies of their own lives to move for an hour or more in a world of half-truths and happy endings."

We can resolve the seeming contradictions in critical responses to the films themselves at least partially by looking at the conflicting forces that were influencing their production. Film studios, now representing a multimillion dollar industry with an enormous investment in sound-film production and exhibition, continued to look to the box office for signs of audience approval and to the formulas that had proven to be most serviceable in the past. Audiences, quickly saturated with the novelty of speech, song, and general din, and faced with world political upheaval and economic strains at home, were looking to the movies for temporary release from both the anxieties and the drudgeries of the real world. Though studios were still guessing about which variations of the formulas might come into vogue, it was becoming clear that the most popular screenplays were those that drew from a combination of the fanciful and the real. These ranged from backstage romances and tales of instant stardom linked to the anxieties of the Depression, such as *Gold Diggers of 1933,* to Rouben Mamoulian's starkly realistic study of an aging burlesque queen in *Applause* (1929). A 1932 Hays organization poll showed American audiences' first choice in films to be slapstick comedies, followed by "thrillers" and then Westerns and other types of adventure. Social, personal, and political films trailed far behind in the polls. Despite this expressed preference for escapist formula fare, social awareness was on the increase and the so-called problem picture was soon to become a popular staple.

Three important factors influenced the nature and direction of the "American problem picture" of the thirties and forties. These were the climate or conditions under which the films were produced, new developments in technology, and the continued evolution of "screen realism."

The Limitations of a Preoccupied Industry

The immediate questions for the Hollywood industry concerned its economic stability and its continued domination of a worldwide market. These issues, of course, were related, and Hollywood's control of both production and exhibition was influenced by events within and outside the industry. But philosophic and critical queries into the true nature and social function of the medium were not foremost in the minds of most American producers.

The 1929 stock market crash and subsequent crises of the thirties plus a resurgence of anxieties about screen morality all strongly influenced both production and exhibition procedures. By 1932, the reduction in foreign markets and general war jitters had resulted in something of an austerity program and a retrenchment in production. Cost accounting and personnel cutbacks were accompanied by an all-out effort to keep up production schedules for fear that independent producers would corner the market. To expand a faltering home market in the mid-thirties, the double-feature program was adopted. To further bolster attendance at an increasing number of mediocre films, various giveaway schemes were instituted at theaters, and dishes and encyclopedias became the exhibitor's supplement to Hollywood's dream.

If economic austerity and sagging attendance were two parts of the threat to Hollywood, a third was the watchful eyes of would-be censors. Pennsylvania censors had banned Eisenstein's *Potemkin* on the grounds that "it gave American sailors a blue-print as to how to conduct a mutiny," and a bill pending in Congress provided for the creation of a Federal Motion Picture Commission, which would make the motion picture industry a public utility. The proposed commission would not only censor all films but also supervise production and regulate distribution and exhibition. The need to bolster a sagging box office and to ward off censorship and control from outside the industry made Hollywood receptive to guidelines. Films with strong moral statements and values thus continued to be a key ingredient of the formula film,

A theater marquee advertises what for many Depression audiences was more important than the film itself.

with a fresh emphasis on affluence and elegance as the rewards for virtue. With a passing reference to "religion," "national feeling," and "repellent subjects," the production code centered its attention on subjects and situations regarding crime and sex. The code had particular applications to murder, drug traffic, vulgarity, obscenity, profanity, and the "low forms of sex relationships" such as adultery; scenes of passion, seduction, or rape; sex perversion; white slavery; and miscegenation. In addition to making specific prohibitions, the code provided its own formula for screen narrative. The sanctity of the institution of marriage and the home were to be upheld, and "correct standards of life shall be presented on the screen, subject only to necessary dramatic contrasts."

All these influences helped to reinforce formula filmmaking in the studios. The star system gave the formula a new focus, and occasionally persistence and vision on the part of a particular director brought attempts to stretch if not break the mold. But of the nearly 600 films produced by the American industry in the peak years of the thirties, the majority were modestly budgeted, highly moral variations of tested themes that satisfied the needs of studios and patrons and perpetuated efficient dream building as established during the silent film era.

Realism Redefined

One important change that was more evolutionary than revolutionary and that involved a quality inherent in the medium itself pertained to the nature of screen realism. From the beginning, the term *realism* referred to an often undefinable quality of a film that lay at the center of both its popular and aesthetic appeal, but interpretations of the term varied widely. The prenarrative concept of screen realism centered on cinematographic recording of actuality. "All very real and singularly exhilarating," reads the *New York Times* review of the first public motion picture showing in 1896. Screen storytelling introduced other criteria: continuity, historical accuracy, and the extent to which a film reflected the laws of science and human nature.

A collection of observations by viewers in 1915 under the heading "Realism on the Reel" illustrates the diversity in the ways screen realism was used. "The restoration of eyesight of a fifteen-year-old girl, blind since birth, is challenged by an optometrist who had seen

Biograph's *A Bit of Driftwood*." Another viewer took exception to a scene showing a heroine repairing a cut telephone wire without scraping the insulation off the ends of the wires. Characters' motivations were challenged—viewers cited a girl who goes to the street dressed in a modern hat but wearing her hair in ringlets, a tightrope walker who fails to check his equipment before a performance, and a minister who strikes another minister, "specially in the house of a millionaire and in the presence of a lady."

Truth and reality as represented in film, then, were anchored in the medium's potential for visual detail and pictorial realism. Griffith had taken special pains to make his epic films historically authentic; Thomas Ince's work, credited for its hard-hitting realism, was tied to authentic settings and believable stories. German films, their settings built completely within the studio confines, extended screen realism to include the social milieu. And these films strongly influenced the complexion of story and setting of the Hollywood film of the late silent and early sound eras. By the time sound films had arrived, the credibility of characters, authenticity of physical detail, and continuity and internal consistency in scripting were all being carefully judged.

The preoccupation of the American industry during the thirties with myth, legend, and the contemporary dream might suggest that films of the period had little social relevance. But many Hollywood films served as social barometers, even offering song, dance, and sophisticated bedroom fun. This social-measuring function was sometimes expressed subtly, through incidental reference, and sometimes consciously, through concerted effort.

The American Problem Picture

Indirect social commentary evolved during the thirties by way of a number of genres and cycles. "Chinup" musicals like *Gold Diggers of 1933* and *Footlight Parade* (1933) extolled the simple rewards and silver linings that made the Depression easier to endure. Warner Brothers' cycle of film biographies — *The Story of Louis Pasteur* (1936), *The Life of Emile Zola* (1937), and *Juarez* (1939) — provided models of individual fortitude and idealism at a time when people's will was dampened if not broken at home and democratic ideals were being challenged in Europe and Asia. Screwball comedies, musicals, and biographies exuded optimism and idealism while giving reassurance about values. And despite tacked-on fairy-tale endings, such films as Capra's *Mr. Deeds Goes to Town* (1936) reflected everyday life more than movies of the twenties and eschewed the social glitter so popular then.

The popular escapist genres and cycles satisfied a social function by indirect means: they assuaged fears, inspired confidence, and reinforced values by way of abstract and general references. Other films, however, attempted to deal more directly with contemporary issues. Their genesis lay in the works of Porter and Griffith and later in the films of Pabst, Eisenstein, and Clair. Now they came in sufficient numbers to constitute a genre of their own—"the American problem picture" or, when sufficiently dedicated to the cause, the social-protest film. These films ushered in an era of, if not social realism, at least social consciousness.

Most prominent among the original problem pictures were those dealing with crime, corruption, and the evils and weaknesses of particular social mores and institutions. This group had been spawned by Warner Brothers' original gangster films, and Warners, too, led the move to explore and sometimes expose society's responsibility for breakdowns in the system that affected individuals. *I Am a Fugitive from a Chain Gang* (1932) launched the movement. Based on an autobiographical account of a man who had been framed for a crime and incarcerated in a Georgia prison, the film attempted to expose the inequities of both our judicial and penal systems and the stark horrors awaiting the unsuspecting citizen. The film was an impressive beginning. Not only did it enjoy both critical and popular support, but it also brought widespread public outcry and eventual reforms in the Georgia chain-gang system.

Warner Brothers continued to reinforce its image as a reformist studio with other exposés, most of which were based on actual incidents. *Wild Boys of the Road* (1933) was a study of the effects of economic crises on adolescents. *Black Fury* (1935) was adapted by the studio from a district attorney's journalistic account of a 1929 case in which a miner had been killed by police in a Pennsylvania strikebreaking scuffle. Paul Muni, who had "suffered" the chain-gang system in *I Am a Fugitive . . .* here became the "victim" of a struggle between management and labor. In 1936, the arrest of members of a secret organization in Detroit led to the production of *Black Legion* (1937), an exposé of this Fascist society. With *They Won't Forget* (1937), the studio moved further into exploring racism; here Mervyn LeRoy directed an account of an actual lynching. This film followed by just a few months Fritz Lang's study of lynch law and mob psychology, *Fury*, which

attempted to uncover the reasons why decent men become irrational and violently take the law upon themselves.

Other studios joined Warner Brothers with an occasional glimpse at society's ills, but production-code pressures, industry economics, and audience disposition

From a Review of *They Won't Forget*

"*They Won't Forget*," which the Warners presented at the Strand yesterday and which wears the fictional cloak of Ward Greene's novel, "Death in the Deep South," re-opens the Leo M. Frank case, holds it up for review and, with courage, objectivity and simple eloquence, creates a brilliant sociological drama and a trenchant film editorial against intolerance and hatred.

In many ways it is superior to "Fury" and "Black Legion," which have been milled from the same dramatic mine. Not so spectacular, or melodramatic, or strident perhaps, yet it is stronger, more vibrant than they through the quiet intensity of its narrative, the simplicity of Mervyn LeRoy's direction, its integrity of purpose, the even perfection of its cast. From Claude Rains and Allyn Joslyn and Gloria Dickson right on down the list of players heading this review, you will not find one whose performance does not deserve commendation. And, as one of the greatest factors in its favor, "They Won't Forget" cannot be dismissed as a Hollywood exaggeration of a state of affairs which once might have existed but exists no longer. Between the Frank trial at Atlanta and the more recent ones at Scottsboro is a bond closer than chronology indicates.

—*Frank S. Nugent*, New York Times *(July 15, 1937)*

▲ From *Black Legion* (1937). Humphrey Bogart and leaders of the hooded society—a secret Fascist organization.

usually ruled in favor of safer and more popular fare. Sensitive issues, particularly those related to sex, race, and religion, were carefully skirted, making social consciousness as reflected in the movies highly selective. Once settled in the posh comforts of the movie palace, most patrons still preferred to give up real-world ties and be lured into the intrigues of favorite screen personalities or whisked away to high adventure in exotic distant lands. One could join the sophisticated social whirl of people who never worked for a living. Or one could ease into the suburban colonial house with white picket fence and join one man's family's crusade to keep the maid from quitting or help in some nondescript local benefit. Many films of this prewar period had the appearance of realist social drama, but were actually charting a circuitous route to dreamland. By using events and issues of the time as touchstones, they could satisfy the viewer's need for escape and identification with real-life "problems" simultaneously.

In 1930, Harry Potamkin, in his "New York Notes" column, stated, "The movie has been a fairy tale and has had its existence as a compensatory mythology. Only a new social mind can stir it to actuality and positive experience." The stir to actuality was clearly under way by the early forties with austere studies in human weakness and want such as Ford's *The Grapes of Wrath* (1940),

Wellman's *The Ox-Bow Incident* (1943), and Billy Wilder's *Lost Weekend* (1945). These pictures showed that in the hands of directors with independence and vision the social-reform film could win both the heart and mind. Though reflected in only a fraction of the films produced, by the middle of the decade social reform was being recognized as an important new avenue for film.

Hollywood During World War II

Despite the growing trend in social realism, the Hollywood film of the thirties provided hardly a hint of the events leading up to World War II. In fact, even the newsreels of the period were dominated by escapist fare and an isolationist posture. Feature films such as *All*

▶ From *The Ox-Bow Incident* (1943). Dana Andrews and Anthony Quinn are two of the lynch victims and Frank Conroy (right) the leader of the mob in this study of mob violence.

Quiet on the Western Front (1930), *The Man I Killed* (1932), *Doomed Battalion* (1932), and *Lost Patrol* (1934) used World War I as a setting for antiwar sentiments. By 1940, isolationist sentiment began to give way, and in the three years following America's entry into the war Hollywood produced nearly 400 features directly related to some aspect of the conflict. This figure represented nearly one-third of the industry's total output. A new commitment to the war effort and patriotic fervor provided the inspiration for films with a variety of styles and stories, but all were dedicated to winning the war. *Tell It to the Marines* (1940), *Flight Command* (1940), *I Wanted Wings* (1941), and *Buck Privates* (1941) were among the early romantic and comic tributes to the American fighting man.

Many films attempted to set the stage for American involvement by dramatizing democratic ideals and sorting out friend from foe. The Nazi invasion of Russia made a new image of our Russian allies necessary and resulted in such films as *Mission to Moscow* (1943), *Song of Russia* (1943), and *North Star* (1943). *Mrs. Miniver* (1942) led a cycle of films dealing with battle-scarred and occupied nations, while anti-Fascist sentiment was expressed in films casting the Gestapo and SS troops as heavies. The ever-serviceable spy formula accommodated films dealing with the Fifth Column activities of spies and saboteurs — for example, the semijournalistic *Confessions of a Nazi Spy* (1939).

Contrasting with the films taking the journalist approach were the war-generated dramas in civilian dress.

Home-front mobilization and participation in the war effort became favorite topics, and they permitted the conscription of a variety of traditional genres. These ranged from civil defense comedies and light dramas involving entertainment of GIs (*Stagedoor Canteen* [1943]) to the family film in wartime dress (*Since You Went Away* [1944] and *I'll Be Seeing You* [1944]). Films dealing with the military services and war campaigns likewise reflected a broad range of styles, with boot-camp and shore-leave comedies and musicals sharing the spotlight with the documentarylike combat films in which individual heroism was a major ingredient. Even the films of the immediate postwar period, which tended to suggest sober reflection on the rationale and aftermath of war, ranged from the sardonic personal statement of Chaplin in *Monsieur Verdoux* (1947) to the studio-crafted *The Best Years of Our Lives* (1946), a homely and sincere American saga, which, according to James Agee, represented "a great and simple, limpid kind of fiction."

World War II saw the Hollywood economy rise beyond all expectations. From 1942 to 1945, the American public spent an average of 23 percent of its total recreation dollar on motion pictures. This contrasts sharply with today's figure of less than 2 percent. A large part of the wartime increase resulted from restrictions on travel and other recreational activities, which provided motion pictures and radio with a virtual entertainment monopoly.

However, it was not only "take and no give." Hollywood's war effort also included contributions of person-

nel, time, and money. In 1943 more than 4,000 Hollywood personnel were in uniform. By the end of the war, film celebrities had made more than 120 overseas tours, the Hollywood Canteen had entertained approximately 3 million armed services personnel, and troops had watched more than 43,000 16 mm feature prints donated by the industry's War Activities Committee. Key Hollywood personnel, such as John Ford, Frank Capra, and William Wyler, were responsible for some of the war's best documentary films — for example, Ford's *The Battle of Midway* (1942), Capra's "Why We Fight" series (1942–1945), and Wyler's *The Memphis Belle* (1944). In addition, Walt Disney produced hundreds of training films using his well-known cartoon characters.

Despite this effort, however, Hollywood's major function during the war was entertaining the home front. There was an initial burst of war films in 1942, but this soon decreased, and between 1943 and 1945 fewer than one-third of the films released by Hollywood dealt with war in any way. The top-grossing films of 1944 and 1945, for example, were two Bing Crosby vehicles, *Going My Way* and *The Bells of St. Mary's.* On the basis of these and other films, Crosby became the top box-office attraction of the war period.

The Directors

How did films of this period differ from other art forms in being produced by an industry rather than individual artists using chisel or brush?

In some ways this question is unfair, since a motion picture by its very nature is a collaborative enterprise. Even D. W. Griffith, one of the most single-minded and personal directors, relied upon others, especially his talented cameraman G. W. "Billy" Bitzer, for advice and help. Indeed, Lillian Gish, in referring to Griffith in his declining years, said,

> There was no one left among his staff to say "no" once in awhile. He needed the gently abrasive minds and personalities of those who had once been close to him. He had thrived on the tactful suggestion, the quiet hint that some other director had done as well, that a better effect could be found.

This comment is relevant to almost every artist who has worked in films. It does not deny the talents and insights of highly talented craftspeople; rather, it illustrates the very nature of the film medium, especially where the feature film is concerned. In filmmaking, collaboration is more than a necessary evil: it is a vital factor contributing to the overall excellence of most motion pictures.

More than 7,500 feature films were produced between 1930 and 1946. Most were characterized by the studios that produced them, but some stand out because a creative, talented director was allowed to place his personal signature on the film. Indeed, as John Baxter has pointed out in *Hollywood in the Thirties,*

> Although the high average standard of Hollywood films during the thirties is directly attributable to the studio system with its pools of talent and techniques, most of the period's major advances in cinema art can be traced to a group of independent producers whose unwillingness to work within the studio system gave them a greater degree of freedom than would have been possible otherwise.

Although the word *most* here is highly debatable, it is certainly true that a few key directors fought the system and in some cases transcended it. Several, including von Sternberg, Capra, and Lubitsch, have already been discussed in relation to the studios they worked for. Some important directors of the period who were not affiliated with a specific studio deserve individual attention.

Howard Hawks

Howard Hawks was one of the most creative craftspeople in Hollywood. He directed several of the outstanding films of the period, including *The Dawn Patrol* (1930), *Scarface* (1932), *Twentieth Century* (1934), *The Road to Glory* (1936), *Only Angels Have Wings* (1939), and *Sergeant York* (1940). Hawks was little appreciated by most critics and historians during the thirties. However, he has come to be recognized as one of the few individuals creating films within and for the studio system who still maintained a personal identity. Hawks's cinema is clean, direct, and functional. He was rarely in the avant-garde in technology or content, but, as he stated himself, "All I'm trying to do is tell a story." One of Hawks's major strengths was an ability to work in a variety of genres, from the gangster film to screwball comedy to Westerns to science fiction. His films contained few profound themes. Instead, they concentrated on tight, continuous narrative action. If one had to identify a consistent Hawks theme it would have to be "masculinity." His concern for men in extreme conditions pervades his most memorable works. In *Road to Glory* (1936) as well as *Only Angels Have Wings* (1939),

*Y*ou've got to choose a story and then know how to attack it. I don't try to get a finished piece of writing as far as dialogue and theme goes. A scenario is terribly important as a basis, but it doesn't have to be followed exactly. Even a play is made by constant changes, alterations during rehearsals. I can give you an example. I made a picture called *Scarface*. We had a new actor called Georgie Raft who had never acted before; he was a pretty lousy actor. I didn't know what to do with him, so I said if he could only be doing something while he was reading his lines, maybe people wouldn't realize how bad he was. So we gave him a half dollar to flip and he dropped it a few times, and then he flipped it and he said his lines and was pretty good. So we used the flipping of the coin all the way through the picture. But it didn't change the story.

—Howard Hawks, CAFS Seminar (February 11, 1970)

Hawks focuses on how men deal with the horrors of war and the perils of flight. He consistently finds the answer in such concepts as professionalism, pride, and *esprit de corps*. Although he made films for many studios and under many producers, his work always retained a unique directness and force that made his efforts commercially successful and artistically distinct.

John Ford

John Ford, too, stands out in this period as a strong, successful, commercial director and an artist with a personal vision. Best known for his Western films, such as *The Iron Horse* (1924), *Stagecoach* (1939), and *My Darling Clementine* (1946), among many others, he was also a versatile director comfortable in a number of genres. This versatility is evidenced by his success with *The Informer* (1935), *The Grapes of Wrath* (1940), and *How Green Was My Valley* (1941). Like Hawks, Ford was known for his pictorial strength and direct visual style. But Ford was also interested in atmosphere and mood, and most of his films, though very formal and structured, have a lyric quality. Ford worked in and needed the studio system. Some critics have questioned Ford's status because of the incongruities in his career. For example, he produced critically acclaimed works such as *The Informer* but also such studio potboilers as *Wee Willie Winkie* (1937) with Shirley Temple. The explanation was that Ford liked to work, and if it came to

▲ From *Stagecoach* (1939). The power and appeal of John Ford's 1939 classic Western are suggested in this view of the stage moving through Monument Valley.

a choice between directing *Wee Willie Winkie* and lying around a pool for six weeks, he chose to work. A key to Ford's ability to stamp his personal signature on his films was the fact that he rarely shot excess footage. He gave a film editor only enough footage to put the film together essentially as he shot it.

Ford did most of his best work in this period for 20th Century-Fox. Before 1939, his reputation was limited primarily to his direction of *The Iron Horse* and *The Informer* (for RKO), but his critical reputation soared with his production of *Stagecoach* (1939), *The Grapes of Wrath* (1940), *The Long Voyage Home* (1940), and *How Green Was My Valley* (1941). If Ford had one consistent problem in his films, it was his sentimentality. He was at his weakest when he attempted the abstract; he was strongest when he was creating a visual tableau of simple and poetic action. Ford was concerned with basic human values — honor, loyalty, discipline, and courage. Henry Fonda as Tom Joad in *The Grapes of Wrath* and Wyatt Earp in *My Darling Clementine* (1946) represented the best of Ford's vision — an affirmation of quiet strength and courage as uniquely American traits.

Orson Welles

A third director came to the era late, producing his first film in 1941. At the age of twenty-five, Orson Welles produced *Citizen Kane* (1941), one of the most significant films of the period and, indeed, of film history. He soon followed it with an equally creative film, *The Magnificent Ambersons* (1942).

So much has been written about *Citizen Kane* that it is difficult to discuss it in a few sentences. Voted by an international panel of film critics in 1972 as the best film of all time, it is regarded by most critics as the American film having had the greatest influence on film development since *The Birth of a Nation* (1915). *Citizen Kane* is famous both for its theme and its artistry. Its story is the ill-disguised and unsympathetic biography of newspaper mogul William Randolph Hearst. This fact alone created tremendous problems both during and after filming. None of the Hearst newspapers carried ads for it, and the pressure Hearst put on RKO eventually made it impossible for Welles to work in Hollywood. Despite this pressure, Welles, in collaboration with cinematographer Gregg Toland, produced a dominating film with scenes of tremendous power. Their artistry lay primarily in the use of "eccentric" camera angles, sweeping camera movement, single-shot deep-focus scenes, and audio-montage, a technique employing overlapping sound that Welles first used in radio.

Welles achieved his style primarily within shots, through careful composition and camera movement, rather than by means of editing. The opening scene of *Citizen Kane* begins with a close-up of a "No Trespassing" sign and then builds as the camera slowly moves along the iron grating of the fence that surrounds Kane's estate, revealing iron flowers, a huge K, and finally the towering and forbidding mansion in the distance. In all his films, Welles's characters usually interact with their environments through their positions within a scene. He uses his camera to reveal these relationships in a completely fluid and highly dramatic manner. However, Welles was not oblivious to the power of montage, and in several instances in *Citizen Kane*, particularly the breakfast scene, the strength of his editing is apparent. Here Welles delivers a series of vignettes showing Kane (brilliantly played by Welles) and his wife moving apart physically as their marriage disintegrates.

As many critics have observed, the structure of *Citizen Kane* is one of the most complex in film history. Welles takes the viewer on a seemingly chaotic trip through time and space, juxtaposing events and people separated by more than sixty years. This clear demarcation from the formula plots of Hollywood provides continuous pleasure and is responsible more than anything else for the film's reputation and appeal.

Welles's second film, *The Magnificent Ambersons*, was not filmed on the grand scale of *Citizen Kane*, but it was almost as effective. The film portrays the disintegration of a way of life at the turn of the century. Welles makes greater use of camera movement here; the camera movement in the grand ball sequence is among the most dramatic and effective ever used. The camera starts outside the Amberson mansion and then moves through the front door, past maids and butlers, through archways, and into great rooms filled with people — all in one sweeping motion.

With this and other tour de force examples, both *Citizen Kane* and *The Magnificent Ambersons* tend to overwhelm the audience with technique. However, both these efforts have come to be appreciated in recent years as much for their vision and social comment as their technical virtuosity. As several critics have correctly pointed out, these films, with respect to content, personal points of view, and individualistic style, are really the forerunners of the "serious" European films of the late fifties and early sixties.

Both *Citizen Kane* and *The Magnificent Ambersons* are studio films. Welles required the studio, accomplished technicians, and a company of actors. He once said, "A Hollywood studio was one of the greatest toys a twenty-one-year-old could have." He was clearly a collaborative filmmaker, requiring the talents of many other people to create his films. Above all, he required the controlled atmosphere that only a studio could provide.

From Orson Welles's *Citizen Kane* (1941). The remarkable deep-focus composition characteristic of many of the film's scenes is beautifully illustrated in this shot of Kane and his wife Susan.

The winter scenes in *The Magnificent Ambersons,* for example, were shot inside a cold storage locker, because Welles wanted both the realism of frosty breath and real snow and the control of studio lighting and camera placement.

Welles made only ten films after 1941. All of them display his unique style, but none carries the thematic strength of *Citizen Kane* or *The Magnificent Ambersons.* As a result, such efforts as *The Stranger* (1946), *The Lady From Shanghai* (1948), and *Touch of Evil* (1958), which contain brilliant individual sequences, ultimately fall under the weight of his style.

Wrap-Up

Owing to the numbers and types of motion pictures that studios produced, plus such factors as their usually large stables of contract directors, writers, and actors, studios were often accused of being merely factories that spewed out chunks of entertainment and did nothing to further film art. Obviously, the studio system produced tension between film as art and film as product. Irving G. Thalberg, production head of MGM, clarified this tension when he stated,

> It is a business, in the sense that it must bring in money at the box office, but it is an art in that it involves, on the part of its devotees, the inexorable demands of creative expression. In short, it is a creative business, dependent as almost no other business is, on the emotional reaction of its customers. It should be conducted with budgets and cost sheets, but it cannot be conducted with blueprints and graphs.

Studios were not the same as factories. In a factory, the same people do the same jobs to produce the same item. In a motion picture studio, innumerable combinations of people and materials produced consistently different items. Certainly close supervision and overall management philosophies resulted in distinct studio styles, but the films produced by the studios are not uniform items like cars or electric toasters produced on an assembly line. In fact, there were some advantages to turning out huge numbers of films, as *New York Times* film critic Vincent Canby has suggested in reference to a contemporary filmmaker:

> Mr. Fassbinder obviously works fast. He doesn't fool around getting things perfect. He tries something difficult and if it works, fine. If not, he'll do it better the next time around. Shakespeare worked this way. So, I'm sure, did a lot of the people in Hollywood in what are called the good old days. Experience doesn't accumulate like dust. You simply can't sit around waiting for it to settle on you. You have to work to get it.

The art/business dialogue was also evident in the phenomenon known as film cycles. Film cycles usually consisted of an initial film or cluster of films within a particular genre that set the pattern for others to follow. With the initial work as a blueprint, a studio would launch a cycle, often using the same production team and talent. Styles and story became as familiar to audiences as stars, and when a cycle proved particularly popular — a good example is the song and dance extravaganzas inaugurated by Warner Brothers with its *Gold Diggers* series — other studios would soon contribute films, thus helping to perpetuate the cycle.

Film cycles usually ran their course within a few years, and were dropped in favor of new cycles. The sensational news accounts of gangland killings provided both stimulus and narrative bases for the gangster series that featured James Cagney, Edward G. Robinson, and George Raft as underworld leaders. By the forties, these had been replaced by private eye films such as *The Big Sleep* (1946), which were usually taken from pulp fiction and characterized by complex plotting and an aura of sophistication. Likewise, the plush musical dramas of the forties — *Meet Me in St. Louis* (1944), *Anchors Aweigh* (1945), and *Blue Skies* (1946) — bore little resemblance to the digest of song and symmetry that made up the Busby Berkeley and Astaire/Rogers films of the previous decade.

Film cycles reflected the means by which Hollywood, still dedicated to formula filmmaking, could meet the social, economic, and technological demands of a rapidly changing industry. The transitory nature of cycles was much less evident in such well-established and venerated genres as the Western. In this category, and to a lesser extent in that of crime melodrama, the molding and fixing of dramatic conventions gave the films the quality of folk myths. The design or framework that had been plain formula in earlier examples by now had become ritual, and the stories, taken from the most cherished aspects of national heritage, had become legend.

Such genres thus resisted the easy accommodation of film cycles and tended to be the least affected by whims and passing fancies.

In summaries of this period in film history, questions always arise about why this particular era so powerfully captured, and continues to hold, the American imagination. What accounts for the mystique of the Hollywood films of the thirties? The answer is not simple. One element, of course, was the monopoly that motion pictures held at the time over entertainment. Radio provided the only strong competition. However, radio was both a nonvisual and a home medium. Motion pictures had a home, but it was the palace rather than the parlor. Often the magic of films had as much to do with the environment in which they were seen as with the films themselves.

In addition to their rococo architecture and plush seats, a majority of the nation's 14,000 theaters were on a double-feature policy, and more than one-third used gimmicks, such as "Bank Night," "Dish Night," "Screeno," and other giveaways to attract customers. For "Dish Night," for example, theater owners would purchase dishes for about ten cents and then give away one piece to each paying customer entering the theater. Exhibitors would sign contracts with dish distributors for fifty-two weeks, indicating the hold this custom had on the industry.

Another factor explaining the power of the movies of this era, and perhaps the most important, was the stars' appeal to the American public. In contrast to today's players, movie stars of the thirties did not really function as "normal" people. Stars' involvement in politics, for example, was severely frowned upon by the studios, whereas today stars are sometimes known more for their political activities than their films. However, when the star system was at its zenith, the public saw the stars only as the studios wanted them to be seen — as gods and goddesses. The images of the stars made the whole system work. These celebrities, and therefore their films, were larger than life. The implications of the star system went beyond adulation and star worship, although these factors initially drew audiences into fantasizing about the glamorous and adventurous life of screen gods and goddesses, both on and off the screen. Previous film roles helped to establish certain expectations in the minds of viewers concerning characterizations and motivations. When these expectations were played upon, they became part of the formula, aiding in the economy of exposition. The appearance of a Clark Gable or a Joan Crawford brought a ready-made delineation of motivation and personal traits. For example, even before his appearance in a film, the very knowledge that the long-awaited new marshal in the crime-ridden Western town was John Wayne or William Boyd would suggest how the crisis would be handled once he arrived on the scene.

Star status led to superstardom for some. With the superstar it was no longer a question of recreating a familiar role, perhaps with some variation to lend a touch of freshness and surprise. Rather, the films themselves became showcases and vehicles in which the superstars performed as themselves with little pretense at characterization. What narrative formula remained served only to perpetuate the star's image.

The motion picture industry was an intensely personal system ruled by men whose taste, while not as refined as some would have preferred, was usually accurate. The people working in the system were conscious of its limitations and restrictions, but they were also conscious that their work was more meaningful than merely cranking out cars on an assembly line. Ed Woeher of MGM expresses the feeling well:

> As a unit manager, what we would do is shoot a picture and prepare one at the same time. You'd always be working on a couple of pictures. It didn't give me too much time for myself, but we were dedicated. I mean we just gave our own good life to the studio and we didn't resent it. In fact, we accomplished something and we were pleased with what we did.

This is a good summary of the era — it was a time when men and women performed assigned tasks with professional skill, creating a product that more than anything else met the needs of society.

9

Film and the Age of Television (1946–1964)

Focus

Hollywood could not fail to be affected by the tremendous changes in society following World War II. The immediate onset of the cold war, along with domestic tensions caused by the problems of returning veterans, gave the American people little opportunity to relax and enjoy the fruits of victory. If there was a trend, dominant theme, or pattern to be observed in the films of the immediate postwar period, it was Hollywood's response to these changes. A new realism appeared, as the movies focused on many of society's problems, including race relations, prejudice, politics, alcoholism, and even Hollywood itself.

Postwar Realism

One of the first "new" films was Billy Wilder's stark portrayal of alcoholism, *The Lost Weekend* (1945). Charles Brackett and Billy Wilder, the film's producer-director team, made use of authentic New York City locations and a journalistic commentary to give this film a semidocumentary feeling. The adjectives Bosley Crowther used in his reviews—for example, "shatteringly realistic," "morbidly fascinating," "graphic," and "candid"—suggest something about the film's style, and set the critical tone for many reviews to follow. Two years later, for the filming of *Boomerang,* director Elia Kazan went to the Connecticut town in which the actual murder of a priest had occurred. The following year *The Naked City* was introduced by its producer as "a motion picture unlike any you've seen." Filmed entirely on loca-

◀ Ray Milland, in alcoholic terror in Billy Wilder's *The Lost Weekend* (1945).

▶ Jeanne Crain stars as a "white" black in Elia Kazan's 1949 production, *Pinky.*

tices heaped on the unfortunate victims of racial prejudice. Major stars with built-in audience appeal played in these movies, sometimes even though they hardly resembled the people they played. *Crossfire* starred Robert Young, Robert Tyan, and Gloria Grahame. *Gentleman's Agreement* starred Gregory Peck; *Lost Boundaries,* Mel Ferrer; and *Pinky,* Jeanne Crain and Ethel Waters. In reviewing *Pinky,* the story of a black girl passing for white who returns to her Southern home, Bosley Crowther wrote what could pass for a sociological analysis of most of these films.

> The hopeless discomfort of poor housing, the ignominy of police abuse, the humiliation of Jim Crowism and the sting of epithets are sharply sized. Likewise, the mean antagonisms of certain bigoted elements in the South are vividly caught when the camera—and the story—takes the heroine into court. . . . With all its virtues, however, this scan of a social problem has certain faults and omissions which may be resented and condemned. Its observations of Negroes, as well as whites, is largely limited to types that are nowadays far from average. . . . No genuinely constructive thinking of relations between blacks and whites is offered. A vivid exposure of certain cruelties and injustices is all it gives.

John Gassner, writing for the *Penguin Film Review* in 1947, stated, "The average film has reduced reality to a glossy picture-card." He also blasted the studios' dedication to realistic detail, noting that "the Hollywood studio spends much money to be certain that the paving stones in the medieval courtyard or the costume of the heroine are historically correct. Surely authenticity with respect to the structure of human personality and human motivations is as important as authenticity in setting."

The films of this period examined other social ills in addition to racial intolerance. Corruption in the world of boxing was one; such films as Robert Rossen's *Body and Soul* (1947), Robert Wise's *The Set-Up* (1949), and Mark Robson's *Champion* (1949) explored this theme. Mental illness and the horrors of mental institutions received graphic illustration in Anatole Litvak's *The Snake Pit* (1948). And *All the King's Men* (1949), directed by

tion, it became the prototype of the New York City manhunt film, with its montage sequences of city life and death, its chase through the lower East Side, and a showdown on one of the towers of the Williamsburg Bridge. Racial intolerance was the most highly developed theme of the period, with films about anti-Semitism and antiblack prejudice receiving about equal treatment. The treatment of anti-Semitism in *Till the End of Time* (1946) was soon followed by Edward Dmytryk's *Crossfire* (1947) and Elia Kazan's *Gentleman's Agreement* (1947). All three films contained obvious messages often delivered in major characters' "speeches." One of the better examples occurs in *Crossfire* (1947), when Robert Mitchum says, "My best friend, a Jew, is lying back in a foxhole at Guadalcanal. I am going to spit in your eye for him, because we don't want to have people like you in the USA. There is no place for racial discrimination now."

Discrimination against blacks was a strong theme in 1949—it was explored that year in Stanley Kramer's *Home of the Brave* and *Intruder in the Dust,* Louis de Rochemont's "re-enactment style" treatment of a Negro trying to pass as white in *Lost Boundaries,* Elia Kazan's *Pinky,* and Sidney Meyers's documentary *The Quiet One.* With the exception of *The Quiet One,* all these films were commercial products, made by major studios or independents and designed to make a profit. As such, they were infused with audience-attracting elements—major stars and melodramatic themes. Themes were explored through highly dramatic and visually explicit scenes depicting the cruelties and injus-

Robert Rossen, revealed the sordid side of politics in the thinly disguised story of Louisiana Governor Huey Long.

The problems of the returning veteran were portrayed most significantly in two films. One was the well-known *The Best Years of Our Lives* (1946), produced on a grand scale by Samuel Goldwyn, and featuring an all-star cast headed by Fredric March, Dana Andrews, and Myrna Loy. The one conspicuous exception to the standard Hollywood lineup was the casting of Harold Russell, a Navy veteran who had lost both hands in the War, as one of the major characters. The film won many awards, including Best Supporting Actor for Russell, and was hailed as giving off a "warm glow of affection for everyday down-to-earth folks." This description would hardly apply to the other veteran film, *The Men* (1950), starring Marlon Brando and produced by Stanley Kramer. Here producer Kramer and director Fred Zinneman dealt with the "raw human anguish" of the paraplegic veteran. Much of the film was shot on location at the Birmingham Veteran's Hospital near Los Angeles, where Zinneman recruited several minor players for the cast. As a result, the film had a documentarylike quality that was greatly intensified by Brando's performance. The role was Brando's first major one, and he brought to it a unique combination of power and pity that fully communicated the problems of the crippled veteran.

Billy Wilder and screenwriter Charles Brackett helped initiate this trend of screen realism with *The Lost Weekend* in 1945, and it is perhaps fitting that their 1950 film *Sunset Boulevard* helped cap the period. This is not

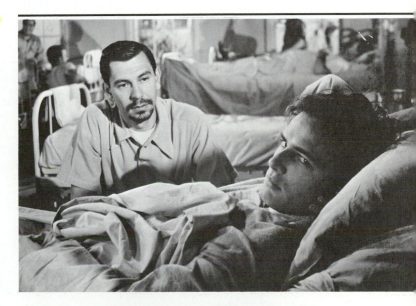

From *The Men* (1950). Jack Webb talks to an embittered Marlon Brando in the paraplegic ward of a veteran's hospital.

to say that screen realism came to a halt. The fifties, as we shall see, were filled with memorable realistic films. However, by 1950 the impact and influence of World War II had abated and films began to reflect the changes taking place in American society. In 1947, for example, 28 percent of all films released in the United States were classified as "social problem and psychology" oriented. By 1954 this category represented only 9 percent of U.S. films.

What makes *Sunset Boulevard* a significant and almost symbolic film, marking the climax of the social realism trend, is its focus on realism itself in the midst of Hollywood's social and economic turmoil. The story of an aging silent film actress trying to recapture former glories is not particularly remarkable in itself. The emotional drama of the plot is greatly intensified, however, by the players that Wilder cast. Gloria Swanson was lured out of semiretirement to play the aging star, a role she must have found frighteningly close to real life. Erich von Stroheim, the great silent film director, played her butler who was also her ex-husband and ex-director. Here, too, the role was all too close to real life. Perhaps the most pathetically realistic scene involved a simple card game with three friends, cynically referred to by William Holden, Swanson's young lover, as "the waxworks." As in the film, the three in reality were former silent stars now living in obscurity—Anna Q. Nilsson, H. B. Warner, and Buster Keaton. Indeed, if one looks at the film's credits, the people listed as playing "themselves" are almost as numerous as those playing fictional roles.

Although many films produced during this postwar period had realism in common, they varied widely in actual content and style. Another shared characteristic, however, was their tremendous success. *The Lost Weekend, The Best Years of Our Lives, Gentleman's Agreement,* and *All the King's Men* all won Best Picture Academy Awards. Social realism was not an underground movement—it was out front in the "A" level of production.

———————————————————•

Film Noir

Another group of films made during this same period were fundamentally realistic in treatment but so bound together in style and content that they were given their own classification—*film noir.*

Literally translated, the term means "black film,"

▲ From Wilder's *Sunset Boulevard* (1950). William Holden and Gloria Swanson dance their lonely way through a ballroom filled with mementos of Miss Swanson's silent screen career.

Dorothy MacGuire and George Brent in Robert Siodmak's *The Spiral Staircase* (1945), one of the "black" films of the forties.

James Cagney as Cody Jarrett in *White Heat* (1949). This role marked Cagney's return to the gangster film and represents one of his most powerful performances. The scene depicted is the classic "top of the world" finale, in which Cagney blows himself up while standing on top of several huge petroleum tanks.

and both the films and their creators have received increasing attention in recent years. The film noir pictures are characterized primarily by their cynical, violent, and brutal themes and by a psychoanalytic tone that tries to get under the surface of the issues. As Paul Schrader points out, "Film noir is not a genre such as the Western or gangster film. It is defined by the subtle qualities of tone or mood." However, this does not really tell us much, so Schrader clarifies the concept by stating that film noir is actually a specific period of film history: "Hollywood films of the forties and fifties which portrayed the world of dark, slick city streets, crime and corruption." The titles of many films in the genre clearly reflect this dark focus: *The Dark Mirror* (1946), *So Dark the Night* (1946), *Somewhere in the Night* (1946), *Nightmare Alley* (1947), *Cry of the City* (1948), *The Naked City* (1948), *He Walked by Night* (1948), *They Live by Night* (1949), *Night unto Night* (1949), *Where the Sidewalk Ends* (1950), *Panic in the Streets* (1950), *Night and the City* (1950), *Dark City* (1950).

The films dealt with the seamy underbelly of city life, crime in the streets, political corruption, and police action. In a sense, film noir seemed to be a creative release

for people in the industry. Previously forbidden themes could now be filmed and highly mannered and sophisticated styles in cinematography and lighting could now be emphasized.

The category was known as "black" cinema because of style and content. Films such as Robert Siodmak's *The Spiral Staircase* (1945), Henry Hathaway's *Kiss of Death* (1947), and Raoul Walsh's *White Heat* (1949) all dealt with "black" characters—psychopaths, to use a more modern term. The major element distinguishing these characters from their 1930s counterparts in such films as *Little Caesar* and *The Public Enemy* was the sadistic nature of their acts and motives. There were few upward-mobility themes. James Cagney in *White Heat* is not the kid trying to make it to the big time like the character he played in *The Public Enemy*. Here he is driven not by his own needs or social pressures, but by an obsessive mother love that strangles and suffocates him. And *White Heat* provided no poetic, sympathetic end, such as the one Cagney met on the church steps in *The Roaring Twenties* (1939). Rather, in *White Heat* Cagney, laughing maniacally, blows himself up atop a huge gas tank.

A New Era

On August 28, 1946, a headline in *Variety* magazine read, "Film Industry's Fattest Six Months in History." This was the apex, the peak, the industry's all-time high. Box-office receipts were $1.7 billion, representing 1.2 percent of all U.S. consumer expenditures. For the last time Americans would spend more than 1 percent of all their money and more than 20 percent of their recreational money on motion pictures. Weekly attendance peaked at 90 million and the number of theaters (21,500) was the largest since 1930.

It was natural for most industry executives to view the end of the war as the beginning of a new age of prosperity. And this feeling was solidly supported by the first postwar box-office figures. However, the situation was not as rosy as it seemed. Problems quickly appeared in a variety of forms. Surprisingly, many of them were not new concerns. The two biggest, antitrust action and television, had been looming on the horizon long before the War.

But Hollywood, basking in the glow of its immensely successful war effort and healthy box-office returns, was caught unprepared. In 1945, the government resumed its antitrust investigation of the major studios (begun in 1931). Labor problems, delayed because few employees had wanted to be accused of hurting the war effort, resurfaced once the War was over, and in 1946 Hollywood suffered through an eight-month union strike that resulted in a 25 percent pay increase for many employees. England announced a 75 percent tax on foreign-film earnings, and other countries followed with similar measures. As a result, despite record high earnings in 1946, the industry began to economize.

A number of small independent studios, such as Rainbow and Liberty, which had been hanging on the fringes of the industry, immediately went out of business. But the major companies felt the impact, too. Universal merged with International Pictures in 1946, Howard Hughes took over RKO in 1948, and David O. Selznick ceased production in 1949. Even MGM, the dominant studio of the time, felt compelled to gather all its stars together for a "show of confidence" group picture. As Andrew Sarris noted, "Studio identification was still meaningful . . . but usually at the lower levels of production. The fact that Metro [MGM] had the best lab work, Fox the best process shooting, Warners the best night quality is interesting, but hardly crucial." Studio employment fell off by 25 percent as contracts were allowed to lapse, and for the first time since the early years of the Depression the industry was in a state of decline.

Despite these problems, however, things did not fall apart completely. The reality of television and antitrust legislation was several years away, and the industry was still confident of its ability to meet the needs of the American public. Thus the studios continued to produce 300 to 400 films a year. These included the usual complement of "A" and "B" features, shorts, cartoons, and newsreels. In 1950, for example, MGM made 41 features, 16 cartoons, 12 "Traveltalks," 9 "Pete Smith Specialties," 8 "People on Parade," and 104 "News of the Day." More theaters appeared, especially in the drive-in category, and by 1950 there were more than 22,000 theaters in the country, including more than 3,000 drive-ins.

Hollywood continued to present themes and styles that had proven popular in the past. *The Green Years* (1946) described a boy's growth into manhood, while *Road to Utopia,* in the same year, continued the Bob Hope/Bing Crosby comedy series. Cary Grant played an angel in *The Bishop's Wife* (1947), Loretta Young a farmer's daughter in *The Farmer's Daughter* (1947), and Edmund Gwenn starred as Kris Kringle in *The Miracle on 34th Street* (1947). Amidst this continuation of past themes, however, new tensions appeared.

Four Problems

Communism

Of the four events, perhaps none caught the industry as unprepared as the investigation into alleged Communist activity throughout society. Like the rest of the country, Hollywood had had to switch its attitude toward Russia several times in the past ten years.

Prior to the War, Russia had originally aligned itself with Germany via the Nazi-Soviet Pact. However, with Germany's attack on Russia in 1941, the Soviets and the United States soon became uneasy allies. Hollywood responded with several pro-Russian films, the most notable being *Mission to Moscow* (1943) and *Song of Russia* (1945). However, the end of a "hot" war and the beginning of a "cold" soon severed tenuous ties, and the Iron Curtain became a forbidding and feared symbol. Most Americans now saw "Uncle Joe" Stalin as a ruthless dictator bent on overthrowing free society. The political machinery in this country geared up for a fight and, prompted and promoted by several publicity-seeking congressmen, began the search for and elimination of known Communists.

The entertainment industry, especially motion pictures, was a good place to begin, primarily because it was so highly visible. In October 1947, the House Un-American Activities Committee (HUAC) began a two-week series of hearings to consider the problem of Communism in the motion picture industry. Representative John E. Rankin of Mississippi set the tone for the hearings by stating, "Unless the people in control of the industry are willing to clean house of Communists, Congress will have to do it for them." Under the chairmanship of Representative J. Parnell Thomas, the committee began to call "friendly" and "unfriendly" witnesses to testify. The industry's initial reaction was anger and defiance. But this reaction soon turned to fear. On November 26, 1947, the industry issued the Waldorf Statement (so named because it was drafted at a meeting in New York's Waldorf Astoria Hotel), which summarized its attitude at the time:

THE WALDORF STATEMENT

Members of the Association of Motion Picture Producers deplore the action of the ten Hollywood men who have been cited for contempt of the House of Representatives. We do not desire to prejudge their legal rights, but their actions have been a disservice to their employers and have impaired their usefulness to the industry.

We will forthwith discharge or suspend without compensation those in our employ and we will not reemploy any of the ten until such time as he is acquitted or has purged himself of contempt and declares under oath that he is not a Communist.

On the broader issue of alleged subversive and disloyal elements in Hollywood, our members are likewise prepared to take positive action.

We will not knowingly employ a Communist or a member of any party or group which advocates the overthrow of the Government of the United States by force or by any illegal or unconstitutional methods.

In pursuing this policy, we are not going to be swayed by hysteria or intimidation from any source. We are frank to recognize that such a policy involves dangers and risks. There is the danger of hurting innocent people. There is the risk of creating an atmosphere of fear. Creative work at its best cannot be carried on in an atmosphere of fear. We will guard against this danger, this risk, this fear.

To this end we will invite the Hollywood talent guilds to work with us to eliminate any subversives; to protect the innocent; and to safeguard free speech and a free screen wherever threatened.

The absence of a national policy, established by Congress with respect to the employment of Communists in private industry, makes our task difficult. Ours is a nation of laws. We request Congress to enact legislation to assist American industry to rid itself of subversive, disloyal elements.

Nothing subversive or un-American has appeared on the screen. Nor can any number of Hollywood investigations obscure the patriotic services of the 30,000 Americans employed in Hollywood who have given our Government invaluable aid in war and peace.

What the industry feared most, of course, was not communism but government regulation. The Waldorf Statement was an attempt by the industry to ward off outside regulation. In the 1920s and 1930s, the industry had produced a set of rules and regulations called a code, but now it produced a series of names called a "list." The blacklist, while not as visible as the code or even the Waldorf Statement, was far more powerful than either. In the twenties and thirties the victims of industry fear were primarily two talented comedians, Fatty Arbuckle and Mabel Normand. In 1947 the toll was much heavier. The headlines were made by the so-called "Hollywood Ten," a group of highly vocal witnesses—deemed "unfriendly" by the committee—first called before HUAC.

Alvah Bessie	John Howard Lawson
Herbert Biberman	Albert Maltz
Lester Cole	Samuel Ornitz
Edward Dmytryk	Adrian Scott
Ring Lardner, Jr.	Dalton Trumbo

However, these people were just the tip of the iceberg —the list itself was huge.

Although the HUAC hearings of 1947 captured more attention, the second set of hearings, conducted in 1951, had a far greater impact, and for one simple reason: business was bad. In 1946, domestic film rentals were at $400 million and more than 90 million people attended motion pictures each week. By 1951, weekly attendance figures had dropped to 64 million. The country was involved in another "hot" war, this time in Korea, and Americans were more security conscious than ever before. The sale of fallout shelters increased rapidly, and Herbert Philbrick became a national hero as television told the story of his life as a spy for the FBI. With the nation's mood becoming more paranoid and aggressive, Hollywood could no longer afford to take a stand against government policy. Ninety witnesses were called at the 1951 hearings and asked to reveal the names of people they knew or suspected of being Communists. Thirty individuals provided a total of 324 names, all of whom were immediately blacklisted.

Red Scare Testimony

The Testimony of Nedrick Young, in the Hearing before The Committee on Un-American Activities, House of Representatives, Eighty-Third Congress, First Session, April 8, 1953, Los Angeles, California. Stenographic transcript, pages 1306 to 1318.

Mr. TAVENNER (HUAC counsel): Mr. Nedrick Young.

Mr. JACKSON (Republican Representative from California): Mr. Young, Will you please raise your right hand? Do you solemnly swear that the testimony you are about to give before this committee will be the truth, the whole truth, and nothing but the truth, so help you God?

Mr. YOUNG: I do.

Mr. TAVENNER: What is your name, please, sir?

Mr. YOUNG: My legal name is Ned Young. The name "Nedrick Young" that appears on the subpoena is a professional name which I have been advised that I will have no longer any use for by a member of your staff.

Mr. TAVENNER: What is your occupation?

Mr. YOUNG: My occupation was that of an actor and writer.

Mr. TAVENNER: Will you tell the committee briefly, please, what your formal educational training has been for your profession?

Mr. YOUNG: My formal educational training consists of an elementary and partial high-school education in the schools of New York and Philadelphia, and a thorough groundwork in the master works of American literature.

My education really began with Emerson and Thoreau, with Jefferson and Lincoln, men who subscribed to ideas that the Chairman of this committee would gladly burn along with the assistance—

Mr. JACKSON: That is an absolute false statement.

Mr. YOUNG: The Chairman of this committee has introduced a bill into the Congress, Bill No. 6335, which provides for the Congressional librarian to brand such books as he deems subversive.

Mr. JACKSON: The introduction of any piece of legislation by the Chairman of this committee is a matter which will be discussed in due course by the Congress of the United States and not by the witness who is presently in the witness chair.

Mr. YOUNG: And which will be discussed by the people of the United States. You made a statement that I took exception to, Mr. Jackson.

Mr. JACKSON: Well, I take exception to your statements.

Mr. YOUNG: A little while ago you referred to Congress as the highest body in the United States.

You are wrong. [gavel] The highest body of the United States is the people.

Mr. JACKSON: Will you please answer the question? Your contempt is of a very low order and will never win any awards if they were handing out presents for contemptuous people before this committee.

Mr. YOUNG: I think that is a pretty low humor and I don't think I like it.

Mr. JACKSON: Will you please proceed?

Mr. YOUNG: Do you seriously think you can pound the truth into dust with that gavel?

Mr. JACKSON: Will you please continue with your answer?

Mr. TAVENNER: Have you completed advising the committee of your educational, formal educational training?

Mr. YOUNG: All that is pertinent to this inquiry, I am certain.

Mr. TAVENNER: Mr. Young, have you been a member of the Communist Party while in Los Angeles?

Mr. YOUNG: Do you have any evidence to this effect, or testimony to this effect? If you have, produce it.

Mr. JACKSON: Answer the question.

Mr. YOUNG: I challenge this committee to produce such evidence.

Mr. JACKSON: Will you answer the question?

Mr. YOUNG: Of course, I won't answer this question.

Mr. JACKSON: Very well, do you decline to answer the question?

Mr. YOUNG: I most certainly do and wish to state my grounds.

Mr. JACKSON: Go ahead.

(At this point Mr. Young conferred with Mr. Esterman and Mr. Marshall.)

Mr. YOUNG: I wish to say, first of all, as an American citizen and as a father, I will not answer any questions that are propounded to me as a result of coercion. I also will most certainly refuse to answer any questions of a committee that refuses to confront me with an accuser, the most primitive American right. Why don't you tell me what evidence you have against me?

Mr. JACKSON: Will you please continue with the reasons for your declination to answer the question?

Mr. YOUNG: I think this is a disgusting Un-American procedure.

Mr. JACKSON: Your observation is entered in the record. Will you please continue with your declination, the reasons for it, if you please.

— from "Hollywood Blacklisting" by Gordon Hitchens in Film Culture *(Summer–Fall, 1970)*

The blacklist was particularly insidious because few acknowledged its existence, yet no one on the list was able to work. The toll in human terms was tragic. Talented artists — some who openly admitted they had once been Party members, others who were simply declared guilty without benefit of a trial or even a public hearing — were quickly dropped from studio rosters. Many went to Europe. Others continued to work in the industry by using aliases and accepting low wages. An example of this emerged publicly in 1956 when a "Robert Rich" won the Academy Award for best screenplay for *The Brave One*. When his name was called, no one came up to accept the award, because "Robert Rich" was in reality the blacklisted writer Dalton Trumbo.

Some anti-Communist films were produced as a response to the climate of fear sweeping the industry and the country. Most of them were cheap potboilers with such obvious titles as *The Red Menace* (1949), *Guilty of Treason* (1949), and *Red Snow* (1952). However, the industry seemed to favor eliminating possible subversive content rather than creating patriotic content. Since this was also a time when the studios needed to cut back on personnel because of poor business, the blacklist became a convenient way of killing two birds with one stone.

The blacklist and its effects lasted more than twenty years, and there are those who say it is still in force in some capacity today. Although out of work for a long period, several blacklisted people made comebacks in the late 1960s. These included Abraham Polonsky, director of *Tell Them Willie Boy Is Here* (1970); Dalton Trumbo, screenwriter for *Hawaii* (1966), *The Fixer* (1969), and *Johnny Got His Gun* (1971); and Howard Da Silva, who, ironically, portrayed Benjamin Franklin in the musical *1776* (1971). Martin Ritt's movie *The Front* (1977) provides a frightening glimpse of this period, made authentic in part by the appearance of blacklisted actors Zero Mostel and Herschel Bernardi.

Television

Another problem was one the industry should have anticipated. Television had existed in an experimental form since the late 1920s and was licensed for commercial use in 1941. However, World War II intervened and the medium did not begin to assume national significance until 1948. By 1949, there were ninety-eight television stations on the air in fifty-eight cities. There were 1,600,000 television sets in homes, but since only 40 percent of the population lived within range of a TV station, early television viewing had a communal pattern — people went to watch the set at neighbors' homes or at local taverns — meaning that the actual viewing public was much larger. By 1950, the number of TV homes increased to 6 million, and, while the number of stations increased only slightly, to 104, these existing stations began to link up with national networks. Suddenly the film industry found itself in competition with corporate giants: NBC, CBS, and ABC, the three major TV networks.

The motion picture industry got a slight reprieve when the Federal Communications Commission imposed a freeze on new TV licenses, from 1948 to 1952. But in 1952 with the freeze lifted, the FCC authorized 2,053 channels in 1,291 communities. The holding action was over, and television began to take off. By 1955, there were more than 32 million TV homes and 458 stations in the nation. Practically every reasonably large community in the country had access to a signal. Motion picture attendance began to drop at an accelerating pace, from a peak of 80 to 90 million weekly in 1948 to 46 million in 1954. And production declined from 369 features released in 1950 to 232 in 1954. The drop was even more dramatic when compared to the 500-per-year feature average that had held steady throughout the 1930s.

Why did people stay home? The answer may seem obvious at first, but consider the following *disadvantages* of television. The home environment was not necessarily more comfortable than the theater. The home environment was not as glamorous or attractive as the theater. The content of television was certainly inferior, especially on the local level, to motion pictures. The quality of the TV image was decidedly poorer than the quality of the film image, with a black-and-white image on a twelve-inch screen subject to all types of interference.

Despite these disadvantages people stayed home in increasing numbers. There were two basic reasons for this. First, television was "free." After the initial $400 to $500 investment, the only price audiences paid was in sitting through commercial interruptions. The second reason, and possibly the more important, was novelty. Television was new, people had money to spend on it, and everyone seemed to feel the urge to buy a set. Television-set ownership increased 696 percent in the 1950s, and with this increase the motion picture industry lost an audience it never regained.

All this activity occurred at a time when Hollywood could least afford competition, and its initial reaction to television was therefore fear and hostility. Studios forbade their film stars to appear on television and clutched their huge backlogs of films to their corporate breasts. However, the industry could not hold out forever. Television was growing too rapidly and film attendance declining too precipitously to allow the industry to stand back and ignore the problem. The first tentative steps in establishing a more cooperative relationship began in 1952, when Columbia Pictures formed a television subsidiary, Screen Gems, to produce programs and commercials. Soon, other relationships were established. ABC and Paramount Theaters merged in 1953. In 1954, Walt Disney and Warner Brothers contracted to produce programs for ABC, and soon afterwards Warner Brothers established its own television subsidiary, Seven Arts. The dam burst in 1956, when Hollywood made more than 2,500 pre-1948 films available to television.

The relationship between television and motion pictures ultimately moved from competition to cooperation. Television did not kill motion pictures any more than it killed radio. What it did was displace a key function of both media. Losing its prime-time evening audience forced radio to create a different formula, which it did remarkably well. The motion picture industry, however, did not adjust as quickly or efficiently, primarily because it had become too big, unwieldy, and inflexible. And when television replaced several of its major forms—the "B" film, the short, newsreel, and cartoon—the industry found it had little alternative but to cut back its production schedule. Television became the "B" movie—the national habit, mass-produced, "spit it out once a week" medium. The sixties saw the relationship between television and motion pictures grow closer. In fact, the motion picture industry has survived only to the extent that it has been able to accommodate and serve television.

The Paramount Decision

The industry might have survived the blacklist and television reasonably intact if its internal structure had remained the same. The vertical integration of the industry in which production, distribution, and exhibition were controlled by the studios allowed the studios to produce 500 films a year because there was always an outlet for them. The key to the system was outright studio ownership of first-run theaters in major cities and lesser control over many other theaters.

The system encouraged and sustained two major selling techniques. The first was block booking, under which, to get certain key films, exhibitors had to take less desirable ones. The other technique was blind selling, whereby exhibitors were asked (required) to take films they had not previewed. Therefore, the studios had an automatic outlet and a guarantee of reasonable success for almost every film they produced. The studios' control often even extended to control of admission prices and the length of a picture's run.

The problem of control was not a new one. It dated from the 1920s and had been under investigation by the Department of Justice since the early 1930s. By 1940,

the courts had asked the studios to stop buying theaters. They agreed, but further action was delayed by the war. Following the war, court action began again, and in 1948 the U.S. Supreme Court, in what is known as the "Paramount Decision" (Paramount was the case being tested), ordered the "Big Five" (MGM, Paramount, Warners, Fox, and RKO) to get rid of their theaters and told the "Little Three" (Universal, Columbia, and United Artists) to stop making binding contracts with theaters. In effect, through this decision, production was "divorced" from exhibition.

The impact of the decision was enormous. Block booking was eliminated and the studios no longer had a guaranteed outlet for their films. The primary impact was on the "B" film. The "A" film, with major stars and strong production values, was not in immediate trouble. However, the studios were forced into making more and more "A" films that would attract audiences, and the "B" film, therefore, was all but eliminated from production schedules.

For the theater owners, the decision was a good one, since it allowed them to pick and choose from a variety of films offered by sources other than the studios. As a result, independent and foreign filmmakers, who for years had beaten on the doors of the industry with little success, suddenly found their product in demand.

The Foreign Affair

Eric Johnston, President of the MPPDA, stated in 1953, "It's a little known fact that nine out of ten United States films cannot pay their way in the domestic market alone. It is only because of revenue from abroad that Hollywood is able to turn out pictures of high artistry and technical excellence." He was, of course, stating the simple fact that the high cost of motion pictures forces manufacturers to go after the largest possible audience. This meant an international marketing plan for virtually every film Hollywood produced.

Following World War II, a tremendous backlog of U.S. films had not been marketed internationally, and this was an obvious gold mine. However, as we have seen, foreign industries, especially in Europe, were trying to recover, and they feared American competition. As a result, foreign governments instituted protective measures in the form of import restrictions and taxes on income earned within the particular country.

England was the first to impose such a tax. In 1947, it levied a 75 percent export tax on earnings of foreign companies. The initial decision was modified somewhat, and in 1948 an agreement was reached whereby United

States film companies could take out $17 million a year. This amount still represented a huge loss, since the take over the past two years had been more than $60 million. France arrived at a similar policy in 1948. Italy imposed a tax in 1949 and then went to a quota system, allowing only 225 American films to be imported in 1951, down from 668 in 1940. And by 1954 the Italian quota had dropped to 209. As Eric Johnston adroitly observed, "This rising foreign competition has come at a time when the financial position of the domestic industry has been adversely affected by a combination of factors."

In addition to restricting American films and earnings, many countries, especially France, England, and Italy, began developing plans to get their films distributed in the United States. In 1951, Italian Film Export was founded for the sole purpose of promoting and distributing Italian films in the United States. With the Paramount decision allowing theaters to choose films from any producer, the market for foreign films increased greatly. By 1954 almost 12 percent of all films released in the United States were foreign. If the goal of all this activity was to achieve some sort of production parity with the United States, it succeeded very well, as the accompanying table indicates.

Besides the four factors just described, other causes of the decline in motion picture attendance included a shift in the population to the suburbs where there were few theaters, a tremendous increase in the popularity of spectator sports, more automobiles, and increased travel.

The result of these many changes was panic and a loss of confidence by the industry. Hollywood became self-conscious, no longer sure that its products would be accepted. In the past, Hollywood's superiority had rested on its absolute mastery of many types of films — comedy, musical, Western, gangster, horror, etc. Some independents and foreign industries might have produced an exceptional film or series of films, but they were limited in the breadth of their output, and Hollywood did everything well. This strength and confidence seemed to suggest that Hollywood's system of production was indestructible and destined to continue forever. André Bazin, the late French film critic and theorist, spoke of an "equilibrium profile" in film that can be applied to Hollywood at its peak. Bazin's term was a geographical one. It referred to the characteristics of a river that flows effortlessly from its source to its mouth without deepening its bed. Hollywood had achieved an equilibrium profile in which films moved effortlessly from the studios to theaters. However, the system was shallow, and the events of the postwar years quickly disrupted the flow of its product.

Feature Film Production

	1950	1955	1960
U.S.	383	254	154
England	125	110	122
France	117	95	119
Italy	98	114	141

Hollywood had been hit over the head with a sledgehammer, not once but four times. Its instinctive reaction was to fight, to try to win back the declining audience. It used a variety of methods to wage its war.

Hollywood's Reaction

The first and most obvious reaction was to introduce a new form of technology. This had worked before, when sound was introduced. The key was to emphasize the technical differences between film and television, and the immediate thinking was "bigger is better." Since most television screens measured, at the most, twenty-one inches across, the industry decided that a bigger motion picture screen would bring audiences back. The idea of enlarging the screen image was not new, of course. People had been tinkering with screen size from the earliest days of film, and it was only because Edison's 35 mm film size was the most widely used format that the standard $4:3$ screen ratio became the accepted norm.

One of the first commercially successful big-screen developments was the Magnascope, developed in 1924 by Lorenzo Del Riccio. In this method, a film was projected through a special lens that magnified scenes up to four times their original size. Magnascope was used in such epic films as *Ironsides* (1926), *The Big Parade* (1926), and *Wings* (1927), and was the principal method of increasing image size for almost thirty years. There were other attempts to increase image size, but since there was no real need to provide something different, little commercial development took place until the early fifties, when the industry was once again searching for a miracle to rescue it from financial ruin.

New Big-Screen Technology

The first attempt used a multiple camera/projector technique. Three cameras recorded individual areas of a scene and the film was then projected through three projectors using standard 35 mm film. Instead of a normal shot being magnified, as with Magnascope, here three films were projected as a single image. Again, there had been some early experimentation with this method, the most famous being the triptych developed in the early 1920s by Abel Gance and Claude Autant-Lara and used with some success in Gance's *Napoleon* (1927). The technique lay dormant, however, until a process known as Cinerama burst onto the scene in 1952. Developed by Fred Waller, the process incorporated stereophonic sound, and the first production, *This Is Cinerama,* was a huge success. There was one major problem, however. The process required a special theater equipped with Cinerama machinery, and its potential was thereby limited from the very beginning. However, the initial attractiveness was so great that soon every major city had a Cinerama theater. The problem now became one of supplying films. In 1955, *Cinerama Holiday* and *Seven Wonders of the World* followed the initial effort. *Search for Paradise* was released in 1957, *South Seas Adventure* in 1958, and the last productions were *The Wonderful World of the Brothers Grimm* (1962) and *How the West Was Won* (1963). By this time the novelty had worn off. Cinerama's major

problem was that it did not lend itself naturally to a narrative approach and audiences soon tired of travelogues with spectacular scenery. In fact, Cinerama literally ran out of scenery to present. At present, the technique lives on only in a few special presentations, such as Walt Disney's Circarama and other similar attractions at various theme parks.

Despite its limited life span, Cinerama caught the industry's attention and stimulated experimentation with other methods of presenting a bigger image. One such method was the anamorphic lens system, in which an image is "squeezed" onto the film and then "spread out" when projected. The theory was originally developed in 1862 and first demonstrated in 1927 by Henri Chretien. Fox bought it sometime later. In 1953, 20th Century-Fox released *The Robe* in a new process it called CinemaScope. The size of the CinemaScope image was $2\frac{2}{3}$ times as wide as it was high (a ratio of 2.66 : 1)

▶ These two stills from the 20th Century-Fox production *How to Marry a Millionaire* (1953) illustrate the "squeezed" and expanded frame images of the CinemaScope process.

and, since it required no special equipment other than the lens itself, the process was compatible with every theater in the country. Other studios began to film in CinemaScope, and by 1954, 75 films were in production. The rush to big-screen films was immediately successful, and seven of the top ten box-office films in 1954 were "new dimension" films — four CinemaScope, one Cinerama, and two 3-D.

Each studio soon developed its own anamorphic system. As there was little difference in technique and content, the real competition centered around coming up with a dramatic, ear-catching name. RKO brought out Superscope in 1954. Republic used Naturama; Paramount coined Panavision. Other names included Panascope, Techniscope, and VistaRama. The anamorphic process held the greatest artistic potential of all the new dimension techniques. The industry recognized the need to get beyond scenery and spectacle and began to use the process as an integral and dramatic part of screen narrative.

Perhaps the best integration of wide screen and narrative construction occurred in 1955, when John Sturges's *Bad Day at Black Rock* and Elia Kazan's *East of Eden* appeared. In both instances the filmmakers considered the requirements of story as well as those of the anamorphic lenses. Both narrative and scenery were integrated to form compelling and dynamic films. With the exception of these films, however, and some intelligent work by Hitchcock with VistaVision in *To Catch a Thief* (1955) and *The Man Who Knew Too Much* (1956), the process remained undeveloped. The primary reasons were cost and the increased necessity to produce films in a size ratio compatible with television.

The third method of achieving a large screen image was accomplished by using wider film. Since the beginning, 35 mm film had been standard, but again there was a great deal of experimentation. The most successful early method was RKO's Grandeur process, which used 70 mm film in two Westerns in 1929 and 1930. However, sound and the Depression stopped further development. It was not until 1955 that motion picture entrepreneur Mike Todd reintroduced wide film with a 65 mm process he modestly called Todd-AO. Todd chose the film *Oklahoma* for his premiere, and the appeal of a popular stage musical, color, and wide screen proved enormously successful. Even more impressive was his next production, *Around the World in Eighty Days,* released in 1956. Using fifty stars in cameo roles and a theme song that quickly became the best-selling record in the country, this film became the year's most popular and received the Academy Award as best picture. Mike Todd was killed in an airplane crash in 1958, but 20th Century-Fox purchased the process and throughout the sixties shot most of its "blockbuster" films with the system, including the disastrous *Cleopatra* (1963) and the successful *Sound of Music* (1965).

One final big-screen method appeared, and it came about strictly because of economic necessity. When the wide-screen movement started, the studios had a backlog of unreleased films shot in the normal 4 : 3 ratio that they wanted to market as profitably as they could. Their solution was to dub in size, just as they had once dubbed in sound. They accomplished this visual dubbing by masking the top and bottom of the projected image, thereby increasing length and reducing height. Using a special gate in the projector, this method achieved ratios ranging from 1.66 : 1 to 1.85 : 1. The result was an artistic disaster. Heads and feet were the main casualties, but whole films became stretched and chopped completely out of shape. George Stevens' *Shane* (1953) was one of the more prominent casualties; it is to the credit of the story, direction, and acting that the film survived at all.

Three-Dimensional Films

The panic of the early fifties also saw the industry renew its age-old fascination with reproducing three-dimensional reality. A crude 3-D process that used two cameras with two lenses and mirrors was introduced in the early 1900s. This technique was replaced in the 1920s by the photographing and projecting of images through different-colored filters (usually red and green). When an audience viewed such a film through special glasses the images separated, creating the illusion of depth. A great deal of experimentation with 3-D took place in the twenties, but with the coming of sound the process was put on the shelf.

In 1952, *Bwana Devil* was made in a polarized filter 3-D process, and despite the fact that it had little but depth to recommend it, this film broke box-office records across the country. Warner Brothers soon followed with *The House of Wax* (1953), and the race was on. Almost all the major studios made several 3-D films in 1953 and 1954. Most of these efforts were Westerns or horror films in which objects or people could be projected at the audience. Soon tomahawks, arrows, bodies, and bullets were flying off the screen and into the audience. A few shorts and cartoons were also produced, but the novelty soon wore off and by 1954 3-D was dying.

There were several reasons for the sudden decline. The obvious were the expense and trouble of projecting the films and the necessity of wearing special glasses. More important, however, was the limited potential of the process for telling a story. Despite all the gimmickry, the essential attractiveness of motion pictures was their ability to tell interesting stories. Hollywood forgot this

An early 1950s audience equipped with 3-D glasses.

basic fact in its mad rush to find a quick and easy formula for winning back its lost audience. The best films involve an audience, but 3-D films simply assaulted theirs.

There were several attempts to revive 3-D in the early 1970s, the most successful being X-rated "sexploitation" films, such as *The Stewardesses* (1971) and Andy Warhol's *Frankenstein* (1973). However, here too the appeal was strictly novelty. The appearance of *Jaws III* in 3-D in 1983 showed that the process was not completely dead; however, one must wonder whether audiences will ever be ready for 3-D. The "flat" experience in film has become an accepted reality, and the attempts to create the *feelings* of depth and space are far more successful and certainly more artistic than attempts to *demonstrate* the reality itself.

New Color Technology

One other technological trend that emerged at this same time was a rush to color. In 1947 only 12 percent of all films made in the United States were in color. In 1954, this figure had increased to 58 percent. Economic need

and competition were again the major factors, since color was beyond the capabilities of television.

The trend toward color motion pictures continued, but by the mid-1960s television *could* produce color, so this became the motivating factor. A film's potential market included television, and virtually 100 percent of all TV programming was in color. Thus, a black-and-white motion picture was at a distinct disadvantage in the bargaining for TV play time.

Independent Production

Although not exactly a direct industry reaction, the rise of independent production outside the major studios was certainly a direct consequence of the events of the early fifties. As the studios cut back their payrolls, they released a large number of writers, directors, and actors who began to form small production companies of their own. The independents also flourished because they were more confident about finding an exhibition outlet than in the past since the divorcement ruling allowed theater owners to choose films from any source.

Following the introduction of sound, few independents had the financial stability to maintain any consistent level of production. Only Sam Goldwyn, Walt Disney, and David O. Selznick were able to produce films outside studio control. And even these independents had to go to the studios for help in obtaining talent and getting films distributed. As we noted, in order to get Clark Gable from MGM for *Gone with the Wind,* Selznick had to give the studio distribution rights to the film.

Following World War II, a number of individuals began careers as independent producers. Stanley Kramer started his career in 1948 and produced a number of notable films in the postwar period including *Home of the Brave* (1947), *Champion* (1949), and *High Noon* (1952).

The most significant development stimulating independent production, however, was the sale of United Artists. Originally formed in 1919 by Mary Pickford, Douglas Fairbanks, D. W. Griffith, and Charles Chaplin, the organization had long been dormant. In 1951, two young men, Arthur Krim and Robert Benjamin, bought the company, and United Artists began to function once again as a major film financing and distributing organization. Two of their early successes included *The African Queen* (1951) and *Moulin Rouge* (1952). These rewarding projects prompted several other independents to enter the field, including Walter Mirisch and Seven Arts. The independent movement continued to grow throughout the fifties, as witnessed by the fact that when the screenwriters went on strike in 1960 they blacklisted 56 independent companies.

Perhaps the greatest indication of the independents' strength, success, and acceptance was that from 1954 to 1962 seven Best Picture Academy Awards went to independently produced films. Helping this growth was a new financial trend in which actors, directors, and even writers "participated" in films by taking smaller salaries in exchange for a percentage of anticipated profits. Quite obviously, this was a gamble, but it paid off so well (William Holden's share of profits on *The Bridge on the River Kwai* [1957] were to pay him $50,000 a year for more than fifty years) that by the middle sixties almost 80 percent of the films made in the United States were independent productions.

Though independent production increased dramatically, the major studios were by no means dead. They still produced a large number of films throughout the fifties and early sixties (278 in 1952 and 211 in 1960). However, the key to their continued dominance in the industry was their role as distributors, not producers. As Stanley Kubrick said in 1960, "The source of the supremacy of the majors was their power to make money.

When they stopped making money they sent for the independent producers." The studios stayed afloat by contracting with the independents for distribution rights, but they had lost much of their original power and meaning.

Another major effort of independent production was a shift to location shooting, especially foreign locations far away from the high-cost labor market and the Hollywood studio environments. By 1958, 60 percent of all feature films were shot in locations other than Hollywood back lots.

A New Morality

In terms of film content, the fifties were a strange decade, a time lacking a distinctive style. It is difficult to pinpoint themes during this period, though circumstances go a long way toward explaining this lack of clarity. The winds of change blowing through the industry were not designed to produce stability. However, one trend that was clearly discernible was a movement toward greater freedom of expression. The movement was spurred by another Supreme Court decision, this time involving a Roberto Rossellini film called *The Miracle* (1952).

Until 1951 the legal place of motion pictures in American culture had been determined by a 1915 Supreme Court decision *(Mutual v. Ohio).* The court said

> The exhibition of moving pictures is a business, pure and simple, originated and conducted for profit, like other spectacles, not to be regarded, nor intended to be regarded by the Ohio Constitution, we think, as part of the press of the country, or as organs of public opinion.

As a result, the censorship of motion pictures was not against the law. By 1950 six states had censorship laws and 150 to 200 communities had a variety of municipal codes and regulations governing the exhibition of certain types of films containing various forms of objectionable content. Despite advances in literary freedom, motion pictures were still under a heavy legal yoke. However, the postwar period brought changes here as well. In 1947, in the Paramount divorcement case, Justice William O. Douglas said in a "dictum," "We have no doubt that moving pictures, like newspapers and radio, are included in the press whose freedom is guaranteed by the First Amendment."

The real breakthrough, however, came in 1952, in the so-called *Miracle* case. The Italian film *The Miracle* was brought into this country by importer-distributor

Joseph Burstyn. It opened in New York in 1951 and subsequently ran into trouble with the New York Board of Regents, which revoked the film's license on the ground that it was "sacrilegious." A struggling independent Burstyn needed the film's income, so for reasons both of economic survival and civil liberty, he decided to fight the decision. The battle continued all the way to the Supreme Court, which in May 1952 declared in a unanimous decision that motion pictures fell under the First and Fourteenth Amendments guaranteeing free speech and free press. The specific ruling applied only to the concept of "sacrilege" and did not, in effect, strike down the right of a state or municipality to censor motion pictures. However, the mood of the Court quickly became apparent; in four other cases over the next six years it overturned bans involving racial themes, crime, and sexual frankness. The impact of these decisions on censorship laws was dramatic. By 1961 only fourteen local censorship boards remained in existence.

External legal restrictions were not the only restraints on motion picture content. The industry had its own censorship system, dating back to 1922, when the Hays Office was set up in response to the threat of federal action. This threat, along with pressure from outside groups — most notably the Catholic Legion of Decency, formed in 1933 — kept the industry's self-regulation system strictly in force. This system included, of course, the Motion Picture Production Code, a self-regulatory

code of standards created in 1930 by the Motion Picture Producers and Distributors of America. The code set forth general standards of "good taste" and specific "dos and don'ts" concerning what could and could not be shown in American movies.

The code remained fairly well intact throughout the thirties and early forties. However, in the postwar period it was amended to permit films on drugs and drug addiction. A further relaxation occurred in the early fifties with the influx of independent and foreign films and the decline of the studio system. The studios had always strictly enforced the code, since, as one of the biggest corporate structures in the country, they feared government regulation the most. The independents, however, had little to lose and needed something different from the standard studio product to attract an audience. They found this difference in sexual and social frankness. One man, Otto Preminger, spearheaded the push of the independents in this direction. Preminger brought the issue of code conflict to a head with two films, *The Moon Is Blue* (1953) and *The Man with the Golden Arm* (1955).

Both films were denied a code "Seal of Approval" (which meant theaters were not supposed to show it) because of content indiscretions. *The Moon Is Blue* was an "adult comedy" starring William Holden, David Niven, and Maggie McNamara, and adapted by F. Hugh Herbert from his stage hit. The crucial issue here was virginity, and especially the use of the word *virgin*. In light of current trends, the film seems quite tame, but then it was seen as a "saucy" sex comedy about a young woman flaunting her virginity.

By contrast, Preminger's *The Man with the Golden Arm,* starring Frank Sinatra, Eleanor Parker, Kim Novak, and Darren McGavin, remains a powerful story of drug addiction. Preminger released both films without code approval, and since theater owners were now free to accept any film, both films succeeded financially. This success, of course, was the key. Had the films failed at the box office, the effect of Preminger's effort would have been greatly diminished. The crucial ingredient here, as in the *Miracle* case, was money. Preminger was no social crusader. He was a realist, a man who thought his films would sell, and since the time to defy the system was right, he pushed the issue.

The rest of the industry quickly saw the light. If this

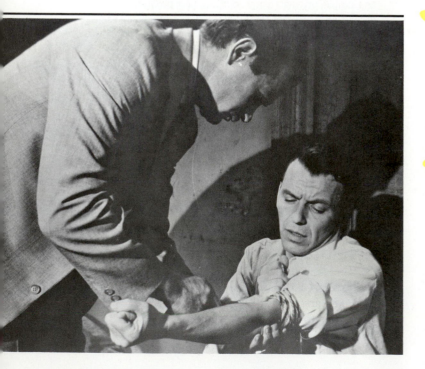

◀ Frank Sinatra prepares to give himself an injection in Otto Preminger's code-busting film *The Man with the Golden Arm* (1955).

was the type of film that would make money, then they would not only allow such films to be made and released, they would make them themselves. In 1956, *Baby Doll* became the first major studio film to receive a "C" (condemned) rating by the Catholic Church's Legion of Decency. Prior to this time the legion, by threat of economic boycott, held enormous power in Hollywood. Legion officials were called in on every film and exerted great influence. If the legion wanted something removed or altered, the filmmaker did it with little argument. This was all changed, however, by Preminger's example. In a few years, both the legion and the code ceased to function as effective filters through which Hollywood's films had to pass. Their "dos and don'ts" and "goods and bads" became fuzzy and watered down to the point of meaninglessness. Eventually, the code was replaced by a rating system and the legion ceased to exist altogether.

System Changes

Perhaps the most significant change taking place in the industry during the fifties was in the traditional Hollywood system of producing motion pictures.

Foretastes of the major upheavals of the sixties were discernible — for instance, in the forced resignation of MGM's Louis B. Mayer in 1951. Mayer had once been the most dominant personality in Hollywood, earning the highest salary in the United States, but now found himself squeezed out by a nervous front office.

The old order was beginning to crumble, and nowhere was this more apparent than in the studio's profit-and-loss statements. In 1950 and again in 1953, 51 of the 70 pictures released by Paramount failed to recoup their negative costs in the United States and Canada. This, of course, was the real issue. In the golden age of the thirties and forties, the studios' primary concern about money had been how to make more of it. Now the issue was how to keep from losing it. Perhaps the biggest concern was how much of the total budget was allocated to studio overhead — usually it was 20–30 percent. In the old days, this money was a legitimate investment, but now it was an intolerable cost. As a result, the studios began to cut back. Feature production declined by almost 50 percent between 1950 and 1960. The number of actors, writers, and directors under contract to studios declined even more drastically, and by 1960 there were fewer than 200 "creators" under contract, compared with more than 1,400 in 1945. Ultimately, the studios retrenched to the point where they killed off certain types of productions altogether. The "B" film was the chief casualty. It had been the staple of the industry, the assembly line product that had underwritten the occa-

sional excursions into art and spectacle. However, as TV took over more and more of the motion picture audience, the "B" film became a liability. If color, wide screens, and big budgets were what Hollywood needed in order to compete, the "B" film was doomed. Some statistics on film costs bear this out. While there was some decline in the number of big-budget films made between 1947 and 1954, the real drop occurred in the films costing $150,000 to $200,000 — the "B" picture category — where production declined more than 18 percent in seven years. Shorts, cartoons, serials, and newsreels felt the crunch even more severely. By 1957 serials and newsreels were no longer part of studio production schedules.

In an effort to cut expenses further, production units were shooting more and more films outside the United States. Instead of constructing castles, streets, or entire villages on a back lot, crews shot the scene or film on location, with substantial savings. Whereas in 1947 more than 90 percent of all films released by Hollywood were made in the United States, by 1954 more than 25 percent were being made outside the country.

Studios themselves were in trouble. Universal, one of the oldest studios, was absorbed into Decca Records in 1955, and RKO stopped production altogether in 1956. Republic Studios, a major producer of "B" westerns, faded and died in 1958.

The overriding philosophical problem was a lack of confidence. Until now, the industry had been strong and confident enough to weather anything — depression, war, competing media — but the combined power of television, the decline in theater ownership, pressure from HUAC, and foreign growth and expansion weakened the studio system's faith in its own product and in its ability to produce what people wanted. As a result, the postwar period became a time of searching — for a new audience, new films, and new formulas.

This search is in evidence everywhere in both the films and the careers of the artists of the period. The regulated efficiency by which the studio system operated in the thirties and forties was no longer possible. The rules for success had changed and little remained the same. Few directors maintained consistent mastery. Orson Welles attempted to recapture the magic of *Citizen Kane* with such efforts as *Touch of Evil* (1958). Frank Capra made only three films in the fifties, none of them successful. Howard Hawks concentrated on a few blockbuster films such as *Gentlemen Prefer Blondes* (1953), *Land of the Pharaohs* (1955), and *Rio Bravo* (1959), all with mixed success. John Ford, while remaining relatively prolific — he made twenty films between 1950 and 1963 — succeeded primarily in creating a patchwork quilt that included *The Quiet Man* (1952), *The Searchers* (1956), *The Rising of the Moon* (1957),

The Horse Soldiers (1959), and *The Man Who Shot Liberty Valance* (1962). Even Alfred Hitchcock was blown momentarily astray by the winds of capricious fortune with such strained efforts as *I Confess* (1952), *The Trouble with Harry* (1956), and *Vertigo* (1958).

However, several directors achieved individual success in the period. These included John Huston with *The Treasure of Sierra Madre* (1948), *Key Largo* (1948), and *The African Queen* (1952); Fred Zinneman with *The Man* (1950), *High Noon* (1952), and *From Here to Eternity* (1953); George Stevens with *A Place in the Sun* (1951), *Shane* (1953), and *Giant* (1956); and Robert Rossen with *Body and Soul* (1947), *All the King's Men* (1949), *Island in the Sun* (1957), *The Hustler* (1961), and *Lilith* (1963).

As a result of the combined difficulties faced by the industry, the fifties became something of a lost period in film history. The films of the time followed few patterns and established few trends, and are therefore usually dismissed by most historians. However, as Andrew Sarris states, this is "forest" criticism, and in order to truly evaluate the time we need to look at a few "trees."

There is little question that the quality of the motion picture as a whole declined. And certain genres, such as comedy, declined more noticeably than others. But this drop in quality is explained in part simply by the huge decline in the number of films made. To analyze the trends or patterns of the fifties, however vague they might be, we need to review some of the major film genres.

The Genre Film

The Musical

Once sound came along, the musical emerged as one of Hollywood's most solid genres. During the thirties musicals were characterized primarily by the individual styles of certain artists, such as Fred Astaire and Busby Berkeley. In the forties, with the development of color film and the emergence of several talented song and dance teams, the musical form matured and developed new strength. Two studios dominated the period: 20th Century-Fox, because it had Technicolor and Betty Grable, and MGM, because it had practically everything and everyone else. Fox's reign was short-lived as the other studios perfected their own color processes and audiences tired of a

Gene Kelly dances his way through the title dance/song number in *Singin' in the Rain* (1952). Kelly codirected this musical masterpiece with Stanley Donen for MGM.

steady diet of Grable with occasional relief supplied by Sonja Henie and Alice Faye.

It was MGM that really brought the musical genre into its own. With former lyricist-turned-producer Arthur Freed and director Vincente Minnelli spearheading the movement, MGM gathered together the best available talent and gave them the freedom and material to produce their best work. Musicals demanded a large studio operation. As one critic noted, "More than any other genre, the successful musical requires the harmonious blending of many talents—design, dance, direction and performance." MGM, with its traditional huge stockpile of talent, was the logical studio to take the musical to new heights. Some of the key musicals produced by MGM in this period include *Meet Me in St. Louis* (1944), *Easter Parade* (1948), *The Pirate* (1949), *An American in Paris* (1951), and *Singin' in the Rain* (1952). Key performers were Judy Garland, Fred Astaire, and Gene Kelly.

Kelly was perhaps the most important individual of the group, since his talents went beyond performing. He was a highly accomplished choreographer as well as dancer, and, in tandem with director Stanley Donen, he produced such musicals as *On the Town* (1949), *Singin' in the Rain* (1952), and *It's Always Fair Weather* (1955). Many other musicals were produced, all similar in style and content. Fred Astaire made several excellent films in the fifties, including *Funny Face* (1957), produced by Donen. And in 1954, Donen himself made one of the most original musicals of the period—*Seven Brides for Seven Brothers*. Based loosely on the legend of the rape of the Sabine women, Donen transformed the reality of rape and conquest into a fantasy world of quilting bees and wedding festivals. This approach characterized most of the musicals of the period. The films were elaborately constructed "fluff," with little if any connection to the real world. Unlike the Busby Berkeley musicals of the thirties, these films had no ties to society and its problems. Instead, they were set in Paris, America of the 1800s, and Hollywood of the twenties.

This fantasy orientation would soon change, however, as the concept of *integration* became dominant. Integration meant that plot and music were interrelated in a semirealistic fashion. With regard to content, musicals moved from backstage gossip and high society glitter to New York street gangs, Nazi Germany, and czarist-ruled, anti-Semitic Russia.

The keys to producing effective musicals were an efficient, highly organized studio system and *original* screenplays written by creative production teams. Following the period for musicals—1945–1955—many of the creative personnel were forced to work apart from each other as the studios declined. Money for expensive productions became harder to justify, and the musical itself began a long, gradual decline. The form did not die, but much of its creativity and originality were lost as the studios turned to safe, tested themes based on biographies or stage adaptations. The era of the musical as a significant staple of the industry ended, oddly enough, with four of its biggest hits—*West Side Story* (1961), *My Fair Lady* (1964), *The Sound of Music* (1965), and *Mary Poppins* (1964). Despite record-breaking grosses for most of these films, the cost of production, including the film-rights purchases, simply became too expensive. Jack Warner paid $5 million alone for the film rights to *My Fair Lady* and spent another $20 million or so to produce the film. Since a film needs to take in approximately 2.5 times its cost in box-office revenue just to break even, this clearly was a risky course to follow. Several disasters, such as *Star* (1968) and *Dr. Doolittle* (1967), finally convinced the studios that the musical could no longer be produced as a genre, but had to be relegated to spectacle status.

The Western

The Western went through a dramatic metamorphosis during this period. On the one hand it became more complicated, socially conscious, and personal; on the other, with respect to the "B" Western, it faded from the scene.

George Fenin and William K. Everson point out in their book *The Western,* that the postwar Western came to be dominated by three elements: sex, neuroses, and racial consciousness. Sex was first, and both Howard Hughes's *The Outlaw* (1943) and David O. Selznick's *Duel in the Sun* (1946) seemed to signal a new era. However, the trend was short-lived and sporadic; the Western heritage seemed to thrive better on violent action and pictorial landscape than on sex. Jane Russell's cleavage in *The Outlaw* may have caused public controversy, but it could not save the film from being a box-office failure.

The maturation process continued as the genre began to explore psychological themes, most importantly the individual against society. This confrontation was symbolized particularly well in Henry King's *The Gunfighter* (1950) and Stanley Kramer's *High Noon* (1952), the film that epitomized the new adult orientation. Gary Cooper became the archetype for what Americans believed was good in a man and good in this country's heritage. Cooper's portrayal of a small-town sheriff—tall, lean, silent, courageously facing a group of killers alone, scorned even by the woman he loved—is, alongside the rebel youth of James Dean, perhaps the best-remembered role of the fifties. Alan Ladd in *Shane* produced a similar although less striking character.

The Western also picked up and followed the theme of racial consciousness. *Broken Arrow* (1950), starring James Stewart and Debra Paget as interracial lovers, broke new ground in the genre's treatment of Indians. Early in film history, the Indian in film had been charac-

terized as a noble savage, romantically symbolized by a proud, silent chief or warrior. The "noble" was soon eliminated, however, and for three decades the Indian was depicted as a pestilence impeding white settlers in the same way that drought or brush fires did. Few individual portraits emerged; rather, the typical Indian on film was a member of a large, screaming horde. *Broken Arrow* portrayed Indians as human, and as having most of the same feelings and ideas as whites.

◀ Gary Cooper as the archetypal Western hero in *High Noon* (1952).

▼ From *Broken Arrow* (1950). This film, directed by Delmer Daves, represented the beginnings of an "adult western" cycle that featured a somewhat more authentic treatment of the Western experience, especially the American Indian. However, as this still shows, the Indian was still being played by movie "stars"—in this instance Debra Paget and Jeff Chandler (as Apache Chief Cochise). James Stewart plays an ex-Army man trying to seek accord between the Indians and whites.

The trend established with *Broken Arrow,* although welcome, was not actually realistic. White actors and actresses were still playing most Indian roles and content became heavily stereotyped in the opposite direction as screens became filled with neurotic traders, evil Indian agents, and blood-thirsty Army colonels. It was not until the late sixties, with such films as *Tell Them Willie Boy Is Here* (1969) and *Little Big Man* (1971), that the Indian issue received even a basic sociological appraisal.

The change in the Western was partially a response to the times and partially a search by several directors for new meaning in the genre. Increasingly, the genre and its basic formula began to serve as a springboard for personal styles and statements. John Ford was a key figure here, if only because he worked in the Western genre more than any other major director of the period. His Westerns are classical and heavily sentimental. He showed little concern for documentary detail or sociological analysis in such films as *My Darling Clementine* (1946), *Fort Apache* (1948), *She Wore a Yellow Ribbon* (1949), *Wagonmaster* (1950), *The Searchers* (1956), *The Horse Soldiers* (1959), or *The Man Who Shot Liberty Valance* (1962). In these films and others, Ford was concerned with a simple message, and he communicated it in a simple yet vivid style. Ford has been criticized for this simplistic vision of the West and, indeed, once one sees past the romantic lines of cavalry riding through Monument Valley, little actually remains of the Western reality. Ford loved the West and greatly enjoyed working in Western films. His films are filled with beautiful images, not realistic detail. And if, in retrospect, his films fall short of our expectations, they still retain the necessary ingredients of dignity and romance.

Anthony Mann is the only director of the period who established a Western style and tradition. He directed eleven Westerns during the fifties. In contrast to Ford's romanticism, Mann's style is much darker; it is heavily psychological, and his films are concerned with tragic, even neurotic, men standing alone as the forces of society swirl around them. Beginning with *Winchester '73* in 1950, Mann began an eight-film collaboration with James Stewart in which he probed and explored the moral ambiguities of men caught in a swiftly changing society. Jim Kitses' book, *Horizons West,* offers an excellent, if somewhat esoteric, analysis of Mann's work.

Many other directors worked in the Western genre during this period. Howard Hawks (*Red River* [1948] and *Rio Bravo* [1959]), Fred Zinneman (*High Noon* [1952]), and George Stevens (*Shane* [1953]) are just a few examples. However, as a genre, the Western too began a gradual decline. Surprisingly, the wide screen, which should have proved beneficial, was not used with any real impact. Perhaps the tension between wide open spaces and the psychological forces of society created a similar tension in terms of style. By 1954, the "B" Western series was gone. Even more dramatic was the decline in Western stars. The genre lost most of its standard characters, replacing them instead with stars who played in Westerns. Gary Cooper, John Wayne, and James Stewart emerged as the dominant actors, but the real Western stars were going to or coming from television. Gene Autry was the first Western star to make the switch in media, and he was followed closely by Roy Rogers and William Boyd, as Hopalong Cassidy. In 1955 *Gunsmoke* and *Wagon Train* appeared, and the TV Western was off and running. This form reached an all-time peak in 1960, when thirty-two different Western programs were aired during prime time across the nation.

As the era ended, several new directors and styles began to appear, bringing a new, personal, almost idiosyncratic style to the Western. The most significant new twist came in Sergio Leone's "spaghetti Westerns," beginning with *A Fistful of Dollars* (1964) and *Once Upon a Time in the West* (1969). By then, however, the genre's reign as a significant and at times dominant force in American film had passed.

The Comedy

Comedy as a film genre suffered from an identity crisis during the fifties as well. Television and the trend toward social realism were perhaps the two biggest factors undermining comedy, particularly the family comedy. Where in the past some of the most popular studio series had been family oriented — examples are MGM's "Andy Hardy," Columbia's "Dagwood and Blondie," and Fox's "Thin Man" — now TV, with *I Remember Mama, I Love Lucy, Make Room for Daddy,* and *Father Knows Best,* among others, usurped this role. Only Walt Disney consistently dealt with family comedies, with such films as *The Parent Trap* (1961) and *The Absent-Minded Professor* (1961). Comedy declined from 19 percent of Hollywood output in 1947 to less than 10 percent in 1954.

In response to the many changes taking place, Hollywood began to concentrate on more realistic comedy, replacing, as film historian and critic Raymond Durgnat notes, the "comedy of manners" with the "comedy of behavior." Instead of the sophisticated high-class comedy of the "Thin Man" series, audiences got drama and tension combined with comedy in *Born Yesterday* (1950) and *The Apartment* (1960). As Milton Berle's zany slapstick continued to lure the motion picture audi-

From *Some Like It Hot*, which represents director Billy Wilder and writer I. A. L. Diamond at their acerbic best. In this sparkling 1959 comedy, Jack Lemmon and Tony Curtis are two musicians who witness the St. Valentine's Massacre and try to elude their pursuers by joining an all-girl band. Marilyn Monroe is memorable as Sugar Kane.

ence over to television, the studios began to explore more mature comedic themes. Marilyn Monroe became a major star in such "adult" comedies as *Bus Stop* (1956) and *Some Like It Hot* (1959). Doris Day and Rock Hudson starred in a series of pseudo-sex comedies beginning with *Pillow Talk* in 1959.

Durgnat describes comedy of this period as falling into two categories: "rosy" and "black." Rosy comedy embraces themes and characters that have inherent plausibility but are nevertheless basically nonsociological. Durgnat points to George Cukor's comedic style as representing the rosy type. Although it is true that Cukor was basically realistic in his approach (for *Born Yesterday* he went back to Washington, D.C., to "study the real thing"), he had no axe to grind, and therefore his comedies are smooth and well rounded, avoiding any real clash with social issues or problems. In another of Cukor's films, *Breakfast at Tiffany's* (1961), Audrey Hepburn plays a "kept woman," yet her character and the situations she becomes involved in are presented not for social analysis, but as comedic ingredients designed to make us laugh.

However, as the era moved to a close, "black" comedy, which made satiric comment and even biting social analysis, began to replace rosy comedy. Billy Wilder's film *The Apartment* (1960) was one of the first major black comedies. Here audiences were shown a callous system in which people were reduced to pawns and manipulated for the pleasure of others. Wilder was one of the major comedy directors of the period. In addition to *The Apartment*, he made *The Seven Year Itch* (1955), *Some Like It Hot* (1959), *One, Two, Three* (1961) and *Irma La Douce* (1963). Even stronger in its "blackness" is Stanley Kubrick's *Dr. Strangelove* (1964), with its biting satire of right-wing military/government paranoia. Here, black comedy, with its characteristic "implausible central idea," makes a serious comment on the cold war and its possible consequences. Likewise, *The Americanization of Emily* (1964) tells audiences that since war is insane, the only sane men are the cowards. This trend would continue in the sixties and seventies, with such films as *The Graduate* (1967), *M*A*S*H* (1970), and Woody Allen's numerous social satires, among many others.

Very few comedy stars maintained their appeal, and even fewer stars emerged. One of the few bright new names was Judy Holliday. She first burst on the film scene by repeating her stage role in *Born Yesterday* (1950), for which she won an Oscar for Best Actress. Next, she starred in *The Marrying Kind* (1952), where she continued her archetypal role of the dumb blonde. She played the same kind of character throughout the fifties in such films as *It Should Happen to You* (1954), *The Solid Gold Cadillac* (1956) and *Bells Are Ringing* (1960). Marilyn Monroe was another major comedienne of the period, doing her best work in collaboration with Billy Wilder in such films as *The Seven Year Itch* (1955) and *Some Like It Hot* (1959).

Holliday's male counterpart was Jerry Lewis. Originally teamed with Dean Martin in a series of zany but

Jerry Lewis in the title role of *The Bellboy* (1960). As was typical of most of his vintage films, there was little plot but many funny gags. This film marked Lewis's directorial debut.

uneven comedies, Lewis broke away from Martin in 1956 and began making his own films. Such efforts as *The Sad Sack* (1957), *The Geisha Boy* (1958), and *Visit to a Small Planet* (1960) helped him establish his own comic identity. Beginning in 1960, he began directing his own films, and thereafter he developed several excellent productions, including *The Bellboy* (1960), *The Nutty Professor* (1963), and *The Patsy* (1964).

Jerry Lewis has evoked a wide variety of critical opinion. He is generally ignored or maligned in this country, while in France he is almost deified. The American reaction to Lewis may stem from the fact that most American audiences regard slapstick as noncerebral and totally farcical. In this context, Lewis emerges as an idiot. He plays a wide variety of idiots, but who in the long run would take an idiot seriously? However, upon closer analysis we see in such films as *The Patsy* (1964), *The Disorderly Orderly* (1964), and *The Nutty Professor* (1963) an increasingly complex character in the chaos, and one with strong elements of pathos. It is this integration of elements that gives Lewis's comedies their special appeal. The chaos always has meaning; it's usually more than simple pie in the face. In his most subtle roles, Lewis plays a misfit in a world that is unnecessarily cruel. The chaos he creates operates as a necessary antidote to a sick society. In this respect Lewis followed in the footsteps of the classic comedians such as Chaplin, Keaton, and Lloyd.

The major comic stars of the thirties and forties — Bob Hope, Danny Kaye, Bing Crosby, Laurel and Hardy, and Abbot and Costello — had difficulty sustaining any consistent form. Of course, age took over Laurel and Hardy and many others, but the decade itself explained the lack of strong comedy films and comic personalities. The fifties were not kind to Hollywood. Fear and confusion replaced confidence at all levels of the studio system and comedy, more than most genres, suffered the most. Comedy appeals to audiences in good times and bad times, but not in between times.

The Science Fiction Film

One other minor genre, the science fiction film, deserves mention here. This genre came to fruition in the Atomic Age. Prior to this time "sci-fi" films were singular and usually adopted from popular works such as H. G. Wells's *The Invisible Man* (1933) and the space serial "Buck Rogers." As the sensibility of the Atomic Age began to pervade society, and as an increasingly large body of sci-fi short stories began to appear, the sci-fi film took on increased stature. Beginning with *Destination: Moon*, in 1950, and continuing with *Five* (1951), *The Day the Earth Stood Still* (1951), *Invasion of the Body Snatchers* (1956), and *The Incredible Shrinking Man* (1957), among others, a whole body of work began to accumulate. Most of the films were low-budget "B" efforts, and most were moderately successful. However, as the reality portrayed on television began to surpass the fiction in motion pictures, the science fiction genre faded for the moment. It was resurrected with blazing success by *2001: A Space Odyssey* (1968) and *Star Wars* (1977) almost twenty years later.

From *Marty* (1955). Originally a television play by Paddy Chayefsky, *Marty* made a spectacular transition to the big screen. Ernest Borgnine won the Academy Award for Best Actor as a Bronx butcher who ultimately finds love with Betsy Blair. Chayefsky won an Oscar for Best Screenplay, Delbert Mann for Best Director, and the film won Best Picture.

From Small to Big

As the preceding section suggests, during the fifties the major genres became more complex and the films in each genre more individualistic. The traditions of the genres, such as the Western or musical, had relatively little effect on new films emerging in response to the times and as expressions of individual directors' philosophies. As the decade wore on, the genres began to fall back into place or die altogether.

To replace and complement the established genres, Hollywood came up with a new classification system, one based on size. The "small film" and the "big film" took their places alongside many of the standard genre productions. The small film—independent, black-and-white, often adapted from TV—flourished briefly in the mid-fifties, beginning with *Marty* (1955). The film, independently produced by the Hecht-Lancaster organization, starred Ernest Borgnine as a butcher who falls in love with a schoolteacher. The film has a distinct neorealist heritage as it looks at two ordinary people living

ordinary lives. *Marty* had a freshness, vitality, and—above all—genuineness that many found lacking in most of Hollywood's products. It won a Grand Prix at the Cannes Film Festival and an Academy Award as Best Picture. These awards, of course, stirred a beehive of activity. A "small" picture in the best sense, *Marty* offered audiences of the fifties who were tired of big-screen and 3-D spectacles a glimpse at deep emotion.

Immediately after the success of *Marty,* producers began a search for small stories to make into small films. They looked to television and the huge number of original sixty-minute dramas being represented there once a week. Here was a bonanza, and soon such TV writers as Rod Serling and the already successful Paddy Chayefsky were being wooed by the major studios. While some of the adaptation succeeded, the old Hollywood game of imitating a popular trend took over as studios tried to create a small-film formula. Unfortunately, despite limited success with Chayefsky's *The Bachelor Party* (1957), Reginald Roses's *Twelve Angry Men* (1957), and Rod Serling's *Patterns* (1955) and *Requiem for a Heavyweight* (1962), the small-film formula did not save Hollywood, although it opened the doors to an interme-

A spectacular scene, the cost of which was one of the reasons that the 1963 production of *Cleopatra* lost money.

dia cooperation that would ultimately prove to be Hollywood's life preserver.

If small didn't do it, Hollywood reasoned, perhaps big would. The spectacle, which had always been part of Hollywood on a limited scale, suddenly erupted in 1956 with *The Ten Commandments* ($13.5 million), *War and Peace* ($6.5 million), *The King and I* ($6.5 million), *Around the World in Eighty Days* ($6 million), and *Moby Dick* ($5 million). The pattern continued throughout the decade with *Ben Hur* (1959), *El Cid* (1960), *Spartacus* (1960), and, the biggest spectacle of them all, *Cleopatra* (1963). By the time the smoke had cleared following *Cleopatra's* failure, the studios were on such shaky ground that even though spectacles were still possible and occasionally profitable, costs had increased so enormously that few organizations could afford the gamble.

In looking back on this postwar period of almost twenty years, it is clear that Hollywood and the whole system of making motion pictures in America went through a radical change in response to several significant events. Prior to this time, Hollywood had thrived on regulated efficiency: there had been rules. More important than rules, however, were existing *expectations*— of the system itself and of the audience. The two were interwoven. The system imposed expectations on producers, directors, writers, and stars based on its expectations of a *mass* American audience in the *habit* of attending motion pictures. However, once both the "mass" and "habit" were gone, the system's expectations—and optimism—went too.

Now the period became one of trial and error, with new forms emerging and old forms dying. Hollywood developed a split personality, desperately trying to hang onto the old while also attempting to adjust to the new. Unlike the twenties, thirties, and early forties, this postwar period is hard to characterize. Society was more complex than ever before, and multiple pressures ultimately caused fundamental changes. Contrary to some ways of thinking, Hollywood and the American film industry (up to this point the two were synonymous) did not die; rather, they were cracked wide open. At times the content of the period is overshadowed by the emphasis on technology and a few special films or people. However, obviously the films of the period had content. Perhaps the most dominant characteristic of the time was its very variety. While few film categories of overriding importance emerged during the fifties, more new people and ideas entered the American film industry during that decade than at any time since the studios had solidified their hold on the industry in the early twenties. In a way the fifties were a testing ground for many of the ideas and people that would characterize the films of the sixties and seventies.

It is a cliché that Hollywood in the fifties was strictly "bubble gum and bobby sox," a period in which few films of any meaning or consequence were made. Certainly, the issues that were treated were disguised and dressed up in the form of Westerns, war films, or science fiction films. Westerns dealt with the past and thus could not really be linked to any current social thought. War films were obviously patriotic. Such films as *The Gunfighter* (1950), *Broken Arrow* (1950), *Shane* (1953), and *High Noon* (1952) in the Western genre, and *The Red Badge of Courage* (1951), *The Caine Mutiny* (1954), and *Twelve O'Clock High* (1950) all dealt with the problems individuals faced because of certain beliefs or standards. Of course, a prime motivator behind this kind of social realism was money; many of the issue-oriented films were simply the result of a "frenzied search for material that would galvanize the public." Otto Preminger's deviance from the Motion Picture Code is one case in point — he did it for profit, not ideals. The use of Tennessee Williams's plays as subject matter for several major films is another example. Although Williams's material lent itself to films owing to the playwright's cinematic style of writing, the themes and the way Williams treated them had great appeal in themselves. He dealt, for example, with impotence in *Cat on a Hot Tin Roof* (1958) and cannibalism in *Suddenly Last Summer* (1959), subjects that previously would have had great problems being filmed.

Problems of youth were increasingly emphasized in such films as *East of Eden* (1955) and *Rebel Without a Cause* (1955), starring James Dean. Other youth-oriented films of this period were *Blackboard Jungle* (1955), *The Dark at the Top of the Stairs* (1960), and *Splendor in the Grass* (1961). The semirealistic emphasis of these films was soon diffused, however, as rock and roll music began to create a youth culture and Hollywood jumped on the bandwagon with a series of musicals starring Elvis Presley, Fabian, and other rock and roll heroes.

The beginning of black consciousness can be seen in two Sidney Poitier films, *Edge of the City* (1957) and *The Defiant Ones* (1958). Although Poitier was a stereotyped, larger-than-life character, later treatment of the more common, ordinary concerns of race relations were made possible in films of this period.

One side issue that contributed greatly to the trend in screen realism was a new acting style known as "the Method." Its origins are found in the writings of the great Russian producer/actor/theoretician Konstantine Stanislavsky, who, in his book *An Actor Prepares,* stated the central thesis of the movement: "You must live the part every moment you are playing it." His major ideas were popularized in the United States by Stella Adler, who taught acting in New York, and by the Actors Studio, organized by Lee Strasberg and Elia Kazan. Marlon Brando was the most famous public communicator of Method acting, and through his strong performances in *A Streetcar Named Desire* (1951) and *On the Waterfront* (1954), he gave what was essentially a very small movement, immense reputation and appeal. Method acting ultimately challenged the star system and its real people/star dualism. This challenge anticipated the trend of the sixties and seventies, where the artificial distance between stars and regular people gradually lessened. Although relatively few players subscribed to the Method, the versatility and impact of such people as Rod Steiger, Ben Gazzara, Paul Newman, Lee J. Cobb, Eli Wallach, Julie Harris, and Marlon Brando would have a major effect on films of the sixties and seventies.

Wrap-Up

As the decade of the 1950s ended, Hollywood and the motion picture industry it symbolized were once more in transition. At the start of the decade the studio moguls still ruled their kingdoms with iron fists. By the start of the 1960s, though, all of them but Jack Warner were gone.

The breakup of the studio system was in high gear. Contract players, once the symbol of a studio's power, were the exception rather than the rule. The game wasn't the same anymore. The players were different and the rules had changed.

At the decade's end, David O. Selznick said to screenwriter Ben Hecht,

Hollywood's like Egypt, full of crumbled pyramids. It'll never come back. It'll just keep on crumbling until finally the wind blows the last studio prop across the sands.

Selznick was wrong only in the way the props would go—they did not blow away; people bought them at auction. Hollywood as it existed for most people—a golden city full of moguls, stars, gods, and goddesses—was gone. However, like the phoenix rising from its own ashes, a new Hollywood would quickly rise up in the old one's place.

10

Postwar Cinema: Europe and the East (1945 – 1963)

Focus

As earlier chapters showed, European filmmakers experienced a period of creative fervor in the wake of World War I. The postwar period was marked by an exploration and a refinement of cinematic styles in conjunction with an examination of the social realities of the time. This period extended into the late twenties, when it was finally absorbed by the revolution that was the coming of sound.

Similarly, the end of World War II brought a new period of aesthetic fervor and enlightenment. This revitalization began in Italy and, with inspiration coming from Sweden and far-off Japan, spread through Western Europe over the next decade, revealing a host of new film creators and works that were to become models of a new realism. A new seriousness of purpose in cinema also arose, propelling several national genres and individual directors into the critical arena as well as the global commercial marketplace.

The common interest, despite a disparity of national styles and individual profiles, was to ask some fundamental questions regarding the nature of the human condition. This meant looking at those value systems that are responsible for "programming" individuals and directing their interrelationships with each other, with the environment, with their institutions, and with their God. To do this, filmmakers abandoned stereotypical plot lines and turned instead to original conceptions. Here they looked beyond the story as an end in itself and let the narrative evolve from the situations and motivations of the characters. In a very real sense the camera was being turned on more than setting, stories, and stars; it was being turned on the individual psyche and conflicts in human thought.

The New Italian Realism

The spectacles of 1912, which probably inspired Griffith's *Judith of Bethulia,* put Italy in the motion picture vanguard during the silent era. The political support (and control) of the Fascist government through the thirties and early forties resulted in sterile romances — the so-called "white telephone films," named after a popular boudoir fixture in many of them — and propaganda films. Though both genres were undistinguished, the training filmmakers received at the large and well-equipped Cinecittà studios on the outskirts of Rome allowed them to refine their technique even if it did not assure them of artistic freedom.

With the liberation of Rome came the release of a creative spirit in cinema. Italian neorealism, a style of filmmaking that is still considered one of the richest and most inspired of any period or country, brought the attention and respect to Italy in the postwar years that neither its silent nor early sound efforts could draw. The movement has been called by one critic "the most important attempt by liberal man to realize himself on film." With what Cesare Zavattini, the leading screenwriter for the movement, called "a hunger for reality," the neorealist approach to filmmaking began in the early forties as a reaction to the militant propaganda of the

Fascist-controlled industry. International recognition came to the movement in 1945 with the arrival of Roberto Rossellini's *Rome — Open City.* Rossellini scraped together camera and film stock and used the city streets as the setting for his tribute to the underground resistance movement during the Nazi occupation. The harbingers of the movement had come earlier in the war years, with Luchino Visconti's *Ossessione* (1942) and Vittorio de Sica's *The Children Are Watching* (1942), which showed the dramatic power of direct and unembellished observation. It was the Rossellini work that gave the movement its form and direction, however, and when released in 1945 it heralded the new age of realist cinema.

Roberto Rossellini

Filming under extremely difficult technical and financial conditions, Rossellini recreated the struggle of Rome's resistance movement against the German occupation forces. The film centers on the attempt by a handful of ordinary citizens to resist Fascist oppression — a housewife, her son, her common-law husband, and a parish priest. It ends with the execution of the priest before a Nazi firing squad as the children of Rome look on.

Plagued by inadequate equipment, inferior film stock, and the lack of financial backing, production was frequently interrupted. When filming was completed, the impoverished conditions under which the film was produced were reflected in the results. But the film's austerity became a virtue and the authenticity of the situations themselves was strengthened by its spontaneous, raw-life look at activities that were a part of the city's life, often shot in secret to avoid Fascist interference. The immediate success of *Open City* encouraged a small group of directors to join in expressing their version of

◀ From *Open City* (1945). This Rossellini work, which ushered in the neorealist movement, was planned during the occupation and based on resistance activities and the Nazi execution of a parish priest in 1944. Anna Magnani and Aldo Fabrizzi (seen here) were the only professional actors in the cast. The screenplay, coauthored by Federico Fellini, was shot in the streets of Rome even as the Nazis were retreating from the city.

the War and the difficult period of reconstruction that followed. This group became the inspiration and guiding force for the neorealist movement, and it was largely responsible for the complexion of Italian film throughout the fifties.

Rossellini's leadership of the new movement was further strengthened in 1946 with the release of *Paisan,* a six-part story covering wartime episodes following the Allied advance up into Italy from Sicily to the marshes of the Po Valley. Each segment of the film, all of which are independent pieces, became an intimate and compassionate tribute to the suffering and anguish of people caught up in war. In addition to revealing Rossellini's sensitivity to the subject, the film also showed his command of a cinematic form that took on the appearance of documentary reportage.

The scarcity of film stock, equipment, studio space, and money for building sets and hiring professional actors was a handicap that Rossellini turned to his advantage. By settling for nonprofessional actors and the streets of Rome, he created a drama that was akin to the social realism of the Soviet directors. Owing to the technical limits of equipment and the necessity to make do with less than polished composition, lighting, and editing, this film seemed to be real life captured in the raw—unpolished, unordered, and unadorned.

Rossellini on Neorealism

*D*uring a congress at Parma on neo-realism there was a great deal of discussion of the term, but it still remains ambiguous. Most of the time it is hardly more than a label. For me it is above all a moral standpoint from which to view the world. Afterwards it becomes an aesthetic standpoint, but the point of departure is definitely moral.

I have also been criticized for not offering any solution—but if I were capable of finding a solution, I wouldn't have made films, I'd have done something else. . . .

—*From an interview with Roberto Rossellini,* Cahiers du Cinéma *(1955)*

Vittorio de Sica

The Rossellini works concerned anti-Fascist activities during the war; Vittorio de Sica concentrated on the tragic human results of war and poverty without using the Fascists as heavies. His *Shoeshine* (*Sciuscia,* 1946), which American critic James Agee called "about as beautiful, moving, and heartening a film as you are ever likely to see," is the story of two street boys who, as part of the black market in Rome, become victims of corrupt state officials. With this film, de Sica joined Rossellini as a leader of the neorealist movement and further expressed the qualities that were becoming the hallmarks of the genre: a deep humanism and sense of compassion together with the feeling of everyday reality. Using real locations, a combination of professional and amateur actors, and Rossellini's direct cinema-journalistic approach, de Sica revealed a method that seemed to have its roots in the Soviet films of the silent era.

The Bicycle Thief (1948), de Sica's next film, represented the true flowering of the form. It is a penetrating yet simple study, set in postwar Rome, of a father and son engaged in a desperate search for a stolen bicycle, which is essential to the man's work as a bill poster. Using amateur actors in the key roles of father and son, de Sica

shot the film entirely in location settings—the streets, churches, and tenements of Rome. And, after working with Cesare Zavattini for nearly a year on the screenplay, de Sica finally shot the film without script in hand to enhance the film's spontaneity. The result has the extemporaneous flavor of his earlier works, but in evidence, too, is a strong sense of the depth of the relationship between the father and son. Scenes showing the father's fear that the boy may be a drowning victim and the son's realization that his father has, in desperation, himself attempted the theft of a bicycle reveal the human spirit at its most engaging. Though criticized for its sentimentality, *The Bicycle Thief* brought the movement a step closer to the ideal that Zavattini himself had articulated: "the reality buried under the myths."

Umberto D (1952), made by de Sica with Zavattini four years later, was the third and final contribution of this writer/director team to the original movement. This film was an intense character study of an old man's struggle to salvage some dignity out of his lonely and impoverished life. The two worked together on *Miracle in Milan* in 1950, but this film was a fanciful social satire that showed the beginnings of a distinct departure from the stark realism of earlier collaborations.

▲   From *The Bicycle Thief* (1948). A father's despair over a stolen bicycle, necessary for his work as a bill poster, provides the simple but haunting theme of this major contribution by Vittorio de Sica (and Cesare Zavattini, the screenwriter) to neorealism. Here even the two major roles of father and son were played by nonprofessionals.

Luchino Visconti

A third key director, Luchino Visconti, was a pioneer in the movement with his *Ossessione* in 1942, and was also responsible for extending the life of neorealism into the sixties with *Rocco and His Brothers* (1960). But it is *La Terra Trema* ("The Earth Trembles" [1948]) that comes closest to the direct and uncompromising ideal set down by Zavattini. Here the subject was the disintegration of a family of Sicilian fishermen under punishing economic strains. The film develops along more expansive lines than the Rossellini and de Sica films. Like Visconti's later works — *Rocco and His Brothers, The Damned* (1970), and *Death in Venice* (1972)—*La Terra Trema* becomes almost operatic, and it shows, in the words of Penelope Houston, "the grandeur as well as the misery of aspiration defeated." Despite the grand design of the film, it still easily meets the basic tenets of the movement. Visconti used location shooting and non-professional actors, and he also encouraged improvisational speech. The resulting Sicilian phraseology and

dialect made parts of the film unintelligible even to many Italians.

Cesare Zavattini

As has been suggested, Cesare Zavattini, scenarist for *Shoeshine* (1946), *The Bicycle Thief* (1948), and *Umberto D* (1952), served as theoretician and spokesman for the neorealist movement and articulated its function and style. He saw the role of the film creator as "being able to observe reality, not to extract fiction from it." Zavattini not only recognized the film medium's compatibility with realistic detail, he also found the potential for real drama in the homely details of everyday life, particularly as lived in the streets and tenement homes of working-class families. Central to his notion of form was the recognition that the invention of a story was "simply a technique of superimposing dead formulas over living social facts." "Reality is hugely rich," said Zavattini, "to be able to look directly at it is enough." He found material worthy

Zavattini on Neorealism

A woman is going to buy a pair of shoes. Upon this elementary situation it is possible to build a film. All we have to do is to discover and then show all the elements that go to create this adventure, in all their banal "dailiness," and it will become worthy of attention, it will become "spectacular." But it will become spectacular not through its exceptional, but through its *normal* qualities; it will astonish us by showing so many things that happen every day under our eyes, things we have never noticed before.

—*Cesare Zavattini,*
"Some Ideas on Cinema,"
La Revista del Cinema
Italiano *(1952)*

of attention through normal everyday life rather than the spectacular. At the same time, he was capable of producing adventures by exploring "dailiness"—the everyday banal details that usually go unnoticed.

The films that evolved from this theoretical base, and from Zavattini's own screenplays in several instances, were the works of independent and creative directors, and they therefore showed individual styles. But certain key features characterized most of the films of the movement. These included a narrative taken from a close study of situations as they occur in life without concern for traditional dramatic elements. Although the films usually told stories, they were not concerned with plot intricacies and neat resolutions.

As described earlier, *Shoeshine* is the story of two shoeshine boys involved in black market activities in Rome; they are imprisoned and one betrays the other. *Bicycle Thief* looks at the relationship between a father and son through the anxieties caused by unemployment, and *Umberto D* focuses on the daily routine of an old man and his dog. What these modest stories convey, beyond their minimal plot lines, is, in Zavattini's words, "the love of reality." They also carry a sense of the social conditions affecting the characters and some insight into those

characters' feelings. Through attention to visual detail, the films also express a sense of the immediate experience—a cinematic journal of the times.

In a sense, Italian neorealism was a reaction to both the slick and sophisticated stories common during Fascist rule and to Hollywood films, which were technically superior but produced a reality that was, in Zavattini's words, "unnaturally filtered." The lack of stylistic refinement became a virtue in the hands of filmmakers seeking to reveal the truth of the unadorned and unexceptional. But the movement was not only a liberation from the studio, the stars, and an externally imposed style. It was a liberation from the past tense.

The French Experience

The French film industry found itself in a state of disarray at the end of World War II. Both the government and the economy were unstable. Government granted financial aid, but only in exchange for films both supportive of national prestige and potentially successful at making money.

During this time, established directors such as Renoir and Cocteau, who had been favorites of prewar cinema, were joined by Robert Bresson, Henri-Georges Clouzot, and Jacques Tati. Bresson's *The Diary of a Country Priest* (1950), like most of his other works, was the product of the scenarist tradition, which required a polished script as a blueprint for a film. In this film Bresson examined the life of a young cleric who is dying of cancer, concentrating on his spiritual search for life's meaning and his struggle to give moral guidance to a country village. The film has some of the flavor of the Italian neorealist works of the same period. Its strength lies in its simple story and artistic direction— particularly its exceptional photographic composition, which, together with choice of setting, provides a strong sense of atmosphere.

Tati and Clouzot were both demonstrating their special talents in the fields of comedy and suspense, respectively. In both *Mr. Hulot's Holiday* (1952) and *Mon Oncle* (1958), Tati followed the Chaplin tradition, exploring the adversarial relationship between modest man and modern world. This director spoofs seaside resort characters and lifestyles in the former film and suburban conveniences and living standards in the latter. In both films, Tati uses his gift of mime to create, as both director and star, choice moments of comic art. Clouzot secured his place alongside Hitchcock as a master of suspense with his *The Wages of Fear* (1953) and *Les Diaboliques*(1955). These films reaffirm the importance of the carefully crafted screenplay that leads, anticipates, controls attention and pace, and keeps the viewer continually on edge.

Each of these directors in his own way demonstrated the importance of the planning and preproduction stages of filmmaking. And each became a master of his material before it became part of a film. Both employed conventional methods in composition and montage and followed rather traditional patterns of structure. For all the merits of these major postwar directors, it was clear that there were few ripples of a renaissance in film here.

Through the early fifties young directors, unable to find financial backing for films because of studio monopolies, turned to criticism of the postwar scenarist films. Several, such as François Truffaut, Claude Chabrol, Jean-Luc Godard, and Jacques Rivette, joined *Cahiers du Cinéma,* the esoteric film journal, to denounce the regression in French cinema since the creative efforts of Renoir, Clair, and Vigo in the twenties and thirties.

The New Wave began as an idea about cinema authorship by film critics and theorists who were dissatisfied with the traditional approaches to cinematic expression and the lack of freedom and individuality on the part of practicing directors. André Bazin, film theorist and founder of *Cahiers du Cinéma,* was the guiding force behind the new spirit, which became a *cause célèbre* in 1954 when François Truffaut, in a *Cahiers* article, denounced the "tradition of quality" represented by the works of the established directors. In what came to be known as the "Politique des auteurs," he attacked the finely crafted studio productions that depended heavily on scenario, which in turn was strongly shaped by dialogue. Truffaut wanted the filmmaker to create his own visual conception of an idea rather than be limited to the production of an already existing screenplay.

Even before Truffaut's dictum, concern was expressed for creating a film with the camera rather than the pen. In 1948 Alexandre Astruc wrote an article describing what came to be called "camera stylo." This authorship rendered through the camera became the foundation of New Wave style, and it was the works of such earlier masters as Clair, Vigo, Renoir, and the American-based directors Hitchcock, Hawks, and Preminger that had provided the inspiration.

By 1959 theory was turning into practice. Top awards at the Cannes Film Festival that year went to three relatively unknown directors—Marcel Camus for *Black Orpheus,* Truffaut for *The 400 Blows,* and Alain Resnais for *Hiroshima Mon Amour.* Also in 1959, some two dozen directors were engaged in the production of first features. Between 1959 and 1963 more than 150

Truffaut Defines the "Politique des Auteurs"

*I*t was a call for a broadening of cinematic concepts. But primarily the idea was that the man who has the ideas must be the same as the man who makes the picture. This being so, I am also convinced that a film resembles the man who made it—even if he didn't choose the subject, didn't choose the actors, didn't exclusively direct them and let assistants do the editing—even such a film would, how shall I put it, profoundly reflect in depth, for instance through the rhythm, the pacing, the man who made it.

—*François Truffaut,*
NY Film Bulletin *(1962)*

---

directors made feature films for the first time. Many of these films were undistinguished and threatened to submerge the work of more creative filmmakers. Those who survived the deluge and became the focus of international attention were those now recognized as the pioneers—Godard, Resnais, Truffaut, and Chabrol—all, except for Resnais, original members of the *Cahiers* staff.

As a reaction to "well-made movies" that had lost contact with the meaning of the modern world, New Wave films attempted to demonstrate the freedom of deliberate artlessness. This was a rebel cinema, which often approached the nihilistic, especially in the hands of Godard. Of the several major national genres, New Wave came closest to reflecting the contradictions, ironies, hazards, and otherwise imponderable and unresolved aspects of life. Although each director, and frequently each film, reflected an individual style, the films all shared a modest, spontaneous look. Although they ranged in theme from social realism to surreal spoof, these films invariably revealed a freedom in style and an extemporaneous quality that made use of location settings, hand-held camera, and improvised dialogue, though they were by no means dependent on these devices.

Unlike the neorealists, the New Wave filmmakers could not be pegged to a common approach or singular style. Their range extended from the naturalistic and humanistic spirit of Truffaut's *The 400 Blows* to the cerebral and formal architecture of Resnais's *Last Year at Marienbad* (*L'Année Dernière à Marienbad* [1961]). Their common ground was a reaction to past and existing styles in filmmaking, and in the case of the major figures — Truffaut, Godard, Chabrol — a common background in film criticism as founders and regular contributors to *Cahiers du Cinéma*. Truffaut expressed an interest in avoiding the big-budget production, with its large technical crews, foreign actors, overabundance of screenwriters, and pressures from distributors, that the others shared. The solution he suggested was "working freely and making cheap films on simple subjects."

François Truffaut

Truffaut not only articulated the theory that gave New Wave cinema its direction and drive, but he also proved to be one of the most versatile and durable of the cinema *auteurs*. His *The 400 Blows*, along with Godard's *Breathless* (*À Bout de Souffle* [1959]), came to be regarded as the key work to launch the movement. Truffaut's subsequent films have shown a wide range of moods and styles. His short, *Les Mistons* (1958), and his first feature, *The 400 Blows*, are models of grace and humor with something of a social conscience. In the former, he examines with affection a group of boys engaged in games and pranks in a sometimes humorous, sometimes painful passage from childhood to adolescence. In the latter, he suggests the strains of his own childhood as he follows the boy from a schoolroom confrontation (he is punished for cribbing an essay from Balzac, whom he idolizes) to his home, where he faces his parent's resentment, to his forays into petty larceny. Truffaut's disturbed childhood, which involved a period of confinement in a reform school as well as association with a local film club, has entered into much of his work. *The 400 Blows* and his more recent *Day for Night*

(1973), though light years apart in virtually every respect, are clearly both autobiographical.

The 400 Blows, which won Truffaut the Best Director award at Cannes in 1959, shows little of the self-con-

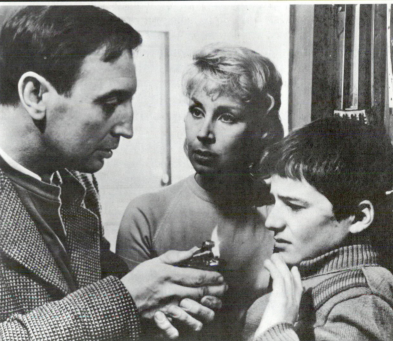

► François Truffaut (1932–1985), critic, theorist, and director of New Wave films.

► From *The 400 Blows* (1959). Reflecting Truffaut's own childhood, this film is the first of several by the director that trace the passage of Antoine (played by Jean-Pierre Léaud in all films) from childhood to adulthood.

scious reaction to previous cinema styles and subjects that characterizes many New Wave films. Rather, it is a cinematic idyll, which combines the poetry, compassion, and realism of such directors as de Sica and the American documentary filmmaker Robert Flaherty. The combination of the lyrical and documentary is characteristic of much of Trauffaut's work. (*The Wild Child* [1970] and *Small Change* [1976] are good examples.) In *The 400 Blows,* Truffaut neither provides pat explanations of Antoine's conflicts and delinquency nor sentimentalizes them. The final freeze frame of Antione's face as he rushes to the sea suggests both kinds of restraint. Truffaut is able to romanticize about the innocence of youth without becoming indulgent. He also incorporates a revolutionary theme—much in the spirit of Vigo's *Zéro de Conduite*—while using quite conventional cinematic technique.

Aside from the works of Godard, the film that came closest to the spirit of nihilism in new French cinema was *Shoot the Piano Player* (1960), which Truffaut made as a kind of homage to the American gangster film. More significantly, however, the film attempted to defy any typing or characterization as to genre, mood, or form, and became a reflection on the contradictory, unexplained, and unresolved incidents of life. Charlie, a former concert pianist who has taken a job as piano player in a bar, tries to help his two brothers escape gangsters. Charlie accidentally kills the bartender; Lena, the waitress with whom Charlie has become involved, is shot in a showdown gun battle; and Charlie's brother Fido, who has been kidnapped by the gangsters, is saved. Truffaut's mimicry of the plots of the American "B" gangster film here is his way of paying homage to the movies while at the same time providing a framework for his shifting style and humor. Truffaut himself has admitted to the self-indulgence of the film, which he made to please himself and other movie buffs.

In *Jules and Jim* (1961), Truffaut celebrated both the freedom of the human spirit and the freedom of the cinema, but in a quieter, less flamboyant way than previously. This film tells the story of the friendship between two men—a Frenchman and a German—and their relationship with Catherine, the impulsive, free-spirited woman they both love. The film sustains a delicate lyric quality that surpasses Truffaut's first feature and is never quite recaptured in his next several works. Camera zooms, slow motion, and freeze frames are employed to reinforce the idyllic mood. Catherine's contradictory, even self-destructive, nature adds a sense of sobering reality to the film. As the third of Truffaut's New Wave efforts, *Jules and Jim* met with both commercial success and critical respect and established Truffaut as one of Europe's outstanding directors. Even

as the New Wave began to subside, Truffaut was only beginning a distinguished career as international *auteur.*

Jean-Luc Godard

Like Truffaut, Jean-Luc Godard came to directing via film criticism. His first feature, *Breathless* (1959), which Truffaut helped script, reflects Truffaut and Godard's shared commitment to the cheaply and simply made film. From here, however, the two directors' cinematic approaches vary widely. Godard clearly uses film for stylistic experimentation, and in his work subject matter has little meaning outside the context of film. *Breathless* is both a celebration of the antihero, here a small-time gangster, and a satire of the American "B" pictures that feature antiestablishment protagonists. In *A Woman Is a Woman* (1961), Godard again produced a tribute to an American film genre—this time the Hollywood musical.

In his work, Godard continually reminds his viewers that they are watching a film. In this he attempts to somewhat counter the tendency in traditional cinema of total absorption, and to keep the viewer at a distance that will permit a more objective view of the work. This technique quickly brought Godard under fire, evoking the charge that his use of the medium was self-conscious. The device is not peculiar to Godard, however. Truffaut and Alain Resnais have both tried, using varying means, to counter the conditioning that puts a viewer in lockstep with narrative development. And Ingmar Bergman draws the viewer out of the story in both *Persona* and *Passion of Anna* by "it's only a movie" techniques. Fellini in *8½* and Truffaut in *Day for Night* carry the device to the ultimate. In both these films, the central conflict is that of the filmmaker trying to make a film.

Although Godard shared New Wave celebrity with Truffaut as a result of his original contributions to the movement, he has not enjoyed the wider appeal that Truffaut gained through his later works. Godard's *Le Petit Soldat* (1960), *A Woman Is a Woman* (1961), and

(continued on page 268)

> Jean-Luc Godard (b. 1930), the radical among New Wave directors.

> From *Breathless* (1959). Jean Seberg and Jean-Paul Belmondo portray young rebels in Godard's tribute to the American gangster picture. This first film by Godard was based on a story by Truffaut. The use of improvisation in many scenes helped to place this film among the foundation works of the New Wave movement.

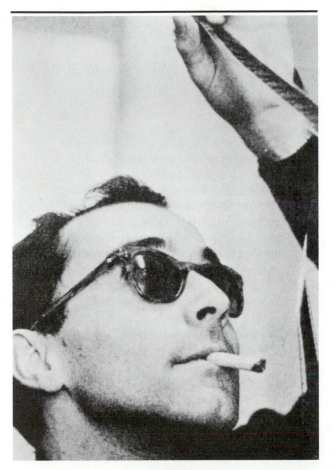

Godard on ''The Process of Cinema''

*W*hat I wanted to do was to depart from the conventional story and remake, but differently, everything that had already been done in the cinema. I also wanted to give the impression of just finding or experiencing the process of cinema for the first time. . . .

I realized, at a certain point, that *Breathless* was not at all what I believed it to be. I believed I'd made a realistic film and it wasn't that at all. . . .

I like *Breathless* enormously—for a certain period I was ashamed of it, but now I place it where it belongs: with *Alice in Wonderland*. I thought it was *Scarface*. . . .

—*From an interview with Jean-Luc Godard*, NY Film Bulletin *(1964)*

My Life to Live (1962) were all original studies of women in which the filmmaker's wife, Anna Karina, performed the leading roles. Though well crafted and insightful, these three lacked the cult appeal of *Breathless* and were given little attention by foreign audiences. His *Les Carabiniers* (1963), a parable on war, had less support, even from home audiences. Still, this film brought Godard further along the road in cinematizing his own attitudes toward his characters and their environments, and in providing more of an intellectual and nihilistic exercise than an emotional trip through conventional narrative.

Alain Resnais

Alain Resnais, an important creative force of the New Wave period, was not a typical New Wave director. Unlike Truffaut and Godard, after attending film school he came up through the ranks as an assistant director and a producer of short documentaries. His early short art documentaries, *Van Gogh* (1948) and *Guernica* (1950), and his study of Nazi concentration camps, *Night and Fog* (1955), established his reputation before he began directing feature films. While directing these shorts, Resnais developed the discipline that characterizes his later work and clearly distinguishes it from that of other New Wave directors. Dedicated to the mastery of material, Resnais works in the scenarist tradition from a highly polished script, using editing as the key to creative design. *Night and Fog,* which moves along a dual time track, was a prelude to the special structuring of film involving the interplay of past and present. This concept is central to the design of his major feature films.

Resnais's highly ordered but unconventional approach to the dramatic unities of time and place has brought his work under the harshest critical assault, in spite of his traditional background and relatively conventional production methods. Responding to Resnais's *Hiroshima Mon Amour* (1959), one critic observed, "He has the skill to say whatever he wants to say on film. Unhappily he has nothing, or almost nothing, to say." Centering on the fusion of present experience and the memory of past events, the film concerns a French actress who falls in love with a Japanese architect while working on a peace film in Hiroshima. A strain in the relationship develops as a result of the girl's memory of her experience at age eighteen, when she was in love with a German soldier during the occupation. (He was shot and she was banished in disgrace.) The cross-cutting between past and present becomes basic to the film's structure, both in the personal story and that of the city itself. As in *Night and Fog,* Resnais uses the interplay of present and past not simply to make direct com-

> ## Resnais on *Marienbad* and the Unconscious
>
> *F*or me *[Last Year at Marienbad]* is also an attempt, still very crude and primitive, to approach the complexity of thought and its mechanism. But I stress the fact that this is only a tiny step forward by comparison with what we should be able to do someday. I find that as soon as we delve into the Unconscious, an emotion may be born.
>
> —*Alain Resnais,* NY Film Bulletin *(March 1962)*

parisons, but also to comment upon the fragile quality of memory. The actress is fearful that she will forget her former lover and the horrors of Hiroshima, just as Resnais himself in *Night and Fog* expresses the fear that nobody "is on the lookout . . . to warn us of the coming of new executioners," because memories are so short. The film was the product of close collaboration between Resnais and scenarist Marguerite Duras, and it illustrates the importance of script in Resnais's approach to filmmaking. It was Resnais as editor, however, who gave the film its final balanced and cohesive form.

Following the enthusiastic reception of *Hiroshima Mon Amour* at the Cannes Film Festival in 1959, Resnais won the Golden Lion award at Venice in 1961 for his second feature, *Last Year at Marienbad.* With this film, a new storm of controversy broke over his unorthodox exploration of mental as well as physical time. Here, as in *Hiroshima,* Resnais and scenarist Alain Robbe-Grillet dealt with the visualization of mental images and gave qualities of the present to experiences of the past. Rather than moving into past tense, Resnais showed the past as present remembrance influenced by present stimuli. The film follows a group of people who roam through a baroque chateau in evening dress. It centers on the relationship between a man and a woman who are uncertain as to whether the events unfolding have occurred in the past, the present, or ever. The importance of mental reality to the film is suggested by scenarist Robbe-Grillet, who says, "When we say that what goes on in our minds is just as real as what goes on in front of our eyes, we are laying the foundation for a cinematic style which can switch to and fro between the things around us and the subject of our conversation." Resnais suggests that the film is about degrees of reality and that it explores the mental as well as the physical dimension of that reality.

From Sweden

Ingmar Bergman

Ingmar Bergman began his career as scenarist in collaboration with Alf Sjöberg, then the leading Swedish director, on the screenplay of Bergman's own short novel, *Frenzy* (1944). His career as director began in 1945 with *Crisis* and continued with virtually a film a year through the sixties. In Bergman's early period as filmmaker, he explored various moods and styles. *Sawdust and Tinsel* (*The Naked Night,* 1953) stands out as one of his important early accomplishments. It is a somber study of humiliation reminiscent of the Murnau and Dupont films of the twenties. Set in a circus world, the story involves the relationship between a circus owner and a passionate girl

performer for whom he has forsaken his family. The film served Bergman as a prelude to the dark poetry that would follow, but first the director revealed a much lighter vein in producing his two most successful comedies — *A Lesson in Love* (1954) and *Smiles of a Summer Night* (1955). Both are high-spirited commentaries on manners and morals, but the latter in particular shows the wit and elegance that contrast markedly with the somber, often anguished mood of the films that were to follow. Though *Smiles of a Summer Night* was Bergman's last successful comedy, it marked the beginning of an extraordinary series of accomplished works that received worldwide recognition and extended the European renaissance to the studios of Svenskfilmindustri, one of the oldest motion picture companies in the world.

Bergman's international debut occurred with the release of *The Seventh Seal* and *Wild Strawberries* in 1956 and 1957. At this time a cycle of Bergman films was shown in Paris, which helped provide the impetus for the New Wave. Truffaut explained the Bergman influence and his stature as *auteur*:

> He was a man who had done all we had dreamed of doing. He had written films as a novelist writes books. Instead of a pen he had used a camera. He was an author of cinema.

Bergman's imagination and mastery of technique began to flower in *The Seventh Seal,* a dark allegory on

▶ From *The Seventh Seal* (1956). Here Max von Sydow as the disillusioned knight returning from the Crusades meets Death on the way and later in the guise of a priest in the confessional. This film made Bergman a celebrity among European directors and began his cycle of films dealing with the conundrum of religious faith.

Bergman as Illusionist

"*M*aking films" is for me a necessity of nature, a need comparable to hunger and thirst. Some achieve self-expression by writing books, climbing mountains, beating their children, or dancing the samba. I happen to express myself by making films.

In making a film, I am thus guilty of fraud; I make use of an apparatus built to take advantage of a human physical imperfection, of an apparatus thanks to which I carry my audience, as if on a pendulum, from one mood to another mood at the opposite extreme: I make it laugh, cry out with fright, smile, believe in legends, become indignant, take offense, become enthusiastic, become bawdy, or yawn with boredom. Thus, I am no better than a fraud, no better than— considering that the public is aware of the deceit—an illusionist.

—*Ingmar Bergman, "What Is Making Film?"* Cahiers du Cinema *(July 1956)*

► From *Wild Strawberries* (1957). Dream imagery—both idyllic reminiscences of youthful romance and horrific visions of failure and death—are central to Bergman's study of old age. An automobile trip to receive an honorary degree provides the simple framework for the self-examination of Isak Borg at age seventy-eight. The film provided veteran filmmaker Victor Sjöström with the most impressive of several acting credits, this one shortly before his death.

man's search for God in a world of suffering and evil. The story is about a fourteenth-century knight who, on his journey home after a decade of crusading, meets Death, but gains a respite in order to resolve his doubts concerning God and the meaning of his existence. Plagued by his inability either to find God or end his belief in him, the knight journeys homeward with his squire, alternately appreciating the exquisite beauty and contentment of a family of wandering players and vicariously suffering the anguish of flagellation and witch burning inspired by the Church. In addition to its original scenario, Max von Sydow's performance as the knight is a distinguishing feature of the film. Also exceptional is Bergman's command of visual composition and his use of realistic detail in developing his metaphysical drama.

Bergman again focused on the search for the meaning of life and death in *Wild Strawberries,* but here he used contemporary setting and incident as the dramatic base, and reserved the allegory for the dreams and fanta-

sies of the central character. Isak Borg, who is summoned to receive an honorary degree for his service to science, is haunted by nightmares and recollections of his past that make him aware of his failures and the emptiness of his life. Here, using veteran Swedish director Victor Sjöström in the central role, Bergman once again had the opportunity to juxtapose the idyllic scenes of human feeling and aspiration with darker scenes of emptiness and fear. The summer retreat of Borg's boyhood and the nightmare in which he witnesses his own death are among the most memorable in film, both for their fine detail and the film's ability to contain them both.

The hope of finding God and meaningful human relationships continued to dominate Bergman's films. *The Virgin Spring* (1959), *Through a Glass Darkly* (1961), *Winter Light* (1962), and *The Silence* (1963) all grappled with these themes, but each became successively more somber and despairing. The miracle of the spring was followed by the faintly hopeful observation that

▲ From *The Virgin Spring* (1959). Bergman used a thirteenth-century Swedish ballad as the basis for the most brutal and yet most inspirational of his early films. It tells of a rather vain young girl who is brutally raped and murdered on her pilgramage to church. The father's ritual killing of the herdsmen responsible is followed by his vow to build a church on the site of her death. Ambiguity in good and evil provides a central motif that led to some of Bergman's most despairing works.

▲ From *The Virgin Spring.* Max von Sydow as the avenging father prepares for a ritual purification and murder.

▶ From *Through a Glass Darkly* (1961). This first of Bergman's "trilogy films"— *Winter Light* (1962) and *The Silence* (1963) completed the set—further intensified the director's study of despair over lost religious faith. The growing insanity of a girl, and its effect on loved ones, provides the narrative, and Bergman's own island retreat provides the setting.

"God is love" in *Through a Glass Darkly,* the first of what is considered Bergman's trilogy. A stark and desolate country parish provides the setting for the second film of the trilogy, *Winter Light,* in which a pastor finds himself in a spiritual vacuum through his inability to accept the love of his mistress, to comfort a despairing parishioner in fear of nuclear disaster, or to regain his own faith. In *The Silence,* which completes the trilogy, the search for God is abandoned. Here Bergman concentrates on the alienation and isolation of two sisters for whom meaningful human contact has been replaced by lustful indulgence. The trilogy, while further establishing Bergman's reputation, also marked his move toward even more subjective landscapes and set the stage for the intense psychological conflicts that were to characterize his later works.

Italian Encore

The original neorealist movement had run its course by the time de Sica's *Umberto D* was released in 1952. Although the neorealist films were still applauded by critics, worshipped by art-house patrons, and studied respectfully by filmmakers around the world, they were a flop with home audiences and criticized by both the Catholic church and the Italian government. When economic and social stability produced an appetite for romantic sensory delights, the reminders of poverty and social injustices that had been so much a part of the recent past were rejected by Italians. By the middle of the decade directors were turning to more fanciful and erotic themes, with such stars as Gina Lollobrigida, Silvana Mangano, and Sophia Loren, as a way of winning the patronage of Italian audiences. Unlike American filmgoers, and subsequently those of Europe, who were kept away from the theaters by television, the gregarious Italians were willing to support the moviegoing tradition as long as they were given the right attractions. And sex and spectacle proved to be the appropriate ingredients for the times.

The arrival of the Italian love goddesses and earth mothers (often one and the same) during the midfifties did not really bring the neorealist movement to an end, but rather marked a critical stage in its evolution. Ermanno Olmi's *Sound of Trumpets* (1961) extended the spirit and much of the style of the original movement, blending them with compassion and a realistic perspective. In this film, the anxiety and exhilaration of entering the adult world was set against the beginning of a deadly life routine. It was a mild but moving protest against the dehumanizing effects of big business told through the story of a shy boy who lands his first job with a large corporation. Visconti's *Rocco and His Brothers* (1960) was a study of the corrupting influence of city life on a family of five brothers who migrate to Milan from their impoverished farm. Both films, one by a pioneer of the movement and the other by a relatively unknown director, were very much in the spirit of the original movement, though both revealed less of the rough-hewn style characteristic of Rossellini and de Sica.

Federico Fellini

The pivotal director in the evolution of the Italian film, however, was Federico Fellini, whose *La Strada* (1954) was to provide the link between neorealism and the "new Italian cinema" to follow. Although Fellini's approach

---

Fellini's Road to Realism

I think all my work is definitely in the neorealist style, even if in Italy today some people don't think so. But this is a long story. For me, neorealism is a way of seeing reality without prejudice, without the interference of conventions — just parking yourself in front of reality without any preconceived ideas.

For me, to make a picture is like leaving on a trip. And the most interesting part of a trip is what you discover on the way.

—From an interview with Federico Fellini, Film Book #1 *(1959)*

---

was basically neorealistic — he used real locations and his scripts developed from a single situation — the focus of the film was on the individual rather than the relationship of the individual to his society. Loneliness, the need for love, the tragedy of selfish cruelty, and ignorance of emotional needs, though hardly original themes, were given a controlled and understanding treatment within unadorned, often stark settings that reflected the personal emptiness experienced by the film's characters. Fellini chose the story of a simple-minded waif who becomes the mate and assistant to a brutish migrant (played by Anthony Quinn), who travels through the country on a motorcycle trailer performing a strong-man act. Complementing Fellini's own contribution to the film was that of his wife, Giulietta Masina, in the role of Gelsomina. Her performance was universally acclaimed as a masterpiece in characterization. In Fellini's next film, *The Nights of Cabiria* (1957), Masina's acting and Fellini's imagery once again combined effectively to tell the story of a lonely streetwalker whose spirit and hope remained unshaken though she is deceived and exploited by several men.

In the same year, 1957, Michelangelo Antonioni made *Il Grido* ("The Cry"), which served as a prelude to his major works of the sixties. By 1960, with the release

From *La Dolce Vita* (1960). This was Federico Fellini's exotic compilation of episodes in the life of an Italian journalist observing and being drawn into the high life of Rome's jet set. The film was greeted by hostile reaction from the Vatican (mainly for its depiction of a phony miracle) and gained wide popularity in the United States. To Fellini it brought worldwide recognition as a major figure among the postneorealist directors.

of both Fellini's *La Dolce Vita* ("The Sweet Life") and Antonioni's *L'Avventura,* the two directors were firmly established as the leaders of a new Italian movement. Though their styles were virtually the antithesis of one another, together the two led a move toward psychological subtlety, social sophistication, and aesthetic experimentalism that was to distinguish their own films and influence their contemporaries.

In *I Vitelloni* (1953), *La Strada* (1954), and *Nights of Cabiria* (1957), Fellini explored human emotions and social forces in contemporary Italy with a fluent, assured mastery of both his characters and their environments. In subsequent films he turned to more expansive and elaborate themes and, in the rococo tradition of the early Italian spectacles, achieved monumental studies of the mores and life styles of a decadent, pleasure-loving society. In *La Dolce Vita* Fellini dropped the single situation and close psychological study to present a grand fresco of depravity and tragedy in Rome's social set. Using a young journalist as a focal point, he leads the viewer through a series of incidents representing societal values, and one by one reveals the corruption and hypocrisy of each. Although the product of realist tradition, Fellini turned to the peculiar, the bizarre, and, if in no other way exceptional, the larger-than-life in his study of "the sweet life." The result was the Rome of Fellini's imagination, more valid as vision than any documentary record.

Fellini's next vision of contemporary Italian life, the movie *8¹/₂,* embraced the director's own struggle and doubts regarding his role as filmmaker and is considered by many to be his most accomplished work. It provides a masterful, if not always lucid, image of the film director's worlds of reality and illusion.

Michelangelo Antonioni

Antonioni had his apprenticeship during the neorealist period, when he wrote film criticism for a local Ravenna newspaper, produced documentary shorts, and wrote screenplays, one for a Rossellini film. Antonioni came into international prominence in 1960 with *L'Avventura,* the first film in his trilogy on emotional bankruptcy and ennui (*La Notte* and *Eclipse* came in the following two years).

In Antonioni's earlier, less celebrated work, *Le Amiche* ("The Girl Friends" [1955]), and *Il Grido* (1957), it was already clear that his approach to the medium differed sharply from Fellini's; now their styles were becoming directly opposite. Where Fellini was increasingly the extroverted, flamboyant showman who leaned toward the extravagant, opulent, and often bizarre, Antonioni was self-disciplined, restrained, and looking to keep every element of a film under complete control and in the service of theme. His trilogy films were successively less plot-oriented (if anyone having seen only the first can imagine that) and more closely focused on the subtlety of character relationships and inner conflicts. With *The Red Desert* (1964), the alienation and disorientation of Giuliana are not only central to the film's statement, they are expressed in visual terms. With his mastery over detail and, in this film, with the aid of color, Antonioni could give a visual representation to the psychological condition, and *mise-en-scène,* or total visual conception of the film, now became a map of the mental landscape.

With *Red Desert,* Antonioni completed his Italian period in filmmaking and moved to production abroad. The move marked a major change in the austere and uncompromising style of this film moralist, who shared with Fellini the major responsibility for the direction of the new look in neorealism.

From Britain: The Kitchen-Sink Realists

Britain's film legacy from the pre-World War II years had been weighted most heavily in the direction of the documentary form. Out of the welter of silent and early sound comedies, spectacles, and intrigues, which were made to compete with the products of the German, Soviet, and French golden ages and the staggering invasion of American films, only a handful of works garnered anything like an international reputation. These were the early works of Alfred Hitchcock and Alexander Korda's mounting of *The Private Life of Henry VIII* (1933). While John Grierson and his associates and disciples were combining social purpose and artistic experimentation in the first documentary movement, feature filmmaking was falling

From *L'Avventura* (1960). Michelangelo Antonioni joined Fellini in affirming the arrival of the New Italian Cinema with this film, made the same year as *La Dolce Vita.* Its unadorned, uncompromising, and frequently enigmatic look at human relationships contrasts with the Fellini work. It is the first of a three-film trilogy on the subject that continued with *La Notte* and *Eclipse.*

victim to the "quota law," which limited the import of Hollywood features in proportion to the number of films made at home. As a result, quickly and cheaply made British films were becoming the ransom for the highly prized American features.

In the decade following World War II, the British feature began to distinguish itself in several diverse genres. Droll satirical comedies made for Ealing Studio by such directors as Alexander Mackendrick (*Whiskey Galore* [1948], *The Man in the White Suit* [1951], *The Ladykillers* [1955]), Robert Hamer (*Kind Hearts and Coronets* [1949]), and Charles Crichton (*The Lavender Hill Mob* [1951]), had popular appeal and achieved moderate critical acceptance. These films also won plaudits and a boost to star status for such players as Alec Guinness, Peter Sellers, and Terry Thomas.

Also distinguishing themselves during the period and establishing a strong tradition in dramatic narrative were such directors as David Lean, Anthony Asquith, and Noel Langley. Their films included several adaptations from classic literature, with Lean's *Great Expectations* (1946) and *Oliver Twist* (1947) gaining prominence. Most prestigious of the dramatic features, however, were the costume spectacles, including two ballet extravaganzas — *The Red Shoes* (1948) and *The Tales of Hoffman* (1950). Laurence Olivier's acting/directing triumphs in *Hamlet* (1948) and *Richard III* (1955) were distinguished follow-ups to his *Henry V* (1944), and these films further extended the genre of literary and stage works. Original screenplays were best represented in the works of Carol Reed (*Odd Man Out* [1946] and *The Third Man* [1949]), whose *The Stars Look Down* (1939) had been a foreshadowing of the social realist cinema to come.

Another group of films was given virtually no notice, but were the most significant in terms of the direction of British cinema in the late fifties and sixties. These were the products of the "free cinema" movement. Following in the tradition in social realism established by the original documentarians, directors and writers who wanted to "celebrate the significance of the everyday" came together between 1956 and 1958 to examine, via film, life in the streets, dance halls, clubs, and markets of the British working class. Their purpose was to fulfill what Lindsay Anderson, one of the directors, saw as the principle to which the movement was dedicated: "If you're going to get attention, you've got to get together and make a row." The row was a reaction to what Anderson called the "emotionally frozen" British features currently in vogue. Anderson's *O Dreamland* (1954) is a harshly satirical commentary on the seedy and hollow pleasures of the "Fun Fair," or amusement park. Karel Reisz dealt with the drab routine of work and play in *We*

Are the Lambeth Boys (1958), a study of a progressive London youth club. Tony Richardson, another free cinema pioneer, worked with Reisz on a look at London youth in a dance hall setting — *Momma Don't Allow* (1956). Another Anderson work, *Every Day Except Christmas* (1957), was a lyrical study of the fruit and flower dealers of Covent Garden Market. Like many of the documentaries of the previous two decades, this film celebrated the work ethic in Britain.

While these filmmakers were developing style through their experiments in social observation, young novelists and playwrights such as John Osborne, Arnold Wesker, Alan Sillitoe, David Storey, and Shelagh Delaney were producing first works of their own. These works represented a challenge by East End and North Country working-class liberals to the more affluent, conservative, and traditional values of Southern and metropolitan populations. The social realist tradition received a fresh stimulus from the dramatic and literary arts, and the free cinema filmmakers moved from documentary shorts to narrative features, with novelists and playwrights creating the scenarios from their own works.

Jack Clayton

The director who launched the movement, sometimes referred to as the "British antiestablishment film," was not a documentarian, however. Jack Clayton had come up through the ranks in feature-film production as production manager and producer. His *Room at the Top* (1959) became the first of the new socially conscious features and set the pattern for several key characteristics of the genre: the drab industrial setting, the class consciousness, the preoccupations and drives that motivate the workers, and finally the young hero who gave human form to social protest. The hero in Clayton's film is Joe Lampton (Laurence Harvey), an ex-RAF sergeant who strives for social status. While realizing his goal — by marrying the daughter of a wealthy industralist — he destroys the woman he really loves and finds his upward mobility a hollow victory. This first feature film by Clayton did more than establish a pattern for protest against the drab and restricted life of the working class in the industrial North; it also depicted the dreariness at the top of the social ladder. Harvey's portrayal of Joe as the scheming and cynical opportunist was not the prevailing view of young rebellion, but does provide the necessary perspective for viewing the class snobbishness and lack of emotional depth of the industrialist and daughter with whom Joe casts his lot. The film's strength rests not only on the sense of social realism Clayton captured with his camera, but also on his choice and handling of actors. And

From *Room at the Top* (1959). The new films from Great Britain, characterized as "antiestablishment," strongly reflected the durability of the English class system. In this Jack Clayton film, Laurence Harvey plays a working-class social climber who sacrifices his relationship with the woman he loves (Simone Signoret) for social status via marriage to the daughter of a wealthy industrialist.

the generally exceptional performances by the cast are highlighted by Simone Signoret's particularly arresting performance as Joe's mistress.

Tony Richardson

Tony Richardson left the London stage to begin his career as a filmmaker and made a major contribution to the new British movement. Working with adaptations from works by John Osborne (*Look Back in Anger* [1958] and *The Entertainer* [1960]) and Shelagh Delaney (*A Taste of Honey* [1961]), Richardson created his own gray world of dingy flats, sleazy seaside midways and music halls, and shabby, smoke-filled pubs. Although Richardson occasionally tried to open up the plays by moving outdoors, the result was something of a forced attempt at naturalism. The drab, airless interiors usually provided

the settings for powerful dramatic moments. These came to life chiefly through the combined talents of scenarist, director, and cast, the latter including such talented performers as Richard Burton, Rita Tushingham, Laurence Olivier, and Joan Plowright. Olivier's portrayal of Archie Rice, the broken-down song and dance man in *The Entertainer*, is both a tour de force for the actor and an expression of Richardson's ability to adapt theater to film without becoming self-consciously cinematic.

In his next work, *The Loneliness of the Long Distance Runner* (1962), based on an Alan Sillitoe story, Richardson moved more clearly into the style of the British realist tradition. This film is a study of an eighteen-year-old boy from the slums who is arrested for robbing a bakery and becomes a top track star of a Borstal reformatory. Through flashbacks Richardson establishes both in action and decor, the grim realism of

From *Saturday Night and Sunday Morning* (1961). This contribution to the British antiestablishment genre by Karel Reisz found its young hero in the Nottingham factory worker, played by Albert Finney in his first major screen credit. The film follows the dreary routine of the young lathe operator through binges, pranks, and sexual escapades.

Colin's life in the slums—Colin sees his mother with a lover before his father is buried; he moves through disarray, noise, and general dreariness in his working-class neighborhood. Here Richardson's earlier training in the free cinema movement, rather than his theatrical background, becomes apparent. Also, he comes closest here to the antiestablishment mood that characterizes the genre. He gives Colin a chance to rebel against the Borstal system and the society that produced it by participating in a competition with members of a public school for a coveted trophy.

Richardson collaborated as codirector with Karel Reisz on *Momma Don't Allow* (1956) for the free cinema movement. Reisz worked again with Richardson in 1961, this time as director on the film Richardson produced that seems now to be the most controlled and uncompromising of the social realist films. *Saturday Night and Sunday Morning,* based on another Sillitoe

story, makes few of the usual appeals to viewer indulgence. It neither proclaims its role as social observer nor impresses with its search for naturalistic detail. With a loose, free-style structure reminiscent of some of the early Italian neorealist films, this film follows the little daily doings of its hero, Arthur, with the unbroken and deadly regularity of a metronome—from factory job to row house "telly" to Saturday night drunk at the local pub to Sunday morning recuperation on the river bank. But Arthur Seaton, a lathe operator from the industrial Midlands, is far from being the embittered young victim of social injustice. Rather, he accepts his dreary routine, occasionally attempting to break the monotony by inventing pranks or engaging in sexual escapades, or, when all else fails, indulging in the escape that itself has become part of the routine—the Saturday night binge. "What I'm out for is a good time," Arthur declares, "all the rest is propaganda." Reisz's control of both his char-

Seeing Ourselves on Film

*T*here is no doubt that *Saturday Night and Sunday Morning* has been a big financial success. And I believe it has been a notable *creative* success, too. Ordinary audiences recognized themselves on the screen for the first time, and that they were not going to see some kind of unreal, overly comic or overglamorized world. Instead they were seeing people whom they could recognize on every street corner. This film expressed something that was close to a whole working-class section of England, and therefore people went to see and enjoy it because of this; because the film was no longer remote, but was something that they lived with every day.

— *Tony Richardson, in* Films and Filming *(June 1961)*

acters and the milieu of Nottingham's factories and pubs gives the film authenticity and dramatic strength despite its low-key style. This style won the movement as a whole, and this film in particular, the name "kitchen sink realism" to describe the utter homeliness of the setting.

Lindsay Anderson

Lindsay Anderson left his work in the free cinema movement to spend several years in the theater. When he returned to begin a career in feature filmmaking, he joined his old co-workers Reisz and Richardson in forming the core of the new movement. *This Sporting Life* (1963), which Reisz produced, is a study of the physical and emotional strains on a British rugby player — Frank, played by Richard Harris — who finds the sport a means of social climbing. His reward, however, is a hopeless relationship with his widowed landlady and exploitation by unscrupulous sports promoters. Like Reisz, Anderson employed many of the documentary techniques he learned in his years with the free cinema movement. The rugby field during a match becomes a brutal challenge not only for the players, but for Anderson's camera, which bobs, weaves, and jostles, newsreel fashion, into the center of the action. Like the work of Reisz and others of the genre, it has an appropriately gray Midlands city setting and equally gloomy prospects for its hero's future. Unlike Reisz, however, who takes a simple and direct narrative approach, Anderson works the narrative through a series of flashbacks to establish Frank's professional and personal commitments and drives. Even Richardson's flashback technique in *The Loneliness of the Long Distance Runner* seems ordered and conventional by comparison with the spontaneous and disassociated flashback sequences here. Though strongly criticized by many, the device gives Anderson the means of exploring the character and makes the film more of a psychological than a sociological study.

The antiestablishment films were not the sole province of the free cinema directors. Several other filmmakers provided variations on the spirit of social protest in the early sixties. John Schlesinger, whose training was in television documentary, contributed *A Kind of Loving* (1962), which matched the work of Reisz or Richardson in achieving a near-documentary style. Sidney Furie's *The Leather Boys* (1963) featured naturalistic acting that included improvised dialogue. An intrigue of the occult, Bryan Forbes's *Seance on a Wet Afternoon* (1964), and Jack Cardiff's adaptation of D. H. Lawrence's *Sons and Lovers* (1960), though hardly at the center of social realist cinema, commanded respect for their visual detail and sense of both the social and physical climate, which had become a significant trademark of British cinema.

By the middle of the decade, the focus had begun to shift unmistakably. Less angry in tone and less devoted to the "kitchen sink" school of realism, such films as *Alfie* (1966), *Morgan* (1966), *Joanna* (1968), *Georgy Girl* (1966), and *Darling* (1965) showed interest in the social environments in which their characters moved but were set in color-bedecked London rather than some dreary Midland town. The characters in these films were vaguely better off and more devoted to play than work than their North Country cousins.

With Richard Lester's *The Knack* (1965) and his Beatles films, *A Hard Day's Night* (1964) and *Help* (1965), the focus shifted even further away from social realist cinema to a form displaying narrative intrigues and eye-catching visual effects that by the 1970s were resulting in films indistinguishable from the Hollywood product.

From the East: Japan and India

In 1951, six years before the Bergman festival in Paris and eight years before the New Wave was signaled at Cannes, a Japanese film was shown at the Venice Festival that caused critics and devotees to sit up and take notice. The film, *Rashomon,* was adapted by its director, Akira Kurosawa, from two Japanese short stories. Set in Kyoto in the year 1200, the film consisted of four conflicting accounts of a single incident: a bandit attack on a samurai's wife and the death of the husband. Each of the characters directly involved (the wife, the bandit, and the dead husband, who speaks through a medium), and a presumably unbiased witness (a woodcutter) gives a significantly different account of the event. Despite its four-part narrative, the film's function was not the telling of a story but the fashioning of an intricate parable on the nature of truth — that which we as individuals perceive, or that which we want others to believe.

With the release of *Rashomon* in Western Europe and the United States, it became apparent that Japan could boast a master director whose sophistication in handling his complex subject matter and whose superb pictorial sense were equal to those of any Western filmmakers. This reputation was further supported by other Kurosawa films — *Ikiru* (1952), *The Magnificent Seven* (1954), *Throne of Blood* (1957), *Yojimbo* (1961) — all of which demonstrated the director's mastery over both contemporary and traditional subjects.

Kurosawa also adapted a number of Western classics to the Japanese film: Dostoevsky's *The Idiot,* Gorki's *The Lower Depths,* Shakespeare's *Macbeth,* and even a nonclassic such as Ed McBain's 86th precinct detective story, which he turned into *High and Low* (1962).

Once the West had discovered Japanese cinema through the works of Kurosawa, it seriously examined films by other Japanese directors. Such distinguished and varied works as *Ugetsu* (1952), by the veteran Kenji Mizoguchi, and *Gate of Hell* (1953), a full-color love story and intrigue by Teinosuke Kinugasa, received respectful attention and even adulation by critics and film-art devotees. Other films, such as Kon Ichikawa's *The Burmese Harp* (1955) and *Fires on the Plains* (1959), and Yasujiro Ozu's *Tokyo Story* (1953) and *Early Spring* (1956) reflect contemporary urban life. Kaneto Shindo's *The Island* (1962) and Hiroshi Teshigahara's *Woman in the Dunes* (1964), both about the survival of primitive ways of life, have continued to enrich the international film scene, as has Kaneto Shindo's tribute to Mizoguchi, *A Life of a Film Director* (1975). Japan's film output had been virtually unknown outside its own borders before 1950, but by the mid-sixties this country was one of the most highly respected sources of film in the world.

► From *Rashomon* (1951). This film by Akira Kurosawa, the first Japanese film seen by many Western audiences, won the Grand Prix at the 1951 Venice Film Festival. In a daring exercise devoted to a search for the meaning of truth, Kurosawa took an incident involving a bandit's attack on the wife of a Samurai and repeated it from the viewpoint of each of the three principals involved as well as that of an "unbiased" witness.

Satyajit Ray from India was another non-Western filmmaker to become enshrined in the pantheon of the world's great directors, and to have his work reach an international market. He made little concession to European and American standards, and his work in many respects seems the most distinctive in style. A slow, serene, lyrical kind of eloquence marks his films, which are dedicated to revealing the everyday life, love, joy, and pain of ordinary Indian people. Despite this distinctiveness in style, a comparison with the spirit of the films of Robert Flaherty and Vittorio de Sica is inevitable. The work that won him wide recognition in the fifties was his Apu trilogy — *Pather Panchali* (1954), *Aparajito* (1956), and *The World of Apu* (1959) — which follows the lives of three generations of an Indian family who struggle with the conflict between ancient tradition and modern life. Ray, like Kurosawa, led his nation into the international film arena and gave screen narrative a new dimension. With *Kanchenjunga* (1962) he further affirmed his status as *auteur* by writing his own scenario and composing his own musical score.

The Quality of Truth in Film

I don't like morals or messages. This story says true things about India. That was enough for me. It had the quality of truth, the quality that always impresses me, wherever I see it and as I have seen it in films such as *Nanook* and *Louisiana Story*, *Earth* and *The Southerner.*''

—*From an interview with Satyajit Ray*, Film Quarterly *(Winter 1958)*

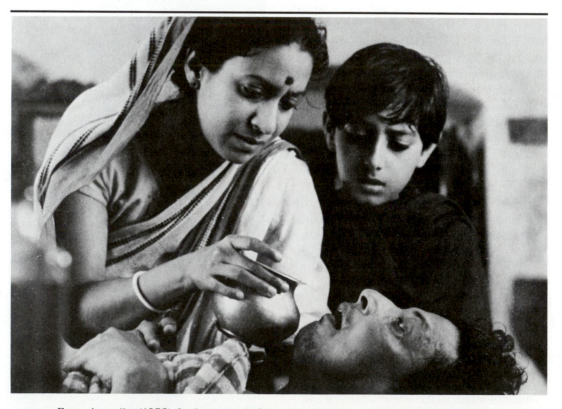

▲ From *Aparajito* (1956). In the second of the three films in which Satyajit Ray follows three generations of a Bengali family, the boy Apu is seen crossing into adulthood on the death of his father, after which he moves to Calcutta as a working student. Despite the film's evocation of an Eastern culture, familial ties and stresses give the work a universal appeal.

*T*he New Wave should not be measured by the failures that followed the first excitement of discovery, but by the successes of the filmmakers who went on . . . That the New Wave directors ultimately created a body of work that will influence all the future filmmakers around the world was not simply because they presented a united front at one point in history. It's because they had the courage and talent — as well as the opportunity — to pursue their particular obsessions.

— *Vincent Canby, "How the Mature New Wave Shapes New Films,"* New York Times *(February 26, 1984)*

Wrap-Up

The beginning of the New Wave cinema from Europe and the East is much easier to pinpoint than its end. In fact, it could be argued that, given some "refinements" or other modifications in form, and the coming and going of individual contributors, the movement continued into the seventies and eighties. But by the mid-sixties a number of things had occurred to suggest that the movement had run its course; if there was not a sense of completion, there were harbingers of change. Owing partly to the inspiration and new directions of the movement itself, other national genres began to rival the Western European output both in critical reception and marketability. From Eastern Europe, from emerging Third World nations, and from the United States (although not necessarily from Hollywood), came new works that were earning prestige and international distribution. At the same time, a general crossing-over, or blending of talents in Western Europe, plus a migration of directors, and the international backing of film projects occurred. These developments ushered in a new ecumenical era in which films could retain a distinctiveness in style but no longer lent themselves to easy classification by national origin.

11

New International Cinema (1963– Present)

Focus

Film has been international or ecumenical in character since its very beginnings. As we have seen, early inventors borrowed freely from one another in developing equipment for recording and projecting the moving image; pioneer filmmakers found inspiration in the works of foreign directors as well as compatriots; and exchanges in technology led to early standardization, which in turn permitted an international traffic. As early as the turn of the century, foreign film exchanges, which provided for the distribution of imported works, proliferated on both sides of the Atlantic.

Somewhat later in the silent period—in modest numbers in the teens and reaching invasive proportions in the twenties—talent in the film industries of foreign countries immigrated to the United States. The result was a blending of European and American techniques and artistry. The importing of directors, producers, screenwriters, designers, and actors from Germany alone was so extensive that it brought about the "Germanization of Hollywood." A harbinger of true international production came in 1928, with the production of the last important film of the silent era, *The Passion of Joan of Arc*. This French-made film had a Danish director, Carl Dreyer; a Hungarian cinematographer, Rudolph Maté; a German designer, Hermann Warm; and an Italian star, Falconetti.

Outside the major Western production centers of France, Great Britain, Italy, Germany, and the United States, filmmaking and the marketing of motion pictures were considerably less developed and more parochial. Countries such as Japan and India had had early starts and vigorous production histories, yet marketing there was limited. Whereas American audiences were aware of an Eisenstein, and European audiences of a Griffith or a

De Mille, long before the arrival of sound, both European and American viewers had to wait for the arrival of Akira Kurosawa and Satyajit Ray in the late fifties to recognize the Japanese and Indian cinemas.

In the West, despite the early exchange of talent, technology, and technique, films through the forties and fifties continued to exhibit an easily identifiable national style. But a new international look began to emerge in the sixties, and by the mid-seventies, a clear evolution in production and distribution patterns was revealed both in the complexion of films and in the prevailing attitudes (or lack thereof) regarding national genres.

The new look of films involved the emergence of major directors of international reputation who had outgrown the bounds of their native cinemas. It was also marked by the emergence (or in many instances the eventual eclipse) of new national industries on the world market, and by a homogenization of talents and national character only hinted at in 1928, when Dreyer produced *The Passion of Joan of Arc*. This move toward integrating industries of many nations involved countries with a long tradition of filmmaking behind them as well as newly emerging ones. And for countries in both categories this often meant an unbreakable link with the American industry.

The Star *Auteurs*

Certain film directors stand alone, not only because they have distinctive styles and fresh ideas, or because their work contains old and profound ideas freshly expressed, but also because they emerge at times propitious for influencing the direction of cinematic art. If they are prolific enough, and unrivaled in their art within their own countries, such filmmakers become one-person national genres. Méliès, Porter, and Griffith came close to holding this distinction in the early days, while the Swedish directors Victor Sjöström and Mauritz Stiller shared the honor, as did Rossellini and de Sica, Truffaut and Godard, and even Fellini and Antonioni some years later.

The worldwide expansion in production has made such prominence and singular identification with a nation's film art less likely today. Still, a number of filmmakers have gained a place in the pantheon of international directors.* This they accomplished

*

Andrew Sarris devised this category originally for the most highly esteemed of American directors in *The American Cinema*.

through the exceptional quality of their work and the universality of its appeal not in one instance but in their films over time. These filmmakers, whose early careers were covered in Chapter 10, include such New Wave luminaries as Bergman, Truffaut, Fellini, and Antonioni, who have gone beyond the bounds of their national industries and have become, like a Cervantes, a Chopin, or a Gauguin, artists who belong to the world. Also included are such directors as India's Satyajit Ray, Spain's Luis Buñuel, and Japan's Akira Kurosawa, who have brought international recognition to their respective styles and, for the first time, the national heritages they reflect.

Ingmar Bergman

Sweden's Ingmar Bergman has become synonymous with his nation's industry and recognized as an important influence in setting the course of cinematic form and function. A number of factors help to explain Bergman's success and prominence. First, he has a long tradition of prestigious filmmaking behind him, with a particularly rich heritage in the works of Sjöström and Stiller, from whom he took inspiration and instruction. Also, through his experience as a theater director, Bergman learned to handle actors, and he has assembled a distinguished company of players who perform on both stage and screen. Finally, in working on his first screenplay, for Alf Sjöberg's *Frenzy* in 1944, and many screenplays for subsequent films of his own, Bergman has become accomplished in the art of the film scenario.

It is difficult to generalize about the characteristics and qualities of Bergman's work. One critic has called him "a metaphysical poet." Bergman himself has described himself as a conjuror and entertainer, but he has also indicated that he is "trying to tell the truth about the human condition," and, as suggested in Chapter 10, the majority of his films have addressed themselves directly to the fundamentals of human existence—the meaning of birth, life, death—and such human values as faith, love, understanding, and fulfillment. The human being's basic solitude in a hostile environment and the loneliness that results from the inability to feel or communicate emotions are pervasive Bergman themes. In such films as *The Silence* (1963) and *Fanny and Alexander* (1983), the bewildering experiences of youth in an adult world are central. Stylistically, Bergman's films are characterized by reserve in the use of cinematic technique, but they also show a technical perfection and a special compositional quality that reveal Bergman as a master of *mise-en-scène*.

In recent years, Bergman's work has continued to display both profundity of theme and stylistic control, which together result in images of extraordinary power and beauty. In *Shame* (1968) he moved beyond the original queries into the metaphysical to examine the impact of war on individuals, and in several more recent works he studies the impact of individual wills and personalities on one another. *Persona* (1966), *The Passion of Anna* (1969), *The Touch* (1971), *Cries and Whispers* (1972), *Scenes from a Marriage* (1973), *Face to Face* (1975), and *Autumn Sonata* (1978) are all intensive studies of human contact and psychic relationships that lead in some instances to personality transfer and in others to emotional bondage. In all these films we find Bergman's relentless probing of the human, particularly the female, psyche. *The Magic Flute* (1970) provides a refreshing shift in mood and style in the midst of these "emotional battles" and reveals more of Bergman as a theatrical showman. This work is a film version of the Mozart opera, produced originally for Swedish television. In *Fanny and Alexander* (1983), which Bergman has called his last film, he returns to personal trauma, this time within the broader, colorful context of family and theater life in turn-of-the-century Sweden. In its combination of fresco setting and biographical roots, this film comes closer than any of his films to the grand manner of Federico Fellini.

Among Bergman's many accomplishments within the Swedish tradition of filmmaking is his impeccable craftsmanship in visually representing his themes and his

The Inspiration for a Film

A film for me begins with something very vague—a chance remark or a bit of conversation, a hazy but agreeable event unrelated to any particular situation. It can be a few bars of music, a shaft of light across the street. Sometimes in my work at the theatre I have envisioned actors made up for yet unplayed roles.

—*Introduction,* Four Screenplays by Ingmar Bergman

ability to provide intriguing if disquieting intellectual exercises. He has also earned the distinction of being one of the most widely analyzed and criticized of film directors, and has to some degree fulfilled his announced purpose as filmmaker: "to please, to distress, to mortify, and to injure."

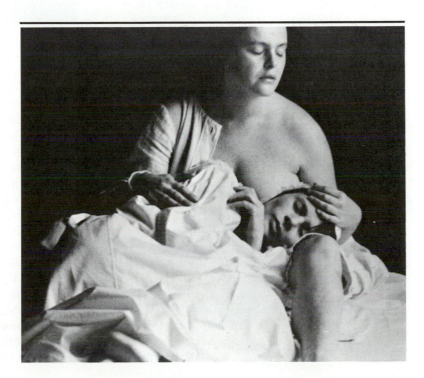

From *Cries and Whispers* (1972). Ingrid Thulin, Harriet Anderson, and Liv Ullmann, three of Bergman's leading performers, are brought together in a penetrating study of the female psyche. Anderson is seen here in the arms of her nurse, played by Kari Sylvan.

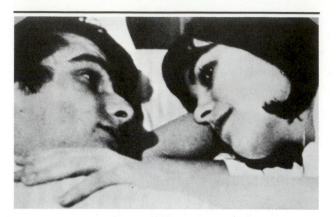

▲ From *Bed and Board* (1970). Having introduced his young hero, Antoine Doinel, in *The 400 Blows* (1959) and in a segment of *Love at 20* (1962), Truffaut once again cast Jean-Pierre Léaud in the now young-adult role in *Stolen Kisses* (1968) and *Bed and Board* (1970). In the latter film the director provides a comic look at Antoine's early years of married life and the challenges of his job, parenthood, and an affair with a Japanese girl.

▶ From *The Wild Child* (1969). Truffaut himself stars as the doctor who brings a young savage to civilized ways and a loving relationship. The film is based on the 1798 case history of an abandoned boy who grew up alone in the wilds. Truffaut's dramatization is an unemotional and documentarylike yet sensitive study of the conflict, gains, and inevitable losses that result when space and freedom are exchanged for the confines of civilization.

François Truffaut, Jean-Luc Godard, and Alain Resnais

After his initial efforts at cinema *auterism,* Truffaut explored a variety of styles. He chose melodrama in *The Soft Skin* (1964), and then made a curiously distant and stylized adaptation of a Ray Bradbury story, *Fahrenheit 451* (1966). His homage to the Hitchcock thriller followed in *The Bride Wore Black* (1967). With *Stolen Kisses* (1968), *Bed and Board* (1970), and *Love on the Run* (1979), Truffaut continued his chronicle of the fictional Antoine Doinel's romantic escapades, begun with *The 400 Blows.* This series, together with *The Man Who Loved Women* (1977), shows Truffaut's dedication to the light, buoyant, unashamedly romantic idyll.

Through these works, Truffaut continued to show his interest in the complexities of human relationships, his whimsical sense of humor, and a familiarity with the characters he portrayed. Simultaneously, he kept his distance from direct social issues and political causes. Many of his films are marked by equivocal and unresolved endings: Antoine's indecision, caught in freeze frame; Jules's adjustment to the deaths of Catherine and Jim; and Victor's progress and relationship to Dr. Itard in *The Wild Child* (1969). While exploring new stylistic approaches in such films as *Day for Night* (1973), *The Story of Adele H.* (1975), and *Small Change* (1976), Truffaut also refrained from imposing conveniently dramatic resolutions on social reality. His look at life and work in a small Paris theater during the Nazi occupation, *The Last Metro* (1980), is an affectionate study of the human spirit rather than an indictment of ideology.

Truffaut's work has escaped the labeling and stereotyping commonly imposed on the work of other filmmakers. Truffaut continues to be recognized not only as a world director, but also one who refused to be typecast

From *The Last Metro* (1980). A stage director must literally stay underground in his theater basement to escape discovery in Truffaut's homage to a theater company's struggle to survive the Nazi occupation of Paris. (The film has echoes of the 1942 Lubitsch *To Be or Not to Be,* about a Polish theater troupe in similar circumstances.) Catherine Deneuve (above) plays the actress-wife who struggles to keep the theater going.

From *Weekend* (1967). Life and death among weekend travelers are incorporated in Godard's chilling metaphors for contemporary social values. In the film's image of modern society, highway carnage gives way to murder and cannibalism among guerrilla fighters. However, the film's grim mood is frequently relieved by mischievous bits of political humor and cinematic "in jokes."

and pinned down by a neat generic label, and his films continue to be treasured after his death.

Jean-Luc Godard, equally daring in his use of the medium, has in recent years focused his attention increasingly on sociopolitical themes. In *Alphaville* (1965), he composed a futuristic Orwellian setting for his study of the dehumanization of a modern society and the corruption of its ideals. *Weekend* (1967) rails against the modern consumer-oriented society and the butchery and violence of modern civilization, which Godard represents metaphorically by guerilla warfare that leads to cannibalism. The serious purpose of these films does not prevent Godard from including the wry commentary on the arts that characterized his early work. In *Alphaville,* Lemmy Caution, the main character, reacquaints us with the private eye, and in *Weekend* Godard uses the kind of storybook characters first introduced by Truffaut in *Fahrenheit 451.*

In making *One Plus One* (1968) and *Le Gai Savoir* (1968), Godard became almost totally absorbed in Marxist polemics, though, like Truffaut, he usually managed to mask his own political position in ambiguity. In *Every Man for Himself* (1980), Godard's only feature film in an eight-year stretch, he turned again to look at survival in the modern world. Like many Marxist studies, this work links sexual degradation and socioeconomic conditions. Godard is probably the least popular among major European directors. But his continued willingness to challenge accepted precepts of film form and function remains unparalleled even through what many critics consider static, long-winded diatribes.

Alain Resnais has remained a respected and reasonably visible *auteur* and cinema stylist throughout the post-New Wave era. *Providence* (1977) and *Mon Oncle d'Amerique* (1980) are his most distinguished films of this period. *Providence* is a highly polished and con-

From *Providence* (1977). In his first English-language film, Alain Resnais cast Sir John Gielgud as a well-known novelist who not only uses life experiences and family relationships as a basis for his last novel, but attempts to control these events to meet both his emotional and literary needs. We see people and events twice removed—through the imagination of the protagonist and again through the filmmaker's camera.

trolled study of an aging novelist who manipulates as well as interprets the reality about him in preparing his final literary work. It shows a new dimension of Resnais's continued fascination with time and memory, and provides John Gielgud with one of his most accomplished screen roles.

Federico Fellini and Michelangelo Antonioni

Fellini, like Bergman, has worked successfully on the psychic front and given visual form to the tortured mental battlefield. As noted briefly in Chapter 10, *8½* (1963), is the study of a film director who is plagued by his own childhood memories and self-doubts in his struggle to come up with a suitable subject for his next film. Fellini is dealing both with autobiography and personal myth here and begins to provide the kind of visual extravagances just hinted at in *La Dolce Vita* but integral to his later work. In *Juliet of the Spirits* (1965), he leads his viewer on an even more subjective but this time less autobiographical and more fanciful tour, and the result is his most visually lavish and also most Freudian work. In this film Giulietta (Masina) has visions of both past and present happenings that provide transport to some of the most exotic images of the surreal ever composed for film. "I'm interested in man, but on all his various levels, in his miscellaneous conditions and dimensions," Fellini has declared.

Fellini is most quickly associated with the broad, elaborately dressed sociological landscape, and this association has earned him the title of "grand showman." In *Satyricon* (1969) and *Roma* (1972), he returns to his favorite setting—the city of Rome. In *Satyricon*, it is the pre-Christian Rome of Petronius and other classic writers. Fellini's approach here is "authentic recon-

From *Juliet of the Spirits* (1965). Giulietta Masina as Juliet searches for meaning in her marriage, which leads to dreams, fantasies, and childhood memories. Sandra Milo, who plays a neighbor, is seen here en route from her bedroom to swimming pool below.

struction, as reflected over two thousand light years." The view, according to Fellini himself, is of "a cynical society, impassive, corrupt, and frenzied." *Roma* is again a distinctly Fellini image; this time the city is seen through the eyes of a boy from the provinces visiting Rome for the first time. Fellini provides a broader landscape and distinctly autobiographical detail in *Amarcord* (1974), in which he relates the adventures of a young man in Italy during the Fascist period of the late thirties. *City of Women* (1980) is a loosely constructed chronicle of loves and conflicts between the sexes in several contemporary Italian settings, and the action in *And the Ship Sails On* (1983) occurs aboard a luxury liner at the outbreak of World War I. Both films reveal once again features that are quintessentially Fellini — autobiography, gentle satire, and an unrestrained (some would say vulgar) visual feast. Like Bergman, Fellini sees himself as conjuror and showman. These qualities have continued to entrance audiences and frustrate critics, and perpetuate the Italian legacy in cinema spectacle begun in the early teens.

Michelangelo Antonioni, however, has become master of psychic drama, and particularly the cinematic representation of the soulless, emotionally barren, and isolated set in the modern world. His characters have lost their sense of the meaning of life, and find themselves tied to social conventions and moral precepts they distrust or reject. They wander into and out of relationships, attempting to resolve doubts about their own identities, their reasons for being, and the meaning of their relationships. In the hands of a lesser talent, such an atmosphere would be stultifying. Antonioni, however, uses his restrained, self-disciplined style to make every

Changes in Perspective

*W*hile making a film, we live, and nevertheless, we are always setting personal problems. Problems which concern our work, but also our private life. If the things we talk about are not those we were talking about right after the war, it is because the world around us had, in fact, changed and, also, we ourselves have changed. Our requirements have changed, our purposes, our themes.

— *Michelangelo Antonioni in* Interviews with Film Directors, *edited by Andrew Sarris (1967)*

detail of sight and sound work toward a complete statement of the emotional conflicts of modern life that lies at the center of all his films.

After the anguish of betrayal and mistrust, Claudia and Sandro of *L'Avventura* learn to adapt to a more stable and realistic, if less idyllic, human relationship. Giuliana in *The Red Desert* articulates the lesson in adaptability she is learning when she stands with her son on the desolate Ravenna factory site at the end of the film. The photographer hero of *Blow-Up* (1966), after struggling to come to grips with what is real and controllable in his life, finally seems to make the necessary adjustment that will enable him to live with some sense of belonging.

What becomes evident in all of Antonioni's films is a new and critical role for the concept of *mise-en-scène*. The film's environment is not merely complementary to the film's meaning; rather, it becomes the key to understanding the characters — their motivation, conflicts, and ultimate adjustment. The action in the first part of

◀ From *Blow-Up* (1966). David Hemmings's obsessive search for reality via the photographic image is set by Antonioni in a frenetic and lonely mod London. The voyeuristic mood of the film as well as the mystery it poses is very much in the spirit of Hitchcock's *Rear Window*.

L'Avventura, for example, takes place on a bleak and forbidding volcanic island. After Claudia and Sandro return to the mainland, the deserted streets, shuttered houses, and cold and impersonal apartments and hotel they frequent continue to suggest emotional aridity. Likewise, the Ravenna landscape of *The Red Desert* is more than just an accommodating setting. Gray marshes, impenetrable fog, stark white corridors — all become a visualization of Giuliana's world and thereby what Antonioni calls "a reality of the moment." The world of mod London in *Blow-Up* is both the controlled, ordered, and revealing world of the photograph and the unpredictable, capricious real world through which the photographer himself moves. In *Zabriskie Point* (1970) the American desert is sufficiently broad, both physically and spiritually, to accommodate the theft of an airplane as an act of youthful rebellion, communal lovemaking, and the spectacular vision of an exploding desert mansion.

Antonioni is not the popular showman Fellini has become, but he is generally recognized as one of the most disciplined and uncompromising of the modern directors. In 1960 *L'Avventura* was greeted with jeers when it was shown at Cannes, but later, in 1964, *The Red Desert* took first prize at Venice. Along with Fellini, Antonioni earned his place as a major force in the Italian cinema of the fifties and sixties, and with *The Passenger* (1975) he reaffirmed his position as an international star among *auteur* filmmakers. This film is a visually complex and thematically obscure work that makes few concessions to the casual moviegoer.

Luis Buñuel

For fifty years Luis Buñuel periodically reaffirmed his sardonic and irreverent wit at the expense of the bourgeois class and the Catholic Church. Like Bergman, he stood apart from the film waves and not in one but in two countries (Mexico and Spain) his work composes a one-man national genre. His film career extended from his original avant-garde *causes célèbres* — *Un Chien Andalou* (1928) and *L'Age d'Or* (1930) — to a Hollywood stint as advisor to both MGM and Warner Brothers in the thirties and forties and several years of feature filmmaking in Mexico in the early fifties. After working for a period in France, he finally returned to his native Spain where, in 1961, he produced *Viridiana,* the film that was to win him renewed infamy and a place among the major world directors.

Although surreal imagery is prevalent in Buñuel's work, and has even become something of a trademark for him, his visual style is less distinctive than that of some of the other major directors, and his use of camera tech-

> ## Potentials and Dangers
>
> *T*he cinema is capable of stirring the spectator as perhaps no other art. But as no other art, it is also capable of stupefying him. Unfortunately, the great majority of today's films seem to have exactly that purpose; they glory in an intellectual and moral vacuum. In this vacuum, movies seem to prosper. . . .
>
> The screen is a dangerous and wonderful instrument, if a free spirit uses it. It is the superior way of expressing the world of dreams, emotions and instinct.
>
> —*Luis Buñuel, "A Statement,"* Film Culture *(Summer 1960)*

nique is generally restrained. It is his sense of irony, realized through grotesque, blasphemous, often hilarious juxtapositions, that clearly distinguishes his work. Buñuel's attitude and humor defy easy classification, however. His ridicule, which seems anarchic, is usually softened by an ambivalence toward his targets. This is particularly true in his dealings with human frailties; a tolerance, if not compassion, is usually detectable. When dealing with social institutions and structures, particularly the Church, less moderation is in evidence. Buñuel is noted for his line, "I have always been an atheist, thank God."

Los Olvidados (1950), the first of Buñuel's major works, is an essentially realistic and, for Buñuel, conservative study of human weakness and social injustice. The focus is on "the young and the damned" (an alternate title for this film) who live in the slums of Mexico. Buñuel actually used records of Mexico City reformatories to prepare his screenplay, and the hard facts of adolescent crime, perversion, and child abandonment that became part of the film won for Buñuel both a petition for his expulsion from Mexico and the Best Director prize at Cannes.

Viridiana (1961), a study of repressive clericalism that he made after his return to Spain, and *The Exterminating Angel* (1962) constitute the major works of Buñuel's middle period. These films also reveal Buñuel's special talents for fashioning cinematic metaphor. In

Viridiana, a young novice nun about to take her final vows visits the estate of a rich uncle who becomes sexually aroused by the girl as she sleeps and attempts to rape her. Though he never actually violates the unconscious girl, he makes her believe he has. Unable to return to the convent, Viridiana decides to use her uncle's estate as a haven for homeless derelicts. Her good deeds are rewarded by drunken feasting and brawling by her charges, who break into the house in her absence. Her final disillusionment is revealed when she goes to the bedroom of her cousin to "play cards" with him. Buñuel links the rape attempt to the playing of Handel's *Messiah,* and the beggars' orgiastic feast to the Last Supper, which makes this one of the most demonstratively perverse of all his films. But despite such ironic outbursts and allegoric references, the film is essentially realistic.

With *The Exterminating Angel,* however, Buñuel moves further into metaphor and a surrealist style. He follows a group of socialites to an after-the-opera dinner at a patron's home. When they discover that they are mysteriously unable to leave the house, the social veneer begins to crack and slowly peel away. Debasing and vicious behavior, which at one point borders on cannibalism, takes over.

Buñuel's assault on human and institutional faults mellowed through the years but is still very much in evidence in his more recent films. *Belle de Jour* (1967) is an attack on contemporary sexual mores. Here Buñuel makes marriage synonymous with impotence and the brothel the place for true passion by way of the fantasies, memories, and real-life relationships of a young wife. He continues to mock organized religion in both *Simon of the Desert* (1965) and *The Milky Way* (1969). Exposure of human frailties and attacks on social mores are once again prime motives in *Tristana* (1970), *The Discreet Charm of the Bourgeoisie* (1973), and *The Phantom of Liberty* (1974).

Though he became gentler and more serene in attitude, Buñuel continued his unruly ways to the end. In *That Obscure Object of Desire* (1977), a middle-aged man becomes obsessed with desire for a pretty young girl he meets on a train. Here Buñuel cast the leading role with two different actresses who appear alternately in succeeding scenes. But unorthodox filmmaking did not keep Buñuel from playing out the longest active career of any major director. Through fifty years of filmmaking, the indefatigable social satirist followed Bergman's own precept—to entertain, injure, and mortify.

▼ From *That Obscure Object of Desire* (1977). At age fifty, an urbane French widower (played by Fernando Rey) becomes infatuated with a Spanish girl on board a Seville-Paris train. In the ensuing relationship, she teases him to the point of utter frustration. In this adaptation of a short novel by Pierre Louys (the fifth movie version of the work!), Buñuel alternates two actresses in the role of the girl, perhaps to show variations in the relationship and in the protagonist's desires.

▼ From *Belle de Jour* (1967). Séverine (Catherine Deneuve) is the wife whose sensual and psychic needs are met by a part-time foray into prostitution. Buñuel's surrealist imagery comes into play as Séverine's fantasies intrude on real events and it becomes increasingly difficult for her to separate the two.

National Cinemas Since the New Wave

France

Several French directors who gained initial prominence during the European postwar renaissance continued to make films that won critical acceptance but limited distribution abroad. Marcel Ophuls hardly achieved cult-hero status, but he is highly respected for his judicious and compassionate investigation of actual events. Ophuls had his apprenticeship in filmmaking with John Huston and worked as a television director in Germany and France. In those capacities, Ophuls received a good grounding in the dramatic reporting of actual events.

Ophuls's two four-and-a-half-hour television films, *The Sorrow and the Pity* (1971) and *The Memory of Justice* (1975), are eloquent testaments to his schooling in both dramatic and documentary forms. The former is a chronicle of the German occupation of France during World War II, and the latter is drawn from the Nüremberg war-crimes trials and from contemporary interviews covering the Nazi era as well as Vietnam and Algeria.

Ophuls's films combine historical study with personal insight. He rejects glib and easy answers to complex social issues, and, by means of old archive and newsreel footage combined with contemporary interviews, he documents the doubt, guilt, and remorse behind the events he covers. His goal is to achieve clarity on the events — with all their complex ramifications — rather than simply documenting the facts.

Costi Costa-Gavras is another filmmaker who brought the drama of real-life political events into vogue, with his *Z* (1969) and *State of Siege* (1973). These political thrillers have been attacked from both the political left and right for popularizing real-life incidents and allowing storytelling to take over from political documentation and analysis. With *Missing* (1982), Costa-Gavras found even wider appeal, by using the star status of Jack Lemmon as the film's protagonist.

Claude Chabrol, Claude Lelouch, Jacques Demy, Louis Malle, and Eric Rohmer are the other major directors who, along with the inexhaustible Truffaut and Godard, helped mold and maintain the image of French cinema through the sixties and seventies. Working within the traditional genres and more conventional forms of dramatic structure and still meeting the production requirements of the industry, they managed to ex-plore and extend the limits of style and story (or statement) open to film. Chabrol combined the tension of the murder mystery with a psychological study in motivation in films from *Les Cousins* (1959) to *Le Boucher* ("The Butcher," 1969). Jacques Demy challenges Hollywood's expertise in the mounting of musical fantasy in *The Umbrellas of Cherbourg* (1964). Eric Rohmer's delicate and graceful studies in human passion continue in *Le Beau Mariage* (1982). Louis Malle's *Murmur of the Heart* (1972) challenges Rohmer's work for its delicacy and grace and notions about what can be treated tastefully on the screen. His *Lacombe, Lucien* (1974) further extends Malle's firm hand and delicate touch in exploring human relationships, particularly between different generations. This continues with his American-made films: a rendering of childhood in a New Orleans whorehouse in languid period setting (*Pretty Baby* [1978]) and a contemporary study of an ex-mobster and young girl adrift in a city on the make (*Atlantic City* [1981]). Malle, like Buñuel and other true *auteurs,* refuses to follow prescribed social and filmmaking dictates. In *My Dinner with André* (1981) he photographs a two-hour conversation on life experiences between two casual friends dining together in a neighborhood restaurant.

The French cinema, traditionally nonconformist and in the vanguard in exploring new ways of using the medium, has continued in the period of European renaissance and beyond to nod respectfully to past masters in film and the other arts, and then go its own way. This independence has been modified but not abandoned in the new era of the seventies and eighties.

Italy

In the wake of increased French-Italian coproduction and American support, several Italian directors, along with Fellini and Antonioni, have been able to preserve some individuality and secure or retain their international visibility among contemporary filmmakers. For several — Luchino Visconti, Vittorio de Sica, Pier Paolo Pasolini, Roberto Rossellini, Pietro Germi — the seminal contribution came just before death. Germi, a social satirist whose career in feature-film production goes back to the forties, shows less concern for subtlety of mood and character delineation than for direct social observation through comic narrative. His *Divorce — Italian Style* (1962) and *Seduced and Abandoned* (1964) dramatize outmoded and pretentious codes, particularly those concerned with filial relations. Frantic attempts to neutralize a marriage in the former film and legalize one in the latter are equally pointed in their reflection of how tortured a sense of honor and propriety can become — and how hilarious it can be.

Straight dramatic narrative as represented in the works of a number of directors makes the stronger showing than these lighter satires, however. Rossellini and de Sica, who pioneered the original neorealist movement, moved into richer, less austere historical impressions with *The Rise of Louis XIV* (1966) and *The Garden of the Finzi-Continis* (1971), respectively, which continued to show mastery over visual detail in their recreations of the mid-seventeenth century French court and the Ferrara estates of Jews in Fascist Italy of the late thirties, respectively. Some directors have revived something of the spirit and style of the original movement. Ermanno Olmi and Luchino Visconti were joined by Vittorio de Seta (*The Bandits of Orgosolo*, 1961) and Mario Monicelli (*The Organizer*, 1964) in taking an unvarnished look at working-class struggles. Pier Paolo Pasolini, who began his feature-film career in the neorealist mode with *Accattone* (1961), moved steadily away from the direct look at social fact to the relatively austere but formalistic and allegorical style of *The Gospel According to St. Matthew* (1964) and *Teorema* (1968). In *Salo* (1976), made just before his death, Pasolini uses sadomasochistic sex as metaphor for totalitarian subjugation. Visconti had also abandoned the direct look and the austerity of *La Terra Trema* in favor of decadent opulence in *The Damned* (1969) and sumptuous elegance and grace in *Death in Venice* (1972). Both films are heavy with visual detail intended to support their density of mood. Olmi's *The Tree of Wooden Clogs* (1978) is a pastoral study of farming families living in Lombardy during the early 1800s.

Also heavily dependent on visual detail in conveying meaning or mood, but more successful than Visconti in total creation of *mise-en-scène,* is Bernardo Bertolucci, who represented new vitality among young Italian directors. He was only twenty-two when he made his first feature, *Before the Revolution,* in 1964. His *The Conformist* (1971) won him acclaim, both for its stylistic control and its intricate working out of the political/sexual theme. With *Last Tango in Paris* (1972), Bertolucci worked with an American star (Marlon Brando) and Hollywood backing and production techniques, but still managed to retain a sense of control over the atmosphere to best accommodate the action and the feeling of film. His *1900* (1977) is an extravagant panorama of the life of three generations of Italians in the pre-Fascist era.

Despite the Italian dedication to film-going, particularly during hard times, skyrocketing admission prices have combined with a flood of television films to eat away

The Life of an *Auteur* on Screen

*T*o make films is a way of life. If we take out the titles of the film and "THE END" and put the film all together we will have the figure of one man, of an auteur, the life of an auteur, transferred in many different characters naturally. But the film is one film.

—*Bernardo Bertolucci, in* The Film Director as Superstar, *by Joseph Gelmis*

at attendance. The films capable of luring Italians back to theaters were such American features as *Star Wars* (1977), *Tootsie* (1982), and *Back to the Future* (1985).

By the early 1980s, many of the major postwar directors were gone. Antonioni had been out of the international limelight since his foray into British and American production. Italian cinema of the early eighties was thus represented by Fellini from the old guard and Lina Wertmüller from the new. Wertmüller, who gained more than passing notice with *Seduction of Mimi* (1970) and *Love and Anarchy* (1971), became something of a celebrity in the United States in the mid-seventies with *Swept Away* (1974) and *Seven Beauties* (1975). Her sexual/political studies in subjugation and compromise generated admiration, scepticism, and scorn, making her one of the most discussed and criticized directors of the late seventies, though not the most universally endorsed.

Wertmüller began her career in film as an assistant to Fellini in the production of *8 1/2.* From him she learned the art of showmanship marked by grotesqueries and exaggerations, and like him she reveals through her work a fondness for the Italian working man. In *Love and Anarchy* he is a peasant whose mission to assassinate Mussolini is subverted by a sexual foray. In *Swept Away* he is a Marxist Admirable Crichton whose sexual/political confrontation takes place on a deserted island. And in *Seven Beauties* he is the murderer of a pimp, having his own sexual encounter with a female commandant of a

◀ From *Seven Beauties* (1975). In this film, director Lina Wertmüller expressed her ongoing interest in the individual's sexual/political confrontations with authority. The film dramatizes the fate of Pasqualino (Giancarlo Giannini), a Fascist wimp, who deserts the Italian Army only to become the ultimate victim of the obscene commandant (Shirley Stoler) of a German concentration camp.

Battle of Algiers (1966), in blending Marxist propaganda with poetry. More recently, Francesco Rosi has been active on the political front with *Three Brothers* (1981), which dramatizes modern urban terrorism and social decay seen from a country setting by three brothers returning to their boyhood home.

Although these filmmakers have reaffirmed film's function as social observer, they have not restored to the Italian cinema its status among the most prestigious and marketable of national genres. Rather, Italy's industry has become the victim of worldwide recession and the timidity of its producers. It has also felt the effects of growing television competition and continued dominance of U.S. imports.

Britain

By the time the protagonist of Michael Sarne's *Joanna* (1968) arrived in mod London to study art and take a black lover, most vestiges of the British social realist cinema were gone. Reisz and Richardson had adjusted their styles to accommodate box-office and big-production methods. From *Morgan* (1966), Reisz went on to the even more rarefied atmosphere of *Isadora* (1968), and Richardson to the richer baroque trappings of such period pieces as *Tom Jones* (1963) and *Joseph Andrews* (1978). Lindsay Anderson, although a long way from documenting the day-by-day activities of Covent Garden and the fun fair, was still devoted to surveying British social institutions. His *If* (1968) moves by way of surrealism to examine the possible results of continued extremes in discipline at a boys' boarding school. Anderson declared that his sympathies were always with the revolutionaries, and *If* came much closer in spirit to Kubrick's *Clockwork Orange* than to Vigo's *Zéro de conduite,* with which it is often compared. But the seventies generally showed a continuation of the move back to period adventure, spectacle, and intrigue.

Nazi concentration camp. All these characters are played by Giancarlo Giannini, Wertmüller's star underdog, who inevitably becomes both a pawn of the political system and a victim of his own and others' sexual drives. Unable to challenge a parasitic system, he capitulates and adjusts to its social requirements.

With few exceptions, the Wertmüller films champion the cause of the little man in the anti-Fascist spirit of Chaplin. They combine comedy with polemics in a kind of formula that her detractors criticize roundly. Wertmüller admits to the repetitiousness of the situations in her films. She says, "I always make the same story—the problems of sex and politics." And, echoing the tenets of the original neorealist movement, she asserts, "Film must be honestly problematical and sincerely social."

Gillo Pontecorvo is another Italian filmmaker dedicated to the social function of the narrative film. His *Burn* (1969), set on a fictitious Caribbean island during an insurrection, follows in the tradition of his earlier *The*

All three ingredients distinguish the films of Ken Russell. Beginning with the adaptation of D. H. Lawrence's *Women in Love* (1969) and continuing with his dramatization of the lives of famous composers — *The Music Lovers* (1971), *Mahler* (1974), *Lisztomania* (1975) — and of the silent film idol *Valentino* (1977), his biographical dramas highlight emotional and sexual drives. In *Altered States* (1980), Russell tells a science fiction tale about sensory deprivation, taking the opportunity to explore the mental landscape.

Diversity of style through a striking sense of visual composition characterizes the films of Nicholas Roeg, another British director who gained prominence in the seventies. His *Walkabout* (1971), *Don't Look Now* (1973), and *The Man Who Fell to Earth* (1976) all concern intrigues in a strange and frequently hostile environment. The distinctive setting and mood of each reveal Roeg's special talent for discovering drama in unfamiliar and life-threatening settings.

In recent years, the kinship of American and British industries and the increased exchange of talent have obscured the distinctive style and singular purpose of British film. This includes not only the angry antiestablishment features of the early sixties, but their mod, offbeat, and elegant successors as well. The seventies saw the collapse of the British studio system, resulting partly from the move to location shooting and partly from a growing economic crisis. Major directors continued to work abroad, some on the growing number of coproductions with France, Italy, and West Germany.

American studio backing of films shot in England with British directors and British and American stars further blurred the boundaries of these national genres. Peter Yates's *Breaking Away* (1979) and Karel Reisz's *The French Lieutenant's Woman* (1981) were both made by British directors but were essentially Hollywood features. With *Chariots of Fire* (1981) and *Gandhi* (1982) boasting both British financing and directors (Hugh Hudson and Richard Attenborough, respectively), the British film was placed, at least momentarily, back in the international spotlight. Scottish writer-director Bill Forsyth (*Gregory's Girl* [1981], *Local Hero* [1983], and *Comfort and Joy* [1985]) brought not only international recognition but a rediscovery of simple charms and a droll, affectionate humor to the British film.

▲ *Local Hero* (1983). Bill Forsyth's affectionate look at human idiosyncrasies takes on a lyrical quality in this film set in a remote Scottish fishing village, with an occasional jump back to the frenetic world of a Houston oil corporation. Burt Lancaster, as the star-gazing corporate head, and Peter Riegert, as a junior executive, discover the enchantments and wonders of the simple life.

Japan

The occasional film by Akira Kurosawa reminds one of Japan's golden period of postwar cinema and keeps its star director visible. *Dersu Uzala* (1975) is a reaffirmation of the director's humanist perspective and technological mastery. Its subject is the friendship between a young Russian and a Siberian hunter who is confronted with the challenge of adjusting to an urban environment. Equally absorbing both for their human story and visually arresting style are Kurosawa's *Kagemusha* (1980), set during the sixteenth-century civil wars in Japan, and *Ran* (1985), his screen variation on Shakespeare's *King Lear.*

Many of Japan's promising young directors have been lured into their country's lucrative softcore pornography market or to television or Western production centers. In the thirty-five years since *Rashomon,* there has been little, save such infrequent successes as Kohei Oguri's *Muddy River* (1982)—a modest black-and-white film about the friendship of two little boys in Japan after World War II—to suggest the Japanese cinema's own postwar glory.

Eastern Europe

That art thrives on its social and political constraints has many proofs in film. From the ashes of revolution arose the new Soviet cinema; Germany's golden age followed the country's defeat in World War I; and the Italian and Japanese renaissances, which formed a prelude to the new cinemas of East and West, rose from the collapse of the Axis powers after World War II.

The limitations under which filmmakers in parts of Europe have labored in recent years have not been linked to such dramatic dissolutions; rather, they have been connected to strong ongoing political pressures. The several nationalized cinemas have found themselves subjected to these constraints since the War. Under the continuing pressure of the state-controlled industries in Poland, Hungary, and Czechoslovakia to conform with the "socialist realism" doctrine, several filmmakers were able to sidestep the approved socialist themes to make personal statements through experimental styles. The result was, in the fifties and sixties, the emergence on the world scene of an Eastern European cinema that involved the importing and exposure of films to Western European and American markets and broad critical acclaim.

First to find recognition in the West was the Polish cinema. That industry was reorganized in the mid-fifties and a vigorous semiautonomous group developed whose

---

Choosing Images

*W*hat Buñuel does, and what I try to do, is to create new images, new series of images which could play the role of symbols. In *Ashes and Diamonds* and *Lotna* I nevertheless willingly use the existing wealth of images, of national metaphors. I do not make films for Japanese or for Parisian audiences; I myself am a part of the public for whom I work, and so I must use images which are accepted and generally understood. That is the only hope I have of saying something new.

—*Andrzej Wajda, in* Film and Filming *(June 1961)*

---

work, although frequently censured by the state, won popular and critical support. The first wave of directors, who had known the traumas of the occupation, the resistance movement, and the decimation of the Warsaw ghetto, followed heroic themes of occupation and resistance in their work. Aleksander Ford's *That Others May Live* (1943) is one of the more prominent examples. After several years of close control and benign, often vacuous themes, the industry was reorganized into independent production units, which brought about a new era in Polish filmmaking. Leading the movement was Andrzej Wajda, with his romantic trilogy—*A Generation* (1954), *Kanal* (1956), and *Ashes and Diamonds* (1958)—which dealt with elements of heroism in the war years. Also establishing himself as a major figure in the late fifties was Andrzej Munk, whose focus was also the war hero, but whose ironic style contrasts with the romantic approach of Wajda. Munk's promising career was cut short in 1961, when he died in a car accident.

The sixties brought a new group of young directors to prominence, among them Roman Polanski and Jerzy Skolimowski, both of whom had strong ties to Western cinema. Although both men received their formal film training at the National Film Academy at Łódź, their films reveal nonheroic themes of Western, and particularly French, cinema. Polanski's first feature, *Knife in the Water* (1962), which won him international recognition, centers on the emotional tension arising out of the interrelationships among a husband and wife and a young man whom they have invited to join them on a sailing holiday. The struggle, which includes the husband's masochistic self-doubt, is far removed from the heroic tradition of earlier Polish cinema.

Jerzy Skolimowski, who coscripted the screenplay for *Knife in the Water* with Polanski, has cultivated a series of nonconformist hero types in his own films. His purpose, however, is criticism of social systems and values, and in the case of *Le Départ* (1967), the values of the hero as well. The film stars Jean-Pierre Leaud (a favorite actor of Truffaut) as a hairdresser whose enthusiasm for sports cars leads to a love affair with a Porsche.

Krzysztof Zanussi, Witold Leszcgynski, Andrzej Kondriatuk, and Roman Zaluski are not known to Western film audiences or to many critics. They are among the new generation of Polish filmmakers who were born during or after the war. Free of the trauma of the Warsaw uprising, they are dedicated to articulating the problems and dreams of their own generation. The majority have a style that is quiet and low-key, and give increased attention to individual experience and less to the social order and the historical hymn to national survival that is predominant in earlier films. Directors of the original New Wave who have continued working in Poland, such as Andrzej Wajda, have also turned to inner worlds and formal problems in cinema. The exhibition of Polish films

On Happy Endings

*I*n Poland, we have gallows humor. Tell me, why do Westerns have a happy ending? Because they were going West and killing Indians and the trains could reach their destination. In Poland, as in the rest of Eastern Europe, we don't have a way out, so we have to laugh at our predicament.

—*Jerzy Skolimowski in*
Film Comment (November/
December 1982)

in Western theaters in recent years has been limited mostly to festivals and national cinema studies.

Polanski and Skolimowski, who led Poland into world recognition, have themselves continued to command broad critical attention and marketability in Western production centers. Polanski has shown a remarkable ability to adjust not only to British and American production methods, but to a diversity of styles as well, ranging from the world of Shakespeare (*Macbeth* [1971]) to that of Thomas Hardy (*Tess* [1980]). Skolimowski made use of the resources of a British studio and star (Jeremy Irons) to create a brilliant metaphor in *Moonlighting* (1982), in which he parallels the life of four Polish laborers stranded in London during the 1981 military takeover with the fate of their homeland. Skolimowski's seriousness of theme is balanced by an ironic sense that he himself calls his "gallows humor."

◀ From *Knife in the Water* (1962). Roman Polanski's first feature film centers on the emotional tension arising out of the interrelationships among a husband and wife and a young hitchhiker who is invited to join the couple on a sailing trip. Most of the action takes place on board the couple's sailboat, and the trio are the only characters in the entire film.

Despite early national support for cinema in Hungary, repressive government control left little room for experimentation. Many filmmakers over the years have left their homeland for the freedom of Western film industries: Alexander Korda to England; Béla Balázs, famed theoretician, to Germany; and Michael Curtiz to Hollywood. In 1945, Balázs returned to Hungary to direct the Academy of Dramatic and Film Arts under a new spirit of esteem for cinema, but nationalization once again proved repressive and films were obliged to reflect proper socialist ideology.

By the early sixties, a liberalization was under way that brought Miklós Jancsó, András Kovács, and István Szabó to prominence. The new Hungarian cinema was characterized by a turning away from the literary tradition that had strongly influenced earlier directors. The new filmmakers used the cinema for inquiry into sociopolitical conditions rather than for the mounting of familiar and revered literary narratives. The behavior of individuals in a historical context became central to the works of Jancsó. His *Confrontation* (1969) became one of the more controversial films. István Szabó, who had his formal film training at the state-run Budapest Academy of Dramatic and Cinematographic Art, began to distinguish himself as a director with *The Father* (1966), a study of a father-son relationship and of a young man's progress from the world of illusion to the world of reality. This film, together with his 1966 *The Age of Illusions,* which follows a similar theme, put Szabó in the forefront of Hungarian directors. And he reaffirmed his claim on that position while showing a maturing style with *Mephisto* (1981). This close scrutiny of human behavior is set in Germany of the twenties and thirties, where an actor rises to fame by capitulating to the Nazis.

New thematic range coupled with vigorous and varied stylistic approaches characterizes the work of these and other Hungarian filmmakers, yet the country remains the least well represented of the major Eastern European nations on the international market.

The film industry of Czechoslovakia was nationalized in 1945 under the control of an artistic council. Although a system of autonomous production units was allowed to continue, decisions on films were finally centralized under the council, and the resulting films generally served as propaganda for the socialist ideology. Meanwhile, FAMU, the Czech Academy of Dramatic Arts, turned out dedicated and free-thinking directors who, by the early sixties, were challenging the artistic council's absolute control and providing the spark for a Czech New Wave. Miloš Forman was one of the first of the Czech directors to emerge on the international scene. His finely drawn studies of individual behavior were often akin to those of the Italian neorealists. *Loves of a Blonde* (1965) and *The Firemen's Ball* (1967) both poke gentle fun at conventions of Czech society, particularly the older generation. Forman's intimate portrait of everyday life revealed humor and compassion seldom seen in the works of the directors who were close to the horrors of the war. His emigration to Hollywood has placed him, since the early seventies, among the most active directors working on big budget productions and in an impressive range of styles: *Taking Off* (1971), *One Flew Over the Cuckoo's Nest* (1975), *Hair* (1979), *Ragtime* (1981), and *Amadeus* (1984).

Among these older directors, the best known and wielding the most influence over the Czech New Wave was Jan Kadar. His international reputation rests chiefly on *The Shop on Main Street* (1965). Set in a Czech town during World War II, the story centers on the moral conflict faced by a carpenter in saving an old Jewish shopkeeper from a concentration camp at the risk of his own life. Another anti-Fascist film from Czechoslovakia to find exhibition in the West and critical plaudits for its director, Zbynek Brynych, was *The Fifth Horseman Is Fear* (1964). This is a study of Nazi oppression centering on a Jewish doctor who treats and facilitates the escape of a political refugee.

Jan Schmidt, like Brynych, is little known outside Eastern Europe, but he has also helped to extend the range and quality of social commentary. His *The End of August at the Hotel Ozone* (1966) is an allegory on the changing of social orders. The movie follows eight girls, led by an older woman, who search the desolate countryside for other survivors of a nuclear holocaust. At the decrepit resort of the title, the party finds an old man living alone, and here the old woman dies. The girls ignore the old man's pleas to allow him to stay, and they kill him when he refuses to give up the phonograph and single record that he treasures. This new civilization as represented by the girls is frightening in its emotional vacuity, and the killing of a human being of the old order trying to preserve one of its relics is bitterly ironic.

Decidedly more human is the work of Czech director Jiří Menzel, who won recognition, including an Academy Award, for his *Closely Watched Trains* (1966). This film blends a haunting Fascist theme with humor in the story of the first sexual encounter of a young railroad station attendant. After a failed suicide attempt, the boy becomes part of the resistance movement and is killed trying to sabotage a train. More sobering and surreal than either Forman or Menzel, but less cerebral and distant in his allegorical treatment, is Jan Němec. His *A Report on the Party and the Guests* (1966) is a study in totalitarian suppression that begins as a pleasant country

▲ From *Closely Watched Trains* (1966). Fascism and first love provide the subject of Jiří Menzel's 1966 offering from Czechoslovakia, which won an Academy Award in the United States. It features an apprentice train dispatcher on his first job at a remote station during the Nazi occupation. This bittersweet study of sexual and political awakening combines comedy and pathos in a starkly authentic setting.

picnic and ends with a terrifying manhunt and, thematically, the linking of conformity with the condoning of persecution and atrocities. The film was suppressed in Czechoslovakia for two years, was cleared for showing by the Dubček regime in 1968, and banned again after Soviet occupation. Since 1968, many Czech films, including one by Menzel, have been suppressed and few have made their way to foreign audiences. Many leading directors are now working abroad, and political surveillance at home keeps new talent in check.

As in Czechoslovakia, Yugoslavia set up a state-run industry in 1945. Here also, international recognition was not to come until the mid-sixties. Of the new Yugoslav directors, Dušan Makavejev is best represented (if not well known) in Western film circles for his *Tragedy of a Switchboard Operator* (1967) and *WR — Mysteries of the Organism* (1971). Most characteristic of the Yugoslav films in general, and the works of Makavejev in particular, is an experimental free-form style, including the blending of interviews and other documentary-type material and staged footage that together develop the film's story.

Stylistically, the most distinctive contribution of the Yugoslav cinema has been in the field of animation. Zagreb Studio, with government support, has gained worldwide recognition in the field since its foundation in 1949. It was established by a group of artists and cartoonists for a Zagreb newspaper who decided to experiment with the film medium. Influenced at first by Disney, they soon abandoned the fantasy world and began to animate real-world situations. Still using folk stories and fables as a narrative base, the filmmaker/artists focused on contemporary social themes with a universal quality and appeal. The satirical edge of much of the work is not sharp or coldly calculating but rather, as the Zagreb animators themselves characterize it, "warmth giving." The Zagreb style is characterized by a kind of visual shorthand, in which drawings are reduced to simple designs and movements. In addition to the basic visual design, experimentation and refinement in animation style includes work with color collages and contrapuntal use of music and sound. Artists at Zagreb refer to animation as "a protest against the stationary condition."

The establishment of cinema institutes and production facilities to support them has given a new boost to film activities in Rumania and Bulgaria as well, albeit within the parameters of "socialist realism." Although not a part of an international market, the studios near Bucharest and Sofia provide evidence of new creative energies in animation and documentary as well as feature-film genres. State control here, as in the other socialist states, results in a combination of benign entertainment and abstract experiments, with any inquiry safely limited to technique.

The burst of free expression that sparked young filmmakers in Eastern Europe began to lose its momentum in the early seventies with a "reunification" (a tightening of controls on production and censorship), and a redirection of whatever creative talent had not been lured to Western European and American production centers. The Lódź Film School in Poland still turns out imaginative and energetic directors. Zagreb Studio in Yugoslavia and Pannonia Films in Hungary continue their leadership in the field of animation. The new cinema of Eastern Europe continues to show new potential, but remains ideologically in tow.

Being Brazilian

*A*t the core of Brazilian film is its function as an expression of national identity. If being American means never having to say you're sorry, then being Brazilian means always having to say you're Brazilian.

—*Pat Aufderheide, "Will Success Spoil Brazilian Cinema?"* American Film *(March 1983)*

The Third World

Latin America

The promise of a Third World cinema movement in Latin America came with a flurry of films in the late sixties and early seventies. Most notable among these in terms of international distribution and recognition were *Antonio das Mortes* (1969) from Brazil, *The Hour of the Furnaces* (1970) from Argentina, *Blood of the Condor* (1970) from Bolivia, and *Memories of Underdevelopment* (1968) from Cuba. Though individual in style and representing both documentary and narrative forms, the majority of films from South America set out in the spirit of Vertov to examine the actual, the familiar, and the contemporary. They succeeded in generating both critical acclaim and a growing anxiety on the part of increasingly repressive governments.

The cinema nôvo, as it was called in Brazil (or cinema liberación, in Argentina), was short-lived. Political restrictions coupled with runaway inflation brought this progressive era of film to a virtual standstill in almost all of South America within a decade of its promising beginnings. In Brazil, where Glauber Rocha was put into the international spotlight, first for his *Black God, White Devil* in 1963 and then for *Antonio das Mortes* in 1969, the cinema nôvo was at an end by 1970. In Argentina, political instability brought increasingly stringent censorship, first with the return of the Peróns in 1973 and then with the coup of 1976. With an inflation rate of

300 percent and frozen admission prices, film-loving Argentinians were going to see *Earthquake, Airport '75,* and *Chinatown* (three of the five top-grossing films for the year 1975), but *Piedra Libre,* the work of Leopoldo Torre Nilsson, the distinguished *auteur* of the original New Wave era, was banned on the day before its release.

In recent years, there have been sporadic signs of vitality in the Brazilian cinema. In spite of a flood of low-budget pornography and crippling inflation, the liberalization in censorship on both domestic and foreign films has led to the production of more substantial and serious work. Hector Babenco's *Pixote* (1981) is the kind of honest and unadorned look at contemporary social ills, particularly those to which children fall victim, that distinguished Buñuel's *Los Olvidados* and de Sica's *Shoeshine.* The film concerns abandoned children who experience the horrors of a reformatory and escape to a sordid world of prostitution, drug abuse, and murder in the city of São Paulo. Though *Pixote* has some of the lyricism of the Buñuel and de Sica works, it takes an even darker view of the corruption of youth. *Kiss of the Spider Woman* (1985) has further extended Babenco's reputation and assured Brazil a place in the sun. The film's story of a homosexual and a political activist who share a cell in a South American prison explores a new dimension in human relations.

Government support in most Latin American nations is coupled with controls on exhibition as well as production. Required bookings of Colombian-produced films, mostly short documentaries, coupled with a rebate system for producers, gives support to production. The degree of latitude enjoyed by Peruvian filmmakers is dependent on whether coproduction is with Venezuela or, what is more usual, the conservative and restrictive Argentinian government.

In Mexico, increasing state control of production has not improved the economic status of the industry or the quality of the films, and Jodorowsky's *El Topo* (1970) remains the high point among that nation's contributions. In Cuba, the nationalized industry continues making films in support of official educational and cultural goals with the "agitprop" newsreels of Santiago Alvarez gaining international attention.

Writing on the current state of Brazilian cinema in 1974 for *International Film Guide,* Jamie Rodrigues reported, "To film in contemporary Brazil is to film on the boundaries: the act itself is fraught with uncertainty and grave personal risk." Exile and imprisonment continue to be the fate of members of filmmaking crews in Bolivia, Uruguay, Colombia, and Brazil. The murder of prominent Chilean and Argentinian filmmakers in 1973,

and in Bolivia in 1980, with the takeover by military juntas, provide a sobering reminder of the constraints on any further flowering of Latin American cinema.

But political turmoil, spiraling inflation, repression, and censorship have failed to extinguish the spirit of the movement. Though militant films cannot be shown anywhere on the continent except in Venezuela, cinema artists and advocates continue working in exile, in secret, or in submission, waiting for an improved climate.

Africa

Feature filmmaking, which until the sixties was nonexistent on the African continent except in the United Arab Republic, has gradually expanded through North Africa and the west coast nations, and below the equator in South Africa. Coming first by way of foreign directors seeking African locations and stories (e.g., Lionel Rogosin's denunciation of apartheid, *Come Back Africa*

From *Antonio das Mortes* (1969). Glauber Rocha's film was a prominent example of *Cinema Novo* in Brazil. Setting the action in his country's poverty-stricken north, Rocha dramatized underdevelopment marked by savagery amid religious fervor while skirting contemporary political issues. Antonio, the protagonist, becomes possessed by the spirit of the local hero whom he has murdered.

[1959]), and then through French/African coproductions, feature-film production began developing in the early seventies. It moved from the Arabic nations of Algeria, Tunisia, and Morocco to the black West African nations of Gabon and Ghana, and to Senegal, where a modest but regular schedule of production is led by Ousmane Sembene, the director whose *Mandabi* (1968) was one of the first African features to reach Western markets and critical attention.

Other west coast African nations — Cameroon, Dahomey, Mali, and Niger — have no organized film industries, and independent filmmakers there are involved in the production of documentary shorts. In central and eastern areas there is even less production activity. In South Africa the political climate and economic conditions have had an adverse effect on production in recent years. Added to these problems has been the arrival of television. The first regular television service in South Africa went on the air in January 1976; with it came an 80 percent cut in film production.

Aside from technical and economic problems, African nations, with their differing language, cultural heritages, colonial histories and degrees of liberal progressiveness, produce films that are limited in their potential for audience identification and acceptance. As with fellow Third World nations across the Atlantic, African filmmakers await a more stable economic and sociopolitical climate for major growth and international recognition.

New Fronts

Since the New Wave encore (or reprieve) by key *auteurs* and the tentative assertion of a Third World cinema, the most significant event in the creative arena of film has been the emergence of prolific and original talents from Germany and Australia. This new generation of directors has been able to command the attention of the more esoteric film circles while enjoying moderate popular success. At least one is on the way to becoming a cult hero as well.

Germany

The migration of much of Germany's talent before and during World War II, and the country's occupation and division at the War's end, left the German film industry moribund. The other Axis powers, Japan and Italy, be-

Fassbinder's Themes

*H*is talents as a filmmaker did not lie in his prowess as a political commentator of Germany today (or on the Forties or Fifties). It lay in his extrapolation of personal fears and furies, loves and losses, tragedies and trials, conflicts of value and vision, catalyzed by a national history unequaled in this century for gruesome vitality and switchback evolution.

—Harlan Kennedy,
"Fassbinder's Four
Daughters," Film Comment
(September–October 1982)

came the centers of a postwar rebirth of cinema, but Germany was not to experience a major renaissance until almost thirty years after its defeat. Confirmation of a new German cinema came in the mid-seventies with growing recognition of such directors as Werner Herzog, Wim Wenders, Hans-Jürgen Syberberg, and Rainer Werner Fassbinder. With an underlying preoccupation with its own political and sociological past and present, the films of these major German filmmakers have generally revealed a dark, cold, sardonic world, both real and imagined. Some, such as Wenders's *The American Friend* (1977) and Wolfgang Peterson's *Das Boot* (1982), evoke the present and recent past — the one a celebration of American *film noir*, the other a grim chronicle of the netherworld of war aboard a German U-boat. Others, like Herzog's *Nosferatu* (1979) and Syberberg's *Parsifal* (1982), revive the legendary images of German folklore already familiar through previous incarnations in this or other art forms. All these films seem to be marked by vibrant, dynamic composition; unconventional narrative style; and frequently by unorthodox production methods.

The late Henri Langlois referred to Fassbinder's emergence as "the beginning of German postwar cinema." After an early career in experimental antitheater in Munich as actor and director, Fassbinder began making films in 1969. The work of Godard was an obvious influence on the direction of his own films. His work

From *The Bitter Tears of Petra von Kant* (1972). Rainer Fassbinder departs exotic settings and decor for this look at the homoerotic relationships among women and the conflict that arises between love and power among the rich and famous.

Fassbinder's 1977 *Despair* is based on Vladimir Nabokov's novel, with a screenplay by Tom Stoppard. In the eight years preceding *Despair*, Fassbinder had directed thirty features, and he was scheduled to direct ten more at the time of his death in June of 1982.

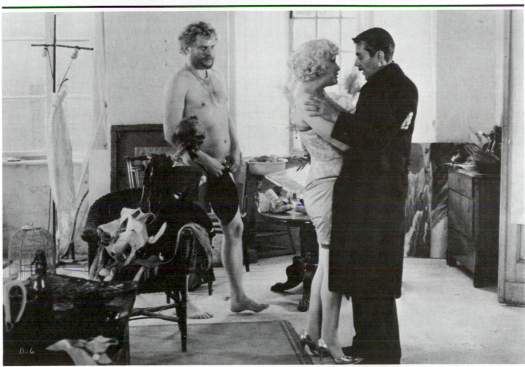

reflects a complete distrust of organization and a fascination with the Hollywood genre films of the forties and fifties, particularly those of Douglas Sirk. His style is marked by leanness and coldness in scripting and a spartan quality in setting that is nonetheless striking in visual composition. It is also characterized, like Godard's work, by leftist themes in which sexual ambiguity is prevalent and in which love becomes an instrument of social repression. Fassbinder himself identified the major theme of all his films as "the alienation of man from his own identity, and how man in this alienation is manipulated in structures of love and friendship." Like Wertmüller's, Fassbinder's films are a mixture of ideology and humanism. His Marxism is imbued with an affection for his characters, who fall victim to a repressive society and to their own *angst*.

Although Fassbinder's *The Merchant of Four Seasons* (1971) and *The Bitter Tears of Petra von Kant* (1972) won him attention in most Western markets, his films found little distribution in the United States beyond the metropolitan art houses. But this lack of broad appeal did not detract from his growing reputation as one of the most promising original talents in Europe in the mid-seventies. His output of forty-one features in sixteen years, in addition to numerous television and theater productions, made him one of the most prolific as well.

Though uneven in quality, this broad body of work secured Fassbinder's place among major international *auteurs*. His final screen credits, before his untimely death in 1982 at age thirty-six, reaffirm his unique and substantial contribution to contemporary cinema. *The Marriage of Maria Braun* (1978), *Lili Marlene* (1980), *Lola* (1981), and *Veronika Voss* (1982) are all chapters in postwar German history, a history marked by hypocrisy, despair, paralysis, and ultimate self-destruction. Besides being an indictment of a world gone wrong, the films stand as a testament to their director's brilliance both as filmmaker and social observer. They also accent the loss of this unique talent, whose creative energy, fed by a love-hate relationship with his own country, gave the world a new dimension in social realist cinema.

The films of Werner Herzog, like those of Fassbinder, portray a world of rebellion and self-destruction, or a world "poised on the outer edge of human experience," in the words of one critic. This is a world populated with the physically deformed, the emotionally crippled, and the mentally unstable.

Aguirre, Wrath of God (1973) was the first of Herzog's films to receive widespread commercial distribution. It tells of a group of 1560 Spanish *conquistadores* who travel up the Amazon River in search of the legendary El Dorado. Here, Herzog was already distinguishing himself as a master of anomalies and absurdist detail. Klaus Kinski plays the mad prophet who leads his band of fortune seekers across a mountain wilderness, dragging the baggage of modern civilization (including a huge cannon) with them. The film is a prelude to his *Fitzcarraldo* (1982), in which a 320-ton steamboat is hauled over a Peruvian mountain pass. In both films the crews' experience in the South American wilds frequently parallel the journey of the films' protagonists; in several instances accidents in the production of the films have been written into the script.

Herzog's place among major directors was secured with *The Mystery of Kaspar Hauser* (1975). Like Truffaut's *The Wild Child,* it is a study of animal innocence in a bourgeois society. Kaspar Hauser's learning of civilized behavior is set in a society that is itself cruel and bestial.

Herzog's unorthodox approach to filmmaking is expressed here in his casting in the title role a forty-five-year-old man who had spent most of his life in a mental institution.

Wild aspiration and madness are at the center of Herzog's mystical medieval drama *Heart of Glass* (1976), about a village that faces ruin when a glassblower dies in possession of the secret formula used to produce the ruby glass at the local factory. The stupefying effect of the film is perhaps in part the result of another unconventional production method — Herzog hypnotized the entire cast during the filming. In *Nosferatu* (1979), a remake of the 1922 Murnau classic and homage to its director, Herzog continues his vision of cursed and tormented souls.

Wim Wenders, like Herzog, pushes the characters of his films to the limits of discovery and madness. Like both Fassbinder and Herzog, Wenders was born during World War II and grew up on Hollywood films of the thirties and forties. The influence of John Ford, Douglas Sirk, and Anthony Mann is readily apparent in his films, and the journey becomes a central motif by which Wenders explores loss of direction, loss of purpose, and loss of identity.

In *The Goalkeeper's Fear of the Penalty Kick* (1972), the journey is that of a soccer goalie who, after murdering the girl with whom he has spent the night, quits the game and takes to the road by bus to rediscover his past. *Kings of the Road* (1976) brings together a pediatrician and a repairman, who travel the border between East and West Germany. The two reflect on the changes in their country, particularly the absorption of American culture, and reveal their anxiety about loneliness and the fragility of human relations. The death and potential rebirth of German cinema are ingeniously portrayed in a scene in which the repairman visits a derelict movie house and, while repairing the sound system, delights the children in the audience with a pantomime, his companion assisting behind the screen.

The American Friend (1977), taken from a Patricia Highsmith novel (as was Hitchcock's *Strangers on a Train*), deals with espionage and international intrigue in New York and European capitals, but has as its focus, beyond the murder and mayhem of the plot, an absorption in loss of identity and direction. (It is like Antonioni's *The Passenger* in this respect.) This film is also a study in the dimensions of friendship, with Wenders's own American friend, director Nicholas Ray, playing a central role. Wenders has said, "All my films are road films." This comment not only reflects his consciousness of American films and New Wave influences but characterizes the themes of his major works, which examine an Everyman's journey through life's mysteries and misadventures.

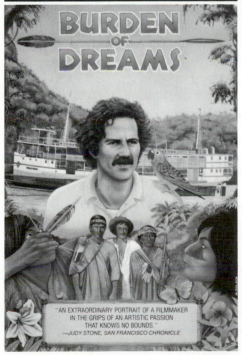

From *Fitzcarraldo* (1982). Inspired by the 1894 account of an Irish rubber baron's Peruvian escapades, Werner Herzog's film centers on the hauling of a 320-ton steamboat through the mountains and jungles of Peru from one tributary of the Amazon to another. Herzog's cast and crew lived for months in the jungle, experiencing many of the hardships encountered by the characters they were portraying. The trials and tribulations of the production, including injuries and fatalities, were recorded in a feature-length documentary entitled *Burden of Dreams* (1982) by Les Blank.

▲ From *The American Friend* (1977). The American friend of the title is a con artist who sells the works of New York painters at Hamburg auctions to dealers who then sell them to wealthy Texans. This international thriller jumps continually from New York, to Munich, to Paris, and to Hamburg in its attempt to reveal the mingling of American and European cultures. Wim Wenders cast American directors Sam Fuller and Nicholas Ray in the film. Ray (seen here) played the "dead" American artist shortly before his own death.

Working in the New Cinema

*I*t's almost like after the revolution, which is always the hardest part. Now we've won: We have a film industry, we have credibility in foreign countries and a small but eager audience, and now it's harder. There are lawyers, agents, fees, false gods, laurels to be won—more to lose. When we get together we tend to remember the good old days in the hills, when we had nothing. We get sentimental, like old soldiers.

—*Peter Weir*, New York Times *(January 16, 1983)*

Australia

Through the late seventies and early eighties, Australian cinema won world recognition and established markets with its intelligent, disciplined, and provocative films. The major works, which have had modest runs, mostly in European and American urban centers, are also refreshingly independent and diverse in style. Phillip Noyce's *Newsfront* (1978), Gillian Armstrong's *My Brilliant Career* (1979), Bruce Beresford's *Breaker Morant* (1980), and George Miller's *Mad Max* (1979) and *The Road Warrior* (1982) all herald a major creative outpouring from a country that has long been active in producing films but has had difficulty in finding audiences

beyond its shores. Miller calls his futuristic tales of a postnuclear-war loner "Westerns in new clothes." Tina Turner made her screen debut in *Mad Max Beyond Thunderdome*, the third in his series. One can see diversity in subject and style by comparing Armstrong's *My Brilliant Career* and Miller's *Road Warrior*. The former is a languid, earth-rich story of the social and intellectual maturing of a young woman writer living on a cattle ranch in New South Wales at the turn of the century; the latter is a hard, glossy vision, in the style of the modern comic strip, of postnuclear punks on the rampage.

Peter Weir has emerged as the most prolific and critically acclaimed of the new Australian filmmakers. His *Picnic at Hanging Rock* (1975) is a mystery that transcends the puzzle of the plot, which concerns the disappearance of some schoolgirls in the Outback at the turn of the century. The true mystery that Weir's camera brings into focus concerns the imposing of one culture on another. *The Last Wave* (1977), *Gallipoli* (1981), and *The Year of Living Dangerously* (1983) have brought Weir to the forefront not only of Australian filmmaking but also to the ranks of world directors. *Gallipoli* is a rich, intelligent, and suspenseful dramatization of the youthful enthusiasm for battle that led up to the World War I debacle near Istanbul, in which waves of soldiers went to their deaths at the hands of entrenched

▲ From *Picnic at Hanging Rock* (1975). The mysterious disappearance of several girls from an Australian boarding school provides the narrative for the mystical film that brought Australian director Peter Weir into the international spotlight.

Turks. Weir's sense of military adventure and mystery combines with his feel for romantic melodrama in *The Year of Living Dangerously*. This film focuses on the love affair and political intrigue encountered by a reporter who travels to Indonesia during the final days of the Sukarno regime. Both the political and love interests are enriched by what Weir himself found intriguing about the subject: "All the smells and sounds of an Indonesian street or market, and the mysteries there."

Brief Encounters

Films appear in the international marketplace without necessarily heralding a national renaissance. Roger Donaldson's *Smash Palace* (1981) is an important contribution from New Zealand in the neorealist tradition of making drama of the most ordinary of circumstances. Here the breakup of a marriage and its effects on the estranged couple and their daughter show how the sub-

ject of *Ordinary People, Kramer vs. Kramer,* and *Shoot the Moon* can be treated in a sensitive but unglamorous style.

In spite of the exceptional quality of such films as *The Lacemaker* (1977) and *Jonah, Who Will Be 25 in the Year 2000* (1976), the Swiss cinema has failed to establish a recognized national genre. And, if one discounts the singular efforts of Buñuel, who died in 1984, Spain has been represented by only the occasional work in broad distribution, the most recent being Victor Erice's *Spirit of the Beehive* (1973). *The Apprenticeship of Duddy Kravitz* (1974) gave Canada its brief spotlight in the seventies, but the country has had nothing approximating a golden age. Top Canadian directors such as Norman Jewison, Arthur Hiller, and Sidney Furie, as well as Canadian-born stars such as Donald Sutherland and Genevieve Bujold, have continued to migrate to Hollywood. Today the Canadian National Film Board and its tradition in documentary remain the center of that nation's film culture and reputation. The board has also provided the training ground for new directors such as Phillip Borsos, whose *The Grey Fox* (1983) adopts the story of the traditional Western but in a high-class cinematic style.

Coproduction and American Accent

If the American industry has been marked by the dissolution of the old studio system, the foreign industry, particularly in Europe, has been marked by retrenchment and consolidation. All the major industries of Western Europe have now faced the television onslaught that has resulted in dwindling patronage, and all have become involved in joint production ventures. Despite the French flair for independence, an era of coproduction has been firmly established between Italy and France, and in its wake a new international cinema with a less easily definable national character has arisen. Despite economic strains in Italy, coproduction between these two nations has been especially successful in recent years and has spurred the exploration of a European film community, or a common market in the financing, marketing, and exhibition of films, that has been in progress since the early sixties. The designs for a consolidated European film industry have included multilateral financial coproduction and distribution networks covering member nations. How such integration would be attained is still open to speculation. Even less clear is the direction such coproduction would take in the nature and quality of films themselves or the effect coproduction might have on the American and European markets. An interest of many, articulated by an official of the National Center of French Cinema, is in how to refuse "to play into the hands of the Americans without becoming anti-American." This *défi Américain* posture is calculated to break the dominance of the American film interests in Europe, particularly in distribution, without jeopardizing European-American coproduction, which inevitably means European settings and talent and American financing.

Attempts to counter American domination of the market have included a version of the old British quota law in Canada, and have extended to an attempt in India to diversify imports and break the monopoly of Hollywood films by canceling import licenses of American distributors. Nevertheless, the resistance to American domination in the film marketplace has done little to dampen the new ecumenical era of coproduction and the American financing of European productions. *The Ten-*

ant brought Roman Polanski together with a Scandinavian cinematographer and a French and American cast, while *Tess* brought the Polish director to France to film Thomas Hardy's English countryside. Jean Jacques Annaud, a director of French television, went to the Ivory Coast to make a film for Allied Artists about French and German colonists in West Africa during World War I — *Black and White in Color* (1976). Akira Kurosawa made *Derzu Uzala* in Russia, winning a Grand Prix in Moscow as well as an Academy Award, while George Cukor worked with American actors, Russian technicians, and the Russian Kirov Ballet in the production of *The Blue Bird*. Herzog's *Nosferatu* is an American/French/West German coproduction; his *Aguirre, the Wrath of God* has a cast and crew from sixteen different countries.

The retrenchment and consolidation of established European industries and the failure of new national industries in Eastern Europe and emerging Third World nations to fulfill their promise are due to a combination of old and new factors. Chronic problems include economic instability combined with the continued invasion of American films. The flood of the ever popular Hollywood product continues, despite attempts at quota laws, import duties, and license revocation. In Japan, exhibition of domestic films dropped fifty percent in 1975, while *Towering Inferno* and *Jaws* set new attendance records. Other problems include continued, and in some cases more stringent, censorship controls, which are politically as well as socially motivated. Socialist and Fascist powers alike are responsible for sanitizing films, or more likely for keeping filmmakers towing the party line. The loss of major film artists to established Western industries (and in some cases to television) continues to plague promising centers of new cinema.

Finally, in many regions, such as India, Africa, and Latin America, television is only now moving from affluent homes of city dwellers to the rural areas. But even where television has been an alternative to moviegoing for some time, improved technical quality, color, and better programming are creating new challenges.

Wrap-Up

Along with the blurring of American national identity and a new international look has come an ebbing of New Wave tides. Economic uncertainty, political pressures, and the television invasion have all made their marks. But in the case of the established Western industries in particular, the continued American dominance of the film marketplace and increasing control by American production studios around the world are the critical factors.

The new international cinema is a cinema with a distinctly American accent. Major American studios take an increasing interest in backing foreign productions and handling the distribution. American film crews work abroad to take advantage of cheaper labor costs and authentic Old World settings. Foreign directors, such as Roman Polanski, Miloš Forman, and Louis Malle are lured to Hollywood by the promise of economic support and artistic and political freedom. Or they go simply for the challenge of working on the American scene with American actors. Some European and Third World directors, such as Bergman, Wertmüller, and Babenco, have chosen to stay put and to make English-language films with American actors occasionally. Such films lack a clear national identity and are often imbued with a distinctly American spirit.

12

New American Films and Filmmakers (1965 – Present)

Focus

Like the 1950s the last twenty years of American film are difficult, if not impossible, to characterize. Trying to piece together the many economic, artistic, technological, and social trends discernible in the fabric of American film is like trying to piece together the parts of a jigsaw puzzle blindfolded.

Part of the problem is a simple lack of historical distance, and compounding it is the speed with which many changes have taken place. Instant trends have been the norm of this period. With the exception of James Bond and an assortment of sharks, homicidal maniacs with knives, flying men in red suits, and Jedi warriors, very few film cycles of any length have been established since 1965. In 1964 – 1965, with the huge success of *My Fair Lady, Mary Poppins,* and *The Sound of Music,* musicals were in. But four years later, with such disasters as *Star* and *Dr. Doolittle,* they were out. Following *The Graduate* (1967), *Easy Rider* (1969), and *Alice's Restaurant* (1969), youth films were booming. Two years later, with Elliott Gould and others leading the way in such films as *Getting Straight* (1970), *The Magic Garden of Stanley Sweetheart* (1970), and *The Land-lord* (1970), the boom was busted. Old-fashioned love flowered once again in 1970 with *Love Story,* but less than two years later *The Godfather* exhibited a different form of affection. *The Exorcist* (1973) started a brief occult cycle, but *Jaws* (1975) soon replaced it with an animal/fish cycle. Next the industry jumped on an "outer space" bandwagon generated by the phenomenal success of *Star Wars* (1977). The space cycle has proved to be the most enduring cycle of all, as box-office receipts for *Return of the Jedi* (1983) and *Superman III* (1983) have documented. This quick overview serves to suggest the many different directions American film has been moving in. Throughout the last twenty years, Hollywood's search for a lost audience, a successful formula, and a return to past glories has continued unabated.

As we have seen, changes in the industry, content, and overall pattern and structure of the American film began in the late forties and early fifties. Like the jack pine tree whose seeds are released only by the intense heat of a forest fire, the roots of the "new American cinema" took hold in the fires of the fifties. And like the jack pine whose seeds explode in all directions, film has exploded over and over during these last two decades, and the explosions have created new styles, new audiences, new markets, and new films.

Burgeoning interest in film on an academic level perfectly illustrates this explosiveness. Film historian Arthur Knight has noted, "Back in 1960 when I joined the staff of USC's Department of Cinema there were many people — teachers as well as students — who suspected that we might be taking money under false pretenses." But by 1969, the American Film Institute (itself a product of the new interest) was conducting an annual survey of film study in colleges and universities.

Some have referred to the period since 1960 as a renaissance in American filmmaking. Clearly, there has been an infusion of new energy and new directions. However, much of the new activity is without clear focus. Film's new directions are still in the process of evolving and, more important for this chapter and book, still in the process of being understood.

outside the United States) had reached the 50 percent level. Industry box-office receipts for 1962 fell to $900 million, the lowest in history. Unfortunately, along came a film called *The Sound of Music* (1965), which Hollywood instantly translated into "The Sound of Money." Grossing more than $135 million, it quickly inspired a trend of big-budget spectacles among the studios that ultimately proved disastrous. Since spectacles take longer to produce than the average feature, the industry found itself with some very expensive films in production just at a time when audiences began lining up for blocks to see such nonspectacle features as *The Graduate* and *Bonnie and Clyde* in 1967. *Star* (1968) and *Dr. Doolittle* (1967), both made by 20th Century-Fox, flopped badly. And Fox's *Tora! Tora! Tora!* (1970), at a cost of $25 million, did even worse. All of a sudden, in 1969, Fox found itself with a film inventory of more than $300 million and a loss of more than $30 million. Paramount was also caught up in big budget – big film thinking, with *Darling Lili* (1969) ($19 million), *The Molly McGuires* (1970) ($17 million), and *Paint Your Wagon* (1969) ($20 million) leading the parade of losses.

By the late sixties, it was clear that the studios were in deep trouble. Traditionally, the system had thrived on size. Huge sound stages and back lots, which had been symbols of prestige and power, were now liabilities draining away badly needed resources. Since the belt

Industrial Change

One of the most significant changes since the 1960s has taken place in the structure of the industry itself. Throughout the fifties and early sixties, the studio system in general and the major studios in particular floundered in a sea of red ink looking for the keys to box-office success. Production costs soared in 1966 to an average $3 million per feature while box-office figures still plunged. The studios were desperate. Independent production companies were now making more than 30 percent of all films, and "runaway" productions (films made

▶ Julie Andrews stars as Maria Von Trapp in the 1965 Rodgers & Hammerstein blockbuster *The Sound of Music.* The film won five Oscars, but ironically Andrews's performance did not win.

United States Theatrical Film Admissions
(1946–1983)

*A*n unbroken annual decline in ticket sales occurred from 1946–1962. Perhaps not by coincidence, 1962 was the year that television had reached 90 percent penetration of U.S. homes, culminating its period of explosive growth. Since 1962, admissions have stabilized in the range of 1 billion per year. The low point was in 1971, at 820 million tickets.

—*Annual Ticket Sales Data: MPAA, Variety.*
Chart © 1984 A. D. Murphy.

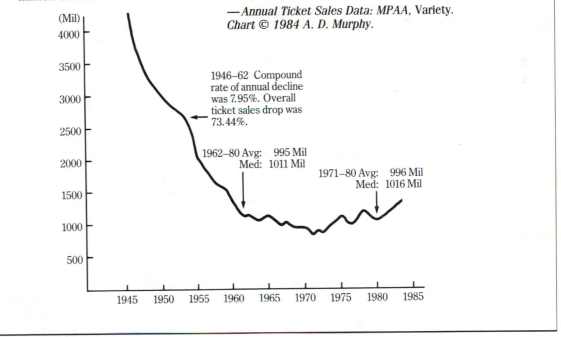

1946–62 Compound rate of annual decline was 7.95%. Overall ticket sales drop was 73.44%.

1962–80 Avg: 995 Mil
Med: 1011 Mil

1971–80 Avg: 996 Mil
Med: 1016 Mil

obviously had to be tightened, studios started firing people, shelving films, and selling back lots to eager real estate developers. The only extensive back lot to survive was Universal's which was saved by TV and tourists, who come to take tours fashioned for their benefit.

Badly weakened, most of the studios succumbed to the fate of most small fish in big ponds — they were eaten by larger fish. In this case the big fish were huge corporate conglomerates that wanted to diversify and thought motion picture studios might make nice acquisitions. Thus, Universal was acquired in 1962 by the Music Corporation of America. Paramount was absorbed by Gulf and Western in 1966; Warner Brothers by Kinney National Services in 1969; United Artists by Transamerica, Inc., in 1967; MGM by real estate magnate Kirk Ker-korian in 1970; and Columbia Pictures by the Coca-Cola Company in 1982.

A faceless, impersonal, remote corporate power began to dominate a historically individualistic industry. Instead of Columbia Studios president Harry Cohn looking out his office window trying to catch some writer leaving early, or Louis B. Mayer alternately raging and weeping in the hopes of coercing some star into accepting a new contract, the industry had Charles G. Bluhdorn, Board Chairman of Gulf and Western, who stated, "I oversee all our divisions. One of them is Leisure Time, and Paramount is just a part of it." Bluhdorn's passion was not movies, but business. Individual studio styles were destroyed, physical plants demolished, and, where previously 20 percent of any film went into studio overhead, now 95 percent was allocated to "on-screen" costs.

Conglomerate takeover has had both positive and negative effects on motion pictures. Both Gulf and Western and Kinney have kept their respective subsidiaries functioning as active production units. Since filmmaking is a highly unstable business, the ability of a conglomerate to "shelter" a studio from the consequences of bad pictures has been critical, and that they have done so is certainly healthy. However, even for "healthy" studios questions arise about the effects of corporate ownership. What, for instance, was the effect on Paramount films of Gulf and Western's 1974 $32 million bullet contract with the U.S. Army? Would a company with such a contract produce films with such strong antiwar sentiments as *M*A*S*H* or *Paths of Glory* or *Dr. Strangelove?* It is certainly true that studio moguls such as Harry Cohn, Louis B. Mayer, and Jack Warner controlled their studios with an iron hand. It is true that Paramount distributed *Reds* (1981), but the decision to do so was based more on producer/director Warren Beatty's personal and professional influence than on corporate policy. Obviously, there are no easy answers regarding matters of conflicting values. It is sufficient to say here that new ownership patterns have brought new concerns and problems as well as new potential.

Another important change involved small independent producers emerging from the fringes of the industry. As the industry slowly evolved over the past twenty years, the production company, often formed to make a single film, and not simply the studio, became the unit of film production. A typical such company was Cannon Films, which was created to distribute the sex potboiler *Inga* (1968) and then hit the big time with *Joe* (1971). Made for less than $300,000, *Joe* grossed more than $20 million. Although companies such as Cannon emerged throughout the entire decade, not until the success of *Easy Rider* in 1969 did the established studios finally become convinced that movies made for less than $500,000 by relatively unknown people could succeed. *Easy Rider* returned a box-office gross of more than $50 million on an investment of $370,000, and inspired a rush to duplicate its success. Of the total $1.8 billion box-office gross of 1969, $1.2 billion came from independent producers.

Some strange production patterns and odd combinations resulted from all this activity. David L. Wolper signed an agreement with the Quaker Oats Company for a series of family movies that included *Willie Wonka and the Chocolate Factory* (1971), and *Reader's Digest* funded *Tom Sawyer* (1973) and *Huckleberry Finn* (1974). The advertising agency Wells, Rich and Greene backed *Dirty Little Billy* (1973), and Mattel Toys pro-

vided funds for *Sounder* (1972). One of the more unusual sources of outside money was for the film *Gunfight* (1971). The Jicarilla Apaches, a tribe of about 1,800 New Mexico Indians, put up $2 million, which they received from income on oil and gas investments. As Chief Charles Vigil stated, "We consider ourselves a corporation like any other."

One of the most successful of the production companies emerging in the seventies was Sunn International. Using a sophisticated marketing strategy, Sunn identified a target audience and proceeded to create a product designed to appeal specifically to that group. In this instance, the target was families and married couples who seldom attended motion pictures, and the product was the nature adventure film. Bypassing the normal distribution process, Sunn rented theaters outright (a strategy called "four walling") and spent huge amounts of money advertising a film to the target audience. With such films as *The Life and Times of Grizzly Adams* (1975) and *In Search of Noah's Ark* (1977), Sunn further demonstrated the ability to make money outside the major studio mainstream.

One reason that independents flourished during the general decline of large studios was that the Hollywood unions were becoming more flexible. This did not come easily, however. Most producers, independent or otherwise, realized that the studios had built up the finest collection of craftspeople and technicians in the world. However, the unions had long been rigid in their rules concerning working conditions and salaries. As one director stated, "Hollywood is great as long as you're working inside a studio. But the minute you go on location, even if it's only ten blocks from the studio gate, the unions will kill you every time." An example from John Sturges's film *The Satan Bug* (1965) clearly illustrates this point. Sturges had a climactic scene involving an auto chase through the downtown freeways of Los Angeles. The Screen Extras Guild wanted to charge him for every car that appeared in the shots, plus a stiff penalty fee, alleging that Sturges was depriving extras of legitimate work.

As a consequence of the unions' strictness, most independents left Hollywood to work abroad, usually in England or Spain, in order to produce their low-budget films. The result of these so-called "runaway" productions was up to 90 percent unemployment in some unions. The unions thus agreed to a new contract in 1970 allowing producers to use a basic nine-person crew and members of one union to help members of any other. In the past, when a lighting person needed assistance, a prop person could not step in to help. Thus, a Hollywood film crew was often two or three times larger than was actually necessary.

With all this independent activity going on around them, the studios found their traditional position as the major film-producing organizations usurped. Now, in most cases, they functioned primarily as financing and distributing organizations for independent producers. One of the most ambitious cooperative ventures took place in 1972, when Paramount put up $31.5 million against 50 percent of the profits to back three young, highly successful directors—William Friedkin (*The French Connection* [1971]), Francis Ford Coppola (*The Godfather* [1972]), and Peter Bogdanovich (*The Last Picture Show* [1971])—in an organization called The Directors Company. The results in general were not good, but the concept remained. In many ways this interaction was similar to what happened in France in the late fifties and early sixties when the French government subsidized hundreds of new filmmakers. The results were not always successful, but new energy and vitality were introduced into a moribund industry.

In most studios during the last twenty years the pattern has been feast or famine. Despite some successes, they have ceased to exist as major production organizations. They stand alongside the independents as peers in production. Nevertheless, the studios continue to dominate the industry. This is because in the motion picture business of the 1980s, the distributor (i.e., the major studio) is still the major risk taker, since it is the primary borrower of funds used to produce films. Studios finance or provide the collateral for nine of every ten films produced in the United States today. If the cost of a movie exceeds production estimates, it is the distributor who has to provide the necessary capital to complete it. Thus distributors receive their return before producers do. Generally one-third of the distribution gross (total receipts minus the exhibitor's share) is retained to cover distribution costs; the remainder is sent to the bank to retire the loan. Studios still control the system, then, because they control distribution and financing. As a result, the so-called freedom of the independent production is largely fictitious. As long as an individual producer has to convince a studio production head to distribute and possibly finance a film, control of the industry and the films produced still rests with a few people.

Therefore, although it is true that the last twenty years have seen enormous changes in the motion picture industry, the more things change the more they stay the same. The emphasis in recent years on the blockbuster film has led to increasing conservatism in the industry and therefore more reliance on the major studios as financing agents. While independent filmmaker George Lucas may operate entirely outside the studio system, he is the rare exception. In effect, Lucas is his own studio, financed by the profits from *Star Wars, The Empire Strikes Back, Return of the Jedi,* and so on. On the other hand, Francis Ford Coppola tried to be his own studio and failed miserably.

In summary, a new/old system continues to dominate motion picture production in this country. While the studios no longer employ actors, actresses, directors, and writers on long-term contracts, and no longer actually produce the majority of motion pictures, they in effect continue to control what is seen on the screen.

A New Star System

The last twenty years have witnessed great changes in the personnel of the film industry as well as in production patterns. The star system, which dominated American films ever since Florence Lawrence received on-screen credit, declined noticeably in the 1970s, partly because old stars were dying and very few new stars were emerging to replace them. Just when Hollywood needed fresh faces and new images most, it found itself undermined by the economy measures of the fifties, which resulted in the signing of few new contracts and the canceling of many old contracts. The 1980s have seen a resurgence of the star's power but in a new manner. Sylvester Stallone and perhaps Barbra Streisand can demand multimillion dollar deals, and are showcased in pictures made especially for them. However, Stallone and Streisand also happen to make those films themselves. They and other stars of equal power, such as Jane Fonda, Paul Newman, and Clint Eastwood, are less stars than creators wearing many hats, including those of writer, director, producer, and actor.

Sociologists and studio heads alike have long understood that leadership patterns define roles to a great extent. Indeed, defining roles in the studios may have been the most powerful effect of the entire studio star system. In the past, Hollywood depended heavily on the consistency of these set roles. The star system institutionalized these roles, and depended on certain faces and names used in carefully constructed patterns: Clark Gable was the rugged he-man; Gary Cooper, the strong, silent individualist; Jean Arthur, the kooky blonde; and Marlene Dietrich, the sultry seductress. Men and women often defined themselves in terms of these screen images, and Hollywood became very comfortable (perhaps unconsciously so) in the knowledge that it was working so well as a "social reflector." Throughout the sixties the studios struggled with and attempted to perpetuate this system. From 1958 to 1967 only twelve of the fifty top-grossing films lacked major stars. However, by 1967 many of the old faces were gone and the new ones were being used badly (Julie Andrews in *Star,* Sidney Poitier in *The Last Man* and *Brother John*). And with fewer films being produced each year, there was too little time for contract players to develop skills or for publicity departments to develop images.

Society had changed also. It had become divided and fractionalized by the 1960s. Youth had a significant hand in this division and, as films began to reflect this orientation, a Richard Burton or Elizabeth Taylor playing a highly manicured role was no longer acceptable to this sizeable part of the American film audience. In 1967 a film called *The Graduate* did much to crystallize and define this audience, and as a result a whole new generation of personalities emerged. *The Graduate* went against most of Hollywood's standard operating procedures. Mike Nichols, its director, was primarily a stage and television personality, and Dustin Hoffman, its major star, was an unknown. The property itself was a minor novel with no built-in audience. Thus with this picture's success most of the old formulas went out the window. Here was a film in which *the theme* was the star and relatively unknown people were acting as attractive vehicles for that theme. The film was the top box-office hit of 1967, and Mike Nichols won the year's Academy Award for Best Director.

Unknowns were in, and almost as if by magic, new faces began to appear. Studios were now willing to gamble on such people as Jack Nicholson, Richard Benjamin, Alan Arkin, Donald Sutherland, and Jon Voight. As one of these new faces, Gene Wilder, stated, "Ten years ago, they wanted the kind of face that only a few hundred people in the world possessed—the Hollywood face. They didn't want people who looked like the people in the audience. Now they realize that they can make money by letting the audience see actors with whom they can identify." Richard Zanuck stated it somewhat more bluntly: "We're hiring the uglies." As a result, many of the films produced in recent years have featured performers who, although not necessarily ugly, have had little inherent box-office value. *Superman* (1978) starred a then unknown Christopher Reeve. The major stars of the two largest grossing films of all time, *Jaws* and *Star Wars,* were a mechanical shark and two robots, respectively. In a recent audience poll, 80 percent of the viewers considered subject matter the most important factor in their decision to see a particular film. As Steven Spielberg said in 1978, "What interests me more than anything else is the idea. If a person can tell me the idea in twenty-five

▼   Dustin Hoffman, staring helplessly at a seduction-minded Anne Bancroft in Mike Nichols's *The Graduate* (1967).

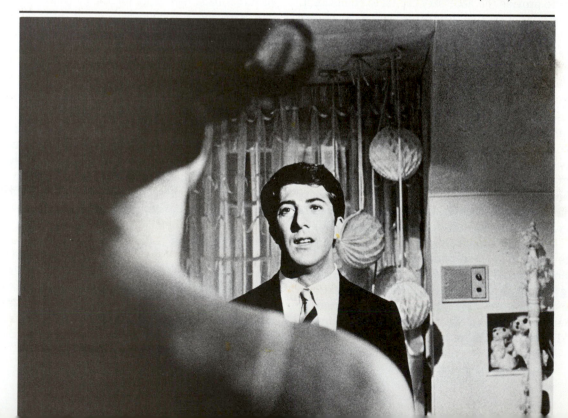

▶ Jon Voight and a radically transformed Dustin Hoffman in *Midnight Cowboy* (1969), John Schlesinger's X-rated compelling character study.

words or less, it's going to make a pretty good movie. I like ideas, especially movie ideas, that you can hold in your hand."

Those stars who continued to work did not perform in the traditional star manner. Dustin Hoffman, for example, did not continue to play confused adolescents following *The Graduate*. Instead, he made a remarkable and thoroughly convincing transformation in *Midnight Cowboy* (1969), playing a Times Square derelict. Hoffman has continued on in this nonpatterned way, as evidenced by his "female" character in *Tootsie* (1982). Christopher Reeve made a similar role reversal, going from playing Superman to playing a young gay playwright in *Deathtrap* (1982). But perhaps no actor of modern times typifies this antitype-cast style than Robert De Niro. He has moved with remarkable grace and skill through a wide variety of roles, including a psychotic taxidriver, a 1940s saxophone player, a young and old Jake Lamotta (1950s prizefighter/boxer), a self-styled "king of comedy," and a Vietnam warrior/ex-warrior. Sean Connery stopped playing James Bond because he did not want to be typed. Of the "old" stars who survived, only those such as Paul Newman and Katharine Hepburn, who had the power to fight for roles that would not stereotype them, met with any reasonable success.

Still, the star system in Hollywood of the eighties is not dead. People continue to go to movies to see certain actors and actresses perform. However, it is now the acting performance itself rather than the individual personality that is the attraction. The careers of several major actresses during the late seventies and early eighties — Meryl Streep, Jane Fonda, Jill Clayburgh, and Jessica Lange — demonstrate this fact. Like their male counterparts — such actors as Dustin Hoffman, Al Pacino, Robert Redford, and Jack Nicholson — these women refuse to be stereotyped as performers. Fonda especially has demonstrated the ability to play a wide variety of roles, ranging from the Vietnam "widow" in *Coming Home* (1978), the meek secretary in *Nine to Five* (1981), to the estranged daughter in *On Golden Pond* (1982). Jessica Lange was able to break away from the "girl in the gorilla's hand" role in *King Kong* into major dramatic roles in *The Postman Always Rings*

Twice (1980), *Frances* (1982), *Tootsie* (1982), and *Country* (1983).

Perhaps the epitome of the performance-as-star phenomenon was Ben Kingsley's Academy Award-winning performance in *Gandhi* (1982). The unknown Kingsley won the award despite very powerful competition, particularly by Paul Newman in *The Verdict* (1982).

The Director as "Star"

The star system has not only changed; it has expanded as well. Now men and women behind the camera are almost as well known and important to the audience as the people in front of it. Although the behind-the-scenes people include writers, cameramen, and set designers, among many others, it is the director who has stepped into the spotlight. Once again, as in the very beginning — with

Méliès, Porter, Griffith, and von Stroheim, among others — the American film has become at least partially a director's medium. The "discovery" of the director as star in the sixties and seventies was not really a discovery at all, but a reassessment and shift in audience attitudes, industry policy, and, perhaps most important, critical evaluation.

Much has been written about the so-called *auteur theory*, in which a film is evaluated primarily on the basis of its director and the film's relationship to the director's total body of work. Emerging from French critical thought in the early fifties, this theory has been both praised and maligned. Whether one agrees with the theory or not, the movement toward recognizing the director as a vital and at times dominant force in the filmmaking process is welcome. In fact, as the movement gained force in the sixties, it not only recognized directors but encouraged them to establish control. Helped by the decline in the studio system, directors *as individuals with ideas they want to express in film* have become a significant force in the American film of the last twenty years.

The words in italics in the preceding sentence are meant to draw attention to an important but often overlooked fact. Directors are not gods who create works of art from pictures inside their heads. They work within a system and with a crew of highly trained professionals. They still function as coordinators, organizers of people and machinery. Directors have always had ideas — some good, some bad. Today, however, they have more opportunities to express those ideas and receive recognition for them than they did twenty years ago. Equally important is a fact well stated by Alan Casty: "An individual artist's style, whether intuitive or conscious, however distinct or even idiosyncratic, bears significant relationships not only to those of his contemporaries, but to a pervasive style of the times, the intricate fabric of a culture." Directors, then, are tied to their cultures, to society at large, and to the industries in which they work. Directors have certain ideas and approach them with their own distinctive styles. Trying to pinpoint and extract a common denominator from these many approaches is impossible. Yet, despite a conservative trend in the eighties, this diversity is precisely what has made the last twenty years one of the most exciting periods in film history. The careers and films of such men as Martin Scorsese, Sidney Lumet, Steven Spielberg, George Lucas, Francis Ford Coppola, Stanley Kubrick, and Robert Altman provide us with various individual glimpses of life and reality as these men perceive them. What is unique in their work is obvious; what they have in common, although not as obvious, can provide us with clues to the general direction American film is taking.

The American cinema of the past twenty years has been characterized primarily by the work of individuals rather than studios, and as such it reflects every aspect of contemporary life. The "problem" picture has become a catch-all category into which many of these films fall, but problems and problem pictures have always been with us. What is significant now is that filmmakers have the freedom to explore *all* problems and present them honestly. This is not to say that all problems are treated or that those treated are dealt with honestly; the key is that the opportunity is there.

Many new directors have emerged in the last twenty years. Of these, several stand out for their consistent contributions to an expanding American cinema. In the subsequent subsections we will discuss the distinguishing characteristics of their work.

Martin Scorsese

Martin Scorsese burst on the American Screen in 1973 with a small gutsy film called *Mean Streets*. Here he displayed both the concern for physical landscape and the intense characterization that would become common themes in his future films. Since then, however, his locales and characters have shifted radically. He moved from the small-town environment of a lonely woman in *Alice Doesn't Live Here Anymore* (1974) to the ugly urban squalor of New York and the demented world of a psychopathic killer in *Taxi Driver* (1976). His next film, *New York, New York* (1977), took his audience even farther away in time and space, to the semisurrealistic world of a musical, set in post-World War II America. Working once again with actor Robert De Niro (who played in *Mean Streets, Taxi Driver,* and *New York, New York*), Scorsese probed deeply into the character of boxer Jake Lamotta with his 1981 feature *Raging Bull.* His *King of Comedy* (1983) was an ambitious but flawed work. It was "gentle," and to some lacked the singular intensity of his earlier work in *Mean Streets* and *Raging Bull.* Still, Scorsese remains a poet laureate of the contemporary American film. And although he has followed in Stanley Kubrick and Robert Altman's path in exploring and experimenting with theme and style, he has emerged as one of the brightest directorial stars of the contemporary scene.

Sidney Lumet

Sidney Lumet came from television, and he brought to such films as *Long Day's Journey into Night* (1962),

Scorsese on Scorsese

*M*y last film *Raging Bull* had been planned for a long time. But we kept on having problems with the script and I couldn't see how to do the central character—a boxer. Then one weekend in September 1978, I was taken seriously ill and I went into hospital. I don't know what happened but somehow during those four days alone in hospital I went through some kind of transformation and I came out of it. Afterwards Bobby De Niro came up to see me in hospital and we talked and somehow, because of what had happened, I not only knew how to do the character but also why I wanted to do it. The leading character in the film is very similar to me.

Raging Bull, which was co-written by Paul Schrader who wrote *Taxi Driver* and my old colleague Mardik Martin, has a lot of violence, but it's a completely different kind of violence from *Taxi Driver.* It's not only physical but psychological, and it doesn't build to a climax in the way *Taxi Driver* does. The climax of *Raging Bull* is something different altogether. I learnt a lot about myself from making the film. And at this point in my career, if I can't learn something from making a film—whether it's about myself or about history or just how the British serve tea—I'm not interested in doing the film. I suppose that if I had to fall back on my knowledge of craft and make an action/adventure or something I would do it to live. But I find it hard to see what you can do to top people like Hawks or Ford. Also we all seem to be agreed that making something like *Star Wars* is a murderous experience; with the use of blue screen as an effects background you can't even have people move an inch while they're talking so even shooting a simple dialogue scene becomes impossibly tedious. This is one reason why all of us are so involved in finding ways of simplifying, ways of making films faster and cheaper.

—*Martin Scorsese,* Anatomy of the Movies

Fail-Safe (1964), *The Pawnbroker* (1965), and *The Group* (1966) a television-oriented sense of space and character. Using tight camera angles and highly expressionistic lighting, Lumet outlined his characters and their concerns with solid brushstrokes. Although perhaps a little too self-conscious in his treatment of socially significant issues (Lumet rarely lets the inherent drama of an event carry the day but usually infuses his films with heavy emotionalism), one finds in American film of the sixties few images to match the old man in *The Pawnbroker,* isolated behind his cage, trapped in an environment of his memories and his own making. Lumet continued to explore this theme of social and personal morality on into the seventies with such films as *Serpico* (1973), *Murder on the Orient Express* (1974), *Dog Day Afternoon* (1975), and *Network* (1976). However, after achieving enormous critical and popular success with *Network,* Lumet wandered away from his previous work and began to experiment unsuccessfully with such efforts as the musical *The Wiz* (1978), *Tell Me What You Want* (1980), and *Deathtrap* (1982). These failures may have contained a message, however, since Lumet returned to old territory with *Prince of the City* (1981), *Daniel* (1983), and *The Verdict* (1983). Whether these efforts are as powerful as his earlier work is open to question, but despite occasional lapses into heavy self-conscious social statements, Lumet continues to create competent films of conscience.

Peter Finch in the role of network newscaster Howard Beale. The character's performance as a mad prophet made his TV ratings soar in the MGM film *Network* (1976), directed by Sidney Lumet.

▶ William Holden in Sam Peckinpah's *The Wild Bunch* (1969). An elegy to aging outlaws, this film is best known for its "beautiful" blood-letting.

Sam Peckinpah

Although not a major directorial force in the eighties, Sam Peckinpah must be acknowledged as a key director of the seventies. Opinion is somewhat divided concerning Peckinpah. In 1968, before Peckinpah made *The Wild Bunch* (1969), Andrew Sarris classified him among the "oddities, one-shots and newcomers." Indeed, Peckinpah was a little of each, as he had produced only three films by 1968: *The Deadly Companions* (1962), *Ride the High Country* (1962), and *Major Dundee* (1964). He had an extensive background in directing television Westerns, and he did so in new ways, combining elements of poetry and realism with statements evoking the lost mythology of the West. Working almost exclusively with the Western genre (one notable exception was *Straw Dogs* [1972]) he became, more than any other director, the apostle of new violence. His film *The Wild Bunch* was perhaps most influential since it used slow motion to heighten and diffuse the impact of violent death. In this it was similar to *Bonnie and Clyde*, made the year before. In a sense, Peckinpah's vision was too

large for the Western tradition and heritage. Although labeled proviolence, he concentrated essentially on men and their conflicts, not simply with each other, but within themselves and with time itself. In one of his lesser known but most cohesive films, *Junior Bonner* (1973), he shows Steve McQueen cast as a man out of place and time, desperately trying to cope with a modern reality. In this film Peckinpah reveals again his traditional concern for and visualization of violence. In this case, however, the violence takes the form of a bulldozer smashing the hero's boyhood home, almost running over a car, and in general wreaking havoc on an old familiar landscape. Even McQueen's role as an aging rodeo star is symbolized by a desperate and useless conflict with a brahma bull. Thus, even though labeled a violent director, Peckinpah's images were seldom violent for their own sake. His violence had a meaning — usually of the new fighting against the old. His films of the late seventies and early eighties, however — such as *Bring Me the Head of Alfredo Garcia* (1975), *Cross of Iron* (1977), *Convoy* (1980), and *The Osterman Weekend* (1983) — revealed no consistent meaning, but emphasized instead Peckin-

▲ Ronee Blakley and Henry Gibson as country music stars appearing at a controversial political rally in Robert Altman's *Nashville* (1975). Altman wove together twenty-four characters into a kaleidoscopic vision of America in the mid-seventies. The film was hailed as the new *Citizen Kane* even before it was released. Although the film was brilliant in many ways, Altman's effort to fuse a coherent truth out of the disparate elements ultimately ran afoul of his "free" cinematic style.

pah's reliance on violence as a "quick fix" for a weak script. These films did little to enhance Peckinpah's reputation as a major creative force in American film.

Robert Altman

Robert Altman's force in the industry, like Peckinpah's, diminished in the eighties. However, at this writing Altman continues to be one of the most important American filmmakers. Robert Altman came to film from television and established himself in 1970 with the film *M∗A∗S∗H*, in which he walked a thin tightrope between comedy and social commentary. The film's anarchic spirit established Altman as a key black-comedy *auteur*. However, instead of continuing in this direction exclusively, he chose to explore a wide range of topics, including comic fantasy in *Brewster McCloud* (1971), the American West in *McCabe and Mrs. Miller* (1971), the south during the Great Depression in *Thieves Like Us* (1973), the contemporary West Coast landscape in *California Split* (1974), the country-music scene in *Nashville* (1975), and the myth of star appeal in *Buffalo Bill and the Indians* (1976). Altman next moved into the

world of the female psyche with *Three Women* (1977) and ended the decade with three idiosyncratic and ambiguous films—*A Wedding* (1978), *Quintet* (1979), and *A Perfect Couple* (1979). In all these films, Altman focused on the realities of the social setting, most significantly experimenting with audio patterns and characteristics, including overlapping dialogue and "underheard" conversation. The eighties have not been particularly kind to Altman. His *Popeye* (1980) met with mixed critical reviews and had modest financial success. However, he soon departed from this big-budget interlude and moved back into the world of the independent low-budget feature with such films as *Come Back to the Five and Dime, Jimmy Dean, Jimmy Dean* (1983) and *Streamers* (1983). Altman continues to pursue his own visions, dreams, and themes with ever-decreasing budgets, and despite occasional flashes of brilliance is as out of step in the eighties as he was in step in the seventies.

Stanley Kubrick

Stanley Kubrick's career started earlier than Altman's, and his interests and themes have been much broader.

He is concerned primarily with man's hypocrisy, and through a relatively small body of work he has developed this theme in a bold and innovative style. Essentially a social satirist, he has looked with a devastating eye at war, both hot (*Paths of Glory* [1958]) and cold (*Dr. Strangelove* [1964]); New England's social and sexual norms (*Lolita* [1962]); technological overkill (*2001: A Space Odyssey* [1968]); futuristic society (*A Clockwork Orange* [1972]); and eighteenth-century English manners and morals (*Barry Lyndon* [1976]). Kubrick works slowly and controls every aspect of his films. What is perhaps most remarkable is the wide range of styles and cinematic forms he has worked with and perfected, ranging from the harshly realistic, semidocumentary style of *Paths of Glory* to the futuristic style dominated by special effects in *2001: A Space Odyssey;* from the baroque, high-design values of *A Clockwork Orange* to the architectural horror of the hotel in *The Shining* (1981). In all his films, Kubrick uses a combination of humor and pathos—laughter leading to deep thought—as he strives to make his audiences see the foolishness and tragedy of humankind.

With an increased emphasis on the director as *auteur,* or at least interpreter, and with directors concentrating on highly personal themes, the problem of meaning in film has become crucial, if at times overstated. Kubrick's films often fall into the trap of meaning versus meaningless. Kubrick may well have been the least understood American director of the past decade. In particular, *2001* inspired an entire body of literature designed to probe the ultimate meaning of his black slab, a symbolic and visual metaphor for the unknown. In this film, Kubrick attempted to combine mysticism and cynicism, and the result was not always clear.

The problem of conveying meaning does not lie completely with either the director or the audience, however. Audiences must become more aware and intelligent, while directors must be aware of their own thoughts and of the audiences they are addressing. Alain Resnais best summarized the obligation of the director when he said, "This is the problem of all communication, whether between two people or ten million. One must know to what extent one can share one's subjective reality with everyone."

The Inheritors

The directors discussed above were important forces in the American film industry of the sixties and seventies. Many other directors emerged in the mid-seventies, and the last ten years have been filled with new names, faces, and forces.

▲ The parts storage area of the spaceship *Discovery* in Stanley Kubrick's *2001: A Space Odyssey* (1968). This set provides evidence of the intricate design work that, along with special effects, was the real star of the film.

It would be impossible to list all the "important" contemporary directors. At this writing, we still lack the critical and historical distance to make more than tentative and incomplete assessments. Such a list compiled in the mid-seventies would have certainly included such names as William Friedkin, Peter Bogdanovich, and Dennis Hopper. At that time, many critics felt that these three directors were major *auteurs* of the period, and they may well have been. However, over time the reputations and performances of these men have diminished. Therefore, although one might be tempted to construct a current "top ten" list composed of such names as Paul Mazursky, Brian De Palma, Ron Howard, Lawrence Kasdan, Irving Kershner, John Carpenter, and Joan Menklin Silver, such a list would serve little historical purpose.

Still, to ignore completely the major directorial efforts of the past ten years would be equally foolish. A review of the last decade shows three directors as standing out for their consistent impact on American film. Not all three have records of sustained brilliance, but all accurately reflect the directions American films have been taking. These three directors are George Lucas, Steven Spielberg, and Francis Ford Coppola.

George Lucas

George Lucas has been important over the last ten years more for the immense impact on the industry of his *Star Wars* (1977) and its sequels than for any artistic contributions. More producer than director (the two *Star Wars* sequels were directed by others), Lucas nevertheless has left a personal imprint on his films, beginning with his early science fiction film *THX1138* (1978) and the nostalgic *American Graffiti* (1973). *Star Wars* and its sequels, *The Empire Strikes Back* (1980) and *Return of the Jedi* (1983), are characterized by dazzling special effects linked to clever, and some say manipulative, narrative.

▶ "Bruce," the mechanical shark in Steven Spielberg's *Jaws* (1975), churning his way through the water in search of new victims. This movement, accompanied by John Williams's Oscar-winning score and manipulated by Verna Fields's superb editing (which also won an Academy Award), succeeded in making a sensational movie out of a best-selling but basically pulp novel.

As executive producer *par excellence*, Lucas has been content to orchestrate rather than direct. The results have been spectacular, as witnessed by the post-*Star Wars* films *Raiders of the Lost Ark* (1981) and *Indiana Jones and the Temple of Doom* (1984). As an executive producer, Lucas is following more in the footsteps of Thalberg and Selznick than De Mille or Hawks. Above all else, Lucas is a master storyteller who combines age-old plots — complete with dragons, knights, and princesses — with futuristic locales and robust visual imagery.

Steven Spielberg

Like Lucas, Steven Spielberg also assumes the dual identity of director/producer, but his work is more carefully and individually shaped. Starting in television in the early seventies, Spielberg made his first feature film, *Sugarland Express,* and it helped to establish him in the industry. However, it was the "chase/water movie" *Jaws* (1975) that catapulted him into the role of superdirector. *Jaws* is a simple suspense movie that was elevated to blockbuster status by an outstanding musical score (by John Williams), clever special effects, superb editing (by Verna Fields), and an intelligent advertising campaign. Not content to have created the all-time box-office champion (up to 1977), Spielberg proceeded to outdo himself critically if not commercially with *Close Encounters of the Third Kind* (1977). This film combined the epic grandeur of the first meeting between humans and ex-

An Oscar for Editing

*W*hen we finally finished *Jaws* at Martha's Vineyard, Steve Spielberg and I went to the cutting room at my house, looked at the takes, and put it together. There were some enormous problems. For example, I had more problems with the damn barrels than I did with the water. In one chase the barrel kept going to the wrong side of the boat, and that was my biggest problem in cutting it right. The worst thing—and we didn't solve the problem until the picture was virtually ready for release—was the scene when the boat is pulled backwards. The boat coming to a stop, we discovered, had never been shot. A fluke. But finally I remembered a shark's-eye view of the boat from underwater that had been scrapped. We used it, so at the end of the pulling backwards we suddenly go underwater, and the boat seems to come to a stop. It's the most arbitrary cut in the world. Why cut underwater? But it was the only thing we had to show the boat stopping.

—*Verna Fields, "Dialogue on Film" (June 1976)*

From *The Color Purple* (1985). Danny Glover and Whoopi Goldberg star as the ill-tempered Mr.——— and Celie, the downtrodden woman who escapes him and outgrows him—until they make a healing peace, late in life.

traterrestrials with the personal story of one man's attempt to deal with the mystery.

Following the disappointing *1941* (1980), *Raiders of the Lost Ark* (1981) further established Spielberg's mastery of special effects and compelling narrative. This was merely a prelude, however, to Spielberg's biggest box-office hit—*E.T.: The Extraterrestrial* (1982). Combining his best narrative and special-effects powers, Spielberg did more than make a movie; he developed a love affair between himself and the American audience unprecedented in film history. As Joyce Jillson said in her book *Real Women Don't Pump Gas,* "Real Women don't want Burt Reynolds. They want Steven Spielberg. No Real Woman gets turned on by a man driving 200 miles per hour. But she'd gladly give her heart to someone who can make millions of Real Men cry." By this

writing, Spielberg has become the world's most successful filmmaker. *E.T.* is the all-time box office hit, *Jaws* is fifth, *Raiders of the Lost Ark* is seventh, and *Indiana Jones and the Temple of Doom* (1984) is eighth. *Gremlins* (1984), which Spielberg produced, is seventeenth, and *Back to the Future* (1985) and *The Goonies* (1985) seem to be headed in the same direction.

With *The Color Purple* (1985), however, Spielberg shifted, at least momentarily, away from his "sequel cycle" of megahits. Some critics felt that Spielberg was merely attempting to become legitimate; others saw in the film a genuinely creative and sensitive handling of a delicate subject. The film most likely represents Spielberg's desire, as a creative artist, to break out of the routine and try something new; he unquestionably has the ability to experiment financially.

Francis Ford Coppola

Like Lucas and Spielberg, Francis Ford Coppola is a man who wears many hats. Director, producer, writer, studio head—Coppola has worn all these titles with grace, and never carelessly though not always easily. Of these three men, Coppola alone has taken the biggest risks and strayed the farthest from the conservative commercial mainstream. After several early films—*Dementia 13* (1963) and *You're a Big Boy Now* (1967)—he directed his first Hollywood film, *Finian's Rainbow,* in 1968. He followed this with the interesting but unsuccessful *The Rain People* (1969) before striking gold with *The Godfather* (1972). This film, along with *The Godfather, Part II* (1974), allowed Coppola and his studio, American Zoetrope, the financial luxury of working on projects that deviated not only from his previous work but from the trends of the mid-seventies, represented by *Jaws. The Conversation* (1974) is a good example of Coppola's divergence from the mainstream. It was critically acclaimed but did not do well at the box office.

All Coppola's previous work set the stage for his magnum opus, *Apocalypse Now* (1979), which perhaps more than any other film symbolizes the last half of the 1970s. Drawing both on the plot and structure of Joseph Conrad's novel *Heart of Darkness,* Coppola sought to paint an epic picture of the tragedy and madness of the Vietnam War. Unlike the two other major Vietnam War

▲ Marlon Brando as Mafia patriarch Don Corleone in Francis Ford Coppola's epic *The Godfather* (1972). Brando won an Oscar for Best Actor, Coppola and Mario Puzo won for Best Screenplay, and the film was named Best Picture. The sequel, *The Godfather, Part II* (1974), also directed by Coppola, was just as compelling but more complex in tone. It won seven Oscars, including Best Picture, Best Director, Best Screenplay, Best Supporting Actor (Robert De Niro), and Best Score (Nino Rota).

▼ From *Apocalpyse Now* (1979), another epic film. Coppola spent four years and much of his money making this after completing the two "Godfather" films. This scene depicts U.S. troops participating in a Holy Communion service, as attack helicopters buzz overhead, and illustrates the many incongruities and absurdities of war.

▲ From Hal Ashby's *Coming Home* (1978). In compelling contrast to Coppola's *Apocalypse Now*, this film presented a personal and powerful look at the effect of the Vietnam War on people at home in the U.S. In this scene, Jane Fonda, an officer's wife, prepares a meal for disabled veteran Jon Voight. Despite occasional lapses into melodrama, the film is one of the best studies of the returning veteran ever made. Jon Voight's Oscar-winning performance compares beautifully with Harold Russell's equally compelling, also Oscar-winning role in *The Best Years of Our Lives* (1946).

films of the late seventies, Hal Ashby's *Coming Home* (1978) and Michael Cimino's *The Deer Hunter* (1978), *Apocalypse Now* dealt as much with the pure visual imagery of war as with the personal trauma experienced by the people caught up in it. Scenes in which Robert Duvall leads a formation of American helicopters while playing Wagner's *"The Ride of the Valkyries"* over loudspeakers set the tone for this basically absurdist view of war. In addition, however, Coppola probed deeply into the minds of some of the men fighting this war, especially the Army captain played by Martin Sheen and Kurz, his protagonist, enigmatically portrayed by Marlon Brando. *Apocalypse Now* met with mixed critical success but, more importantly, it drained Coppola of most of his *Godfather* money and much of his creative energy as well.

The eighties have not been kind to Coppola as he struggles to regain control of his artistic and financial empire. *One From the Heart* (1980) eroded his critical reputation and further sapped his finances. His attempts to work in a low-budget "small-film" format with *The*

Outsiders (1983) and *Rumblefish* (1983) left him floundering. A measure of financial success returned with his work as executive producer for *The Black Stallion* (1979) and *The Black Stallion Returns* (1983). And critical and financial success, though mixed and limited, finally returned with *Cotton Club* (1984). Unlike Lucas and Spielberg, who seem content with more focused identities and themes, Coppola delights in his multiple personality, and his reach therefore often exceeds his grasp.

The directors discussed above represent only the tip of the creative and industrial iceberg of American film over the last ten years. As noted earlier, many will argue that other directors are more deserving of individual attention and extensive analysis. Certainly directors such as Brian De Palma (*Carrie* [1976], *The Fury* [1978], *Dressed to Kill* [1980], *Blowout* [1981], and *Scarface* [1983]), Paul Mazursky (*Blume in Love* [1973], *Harry and Tonto* [1974], *Next Stop Greenwich Village* [1976], *An Unmarried Woman* [1978], *Tem-*

pest [1982], *Moscow on the Hudson* [1984]), Hal Ashby (*Harold and Maude* [1972], *The Last Detail* [1973], *Shampoo* [1975], *Coming Home* [1978], *Being There* [1979]), Lawrence Kasdan (*Body Heat* [1982], *The Big Chill* [1984], *Silverado* [1985]), John Landis (*National Lampoon's Animal House* [1978], *The Blues Brothers* [1980], *American Werewolf in London* [1980], *Trading Places* [1983]), and John Badham (*Saturday Night Fever* [1977], *Dracula* [1980], *Whose Life Is It Anyway?* [1981], and *Blue Thunder* [1983]) deserve our attention, among others. However, attempting to discuss every important director over the last ten years would lead us to lose perspective — to focus on the trees of the period to the exclusion of the forest. One characteristic of the 1970s in particular was that reputations were established on the basis of one or two pictures (an example is Michael Cimino's swift plummet with his disastrous remake of *Heaven's Gate* [1980]). As noted, directors such as Peter Bogdanovich and William Friedkin, who ruled the early seventies much as Lucas, Spielberg, and Coppola ruled the late seventies, faded into virtual obscurity. Following the explosive rise and fall of the youth-film movement of the late sixties, the seventies and early eighties were primarily characterized by increasing critical and financial conservatism resulting in a blockbuster mentality. The prevailing atmosphere allowed few opportunities for the small film and even fewer opportunities for directors intent on experimenting and developing their personal styles.

Spielberg on Spielberg

I don't think that the new directors are going to bring anything different to American film. But I think that they are going to bring the audience back into the theater by making popular, entertaining movies the way they used to be made. And they are not going to be embarrassed if the movies make money or if Andrew Sarris or Molly Haskell is angry at them because of the money they make. They think criticism is interesting and important, but they don't take it all to heart. I love reading my reviews, but if I made films for the critics, I certainly wouldn't be making *Close Encounters* and *Jaws.* I think that a lot of the people I'm meeting today are more concerned with getting people into the theater and hearing them laugh and scream and clap. Then, once in a while, they'll go out and make *Red Desert.*

—*Steven Spielberg,*
"Dialogue on Film"
(September 1978)

New Technology

Three major technological developments have dominated the past two decades: the invention of the Cinemobile, increased portability and miniaturization of equipment, and computerization. The first two were born out of the need and desire of filmmakers to shoot films outside the studio. With location shooting and "runaway" productions becoming the norm, the need developed for a portable, compact film studio that could effectively duplicate the studio at a reasonable cost. That need was filled by an Arab immigrant Fouad Said, who in 1967 developed the Cinemobile Mark IV, a movie studio on wheels. Approximately thirty-five feet long, the Cinemobile contains dressing rooms, bathrooms, space for a crew of fifty, and large amounts of equipment. The mobile unit proved immediately effective. Producer Al Ruddy, for example, used the Cinemobile extensively in

the making of *Little Fauss and Big Halsy* (1971). He related a typical incident in which he wanted to shoot a motel scene and found it would cost him between $6,000 and $8,000 to use a Paramount sound stage. Instead, he rented rooms at a Los Angeles motel for $100 and used the Cinemobile, thus saving money and creating a greater sense of reality. In 1971, Cinemobiles were used in some seventy pictures, more than 50 percent of Hollywood's total output for the year.

The second technological development, increased portability and miniaturization of equipment, although not as dramatic or conspicuous as the Cinemobile, was probably more important in the long run. This general development, along with decreased costs, was welcomed by professionals and amateurs alike. Sixteen-millimeter filmmaking became a standard subject taught in colleges and universities, and the home-movie market spurted tremendously with the development of Super 8 mm film

◀ The Cine II, a modern, updated version of the Cinemobile Mark IV.

and cassette packaging. Documentary filmmakers received a tremendous boost with the development of low-cost, portable 16 mm sound cameras and sound equipment. And Hollywood itself found new possibilities in on-location shooting with portable 35 mm cameras, while a cinéma vérité style (in which the subject is seen from the perspective of participants in a scene) became standard.

The third and in some ways most dramatic technological development has been an increase in computerization. As with almost every phase of American life, motion pictures have been affected by the computer. The business of filmmaking, like business in general, has accepted the computer without question. Involved in everything from market research to production budgets to box-office figures, computers have become vertically integrated into the world of motion picture production, distribution, and exhibition.

With respect to the art and craft of making films, George Lucas has pioneered the increasing use of computers. His Edit Droid applies computer technology to motion picture editing. Until now, film editing has been basically a physical "cut and paste" effort: the editor shifted various lengths of film footage as if rearranging a manuscript. But the Edit Droid simplifies the task. A film editor using the device can rearrange footage almost as easily as a text editor at a word processor can juggle words and phrases, inserting and deleting frames and moving a sequence around.

Lucas also developed an audio signal processor (ASP), which does for sound tracks what the Edit Droid does for film footage—the processor mixes, edits, and synthesizes music, speech, and sound effects. One of the first uses of ASP was to change the pitch of a scream in *Indiana Jones and the Temple of Doom* (1984).

A third development involves a computer graphics machine called Pixar, which is capable of producing a wide variety of scenes and images. Pixar's software can in effect replace traditional methods of animation and model making, which often require thousands of individual drawings.

Additional developments include experimentation with videotape as a substitute for film, used early by Frank Zappa in his film *200 Motels* (1971) and later by Coppola. The flexibility and economy of instant playback and erasure are strong factors in favor of tape, and the use of videotape as a tool for rehearsal is increasing. However, the image quality that results from transferring tape to film for theatrical release is at present too poor to make videotape a practical substitute for film.

Films of the Time: An Overview

As with individual directorial styles, any attempt to describe the films of the past twenty years is doomed to failure. There were too few trends and too many individual successes to permit generalizations. Still, some patterns are discernible.

The Early Sixties

The early years of the sixties saw Hollywood still seeking the magic formula that would bring back the habit audience. But the studios were afraid to gamble, and films were therefore limited to what were considered guaranteed box-office hits, especially Broadway musicals and best-selling novels. *Big* was considered synonymous with *better,* and, as noted, the blockbuster became a standard product. After the experimentation of the mid-

Film on Video

*V*ideo has come to dominate the moviemaking process. A movie begins production. Casting sessions are taped. Tapes of an actor's other performances are looked at. Rehearsals are taped. The director views more cassettes of movies for a key to a look, a special shot, or the solution to a technical problem.

Photography begins. What the lens sees is viewed on a video playback monitor. Each shot is carefully worked on before it goes to film. That day's shots, all of the takes, whether printed on film or not, can be viewed *that night* at home.

Editing begins. The first assembly is transferred to tape in order to have a record of all the scenes that you have to work with. Each successive cut gets a tape made for comparison and as a way of keeping a memento of favorite moments and scenes that eventually have to be lost. Some films are cut and mixed on tape and then the negative is conformed as a final step. The music composer works from a time-encoded dub of the final cut. The color timers work on a Hazeltine.

Marketing begins. The studio makes a rock video for MTV. Clips are sent out to reviewers and talk shows. Television ads are run coast to coast. Then the director gets his wish: The movie is run in a theater in front of a paying audience. Finally, but not for long, 70 mm and Dolby stereo. Six months later, it's for sale for $39.95 on cassette. Six months after that, it's on cable television. Now you walk into your local video store and it's just another movie for rent. Seeing your movie on a movie screen has become a rare treat; it's now only *part* of the process.

—*Allan Arkush,* American Film *(June 1985)*

---

fifties, there was little further development of the small film. Musicals were very popular in the period between 1960 and 1965, and *West Side Story* (1961), *My Fair Lady* (1964), *Mary Poppins* (1964), and *The Sound of Music* (1965) were all major films. Spectacle films with all-star casts and thousands of extras made another strong showing—for example, *Spartacus* (1960), *El Cid* (1961), *Lawrence of Arabia* (1962), *The Longest Day* (1962), *Cleopatra* (1963), and *The Great Escape* (1963). Even Westerns and comedies were infected by the big-is-best principle, and *How the West Was Won* (1963) and *It's a Mad, Mad, Mad, Mad World* (1963) displayed size but little else.

The "problem" picture suffered, however, since Hollywood could not really afford to take chances with message films. A few such films were produced, though, such as Stanley Kramer's *Inherit the Wind* (1960), a film version of the play dealing with the Scopes monkey trial, and *Judgment at Nuremburg* (1961), a highly dramatized version of the war-crimes trial with an all-star cast. *A Man for All Seasons* (1966), from a play by Robert Bolt, dramatized Thomas More's conflict with Henry VIII and the establishment of the Church of England.

One other observable trend besides the big-is-best pattern was the development of the spy-thriller genre. It began with the James Bond series and quickly became entrenched with other series (Matt Helm played by Dean Martin, and Our Man Flint played by James Coburn). In a sense, these were not really spy melodramas at all, but more in the line of thirties' screwball comedies that treaded a thin line between reality and fantasy. The fantasies primarily involved new ways of killing people and old ways of seducing them.

Toward the end of the sixties, the series film made a brief comeback when the highly successful film *Planet of the Apes* (1968) spurred three sequels, each worse than the one before. The major reasons inhibiting more cycles during this period were the changes in both audiences and creators. The audience for films was becoming increasingly fragmented and splintered. In fact, a mass audience as such no longer existed; instead there were small separate audiences, none of which was economically strong enough to support lengthy cycles. Further, the emerging filmmakers, as we have seen, took pains not to be typed or tied to a particular genre. They made films that interested them, and worked with little interference. They were free from the studio structure that forced them into making films they did not want.

The relationship between these new creators and the new audiences was fluid, to say the least. The films of the sixties and early seventies reflected a constant shift between highly personalized work and safe commercial successes. For example, although 1963 was one of the biggest years for the blockbuster film, small films, such as *Hud* and *David and Lisa,* also made an impact. Everyone was searching—studios for formulas, independent filmmakers for fresh ideas, and audiences for new films.

This search seemed to reach its end in 1967 with the appearance of *The Graduate* and *Bonnie and Clyde.* Suddenly, the "New American Film" was here. The youth audience was "discovered" and films appeared that would prove to be barometers of things to come. The new violence was graphically expressed in *Bonnie and Clyde* and *In Cold Blood. Cool Hand Luke* continued to explore the antihero, the amoral yet highly sympathetic character introduced by *Hud* four years earlier. And *In the Heat of the Night,* also released in 1967, explored racial tension and conflict in a realistic way for the first time since the late forties.

1968–1969

The *"now"* film was in vogue. *Now* was a label for American society in turmoil, a society that was antiauthority, violent, and sexual. If a film was not *now,* it was doomed. The year 1968 was a holding year, since most *now* films were still in production then, but 1969 witnessed an explosion that would alter the face of American film. All the forces that had been developing throughout the decade seemed to burst forth at once that year. The old restrictive Motion Picture Code was replaced by a liberal rating system, and a new sophistication in content quickly resulted.

Butch Cassidy and the Sundance Kid did not express a particularly new or radically different theme, but it continued to explore the antihero, making criminals into folk heroes much like those in *Bonnie and Clyde. Alice's Restaurant* carried on the youth-film movement; here Arthur Penn looked at American society with a critical, satiric eye, perfectly catching the mood of young America.

However, of all the films released in 1969, four stand out as marking a significant change in the direction of

From *Bonnie and Clyde* (1967). Here the three remaining members of the Barrow gang, Bonnie (Fay Dunaway), Clyde (Warren Beatty), and C. W. (Michael Pollard), are attacked as they try to escape a police ambush.

American film. The first was the Swedish production of *I Am Curious, Yellow.* It was initially banned as obscene in 1967 by U.S. Customs, but this ruling was overturned in 1969, and the film was distributed to an eager audience. The explicit sex in the film included male and female frontal nudity and simulated copulation in a variety of positions—all revealed in great detail. This motion picture became one of the all-time top grossing foreign films, suggesting that a large majority of the American audience wanted to see sex on the screen in more detail and with greater frequency than in the past.

Midnight Cowboy also dealt with sexuality in graphic terms. It broke new ground as the first X-rated film to win an Academy Award (the rating meant that those under seventeen were not admitted). This was one of the top-grossing films of 1969, and it too furthered the realistic and graphic treatment of sex.

The Wild Bunch did for violence what *Midnight Cowboy* and *I Am Curious, Yellow* did for sex. Peckinpah's film set a new standard for violence with much of its explicit and prolonged blood-letting portrayed in slow motion. This particular technique seemed to divide the critics more than anything else. Some felt it heightened and intensified the film's violence while others saw it as a diffusing device. The precedent, however, was set.

The fourth important film of the year was *Easy Rider,* and it set a precedent of another type altogether. Artistically, this film had few bright moments, but its real

The Perils of Youth

*I*t is worth remembering that the two films that were supposed to change completely the American movie industry simply didn't. The back-to-back success of *Easy Rider* (1969) and *Woodstock* (1970) ushered in the "youthquake" which, it was generally agreed, would shake Hollywood so profoundly that in no time it would be turned upside down: The kids just out of film school would soon be in charge of that vast picture-making apparatus which was then under the stewardship of men in their fifties and sixties. Mind you, this was all right with the older generation. As long as they could profit from it, they were willing to let youth have its fling.

And so a number of very young men—some of whom were ready and some of whom were not—were given assignments, budgets, and production schedules and told to go out there and make movies for people their own age. The result? A lot of unreleased features, a few that were allowed to escape, and one or two that eventually began some careers.

—*Bruce Cook,* American Film *(December 1979)*

significance was that it continued, and in a sense represented the peaking of, the theme of alienated youth. Most important of all, however, was the fact that this theme earned the film more than $50 million on a cost outlay of less than $400,000.

Suddenly, studio doors and pocketbooks were opened to eager young filmmakers anxious to make the "great American film." In some respects the time was

Dennis Hopper and Peter Fonda ride the open road in *Easy Rider* (1968). This film spawned the youth movement of the late 1960s.

similar to that of the French New Wave in the early sixties in that many came, but few conquered. Even the head guru himself—Dennis Hopper, director of *Easy Rider*—was unable to duplicate his initial success. Nevertheless, Hollywood was revitalized. A new era was beginning and a new breath of freedom was felt. But the euphoria was shortlived. Hindsight shows us what really happened: a lot of gambles, risks, and long shots paid off all at once. Audiences and especially the youth audience (ages eighteen to twenty-nine), responded to these new films, and the steady nosedive attendance figures had been taking for the past twenty years not only leveled off, but actually reversed. However, the new wave quickly broke on the rocky shore of a fickle audience and a nervous industry.

The Early Seventies

The next several years saw many attempts to duplicate the successes of the late sixties, but no real permanent change took place. The youth film, with its new heroes and new myths, proved to be a minicycle like many others before it. Disenchantment soon set in, and Arthur Penn, one of the movement's leading apostles, was one of the first to speak:

> Some movies are creating the myths of the young. They promote the notion that freedom from all authority is an unqualified good, that mobility as a life-style is superior to permanence, that the older generation is totally corrupt, that cool is the only legitimate response.

A new sense of visual style had accompanied the new content. A shift occurred from a literary to a visual base, as evidenced in such films as *Reflections in a Golden Eye* (1967), *2001: A Space Odyssey* (1968), *If* (1968), *Slaughterhouse Five* (1970), and *A Clockwork Orange* (1971), among many others. The industry, witnessing the success of these films, soon got on a style bandwagon and began to ignore plot. Now normal space-time relationships were juggled and black and white was mixed with color. At times this "new" style was handled well, but ultimately it was looked on as simply another formula for commercial success. Ordinary films were suddenly infused with—and some would say confused by—stylistic significance. In 1968, *Newsweek* reported,

> *Two for the Road,* otherwise an ordinary Audrey Hepburn vehicle, has as much back and forth juggling of chronology as any film made by Alain Resnais—not to mention a comic acidity about marital discord that is as candid as anything the Swedes have said.

How naive this all seems today in the light of the huge commercial success of *Love Story* (1970), *Airport* (1970), *The French Connection* (1971), *The Godfather* (1972), and so on. The industry was again clutching at straws, tacking on style and pointing to it with pride because it made their films "legitimate." Like the Europeans, we too had "cinema." The British director Richard Lester stated that television's abrupt leaps from news about Vietnam to Gomer Pyle to toothpaste ads had expanded people's vision. "TV is best," according to Lester, "at those sudden shifts of reality." But such technical capabilities had no meaning. The key to Lester's comment focused on the absurdity of the switches, not the ability to create them or even the ability of the audience to understand them.

However, despite the confusion, something lasting did come from all of the ferment and freedom. In searching for new answers to many old questions and values, new directors began to explore a wide variety of subcultures. As Michael Laughlin, producer of *Two Lane Blacktop* (1971), said, "The movie business used to be dominated by middle Europeans who imposed a fantasy landscape. Now screenwriters . . . are not afraid to write scenes about Americans in bowling alleys, or about waitresses." Laughlin overstates his point, of course, since Hollywood was always open to a limited amount of social realism. But now the system was open to more voices exploring many different areas of society. Many different types of people were now illuminated on the big screen. Thus, Robert Altman was able to direct *M*A*S*H* (1970) and *McCabe and Mrs. Miller* (1971); Mike Nichols was able to do *Carnal Knowledge* (1971); John Cassavetes was able to find an audience for *Husbands* (1970) and *Minnie and Moskowitz* (1971); and Robert Rafelson could direct *Five Easy Pieces* (1970).

An important result was a new variety in American films. Despite the so-called vacuum-cleaner syndrome of 1970 and 1972, when *Love Story* and *The Godfather* "sucked up" most of the business, the differences among the films that achieved success is remarkable. A survey of the top-grossing films of 1971 reveals this variety clearly. Love led the way *(Love Story),* closely followed by nostalgia *(The Summer of '42),* Walt Disney *(The Aristocats),* sex *(Carnal Knowledge),* rats *(Willard),* science fiction *(The Andromeda Strain),* the West *(Big Jake),* and blacks *(Shaft).*

In these films and many others, the new American cinema flourished. Like all movements in film, the outcome was mixed, but overall the freedom to innovate and explore new themes and styles, formerly confined to underground, experimental, or foreign films, had surfaced, and mainline American movies were now looking at society in new ways.

Nostalgia Films

Besides the continued exploration of sex, violence, and race, if any one trend characterized the early seventies, it was the replacement of the *now* film with the *then* film. Nostalgia entered the motion picture industry with *The Summer of '42* in 1971 and reached a peak in 1974 with *The Great Gatsby,* heralded by a tremendous publicity effort. This was nothing new; the period picture had long been a Hollywood staple. Film is capable of reproducing the visual sense and style of a time, and nostalgia has always been a perfect theme for filmmakers looking for new areas to explore. But in the early seventies the motion picture was consistently being used to recreate historical realities and fiction. Witness *The Great Gatsby,* which tried to duplicate the splendor of Fitzgerald's twenties; George Lucas's *American Graffiti* (1973), in which Lucas relived his high school fantasies; Robert Altman's *Thieves Like Us* (1973), which reflected the atmosphere of the rural South during the Depression; or *Badlands* (1974), which took the audience back fewer than twenty years for a look at two troubled teenagers on a killing spree.

1974

The 1974–1985 span was a period of tremendous activity, a tumultuous time that seemed to offer a tremendous new hit every year accompanied by a new and seemingly inexhaustible supply of special effects. It was also a time of general creative decline, for the cost of making films escalated dramatically and both studios and individual directors concentrated on achieving blockbuster commercial successes. J. Hoberman, writing in *American Film* in 1985, said, "In 1975 the average cost to produce and market a film was $3.1 million. A film had to sell more than five million tickets to break even. In 1984, the cost to make and release an average film had escalated to $14.4 million and the number of tickets sold to reach the break-even point had risen to fifteen million." No stable trend and no lengthy cycle — except the search for the next *Star Wars* — has, at this writing, emerged.

Nineteen seventy-four was the year of the disaster movie, initiated by the enormous success of *The Poseidon Adventure* (1973). Included among the films of this type were *Airport 75, Earthquake,* and *The Towering Inferno.* This trend was short-lived, however, for audiences grew tired of being guinea pigs for ambitious special-effects artists who filled vapid plots and surrounded dull acting with all sorts of magical tricks. Aside from this minicycle, 1974 was a year of great diversity. Releases included Francis Ford Coppola's intense character study

The Conversation, Sidney Lumet's witty *Murder on the Orient Express,* and Roman Polanski's searing picture of the 1930s Los Angeles underworld in *Chinatown.* Other notable efforts of 1974 were Art Carney's wistful portrayal of the problems and beauty of old age in *Harry and Tonto,* and John Cassavetes's exploration of the human condition in *A Woman Under the Influence.*

1975

Jaws so dominated 1975 that few people remember that a number of powerful social dramas were produced that year, including Robert Altman's *Nashville,* Sidney Lumet's *Dog Day Afternoon,* Miloš Forman's *One Flew Over the Cuckoo's Nest,* and Martin Scorsese's *Alice Doesn't Live Here Anymore.* With *Jaws* the era of the huge rental film began in earnest. As one critic put it, "where *Nashville* exploded the [disaster film] genre, *Jaws* imploded it." The picture opened simultaneously in five hundred theaters after an unprecedented advertising blitz, and it went on to become the top-grossing movie of all time (until 1977). More importantly, *Jaws* set the direction of the industry for the next decade. As Robert Evans, then head of production at Paramount, said in 1974, "The making of a blockbuster is the newest art form of the twentieth century."

1976

The year 1976 saw a lull in the growing storm begun by *Jaws. One Flew Over the Cuckoo's Nest* was the top film of this year and *Network, Taxi Driver,* and *All the President's Men* were released then, too. Some saw 1976 as the sixties' "last hurrah." *King Kong* made a much publicized appearance then, and, though it had moderate success, demonstrated that publicity cannot determine success. Sylvester Stallone's outstanding *Rocky* bore out this fact even more impressively, since it had little publicity except word of mouth. This film stimulated a brief spate of "little people" films similar to Frank Capra's populist films of the thirties. The character of Rocky was in many ways the reincarnation of Mr. Deeds, Mr. Smith, and John Doe cleverly packaged in patriotic bicentennial bunting. Still, with the overpowering success of *Star Wars,* the "little people" were soon more likely to be robots or space mutants than human beings.

1977: The Big Sequel Storm

Star Wars was *the* film of 1977 and of film box-office history. This success, and a 1976 production called *Logan's Run,* immediately revived the long dormant

From the 20th Century-Fox production *Star Wars* (1977). Imperial stormtroopers interrogate Ben Kenobi (Alec Guinness) and Luke Skywalker (Mark Hamill) about their robots.

From *Rocky* (1976). Sylvester Stallone stars as Rocky Balboa, a small-time fighter who gets his "million-to-one shot" for fame and, more important, his self-respect. This film was Stallone's personal project, and both his on- and off-screen heroics captured the hearts and pocketbooks of the audience. The original has inspired three sequels to date, all very successful at the box office.

science-fiction genre and began a new cycle. But this new cycle was based less on content or style than on formula and financial success. It was characterized by the obsessive use of sequels and reissues. The blockbuster psychology of the studios made it almost impossible for a filmmaker to be offbeat and personal.

The urge among certain filmmakers to duplicate their previous successes created a sequel bandwagon that continued unabated into the eighties. The year 1977 also saw the birth of two additional sequel sires in addition to *Star Wars*. One was *Rocky* (actually released late

in 1976) and the other was *Smokey and the Bandit*, starring Burt Reynolds. As the number two and three rental films of the year, they inspired (some would say conspired) to spawn a succession of baby Rockys and Smokeys that would be going strong well into the mid-eighties.

Although relatively few in number, the feature-film follow-ups have exerted an extremely potent box-office appeal. In 1981 and 1982, sequels and follow-ups to major films (nine and eleven titles respectively for those years) accounted for 12 percent of all domestic rentals. This is a startling performance given that more than 500 new and reissued pictures appeared in the marketplace during each of these years.

The key sequel films for these years included *Superman II, For Your Eyes Only, The Great Muppet Caper, Halloween II, The Final Conflict, Friday the 13th Part 2, Rocky III, Star Trek II: The Wrath of Khan, Friday the 13th Part 3, Airplane II: The Sequel, Halloween III, Grease 2,* and *Trail of the Pink Panther.*

The sequel syndrome of the 1980s remained a continuing phenomenon in 1983, when *Return of the Jedi, Superman III, Octopussy, Jaws 3-D, Porky's II, Smokey and the Bandit Part 3,* and *Psycho II* dominated box-office statistics. Some cracks were beginning to appear — for example, *Superman III* generated less return revenue (people seeing a film twice and even three and four times) and met with decidedly less than universal critical acclaim. In 1984, however, series and sequel films continued to do well with the issue of *Indiana Jones and the Temple of Doom, Star Trek III: The Search for Spock, Cannonball II, The Muppets Take Manhattan, Oh God, You Devil,* and *Friday the 13th, Part 4.*

The year 1977 also saw the emergence of the contemporary dance musical. This was the year that *Saturday Night Fever* cashed in on the disco craze in a big way.

1978–1979

Grease was the big film of 1978, followed in turn by *Close Encounters of the Third Kind* (actually released in late 1977) and *Animal House. Jaws 2* and the reissue of *Star Wars* made the top ten box-office hit list as well. There was no pattern to the top films of 1978. Science fiction fared best but widely and wildly diverse forms of comedy emerged too. The latter were represented by such divergent efforts as *Animal House, Heaven Can Wait, The Goodbye Girl, Hooper, Foul Play,* and *Up in Smoke. Julia* and *Coming Home* were the two most popular dramas, and *The Deer Hunter* won the Academy Award for Best Picture. *Superman* led the way in 1979, followed by the first wave of *Star Wars* imitators. The latter included *Alien, Buck Rogers, Star Trek,* and *The Black Hole,* among others.

By the late seventies, more than 60 percent of all movie tickets were being bought by people under twenty-five. An enormous youth market had once again emerged. Its appetite was well met in 1979 with such efforts as *Meatballs, Breaking Away, A Little Romance, My Bodyguard,* and *The Champ.* Some "adult" comedy survived in the form of *10* and *The Jerk. Rocky II* proved that the little man as champ was just as powerful as the little man as loser. And *Apocalypse Now* finally emerged out of Coppola's editing suite in 1979, stirring a wide spectrum of emotions in the American audience.

1980–1981

In 1980 *The Empire Strikes Back* more than doubled the box-office rentals of the number two film, *Kramer vs.*

▲   From Steven Spielberg's *Raiders of the Lost Ark* (1981). Here Harrison Ford, as Indiana Jones, runs for his life.

Kramer — but this was not surprising. What *did* surprise was that the adult drama *Kramer vs. Kramer* earned more than $60 million in box-office gross. Comedy once again dominated the box office that year with such diverse efforts as *The Jerk* (a 1979 release), *Airplane, Smokey and the Bandit II, Private Benjamin,* and *The Blues Brothers.* The horror/slasher genre continued its *Halloween* (1978) phase with such efforts as *Friday the 13th, The Fog, Dressed to Kill,* and *Prom Night.* Several individual films in 1980, while not big moneymakers, were notable for their continued effort to "march to the beat of a different drummer." These included *Ordinary People, The Elephant Man, Being There,* and *Fame.*

Raiders of the Lost Ark ran away with 1981 and established George Lucas and Steven Spielberg as the most dominant producer/directors of the time. *Superman II* ran a distant second in box-office appeal and yet another set of diverse comedies followed closely. These included *Stir Crazy, 9 to 5, Stripes, Arthur, The Cannonball Run,* and *Four Seasons.* Fantasy/science fiction continued to have a strong showing with *Excalibur, Flash Gordon, Time Bandits,* and *Clash of the Titans.*

1982

E.T. and Steven Spielberg were the major stories of 1982. Earning $187 million, *E.T.* more than *tripled* the next highest box-office gross, *Rocky III.* And in addition to producing and directing *E.T.,* Spielberg also produced the number eight box-office hit — *Poltergeist. On Golden Pond,* with its box-office draw assured in the persons of Katharine Hepburn, Henry Fonda, and Jane Fonda, finished a close third to *Rocky III.* After that a mixed bag appeared, consisting of such films as *Porky's, An Officer and a Gentleman, The Best Little Whorehouse in Texas,* and *Star Trek II: The Wrath of Kahn. Chariots of Fire* and *Diner* were the surprise films of the year, with *Chariots of Fire* winning the 1982 Academy Award for Best Picture. And for the first time in several years, comedy did not dominate the top films. In fact, with the exception of Richard Pryor, the late John Belushi, director Blake Edwards *(Victor/Victoria),* and *Porky's,* comedy was pushed aside by the old-fashioned melodrama of *On Golden Pond, Rocky III, An Officer and a Gentleman,* and *Chariots of Fire.*

1983–1984

With *Return of the Jedi,* the huge moneymaking *Star Wars* phenomenon continued in 1983. Also, more sequels and reissues were released that year than ever before. *Tootsie* was a huge box-office and critical success. Comedy returned in full force with such films, in addition to *Tootsie,* as *Mr. Mom, Risky Business, National Lampoon's Vacation,* and *Trading Places.* And Mike Nichols returned to the screen with *Silkwood.* Brian De Palma continued his assault on the American public with the highly violent *Scarface. Terms of Endearment* won the hearts of the public and most of the Academy Awards as well. Finally, *The Big Chill,* also released in 1983, was to the eighties what *American Graffiti* was to the seventies, a nostalgic, often humorous, and always entertaining look back in time.

The year 1984 was led by *Indiana Jones and the Temple of Doom* and *Gremlins.* Both carried on the sequel pattern to the point of formula and confirmed Steven Spielberg as the man with the Midas touch.

A New Conformity

The real profile of the American feature film in the late 1970s and early 1980s reveals a patternless sprinkling of isolated successes. As several contemporary critics have noted, among the Hollywood studios and independent production companies, strategy in production has replaced style, and the emphasis in commercial filmmaking has focused almost totally on achieving great box-office success. In four of the last five years of the 1970s, one huge box-office success spawned a host of attempts at duplication (*Jaws* in 1975, *Star Wars* in 1977, *Grease* in 1978, and *Superman* in 1979).

When one looks at films today, the word *conformity* comes to mind. The conformity relates not so much to style as to the attempt to reproduce commercial success. One of the significant effects of this trend has been the decline of the foreign film. The 1960s saw a tremendous surge in foreign films, but by 1972 Ingmar Bergman's *Cries and Whispers* could not find an American distributor. Today, the foreign film that successfully cracks the U.S. theatrical market is a rare commodity. Most illustrative of this trend is the recent history of films made in France and Italy, traditionally two leading suppliers of import films to America. None of the locally popular films

---

An Unfriendly Opinion

*T*he most shattering impact on the Hollywood scene in the last ten years has come from a small group of talented men who have rolled up huge grosses and personal fortunes by subordinating content to technique, appealing to the youngest and most retarded elements in the potential movie audience, and glorifying the fine art of merchandising. Their superhits, when screened by future scholars, will suggest that among the great issues of our day were the malevolent forays of the great white shark, the imperialist assaults of an alien galaxy, the international struggle for possession of a biblical scroll booby-trapped with deathrays, the unfriendly occupation of innocent buildings and children's bodies by ghostly intruders, and the continuing conflict of attitudes about social relations with interplanetary visitors.

—*Ring Lardner, Jr.,*
American Film *(June, 1985)*

Bill Murray and Dan Ackroyd in the top box-office film of 1984, *Ghostbusters.* This film, which carried on the tradition of the popular television comedy show "Saturday Night Live," was something of a sleeper that became the summer hit of 1984.

have shown up on American marquees. Nor have many, if any, of Italy's myriad comedy hits. The current practice of major U.S. distributors is to set up a separate "classics" division to handle what they term the "arty" imports. Independent distributors concentrate primarily on importing European art films or fantasy and sex films, allowing the popular hits to remain at home.

The key to understanding the conformity and noticeable lack of individuality in American films of the early 1980s is simple economics. The average cost of producing a feature film rose from $1 million in 1972 to more than $14 million in the mid-1980s, making the small film financed, made, and distributed outside the major studios all but obsolete. As the studios themselves have become small parts of large conglomerates, motion pictures have become solely the means to an end (profits) rather than the end in themselves.

Filmmaking today is controlled by a few major studios that are in turn controlled by conglomerate owners. As suggested throughout this overview, the individuals who run these and other film conglomerates, such as MCA and Transamerica, have decided to devote their money to large blockbuster films and to eliminate small films. The top ten box-office films for 1982 reveals this pattern very clearly. The big film of the year, *Rocky III,* speaks for itself as the repeat of a simple plot and formula. *Star Trek II* continued the science fiction theme, and *Poltergeist* gave Steven Spielberg a sweep of the big-money stakes of 1982. *Annie* and *The Best Little Whorehouse in Texas* were based on Broadway plays in the hopes of a repeat success, and *On Golden Pond* had not one but three surefire, run-to-the-bank stars (Henry Fonda, Katharine Hepburn, and Jane Fonda). Only *Chariots of Fire* showed any degree of individuality.

As the cost of making films rose, the stylistic and thematic freedoms of the early 1970s gave way to the action-dominated and star-populated conformity of what their producers hope are sure bets. It is true that small, personal films such as *The Elephant Man* (1980), *Diner* (1982), and *Local Hero* (1983) do get made, but they represent a dying breed. The current trend is toward content-theme cycles of increasingly shorter duration.

Releases on similar themes nearly have "seasons," as on television. The key is to start a new trend or get on the bandwagon quickly, before the audience gets bored.

A perfect illustration of the bandwagon effect is the horror-film cycle of the late 1970s and early 1980s. After steady and in some years spectacular increases in box-office rentals, horror films in 1983 suffered badly — domestic rentals for the genre fell by 50 percent. Only nineteen horror films in 1983 earned $1 million in domestic rentals. Compare this figure with sixty-one in 1982, twenty-two in 1981, and twenty-six in 1980. The decline in horror-film production since 1980 indicates the general public's disenchantment with the form. This is the inevitable result of relentless imitation in the exploitation film market.

In by-gone days, there were a few "guarantees" of success. One could count on such studios as MGM; such stars as Gable, Cooper, Tracy, Newman, McQueen, and Hoffman; such directors as Ford, Bogdanovich, Peckinpah, Altman, and Kubrick; and such audience habits as going to the movies regularly. Nowadays, no such guarantees exist. It is difficult to say where motion pictures stand at the present. Ultimately they are in the hands of the people who make them and the people who view them. This constant interaction reflects change and growth, and if anything is a constant for this medium it is change.

As J. Hoberman, film critic for the *Village Voice* wrote in *American Film* in 1985, "If nothing else, the events of the past ten years demonstrate the cyclical nature of American popular culture. The cop shows that disappeared in the mid-seventies are back in the mid-eighties. . . . The black stars and themes that faded away around the same time have also returned, just as the science fiction spectacle and perhaps even the youth film seemed, in early 1985, marked for decline."

The Genre Film

The great emphasis on sequels and blockbuster films has forced the decline of the genre film even further. A few types, such as the Western and the musical, have so far survived, though with mixed success. *Fiddler on the Roof* (1971), *Cabaret* (1972), *Jesus Christ Superstar* (1973), *Tommy* (1975), *Saturday Night Fever* (1977), and *Grease* (1978) were among the few successful musicals of the seventies, and their success was probably due as much to the mixture of social commentary and nostalgia they contained as to the music itself. The industrial importance of the "old" musical as evidenced by *The*

▼ From Barry Levinson's *Diner* (1982). In this comedy/drama, friends — played by (left to right) Kevin Bacon, Mickey Rourke, Daniel Stern, and Paul Reiser — make the difficult transition to manhood during the early 1960s. This is a marvelous example of the "small" film in the *Marty* tradition.

Sound of Music (big box-office dollars) and *Star* (few box-office dollars) is gone. Most independents do not have the time, money, or inclination to make musicals, and the studios do not want to gamble the kind of money it takes to create a big musical. The failure of *The Wiz* (1978) and *New York, New York* (1977), despite their major directorial stars, Sidney Lumet and Martin Scorsese, reinforced this reluctance. Even the relative success of *The Blues Brothers* (1980), *All That Jazz* (1979), and *Annie* (1982) has done little to resurrect the genre. However, the music video phenomenon of the mid-eighties has spawned several late-blooming spin-offs that have captured the youth audience — *Flashdance* (1983), *Footloose* (1984), and *Purple Rain* (1984).

The Western genre became diffused as men such as Peckinpah, Altman, and Penn infused the Western with their own personal styles and themes. Such films as *Tell Them Willie Boy Is Here* (1970), *Little Big Man* (1971), *McCabe and Mrs. Miller* (1971), and *Doc* (1971), among others, severely questioned the traditional morality of the Western. As Penn noted about *Little Big Man,* "It challenges the nation that the heroes of America are the ones you read about in the history books. . . . It exposes the rotten values of commercialism." The only exceptions to this trend were the films of John Wayne, such as *True Grit* (1969), *Rooster Cogburn* (1975), and *The Shootist* (1976). In these films, however, Wayne was essentially portraying his old screen image in a series of Western morality plays stressing the power of one man against the forces of evil in society. The closest thing to box-office hits in the Western genre — as broadly defined in the eighties — were Sidney Pollack's *The Electric Horseman* (1980) and *Urban Cowboy* (1980). *The Long Riders* (1980), directed by Walter Hill, received widespread critical acclaim but grossed less than $6 million. *Legend of the Lone Ranger* (1981), although a more interesting film than generally assumed, was a major financial disaster. A recent small Western cycle consisting of Clint Eastwood's *Pale Rider* (1985) and Lawrence Kasdan's *Silverado* (1985), however, proves that old genres never die. Rather, they are consumed by a new generation wholly free of traditional genre expectations.

The comedy genre has gone much the same way. The sixties witnessed the decline of Jerry Lewis and the rise of Peter Sellers. Also missing, besides Lewis, was the black comedy of Billy Wilder. Robert Altman with *M*A*S*H* (1970) might have seemed to be Wilder's heir apparent, but Altman was unwilling to be confined to a single genre.

In the seventies, Mel Brooks and Woody Allen dominated screen comedy and Steve Martin and Richard Pryor entered the arena late in the decade. In addition,

Wilder Comments

*N*eat constructions are out. Third acts are out. Payoffs are out. Jokes don't have toppers; they just have an interesting straight line, and let the audience write their own toppers. We come from a whole different school. A comedy like *Shampoo* I don't think was constructed at all. What makes it successful, I guess, is that it's slapped together with verve and overt language and naked behinds and God knows what. It is a kind of supergusto sex chutzpah, whatever you want to call it, that makes it come off. It's not constructed in the way we learned. Construction is frowned upon, it's not being done, it's old-fashioned. I guess it is, but that's the way we've been doing it, and that's the way we're going to do it until they take the cameras away. The idea that people in a picture can sit around a campfire and break wind and scream for fifteen minutes seems very strange to us.

—*Billy Wilder, with I. A. L. Diamond, Dialogue on Film (July–August 1976)*

Burt Reynolds and Neil Simon produced their own unique brands of light "screwball" comedy.

Brooks and Allen have been the most consistent comedy *auteurs* of the past ten years, primarily because they write, direct, and act in their films. Allen balances off Brooks's wild slapstick humor with his own particular blend of wry commentary and point-of-view humor. These characteristics are showcased most successfully in his *Sleeper* (1973), *Annie Hall* (1977), *Manhattan* (1979), *Broadway Danny Rose* (1983), *The Purple Rose of Cairo* (1984), and *Hannah and Her Sisters* (1986). Both Brooks and Allen satirize contemporary society, but there the similarity ends. Brooks makes fun of monster movies, cowboys, and silent films while Allen makes fun, as he himself admits, of "God and Mother and human relationships failing." Allen's work has become increas-

From *Sleeper* (1973). Here Woody Allen escapes from his pursuers.

ingly idiosyncratic over the years, and some critics consider it too self-centered (witness *Stardust Memories* [1980] and *Zelig* [1983]). Brooks's last several efforts to date, such as *High Anxiety* (1977), *History of the World: Part I* (1981), and *To Be or Not to Be* (1983), have lacked the zany energy of his early films such as *Young Frankenstein* (1974), *Blazing Saddles* (1974), and *Silent Movie* (1976).

Steve Martin scored a huge success with *The Jerk* (1980), but failed critically and commercially with *Pennies from Heaven* (1981), *Dead Men Don't Wear Plaid* (1982), and *The Man with Two Brains* (1983). Martin's humor, like that of Jerry Lewis, has attracted a rather small group of afficionados. In the current "hit or miss" industry philosophy the "small" comedy has little chance of surviving.

Despite this bleak picture, "big" comedies have done well. The year 1981 was especially good for comedy, with six of the top ten box-office films of the year falling somewhere in the genre. Leading the way was *Stir Crazy* starring Richard Pryor and Gene Wilder, followed closely by *9 to 5* and *Stripes*. Dudley Moore chipped in with *Arthur*. Burt Reynolds continued his

assault on the American audience with *The Cannonball Run,* and Alan Alda made a successful transition from television ("M*A*S*H") with *Four Seasons.*

The science fiction genre exploded on the scene in 1977 with *Star Wars.* As discussed, due primarily to the efforts of George Lucas and Steven Spielberg, science fiction has developed a mass appeal, style, and consistency undreamed of in the days of Buck Rogers serials. Indeed, the top four box-office hits of all time are *Star Wars, E.T., The Empire Strikes Back,* and *Return of the Jedi,* with *Superman* and *Close Encounters of the Third Kind* close behind. These films and others such as *Star Trek* (1979), *Alien* (1979), *Superman II* (1981), and *Superman III* (1983) have in fact transcended the genre of science fiction and become their own genre, made up of part science fiction, part Western, part light comedy, and part melodrama.

Of all the genres, that of the horror film has prospered most during the last ten years, as earlier sections suggested. This genre took on new life beginning in 1973 with William Friedkin's *The Exorcist* but did not begin to dominate until John Carpenter's *Halloween* (1978) took off. By 1982 the horror film had become a major force in the industry. Content and style ranged over a wide arena, from cheap "hack and splatter" films filling drive-in movie screens to efforts by major directors such as Stanley Kubrick's *The Shining* (1979) and Steven Spielberg's *Poltergeist* (1982; Spielberg produced this film). In 1982 alone sixty-one horror films were released domestically. Led by *Poltergeist,* these films generated a record $230 million plus in film rentals. As noted, however, public taste and product glut led to a more modest output in 1983.

The black film emerged from obscurity in the seventies and established itself as a consistent if not major genre. This form was born out of the economic motive to exploit both a sizeable but relatively untouched portion of the American audience and the striving of blacks to see accurate images of themselves on the screen.

Recent population demographics reveal that half the black population lives in fifty cities. As white America moved to the suburbs, urban areas, with their huge downtown theaters, drew a new population requiring new motion pictures. A few individual efforts appeared in

► From *Sounder* (1972). Cicely Tyson helps Keven Hooks get ready to leave home for a distant school.

the late sixties, such as Melvin Van Peebles' *Sweet Sweetback's Baadasssss Song* (1970), but the real boom began in 1971–1972 with Gordon Parks's *Shaft* (1971) and *Cotton Comes to Harlem* (1972). Thirteen black films appeared in 1970, eighteen in 1971, and then the movement really exploded, with sixty films in less than two years. Black films fell into virtually every genre, including comedy, horror, musical, and Western. However, it was the detective gangster genre that held the most potential. Here the urban black experience could be reflected easily, and such 1972 films as *Super Fly, Hit Man, Trouble,* and *Trick Baby* exploited this orientation with tremendous success.

With this exploitation, primarily by white producers using black actors, came strong concerns over the image being reflected and projected. The dope-pusher/super-stud/superspade formula worried many black leaders, and they called for an effort to balance the image. New images soon resulted in such films as *Sounder* (1972) and *Lady Sings the Blues* (1973), and the black film began to settle down and round out. By 1974 the blatant exploitation via cheap formulas seemed to have run its course.

James Murray, in his book *To Find an Image,* identified three goals for black cinema: (1) to correct white distortions, (2) to reflect black society, and (3) to create a positive black image. Accomplishing these goals requires exploration, not exploitation. There has to be a sense of purpose behind black films other than making money. Above all, there must be time and thought. Quickie productions designed simply to "take the money and run" accomplish none of Murray's goals and are ultimately self-defeating. Still, since 1974 further development of black cinema has unfortunately been limited to exploitation films running in inner-city theaters and a few comedies starring Bill Cosby, Harry Belafonte, and Sidney Poitier. The "black film" became the "black and white film" as the successful ones began to appeal to an all-color market. Poitier hit the jackpot by directing *Uptown Saturday Night,* (1974) followed by *A Piece of the Action* (1977) and *Stir Crazy* (1980). Television, meanwhile, has provided much of the mass-audience exposure of black characters, in such series as "The Jeffersons," "Good Times," and "The Cosby Show." The motion pic-

ture industry has shown unwillingness to risk money in competition with these programs.

Unfortunately, no similar effort has been made with respect to the American Indian. Some individual attempts to provide a more accurate image are *Tell Them Willie Boy is Here* (1970), *Soldier Blue* (1970), and *Little Big Man* (1970). But, as noted, economics is the key motivator for motion pictures. The primary objective of makers of black films was to make money. The population was there, the theaters were there, and the only things missing were the films. But the native American population is not only considerably smaller than the black population, it is also widely scattered and predominately rural. The economic potential simply does not exist for a native American cinema.

Except in some genres, successful American films of recent years, and especially of the seventies, have been isolated efforts. As Paul Mayersberg stated, "Among the Hollywood studios, strategy in production is replacing style." Genres no longer hold much appeal for the American audience. More attractive by far are individual films regardless of the genre they operate in.

Sex and Violence

Although the genre film has declined, a preoccupation with sex and violence has steadily grown in contemporary films. Beginning with Edison's *The Kiss* and Porter's *The Great Train Robbery*, films have always used sex and violence as staple ingredients. Still, the freedom to treat these elements of society has been very restricted — both by legal regulation and social attitudes.

Sex

There was little indication at the beginning of the sixties of the revolution to come. Sex was a game played with clothes on and hands off. Doris Day and assorted male leads, most prominently Rock Hudson and Cary Grant, were the most representative nonlovers of the period. Such films as *Lover Come Back* (1962) and *That Touch of Mink* (1961) are examples. The "cute sex" philosophy they exuded was probably best summed up by Bosley Crowther in his review of *The Facts of Life* (1961), starring Bob Hope and Lucille Ball. Crowther called this romp "grandly good-natured, winsome and wise," and closed with, "Anyone who is worried about the state of the nation and of homelife should see it and be refreshed."

Meanwhile, some minimal realism began to creep in, especially in Billy Wilder's films — *The Apartment* (1960), *Irma la Douce* (1963), *Kiss Me, Stupid* (1964), and *The Fortune Cookie* (1966). However, the real effort at sexual realism was being made at the so-called underground level by such people as Radley Metzger, Russ Meyer, Andy Warhol, and others. In such films as *The Immoral Mr. Teas* (1959), *Not Tonight Henry* (1963), and *Three Nuts in Search of a Bolt* (1962), waist-up nudity in a burlesquelike atmosphere became common.

In 1968, when the rating system replaced the Motion Picture Code's "Seal of Approval," the emphasis on sex increased. *I Am Curious, Yellow* and *Midnight Cowboy*, discussed earlier, were trend setters in this regard. But the one film that probably did more to legitimize or at least popularize "soft-core" pornography was *Vixen* (1968), directed by the self-proclaimed "king of the nudies," Russ Meyer.

Meyer has been making "skin flicks" since 1959, and the crucial distinction between his films and others of the same kind is that his make money. Meyer's films are primarily exercises in voyeuristic fantasy. They have been described as "good-hearted" and as having a "bar-racks-room heartiness." The nudity in his pictures always carries a strange prudishness, revealed in the almost exclusive waist-up composition. Audiences laugh at Meyer films, and the response is legitimate, consciously elicited by the work. *The Immoral Mr. Teas* (1959), for example, revolves around a man who has the uncontrollable ability to undress women mentally. Meyer takes the audience through episode after episode in which Teas "sees" nude women in doctors' offices, behind secretaries' desks, and so on. But above all Meyer's films differ from most pornographic productions in their high production value. *The Immoral Mr. Teas* returned more than $1 million on a $24,000 investment. *Vixen* (1968) was the real eye-opener, for it earned more than $6 million against a $72,000 cost. These figures (both the monetary and the physical) caught the eye of 20th Century-Fox President Richard Zanuck, who signed Meyer to direct *Beyond the Valley of the Dolls* (1970). This film represented the big breakthrough with regard to sex on the mainstream screen. What had formerly been strictly an underground, stagfilm movement suddenly surfaced.

The barriers were down. Sex became legitimate in every sense of the word, and when *Playboy* began to show pubic hair — its own revolutionary development — films quickly followed. The mood of the industry and the public changed rapidly. In 1969 *Midnight Cowboy* was given an X rating for "suggesting" certain taboo subjects such as fellatio, but less than three years later Peter Bogdanovich's *The Last Picture Show* showed full frontal female nudity and received an R. Ann-Margret was nominated for an Academy Award in *Carnal Knowledge* (1971) for, among other things, allowing herself to be photographed walking in the nude from the bedroom to the bathroom. Jane Fonda won an Academy Award for playing a prostitute in *Klute* (1971). And Glenda Jackson also won an Academy Award for *Women in Love* (1970), in which she appeared nude. Male nudity was shown for one of the first times in *Women in Love* as well. In general, however, the nude male body has not been heavily exposed in films.

While nudity and sexual themes entered the scene, most actual sexual activity was suggested rather than shown. Hard-core films still played to small art houses in large cities. However, in 1972 a movie entitled *Deep Throat* changed all that, and the hard-core trend went mainstream. The sex shown in *Deep Throat, The Devil and Miss Jones* (1972), and *Behind the Green Door* (1972), to name probably the three most successful films, was graphic and not simulated. Although most of these films played in specialized houses that showed nothing but X-rated films, such houses were now located in Des Moines, Iowa, as well as New York City. By 1972 an estimated 700-plus theaters nationwide were playing nothing but "porn" films, an increase of 60 percent over 1968 numbers. The pendulum had definitely swung.

Sex became so prevalent in films that by 1974 42 percent of the films rated by the MPPA since 1968 had received an X tag. However, as the decade wore on, the R film (restricted to those under 17) became commercially viable and the X rating was relegated to the hardcore pornography film. Increasing sexual freedom within the mainstream of the industry during the late seventies was reflected in the successful appeal by the makers of *All the President's Men* (1976) to receive an R rating despite its one four-letter expletive. Crucial, too, to the industry were two Supreme Court decisions on obscenity. The first, in 1973, made defining obscenity the responsibility of local governments and courts, which were to base those definitions on "community standards." The second was the pivotal ruling that *Carnal Knowledge* was not obscene. The threat of legal retribution for sexual openness that had hung over the film industry like a two-edged sword was now diminished, although filmgoers, exhibitors, and religious groups continued to register complaints throughout the decade.

Like youth films, bike films, and other such trends, the porn film was a cycle. Soon audiences grew tired of watching copulating bodies, and the cycle began to die. Andrew Sarris pinpointed one of the reasons for this decline when he noted that "the fantasy of superhuman restraint has been replaced by the fantasy of superhuman release." Like all fantasies, this one had a limited life span. Viewers could achieve the same results with home movies, and indeed most porn films have resembled home movies. The realistic and artistic integration of sex into films, both thematically and visually, is not easily achieved. There is a natural tendency to exploit any new phenomenon. Nevertheless, at least today's filmmakers have the freedom to use sex however they wish. Though their treatment may be questionable and the audience's response not as elevated as they would prefer, at least they have the opportunity to try.

Violence

Violence in films has had a history similar to sex in some respects. Without question, violence has played a large role in film history. And the arguments concerning its effects are almost as numerous as those concerning sex.

In the seventies, as films began to explore the various subcultures of American society more realistically, violence emerged as a natural part of that exploration. Further, as the focus of film shifted from the boy next door to the gang on the street, the amount and nature of violence changed radically too. But the increase in violence was related to other factors besides theme. The studios needed a new gimmick to attract audiences, and film favored violence because it could be depicted graphically in all its forms. As one producer stated,

> You can't say it's a bad thing per se—it all depends on how it's integrated into the story. Violence has always been an element in drama, from Shakespeare to Japanese tragedy. Violence doesn't guarantee success in movies, but it reaches the audience on an emotional level, and that's very important.

As with sex, however, Hollywood played by certain rules with respect to violence. Thus graphic bloodletting was usually discouraged, and most killing and violence was "clean." Early, for example in *Guadalcanal Diary* (1943), entire platoons of men simply fell over in their foxholes as if they had gone to sleep. But all such rules were graphically broken by *Bonnie and Clyde* in 1967 and destroyed altogether in the next three years by such films as *Bullitt* (1968), *Madigan* (1968), *The Wild Bunch* (1969), *The French Connection* (1971), and *Shaft* (1971). Violence was now "dirty," and audiences saw bullet holes, blood, and torn flesh on the screen.

One of the many reasons for the change was simply that such directors as Peckinpah, Don Siegel, and Roger Corman were expressing their personal styles and visions within the new context in which thematic and stylistic freedom prevailed. These men saw society as violent and filled with conflict. Whether the setting was the Old West or an urban ghetto, they saw people as violent, expressing their essential nature in violent ways. Meanwhile, society itself was changing. Television showed the Vietnam War nightly, exposing most people to more graphic violence than they had ever seen before. As Philip D'Antonio, the producer of *Bullitt* and *The French Connection,* said, "People are used to seeing the war on television. They know what the real thing looks like. So how can you fake it? Audiences won't buy that anymore." In the horror-genre cycle of the early eighties, new expressions of violence broke any remaining taboos. Heads were severed, eyes were gouged out, stomachs were split open, and in general the human body was subjected to every imaginable form of mutilation until the effect became almost comic.

Whether audiences would "buy" this sort of explicit violence was, and remains, the real issue. As long as they are willing to accept it, filmmakers are going to produce it. Some filmmakers, such as Samuel Z. Arkoff, board chairman of American International Pictures, may demonstrate a social conscience and set "a limit on the number of blood bags used," but the dominant attitude is summed up by Joe Eyman, producer of *Prime Cut* (1972): "The effect on society? I don't give it a thought. Psychiatrists don't have the answers, why should I?"

Film and Television

In returning to the relationship between film and television in the mid-seventies, we find the patterns begun in the fifties intensified and solidified. Motion picture attendance still decreased steadily while the number of TV sets increased. However, as described in an earlier chapter, what started out as competition evolved into cooperation and ultimately coexistence. And what once appeared to be the destroyer of film has turned out to be a savior. Without television, Hollywood would simply not have survived, even in a diminished way. Of the more than 20,000 jobs in Hollywood today, 50 percent are in television. Ninety percent of all prime-time TV (8–11 P.M., Eastern standard time) is film material. And motion pictures make up a significant part of this prime-time programming. As William Fadiman noted in *Hollywood Now,* "More people than ever before are seeing Hollywood films, but most of them are not paying Hollywood for the privilege." Motion pictures account for more than half of all network prime-time programming and up to 80 percent of the air time on nonaffiliated independent stations. Universal Studios turned out eighty feature films in 1972, breaking an industry record set back in 1927. Fewer than twenty-five of these, however, were for theatrical release.

We have seen that television has become the "B" movie, providing for the industry what "B" movies have always provided — a substantial, reliable, steady income. New markets in the area of cable and pay TV currently hold great potential, and it is quite clear that television and motion pictures are firmly and permanently linked together. This linkage is causing concern in the board rooms of the major studios. The case is simply one of numbers. Five years ago, 80 percent of a film's revenues came from its box-office performance. But by 1990 domestic theater attendance could drop more than 50 percent to about 500 million, according to Jay M. Gould, president of Economic Information Systems. An audience loss of that size could force moviemakers to rely on television sales and other nontheater markets for as much as 50 percent of their revenues.

For the film companies, the predicted shift in revenue sources means bad news: they split the box-office gross with theater owners nearly right down the middle, but they take a smaller percentage of sales in other markets. For example, in pay TV (where viewers pay per viewing), the studios generally keep only about 20 percent of the revenues. And HBO, a major cable programmer, virtually dictates how much it will pay for a film. In short, studios can no longer depend on a steady income from theatrical distribution rights, for in fact forms of distribution have undergone radical change in the past few years.

The new markets are already altering release patterns. For example, a decade ago, *Prizzi's Honor* (1985) would have opened in movie theaters and a year later would have been reissued. Next, it would have made its debut on network TV and then been syndicated to independent television stations. The whole process would have lasted 1 to 4 years. But today *Prizzi's Honor,* just out of first run, is already on video cassettes, and will be on pay TV within a year. This pattern has virtually killed the theatrical reissue business except for the biggest hits such as *The Empire Strikes Back, E.T.,* and *Return of the Jedi.*

For the immediate future, the most critical new market is pay TV. Soon it will no longer be enough for the studios to ally themselves with competing services to take on Home Box Office (HBO); their success will rest on heavy capital investments. Consequently, motion pictures and television will continue to be inseparably linked. As one industry analyst put it, "Clearly, the tremors shaking Hollywood have nothing to do with the San Andreas Fault. It is the movie business undergoing upheaval and change, the end of another era. In the beginning was D. W. Griffith and Mack Sennett. After the silents came the talkies, after the dream merchants and starmakers came the bankers and accountants, and after the studio lords came the upstart independents. There was Cinerama, Todd-AO, 3-D, Technicolor, and Dolby stereo emerged. Now come satellites, pay-per-view, dish antennas, and video cassettes. If it wants to survive, Hollywood must get into the technology parade before it passes by."

Regulation and Content Control

With respect to the regulation of the moral content of films, the big story was the rating system introduced in 1968. In 1966 the old production code gave a seal of approval to *Who's Afraid of Virginia Woolf?,* granting an exception to the language used and thereby effectively killing what power it had left. The code could no longer stand up as a moral guardian against the onslaught of increasingly sophisticated films. Economic reasons entered the picture as well. The industry was fighting to keep its head above water, and the chief culprit, as noted above, was television. This time technology had not really worked to increase revenues, and now with color television a reality, working more adult themes seemed to be the only possibility left to motion pictures for gaining a competitive edge. On November 1, 1968, therefore, the G, M, R, X rating system went into effect. The labels were soon changed to G, PG, R, and X, but the definitions remained the same: G meant general audiences; PG indicated that parental guidance may be necessary; R meant the film was restricted to those over age seventeen or accompanied by an adult; and X meant the film was banned for everyone under seventeen.

In 1984, in response to increasing pressure from parents and some theater owners, the MPPA added a new rating—PG-13. This rating meant that a film so rated contained material that "may be inappropriate for young children." Over the years since 1968, the number of PG-rated films had grown and the rating, according to one industry observer, "had been stretched to insignificance." The major concern was that the PG rating was being applied to films containing "lots of violence and big body counts," and many felt it was time to draw the line. The film that "broke the code" was Steven Spielberg's *Indiana Jones and the Temple of Doom* (1984). The PG-13 rating, by the way, does not require theaters to keep preteens out; it simply raises a red flag of warning for parents.

The industry intended the ratings to be primarily a labeling system, but quite clearly the effect of the system has been otherwise. The rating system has in effect been used to alter content or prohibit certain people from seeing the material. Those deciding on a rating of necessity make decisions and judgments concerning content, particularly in the PG and R categories. Thus, in applying the ratings, the industry still regulates content, for the difference between a PG and an R often has significant economic ramifications. Losing a large portion of a film's potential audience can be devastating, so most filmmakers who work with sexual themes seek the R or even the PG rating and are willing to tailor their films to the industry's board of review in order to obtain them. Industry statistics reveal that the vast majority of films in the seventies received either PG or R ratings.

To summarize, it is clear that industry self-regulation still exists. Complaints are still heard as to the power wielded by boards of review, but as a device to offset outside regulation the rating system has for the most part worked well.

Wrap-Up

Where have we arrived since the mid-sixties? What is a *now* movie? Where will violence and sex take the American film? We can offer few overall generalizations. One concept, however, remains as valid today as it has been for the past fifty years. Ninety percent of the motion pictures made during the past twenty years are products of an industry. Films, in order to survive in this country, must still make their way in the open marketplace. For this reason, despite new audiences, new filmmakers, new films, and new conditions in the industry, the same old concepts—cycles, trends, and market appeal—dominate. Films are a form of mass communication. Their creators will continue to make them and will continue to build in certain characteristics as long as their audiences are willing to respond to their products.

In 1967, *Time* magazine analyzed the new trend in motion pictures supposedly begun by *Bonnie and Clyde* and *The Graduate*. In the article, *Time* made what turned out to be a prophetic statement about the direction of the new American cinema:

> For all the new talent, new money and new freedom available it is not certain that Hollywood can or will sustain the burden of living in a renaissance. Technical innovation does not in itself guarantee quality. There is some evidence already that the relaxation of censorship, for example, only replaces euphemistic cliches with class cliches. Love scenes are not necessarily better because they are nuder. By getting closer to graffiti, movie dialogue does not necessarily get closer to truth.

As this quote suggests, the time up to the mid-seventies did not represent a true renaissance. Rather, it revealed a shifting of the sands, during which some old structures were covered up while some new ones were revealed. The studio system, with its emphasis on big films and the bottom line, still survives in this country. The spirits of Louis B. Mayer, Irving Thalberg, Henry Cohn, Darryl Zanuck, David O. Selznick, and Sam Goldwyn still exist, though the names are new—Steven Spielberg, George Lucas, and Francis Ford Coppola, to mention only a few. The changes are more subtle than a renaissance, involving gradations of style and taste. Perhaps the late actor Robert Taylor summed it up best:

> If today is still the 20th century, the Hollywood of the 1930s and the early 1940s was 200 years ago. In a sense it was baroque. There was a style of living and making motion pictures which no longer exists. It has been coldly modernized into something very factual, very efficient—and I'm afraid, not very much fun.
>
> It ended in the late 1940s with the unexplained but seemingly premeditated murder of glamour. Television, taxes, actors pricing themselves to the skies. . . .
>
> I can't explain the demise. Perhaps if someone could correctly explain the phenomenon of rock 'n' roll, Beatle haircuts and beatnik wardrobe, we will start to understand. In any case, it was 200 years ago. . . .

Experimentation and New Directions

Focus

Any summary of the directions the motion picture may be taking today remains bound to those same forces that have made film a unique blending of art, industry, technology, and social interaction from its beginnings. Born of science, nurtured by both art and industry, traumatized by still another technological wonder — television — film has continued in the last quarter of its first century to be guided by both scientific and aesthetic invention and by the requirements of society and its own industry.

But film today is more than production methods, technology, and aesthetics. Both the functions film serves and the nature of the film experience itself have undergone dramatic changes in the past two decades. The coming of television, new experiments in style and content, shifts in exhibition patterns, and an awareness of "cinema" that now extends beyond the actual viewing experience are increasingly important to an understanding of film. Some of these changes are more significant than others: audience conditioning to the medium, the expanding role and changing stature of film in our society, the breaking away from stereotypes in the changing images of women and minorities, and the increasing variety of viewing styles becoming available. Today, film as art falls into the purview of scholars in fields outside the traditional arts that gave it birth and early sustenance. Movies have become a variety of things for an increasing number of people in diverse areas of production, consumption, and inquiry. Not only have the form and function of films themselves been affected, but the very nature of today's viewing experience has changed. The experience itself will be a significant part of the future study of film history.

The Experimental Film

The experimental film has led the way in suggesting new directions in film styles and functions. The exploration and development of new forms and content for movies started when Méliès discovered the trick possibilities of the camera in constructing his magical "artificially arranged scenes." They continued with experiments in narrative construction by Porter and Griffith, the refinements in montage construction by Soviet filmmakers, and the introduction of expressionist design by the Germans. The avant-garde movement, discussed in Chapter 6, established the experimental film, along with the narrative and documentary forms, as an identifiable class. And yet the movement is highly elusive and almost impossible to characterize. Simply finding an acceptable definition is difficult. The movement has been called the Underground, the experimental film movement, the avant-garde, the New Wave, the New American Cinema, and more. But all these labels have built-in limitations. In a sense, the movement has all the characteristics they suggest, and yet is more than these separate parts. The very nature of film experimentation takes filmmakers into areas where none have gone before. Further, the movement's dedication to exploring new styles, breaking old rules, and upsetting expectations and traditional patterns makes it difficult to pin it down by time periods and categories. As Gregory Markopolous, one of the pioneer experimental filmmakers, has stated, "The

The New Cinema

*T*he New American Cinema is a spiritual medium; and more physical than Hollywood ever dreamed. In it the conscious and the deep images are reunited, man himself is reunited with passion and no apologies. It seeks to project genuine experience and direct vision. The new cinema attempts to restore subjectivity to its proper realm, and urges the balance of human nature.

—*Ken Kelman, "Anticipation of the Light,"* The New American Cinema

foundation of the New American Cinema is molded out of invisibility and decorated in invisibility. With such a foundation, films are begun like quick-fire even as others are being completed."

Since the movement escapes complete definition by label, time, or category, perhaps the best way to describe it is as a process—as something that is constantly evolving, changing, developing, and becoming. And be-

hind this process are individual filmmakers. If we can hope to find a definition somewhere, it is with these men and women. The basic and original motivation for all avant-garde film is the filmmakers' need to express their personal artistic visions in ways appropriate to them.

The Pioneers

Historically, the modern experimental film in the United States began with Maya Deren, who formed a link between the European avant-garde of the twenties and the New Wave that appeared after World War II. Although Deren made only six films in a career beginning in 1943 (she died in 1961), she was the first American to reach a large audience with "personal" films. Some of her most influential films were *Meshes of the Afternoon* (1943), *At Land* (1944), *A Study in Choreography for Camera* (1945), and *Meditation on Violence* (1948). Her real importance, however, was as a lecturer, writer, and organizer for the fledgling avant-garde movement.

The contemporary avant-garde movement as it emerged in the late fifties and early sixties was born out of frustration—with a system of production that stressed uniformity of content and style, and with the continual need to beat on the doors of a closed shop. The lack of aesthetic variety and the absence of opportunity, coupled with access to a new inexpensive 16 mm and 8 mm technology, created a revolution.

"Any direction at all" was the signpost followed, and yet critics and historians have been able to discern three major types of films in the work of the avant-garde: social protest, social anarchy and liberation, and abstract. Regardless of label, all the films made were protesting something, be it the prevailing politics, sexual mores, aesthetic values, or other aspects of the mainstream culture. Whether the film was Jack Smith's *Flaming Creatures* (1963), Shirley Clarke's *The Connection* (1960), or Andy Warhol's *The Chelsea Girls* (1966), a protest or challenge was being made through film.

At first the chief protest was partially economic. The movement stressed cheaply made films and seemed to find some sort of justification in this alone. John Cassa-

Breaking Out

*I*n cinema, this search is manifested through abandoning of all the existing professional, commercial values, rules, subjects, techniques, pretensions. We said: We don't know what man is; we don't know what cinema is. Let us, therefore, be completely open. Let us go in any direction. Let us be completely open and listening, ready to move to any direction upon the slightest call, almost like one who is too tired and too weary, whose senses are like a musical string, almost with no power of their own; blown and played by the mystical winds of the incoming age, waiting for a slightest motion or call or sign. *Let's go in any direction to break out of the net that is dragging us down* [emphasis added].

—*Jonas Mekas "Where We Are—The Underground?"* The New American Cinema

vetes, for example, made his first film, *Shadows* (1960), for $15,000, and this fact seemed to ensure the film's integrity and purity as part of the movement. This philosophy still exists to some degree, but personal vision is not always cheap, and certain filmmakers have found that an experimental film can be expensive—witness Stanley Kubrick's *2001: A Space Odyssey* (1968) and *A Clockwork Orange* (1971), with their unorthodox language and narrative pattern, dazzling special effects, and purposely cold and remote looks at their respective subjects.

Geographically the movement was scattered, but the primary focus and orientation were on the two coasts, specifically in New York and San Francisco. These two cities were important because they contained several key individuals and organizations that would give the movement power and visibility. The organization came from various film societies and individuals, but the real key was the establishment in 1960 of the magazine *Film Culture* by Jonas Mekas. Although based in New York, it quickly became a rallying point and voice for the entire movement.

From *At Land* (1944). In this film by Maya Deren, the leader of the American experimental movement of the forties and fifties, Deren herself portrays a girl who comes from and returns to the sea. The character's land adventures include a crawl past dining guests along a food-laden banquet table.

The "Outposts of Culture"

*F*inally, the collectivity of Independent cinema is not worth writing about. Only individual films. . . . Add it all up and you have an interesting footnote to the history of world cinema. Much ado about nothing? Hardly. Someone has to man the outposts of culture, and the Independent Film is uniquely qualified to express the chaos and confusion of our time.

—*Andrew Sarris, "The Independent Cinema,"* The New American Cinema

Other important organizations included Amos Vogel's "Cinema 16" programs in New York and Frank Stauffacher's "Art in Cinema" series on the West Coast, events that were the movement's first real showcases. Starting in 1947, they provided recognition for new films and new filmmakers. As the movement began to pick up speed in the sixties, many more societies and festivals sprang up, and the original two lost most of their power. A key event was the New York Film Festival's official recognition of the New American Cinema in 1966, when it showcased many previously unknown films.

Owing to widespread festival recognition, distributors began to acquire and promote many of the new avant-garde films. Grove Press, Newsreel, and the Filmmakers Cooperative became vital elements in helping the movement to grow and develop.

The Postwar American Underground

Critics of the American avant-garde of the sixties generally acknowledge Kenneth Anger, Gregory Markopolous, and Stan Brakhage as three of the movement's key filmmakers. These three represent the diversity that makes up the very fabric of the avant-garde movement.

Kenneth Anger made his first "public" film in 1947. Called *Fireworks,* it was typical of the movement in its total rejection of a Hollywood style. Anger himself, however, dropped this style and began to create "polished" films that explored various areas of the American popular myth. Perhaps his best-known work is *Scorpio Rising,* made in 1963. In this film, Anger examines the myth of the motorcyclist, and in the process he creates a ritual-like film that looks at all aspects of the myth — the dress of the cyclists, their cultlike worship of the bike, their orgies of power and speed, and the relationships between the cyclists and mythic heroes such as Marlon Brando and James Dean. All Anger's films except *Fireworks* have strong associations with Hollywood, characterized primarily by careful attention to detail and an almost classic approach to the construction of elaborate montage units.

Gregory Markopolous is another pioneer in the movement. Although he studied under the "classic" director Josef von Sternberg at UCLA, his films consciously destroy all the standard Hollywood narrative ingredients. For example, his film *Galaxie* (1966) consists of thirty portraits of various friends, using one roll (100 feet, or three minutes) for each individual. The film consists of the rolls attached to each other, with all editing done in the camera. Working in the camera has become a Markopolous trademark. In *Ming Green* (1964), he photographed his flat in New York and, by overlapping images and juxtaposing objects, created a remarkable portrait of a common environment. Unfortunately, Markopolous's technique of working in the camera has been conceived as an "easy" way of making films by many avant-garde filmmakers. There is nothing "easy" or lazy, however in Markopolous's work. His effects are carefully designed to present his point of view and to create images of the reality he wants to present.

Stan Brakhage has worked consistently in experimental film for more than twenty years. Brakhage probably epitomizes the "underground experimental filmmaker" to most audiences, since his style departs most radically from accepted film technique. Brakhage's films display no story, no acting, no narrative editing, and no conscious camera composition. Instead, this filmmaker seems obsessed with the purity of film recording. His films usually "look at" a subject, and only when he feels that this revelation has been accomplished does he begin to structure the experience. His most ambitious and well-known work is *Dog Star Man,* which took him more than four years to complete (1961–1965). The basic structure involves a man and a dog climbing a mountain to cut down a tree. As the man climbs, his mind becomes flooded with memories of his past. The camera constantly shifts perspective, and the reality of the film be-

The Freedom of the Underground

*S*ome underground films are good. Some are bad. A few are great. But whatever they are, underground films are the film artist's unmitigated vision. No banker, no producer, no patron has dictated what they must be or can later change them. Underground films are banned, but they are never cut.

Therefore, the underground is free to look outward with an unblinking eye and inward in complex and mystical ways. It is free to be poetic and to be obscure. It is even free to go mad.

The underground film has a vitality, an arrogant originality and an integrity that today is almost unique in cinema. It has unleashed the artist in the young and still unexplored medium of film. . . .

— *Sheldon Renan,* An Introduction to the American Underground Film

comes a constantly changing visual pattern of clouds, sun, dog, internal organs, sky, and so on. Brakhage is a pivotal figure, for with his work experimental film moved away from a literary base to express a highly personal vision.

This move toward a more subjective statement reveals a shift from pictorial to a more emotional landscape. Directors such as Markopolous, Anger, and Brakhage are film poets who have set aside accepted concepts in cinematic technique and subject matter. We can see the break in treatments ranging from the film journal of the New York City subway (Carson Davidson's *Third Avenue El* [1955]) to the surreal sexual imagery of Kenneth Anger's *Fireworks* and Brakhage's *Flesh of the Morning* (1956). Stylistic experimentation in the movement has run the gamut from the collages of Stan Vanderbeek and the unedited marathons of Andy Warhol to the nonphotographed images of Brakhage.

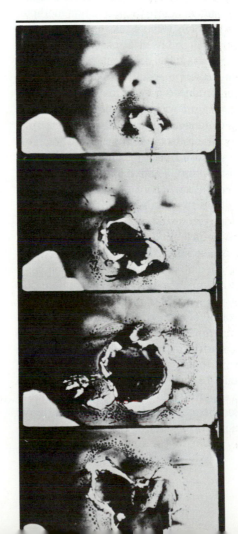

From *Dog Star Man* (1965). A man's vision of his past leads the viewer into Stan Brakhage's subjective world, which contains this radically transformed image of a baby's mouth.

The New Avant-Garde

The experimental, or avant-garde, cinema has always been an unruly movement, dedicated to the extension or outright rejection of styles, structures, and themes of conventional motion pictures. Many independent filmmakers of the seventies and eighties have reacted not only against Hollywood formula films, but also against what have become conventions of the avant-garde. Working in cheap, highly flexible super 8 mm film, such "punk" filmmakers as Amos Poe, Eric Mitchell, and Vivienne Dick have challenged, ignored, or extended the film experiments of Warhol, Brakhage, Anger, and Markopolous. Mitchell has followed the style of early Warhol in the long take of extemporaneous nonaction in search of a statement. (In *Kidnapped* he turns the camera on friends and waits for something to happen.) Dick has drawn from the various *cinéma vérité* styles to make more directed political statements and is among the leaders of the new feminist film movement. Poe began his moviemaking career by filming rock bands, but found his inspiration in the works of Jean-Luc Godard. He produced a remake of Godard's *Breathless* (1975) and also undertook a new version of *Alphaville*. These ambitious and high-budget projects bring directors such as Poe into feature-film styles and mainstream production methods. He is only one of many experimentalists who have contributed to, if not joined, commercial feature-film production. Scott Bartlett was hired as a technical consultant for Ken Russell's *Altered States*. John Whitney, the pioneer in computer-produced films, provided both *Westworld* and *Futureworld* with much of their technical wizardry; a cadre of young independents assisted George Lucas in the special-effects creations of his *Star Wars* and *The Empire Strikes Back*.

Such early innovators as Scott Bartlett and Jordan Belson have joined the new breed of experimentalists in turning to computer and video technology and adapting ideas and techniques from the electronic media to film. Stan Vanderbeek has produced a series of "poem fields," which are films produced through computer programming. Electronic effects used in television, which allow for the creation of intricate abstract designs, are also being explored.

The avant-garde of the eighties continues to influence mainstream filmmakers and to blur the distinction between film and television. Because of differences from commercial film in funding, distribution, and sense of mission it remains a reasonably discrete movement in noncommercial, experimental cinema. And it continues to extend and challenge the medium's capabilities in technology, sociopolitical observation, and personal expression.

Animation

The story of screen animation has been closely tied to the fortunes of the industry as a whole. As discussed, the general decline of the studio system led to the extinction of most forms of the commercial short—the serial, newsreel, travelogue, "specialty," and comedy short. The only form to survive with any degree of vigor has been the animated cartoon.

Following World War II, animation took on new forms and styles. The war itself had a big impact, for, as we have seen, the Communist domination of Eastern Europe fostered the establishment of several state film schools. These schools ultimately resulted in the development of new styles of animation. But the key event in the evolution of animation was an employees' strike at the Walt Disney's studio in 1941. When this strike was finally settled, there were a number of defectors from the studio. One was Stephen Bosustow, who in 1945 founded a new animation studio, United Productions of America (UPA). Gathering a number of former Disney animators, UPA began producing cartoons in a wide variety of styles. The new studio permitted a great deal of personal freedom, the very thing Disney forbade. The general UPA style involved a move away from realism, utilizing greater economy in characterization and story. Most of the UPA cartoons used stick figures against sparse backgrounds. The philosophy of the films was decidedly realistic, however, in distinct contrast to the romanticism Disney adhered to.

UPA's most famous character, Mr. Magoo, was developed in 1949. Magoo films were produced with great regularity and were popular for more than twenty years. Other well-known UPA characterizations were Gerald McBoing Boing and Madeline, both created by Bob Cannon. Outstanding individual films included Bill Hurtz's *Unicorn in the Garden* (1953) and John Hubley's *The Hole* (1962) and *The Hunt* (1964).

Arguably as important as UPA in its overall impact was a less formal school of animation characterized by a strong streak of violence. Beginning with the Tex Avery and Chuck Jones character Bugs Bunny, this new school grew rapidly, presenting such cartoon characters as Tweety Pie and Sylvester, Daffy Duck, Elmer Fudd, and, perhaps its best-known figures, Tom and Jerry. This new school dominated the theatrical cartoon in the fifties and early sixties. However, the financial crunch finally caught up with the form in the early sixties, and the cartoon was ultimately pushed into television. William Hanna and Joseph Barbera led the way there, and throughout the sixties and seventies this pair dominated

Mr. Magoo, the most famous character to come out of the UPA animation studio, gained star status among cartoon characters in the early fifties with the assistance of Jim Backus's voice.

the television cartoon market. At its peak in the mid-sixties, the team produced more than 25,000 feet of cartoon material a week and created such popular characters as Ruff and Reddy, Quick Draw McGraw, Yogi Bear, Huckleberry Hound, and the Flintstones.

Television animation took two forms—children's cartoons and advertising—and, with few exceptions, this pattern has remained consistent. That children's programming was dominated by animation drew heavy criticism beginning in the early seventies, and slowly live performances and performers began creeping back into the Saturday-morning scene. Still, the television cartoon remains the dominant form in children's programming, and the reasons are quite obvious. The cartoon allows for spectacular events and characters at less cost and under greater control than any other film form.

As an advertising vehicle, animation began to fade in the early seventies, when market researchers started recognizing the need to "talk straight" about products via spokespeople who looked real and communicated directly with the television audience.

Animation found uses outside the mainstream, however, specifically in the avant-garde experimental movement of the sixties. Several new filmmakers began to

work with animation to produce highly abstract and personal films. The Whitney brothers, John and James, used computers to create abstract forms and patterns along with synthetic sound in such films as *Celery Stalks at Midnight* (1951–1958) and *Permutations* (1967). Robert Breer, Stan Vanderbeek, and Jordan Belson all used animation to help create their niches in the new American cinema. Other independent filmmakers working in animation include Ernest Pintoff, who produced the hilarious parody on contemporary film thought in *The Critic* (1963), and long-time animator John Hubley, who, along with his wife Faith, produced *Moonbird* (1960), one of the most fascinating and touching of all animated shorts. This film is built around nighttime conversations of the couple's two young sons, during which the boys spin a fantasy game, catching a moonbird. Using stick figures against an abstract background, the Hubleys achieve unique and revealing insights into the fantasy world of children.

In all this activity, the styles varied greatly. However, there was an overall tendency toward simple, clear lines and shapes, since most of the creators were chiefly interested in expressing a particular point of view.

Much of this experimental work in the United States was twenty years behind that of Canada. There, in the late forties, Norman MacLaren worked in animation to produce such classics as *Begone Dull Care* (1949) and *Neighbors* (1952), which makes use of the repetition of individual film frames and the elimination of others to produce a slightly jerky (cartoonlike) movement of characters. MacLaren developed a number of styles, ranging from the purely abstract *Vertical Lines* (1960) to his famous pixilation style epitomized in *Neighbors*. Here he used live actors and real settings, but created animated movement by using stop-action photography and manipulating the speed of the film. MacLaren remained a singularly strong force in developing new animation forms and films.

Additional work in animation took place in England, chiefly through the work of John Halas and Joy Batchelor, who produced the controversial *Animal Farm* in 1954. But the most significant and popular work to come from England was George Dunning's *The Yellow Submarine* (1968). This feature-length film about the Beatles literally deluged audiences with images in a variety of styles, including abstract, cartoon, and pixilation. Quickly achieving cult status, it became for many audiences a unique psychological "trip."

Important animation innovations were also taking place in Eastern Europe. Jiří Trnka of Czechoslovakia brought puppet animation to its highest form. He used puppets because they had "more presence" and created complex forms of great charm and genuine involvement. His major work was *A Midsummer Night's Dream,* produced in 1959.

Yugoslavia was the other Eastern European country to produce new innovations in animation, with the founding of the Zagreb Studio in 1956. Headed by Dušan Vukotić, the school emphasized a clean, functional style obviously influenced by UPA. However, Zagreb's animators went beyond their American counterparts in developing the cartoon form as a rich vehicle for satire, parody, and political comment, with such films as *Concerto for a Sub-Machine Gun* (1959), a parody of the American gangster film, and *Ersatz* (1961), the first non-American cartoon to win an Academy Award.

Recent developments in theatrical animation have involved feature-length films. Of the 125 such films produced since 1917, almost 100 were made after 1945. Although the Disney studios were turning increasingly to the production of live-action films in the late sixties, animated features such as *The Yellow Submarine* were exploring new styles and functions in feature film anima-

tion and sparking renewed interest in the form. The most important animated features to emerge in the seventies were Ralph Bakshi's *Fritz the Cat* (1972), *Heavy Traffic* (1973), and *Wizards* (1977). In somewhat contradictory fashion, Bakshi uses animation to portray a real world of drugs, sex, and life in an urban ghetto. In *Fritz the Cat* all of the characters are animals, but *Heavy Traffic* uses the human form as well. Obviously influenced by both the content and style of the new underground comic books, his first two films departed strikingly from the child orientation of most American film animation, as evidenced by the X rating both films earned from the industry. These works are basically satiric in intent, but they strike with an axe rather than carve with a knife. They are both visually and orally blatant and present a view of life "as it is" in the city ghetto. Although many critics consider these films to be in bad taste, there is little question that they are major works that have influenced the development of the form.

New directions in screen animation are clearly tied to developments in computer graphics. Computer ani-

▲ From Ralph Bakshi's *Heavy Traffic* (1973). This typically "heavy" scene represents a new use for animation. Contemporary urban strife takes the place of the more fanciful cartoon and fairy-tale imagery usually associated with American animation.

Feature Films and Computer Graphics

*T*he special-effects rage continues, but instead of a computer-graphics boom, the movies have entered a cautious, "show me" phase in which only a few feature films that might rely heavily on computer graphics have even reached the talking stage. . . . What happens next depends largely on how successful the computer-graphics companies are in impressing the people who bankroll the movies.

—*Marc Kirkeby,
"Computer Graphics" by*
American Film *(January–February 1983)*

mation can affect film production in a number of ways. First, the computer's capacity to store, retrieve, and modify design details can provide the animator with electronically produced and painted images. This eliminates the expensive and time-consuming process of cell animation, which requires that the series of transparent overlays to be combined to create the scene be manually manipulated and modified. A second way of applying computers to animation involves combining live action with animation. Though the combination is hardly new, the computer allows computer-generated settings and live-action "action" to be integrated more effectively than before. Finally, the computer's potential for programming a scene as observed from two slightly different perspectives has important implications for 3-D animation.

It is also possible that computer-generated models of live-action subjects will soon be used to create images that are somewhere between live action and animation. Filmmakers might someday be able to scan live models and "program" them into action, permitting computer-aided performances by favorite stars not present on the movie set.

Walt Disney Productions, an early experimenter in both sound and color, has also led the way in computer animation. Joining forces with a computer graphics com-

pany, Disney produced *Tron* (1982), an innovative if commercially unsuccessful animated feature in which the computer becomes a central character in the narrative as well as the creator of many of the film's images.

Animation today exists in many forms all over the world. It is used for many purposes, including formal instruction, popular entertainment, social comment, and abstract personal expression. At one time it was threatened with extinction in the use of commercial shorts. However, animation has grown far beyond this limited function and is one of the most versatile of film forms today.

Technology and Exhibition

The importance of technology to the development of cinematic form has been repeatedly illustrated throughout this book. Every major technological breakthrough has been preceded by a considerable period of anticipation and experimentation and followed by a period of exploitation and integration. Sound was anticipated in the piano accompaniment to the earliest of films; color was more than a dream to silent filmmakers, as the use of hand-tinting and colored film stock in the works of Porter and Griffith shows. Curved and multiscreen projection goes back to Hale's Tours and the triptych screen of Abel Gance for *Napoleon*. James Card, former curator of Motion Pictures at the George Eastman House in Rochester, New York, reports that color, wide screen, sound, and other special effects were displayed at the Paris Exposition in 1900. The Lumière brothers showed hand-tinted films on a 48 × 69 foot screen, and the Cinéorama process using ten synchronized cameras and projectors was exhibited by its creator, Raoul Grimoin-Sanson.

Although a receptive climate existed for such major innovations, the problems of technology had to be solved before they could become accepted and viable embellishments. Sound awaited synchronization and amplification; color, the three-color process of photography; and wide screen, the anamorphic lens.

Once the technological limitations were removed, each innovation saw a period of exploitation, in which it was self-consciously worked and overworked for its own sake with little regard for its contribution to total design. And in each case this period ultimately gave way to one of integration, in which the process or device came under artistic control and through selective and creative uses became a part of the film's overall style and function. This shift from exploitation to integration was echoed by

René Clair, when he said, "The talking film exists. . . . It is too late for those who love the art of moving pictures to deplore the effects of this barbaric invasion. . . . The talking film is not everything. There is also the sound film."

There is little question today that sound has become a creative element in film. However, the potential for using the color process in selective and controlled ways, beyond basic photographic realism, is open to debate, since until very recently few attempts have been made to use color to go beyond a faithful representation of actuality. As for screen shapes and sizes, the formative period is still upon us. Although basic wide-screen processes such as Panavision have come to provide an unobtrusive and agreeably flexible aspect ratio, broader implications of film projection and the film-viewing experience have not been fully realized. And what has been termed "expanded cinema" is still in a period of anticipation and experimentation.

Multiscreen Projection

Multiscreen projection, as noted by James Card, had its unveiling at the Paris Exposition in 1900, nearly thirty years before Abel Gance's *Napoleon* was shown in "Polyvision" on a triple screen at the Paris Opéra. Not until the arrival of television, however, did the use of multiple images became more than a novelty. It was probably that medium's tendency to cultivate our appetite for simultaneous action that helped spur exploration. It is even more likely that the search for visual-aural experiences *not* available on the small screen brought about the flurry of multiprojections in the sixties. The 1964–1965 New York World's Fair became a major showcase for multiscreen projection. Eastman Kodak's *The Searching Eye;* Disney's *Circarama,* transplanted from Disneyland in Anaheim; and IBM's computer-style show were fair favorites. And the Johnson's Wax Pavilion offering— *To Be Alive,* a documentary short by Francis Thompson and Alexander Hammid that utilized a triple screen—became a feature attraction of the entire exposition.

With the opening of Expo '67 in Montreal came an explosion in film-exhibition techniques. Refined optics, electronics, and computer programming contributed to not only multiscreen projection but multimedia and multidimension programs as well. The less bizarre variations of multiple image, which used a single flat or slightly curved viewing surface, showed the greatest flexibility and potential for conventional film functions. Multiple images, single composite images, the simultaneous repe-

In *Napoleon* (1927), Abel Gance introduced an early multi-image process called "Polyvision." In addition to allowing the entire oversize screen to carry a single panoramic action, he produced individual images for each of three or six sections of the screen to run simultaneously, thus providing complementary or contrasting action. The film also was adorned with color scenes produced with tinted stock.

tition of an image, the contrasting of images, and even the variable masking or framing of images to keep sections of the overall viewing surface dark were all demonstrated with varying degrees of success. *We Are Young,* a twenty-minute presentation of the Canadian Pacific Cominco Pavilion, used six screens in two rows of three to examine the dilemmas of youth in the modern world. The most ambitious and popular exhibit of the fair was a multipart show by the National Film Board of Canada called *Labyrinthe.* It featured a double triptych, or five-screen cross, at one point and a huge well, ringed by balconies, for viewing at another. In the film presentation entitled "Man and His World," images were projected on both a screen extending the forty-five foot height of the well and on the bottom of the well, and the actions on the two screens were interrelated.

The film industry adopted Expo's multiple-image experiments the following year in, for example, Norman Jewison's *The Thomas Crown Affair* (1968) and Richard Fleischer's *The Boston Strangler* (1968). Jewison used multiscreen images to create the kind of simultaneity that Pudovkin described in his montage theory and revealed in his films — the cross-cutting between simultaneous actions that goes back to *The Great Train Robbery* (1903). With the Jewison film, the actions were shown simultaneously rather than sequentially — two or more actions representing the complex preparations and execution of a modern-day robbery. John Frankenheimer had also made use of multiple image in the racing scenes of *Grand Prix* (1966). Still, these examples did not turn out to be trend setters, and the use of multiple images in feature films since has been scarce. On the home screen, however, the technique has become a standard device in telecasting sporting events, variety specials, and many other types of program.

Stereoscopic Film

In an article called "Moving Pictures in the year 2000," written for *Moving Picture News* in 1911, a journalist describes her vision of figures "flitting about, spirit fashion, propelled and reflected by some electrical or gaseous method, through the abstract space." Though film images continue to be two-dimensional, a number of new techniques give the impression of in-depth viewing. A range of these techniques, such as Cinerama and CinemaScope, employ curved and multiscreen forms. More conventional techniques of composition and deep focus, which give the impression of depth to the standard 35 mm flat image, are also prevalent. True stereoscopy came with 3-D movies, which went commercial in 1952. *Bwana Devil,* the first feature-length stereoscopic

▲ Numerous "multiscreen" showings awaited fair goers at the 1967 International Exposition, Expo '67, in Montreal. These ranged from single expanded screens with single or multiple images to projections on a variety of surfaces, at varying angles, in special settings.

film —"A lion in your lap! A lover in your arms!" read the ads — was followed by several horror and adventure tales in 1953, all of which exploited the stereo effect by having objects pop out of the screen and into the laps or past the ears of spectators. The craze was already on the wane by the following year, and Hitchcock's *Dial M for Murder,* though photographed in 3-D, was released in a conventional print version. A revival attempt in 1972, which included the sexploitative *The Stewardesses* and reissuance of Warner Brothers' more durable offering from the original 3-D era, *House of Wax,* failed to make headway. *Jaws 3-D* (1983) failed to give much promise for new stereoscopic films of the eighties. Pedestrian and exploitative plots, plus the annoyance and eye fatigue from wearing polarizing glasses, left audiences unimpressed.

The future for stereoscopic film will likely come by way of the holographic image, which employs a laser beam to produce an in-depth image in the form of the original object being projected. The fact that the hologram is a true stereoscopic image means that any change in perspective, such as moving from the left to the right of an object (or, theoretically, through it) reveals a new

*W*hat wonderful dimensions the idea may arrive at by the commencement of the next century I am not prepared even to hint at. Whether the canvas will be done away with and the figures will be seen flitting about, spirit fashion, propelled and reflected by some electrical or gaseous method, through the abstract space, we do not know. Whether by some trick of phonography or ventriloquism the figures will aid their pantomimic expression by deep sonorous tones of dramatic marvel, proceeding apparently from the life-like shadows of things that have been seen, is a secret locked away in the treasure troves of the future.

—*Margaret I. MacDonald,
"Moving Pictures in the
Year 2000,"* Moving Picture
News *(April 22, 1911)*

facet or angle of the object without the aid of moving camera or editing. Holographic motion pictures have already been produced, but at this writing these represent crude first steps. Problems still to be solved involve sufficiently lighting large objects or areas, reproducing holograms for large audiences, and reproducing holograms in color. Still, an important first step has been taken, and predictions for when a holographic movie system will be viable run as early as ten years hence.

There seems to be little doubt that both filmmakers and audiences will be able to absorb the addition of a third dimension to film viewing. Sergei Eisenstein, in writing on "The Future of Film," observed that

unlike sound, the application of colour and stereoscopy to the film will effect no radical departure: they involve no structural changes, but merely mark further stages in the evolution toward perfection. . . . Stereoscopic films will at first give the onlooker a feeling of strangeness, but this will pass away after sixty feet of film have been shown.

New Systems and Functions

In addition to multiprojection and stereoscopy, a number of systems and devices have the potential for modifying film's function, or at least the way we experience the medium. Shortly after the appearance of 3-D movies, two different systems promising the added realism of olfactory stimulation appeared in a few major cities of the United States—"Smellovision" and "Aromarama." Neither system caught on, nor has anything resembling Aldous Huxley's futuristic vision of "the feelies" yet become a reality (an exception is the "multidimension feel of Sensurround," which makes up one part of *Earthquake* [1974]). Such systems might seem unlikely ever to move beyond the novelty stage, but with the serious interest today in multisensory experience and multimedia, the possibilities of broader sensory appeal involving film cannot be ignored. Under the influence of Marshall McLuhan's call that we liberate ourselves from the dominance of print media in favor of multisensory experience, museums, galleries, and exhibition and communication centers of all kinds are attempting to create media environments and kinetic experiences by combining movies with a host of visual, aural, and tactile stimuli.

In the "happening" of the 1960s, music, light shows, and some form of performance (dance, poetry reading, mime) were combined. Now, as an extension of that concept, what is called the intermedia kinetic experience is offered as an electronic world in which multiple films are combined with other forms — the orchestration of projected light, multitrack music and sound sources, kinetic sculpture, and live dance and acting. Thus the discrete nature of the film-viewing experience is being abandoned by showman and museum curator alike in an attempt to integrate movies with other sensory stimuli to form mixed-media shows and exhibits.

The notion of combining film with live action goes back to the silent Japanese movie theater, where the Hanashika—"the man who tells the story," or live narrator — was as popular with audiences as the stars themselves. Early U.S. vaudeville shared billing with movies, as do more recent variety and stage-show routines, but film and live action have rarely been integrated in Western theater over the years. A notable exception is the projection of film images as part of the setting or for special visual effects in legitimate stage productions. This technique was helping German producers solve problems in staging as early as the 1910s, and it has been revived, on occasion, in European and American theaters. *Laterna Magica,* a mixing of live stage action with screen action, was devised in Czechoslovakia and first presented at the Brussels World's Fair in 1958, with repeat performances at both the New York and Montreal fairs. Other "living screen" processes have been devised in the effort to blend large-scale exterior and spectacle film sequences with intimate live drama without interruption. These use a variety of screens in various combinations manipulated during performances by stagehands. Such blendings of film and theater, however, have not developed beyond demonstration models. However, the use of rear-projection cinematography for scene building or filmed interludes as part of stage productions has been on the increase.

Computers and Film

The age of electronics has begun to influence cinematic form in a variety of ways. Another Expo '67 attraction devised by the Czechs was *Kinoautomat,* an audience-participation scheme that employed a computer. Audiences were invited to choose among plot developments at key intervals. The stars of the film would themselves come on stage to present the audience with the choice of plot alternatives, and a computer would then tally the audience members' choices and select the winning variation. The long-range implications for such a system seem doubtful, but other uses of computer programming in cinematography go beyond gimmick and showy exploitation.

The computer has provided the means by which such experimentalists as Stan Vanderbeek and John Whitney are able to create complex abstract patterns in motion. More recently, the producers of both experimental and feature films have recognized the possibilities in combining computer programming and videotape to provide immediate access to images just shot and to store and retrieve images easily during the editing process. Such a system makes it possible to call up a series of shots in a desired sequence; to add, delete, reorganize, and lengthen or shorten the shots; and even to select special optical effects without ever actually touching the film.

"Electronic cinema" is a term used by Francis Ford Coppola to describe his use of video and computer in several stages of film production. In *One From the Heart* (1982), he used a word processor to store and retrieve script detail. He also used "electronic storyboarding," whereby he placed sketches of action, together with dialogue, onto videotape, which facilitated the "previsualization" of a scene. Video recordings of rehearsals and final takes gradually replaced the storyboard sketches so that finally, in the editing, Coppola could gain immediate access to and control over all aural and visual material. By working at a computer terminal rather than an editing bench, he was able to orchestrate the final version of the film electronically, eliminating the laborious and time-consuming practice of physically rearranging and combining shots to attain a final "cut." From both a practical and aesthetic perspective, the possibilities that video and computers offer to the film production seem limitless.

Still another application of computers in the world of film is turning black-and-white films into color videotape. The system was first introduced in 1983; since then MGM/UA has contracted to have some of its black-and-white feature films converted to color. Demonstration cassettes have already been produced with scenes from Laurel and Hardy shorts; *Broadway Melody,* with Fred Astaire and Eleanor Powell; Hitchcock's *Rebecca;* and *Mutiny on the Bounty,* with Charles Laughton and Clark Gable.

◀ From *One From the Heart* (1982). Frances Ford Coppola experimented with the video technology to edit and provide special effects for his 1982 film by transferring it to videotape. Using video technology, he could select scenes, arrange them in the desired sequence, and time them without having to touch the actual film footage until the final cut was assembled.

Changes in Exhibition

Technology has also revolutionized film exhibition. Video cassette systems are now widely available for home use and are being promoted as "complete home-entertainment centers." They make it possible to record and play back images in a form of home movies and record and play back a wide variety of prepackaged films on tape. Video disk systems are substantially less expensive than tape equipment and are also more flexible. Disk systems not only provide viewable images at fast-forward and fast-reverse speeds, but also permit viewers instant access to a certain scene, just as one can select a particular band on an LP record.

Another new technology currently in the experimental stage is "high-definition video" (HDV), which produces a high-definition video image (1125 scan lines) that far surpasses the 525-scan-line system of standard U.S. television. Because the images on the screen are so much sharper, technicians should be able to shoot film on HDV and then transfer it to celluloid without a significant loss of density and resolution.

Without question, technology will play a critical role in the development of films of the future. Stereophonic sound on video cassette and disk is now available, and home disk-recording systems and stereoscopic film are

in the experimental stages. But the mastery of scientific devices alone will not ensure effective application. The challenge for future filmmakers will be — as it was for Porter, Méliès, Griffith, Clair, and other pioneers in revolutionary technique — finding means of using these creatively.

Extending the Film Experience

The Viewing Situation

The very nature of the film-viewing experience is an important aspect of film evolution. We relate differently to movies today than the first film viewers did because we see them more frequently, under more diverse viewing conditions, and in a greater variety of styles.

Film viewing began with Edison's Kinetoscope, by which an individual peered through the eyepiece of a

A multicinema complex in a mall. With the shopping mall becoming the center for both consumer and social activity, movie theaters have found a congenial home and ready audiences.

penny-arcade contraption for several seconds. Projection brought film to the theater—first the makeshift storefront variety, then the nickelodeon, and later the grandiose palaces. By the thirties, this trend had already begun to reverse itself, as streamlined, functional suburban or neighborhood theaters supplemented and gradually replaced the cavernous first-run houses. With the advent of television and the dwindling of audiences came the closing of many of the neighborhood theaters. These, together with the remaining palaces, were replaced by small, comfortable though utilitarian cinemas, often located in large shopping centers. Today the trend continues, with multiple theaters being designed to share a common lobby and other facilities, and individual auditorium capacities ranging from 150 to 500 seats. Some are cinema complexes incorporated into the grand design of enclosed malls, where consumers can combine a full range of activities—shopping, professional consultation, dining—with a visit to the movies without ever seeing the light of day. Such a fully climate-controlled existence extends to fully automated theaters, which, in addition to their film offerings, provide sitter services or serve as rendezvous points. Some small theaters, especially those in mall complexes, have "dollar nights," which make dropping in to see a film a casual experience, one the viewer can decide on at short notice while shopping. Thus moviegoing takes on the form of "impulse buying."

At the other end of the spectrum, though, major cities today offer film experiences that rival other cultural arts events. Often a city's civic or cultural center contains a film theater, and here filmgoers mingle with symphony, opera, and ballet devotees. Lincoln Center in New York is the home of the New York Film Festival

▶ With the addition of new theaters and the division of larger, older ones, cinema complexes now provide as many as ten or twelve screens.

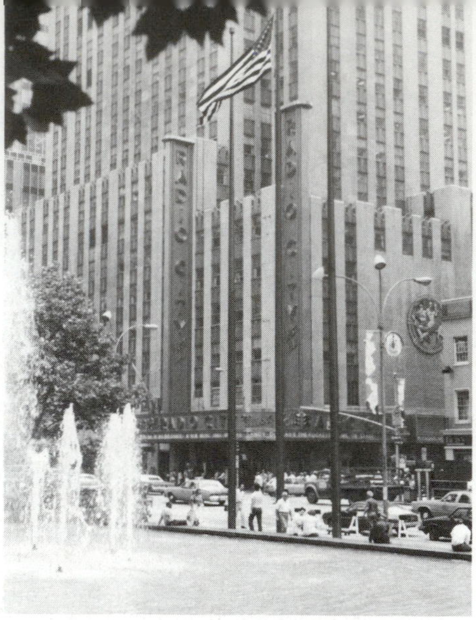

a

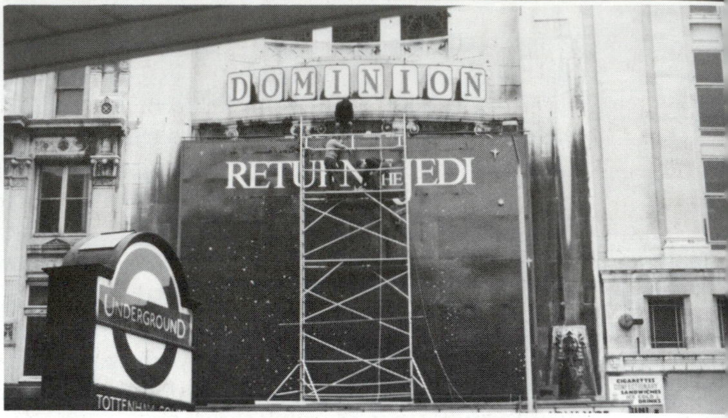

b

City theaters. Large metropolitan centers still provide a few showcase cinemas for big-budget releases, but few "palaces" remain, and many of the older theaters have been divided to accommodate two or more screens. Shown here are (a) Radio City Music Hall in New York, (b) the Dominion Theater in London's West End, and (c) a "triplex" in Boulogne, France.

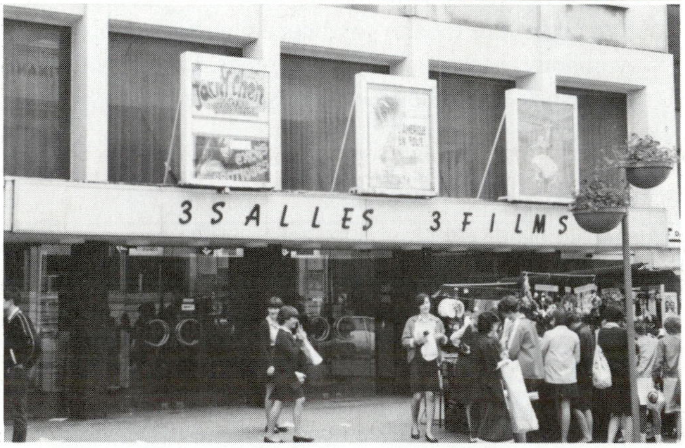

c

Downtown theaters. In urban centers that support downtown, or "inner-city," theaters as well as the outlying, newer mall theaters or cinema complexes, a variety of architectural styles are represented. In this group is (a) a traditional downtown theater (named after a native son who became a U.S. president), which shows films in their second run; (b) an "art house," which features foreign and early American film classics; and (c) a city-owned "legit" house, which books music, theater, and dance groups as well as its mainstay of film programs.

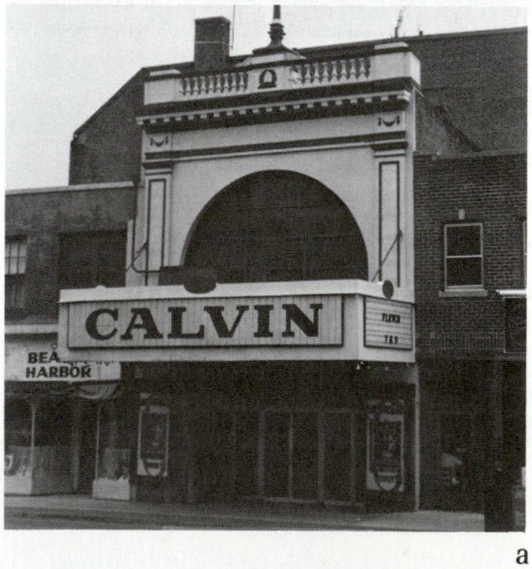

a

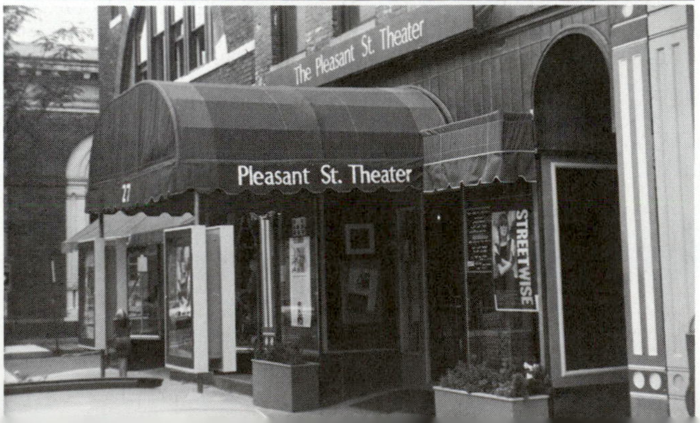

b

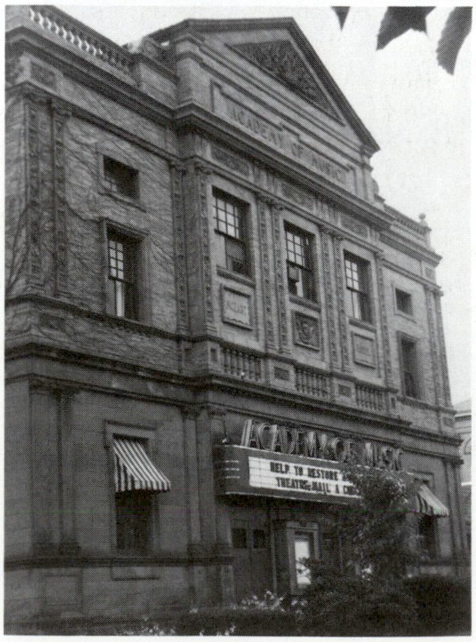

c

▲ The drive-in in decline. In their golden years in the late fifties, there were more than 4,700 drive-in theaters in the United States. Although still enjoying popularity in the more temperate climate of the South, the drive-in is in eclipse in the North, the victim of rising real estate values and competition from cable, video cassettes, and mall theaters, which make the relatively short drive-in season unprofitable. Difficulty in obtaining first-run films has made most drive-ins showplaces for horror and sex-exploitation fare.

each September and holds other special film programs as well. In Shanghai, at one of the world's largest cultural centers, film showings, performances by the Peking Opera, and as many as twenty other arts activities might be going on simultaneously. The National Film Theatre in London, part of the complex that includes Festival Hall on the South Bank of the Thames, presents regular contemporary and retrospective screenings and film lectures. More recently, the American Film Institute Theater has been established as part of the John F. Kennedy Center in Washington, D.C. Like other civic centers, the institute theater serves as a repertory film theater that gives special, though by no means exclusive, attention to director and genre retrospectives.

Whether as part of such cultural-center offerings in large metropolitan areas or as local art-house fare, more films from a greater variety of genres and periods are available today, and in an ever-increasing range of settings. And the in-flight movies on commercial airlines extend the range even further. But the developments in regular commercial circuits are miniscule compared with the effects that 16 mm film, television, and video games have had on the nature of film viewing today. As 16 mm projection equipment grows more portable and flexible, virtually any room or hall that can be darkened can become a movie theater. The rapid expansion of nontheatrical 16 mm film distribution throughout the sixties, coupled with the rise in film societies, particularly on college campuses, has made an even greater variety of film available in even more casual surroundings. And the

video cassette boom of the eighties is conditioning a new generation of film viewers.

Television has already made many films more widely available, including a good deal that were originally intended for theatrical distribution. With the explosion of film packaging by way of disk and cassette systems, access to films of all kinds today seems virtually limitless.

Conditioning

With films serving a variety of functions in an ever-increasing array of settings, the general population has grown increasingly familiar with the "film form" and has gained a definite "film sense," sometimes referred to as "cinema literacy." Audience training began when filmmakers started moving the camera. The close-up inspired some early anxiety about showing only half the actor, but viewers quickly understood and accepted it. Since then, viewers have come to understand a wide variety of cinematic techniques involving camera, editing, decor, sound, and combinations of these, particularly through exposure to television. Flash forwards, which propel the viewer into actions of future scenes, slow motion, and jump cuts, which jump directly from scene to scene without benefit of fade-outs, are accepted by viewers who have given little thought to the theory behind their use. In the same way, viewers have gradually accepted the de-emphasis of plot intricacies in favor of *mise-en-scène* and character analysis. Though still inter-

*I*f the principal point of an action movie has always been to afford the viewer the vicarious pleasure of being in the thick of it, then the experience that allows the viewer to enter the action and to control it, as a video game does, must be more satisfying than an experience that excludes the viewer, all other things being equal. It's true, unfortunately, that all other things often are equal these days, since most action films aren't especially strong on characters or plot.

— *Vincent Canby,* New York Times *(May 15, 1983)*

ested in story, most viewers are satisfied with less elaborate synopses and have, under the influence of television, learned to accept (if not prefer) more intimate and less decorative and action-packed styles.

We relate differently to motion pictures today than early viewers did because we have been conditioned to a wide range of cinematic techniques in the service of a broad range of functions. Many of today's features depend heavily on the immediate sensations derived from scenes of violence and sexual stimulation. Screen violence, which proved to be acceptable in such prestigious films as *Bonnie and Clyde* and *The Wild Bunch* in the sixties, continued unabated in the seventies with *The French Connection, Dirty Harry, Straw Dogs, A Clockwork Orange, Taxi Driver,* and Alfred Hitchcock's grisly but masterful *Frenzy.* The controversy over dramatic necessity versus gratuitousness in matters of sex and violence, which goes back to the earliest critical examination of the movies, is, as this book goes to press, no closer to resolution than it ever was. Sudden, turbulent, and often death-dealing action has been part and parcel of screen storytelling from the beginning, but in recent

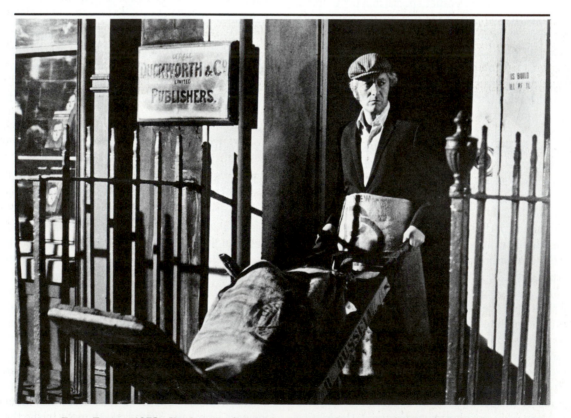

▲ From *Frenzy* (1972). Hitchcock used the bustle of contemporary London and its Covent Garden Market as the setting for murderous intrigue. This was a final return for the "master of supsense" to the scene of many of his earlier crimes, and in this film he carried on his tradition of placing the action in famous and busy locales.

years the depiction of it has become more graphic and more pervasive—in short, simply a cinematic way of life.

With the sweeping away of many sexual taboos in film in the past decade, other taboos are revealed, and the challenge of dealing candidly with them remains. Homosexuality and incest, probably the topics most sensitive to public exposure and surely the most forbidden in film history, are currently not only receiving frank treatment, but are being handled in morally ambiguous and/or morally neutral ways. As a result, these topics are being rendered unobjectionable if not downright appealing. For example, Louis Malle has managed to make the love-making between a fifteen-year-old boy and his mother in *Murmur of the Heart* (1971) seem natural and even poetic. Our surprise comes not from the activity portrayed, but, belatedly, from our own benign reaction to it.

Violence and sexual candor in films are today as much matters of the style and structure of the film as of the content. Often, films that do not even explicitly address these subjects are nevertheless pervaded by a mood of violence and eroticism. More than ever, any attempt to separate the subject matter of a film from its style is self-defeating. *Mise-en-scène,* used by film theorists to refer to what the Soviet filmmaker Pudovkin called the "total atmosphere of the film," is often a critical link. It has become an increasingly significant element in a great variety of film styles today, and not simply to tie together the scenery and the action, but to allow the action to flow as a natural extension of the film's total atmosphere. Bergman, Fellini, Godard, and more recently Altman, Scorsese, and Coppola, all show characters to be part of their environments. The compelling aesthetic reason behind *mise-en-scène* goes back as far as some of the Biograph one-reelers and was reinforced both by the "Kino Eye" concept of cinematography in the twenties and the postwar neorealist movement in Italy, both of which allowed the environment in which the action took place to be central to that action's meaning. Today, tehnological developments and economic pressures as well as aesthetic tenets have given new life to the concept of *mise-en-scène.* The demise of the back lots and the availability of more portable and flexible equipment have tended to put the camera where the action is, or is purported to be—and the action is part of the larger setting or the milieu.

Today's filmmakers refine the total atmosphere of the film to a much greater extent than merely recording or representing physical detail. Free-association styles, identified by jump cuts, slow motion, flash forward, and pop focus are all used today to provide the viewer with a new dimension in reality in which the presence of the camera is acknowledged. Today, in a new dimension in realism, the presence of the camera is acknowledged. In several notable examples—*8½* (1963), *Blow-Up* (1966), *Persona* (1966), *Medium Cool* (1969), *Day for Night* (1973), and *Videodrome* (1983)—the media have become at least a part of the message. But more important than film's ability (sometimes self-indulgent) to create a self-portrait of the medium is the tendency to use that ability to suggest mental reality or psychological truth. The experience may be one of terror, as in *Jaws* or *Poltergeist;* exhilaration, as in *Chariots of Fire;* or simply wonder, as in *Quest for Fire* or *E.T.* For better or worse, more films today provide immediate experience rather than a "by-the-numbers" exercise in plot construction.

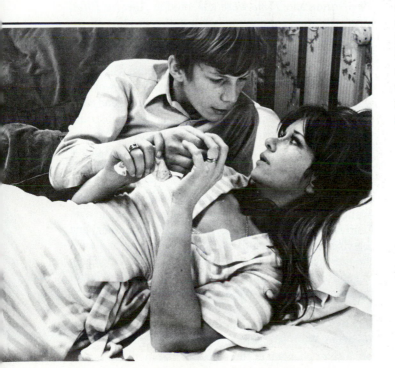

From *Murmur of the Heart* (1971), Louis Malle's gentle satire of family life and the growing up of privileged youth. Malle is one of several European directors who have successfully made the transition to the Hollywood scene. Some of his films are *Pretty Baby* (1978), *Atlantic City* (1980), and *My Dinner with André* (1981).

The promotion of *King Kong* (1976) and *Jaws 2* (1978), a remake and a sequel. The life of successful films is often extended through these two means. Though frequently pale imitations (as in *King Kong*) or merely extensions *(Jaws 2)* of famous originals, remakes and sequels profit from the use of familiar names and "stars" in press and television marketing. Billboard ads, like those shown here, though once a major marketing tool, are now used only for a few spectacle films. Where they are used, billboard ads are sometimes put up as much as a year before the release of the films they promote.

Film Study

The film experience extends beyond the viewing of movies. Among literate and culturally advantaged groups, film literature, which includes both serious critical work and promotional material, colors attitudes about the medium and specific films. Simply put, more and more is written and spoken about film—and more seriously—than ever before in history.

The explosion in film literature began in the mid-sixties while movie attendance was still on the decline. Though fewer people were going to the movies, more were interested in reading about them, partly because television had made available a storehouse of past films, and partly because the paperback revolution made books about movies and their directors cheaper to buy. The boom in film literature greatly expanded the scope and basic format of the writings. Reprints of the established works of historians and theorists have appeared in the past several years along with a wide assortment of both popular and esoteric works. Those focusing on a particular director are particularly popular in this age of *auteurism* and cultism. Such works include biographies and film analyses as well as interviews with and essays by the filmmakers themselves. Film scripts, though not yet

published in a format that accurately conveys what we see and hear on the screen, are in demand, and both "modern" and "classic" films are being brought to print. Also, new writings in history and theory are appearing with increasing frequency, both as discrete works and as selections, mixed with earlier essays, in anthologies. Most popular are the coffee-table tomes that use frame enlargements, production stills, and other photographic materials to provide embellishment and documentation.

Writings in film criticism reflect an increased seriousness toward cinema and are even keeping motion pictures before the nonmoviegoing public. Today both popular weekly and monthly magazines and the more literate journals regularly review and discuss films. And large-circulation magazines are providing serious film analysis rather than mere statistics and plot synopses.

This abundance of critical writing in periodical literature has in turn inspired a whole new kind of film book. In 1958 James Agee's reviews and comments written for *The Nation* and *Time* were collected in *Agee on Film*. Since that time, the compilation and reprinting of reviews and analytical essays by major critics and theorists have resulted in a legacy of literature on individual films and have given the reading public, even those who never see the movies, a new kind of exposure to the world of film. Fewer films, closer scrutiny by the critics, and elaborate advertising campaigns by producer and/or distributor combine to thrust a handful of pictures into the limelight. As a result, movies often become a part of our experience long before we get to the theater—if we get there at all.

These writings on film plus the increase in film events help to keep the medium before the public eye. Festivals, televised awards presentations, personal and televised appearances of stars and directors, and even the increased presence of "on location" film crews help to keep audiences aware not just of moviemaking, but of the existence and progress of individual films.

Conditioning today extends in a subtle but pervasive way beyond publicity, criticism, and the learning of film language. We relate differently to motion pictures today because of changes in the status of the medium.

More serious film fare and the more serious attitude taken toward it by critics and the public are in themselves indicative of the new respectability of movies. But added to them is a kind of institutionalizing that puts cinema today in a far different class from that it occupied in the days of the Rialto, the Bijou, and the Dream. Film's cultural standing has risen with community and educational groups, a development that has been reinforced in the past several years by a proliferation of film societies, academic offerings, and archival and research activities. The college film course has extended beyond such institutions as UCLA and New York University, which pioneered in film scholarship. Today there are more than 3,000 courses at some 600 colleges and universities across the country; adult education and high school offerings further increase the number. In addition to the formal curriculum is an ever increasing number of community and college film societies dedicated to the study of motion pictures. Nearly 2,000 such societies are affiliated with the American Federation of Film Societies, and the majority have been in existence for less than ten years.

Film research centers and archives represent a growing area of film activity today, and indicate film's new status as art and as subject of serious inquiry. The Museum of Modern Art in New York, La Cinémathèque Française in Paris, and the National Film Archive in London pioneered in the collection and preservation of film, film literature, and other related materials. The Museum of Modern Art is the home of a film library founded in 1935 by Iris Barry for the purpose of preserving a filmed record of the technical and aesthetic history of the art. The museum collection today contains more than 8,000 titles, many of which are part of a circulating program available to schools and film societies. The National Film Archive in London was also founded in 1935, and, like the museum in New York, it features viewing services as well as a book library, a still photograph collection, and a film-information service.

Today, there are other national archives and institutes plus several independent and regional centers. In the United States, these include the George Eastman House in Rochester, New York; the American Film Institute in Los Angeles and Washington; and Anthology Film Archives in New York.

The George Eastman House has been engaged, since 1949, in the collection and exhibition of films, photographs, and movie equipment and memorabilia. Under the direction of George Pratt, its curator, this archive today provides a special study collection and book library for film research.

Anthology Film Archives is unique in its attempt to present films in their original versions and to refine the film-viewing experience itself. Special projection facilities, auditorium design, and individual controls have been built into the ninety-seat theater to provide optimum viewing conditions. Seat hoods and blinders between seats eliminate distractions, and remote sound and focus controls provide for individual viewer needs. Projectors are also equipped to show films in their original screen ratios and running speeds.

The American Film Institute, established in 1967 under the National Foundation of the Arts and Humanities, is the newest national archive among the major film-producing countries. Since its foundation, it has continued its programs devoted to director training, film preservation, and what it calls its "scholarly and reference services." The preservation program has centered on a cooperative effort with the Library of Congress in transferring vintage films from decomposing nitrate to more stable acetate stock. Research and publication activities include a projected nineteen-volume catalog of American films.

Wrap-Up

In 1925, when David Wark Griffith was invited by *Collier's* magazine to predict what moviegoing would be like 100 years in the future, he proved to be remarkably prophetic. Although a national film institute was not a part of his vision, he did foresee "a great deal more of the so-called intimate drama presented on the screen." In addition, he envisioned "actors appearing in twice the size you see them now," "film so sensitive that it will record the natural tints and colors as the picture is being photographed," and "motion-picture shows on regular schedule between New York and Chicago and between New York and London." Griffith also predicted that stereoscopic films by the year 2024 "will long since have been discovered and adopted." What can hardly be minimized as a flaw in Griffith's gift of prophecy was his prediction regarding sound: "I am quite positive that when a century has passed, all thought of our so-called speaking pictures will have been abandoned."

Today, we find that in large part the Griffith prophecy has already been fulfilled. Despite his lapse regarding sound, he led the way in opening new frontiers in filmic representation, both by deed and inspired declaration. The fact that no new prophet is at hand to extend the vision may itself be significant. This fact perhaps mirrors the uncertainty that surrounds the direction the medium is taking, both as an industry and art, at a time when it is becoming a pervasive communicative and aesthetic form.

Documentary: Reality Redeemed Through the Art of the Film

Focus

The documentary film was brought to the screen by the Lumière brothers in 1895. Their premiere program included one-shot documents, simple *actualities* that recorded a world in motion. Workers leaving the Lumière factory, photographers disembarking from a boat to attend a conference at Lyon, and the arrival of a train are all documents of French life in 1895 that are preserved for us to see.

Still, it was the film medium's potential for storytelling that seized the attention and imagination of audiences and producers. In 1915, while D. W. Griffith was shooting the material for heart-pounding sequences in *The Birth of a Nation,* travelogues of the time were little more than well-shot home movies. While techniques were evolving to communicate narrative plots in brilliant and complex visual form, American newsreels were lurching through jumpcuts and missing action shots, utterly dependent on titles to tell the story.

In the Soviet Union in 1922, Vertov applied those narrative techniques to the newsreel in *Kino Pravda* editions. Throughout the twenties, others would join in developing a new film form — the documentary — which would redeem the nondescript educational, scenic, travelogue, and newsreel models. The documentary got film "back to its fundamentals," as Hans Richter said, "in the free use of nature, including man, as raw material." In the 1920s filmmakers learned to use all the film techniques to redeem reality. It was important, said documentary producer John Grierson, to see "the world under our noses."

Recording unstaged events in the real world was sometimes dangerous, however. Two French cameramen were on hand for the coronation of Nicholas II in 1896. They managed to survive the stampede of Russian peasants retrieving imperial gifts thrown in their general direction—only to have the police seize their film.

Dickson attached a camera to a microscope to film Edison's *Unseen World* series (1903), and microphotography was soon being used to produce medical instructional films. By 1906 news events, travelogues, and scientific and instructional films were clearly established. And by 1907 in Europe and 1909 in the United States, a newsreel style was evolving. Pathé Frères started producing regular newsreels in 1910.

All these events added up to the development of a specialized sector of the film industry. The movement was supported by people's interest in facts, events, and news from all corners of the world. In England, Charles Urban was experimenting with a color process, Kinemacolor, which was said to reproduce lifelike colors. Urban filmed the investiture of the Prince of Wales in 1911, and audiences throughout the world were thrilled by the pageantry.

As early as 1911, one British company was distributing educational shorts to schools, universities, teaching hospitals, and other institutions. "By educational films we do not particularly mean travel and such subjects," said an American tradesman, "but of a nature that brings science from its high pedestal right into the ranks of the layman." What was so special about the film medium? Moving pictures could "explain points difficult to render in the verbal," he said.

And so the Mothers Club of Alameda, California, presented their local school officials with projectors to show materials suitable for geography and history classes. By 1920 even American university presidents were speaking in praise of the new educational technology. In 1926 at least seventy-five U.S. companies were producing educational films.

Margaret MacDonald encouraged instructional film production in the trade magazine *Moving Picture World*. She had personally traveled to the Arctic to observe Eskimo culture, and upon her return she wrote, "All of this would prove very interesting and instructive placed before the public on the moving picture film, and would be productive of an interest in our brothers of the Far North who are so anxious to know and do the best that the white man has to teach him."

MacDonald's dismal ethnocentrism aside, Paul Rainey's *African Hunt* (1912), a feature-length (eight reel) film, was more in keeping with popular travelogues. *Wild Men of Africa* (1921) was typical of the genre. A Dr. Leonard Vandenbergh had "put the motion picture camera to one of its most productive uses by going into Africa with it and bringing back in film what his lens found there." And what did his lens find? "[We see] how the tribesmen of the dark continent live, what they look like, what their social and religious practices are, and the

---

The Medium of Choice

*T*he publicity bureau of the St. Paul Association of Commerce is formulating plans for a country-wide advertising of the advantages of St. Paul. The motion picture, of course, is to be the medium.

—Motion Picture News
(June 10, 1911)

---

nature of the country they inhabit." Those were the facts. But what did the information *mean?* In the words of a *New York Times* critic, the tribesmen of Darkest Africa "are not an attractive people. They have no physical charm, and their customs are revolting to anyone familiar with social refinements. They could hardly be called romantic, these crude, cruel, animalistic savages, whose chief recommendation to sympathy is their simplicity and helplessness."

Many religious groups had been skeptical and often hostile toward the movie business. But in little more than a decade after the first public motion picture showing, the Moody Bible Institute was using film to illustrate songs for outdoor evangelist meetings. Other groups were producing their own films for use in converting the ungodly. Even D. W. Griffith would later serve as a consultant to a religious film production company.

A demand was also growing for industrial promotional films. A Seattle Company filmed the Yakima Valley to promote agricultural sales in New York City. J. J. Hill of the Great Northern Railway had scenes shot from Ellis Island in the East to Portland in Oregon for showing "in those European countries where are to be found the most desirable settlers."

Robert Flaherty

*T*he experiments of an American, Robert Flaherty, yielded what would eventually be called the first documentary film. That film was *Nanook of the North* (1922), the first feature-length, nonfiction film of sufficient stat-

From *Nanook of the North* (1922). Of Flaherty's pioneering work, the critic Robert Sherwood said, with understated eloquence: "Here was drama rendered far more vital than any trumped-up drama could ever be by the fact that it was all real."

ure to give form to the ambiguous and haphazard nonfiction film industry. Flaherty did not simply set off for the Arctic with a visionary goal to make a film about Eskimos. He was born in northern Michigan and raised in northern Minnesota and in the forests of Ontario. At the age of ten he received a pair of genuine Indian moccasins, to him a gift of unparalleled treasure. Grade school and later academia proved no substitute for the wilderness for Flaherty, so to earn a living he turned to exploring and prospecting for the Hudson Bay Company. In 1913 his employer, Sir Alexander Mackenzie, urged upon him "one of these newfangled things called a motion picture camera" as Flaherty was preparing to set out on an Arctic prospecting venture. Flaherty stopped at Rochester for three weeks of instruction—this was to be his only formal film training—and then he was on his way. He had an affinity for adventure, but he also had another quality known to any woodsman or explorer—humility in the face of an unknown environment. As Calder-Marshall noted in his biography of Flaherty, "He knew that in their country, Eskimo knew best." Flaherty had a knack for building authentic perceptions, not so much from his own predispositions as from the perspective of people who knew the land.

That sensitivity to Eskimo knowledge enabled Flaherty to put on film images of Eskimos that were simultaneously specific and ambiguous. Rather than forcing his own preconceptions on the Eskimo experience, he seems to have gone north with the purpose of documenting the Eskimo way of life and the environmental demands that shaped the values and behaviors unique to the Eskimo people. And the motion picture camera that he received so casually was to become the prime motivation for his subsequent returns to the Arctic.

While surveying the Belcher Islands for the Hudson Bay Company, Flaherty filmed some 70,000 feet of Eskimo scenes. However, he lost the negative in a fire caused by his own cigarette, and was left with a duplicate he could not reproduce owing to the technological limits of the time. He showed the print to his friends, and was depressed to observe that they put up with the film only to see where *he* had been and what *he* had done rather than to observe Eskimo life. Said Flaherty, "That wasn't what I wanted to show them, not from the civilized point of view, but as they [the Eskimo] saw themselves, as 'we the people.' I realized then that I must go to work in an entirely different way."

As he and his wife discussed the problem, a new

approach evolved—follow one man and his family in order to compose a "biography" of an Eskimo. But where to get the financial backing? Europe was in the throes of carnage in the form of war, revolution, and epidemics. Hollywood studios had no interest in a project of his kind. Banks could see no promise of return. It was Revillon Frères, the rival of his former employers at the Hudson Bay Company, who made his project possible in return for the exposure the company would gain through the film's exhibition. The agreement was made in 1920. Thus an industrial sponsor had been found for a project promoted by an amateur—but an amateur with special knowledge about cameras suitable for Arctic temperatures and in possession of a new tripod with a gyro head to facilitate smooth pans and tilts. Flaherty took lighting, processing, printing, and projection equipment along.

When he arrived on location, he found that the people were no longer wearing traditional Eskimo clothing, so he ordered in the gear that had recently passed from use. Many events presented in the film were restaged from memory, his own and the Eskimo people's. Thus Flaherty's was not the method of direct cinema, but a studied, formal style that would allow the rest of the world to meet the people with whom he himself had developed a rapport. The film told the story of Nanook, a name soon to be known worldwide.

A year later Flaherty returned from the Arctic to edit the footage. That done, he faced a problem as acute today as it was then: to secure a distributor. Only the studios distributed films in those days. Paramount and First National were not interested. Pathé, however, interested the Roxy theater chain, and *Nanook of the North* opened in New York City, billed second to Harold Lloyd's *Grandma's Boy* (1922).

Pathé mounted an expensive and tasteful promotion campaign for *Nanook of the North*. The film was praised by the critics. Several short comedies set in the Arctic were soon manufactured to trade in on the topicality of Flaherty's film. Exhibitors were largely neutral, though they praised Arctic pictures, which helped, at least psychologically, to make the patrons in hot summer months feel cooler in the often hot and stuffy movie houses.

Nanook of the North was praised wherever it played. Its audiences everywhere came away with a sense of having been in touch with the truth of Nanook's experience. And yet nothing of a sensational nature appeared in the entire film, and that made it unique. Up to now, it was the sensational aspects that were diverting in nonfiction films. But from this film audiences learned how much they and Nanook's little family had in common. And the film has proved timeless—it reminds us even now that the basics of survival and human relationships are fundamental and universal.

A New Kind of Picture— *Nanook of the North*

*I*t isn't a story with a plot, but it's human. It's real life with real people—different, vital, vigorous and wonderful—all done on an actual background of glittering snow and ice. Its thrills are not machine made. Its appeal is not of the studio. Its scenes are so vivid and so informing that it possesses more real drama than most pictures made with drama as their aim.

—*Arthur James,*
Moving Picture World
(June 24, 1922)

Sometime after the film had swept the world, Mrs. Flaherty remarked on the irony of buying an ice cream bar wrapped in paper on which Nanook's smiling face appeared: Nanook himself had died of starvation while on the incessant hunt for food.

Never had a nonfiction film commanded such international acclaim. Now the studios were interested. Jesse M. Lasky commissioned Flaherty to "go off somewhere and make me another *Nanook.* Go where you will; do what you like. I'll foot the bill. The world's your oyster." In 1926 Paramount released *Moana,* advertised as "The love-life of a South Sea Siren." It was a box office flop. However, John Grierson, writing for the *New York Sun,* gave *Moana* a glowing review. He ascribed "documentary value" to the film, using the word *documentary* in the sense of *documentaire,* a French word denoting serious anthropological/expeditionary/academic films.

Flaherty tried a collaborative effort with F. W. Murnau, but the result, *Tabu* (1931), was a theatrical film showing little of Flaherty's vision. Flaherty ended up in Europe, where he met Joris Ivens and others. And in the Soviet Union he met Pudovkin and Eisenstein. They discussed some ideas for projects, but the effects of the Soviet political limitations were too much like the Hollywood constraints he was fleeing.

In England, Flaherty finally met former *New York Sun* film critic John Grierson, who was in charge of a governmental documentary production unit. The two collaborated on a project, *Industrial Britain* (1933), but the purposes, styles, and approaches of the two were so different that Flaherty went off on his own, this time to the harsh Aran Islands off the Irish coast. He crafted *Man of Aran* (1934) in a style similar to *Nanook of the North,* but added music and sound effects in postproduction. The film is still aired on occasion by Irish state television.

Flaherty's last work was *Louisiana Story* (1948). Standard Oil sponsored this work for little more than a quarter million dollars. The film is actually soft-sell public relations, as we meet a Cajun boy of the bayous whose backwoods Eden comfortably accommodates the drilling crews in search of oil. *Louisiana Story* is a lovely, lyrical film, but its corporate message is also disturbing if only because it is so subtle and understated.

John Grierson

In 1922 Walter Lippmann warned that the mass media were already creating a "pseudo-environment." At the University of Chicago he stated his concern that the modern citizen was sinking under the load of mediated information being generated by the increasingly complex problems characteristic of industrial society. How could democratic government function when citizens were unable to see a problem and all its important facets clearly? John Grierson would take the lead in showing how the documentary film could contribute to an informed citizenry.

Lippmann challenged his students to "follow the dramatic patterns of the film through the changing character of our time." In response, Grierson, who had come to the United States from Britain on a Rockefeller grant in 1924, dropped his studies in print journalism and went to Hollywood where he managed to gain access to Paramount's box-office records. He wanted to see if he could discern correlations between audience response (box of-

fice) and thematic trends as well as movie star personalities.

Upon returning to New York, Grierson joined Robert Flaherty in seeking an American release for Eisenstein's *Potemkin*. He said, "What I know of cinema I have learned partly from the Russians, partly from the American Westerns, and partly from Flaherty, of *Nanook*. The Westerns give you some notion of the energies. The Russians give you the energies and the intimacies both. And Flaherty is a poet."

Back in England, Grierson organized a film collective based on Soviet models but under the sponsorship of Britain's Empire Marketing Board (EMB). As economic depression gripped the globe, many of the world's leading filmmakers crossed paths on Grierson's doorstep. Dropping in from time to time were the likes of D. W. Griffith, Josef von Sternberg, Sergei Eisenstein, Vsevolod Pudovkin, and Robert Flaherty.

The poetic lyricism of *Nanook* and *Moana* is evident in *Drifters* (1929), the first film Grierson and his team made. But if there is a measure of Flaherty in this first venture, so is there also a measure of Eisenstein and Pudovkin. *Drifters* is a reflective, rhythmical document of herring fishermen as they go about the business of their sometimes dramatic and dangerous livelihood.

▶ Robert Flaherty and his editor, Helen Van Dongen, examine footage from *Louisiana Story* (1948). Van Dongen's task was especially formidable here, since Flaherty was well known for shooting thousands of feet of film to capture his often elusive perspective.

John Grierson (right) reviewing posters for the Canadian Film Board's series *Canada Carries On*. Grierson came to Canada in 1939 as the first commissioner of the Film Board and brought to the board his energy and commitment to the documentary ideal.

omy to cease film operations, and the Grierson group was taken in by another government agency, the General Post Office. Remarkable films were produced under this sponsorship: Edgar Anstey's *Granton Trawler* (1934), Evelyn Spice's *Weather Forecast* (1934), Paul Rotha's *The Face of Britain* (1934–1935), Basil Wright's fascinating *Song of Ceylon* (1935), Alberto Cavalcanti's *Coal Face* (1935), Anstey's *Enough to Eat* (1936), and Harry Watt's *North Sea* (1938).

From a political base rather than the poetic romanticism epitomized by Flaherty's work, the Grierson group worked for two kinds of social change. One objective was to elevate and celebrate in film art the dignity and grace of the worker. The other was to influence the formation of public policy, an objective that seems to have become more important as the Depression held the world in its grip. Two examples illustrate these real-world political objectives, so different from the Flaherty goal — *Night Mail* (1936) and *Housing Problems* (1935).

Basil Wright and Harry Watt worked together on *Night Mail,* a celebration of mechanical processes and the working men and women who made it all work. We watch as a mail train is prepared for its night run to Glasgow in Scotland. We become part of the process as mail sacks are grabbed by mechanical devices, the contents sorted by genial postal workers, and other sacks of mail sprung from the charging train — so punctually that villagers can set their watches by the train's passing and read their mail with morning tea.

The editing technique is lifted directly from a Vertov newsreel. But *Night Mail* is not silent. Location sound from locomotives, steam, and steel as well as gentle words exchanged by workers, who take pride in their work, punctuate the exciting visual line of development. For the epilogue, a young poet, W. H. Auden, provided alliterative poetic narrative and Benjamin Britten composed the musical score.

Edgar Anstey and Arthur Elton completed *Housing Problems* in 1935. Its purpose was not to honor the

As Grierson organized his unusual group of students, educators, journalists, and sociologists, he taught them filmmaking by showing and discussing James Cruzes' epic Western *The Covered Wagon* (1923), and Eisenstein's *Potemkin* (1925). He chose the former as a model because the American Western managed to convey an astounding sense of realism. After all, many of the players in the film (like the wagons) had actually gone West in wagon trains, or were first-generation descendants of California immigrants. And he chose *Potemkin* because Eisenstein's theory was rich in productive applications, and therefore highly valuable, as Grierson said, in "the observation of the ordinary or the actual," which could aid in "civic education." It is fitting, therefore, that *Drifters* was released to British theaters in the company of *Potemkin,* which had finally been wrested from the clutches of a conservative film censor.

Thereafter, Grierson became a producer, supervising disparate projects and a number of filmmakers. In 1933, the EMB was forced by the faltering global econ-

The World Under Our Noses

*T*he main thing to remember is not that all the films were gems. They were, many of them, amateur and second-rate, but they were revolutionary because they were putting on the screen for the first time in British films and very nearly in world films . . . a working man's face and working man's hands and the way the worker lived and worked. It's very hard with television nowadays and everything to realize how revolutionary this was. . . . We were on the razor's edge. We were always financed by the Establishment and the Establishment basically regretted that they'd started this thing.

—*Harry Watt, in* The Rise and Fall of British Documentary, *by Elizabeth Sussex*

A Radical Notion

I was very interested in this question of putting the working class on the screen, bringing the working class thing alive in another form than we were getting on the [political] soapboxes of Glasgow Green. That wasn't good enough for me, the soapbox. You see, I worked in a factory down the Clyde and I didn't think we could live off platforms, platform relationships. . . . But then, of course, Flaherty was a turning point—*Nanook* hit Glasgow round about 1922, I think. I was on to it by 1924, that film could be turned into an instrument of the working class.

—*John Grierson, quoted in* The Rise and Fall of British Documentary, *by Elizabeth Sussex*

worker, but to expose the problem of slum housing, provide incontrovertible evidence, and suggest a workable solution so that living conditions for the working class could be improved. Its style presages the television documentary—that is, on the rare occasion when it is allowed a point of view in the United States. The appeal is not to emotion, as in the cinematic *Night Mail,* but rather to logic and action via the public conscience. A narrator provides factual data while the visuals stand as proof. Testimony is provided by rather self-conscious residents speaking to the camera in rather awkward actualities. But no music is used, apparently in the belief that music would make the film seem unduly manipulative. Rather, the problem is presented methodically, compelling evidence is offered, and the solution—urban green belts and new towns—is shown to be feasible.

Said Grierson, "We were, I confess, sociologists, a little worried about the way the world was going. . . . There were no large films, and none pretentious, but there were hundreds of them a year, short and simple, humble and honest, progressively covering the whole wide field of practical civic interest."

The documentary became a new channel for communicating persuasive messages, and occasionally brilliant examples of film art emerged from their ranks. In France, Jean Vigo's *A pròpos de Nice* (1930) juxtaposed shots of the wealthy with shots of the poor, even rendering naked the expensively dressed promenading dowager. Vigo said he was presenting "the last twitchings of a society that neglects its own responsibilities to the point of giving you nausea and making you an accomplice in a revolutionary solution." Joris Ivens's *Borinage* (1933), which concentrated on a Belgian slum, marked the radicalization of the Dutch filmmaker whose *Rain* (1929) had so exquisitely traced the patterns, textures, and light of a rainy day in Amsterdam. *New Earth* (1934) railed against the human costs imposed by a government project to reclaim land from the sea, and *The Spanish Earth* (1937) made the case for the Spanish people and against the Facist struggle for power under Franco.

Thesis/Antithesis

[*M*y] film is only a documentary. I showed what everyone was witness to or had heard about. And everyone was impressed by it. I am the one who registered it on film. And that is doubtless why people are angry with me: for having seized it, put it in a box. . . . What did I do that was political? I was not a Party member . . . I should have been able to foresee that one day things would change? At that time, one believed in something beautiful. In construction. In peace. . . . It is history. A pure historical film. . . . It reflects the truth that was then, in 1934, history. It is therefore a documentary. Not a propaganda film. . . . I found myself, me, at the heart of an event which was the reality of a certain time and a certain place. . . . I had sought to make a striking and moving film. A poetic and dynamic film.

—*Leni Riefenstahl, in* Cahiers du Cinema *(1966)*

*I*n this monstrous, primeval rite, the mass—anonymous and hypnotized—never acts, but only responds to the Fuehrer's initiatives, delivered in an authoritarian, hysterical, obsessive fashion. The film's caressing, sensual pans of Hitler's face are world famous. Everything is designed for seduction (Hitler's term for propaganda): the sensory overload of high-pitched oratory, the massed bands and banners, the dynamism of goosestep and drums, the incantatory rhythms of montage, sound and visuals.

Precisely because of its powerful appeal to such factors and its perfect orchestration of filmic and psychological components, "Triumph of the Will" must be classified as a profoundly subversive work and its creator as Nazism's most effective propagandist . . . only a fanatic Nazi could have created such a work.

—*Amos Vogel, "Can We Now Forget the Evil That She Did?"* New York Times *(May 13, 1973)*

Leni Riefenstahl

Leni Riefenstahl brought epic scale to the documentary genre. She marshalled all the possibilities of film craft to introduce Nazi party leaders to the German people. *Triumph of the Will* (1935) was "only" a documentary, said Riefenstahl. Actually it is a hypnotic rendering of the Nazi Party rally organized at Nuremberg in 1934, one of the most impressive pseudo events ever staged for the cameras. No one can dispute the impact of the startling compositions and editing, the grand design imposed over

the event, and the structure of certain sequences—if not the entire feature-length opus.

Riefenstahl was furious, because after the war she was placed in an internment camp. What had she done except to make "a pure historical film" that turned out to be "poetic and dynamic" because of her artistic sensibilities and vision? She had used her talent to advance an unparalleled evil, the evil of the Holocaust. It became clear that some of the camps were designed as streamlined factories intended to incinerate the bodies of individuals and entire races—by the millions.

Even during the war years, Riefenstahl's images were used by anti-Nazi filmmakers. In the decades after-

Lorentz on *The Plow That Broke the Plains*

*T*hus, with some outstanding photography and music, *The Plow That Broke the Plains* is an unusual motion picture which might have been a really great one had the story and construction been up to the rest of the workmanship. As it is, it tells the story of the Plains and it tells it with some emotional value—an emotion that springs out of the soil itself. Our heroine is the grass, our villain the sun and the wind, our players the actual farmers living in the Plains country. It is a melodrama that only Carl Sandburg or Willa Cather perhaps could tell as it should be told.

—*Pare Lorentz*, McCall's *(July 1936)*

ward, many searched them in hopes of finding a clue, an as yet unnoticed revelation about the nature of the evil its symbols have come to represent. Riefenstahl's images are still powerful and frightening.

Perhaps it was true that Riefenstahl was not a Nazi Party member. In her next film, *Olympia* (1937), Hitler is incidental to the Olympic events her cameras record. And despite Hitler's refusal to acknowledge the black American gold medalist, Jesse Owens, she included the hero in her *Olympia,* though the footage was not always retained in released prints.

If Riefenstahl thought of her Nuremberg film as "poetic and dynamic," others used those words without hesitation to describe *Olympia.* Rather than recording "the thrill of victory/the agony of defeat," she saw a ballet in the Olympic games. Today, live television could record a diver's descent in perhaps three shots. But she used multiple shots and numerous camera positions, several divers, slow motion, a musical score, and a lyrical editing style to celebrate the glory, the poetry, and divine grace and sheer beauty of the human form as it leaps, leaps and arches, falls, leaps again and again, and is eventually permitted to complete, complete, and again complete the dive.

Pare Lorentz

As Riefenstahl was working on her two great films in the 1930s, and as Grierson's energy was propelling documentaries throughout the British Commonwealth, an American, Pare Lorentz, managed to convince the Franklin Delano Roosevelt administration to enlist the power of the documentary to help win acceptance for government programs.

Film production under government auspices has always been controversial in the United States. In 1908, for example, a film unit was established by the Department of Agriculture, and kept as a secret from Secretary James Wilson. He believed that motion pictures were "the work of the devil, a disreputable medium of expression." (It had been Agriculture photographers who filmed the Wright brothers' historic flight in 1903.)

Pare Lorentz made *The Plow That Broke the Plains* in 1936 for the Farm Security Administration, but by then the Departments of Agriculture, Interior, Labor, War, and Commerce and other agencies already had an established tradition in film production. Still, the government films that had been produced were meant to inform and instruct. Lorentz, however, wanted his countrymen to open their eyes and ears, stir a common will, and get on with planning and implementing New Deal programs.

Lorentz shared Grierson's concern for the way the world was going. A serious music and film critic, he came to filmmaking like Flaherty and Grierson, as an amateur. He had been impressed with the editing of Soviet feature films, and he had been greatly pleased by the ways in which René Clair had used sound in *Le Million* (1931) and Fritz Lang had used it in *M* (1931). These filmmakers had known that just because a face was on the screen with its mouth moving, the sound coming from that mouth did not have to be placed synchronously on the sound track. One could juxtapose one element (visual) against an entirely different element (sound). Meaning could occur in the mind of the beholder, much as it did in response to Eisenstein's montage of differing and apparently unconnected visual elements. Sound—asynchronous, contrapuntal sound—did not necessarily threaten the rich visual heritage of the silent film period, a fact that Grierson's organization had demonstrated effectively. For *The Plow That Broke the Plains,* Lorentz hired Ralph Steiner, Paul Strand, and Leo Hurwitz, all of whom were accomplished still and motion photographers and, equally important, socially committed individuals who, like those in Grierson's collective, wanted to put their art in the service of social change.

Friction developed among the four individual creative talents, however, and Lorentz fired his crew before he had all the footage he needed for the film. He went to Hollywood, hoping to buy stock footage from studio and archive sources. But in 1930 he had co-authored a book that was highly critical of the industry's censorship policies, and Hollywood now tried to prevent access to the material he needed.

Lorentz learned how to edit for himself, cutting first for purely visual sequence, then working with the composer Virgil Thomson to reflect the attitude and intended meaning in the score, and then re-editing to achieve the greatest possible organic impact from the two elements. Finally, he went through again to refine the narrative thread.

Having been so closely involved in all phases of its production, Lorentz took his first film to friends whose judgment he trusted. In Hollywood he showed *The Plow That Broke the Plains* to King Vidor. Rouben Mamoulian and Lewis Milestone joined Vidor in assuring Lorentz that he had made an unusually fine film. A private screening was arranged for President Roosevelt, but Lorentz did not want his work to become a football during an election year. *The Plow That Broke the Plains* opened to the public in the company of British, Soviet, French, and German films at the Museum of Modern Art in New York.

But what good is such a film if only a few art patrons see it? The perennial problem of distribution faced the new filmmaker. Studio chiefs feared competition with New Deal schemes, and opposed Roosevelt's re-election; some studios even threatened to fire employees who voted for Roosevelt. No industrial distributor would

▲ Paul Lorentz's *The River* (1937) represents documentary film at its best and most compelling. The often stunning combination of music, monologue, and visual elements communicated a powerful message with what can only be described as poetic force.

*W*e built a hundred cities and a
     thousand towns.
But at what a cost!
We cut the top off the Alleghenies
     and sent it down the river.
We cut the top off Minnesota
     and sent it down the river. . .
We left the mountains and the hills flat
     and burned
     and moved on.
                    —*from* The River

Lorentz on *The River*

*L*et me see if I've got
this straight. This is a government boat
and I'm making pictures for the government—the one that owns this boat and
that you're working for and I'm working
for. The same government that has to
have thousands of feet of motion pictures
of this flood for the Army Engineering
Corps and the Department of Agriculture.
If they don't get these pictures from me,
they're going to have to buy them from
commercial newsreel men, and meanwhile
I am being paid to take them and I can't
get on a government boat to do it without
permission from Paramount.

> —*Pare Lorentz, to a Para-
> mount official supervising
> the shoot at Cairo, Illinois,
> quoted in* Pare Lorentz and
> the Documentary Film, *by
> Robert L. Snyder*

touch Lorentz's film. So Lorentz hand carried his film
from city to city as King Vidor had done with *Hallelujah!*
(1929)—arranging for showings to the local press and
urging reporters and critics to let readers know that
"this picture cannot be shown in your town." The occasional theaters who booked the film employed the old
advertising cliché, "The picture they dared us to show!"
Throughout, Congress debated, the studios complained,
the Hays Office threatened, and various courts ruled.

Though the number of problems he had to cope with
would have discouraged most people, Lorentz could not
shake his new film idea on another environmental problem. He wanted to document the human misery caused
by poor land management and consequent flooding
within the Mississippi River system. In 1937 this eco-
system embraced more than half of the total United
States population. *The River* (1937) was his second
project.

This time he defined his topic precisely and developed a careful plan. He did exhaustive research and chose
locales before filming began. For *The River* Lorentz
knew just what he was making: a study of the ecological
relationship among the land, the river system, and the
people. Shooting proceeded with dispatch and economy,
but just as filming had been completed news arrived of an
Ohio River flood of major proportions. The crew shot the
flood, and this unplanned footage gave direct and raw
substance to the studied compositions and cutting of
Lorentz's artistic argument. The actuality material was
the most difficult to get, however, and Lorentz obtained
it only by persevering with extraordinary determination.

Today these films made by Lorentz may seem too
heavy, the music too obvious in its parallels or contrasts
with visual components, and the narration, peppered
with alliteration, too pretentious. But they make it clear
that the ecology film did not originate in the 1960s—
even though their pride in large smoke-billowing factories appears out of character in the post-industrial era of
Love Canals and nuclear and toxic wastes.

Ingmar Bergman said that "film is mainly rhythm; it
is inhalation and exhalation in continuous sequence."
Lorentz had that knowledge too. *The River's* visual,
musical, and verbal elements earned it the Best Documentary award at the 1938 Venice Film Festival, where
Riefenstahl's *Olympia* was one of the competitors. The
integration of sight and sound elements in *The River*
was compared to Walt Disney's craft with animation.
Ironically, though *The River* was nominated for an Academy Award, Disney objected because there was no documentary category at that time, and because he
considered it unfair to let the government compete with
industry. Yet Disney encouraged the exhibition of *The
River* along with his first full-length animation, *Snow
White and the Seven Dwarfs* (1938).

It Was Done Simultaneously

*V*irgil [Thomson] made piano sketches of each section of the movie, each large sequence, and then the crew and I tried to edit it down to a preconceived time, at which point Virgil would get some ideas, genius ideas, and we would work back and forth so that you didn't have a completed score out on top of a completed movie or vice versa. The words were then written to the music and to a concept of music.

—*Pare Lorentz, quoted in* Pare Lorentz and the Documentary Film, *by Robert L. Snyder*

The River marked a turning point in the American documentary. The United States Film Service was established. Distributors found a mass audience for such films (*The River* was so popular that it often outlasted the main entertainment feature with which it had been paired). The Academy Awards were broadened to include the documentary genre, and *The River* was the first documentary to be shown on television, by the BBC. Overall, the film's success at Venice helped to create a more favorable environment for documentary production. Perhaps less desirable, however, was the fact that film became a recognized tool for political persuasion.

It is interesting to note in passing that *Night Mail* and *The Plow That Broke the Plains* were made in the same year, 1936. These two films, one British and the other American, share a similar style. Both are highly rhetorical, and their composition and editing were greatly influenced by theories of montage. Both use location sound reinforced with postproduction effects. Composers Benjamin Britten and Virgil Thomson both wrote their respective scores with the filmmakers as the latter shaped the visual and verbal elements. And in both, a formal narrator spoke unashamedly poetic verse. Despite the theoretical and high-culture influences, the purpose and argument are always immediately apparent in both films. In this they contrast with the work of Vertov and even Eisenstein, who were barred from filmmaking because of their "barren intellectualism."

Film in the Streets

Both the Grierson and Lorentz schools were Establishment-oriented, as Harry Watt admitted. But in a period of terrifying unemployment, bloody labor strikes, civil disobedience, and national hunger marches, one might have expected the documentary to become a weapon for revolutionary social change, and it did.

The Workers Film and Photo League was formed by unemployed workers and intellectuals whose goals were more radical than the policies of the New Deal. In the 1930s the league managed to produce its own newsreels and documentaries, often re-editing existing footage into the new material. The league used the films to inform, recruit, and rally support for alternatives to a system run by politicians and big business — a system members considered moribund. *People of the Cumberland* (1938), *Heart of Spain* (1937), and *Native Land* (1942) are examples of deeply affecting filmmaking produced by a new coalition of leftists known as The Frontier Film Group. Narrated by Paul Robeson, *Native Land* was a major project, begun in the despair of the Depression but not released until 1942. By then, the battles were in Europe and Asia, not at the Republic Steel plant where strikers were killed, or where corporate spies infiltrated a union to steal membership lists.

Originally planned as a Frontier project, *The City* (1939) was directed by Willard Van Dyke and sponsored by the American Institute of Planners with a grant from the Carnegie Foundation. Ralph Steiner helped Van Dyke shoot, and Aaron Copland composed the score. Except for the last part, which presents the planners' solution, *The City* remains a remarkable piece of filmmaking. It was made in the Grierson/Lorentz style, which works to great effect when the subject is a process. Thus it is the *process* of the night mail train, the *process* of land erosion or of river flooding, the *process* by which cities become unacceptable places for human habitation that is rendered so effectively by this kind of stylish filmmaking. When the subject is a specific strike, a specific lynching, or a specific case of miscarried justice in the life of an individual person, then cinematic craft can get in the way. Flaherty's style in *Nanook,* after all, was free from the inventive bedazzlements of montage and an integrated symphonic score. Like some of the Workers League films, *Nanook* still manages to compel our attention and affect our hearts.

The Compilation Documentary

In 1896 it was exciting just to see a moving image, just one fifty-foot long shot of any scene from life. By 1910 Pathé was producing theatrical circuit newsreels. And by 1912 Frederick Talbot had described how all the accumulating news shots were spliced together to "form a continuous miscellaneous moving mirror of the world's happenings."

The trouble with the newsreels was that, as Grierson had complained, they were "just a speedy snip-snap of some utterly unimportant ceremonies." But Vertov and Esther Shub in the Soviet Union made another kind of film—"compilation" documentary, compiled from existing shots taken for one purpose and through editing made to serve another purpose (so went Jay Leyda's definition of the genre of his book, *Films Beget Films*). Schub made her first major work, *The Fall of the Romanov Dynasty* (1927), from footage found in personal collections, bought from foreign newsreel companies, and even taken from Romanov home movies that had been buried for safekeeping. The compilation documentary was well established by the 1930s.

The newsreel, complained compilation filmmaker Louis de Rochemont, never got behind the news. "What has led to a given event? What does it portend? . . . Some day I'm going to revolutionize the newsreel." Although de Rochemont did not revolutionize the newsreel, beginning in 1935 he produced *The March of Time,* a compilation documentary series, for Henry Luce and the Time-Life Company. The series was to the film medium what *Time* magazine was to print: an attempt to provide an analysis of current events and to suggest causes leading to complex problems in need of solution.

De Rochemont felt free to include re-enactments of events that had not been filmed, thus mixing truth and fiction. Nevertheless, in contrast with the newsreels, the *March of Time* series covered issues in depth contrasted with the newsreels. A good number of political figures were incensed by various episodes in the series, but as long as the Time-Life foray into controversy did not impinge on profits, de Rochemont continued with his work. The series was to influence film and television magazine styles.

The point of view assumed in the series was often equivocal, a fact noted by one critic who said, "I wish that these editors of *March of Time,* since they have at their disposal these fictions which excite and enrage people, would use them for some purpose—I wish they would say—outright beyond question—that somebody was right or wrong." For example, *Land of Cotton* (1936) tries to report on the plight of Southern sharecroppers who are losing what little they own. Landowners and foreclosing bankers are named as the causes. Audiences see actual footage of grass-roots organizing and speech making. A re-enactment of a sensational kidnapping and some beatings makes one think filmmakers from the Workers Film and Photo League had infiltrated Time-Life. By the end, however, the landowners, the bankers, and the Time-Life narrator all blame the Depression for the sharecroppers' problems. Guilt is displaced. At the end it is nobody's fault. But, then, one ought not expect editorializing from a corporate entity that might imply the need for radical social change.

World War II

As the nations of the world raised their armies, so did they raise their national film units. Gearing up for war made it necessary to stir up the hot blood of nationalism. Hitler was, after all, pressing Europe to the wall. Survival was at stake on battlefields and shipping lanes, just as it was in the battle for hearts and minds, for national unity and the will to persevere. In this battle for survival, film was the medium of choice.

Grierson and Lorentz had given the mainstream documentary a point of view, turning the film form into a medium for shaping public opinion and policy. Everything that had been learned in the past ten years would now serve the urgent struggle against the Axis powers of Germany, Italy, and Japan. This time there were social scientists on hand to measure the effectiveness of the propaganda designers. One general reportedly said that victory would probably go to the side with the greatest supplies of film stock, camera gear, and filmmakers.

Britain had been at war for more than two years by the time the United States was provoked into declaring war. Not only had British and Canadian soldiers been dying in Europe, but the German Luftwaffe had been pounding British cities in massive air raids that took a terrible toll. Grierson had moved on to Canada, where he organized the National Film Board. But he left behind capable filmmakers to carry on in his stead.

The Scenario of *Listen to Britain*

*F*ade up on trees, wind blowing. Grain fields. Sound of Spitfires; planes pass overhead. Family harvesting potatoes in garden; pause, look up. Two soldiers in helmets look up. Four planes pass. Tractor moves into frame. Harvest time. Soldiers man anti-aircraft position dug into the field.

As a large crowd dances, we hear "Roll Out the Barrel." Back to anti-aircraft crew. CUT to miners. CUT to train; stops; inside Canadian soldiers sing "Home On the Range." Train pulls out. CUT to airplane assembly plant. Completed aircraft flies off into the night. CUT to sign, "Ambulance Station 76," as woman plays piano and sings "The Ash Grove." Women ambulance personnel listen, waiting for the alarm. CUT to Big Ben and BBC World Service as morning light signals a new day. Workers arrive at factory. CUT. Piano playing children's ditty as children dance in a game; mother watches from window. Turns to look at something in the room: picture of man in uniform. She turns back to children as mechanized unit rolls through the old village. CUT to industrial sequence. Then to women in factory singing to music from public address loudspeakers in factory — "Yes, My Darling Daughter." Machine gears move in time with the popular song. CUT to railroad station, filled with groups of military waiting for departures. CUE Flannigan & Allen, music hall singers, then CUT to factory where they sing for lunchtime entertainment. FADE to Mozart piano concerto at National Gallery. A variety of Londoners, including veterans in bandages, and the Queen Mother. Music continues as CUT to outside, streets. Long shot of Trafalgar Square, statue of Lord Nelson visible. CUT to shot of Lord Nelson. CUT back to industrial material as Mozart is lost to clamor. Tanks being assembled.

CUT to marching band, casually moving through a village leading troops dressed for battle. March music CUT as molten steel is poured. Sneak in "Rule Britannia" over industrial montage. Smoke stacks. Wheatfields. And as "Britannia" comes to end, so does the film from among the clouds, looking down over the British Isles. End.

Harry Watt and Humphrey Jennings encouraged British resolve on the homefront and sympathy in America with *London Can Take It* (1940). Stuart Legg, with *Churchill's Island* (1941–1942), brought the same messages to the screen. Harry Watt's *Target for Tonight* (1941) was immensely popular and satisfying, because it took the viewer with the Royal Air Force on a bombing raid over enemy territory, the German heartland. Thereafter, production was increased, until by 1945 the Crown Film Unit had become a large production center.

Humphrey Jennings left perhaps the most interesting personal film legacy of the war years. *Heart of Britain* (1941), *Listen to Britain* (1942), *Fires Were Started* (1943), *Lili Marlene* (1944), and *A Diary for Timothy* (1945) are some of his works.

Jennings's *Listen to Britain* is similar in style to *Triumph of the Will.* It was constructed from visual and location sound materials that communicate effectively without that bane of the form, the narrator. This is an eighteen-minute piece of exquisite cinematic poetry that carefully attends as the camera records activities taking place throughout the British Isles in a twenty-four-hour period. We see a farmer, a foundry worker, a coal miner, and the Queen Mother. All social classes are shown, linked together through musical themes—from "Roll Out the Barrel" in a large dance hall to a Mozart piano concerto at London's National Gallery.

Though *Listen to Britain* is similar to *Triumph of the Will* in style, the social values and nonverbal messages of the two films contrast sharply. The British military units almost saunter through a village, while the jack-booted goose-stepping Nazis seem dwarfed by their swastikas. The British film celebrates individual differences, whereas Riefenstahl's film supports the idea of "one folk, one leader," with the two interchangeable.

In the United States, RKO-Pathé's *The Last Stronghold* (1940) and Paramount's *The World In Flames* (1940) and *The Ramparts We Watch* (1940) were compilations intended to win American support for the reeling European Allies. A few months after the attack on Pearl Harbor, studio energy and talent were tapped for some unusual documentary productions.

Frank Capra was made a colonel, and under his direction and supervision, a series of seven films were produced known as the "Why We Fight" series. Since the United States was until so recently a confirmed isolationist, it was deemed necessary not only to train the volunteers and draftees physically for war, but also to make sure the troops understood why such national sacrifices had to be made. The series was intended to motivate the men to serve as soldiers.

Prelude to War (1942) explained why America could not remain neutral—indeed, why neutrality had been a mistake. Characteristically compilation films provide a field day for narrators, and this was certainly true for "Why We Fight." Moses, Confucius, Jesus, Lafayette, and Lincoln were all aligned against enemy mobs mindlessly screaming *"Sieg Heil"* in Germany, *"Duce"* in Italy, and *"Banzai"* in Japan. *The Nazis Strike* (1943), *Divide and Conquer* (1943), *The Battle of Britain* (1943), *The Battle of China* (1944), *The Battle of Russia* (1944), and *War Comes to America* (1945) followed.

For their purpose and time, the scripts in this series were quite strong. Editing and special effects (animation by the Disney Studios) were often brilliant. In the last of the series, a shot tilting up a virgin pine tree dissolves to a tilt up the front of a New England church. Occasionally a sequence stands alone, but for the most part the archival material illustrates the message spoken by the narrator. In *War Comes to America,* Humphrey Bogart recites a litany of sentimental American traits, traits that in large measure were clichés that had been established by Hollywood itself.

Psychologists analyzed the films for their effectiveness. They found that the films significantly increased viewers' knowledge about why America had to fight. However, "the films had no effect on items prepared for the purpose of measuring effects on the men's motivation to serve as soldiers, which was considered the ultimate objective of the orientation program," concluded the experts.

Like Capra, John Ford turned from fiction to documentary (*The Battle of Midway* [1944]) as did William Wyler (*Memphis Belle* [1944]). John Huston's *The Battle of San Pietro* (1944) used charts, actual footage, and staged material to explain the battle in Italy at San Pietro. Huston scandalized military officials, who were appalled by the shots showing American bodies being placed in body bags. That certainly was no way to win a war, they said. (What a contrast to television's coverage of the war in Vietnam!)

In the years following 1945, the purpose of documentary film shifted from inciting national purpose and motivating a will to victory toward probing the meaning of recent events. Compilations from Poland, Yugoslavia, the Soviet Union, England, Sweden, the German Democratic Republic, and the United States searched for answers in the images from archival storage: What manner of man was he? What was the nature of the Nazi evil? How does one use the knowledge that the power of the modern state can organize and begin to eliminate entire races of people? And what portent for the future was contained in the mushroom clouds over Hiroshima and Nagasaki?

At the Nuremberg trials, film of the horrors committed was included as graphic evidence against the Nazis charged with crimes against humanity. In *Nuremberg* (1945), Pare Lorentz and the Signal Corps Pictorial Center condensed the trials, including archival material (much of it shot, cataloged, and stored by the Nazis, including damning material taken by the Gestapo for their own records). Intended for use in the re-education of the German people, *Nuremberg* shows the former heros in *Triumph of the Will* as prisoners, and further shows indictments against them being read. As prosecutors make their cases, the horrible footage is presented. No rhetorical tricks are played. Rather, the film makes a coldly logical presentation with no editing, sound, or narrative to manipulate the viewer. *Nuremberg* was shown throughout the American- and British-occupied sectors of Germany until 1950, when it was withdrawn at the request of West German officials.

As *Nuremberg* cut between the courtroom of the present to the past, so *Night and Fog* (1955), by the French filmmaker Alain Resnais, cut between the present in color and the past in black and white. Color film records his camera's slow movement through the ruins of war. Weeds grow along the rusting track that carried the freight of human cargo. Barracks are empty. Empty too are the rooms where people were gassed, as are the crematorium, hospital, and even the prison within the prison. Empty guard houses still stand along the rusting fences of barbed wire ten years after the end of the war. That same archival footage of the horrors appears again here, along with the now familiar images from *Triumph of the Will.* Resnais has silenced the martial music, and plays the images off a flute and percussion, synchronizing the marching images to dissonant sounds, not a military beat. The effect is unforgettable. The viewer staggers under the film's questions: "Who is on the lookout from this strange tower to warn us of the coming of new executioners? Are their faces really different from our own?"

As for Japan, the documentary lens turned away. Japanese Americans were released from their American detention camps, and in time the American people stopped using the word *Jap.* Racism and the atomic bomb were at least two reasons for avoiding Japanese questions in compilation reviews. A third reason was the Pentagon. For security reasons, Japanese footage of the bombs' aftermath was withheld along with Allied footage shot after the Japanese surrender. Had that material been made public, funding for further nuclear research might have been jeopardized. *Hiroshima-Nagasaki, August 1945,* released in 1970, was the first documentary to probe the images of ruins and bodies, burned and sick unto death from radiation. The film had a fortuitous origin. An English-language newspaper from Japan had carried a small notice to the effect that the U.S. government was returning Japanese footage taken prior to surrender. Eric Barnouw at Columbia University secured a duplicate of the material and began to organize it. Two music students assigned to work-study in the film department composed the plaintive music. Columbia was deluged with purchase orders.

In 1948 a short documentary from Sweden known in this country as *Symphony of a City* (*People of the City,* 1947) was awarded an Oscar. In this film, Arne Sucksdorff compressed a day in the life of the city. He composed it of charming episodes of his own children adventuring through the streets and entering an austere church in which they seem strangers. An image appears of the statue of an angel blowing a trumpet, which cues a trumpet fanfare, and then the film cuts to a parade of the Royal Guard outside the palace. The children continue their adventures. The day is coming to an end when the older boy pauses to push the fallen bow within range of the blind violinist (who then finds it on his own). As the boy and old man walk down the street, a solo violin provides the outré music. Composition, light, textures,

visual details, reflections, structures, the location sound (there is no dialogue) — all the elements of film are carefully and beautifully selected and blended into a wonderful and perfect whole.

Gulls! (1944) is a study of bird species' fight for survival on an over-populated island in the Baltic Sea. The film is careful not to anthropomorphize the birds, and death strikes without warning, capriciously. Compared with Disney's *Beaver Valley* (1950), *Gulls!* is real rather than comforting, and deserving of its U.S. title, *Struggle for Survival. The Great Adventure* (1953) shows Sucksdorff's children again, this time learning about the wildlife sharing the land near a small farm. *Symphony of a City* and *The Great Adventure* reflect Flaherty's approach to documentary filmmaking as displayed in *Louisiana Story* (1948). Both Sucksdorff and Flaherty work from scenarios. They take shots in controlled circumstances, much as in a studio production. Neither attempt to catch life unawares; both re-order life, dictate the action, and rehearse the characters and the camera movement. Once television came into its own, this kind of questionable documentary filmmaking would fall into the category labeled docudrama. In fact, television and the direct cinema made possible by technological breakthroughs put an end to the poetic style of Sucksdorff and Flaherty.

Engineers picked up where they had left off in developing television technology before the war, and by 1948 the demand for television stations, programs, and sets was out of control. So chaotic was the situation, in fact, that the Federal Communication Commission (FCC) imposed a freeze on station allocation until a plan could be developed. In 1952 new licenses were again issued and the climb towards 98 percent saturation was resumed. In this same year, NBC provided its affiliates with the compiled series "Victory at Sea" (1952–1953). Here was film, originally shot for the large screen, now being distributed through a new medium directly into the home. But at CBS Edward R. Murrow and Fred Friendly were trying to figure out what documentaries for television — not film — should look and sound like. "See It Now" (1951–1958) was the series in which they explored the possibilities.

These were the days before videotape, when programs and even commercials were either live or on film. In this context, to watch a kinescope (a film recording made from a television picture tube) of a "See It Now" program is to see the idea of direct cinema coming to life. For example, "A Report on Senator McCarthy" (1954) has Murrow live on camera for the introduction. Then he turns to the primitive monitors for the first film clip of evidence as, live on network television, he begins to expose the Wisconsin senator's witch-hunting methods.

The Murrow Style

*T*his is no time for men who oppose Senator McCarthy's methods to keep silent, *or* for those who approve. We can deny our heritage and our history, but we cannot escape responsibility for the result. As a nation we have come into our full inheritance at a tender age. We proclaim ourselves, as indeed we are, the defenders of freedom—what's left of it—but we cannot defend freedom abroad by deserting it at home. The actions of the junior senator from Wisconsin have caused alarm and dismay amongst our allies abroad and given considerable comfort to our enemies. And whose fault is that? Not really his; he didn't create this situation of fear, he merely exploited it and rather successfully. Cassius was right. "The fault, dear Brutus, is not in our stars but in ourselves."

—*Edward R. Murrow,*
"A Report on Senator
McCarthy," *CBS News*
(March 9, 1954)

When CBS had only audiotape, that's what they played, and the audience watched the tape recorder's reels turn. Most producers today would not use audio material unless they could find some visual material to coincide with it despite the communication value of the latter. But in those early days flashy technology didn't exist, and the television pioneers concentrated on the material and focused on creating memorable scripts.

By the early 1950s it was not difficult to believe that Communists had infiltrated any American institution. Eastern Europe was locked behind an "iron curtain." China had gone Communist and Greece almost went red. And in Korea American soldiers were dying on battlefields less than a decade after victory against Germany and Japan. The Soviets were in possession of nuclear weapons, believed by many to have been delivered by American traitors. McCarthy, as Murrow said, was merely exploiting the times.

In this first network news documentary series, the narrator was once again installed as the voice of authority. The network news documentary became a vehicle for news anchors and vigorous reporters. Literate scripts made the transition from the classical period of Grierson/Lorentz to television too, but actually their origins lay less in the film tradition than in journalistic traditions established by serious radio network news broadcasters. However, the dynamic editing and inventive sound constructs used in radio were abandoned by the television documentary, because good newspeople tried to be objective.

The new medium's documentary only waited for technology to provide the final form so perfectly suited to television: the live event. Television's purest form is the Super Bowl shown live. A presidential speech to the nation (and Lyndon Johnson shocks viewers when he announces he will not seek re-election); preparations for and the execution of national funerals (and Jack Ruby kills the assassin on live television); the nonstop broadcasts during Watergate summer, 1973—live, unrehearsed, spontaneous broadcasts in which anything can happen are the authentic documentaries that only television can provide. The form permits little reflection, eloquence, or metaphor. The result contains only those qualities inherent in the events and personalities being broadcast. But then, this is the post-rhetorical era: we do not believe in words anymore. We question even the images now.

Direct Cinema

Until the 1960s, television was imprisoned in the studio. News and television documentary film units sent increasingly lightweight single-system sound cameras into the world. Processed and edited, the film could get on the air that evening. Those early units used film, not video, and the television film crews simply shot for a small screen, using lots of close-ups and medium shots, rather than for the epic theater screen.

In *Louisiana Story* (1948), Robert Flaherty dropped in on the idyllic backwoods life of a small boy living in harmony with nature and oilmen in the bayous. In a similar manner, Sidney Meyers dropped in on a young black boy trying to survive in a New York City ghetto with *The Quiet One* (1949). And Sucksdorff carried on in a planned, formal style in his *The Great Adventure* (1953). But as synchronous recording became easier and film stocks became more sensitive, meaning that they needed less light while still retaining a sharp

Forecast

*T*elevision is a new, hard test of our wisdom. If we succeed in mastering the new medium it will enrich us. But it can also put our mind to sleep. We must not forget that in the past the inability to transport immediate experience and to convey it to others made the use of language necessary and thus compelled the human mind to develop concepts. For in order to describe things one must draw the general from the specific; one must select, compare, think. When communication can be achieved by pointing with the finger, however, the mouth grows silent, the writing hand stops, and the mind shrinks.

—Rudolf Arnheim, "A Forecast of Television," 1935

*S*hakespeare's been dead for 354 years. The world's no longer a stage—it's a TV documentary!

—An impromptu remark recorded in Haskell Wexler's Medium Cool *(1969)*

Sidney Meyers's *The Quiet One* (1949) examines a world of youth radically different from that depicted in Flaherty's *Louisiana Story*. Meyers's purpose is, however, more focused; with James Agee's simple and moving commentary, Meyers creates a more distinct and powerful message.

The Case Against Narration

*W*here would CBS Reports or NBC White Paper be without narration? For programs like those, narration props up weak film, justifies aimless film, rationalizes disjointed film, unifies disparate film, adds intelligence to dumb film.

Where would National Geographic be without narration? Where would travelogues, industrial films, and educational films be? For them narration provides the thread to hang the pictures, the opinions with which to color the pictures, the facts, reasons and measurements that give the pictures their logic. . . .

Give viewers the signal, "Here comes narration," and the program is shunted to the right side of the brain, which sits back expecting to listen to the documentary. Give the same viewers another signal, "Here comes a story for you to see for yourself," and up comes the other side of the brain, leaning forward expecting somehow to participate.

—Robert Drew, from "Narration Can Be a Killer," International Documentary *newsletter (Fall 1983)*

---

image, shots became more spontaneous. Now film-makers could start to film despite their uncertainty about what would eventually be recorded. Alan King's *Skid Row* (1956) and Lionel Rogosin's *On the Bowery* (1957) advanced toward a new style—direct cinema.

Like Riefenstahl and Jennings's work, direct cinema banishes the narrator. If present, the voice may provide connecting facts, but it is never permitted to interpret what is seen and heard. Unlike Riefenstahl, Flaherty, Sucksdorff, or Meyers, however, no direct cinema film-maker would ever stage an event. Be unobtrusive, the idea goes, and soon people will forget you are filming. Observe coolly, refraining from propaganda. Simply offer the viewers your record and let them project (or deduce) its meaning. The approach has been called *kino pravda,* or cinema truth. Direct cinema rejects heavy-handed manipulative editing that shapes the material to fit often preconceived notions; it strives instead to reveal the truth naturally, without artifice.

Life magazine had proven that a still photographer could catch life unawares, and that people took pleasure in seeing the captured moment. "Why can't moving pic-ture film do that?" someone at Time-Life asked. Robert Drew, Richard Leacock (the photographer for Flaherty

on *Louisiana Story*), and D. A. Pennebaker solved some of the technical problems in capturing life in motion. Later, Drew and Leacock managed to convince two U.S. senators, Hubert H. Humphrey and John F. Kennedy, to let them follow them as they campaigned through Wisconsin for the primary election.

Primary (1960) records the large events, but it also captures the small moments that reveal so much about the human beings writ large as candidates. From the glad-handing appearances in the large auditorium to the drumsticks and hot dogs curbside in a small town, the toil and grime of the campaign had never been revealed so powerfully before. For example, we see the smiling face of the Happy Warrior turn into a mask of pain as the weary Humphrey sinks back for a nap while the driver pilots the large car toward the next destination.

It looked and sounded as though the candidates had been wiretapped in sight and sound. Drew and Leacock had captured the small, private moments for everyone to witness. Narration by W. H. Auden, scores by Britten or Thomson, editing by students of Soviet montage—all these were too didactic. *Night Mail* and *The River* styles were out; so was compilation. With the decade of the 1960s came the era of direct cinema: events observed

"The Selected Second"

I remember one day poring through hours of film I'd shot in nursing homes. . . . There was one interview with an old man whose legs had been amputated because of an advanced case of diabetes. He was dying, and time seemed to stretch out for him as he waited for an exit from the world. For 10 minutes I interrupted the wait, asking him questions about his life, his family, conditions at the nursing home, and how often he had visitors. They were, I thought then, 10 depressing, emotionless minutes. The old man seemed to keep a stone face. But the camera saw something I didn't. I had asked the old man how frequently his children came to visit him, and he replied that they never came, but that that didn't bother him because he had his friends at the nursing home. I had paused . . . and continued on. But my cameraman, Dick Roy, had used his zoom lens at that moment to slowly fill the screen with a shot of nothing but the old man's eyes. Weeks later, for the first time, I could see those eyes up close on film brimming with tears. . . . There was fear in the eyes, and bitterness, and sorrow, and hurt, and a hundred other emotions that well up when a human being is abandoned by his loved ones at his weakest hour. So I used that film in the program and cut out thousands of feet, dozens of minutes of nothingness that didn't quite tell what it means to be endlessly dying in an antiseptic box.

—*Dick Hubert, "The Selected Second,"*
Harpers *(January 1974)*

directly, without layers of film artifice to separate the viewer from the actual event.

Drew attracted a group of like-minded filmmakers and technicians much as Grierson had. Time-Life lent the group to ABC Television, and Drew came back with another one of these intriguing synchronous picture and sound pieces, *Yanki No!* (1960). It documented intense anti-U.S. sentiment in Latin America. *The Chair* (1963) showed what happened as a commutation appeal was made in behalf of a condemned prisoner.

A Happy Mother's Day (1963) exposed the media hype and circus atmosphere surrounding the birth of healthy quintuplets. But ABC and its sponsor, a baby-food manufacturer, didn't much care for the images and sounds recorded by the reality observers. They edited out the embarrassing exposure of a small town's greed to cash in on its famous new residents and showed the revised version as *The Fischer Quintuplets.* As a result, the relationship between Drew and ABC unraveled.

In 1966, *Don't Look Back* gave people a peek into the life of a rising young folksong writer and performer, Bob Dylan. And *Monterey Pop* (1968) prepared the way for the music "rock doc" and for *Woodstock* (1970).

Albert and David Maysles were attracted to the same kind of filmmaking with *What's Happening! The Beatles in the U.S.A.* (1964). They followed with *Salesman* (1969), filming a cigarette-smoking Bible salesman as he called door-to-door, got pumped up at sales meetings, and, alone in a cheap motel, called home to his family. The trouble with this film was that nothing noble was revealed in the salesman's character. The pathetic Good Book pitchman could have died, and, in contrast to Arthur Miller's Willy Loman in *Death of a Salesman*, would have elicited no feeling in us at all.

The Maysles brothers were running their cameras one night at a rock concert on the West Coast in 1970. Members of the motorcycle gang the Hell's Angels had been hired to keep order. Suddenly, during a set by the

Rolling Stones, a fan got into a scuffle with an Angel near the front of the stage and was killed. Later the Maysleses filmed as Mick Jagger sat in front of the editing console, watching the murder with hardly a word, with hardly an expression on his face. The result was the film *Gimme Shelter* (1970).

Critics charged the filmmakers with going too far in *Grey Gardens* (1976), by making targets of two odd old ladies (relatives of Jackie Onassis). But the Maysles brothers more than redeemed their reputations with *Christo's Running Fence* (1977). The 25-minute film documents the process as Christo gets permission to run a 24.5-mile white fence across Northern California farmland and into the sea. The Maysleses' work shows how area residents were won over by the artist and even became willing participants in the "fence" building.

In the 1960s Frederick Wiseman entered the scene. This lawyer-turned-filmmaker never interviews anyone on camera and suffers no words of narration. His long list of films include *Titicut Follies* (1967), which takes viewers inside a mental institution in Massachusetts (an

act, said the courts, that violated the patients' right of privacy); *High School* (1968); *Law and Order* (1969); and *Hospital* (1970). Premiered on PBS Television were *Basic Training* (1971), *Essene* (1972), *Primate* (1974), *Welfare* (1975), *Meat* (1976), *Canal Zone* (1977), *The Store* (1983), and *Racetrack* (1986). Wiseman's work bears out a remark Leo Tolstoy is said to have made in the early 1900s: it is only necessary to film everyday people; with film, invented stories are unnecessary. No one has exposed in such detail the warp and woof of American institutions as has Frederick Wiseman.

In France, Marcel Ophuls's *The Sorrow and the Pity* (1970) added a twist to the direct cinema style from America. This four-and-a-half-hour documentary probed the memories of French people in a small town and of the Germans who had occupied the same town during World War II. The film was shown by Swiss, German, Dutch, Belgian, Hungarian, and Swedish television systems, but not by the French system. The village in the film had not been populated with valiant resistance fighters, but only people trying to survive. A government official ex-

▲   In such films as the Maysles brothers' *Gimme Shelter* (1970), the *cinéma vérité* philosophy and aesthetic became fully articulated. The "unobstructed" camera in this film communicates the reality of a rock concert in compelling and often frightening images.

Direct Cinema

*W*hat I think Eisenstein took as the essence of film in the editing process would have destroyed the benefit of spontaneous juxtapositions that occur in filming — in life itself. I think the camera picking up material in an individual shot has great power. It has an ability to convey a truth that will allow the viewer more freedom to make a judgment for himself, therefore to be given something that has the right to be more believable.

—Albert Maysles

I think the danger again lies whenever you talk about "truth." When you are dealing with reality it seems to make everyone question it, where they wouldn't question a fiction film.

—David Maysles

*O*ur films are spontaneous eruptions that we find ourselves catching with our cameras. To classify these things is some kind of sin. Nevertheless, people force us into giving it a name. So the name "direct" came into being — if only because people are set off on a rampage by the use of the word *verite*. I think the word "direct" is more dispassionate. We go directly to things as they take place, and almost in spite of ourselves we are bound to come up with something that's more truthful.

—Albert Maysles

*W*e had a hundred different formulas for the structure of the film *[Gimme Shelter]* at different stages. It just finally evolved into what it is.

—David Maysles

Source: Robert Phillip Kolker's "Circumstantial Evidence," Sight and Sound (Autumn 1971)

plained, however, that "certain myths must not be destroyed."

In 1975 Paramount distributed *The Memory of Justice,* also by Ophul. This was another long probe lasting four and a half hours. It examined archival footage of the Nuremberg trials, the French war in Algeria, and the American nightmare in Vietnam. The film asks why, if history repeats itself, do we have such trouble seeing the similarities among events. This documentary is not entertaining, but seeing it is itself a memorable experience.

Ophuls's work is not true direct cinema. Rather, it blends direct observation and archival footage with *cinéma vérité* — where behind-the-camera questions provoke the people being filmed. In direct cinema the crew tries only to remain invisible and record an event without affecting the process or outcome. But in *cinéma vérité* the filmmaker unhesitatingly allows a microphone or sound technician to intrude into a shot, and will even allow his or her voice to be heard to engage the people in the frame. Some television news teams use this practice when a public official refuses to grant an interview: the team appears on location, the camera and microphone on and recording as the secretary says the official is not in. Undeterred, the reporter knocks on the office door, the official opens the door, sees who is there, notices a record is being made — and is forced into responding.

In *Memory of Justice,* Ophuls tries to locate an infamous concentration camp "medical" officer. He has reason to believe the old Nazi is living in a small German village. He stops a farmer along the road who is smiling, polite — until, as the camera continues to record from inside the car, he understands what it is Ophuls wants to know. His face turns vicious; his voice reveals his rage as he stomps back to his tractor. The provocation from behind the camera strips the veneer away to reveal what is true. The farmer is angry. If one has no sympathy for Nazis or for those who would help to conceal their whereabouts, the scene is a chilling revelation of an unrepentant heart.

Cinéma vérité is not an approach that people accept readily. It may reveal a level of truth that has been hidden, but it seems to many a baldly manipulative style, one that tricks subjects into inadvertent disclosure. Some consider the trick to be unfair even when the target is guilty — say, a public official who is bribed by undercover agents as they record the exchange for evidence. (If Mike Wallace of "60 Minutes" appeared at your door, would *you* open it?)

The primary distribution system for documentary film is television — public and commercial, broadcast and cable. *Cinema vèrité* is seldom broadcast on television, and direct cinema is only shown on occasion. For the most part, the television documentary still depends on the narrator in the person of a news anchor or reporter. The style has not changed much since "See It Now." And because most people's documentary experience is with television, an odd expectation has evolved. It is expected that a documentary *will* be objective, that it will *not* argue a point of view. Joris Ivens recently asserted that a documentary filmmaker, whatever the style, *must* take a position if any dramatic, emotional, or artistic value can emerge. "I was surprised," he said, "to find that many people automatically assume that any documentary would *inevitably* be objective. Perhaps the term is unsatisfactory, but for me the distinction between the words *document* and *documentary* is quite clear." When viewers raised on television see a Grierson or Lorentz film or some other nontelevision-produced indictment against, say, acid rain or nuclear or toxic wastes, they

become uncomfortable. There is a tendency among them to reject the documentary out of hand because it is "biased," has a "point of view," is actually "propaganda." "A sad thing happened to documentary films when they moved from theater screens to the television tube — they died, and nobody mourned," said one critic.

Critics often blame cautious network or local station executives for bland, safe, or "objective" documentaries. Others blame sponsors for their reluctance to buy time in or adjacent to controversial or unpopular programs. However, there are reasons to explain both positions. NBC's "Pensions: The Broken Promise" (1972) is a dramatic example of what can happen when a film takes a stand on a controversial issue.

The "Pensions" thesis warned that many of the 25 million Americans covered by private (union and corporate) pension plans would find themselves without anticipated benefits when they retired. The film showed examples — from a vice president fired shortly before his retirement to a union member promoted to a job represented by another local — of workers losing their accumulated pension benefits. Concluded narrator Edwin Newman, "The situation, as we've seen it, is deplorable."

The film aired on the evening of September 12, 1972. Viewers could have chosen "Marcus Welby, M.D." on ABC or a made-for-TV gangster movie on CBS. Fifteen million people watched "Pensions." The documentary won a Peabody Award as "a shining example of constructive and superlative investigative reporting." Meanwhile, the Federal Communications Commission (FCC), acting on a complaint, issued a citation, charging NBC with the broadcast of "a one-sided documentary" that violated the Fairness Doctrine. (The Fairness Doctrine requires that a broadcast documentary present controversial issues and major points of view fairly.) The commission gave the network twenty days to present its plan for counterprogramming to show "the other side" of the issue. But where might one find anyone who would publicly declare that earned pensions should *not* be paid?

NBC appealed the FCC judgment to the U.S. Circuit Court of Appeals in Washington, which sustained the FCC's judgment. NBC appealed to the U.S. Supreme Court. Three and a half years later the justices ruled in favor of NBC, apparently agreeing with briefs filed in support of NBC by CBS and the *New York Times.* The *Times* had argued that the injustices suffered by those entitled to their promised pensions "are no more controversial than are acts of theft or embezzlement."

This bizarre case had been initiated by a complaint filed with the FCC. One might have expected a representative of a pension plan indicted by NBC to have filed

The Problem: To Find a Sponsor

*I*n 1975 CBS had interested Lanacane, Grecian Formula, Odor-Eaters, Aqua-Tech, Lenox Air-Conditioning, Williams Lectric Shave, Datsun, Mr. Coffee, and Block Drugs in sponsoring *The Guns of Autumn.* The documentary took aim at hunters, some of whom were shown stalking their prey in fenced game farms. The gun lobbies scared off all the sponsors except Block Drugs — which issued a statement saying that cancellation would mean that the company was trying to censor "a major news medium, and that would be contrary to fundamental American traditions."

—John Culhane, "Where TV Documentaries Don't Dare to Tread," New York Times *(February 20, 1977)*

Edward R. Murrow maintained that television could teach, illuminate, "yes, even inspire. But," he continued, "it can do so only to the extent that humans are determined to use it to those ends. Otherwise it is merely wires and lights in a box."

People in 5.4 million American homes watched the CBS documentary *Selling of the Pentagon* (1971) while 10.6 million were tuned to a movie on NBC and 17.3 million spent the time with a medical series episode. And yet research establishes that a documentary need not be seen directly by all those who will eventually act in response to the information it presents. Comparatively few people in Britain saw the Grierson-produced documentary about housing problems, but newspaper reporters saw it and they wrote about what they saw. Public opinion was mobilized. The misery of the affected was reduced.

"Where we've had impact it isn't in numbers of viewers," says Marlene Sanders at ABC Television in 1977. "You measure it in whether there are changes in the society as a result. And one of the first changes is that the other media pick up the subject — as they did when I did 'Right to Die.' And since then, California has passed a law on living wills."

Documentary filmmakers will continue to be a little worried about the way the world is going, just as Grierson was. It is that concern that remains constant and fires the resolve to make others see and better comprehend the world: reality redeemed.

the complaint. However, the complainant was a special interest group, Accuracy in Media (AIM). AIM saw the program as a liberal effort to influence legislation pending in Congress. In fact, the program did inspire action, and legislation was passed to restore honor to pension promises.

"Pensions" cost NBC a fortune in legal fees alone. Concluded Julian Goodman of NBC, "It is easier for broadcasters to steer clear of controversial issues because of the high price tag that can be placed on freedom of expression. It is easier to give in. But it is not in the public interest."

Where television news documentaries seem bland, objective, and lacking a point of view, the Fairness Doctrine may be a contributing cause. This doctrine evolved to protect viewers from one-sided station owners and to guarantee that all sides of controversial issues, local and national, would get a fair hearing. However, given the expansion of the system through cable companies, some argue that the FCC doctrine has outlived its usefulness.

Wrap-Up

The initial value of the motion picture was its mechanical ability to record and project real images in a way that suggested movement. Newsreel stories in one shot or travelogues reporting events in the world's freak shows were not sufficient in purpose or method. It took Flaherty to work out an approach to filmmaking that would serve a more substantive purpose. Today the direct cinema filmmaker appreciates his work, but could not accept Flaherty's penchant for setting up and orchestrating events.

The formal structures created by some of Grierson's people, Lorentz, and Steiner and Van Dyke, may seem beautiful or interesting, but brazen in argument and style. The compilation film, too, is suspect and out of favor for the same reason the provocative *cinéma vérité* style is suspect: these treatments of reality are too creative, manipulative.

Direct cinema remains credible. It is the style that millions of Americans found compelling in the series *An American Family* (1973) and again in *Middletown* (1982) on PBS. Audiences continue to accept the Murrow style: a narrator who provides continuity for a variety of interviews, and some archival, direct observation, and occasionally a little *vérité* material.

Whatever the style, every filmmaker has the problem of finding a sponsor, whether an independent who is able to sell footage of Guatemala rebels to CBS so that Pamela Yates can make the film *she* really wants to make, *When the Mountains Tremble* (1983). The problem is posed for the independent filmmaker and television station or network, commercial or public: someone has to care enough to put up the money to produce. And then there is the problem of distribution. If the film cannot be sold to television (or by television to a sponsor), then how does the film become available to people? All the networks are jittery about buying independently produced material, and when budgets are pressed, documentary units are the first to be sacked. Public television's series, *Frontline* and *A Matter of Life and Death* (1983–1984), are exceptions. These series have provided distribution to filmmakers who, like Grierson, are concerned about social issues.

BIBLIOGRAPHY

Reference Works and General Histories

Bordwell, David, Janet Staiger, and Kristin Thompson. *The Classical Hollywood Cinema: Film Style and Mode of Production to 1960.* New York: Columbia University Press, 1985.

Brownlow, Kevin. *The Parade's Gone By.* New York: Alfred Knopf, 1968.

Cook, David. *A History of Narrative Film.* New York: W. W. Norton, 1981.

Dickinson, Thorold. *A Discovery of Cinema.* London: Oxford University Press, 1971.

Everson, William K. *American Silent Film.* New York: Oxford University Press, 1978.

Griffith, Richard, and Arthur Mayer. *The Movies.* New York: Simon & Schuster, 1970.

Hampton, Benjamin. *A History of the Movies.* New York: Covici, Friede, 1931.

Houston, Penelope. *The Contemporary Cinema.* Baltimore: Penguin Books, 1963.

Jacobs, Lewis. *The Rise of the American Film.* New York: Harcourt, Brace, 1939.

Katz, Ephraim. *The Film Encyclopedia.* New York: T. Y. Crowell, 1979.

Knight, Arthur. *The Liveliest Art.* New York: New American Library, 1959.

New York Times Film Reviews 1913–1968. New York: New York Times and Arno Press, 1969.

Pirie, David, ed. *Anatomy of the Movies.* New York: Macmillan, 1981.

Pratt, George C. *Spellbound in Darkness.* Rochester: New York Graphic Society, 1966.

Quigley, Martin. *Magic Shadows.* Washington, D.C.: Georgetown University Press, 1948.

Ramsaye, Terry. *A Million and One Nights.* New York: Simon & Schuster, 1926.

Rotha, Paul, and Richard Griffith. *Film Till Now.* New York: Twayne, 1960.

Salt, Barry. *Film Style and Technology: History and Analysis.* London: Starward, 1983.

Sarris, Andrew. *The American Cinema.* New York: E. P. Dutton, 1968.

Sklar, Robert. *Movie-Made America: A Cultural History of American Movies.* New York: Random House, 1975.

Chapter 1   Technology, Industry, and Form (Beginnings to 1907)

Dickson, W. K. L., and Antonia Dickson. *A History of the Kinetograph, Kinetoscope and Kinetophonograph.* New York: Arno Press, 1970.

Fell, John, ed. *Film Before Griffith.* Berkeley: University of California Press, 1983.

Haas, Robert Bartlett. *Muybridge: Man in Motion.* Berkeley: University of California Press, 1976.

Marek, K. W. *Archaeology of the Cinema.* New York: Harcourt, Brace, 1965.

North, Joseph H. *The Early Development of the Motion Picture, 1887–1909.* New York: Arno Press, 1973.

Slide, Anthony. *Early American Cinema.* Cranbury, N.J.: Barnes, 1970.

Tarbox, Charles H. *Lost Films, 1895–1917.* Los Angeles: Film Classic Exchange, 1983.

Vardac, Nicholas. *From Stage to Screen.* Cambridge, Mass.: Harvard University Press, 1949.

Chapter 2   Industrial Development and Emerging Film Styles (1908–1916)

Arvidson, Linda. *When the Movies Were Young.* New York: Benjamin Blom, 1968.

Fell, John. *Film and the Narrative Tradition.* Norman: University of Oklahoma Press, 1974.

Frazer, John. *Artificially Arranged Scenes: The Films of Georges Méliès.* Boston: G. K. Hall, 1980.

Gish, Lillian. *The Movies, Mr. Griffith and Me.* Englewood Cliffs, N.J.: Prentice-Hall, 1969.

Henderson, Robert M. *D. W. Griffith: The Years at Biograph.* New York: Farrar, Straus, 1970.

O'Dell, Paul, with Anthony Slide. *D. W. Griffith and the Rise of Hollywood.* New York: Barnes, 1971.

Slide, Anthony. *Early American Cinema.* Cranbury, N.J.: Barnes, 1970.

Smith, Albert E., and P. A. Koury. *Two Reels and a Crank.* New York: Doubleday, 1952.

Chapter 3   American Silent Film (1917–1927)

Balshofer, Fred J., and Arthur Miller. *One Reel a Week.* Berkeley: University of California Press, 1967.

Blesh, Rudi. *Keaton.* New York: Macmillan, 1966.

Brooks, Louise. *Lulu in Hollywood.* New York: Alfred Knopf, 1982.

Brownlow, Kevin. *The Parade's Gone By.* New York: Alfred Knopf, 1968.

———. *Hollywood: The Pioneers.* New York: Alfred Knopf, 1979.

———. *The War, the West and the Wilderness.* New York: Alfred Knopf, 1979.

Chaplin, Charlie. *My Autobiography.* New York: Simon & Schuster, 1964.

Everson, William K. *American Silent Film.* New York: Oxford University Press, 1978.

Kerr, Walter. *The Silent Clowns.* New York: Alfred Knopf, 1975.

Lloyd, Harold. *An American Comedy.* New York: Dover, 1971.

O'Leary, Liam. *The Silent Cinema.* New York and London: Dutton/Vista, 1965.

Pratt, George C. *Spellbound in Darkness.* Rochester: New York Graphic Society, 1966.

Robinson, David. *Chaplin: His Life and Art.* New York: McGraw-Hill, 1985.

Weinberg, Herman G. *The Complete "Greed" of Eric von Stroheim.* New York: E. P. Dutton, 1973.

Chapter 4   The German Silent Film (1919–1932)

Eisner, Lotte. *The Haunted Screen: Expressionism in the German Cinema.* Berkeley and Los Angeles: University of California Press, 1969.

———. *Fritz Lang.* New York: Oxford University Press, 1977.

Kracauer, Sigfried. *From Caligari to Hitler.* New York: Noonday, 1959.

Manvell, Roger, with Heinrich Fraenkel. *The German Cinema.* New York: Praeger, 1971.

Prawer, S. S. *Caligari's Children: The Film as a Tale of Terror.* New York: Oxford University Press, 1980.

Chapter 5   The Soviet Silent Film (1918–1930)

Barna, Yon. *Eisenstein.* Bloomington: Indiana University Press, 1974.

Eisenstein, J. M. *The Film Sense.* New York: Harcourt, Brace, 1947.

———. *Film Form.* New York: Harcourt, Brace, 1949.

Leyda, Jay Kina. *A History of the Russian and Soviet Film.* London: Allen & Unwin, 1960.

Leyda, Jay, and Zina Voynow. *Eisenstein at Work.* New York: Pantheon Books, 1982.

Marshall, Herbert. *Masters of the Soviet Cinema: Crippled Creative Biographies.* London: Routledge & Kegan Paul, 1983.

Pudovkin, V. I. *Film Technique and Film Acting.* London: Vision Press, 1959.

Seton, Marie. *Sergei M. Eisenstein.* New York: Grove Press, 1960.

Chapter 6   Other International Influences (1919–1927)

Hull, David Stewart. *Film in the Third Reich.* Berkeley and Los Angeles: University of California Press, 1969.

Martin, John. *The Golden Age of French Cinema, 1929–1939.* Boston: Twayne, 1983.

Sadoul, Georges. *French Film.* London: Falcon Press, 1953.

Welch, David. *Propaganda and the German Cinema, 1933–1945.* New York: Oxford University Press, 1983.

Chapter 7   Sound: A New Beginning (1927–1933)

Corliss, Richard. *Talking Pictures.* Woodstock, N.Y.: Overlook Press, 1974.

Geduld, Harry. *The Birth of the Talkies.* Bloomington: Indiana University Press, 1975.

Chapter 8   Studio Styles (1933–1945)

Baxter, John. *The Cinema of John Ford.* Cranbury, N.J.: Barnes, 1971.

Bergman, Andrew. *We're in the Money.* New York: Harper & Row, 1975.

Capra, Frank. *The Name Above the Title.* New York: Macmillan, 1971.

Carringer, Robert. *The Making of Citizen Kane.* Berkeley: University of California Press, 1985.

Dooley, Roger. *From Scarface to Scarlett: American Films in the 1930s.* New York: Harcourt, Brace, Jovanovich, 1984.

Haver, Ronald. *David O. Selznick's Hollywood.* New York: Alfred Knopf, 1980.

Koszarski, Richard. *Hollywood Directors: 1914–1940.* New York: Oxford University Press, 1976.

Millichap, Joseph R. *Steinbeck and Film.* New York: Frederick Ungar, 1983.

Roddick, Nick. *A New Deal in Entertainment: Warner Brothers in the 1930's.* London: British Film Institute, 1983.

Richie, Donald. *The Japanese Cinema.* New York: Doubleday, 1971.

Rondi, Gian. *Italian Cinema Today.* New York: Hill & Wang, 1965.

Seton, Marie. *Portrait of a Director: Satyajit Ray.* Bloomington: Indiana University Press, 1971.

▶ Chapter 9   Film and the Age of Television (1946–1964)

Ceplair, Larry, and Steven Englund. *The Inquisition in Hollywood.* Garden City, N.Y.: Anchor, 1980.

Dowdy, Andrew. *The Films of the Fifties: The American State of Mind.* New York: Wm. Morrow, 1973.

Koszarski, Richard. *Hollywood Directors: 1941–1976.* New York: Oxford University Press, 1977.

Leaming, Barbara. *Orson Welles.* New York: Viking, 1985.

MacCann, Richard Dyer. *Hollywood in Transition.* Cambridge, Mass.: Houghton Mifflin, 1962.

Pauly, Thomas H. *An American Odyssey: Elia Kazan and American Culture.* Philadelphia: Temple University Press, 1983.

▶ Chapter 10   Postwar Cinema: Europe and the East (1945–1963)

Armes, Roy. *French Cinema since 1946,* 2 volumes. New York: Barnes, 1966.

Bondanella, Peter. *Italian Cinema: From Neorealism to the Present.* New York: Frederick Ungar, 1983.

Cowie, Peter. *Antonioni, Bergman, Resnais.* New York: Thomas Yoseloff, 1964.

———. *Swedish Cinema.* New York: Barnes, 1966.

Donner, Jorn. *The Personal Vision of Ingmar Bergman.* Bloomington: Indiana University Press, 1964.

Durgnat, Raymond. *Luis Buñuel.* Berkeley and Los Angeles: University of California Press, 1968.

Fellini, Federico. *Fellini on Fellini.* New York: Delacorte Press, 1976.

Godard, Jean-Luc. *Godard on Godard.* Translated by Tom Milne. New York: Viking, 1972.

Houston, Penelope. *Contemporary Cinema.* Baltimore: Penguin Books, 1964.

Insdorf, Annette. *François Truffaut.* Boston: Twayne, 1978.

Manvell, Roger. *New Cinema in Europe.* New York and London: Dutton/Vista, 1966.

Mellen, Joan. *The Waves at Genji's Door: Japan Through Its Cinema.* New York: Pantheon Books, 1976.

Quinlan, David. *British Sound Films: The Studio Years 1928–1959.* Totowa, N.J.: Barnes & Noble Books, 1984.

▶ Chapter 11   New International Cinema (1963–Present)

Auty, Martyn, and Nick Roddick, eds. *British Cinema Now.* London: British Film Institute/University of Illinois Press, 1984.

Corrigan, Timothy. *New German Films: The Displaced Image.* Austin: University of Texas Press, 1983.

Goulding, Daniel J. *Liberated Cinema: The Yugoslav Experience.* Bloomington: Indiana University Press, 1985.

Hands, Peter. *The Czechoslovak New Wave.* Berkeley: University of California Press, 1985.

Kolker, Robert Phillip. *The Altering Eye: Contemporary International Cinema.* New York: Oxford University Press, 1982.

Liehm, Antonin J. *Closely Watched Films: The Czechoslovak Experience.* White Plains, N.Y.: International Arts, 1974.

Mora, Carl J. *Mexican Cinema: Reflections of a Society 1896–1980.* Berkeley: University of California Press, 1982.

Phillips, Klaus, ed. *New German Filmmakers: From Oberhausen Through the 1970's.* New York: Frederick Ungar, 1985.

White, David. *Australian Movies to the World.* Sydney: Fontana Papers and Melbourne/New York: Frederick Ungar, 1984.

Witcombe, R. T. *The New Italian Cinema.* New York: Oxford University Press, 1982.

▶ Chapter 12   New American Films and Filmmakers (1965–Present)

Bliss, Michael. *Brian De Palma.* Metuchen, N.J.: Scarecrow Press, 1983.

Carney, Raymond. *American Dreaming: The Films of John Cassavetes and the American Experience.* Berkeley: University of California Press, 1985.

Goldman, William. *Adventures in the Screen Trade: A Personal View of Hollywood and Screenwriting.* New York: Warner Books, 1983.

Jacobs, Diane. *Hollywood Renaissance.* New York: Delta, 1977.

———. *But We Need the Eggs: The Magic of Woody Allen.* New York: St. Martin's Press, 1982.

Kim, Erwin. *Franklin J. Schaffner*. Metuchen, N.J.: Scarecrow Press, 1985.

Kolker, Robert Phillip. *A Cinema of Loneliness: Penn, Kubrick, Coppola, Scorcese, Altman.* New York: Oxford University Press, 1980.

Lloyd, Ann. *Movies of the Sixties.* London: Orbis, 1983.

Monaco, James. *American Film Now.* New York: Oxford University Press, 1979.

Pollock, Dale. *Skywalking: The Life and Films of George Lucas.* New York: Harmony Books, 1983.

Smith, Julian. *Looking Away: Hollywood and Vietnam.* New York: Scribner, 1975.

Chapter 13 Experimentation and New Directions

Curtis, David. *Experimental Cinema.* New York: Universe Books, 1971.

Manvell, Roger. *The Animated Film.* London: Sylvan Press, 1954.

Renan, Sheldon. *An Introduction to the American Underground Film.* New York: E. P. Dutton, 1967.

Sitney, P. Adams. *Visionary Film,* 2nd edition. New York: Oxford University Press, 1979.

Stephenson, Ralph. *The Animated Film,* revised edition. New York: A. S. Barnes, 1981.

Youngblood, Gene. *Expanded Cinema.* New York: E. P. Dutton, 1970.

Chapter 14 Documentary: Reality Redeemed Through the Art of the Film

Barnouw, Erik. *Documentary: A History of the Nonfiction Film.* New York: Oxford University Press, 1974.

Barsam, Richard. *Nonfiction Film.* New York: E. P. Dutton, 1976.

Bluem, A. William. *Documentary in American Television.* New York: Hastings House, 1965.

Bohn, Thomas. *An Historical and Descriptive Analysis of the "Why We Fight" Series.* New York: Arno Press, 1977.

Calder-Marshall, Arthur. *The Innocent Eye.* London: W. H. Allen, 1963.

Grierson, John. *Grierson on Documentary.* London: Faber & Faber, 1966.

Jacobs, Lewis, ed. *The Documentary Tradition.* New York: Hopkinson & Blake, 1971.

Levin, Roy. *Documentary Explorations.* Garden City, N. Y.: Doubleday, 1971.

Leyda, Jay. *Films Beget Films.* New York: Hill & Wang, 1964.

Mamber, Steven. *Cinema Vèritè in America.* Cambridge: M.I.T. Press, 1974.

Rotha, Paul. *Documentary Film,* 3rd edition. New York: Hastings House, 1952.

ILLUSTRATION CREDITS